PENGUIN REFERENCE

The Pocket Roget's Thesaurus

George Davidson is a former senior editor with Chambers Harrap. In addition to writing dictionaries and thesauruses, he is the author of several books on English grammar, usage, spelling and vocabulary. He lives in Edinburgh.

The Pocket

Roget's Thesaurus

George Davidson

PENGUIN BOOKS

PENGUIN BOOKS

Published by the Penguin Group
Penguin Books Ltd, 80 Strand, London WC2R ORL, England
Penguin Group (USA) Inc., 375 Hudson Street, New York, New York 10014, USA
Penguin Group (Canada), 10 Alcorn Avenue, Toronto, Ontario, Canada M4V 3B2
(a division of Pearson Penguin Canada Inc.)
Penguin Ireland, 25 St Stephen's Green, Dublin 2, Ireland
(a division of Penguin Books Ltd)
Penguin Group (Australia), 250 Camberwell Road, Camberwell, Victoria 3124, Australia
(a division of Pearson Australia Group Pty Ltd)
Penguin Books India Pvt Ltd, 11 Community Centre,
Panchsheel Park, New Delhi – 110 017, India
Penguin Group (NZ), cnr Airborne and Rosedale Roads, Albany, Auckland 1310, New Zealand
(a division of Pearson New Zealand Ltd)
Penguin Books (South Africa) (Pty) Ltd, 24 Sturdee Avenue, Rosebank 2196, South Africa

Penguin Books Ltd, Registered Offices: 80 Strand, London WC2R ORL, England

www.penguin.com

First published 1852
Abridged edition first published in Great Britain by Penguin Books 1988.
Based on *Roget's Thesaurus*, revised and edited by Betty Kirkpatrick,
first published by Longman Group UK Limited 1987
Revised edition published 2000
New edition, revised and edited by George Davidson, first published 2004
This Pocket edition first published 2005

1

Set in 6/7 pt PostScript ITC Stone Serif and ITC Stone Sans
Typeset by Rowland Phototypesetting Ltd, Bury St Edmunds, Suffolk
Printed in England by Clays Ltd, St Ives plc

Contents

Introduction

Roget's Thesaurus began life two hundred years ago as a small notebook of useful words and phrases that Peter Mark Roget, an English physician, created purely for his own use as a writer and lecturer. However, recognizing that other people might also find such a book useful, Roget later spent the early years of his retirement expanding the material he had in his notebook into a much larger book, which was published in 1852 as the *Thesaurus of English Words and Phrases*.

The original purpose of the *Thesaurus* was, as Roget put it, to 'facilitate the expression of ideas and assist literary composition', and this is still the book's main purpose. Whatever you want to say, the *Thesaurus* will help you find the exact word or words you need to say it.

Helping you to express yourself clearly is not, however, the only use the *Thesaurus* can be put to nowadays. If you enjoy crossword puzzles and other word games, the *Thesaurus* is also a valuable source of ideas and solutions.

As it has absorbed new vocabulary over the past hundred and fifty years, *Roget's Thesaurus* has grown to be a very large book, and the need for smaller, shorter versions has long been recognized. For this reason, there are now both *Concise* and *Pocket* versions of *Roget*.

The first edition of this *Pocket Roget's Thesaurus* was published some twenty years ago. This new edition has been fully updated with the vocabulary of the late twentieth and early twenty-first centuries, such as telecommunication, computer and Internet technology. While a book of this size cannot, of course, hope to be as exhaustive in its word coverage as a larger *Thesaurus*, the *Pocket Roget* nevertheless covers a wide range of vocabulary, from the technical to the informal and from slang to literary words and archaisms.

How to use this book

Unlike a dictionary, in which the words are listed alphabetically, a thesaurus groups words and phrases according to their meanings. Each of the 882 Units in the *Thesaurus* covers a particular area of vocabulary such as 'existence', 'reality', 'space', 'sharpness', 'usefulness', 'stealing' or 'virtue'. (See page xi for a complete list of all the Units in the *Thesaurus*.)

Some words and phrases are listed in only one Unit, whereas others may be found in two or more Units. For example, *downcast* is found in Unit 743 (dejection), *downfall* in Units 275 (descent) and 652 (failure), and *downgrade* in Units 277 (lowering), 673 (cancellation) and 860 (punishment).

There are two ways of looking for a word in the *Thesaurus*: via the list of Units or via the index:

i) To find a word or phrase via the Units list, scan through the list on pages xi to xviii until you find one that covers the general area of vocabulary that you are interested in, such as 'roughness', 'toughness', 'thought', 'fear' or 'fashion'. (This will become quicker, the more familiar you become with the book. Often you will not have to scan through the list at all, because you will know from past experience where to look.) Turn to the Unit you have found and look through it to find the word or phrase you are looking for.

Notice that in each Unit words and phrases are grouped in separate paragraphs according to their part of speech: noun, verb, adjective, adverb or preposition (although there will not be items from all five parts of speech in every Unit). Within each part-of-speech paragraph, words and phrases are grouped according to their sense. The first word or phrase in each sense group is printed in italic type.

If by chance you do not find a suitable word or phrase in, say, the list of nouns in the Unit you are looking at, look at the verbs and adjectives lists as well, where you may find an entry that suggests an alternative way of expressing what you want to say.

Another thing to notice is that many of the Units are preceded or followed by Units of opposite or related meaning; for example Unit 1 (existence), Unit 2 (non-existence); Unit 615 (haste), Unit 616 (lack of haste); Unit 513 (writing), Unit 514 (print), Unit 515 (correspondence), Unit 516 (book). This again allows you to broaden your search easily and quickly into related areas of vocabulary.

Yet another way of expanding your search is by using the cross-references that are found at the beginning of many of the Units. For example, at Unit 62 (end), there are cross-references to Units 60 (sequence), 133 (effect) and 323 (death).

ii) To find a word or phrase using the index, you simply have to think of a related word or phrase and look it up in the index. If the word or phrase you look up is not there, think of another related word or phrase and look for that. As a rule, the simpler or more general the word or phrase you look up, the more likely it is to be in the index.

Once you have found the word or phrase you want, you will see a list of one or more numbers, often separated out by part of speech (noun, verb, adjective, adverb or preposition). These numbers refer to the Units in the text of the *Thesaurus*. By looking up these Units, you should quickly find the word or phrase you need. If necessary, expand your search in the ways described above.

The fact that a word or phrase is not to be found in the index does not mean that it is not included in the text. Not every word or phrase in the text has been listed in the index. See page 185 for further explanation of this point.

Words and phrases are entered in the index in strict alphabetical order. For further explanation of this point, and some explanatory examples, see page 185. Remember that since words and phrases have separate entries in the index, there may be more than one place for you to look: for example, *bound*, *bound for* and *bound to* are three separate index entries.

Commas

In the text of the *Thesaurus*, a comma that belongs within a phrase (such as *Tom, Dick and Harry*) is printed smaller than the commas printed between separate words and phrases in the word lists.

Abbreviations

The following abbreviations are used in the *Thesaurus*:

sb = somebody; *sb's* = somebody's
sth = something
colloq. = colloquial
derog. = derogatory
dial. = dialect
offens. = offensive
tdmk = trademark
US = United States (i.e. American English)
vulg. = vulgar

The System of Classification

1 existence
2 non-existence
3 reality
4 unreality
5 essence
6 extraneousness
7 state
8 circumstances
9 relatedness
10 unrelatedness
11 reciprocity
12 family relations
13 sameness
14 oppositeness
15 uniformity
16 diversity
17 similarity
18 dissimilarity
19 accord
20 disparity
21 imitation
22 originality
23 quantity
24 degree
25 equality
26 inequality
27 average
28 compensation
29 greatness
30 smallness
31 superiority
32 inferiority

33 increase
34 decrease
35 addition
36 subtraction
37 remainder
38 mixture
39 purity
40 union
41 separation
42 connection
43 adhesion
44 non-adhesion
45 combination
46 disintegration
47 whole
48 part
49 completeness
50 incompleteness
51 inclusion
52 exclusion
53 component
54 foreign body
55 order
56 disorder
57 arrangement
58 disturbance
59 precedence
60 sequence
61 beginning
62 end
63 middle
64 consecutiveness

65 discontinuity
66 assembly
67 dispersion
68 class
69 generality
70 speciality
71 rule
72 conformity
73 nonconformity
74 number
75 calculation
76 list
77 zero
78 fraction
79 one
80 plurality
81 two
82 three
83 four
84 five and over
85 accompaniment
86 multitude
87 few
88 repetition
89 infinity
90 time
91 timelessness
92 period
93 duration
94 transience
95 eternity
96 immediacy

723 dearness
724 cheapness
725 generosity
726 thrift
727 extravagance
728 meanness
729 feeling
730 sensitivity
731 insensitivity
732 strong emotion
733 impassivity
734 joy
735 sorrow
736 pleasantness
737 unpleasantness
738 satisfaction
739 dissatisfaction
740 relief
741 aggravation
742 cheerfulness
743 dejection
744 humour
745 seriousness
746 rejoicing
747 lamentation
748 hope
749 hopelessness
750 fear
751 courage
752 cowardice
753 rashness
754 caution
755 desire
756 indifference
757 liking
758 dislike
759 wonder
760 lack of wonder
761 recreation
762 boredom
763 beauty
764 ugliness

765 beautification
766 decoration
767 blemish
768 refinement
769 vulgarity
770 fashion
771 affectation
772 ridiculousness
773 derision
774 repute
775 disrepute
776 aristocrat
777 commoner
778 title
779 pride
780 humility
781 insolence
782 servility
783 vanity
784 modesty
785 showiness
786 celebration
787 formality
788 informality
789 sociability
790 unsociability
791 courtesy
792 discourtesy
793 friendship
794 enmity
795 love
796 hate
797 marriage
798 divorce;
    widowhood
799 celibacy
800 endearment
801 curse
802 resentment; anger
803 irascibility
804 sullenness
805 benevolence

806 malevolence
807 philanthropy
808 misanthropy
809 pity
810 pitilessness
811 gratitude
812 ingratitude
813 forgiveness
814 atonement
815 jealousy
816 envy
817 right
818 wrong
819 entitlement
820 lack of entitlement
821 duty
822 exemption
823 respect
824 disrespect
825 approval
826 disapproval
827 flattery
828 disparagement
829 vindication
830 accusation
831 probity
832 improbity
833 disinterestedness
834 selfishness
835 good
836 evil
837 virtue
838 wickedness
839 innocence
840 guilt
841 penitence
842 impenitence
843 self-restraint
844 self-indulgence
845 fasting
846 gluttony
847 sobriety

1 EXISTENCE

See also 3 (reality); 322 (life).

n. *existence*, being, life, essence; *actuality*, reality, substance, fact, concreteness; *coexistence*, co-occurrence; *presence*, duration, entity; *universe*, cosmos, creation, world; *coming into being*, realization, materialization, actualization; *creation*, evolution, natural selection, intelligent design; *survival*, endurance, persistence, continuance; *metaphysics*, ontology, existentialism.

adj. *existing*, being, existent; *actual*, real, substantial, factual, genuine, attested, documented, historical, material, physical, concrete; *present*, ongoing, current, prevalent, rife; *surviving*, extant, enduring, lasting, abiding; *metaphysical*, ontological, existential.

vb. *exist*, be, have being, live, breathe; *be present*, be found, be situated, prevail, obtain, occur; *coexist*, co-occur; *survive*, subsist, remain, endure, continue, last, abide; *come into being*, come about, evolve, arise, take shape; *just exist*, vegetate, stagnate, languish.

adv. *actually*, in (actual) fact, in point of fact, really, truly; *presently*, currently, at the moment; *in* one's *lifetime*, in all one's born days, man and boy.

2 NON-EXISTENCE

See also 4 (unreality); 323 (death).

n. *non-existence*, nonentity, absence, unreality; *nothingness*, emptiness, vacuum, void, limbo, blankness; *extinction*, death, oblivion, annihilation, nirvana; *nothing*, nil, love, zero; *nullification*, annulment, cancellation, obliteration; *disintegration*, dilapidation, decay, obsolescence; *nihilism*, negativism.

adj. *non-existent*, absent, missing, minus; *vacant*, empty, blank, null, void; *unreal*, insubstantial, abstract, ideal; *extinct*, dead, defunct, dead and gone, past, obsolete; *nihilistic*, negative, destructive.

vb. *not exist*, be null and void, be over and done with; *cease to exist*, die, pass away, perish, die out; *disappear*, vanish, evaporate, fade (away), melt (away), dematerialize; *extinguish*, annihilate, demolish, wipe out, snuff out, quell; *nullify*, abolish, annul, cancel, obliterate, invalidate, neutralize, negate, veto; *disintegrate*, decay, decompose, go to rack and ruin.

3 REALITY

See also 1 (existence); 282 (material world).

n. *reality*, existence, the here and now; *objectivity*, corporeality, substance, tangibility, palpability, solidity, concreteness; *real world*, universe, creation, physical world, earth, matter; *actuality*, fact, historicity, validity, authenticity; *realism*, naturalism, verisimilitude, cinema vérité, documentary, kitchen sink drama, slice of life; *plausibility*, feasibility, practicality; *realities*, the facts of life, home truths, basics, fundamentals, the bottom line (*colloq.*), the nitty-gritty (*colloq.*), brass tacks, the crunch (*colloq.*); *materialism*, realism, empiricism, pragmatism.

adj. *real*, existing, substantial; *objective*, corporeal, tangible, palpable, solid, concrete, physical, material, natural; *actual*, factual, historical, true, valid, authentic; *realistic*, naturalistic, true-to-life, lifelike; *plausible*, feasible, practicable, likely; *practical*, down-to-earth, matter-of-fact, no-nonsense, realistic; *basic*, fundamental, crucial, primary, cardinal; *materialist*, realist, empirical, pragmatic.

vb. *be real*, weigh, bulk large, loom; *objectify*, embody, incarnate, personify, body forth; *validate*, substantiate, corroborate, authenticate; *actualize*, materialize, realize.

adv. *really*, in reality, in fact; *in practice*, in all likelihood, when it comes to the crunch (*colloq.*), when the chips are down (*colloq.*), when push comes to shove (*colloq.*).

4 UNREALITY

See also 2 (non-existence); 370 (vision); 457 (imagination).

n. *unreality*, non-existence, insubstantiality, incorporeality, abstractness, intangibility, impalpability; *subjectivity*, fantasy, make-believe, fiction, dream world, maya, vision, hallucination, delusion, nightmare, night terror, castle in Spain, pipedream; *illusion*, figment of the imagination, mirage, optical illusion, trompe l'oeil, fata morgana, ignis fatuus, will-o'-the-wisp, jack-o'-lantern; *simulacrum*, shadow, phantom, chimera, ghost, spectre, ectoplasm; *bubble*, a fool's paradise, fairy gold, tinsel, nine days' wonder, gossamer, cobweb; *a nothing*, a nobody, non-person, unperson, hollow man, man of straw, broken reed, paper tiger, puppet; *vain hope*, empty promise, false dawn, pie in the sky (*colloq.*); *empty talk*, hot air (*colloq.*), cock and bull story, bullshit (*colloq.*).

adj. *unreal*, non-existent, insubstantial, incorporeal, intangible, impalpable; *abstract*, ideal, rarefied, bloodless; *subjective*, imaginary, fantastic, make-believe, fictional, dreamlike, hallucinatory, delusory, illusory, chimerical, ghostly, shadowy; *ephemeral*, fleeting, elusive, evanescent; *vague*, hazy, nebulous, tenuous; *spurious*, specious, phoney, flimsy, hollow, meretricious; *token*, nominal, honorary.

vb. *be unreal*, belie, deceive, delude; *idealize*, rarefy, etiolate; *imagine*, fantasize, hallucinate, daydream, hear/see things; *dissolve*, fade, melt, blur, cloud, mist; *falsify*, fudge, distort; *invent*, dissemble, fib, spin a yarn (*colloq.*), waffle (*colloq.*); *invalidate*, refute, puncture, expose, give the lie to.

adv. *ideally*, in theory; *in name*, superficially, to all appearances.

5 ESSENCE

See also 576 (importance).

n. *essence*, substance, gist, heart, stuff; *essential part*, prime constituent, main ingredient, property, attribute; *core*, kernel, backbone, nub, nucleus, marrow, pith, sap, lifeblood; *quintessence*, embodiment, incarnation, personification, epitome, soul; *character*, make-up, constitution, complexion, temperament, stamp, breed, stripe, humour, hue.

adj. *essential*, intrinsic, immanent, inherent; *innate*, inborn, inbred, deep-seated, deep-rooted, ingrained, bred-in-the-bone; *quintessential*, fundamental, constitutional, structural, organic; *integral*, inseparable, ineradicable, built-in.

vb. *be essential*, inhere, belong, be part and parcel of; *characterize*, stamp, inform, mark; *embody*, incarnate, personify, epitomize.

adv. *in essence*, essentially, intrinsically; *at heart*, at bottom, basically, fundamentally.

6 EXTRANEOUSNESS

See also 10 (unrelatedness); 54 (foreign body).

n. *extraneousness*, exteriority, externality; *exterior*, outside, surface, periphery, circumference; *objectification*, externalization, projection; *foreignness*, alienness, unrelatedness, irrelevance, contingency.

adj. *extraneous*, exterior, external, outer, superficial; *foreign*, alien, unrelated, unconnected; *irrelevant*, peripheral, tangential, contingent, incidental, circumstantial.

vb. *be extraneous*, externalize, realize, body forth, objectify; *be irrelevant*, miss the point, talk off the subject, digress.

adv. *outwardly*, on the outside, superficially, prima facie; *off the point*, beside the point, neither here nor there.

7 STATE

See also 5 (essence); 8 (circumstances).

n. *state*, condition, situation, circumstances, lot, plight, estate; *position*, status, standing, footing, rank; *sphere*, realm, world, orbit, walk of life, department (*colloq.*), line of country (*colloq.*); *mode*, manner, modality, modus operandi, modus vivendi; *state of mind*, frame of mind, mood, temper, disposition, attitude, culture, morale, fettle, spirits; *physical condition*, form, shape (*colloq.*), repair, trim, nick (*colloq.*).

adj. *stative*, situational; *modal*, conditional.

vb. *be situated*, stand, lie, sit, be found; *situate*, contextualize, locate.

adv. *as things stand*, in the present situation, in the circumstances.

8 CIRCUMSTANCES

See also 7 (state).

n. *circumstances*, situation, state of affairs, status quo, set-up (*colloq.*); *position*, state of play, lie of the land, story so far; *conditions*, environment, surroundings, setting, milieu, context, background; *occasion*, occurrence, event, episode, incident, happening, coincidence; *stage*, point, juncture, stepping-stone, milestone, turning-point, crisis, crossroads.

adj. *circumstantial*, relative, contingent, conditional, provisional, incidental;

surrounding, environmental, contextual, situational.

adv. *in the circumstances*, as things stand; *in the event*, as it happened; *provisionally*, conditionally.

9 RELATEDNESS

See also 11 (reciprocity); 12 (family relations); 19 (accord); 24 (degree).

n. *relatedness*, relevance, pertinence, bearing, point, appositeness; *relationship*, affinity, kinship, affiliation, bond, tie, rapport; *connection*, relation, link, tie-up, association; *relativeness*, ratio, proportion, scale; *interrelatedness*, correlation, reciprocity, interdependence, cross-reference, complementarity; *correspondence*, agreement, similarity, parallel, comparison, analogy.

adj. *related*, relevant, pertinent, apposite, appropriate, germane, à propos; *corresponding*, connected, similar, parallel, comparable, analogous; *interrelated*, correlative, reciprocal, interdependent, complementary, mutual, respective; *relative*, proportional, commensurate.

vb. *be related*, belong, pertain; *touch*, concern, regard, involve, interest; *relate*, link, connect, tie up, tie in, bracket together; *correlate*, juxtapose, reconcile, compare, contrast, draw a parallel between, cross-refer; *correspond*, approximate, agree, match, accord, fit, tally; *be relevant*, address the question, stick to the point.

adv. *relatively*, proportionally, in proportion, to scale; *in contrast*; *by/in comparison*, comparatively; *respectively*, mutually.

prep. *relative to*, with respect to, with regard to, as regards, with reference to, concerning, in relation to, re, vis-à-vis.

10 UNRELATEDNESS

See also 6 (extraneousness); 20 (disparity).

n. *unrelatedness*, irrelevance, inappositeness, inappropriateness, extraneousness, red herring (*colloq.*), non sequitur; *unconnectedness*, separateness, dissociation, independence; *randomness*, arbitrariness, coincidence, long shot, shot in the dark, fluke; *disproportion*, disparity, imbalance, asymmetry, distortion.

adj. *unrelated*, irrelevant, inapposite, inappropriate, extraneous, foreign, alien; *unconnected*, incidental, tangential, peripheral, inessential, unimporant, immaterial; *random*, arbitrary, chance,

coincidental; *disproportionate*, unbalanced, distorted, asymmetrical.

vb. *be unrelated*, have no bearing on, have nothing to do with; *digress*, miss the point, avoid the issue, get sidetracked.

adv. *beside the point*, off the point; *by the way*, incidentally, in parenthesis.

11 RECIPROCITY

See also 9 (relatedness); 129 (exchange).

   n. *reciprocity*, correspondence, interrelation, interdependence, mutuality, interconnectedness, complementarity; *counterpart*, equivalent, opposite number, alter ego, mirror image; *interaction*, interchange, interplay, exchange; *alternation*, exchange, give and take, tit for tat, seesaw, vicissitudes, ups and downs, swings and roundabouts.

   adj. *reciprocal*, interrelated, interdependent, mutual, interconnected, complementary; *equivalent*, interchangeable, corresponding; *alternating*, seesaw, dingdong (*colloq.*), retaliatory.

   vb. *reciprocate*, exchange, swap (*colloq.*), return in kind, give as good as one gets, retaliate; *interact*, interconnect, interrelate, interchange; *alternate*, seesaw, fluctuate, take turn about; *correspond*, match up, tally.

   adv. *in turn*, turn and turn about, Box and Cox; *all things being equal*, on balance; *conversely*, on the other hand; *vice versa*, mutatis mutandis.

12 FAMILY RELATIONS

See also 9 (relatedness); 154 (parent).

   n. *family relationships*, kinship. tribalism, nepotism, inbreeding, incest; *ancestry*, blood, lineage, descent, matriarchy, patriarchy, genealogy, distaff side, spear side; *family*, clan, folks (*colloq.*), kith and kin, one's own flesh and blood, next of kin, relatives, in-laws, nuclear family, extended family; *parenthood*, motherhood, fatherhood, parenting, fostering, adoption, artificial insemination; *parent*, mother, father, donor, surrogate mother, godparent, stepparent, grandparent; *offspring*, issue, son, daughter, bastardy, illegitimacy, natural child, love child, test-tube baby; *sibling*, brother, sister, half-brother, half-sister, stepbrother, stepsister, twin; *aunt*, uncle, niece, nephew, great-aunt, great-uncle, great-niece, great-nephew, cousin, second cousin; *heredity*, chromosome, gene, DNA, genetic engineering, genetic modification, gene technology, biotechnology, GMO, cloning, clone.

adj. *familial*, kindred, cognate, agnate, consanguineous, incestuous; *ancestral*, tribal, genealogical, matriarchal, patriarchal, matrilineal, patrilineal; *filial*; *sibling*, sisterly, brotherly, fraternal; *avuncular*; *hereditary*, inherited, congenital, genetic, inbred; *genetically modified*, GM; *adopted*, adoptive.

vb. *be related to*, be descended from, take after, *father*, sire, beget, adopt, foster; *wed*, intermarry, interbreed; *be inherited*, run in the family, be in the blood.

13 SAMENESS
See also 15 (uniformity); 17 (similarity); 21 (imitation).

n. *sameness*, identity, equivalence, similarity, coincidence, congruence, agreement; *likeness*, double, Doppelganger, alter ego, second self, clone, lookalike, spitting image (*colloq.*), chip off the old block (*colloq.*), dead ringer (*colloq.*); *copy*, duplicate, replica, carbon copy, facsimile, analogue, fellow, mate, match, twin, Tweedledum and Tweedledee; *uniformity*, monotony, the same old story, same song, second verse, the same old same old, nothing new under the sun.

adj. *same*, identical, selfsame, indistinguishable, interchangeable; *similar*, equivalent, like, analogous, congruent; *uniform*, unvarying, monotonous, samey (*colloq.*), one-size-fits-all.

vb. *be the same*, be identical, come to the same thing, be tantamount to; *merge*, coincide, coalesce; *mirror*, repeat, parrot, echo; *copy*, duplicate, replicate, match, twin, clone; *look alike*, be (as) like (as) two peas in a pod.

adv. *similarly*, by the same token, in the same way, likewise; *ditto*.

14 OPPOSITENESS
See also 18 (dissimilarity); 215 (contraposition); 632 (opposition).

n. *oppositeness*, contrariety, contraposition, polarity, contradiction, incompatibility; *opposite*, converse, opposite pole, other extreme, antipodes, antithesis, antonym, negative, counterpoint, foil, antidote; *opposition*, antagonism, hostility, antipathy, conflict, clash; *reverse*, mirror image, the wrong side, the other side, verso, countercurrent, contraflow; *diametric*

opposites, day and night, chalk and cheese, oil and water, yin and yang.

adj. *opposite*, contrary, contradictory, incompatible, inverse, converse; *diametrically opposite*, antithetical, antipodean, contrapuntal, negative; *opposed*, antagonistic, hostile, antipathetic, adversarial; *reverse*, counter, anticlockwise.

vb. *be opposite*, contradict, contrast; *oppose*, antagonize, clash with, conflict with, challenge; *reverse*, negate, counteract, contravene, run counter to, turn the tables on.

adv. *on the contrary*, in contrast; *conversely*, on the other hand; *back to front*, inside out, upside down, topsy turvy.

15 UNIFORMITY
See also 13 (sameness); 17 (similarity); 72 (conformity).

n. *uniformity*, evenness, consistency, homogeneity; *continuity*, regularity, constancy, stability; *identity*, accord, agreement, consensus, unison, unity; *conformity*, regimentation, standardization, normalization, mass-production; *mould*, pattern, stamp, stereotype, production line, conveyor belt; *sameness*, drabness, monotony, routine, daily round, groove, rut.

adj. *uniform*, even, consistent, homogeneous, alike, of a piece; *continuous*, constant, regular, unbroken, uninterrupted, rhythmic, stable, unchanging, unvarying; *identical*, mass-produced, unisex, off-the-peg, standard, one-size-fits-all, stereotyped, typecast; *same*, monotonous, repetitive, dull, drab, monochrome, self-coloured; *undifferentiated*, unrelieved, monolithic.

vb. *make uniform*, level, even off, homogenize, grade, size; *regularize*, stabilize, normalize; *standardize*, stereotype, systematize, typecast, mass-produce; *align*, bring into line, rehabilitate, re-educate, drill, regiment.

adv. *uniformly*, across the board; *in line*, in keeping.

16 DIVERSITY
See also 18 (dissimilarity); 38 (mixture).

n. *diversity*, variety, heterogeneity, dissimilarity, contrast, relief, variegation; *non-uniformity*, inconsistency, irregularity, discontinuity, unevenness; *changeability*, instability, variability, versatility; *assortment*, medley, mixed bag, miscellany, motley crew, ragbag, patchwork, mosaic, kaleidoscope, rainbow, coat of many colours, chequered career, everything but the kitchen sink (*colloq.*).

adj. *diverse*, varied, heterogeneous, variegated, chequered; *non-uniform*, inconsistent, irregular, discontinuous, uneven; *changeable*, unstable, variable, kaleidoscopic; *assorted*, mixed, motley, divers, sundry, various, miscellaneous; *versatile*, all-round, multipurpose, multifaceted.

vb. *make diverse*, vary, contrast, variegate, chequer; *mix*, stir up, shake up, jumble, shuffle; *diversify*, have many strings to one's bow, have many irons in the fire, branch out, spread one's wings, broaden one's horizons.

adv. *all anyhow*, in a muddle, higgledy-piggledy (*colloq.*).

17 SIMILARITY

See also 13 (sameness); 15 (uniformity); 19 (accord); 21 (imitation).

n. *similarity*, sameness, synonymy, symmetry, similitude, resemblance, likeness, affinity; *correspondence*, equation, comparability, analogy, simile, parallel, alliteration, assonance, assimilation; *semblance*, simulation, imitation, dissimulation, disguise, camouflage; *counterpart*, twin, copy, clone, soulmate, kindred spirit, two of a kind, birds of a feather; *sameness*, equivalence, approximation, much of a muchness (*colloq.*), six of one and half a dozen of the other.

adj. *similar*, same, synonymous, symmetrical, like; *corresponding*, comparable, analogous, parallel, equivalent, approximate, akin; *simulated*, imitation, artificial, cultured, synthetic, ersatz, faux.

vb. *be similar*, resemble, take after, favour, suggest; *reflect*, mirror, echo, evoke, savour of, smack of, be redolent of; *make similar*, equalize, homogenize, assimilate, camouflage, disguise; *compare*, liken, draw a parallel between; *imitate*, emulate, copy, reproduce, duplicate, clone; *correspond*, accord, tally, match, coincide, agree.

adv. *all the same*, at the same time; *similarly*, by the same token, likewise; *in the style/manner of*, à la; *as it were*, so to speak; *in the same boat*, in a similar situation.

18 DISSIMILARITY

See also 14 (oppositeness); 16 (diversity); 20 (disparity); 418 (discrimination).

n. *dissimilarity*, difference, disparity, diversity, discrepancy, divergence; *unlikeness*, incongruity, incompatibility, contrast, asymmetry, no comparison, nothing in common, another matter/story, a different kettle of fish (*colloq.*), clear blue water between; *differentiation*, discrimination, distinction, nuance, nicety, nit-picking (*colloq.*).

adj. *dissimilar*, different, disparate, divergent, diverse; *unlike*, incongruous, incompatible, contrasting, poles apart; *distinctive*, unusual, peculiar, out of the ordinary, singular; *discriminating*, discerning, selective, choosy (*colloq.*).

vb. *be dissimilar*, differ, diverge, deviate, depart from; *be unlike*, contrast, conflict, be at odds, be at variance; *differentiate*, distinguish, discriminate, split hairs, nit-pick (*colloq.*), separate the sheep from the goats, tell the men from the boys.

adv. *at different times*, variously; *in contrast*.

19 ACCORD

See also 15 (uniformity); 17 (similarity); 25 (equality); 436 (assent).

n. *accord*, agreement, concord, concert, chorus, harmony, understanding, reconciliation, arbitration; *consensus*, unanimity, unison, unity, cooperation, solidarity; *consistency*, uniformity, coherence, congruity, conformity; *aptness*, fitness, appropriateness, suitability, compatibility, timeliness, right moment, mot juste; *adaptation*, accommodation, adjustment, alignment, synchronization, fine tuning.

adj. *agreeing*, harmonious, reconciled; *unanimous*, united, concerted, joint, cooperative; *consistent*, uniform, coherent, congruent, of a piece; *apt*, appropriate, suitable, fitting, compatible, consonant, commensurate, timely, opportune; *adaptable*, accommodating, flexible, easygoing, conciliatory; *well-adjusted*, balanced, close-fitting, snug, made-to-measure.

vb. *accord*, agree, concur, consent, chorus, chime in, harmonize, reach an understanding; *cooperate*, get along, pull together, hit it off (*colloq.*), be on the same wavelength (*colloq.*), see eye to eye; *fit*, suit, fit the bill (*colloq.*), tally, square, match, dovetail, marry, coincide; *adapt*, adjust, accommodate, align, true up, synchronize, fine-tune.

adv. *in accord*, in chorus, in concert, in step, in phase, in tune, in unison; *in keeping*, in place, in context; *at home*, at ease, in one's element.

20 **DISPARITY**

See also 10 (unrelatedness); 18 (dissimilarity); 26 (unequality).

n. *disparity*, inequality, imbalance, difference, dissimilarity, divergence; *discrepancy*, inconsistency, gap, margin, overlap, shortfall, surplus, differential; *maladjustment*, mismatch, mésalliance, crossed line, cross-purposes, discord, dissonance, false note; *misfit*, odd man out, eccentric, freak, sport, a square peg in a round hole, a fish out of water; *unsuitability*, incompatibility, inappropriateness, untimeliness, irrelevancy.

adj. *disparate*, unequal, disproportionate, dissimilar, different, divergent, inconsistent; *discordant*, dissonant, jarring, grating, out-of-tune; *maladjusted*, unbalanced, deviant, eccentric, freakish, odd, ill-matched, ill-assorted; *unsuitable*, unfitting, unbecoming, inappropriate, untimely, inopportune, incompatible, irrelevant.

vb. *be disparate*, differ, diverge, contradict; *conflict*, clash, jar, grate, stick out like a sore thumb (*colloq.*); *misplace*, mistime, mishit, talk out of turn, drop a brick/clanger (*colloq.*).

adv. *out of step*, out of line, out of phase; *at odds*, at variance, at cross-purposes; *out of* one's *element*, out of place, out of keeping, out of season.

21 **IMITATION**

See also 13 (sameness); 17 (similarity); 151 (reproduction).

n. *imitation*, mimesis, onomatopoeia, emulation, plagiarism; *copy*, reproduction, duplicate, facsimile, photocopy, carbon copy, replica, clone; *fake*, forgery, counterfeit, sham, simulation, disguise, camouflage; *mimicry*, mockery, travesty, satire, caricature, burlesque, parody, pastiche, impersonation, spoof (*colloq.*), send-up (*colloq.*), takeoff (*colloq.*); *imitator*, follower, emulator, disciple; *copyist*, plagiarist, impersonator, mime, echo, sheep, ape, parrot, copycat; *forger*, counterfeiter, fake, impostor, poseur, charlatan, mountebank; *mimic*, satirist, caricaturist, parodist.

adj. *imitative*, mimetic, onomatopoeic; *derivative*, second-hand, unoriginal, copycat, follow-my-leader; *take*, counterfeit, false,

sham, phoney, pseudo, artificial, synthetic, mock, ersatz, faux, cultured.

vb. *imitate*, emulate, follow, model oneself on, pattern oneself after, follow in the footsteps of; *copy*, reproduce, duplicate, clone, photocopy, borrow, crib, plagiarize; *fake*, forge, counterfeit, sham, simulate, impersonate; *repeat*, echo, ape, parrot, chorus, follow the herd, jump/climb on the bandwagon (*colloq.*); *mimic*, mock, caricature, satirize, burlesque, parody, travesty, send up (*colloq.*), take off (*colloq.*).

adv. *word for word*, verbatim, parrot-fashion; *ditto*; *to the life*.

22 **ORIGINALITY**

See also 70 (speciality).

n. *originality*, creativity, imagination, innovation, inventiveness, thinking out of the box (*colloq.*); *novelty*, individuality, uniqueness, freshness; *original*, source, model, pattern, mould, matrix, blueprint, prototype, archetype, paradigm, test case, precedent; *originator*, inventor, creator, innovator, deviser; *authenticity*, genuineness, the real thing, the genuine article, the real McCoy (*colloq.*).

adj. *original*, creative, imaginative, inventive, innovative; *novel*, individual, unique, one-off, unparalleled, unprecedented, unheard-of, off-beat (*colloq.*), sui generis, inimitable, incomparable; *seminal*, prototypal, archetypal, stereotypical, standard, classic; *authentic*, genuine, real, echt, kosher, bona fide.

vb. *originate*, create, invent, devise, imagine, dream up, conceive, generate; *patent*, blueprint, copyright, trademark; *model*, mould, pattern, stereotype; *exemplify*, typify, represent.

adv. *from the beginning*, from scratch, ab ovo.

23 **QUANTITY**

See also 29 (greatness); 30 (smallness); 168 (size); 177 (measurement).

n. *quantity*, amount, amplitude, magnitude, bulk, mass; *dimensions*, longitude, length, latitude, breadth, width, girth, altitude, height, depth; *area*, extension, volume, capacity, weight, heaviness; *strength*, pressure, potential, tension, torque, stress, strain; *definite quantity*, quantum, measure, dose, ration, portion, helping, share, slice of the cake; *small quantity*, thimbleful, cupful, pinch, teaspoonful, ounce, milligram; *large quantity*, bucketful, sackful, armful, bundle, lorryload, hundredweight, kilo, stack, mountain.

adj. *quantitative*, high, long, wide, deep, broad; *large*, ample, bulky, massive, extensive, capacious, voluminous; *small*, compact, light, shallow, neat, diminutive.

vb. *quantify*, measure, estimate; *apportion*, ration, allot, distribute.

adv. *to the tune of; in the region of*, approximately, in the right ballpark (*US colloq.*).

24 DEGREE

See also 9 (relatedness).

n. *degree*, extent, proportion, scale, ratio, rate, frequency; *stage*, level, step, rung, point, remove; *rank*, status, class, standing, footing; *gradation*, calibration, differential, interval, nuance; *hierarchy*, taxonomy, series; *gauge*, grid, graph, sliding scale, ladder.

adj. *gradational*, serial, hierarchical; *proportional*, relative, comparative; *gradual*, staggered.

vb. *graduate*, calibrate, measure off, grade, scale, size; *class*, sort, rank, rate.

adv. *by degrees*, gradually, bit by bit, step by step, little by little; *in some degree*, to some extent, somewhat.

25 EQUALITY

See also 19 (accord); 28 (compensation).

n. *equality*, equivalence, equal footing, identity, sameness, symmetry; *parity*, par, quits, level pegging, six of one and half a dozen of the other; *equilibrium*, balance, poise, even keel, equation, balance of power, balance of terror, mutually assured destruction; *stability*, status quo, stasis, stalemate, deadlock, hung jury; *draw*, tie, dead heat, photo finish (*colloq.*); *equalizer*, complement, makeweight, counterweight, ballast, stopgap; *equal*, peer, match, mate, twin, fellow, counterpart, opposite number, oppo (*colloq.*); *egalitarianism*, democracy, equal rights, equal opportunity, positive discrimination, justice.

adj. *equal*, same, equilateral, equidistant, coextensive, identical; *even*, stable, static, self-righting, self-regulating, homoeostatic; *symmetrical*, half-and-half, fifty-fifty, parallel, one-to-one, one-on-one, dingdong (*colloq.*); *egalitarian*, democratic, equitable, just, fair, impartial.

vb. *be equal*, tie, draw, even out, tally, balance; *equalize*, synchronize, level up/

down, round up/down; *compensate*, make good, offset, rob Peter to pay Paul; *stabilize*, strike a balance, redress the balance.

adv. *equally*, by the same token; *on equal terms*, pari passu; *neck and neck*, abreast.

26 INEQUALITY

See also 20 (disparity).

n. *inequality*, disparity, difference, discrepancy, disproportion; *imbalance*, overload, overkill, top-heaviness, shortage, shortfall, deficiency; *handicap*, disadvantage, loaded dice, advantage, privilege, head start; *unevenness*, asymmetry, tilt, camber, list, lopsidedness, odd number, casting vote; *inequity*, injustice, discrimination, prejudice, bias.

adj. *unequal*, disparate, different, disproportionate; *unbalanced*, overweight, underweight, top-heavy, overshot, undershot; *uneven*, asymmetrical, askew, awry, lopsided, skewwhiff (*colloq.*); *inequitable*, undemocratic, unfair, unjust, discriminatory, biased, prejudiced.

vb. *be unequal*, be above/below par, overcompensate, overshoot, fall short; *outweigh*, outrank, outclass, outstrip, outvote; *unbalance*, upset, capsize, destabilize; *bias*, prejudice, skew, disadvantage, handicap, tip the scales.

adv. *off balance*, on the light/heavy side; *at a disadvantage*, up against it, with the odds stacked against one, on the back foot; *at an advantage*, out in front.

27 AVERAGE

See also 63 (middle); 69 (generality).

n. *average*, mean, median, norm, par; *moderation*, middle course, golden mean, happy medium, the best of both worlds; *midpoint*, midway, halfway, halfway house, middle age, middle class, middle distance, midlife crisis; *averageness*, mediocrity, ordinariness, lowest common denominator, the middle of the road, common run, the common man, the man in the street, Joe Bloggs (*colloq.*); *neutrality*, impartiality, mugwumpery, silent majority, floating vote, don't knows.

adj. *average*, mean, median, normal, standard, par for the course; *moderate*, middling, middle-aged, middlebrow, middle-class, middle-of-the-road; *mediocre*, ordinary, commonplace, run-of-the-mill, passable, adequate, so-so (*colloq.*); *neutral*, impartial, tepid, lukewarm, Laodicean.

vb. *average out*, balance out, even out; *take an average*, go halves, split the difference; *be moderate*, strike a balance between, see both sides of the question, sit on the fence (*colloq.*).

adv. *on average*, in general, as a rule, on the whole; *all in all*, on balance, all things considered, at the end of the day; *up to the mark*, up to scratch (*colloq.*), up to snuff (*colloq.*).

28 **COMPENSATION**
See also 25 (equality).

n. *compensation*, amends, atonement, reparation, redress, restitution; *exchange*, quid pro quo, swap (*colloq.*), give and take; *allowance*, security, insurance, assurance, hedge, cover, collateral, safety net, failsafe; *counterweight*, weighting, ballast, makeweight; *refund*, indemnity, costs, damages, reimbursement, repayment.

adj. *compensatory*, reparatory, expiatory.

vb. *compensate*, offset, counterbalance, make amends, atone, make up for, make good; *repay*, refund, redeem, indemnify, reimburse, square up (*colloq.*); *insure against*, secure oneself, cover oneself, hedge; *allow for*, take into account, set against.

adv. *on the other hand*, nevertheless, having said that; *instead*, in lieu, in exchange.

29 **GREATNESS**
See also 23 (quantity); 47 (whole); 49 (completeness); 66 (assembly); 168 (size).

n. *greatness*, size, bulk, mass, amplitude, girth, intensity, magnitude, enormity, immensity, infinity; *superiority*, power, might, grandeur, eminence, majesty, authority, distinction, charisma, fame, renown, celebrity, prestige; *greatest part*, lion's share, majority, macrocosm, magnum opus; *maximum*, optimum, ceiling, high point, zenith, peak; *great quantity*, profusion, abundance, host, wealth, plethora, spate, flood, torrent, rush, stream; *lots*, heaps (*colloq.*), loads (*colloq.*), shedloads (*colloq.*), masses (*colloq.*), stacks (*colloq.*), bags (*colloq.*), pots (*colloq.*), lashings (*colloq.*), oodles (*colloq.*), tons (*colloq.*), miles (*colloq.*), reams (*colloq.*), millions (*colloq.*), billions (*colloq.*), trillions (*colloq.*), gazillions (*colloq.*), squillions (*colloq.*), zillions (*colloq.*).

adj. *great*, big, bulky, massive, huge, vast, outsize, enormous, immense, infinite, economy-size, king-size, industrial (*colloq.*);

greatest, main, major, best, maximal, optimal; *substantial*, sizable, considerable, respectable, hefty (*colloq.*); *giant*, gigantic, Brobdingnagian, colossal, monumental, monolithic, hulking, strapping, whopping (*colloq.*), whacking (*colloq.*); *ample*, generous, voluminous, capacious, spacious, roomy; *superior*, powerful, mighty, eminent, grand, majestic, authoritative, distinguished, noble, august, charismatic, famous, renowned, celebrated, prestigious; *extraordinary*, outstanding, remarkable, exceptional, prodigious, overwhelming; *plentiful*, abundant, thick on the ground; *full of*, filled with, loaded with, riddled with, crawling with, swarming with, teeming with, lousy with (*colloq.*).

vb. *be great*, bulk (large), loom, soar, tower; *prevail*, predominate, rule, dominate, sway; *maximize*, enhance, increase, improve; *abound*, crawl, swarm, teem, brim, overflow.

adv. *greatly*, widely, extensively, amply; *on a large scale*, in a big way (*colloq.*), big time (*colloq.*); *largely*, mainly, for the most part, to a great extent, mostly; *very*, very much, seriously, hugely, vastly, enormously, immensely; *substantially*, considerably, materially; *to the utmost*, maximally.

30 **SMALLNESS**
See also 23 (quantity); 87 (few); 169 (littleness).

n. *smallness*, littleness, diminutiveness, minuteness; *insufficiency*, scantness, paucity, scarcity, sparseness, a drop in the ocean/bucket; *pettiness*, paltriness, meanness, insignificance, small beer, small fry; *diminution*, contraction, abridgement, reduction, decrease; *smallest part*, minority, microcosm, atom, particle, mote, grain, granule; *minimum*, pittance, low point, floor, nadir, rock bottom; *small quantity*, modicum, fraction, pinch, handful, spoonful, bite, sip, scrap, morsel, crumb, whit, jot, whisper, ray, flicker, trace, tinge, vestige, dash, splash, drop, dribble, trickle, sprinkling; *trifle*, bagatelle, bauble, mite, bean, dime, cent, sou.

adj. *small*, least, little, tiny, diminutive, minute, microscopic, infinitesimal, Lilliputian; *dwarf*, midget, miniature, toy; *insufficient*, scant, scarce, few, rare, sparse, minimal; *narrow*, cramped, confined; *petty*, paltry, mean, insignificant, derisory, minor, trivial, trifling; *slight*, undersized, puny, feeble, meagre, thin, weedy (*colloq.*); *modest*, lowly, humble, unobtrusive, self-effacing.

vb. *become small*, lessen, decrease, diminish, shrink, contract; *make small*, abridge, abbreviate, shorten, reduce, curtail, minimize, downscale.

adv. *slightly*, somewhat; *partially*, nearly, almost, virtually; *scarcely*, hardly, barely, narrowly; *at the very least*, minimally; *merely*, simply, only.

31 **SUPERIORITY**

See also 576 (importance); 651 (success); 665 (master).

n. *superiority*, precedence, primacy, seniority; *pride of place*, prominence, advantage, privilege, prerogative; *lead*, head start, edge, leverage, the upper hand, whip hand, trump card; *domination*, rule, sway, ascendancy, hegemony, leadership, supremacy, sovereignty; *quality*, excellence, perfection, high calibre; *elite*, chosen few, happy few, crème de la crème, top people, upper crust, the brightest and best, the pick of the bunch (*colloq.*); *top*, acme, peak, summit, Everest, the top of the heap (*colloq.*), the top rung of the ladder, vantage point; *superior*, elder, senior, captain, head boy/girl, leader, chief, commander, premier, prime minister, first minister, first lady, prima donna, cock of the walk, top dog, alpha male/female, the great and the good; *champion*, prizewinner, victor, world-beater, record-breaker; *paragon*, model, star, whiz kid (*colloq.*), high-flier, mastermind, superman; *manager*, boss, foreman/-woman, gaffer (*colloq.*), governor (*colloq.*); *big battalions*, big boys (*colloq.*), big guns (*colloq.*), top brass, heavyweight (*colloq.*).

adj. *superior*, elder, senior, principal, foremost, prominent; *excellent*, top-level, top-flight, top-notch (*colloq.*), first-class, first-rate, prestigious, five-star, blue-chip, A-1; *outstanding*, matchless, peerless, unparalleled, unrivalled; *leading*, influential, chief, ruling, supreme, paramount, sovereign, royal; *champion*, victorious, world-beating, winning, triumphant.

vb. *be superior*, prevail, predominate, carry the day, win, triumph; *outdo*, defeat, best, wost, outbid, outplay, outshine, outwit, surpass, be one up on, lick/beat hollow (*colloq.*), hammer (*colloq.*), trounce, knock into a cocked hat; *overshadow*, eclipse, put in the shade, steal sb's thunder, put sb's nose out of joint (*colloq.*); *lead*, head, front,

captain, boss, direct, manage, run, spearhead; *culminate*, peak, climax, go through the roof/ceiling (*colloq.*).

adv. *above par*, above average, out of the top drawer, out of the common run; *to crown/cap it all*; *principally*, chiefly, mainly, above all.

32 **INFERIORITY**

See also 577 (unimportance);
583 (worthlessness); 652 (failure);
666 (servant).

n. *inferiority*, dependence, subordination, supporting role, obscurity; *disadvantage*, handicap, uphill struggle, losing battle; *poor quality*, second best, seconds, rubbish, trash, tat (*colloq.*); *subjection*, subjugation, conquest, servitude, bondage, yoke; *dregs*, scum, riffraff, the lowest of the low; *bottom*, record low, minimum, nadir, trough, rock bottom, the bottom of the heap (*colloq.*); *inferior*, junior, subordinate, the rank and file, second string, assistant, auxiliary, follower, dependant, servant, retainer, underling, hireling, henchman, myrmidon, pawn, tool, creature; *loser*, runner-up, also-ran, non-starter (*colloq.*), underdog, no-hoper (*colloq.*), has-been (*colloq.*), poor relation.

adj. *inferior*, junior, lower, minor, dependent, subordinate, subject; *secondary*, subsidiary, auxiliary, ancillary, assistant, backup; *second-class*, second-rate, poor-quality, mediocre, substandard, imperfect, shopsoiled, shoddy, defective, tatty (*colloq.*), trashy (*colloq.*), crummy (*colloq.*), poor man's; *common*, low, vulgar, menial.

vb. *be inferior*, submit, yield, bow, knuckle under (*colloq.*), retire defeated, come off second best, lose face, take a beating/hammering (*colloq.*); *efface oneself*, hang back, take a back seat (*colloq.*), play second fiddle (*colloq.*), keep a low profile; *fall short*, not make the grade, leave something to be desired, not come up to the mark, not come up to scratch (*colloq.*), not be a patch on (*colloq.*), not be in the running; *sink*, slump, bottom out, go through the floor (*colloq.*), hit rock bottom.

adv. *below par*, below average; *under sb's heel*, under sb's thumb.

33 **INCREASE**

See also 35 (addition).

n. *increase*, addition, increment, augmentation, supplement, complement, accretion, accumulation, appreciation, intensification; *growth*, development, advance, progression, acceleration, crescendo, rise, buildup, inflation; *spread*, expansion, enlargement, proliferation, multiplication; *sudden increase*, escalation, explosion, bulge, boom, boost, spiral, climb, rising tide, quantum leap; *extra*, bonus, profit, rake-off (*colloq.*).

adj. *increasing*, growing, escalating; *progressive*, cumulative, incremental; *additional*, supplementary, extra; *spiralling*, inflationary.

vb. *increase*, add, accrue, accumulate, appreciate, augment; *grow*, develop, burgeon, sprout, thrive, prosper, boom, advance, progress, accelerate, rise, inflate, wax; *spread*, expand, enlarge, mushroom, proliferate, multiply; *escalate*, climb, spiral, rocket, take off; *intensify*, redouble, treble, step up, hot up (*colloq.*); *boost*, swell, stoke, reinforce, bolster, pad out, flesh out, beef up (*colloq.*).

adv. *increasingly*, more and more; *on the increase*, on the up and up; *into the bargain*, with interest, with knobs on (*colloq.*).

34 **DECREASE**
See also 36 (subtraction).

n. *decrease*, diminution, abatement, reduction, deduction, subtraction, loss, depreciation, decline; *contraction*, shrinkage, cutback, rundown, retrenchment, deceleration; *recession*, slump, depression, squeeze, freeze, restraint, deflation; *gradual decrease*, diminuendo, decrescendo, ebb, leakage, evaporation, erosion, attrition; *sudden decrease*, fall, dip, drop, plunge, slide, tumble, crash.

adj. *decreasing*, diminishing, dwindling; *reductive*, subtractive; *depressive*, deflationary.

vb. *decrease*, diminish, reduce, deduct, subtract, lose, depreciate, decline; *contract*, shrink, cut back, retrench, tighten one's belt, deflate, depress, squeeze, freeze; *lessen*, dwindle, ebb, recede, abate, subside, wane, slacken, decelerate; *fall*, dip, drop, plunge, slide, slump, tumble, crash; *cut*, axe, slash, curtail, decimate.

adv. *decreasingly*, less and less; *in decline*, on the wane.

35 **ADDITION**
See also 33 (increase).

n. *addition*, increase, increment, appendage; *extra*, add-on; *adjunct*, attachment, annexe, extension, arm, wing; *appendix*, supplement, postscript, coda,

codicil, addendum, footnote, rider, pendant; *insertion*, interjection, interpolation, parenthesis, filling, padding; *reinforcement*, auxiliary, supernumerary, reserve, backup; *accretion*, agglomeration, agglutination, concatenation; *additive*, admixture, ingredient, seasoning; *accompaniment*, extras, trappings, accessories, trimmings, frills (*colloq.*); *bonus*, perk (*colloq.*), overtime, profit, gain, interest, percentage, golden handshake, windfall; *sequel*, follow-up, encore, epilogue, afterthought.

adj. *additional*, accessory, supplementary; *extra*, spare, reserve, auxiliary, ancillary, supernumerary.

vb. *add*, affix, annex, attach, append; *supplement*, augment, swell, reinforce, pad out, flesh out, top up, beef up (*colloq.*); *insert*, interject, introduce, interpose, interpolate, throw in, chip in (*colloq.*); *add on*, tack on, join on, slap on (*colloq.*), superimpose, overlay, graft.

adv. *in addition*, moreover, furthermore; *plus*, with interest, over the odds; *into the bargain*, to boot; *to the good*, in profit, in the black.

36 **SUBTRACTION**
See also 34 (decrease).

n. *subtraction*, deduction, removal, withdrawal, elimination, deletion, expurgation, bowdlerization; *curtailment*, cutback, contraction, retrenchment; *reduction*, discount, rebate, loss, decrement, tare; *abridgement*, abbreviation, condensation, summary, precis; *amputation*, excision, decapitation, castration; *erosion*, abrasion, attrition.

adv. *less*, minus, without; *at a discount*, at a loss; *out of pocket*, down, in the red.

vb. *subtract*, deduct, remove, withdraw, eliminate, delete, censor, blue-pencil, expurgate, bowdlerize; *curtail*, decrease, cut, cut back, prune, pare, whittle, trim, slim down, dock, chop, axe, slash; *reduce*, abridge, abbreviate, condense, summarize; *amputate*, excise, decapitate, behead, castrate, geld, spay; *erode*, abrade, wear away, grind down.

37 **REMAINDER**
See also 60 (sequence).

n. *remainder*, residue, remains, remnant, relic; *surplus*, balance, profit, net; *trace*, track, trail, footprint, spoor, vestige; *ruins*, shell, shadow, wreck, husk, skeleton, fossil, ashes; *debris*, detritus, slough, scurf, refuse, litter, rubbish, sewage, excrement; *sediment*, dregs, lees, grounds, scum, dross; *leavings*, leftovers, scraps, scrapings, offscourings, gleanings, stubble, chaff; *rump*, stump, offcut, tail end, fag end (*colloq.*), odds and ends, odds and sods (*colloq.*); *wake*, aftermath, aftereffect, fallout, hangover, by-product, spin-off; *survivor*, orphan, widow, widower, relict, heir, successor.

adj. *remaining*, leftover, residual, vestigial; *surplus*, spare, odd, net, outstanding, superfluous; *sedimentary*, alluvial; *surviving*, alive, extant.

vb. *remain*, survive, outlast, persist, endure.

adv. *to spare*, in hand, to play with (*colloq.*); *on the shelf* (*colloq.*).

38 **MIXTURE**
See also 16 (diversity); 45 (combination).

n. *mixture*, combination, compound, concoction, infusion, confection; *amalgam*, alloy, blend, fusion, merger; *assortment*, mixed bag, motley crew, miscellany, melange, medley, kaleidoscope, mosaic, patchwork, pot pourri, cocktail, punch; *mishmash*, hotchpotch, ragbag, farrago, job lot, jumble, gallimaufry, ragout, witches' brew, everything but the kitchen sink (*colloq.*); *mixer*, blender, liquidizer, melting pot, crucible; *hybrid*, cross, mongrel, chimera, half-breed, mulatto, Creole, androgyne, hermaphrodite, bisexual, transsexual; *admixture*, tinge, trace, dash, sprinkling, hint, soupçon.

adj. *mixed*, combined, composite; *assorted*, miscellaneous, heterogeneous, catholic, eclectic, syncretic; *variegated*, dappled, mottled, brindled, piebald, skewbald, motley, rainbow, kaleidoscopic, psychedelic, technicolour; *hybrid*, mongrel, half-caste, crossbred, bionic androgynous, bisexual, transsexual, hermaphroditic.

vb. *mix*, combine, amalgamate, fuse, merge; *blend*, shake, stir, dilute, brew, knead, mash, liquidize, homogenize; *mingle*, intersperse, interlard, interlace, interweave, intertwine; *suffuse*, pervade, imbue, impregnate, infuse, permeate; *tinge*, season, spice, sprinkle, lace, spike, adulterate; *intermarry*, interbreed.

adv. *among*, amidst; *pell-mell*, higgledy-piggledy (*colloq.*).

39 **PURITY**
See also 586 (cleanness).

n. *purity*, homogeneity, integrity, immaculateness; *wholeness*, whole food, health food, macrobiotics; *essence*, distillate, concentrate, extract; *cleanliness*, antisepsis, hygiene, sanitation, pasteurization; *sterilization*; *purification*, clarification, filtration, distillation; *purgative*, laxative, cathartic.

adj. *pure*, simple, single, unalloyed, irreducible, homogeneous; *integral*, intact, immaculate, pristine, virgin; *natural*, whole, raw, unadulterated, unprocessed, untreated, free, macrobiotic; *clean*, antiseptic, hygienic, sterile, unpolluted, sanitized; *undiluted*, neat, straight; *purebred*, thoroughbred, pedigree.

vb. *purify*, simplify, refine, distil, clarify, concentrate; *filter*, sieve, sift, winnow, weed; *clean*, wash, sterilize, disinfect, pasteurize, purge, flush out, cleanse the Augean stables.

adv. *purely*, simply, merely; *neat*, straight, on the rocks.

40 **UNION**
See also 42 (connection); 43 (adhesion); 66 (assembly).

n. *union*, combination, conjunction, confluence, convergence, merger, fusion, synthesis; *alliance*, coalition, association, league, brotherhood, guild, trade union, syndicate, cooperative; *meeting*, reunion, gathering, congress, conference; *joint*, link, bond, connection, tie-in, hookup, linkup, ligature, suture, seal, bracket, seam, splice, weld, coupling, yoke; *junction*, intersection, node, nexus, crossroads, interface, hinge, pivot; *consolidation*, compaction, coagulation, coalescence, conglomeration, concretion; *coordination*, cooperation, communication, teamwork, solidarity, symbiosis; *marriage*, wedlock, matrimony; *sexual union*, coitus, coition, coupling, pairing, mating, copulation, sexual intercourse, carnal knowledge, intimacy, nooky (*colloq.*), fucking (*vulg.*), screwing (*vulg.*).

adj. *united*, combined, composite, conjoined, coordinated, linked, interlinked, integrated, joined up, on-line; *allied*, associated, joint, symbiotic, corporate, communal, cooperative; *connective*, conjunctive, adhesive, cohesive, copulative; *compact*, close-set, dense, solid, firm, immovable, inextricable; *married*, wed, matrimonial, marital; *coital*, sexual, venereal, intimate.

vb. *unite*, combine, conjoin, compound, coalesce, blend, fuse, merge, incorporate,

amalgamate, converge; *ally*, associate, join
forces, team up, organize; *join*, bond, link,
connect, bridge, span, straddle; *couple*,
harness, hitch, yoke, pair, bracket, lump
together; *cement*, solder, seal, splice, tie, knit,
sew, bind, lash, stitch, lock, bolt, clamp,
staple; *attach*, secure, fasten, nail, hook, pin,
screw, stick, gum, plaster; *hinge*, dovetail,
mitre, rabbet; *moor*, tether, hobble, fetter,
shackle, manacle, handcuff; *marry*, wed, get
hitched (*colloq.*), get spliced (*colloq.*); *copulate*,
mate, pair, couple, mount, cover, serve, have
sex with, know, enjoy, possess, make love to,
sleep with, bed, lay (*vulg.*), screw (*vulg.*), fuck
(*vulg.*), have it off with (*colloq.*), make it with
(*colloq.*), get one's oats, get one's leg over
(*colloq.*).

adv. *arm in arm*, hand in hand; *side by side*,
shoulder to shoulder, as one man; *hand in
glove*, in league, as thick as thieves.

41 SEPARATION
See also 44 (non-adhesion);
46 (disintegration); 67 (dispersion);
790 (unsociability).

n. *separation*, disintegration,
fragmentation, decomposition, dissection,
analysis; *division*, partition, demarcation,
cleavage, dichotomy, divergence,
polarization, parting of the ways; *breach*,
break, rupture, fracture, split, fission,
severance, divorce; *dissociation*, dissolution,
disbandment, demobilization, breakup,
dispersion, diaspora; *cleft*, crack, fissure, rent,
crevasse, chasm; *separatism*, segregation,
apartheid, purdah, secession, ghettoism,
isolationism, insularity, non-alignment;
seclusion, quarantine, ghetto, enclave, oasis,
reserve; *schism*, sect, faction, splinter group,
breakaway group, offshoot, branch; *exclusion*,
embargo, boycott, blacklist, blackballing,
ostracism.

adj. *separate*, distinct, discrete, unattached,
disengaged, free, free-standing; *solitary*,
alone, aloof, detached, insular, self-
contained, self-sufficient, independent; *apart*,
asunder, cleft, cloven, broken, torn, rent;
separatist, segregationist, isolationist,
secessionist, sectarian, dissident, breakaway;
divisive, controversial, contentious,
polemical.

vb. *separate*, disintegrate, fragment,
decompose, dissolve; *break*, breach, rupture,
fracture, splinter, split, crack; *dissociate*,
disband, disperse, scatter, diverge, divorce,
polarize, go one's separate ways; *divide*,

halve, split, sever, partition, hive off; *seclude*,
sequester, quarantine, segregate, isolate,
insulate, cut off; *exclude*, expel, bar, blacklist,
blackball, ostracize, send to Coventry, cold-
shoulder (*colloq.*); *part*, rend, cleave, sunder,
tear, slash, gash, score, slit, scratch, lacerate,
chip, shred; *cut down*, hack, chop, dock, clip,
shear, prune, fell, scythe, mow.

adv. *apart*, asunder, in two, in twain; *in
pieces*, in bits, to shreds, to tatters, to
smithereens (*colloq.*), limb from limb.

42 CONNECTION
See also 40 (union).

n. *connection*, association, relation, link,
tie, nexus; *bond*, affinity, sympathy, fellow
feeling, rapport; *bridge*, aqueduct, span, arch,
stepping-stone, neck, isthmus, causeway,
ladder, companionway; *channel*, route,
passage, corridor, tunnel, duct, pipeline;
linkup, hookup, tie-up, hot line (*colloq.*),
switchboard, bleeper, intercom, walkie-talkie;
intermediary, link-man, go-between,
middleman, broker, matchmaker, negotiator,
pig-in-the-middle (*colloq.*); *fastener*, buckle,
hasp, clasp, brooch, bracket, bolt, padlock,
latch, nail, peg, dowel; *glue*, adhesive; *cable*,
rope, leash, halter, harness, rein, chain,
fetter, manacle, shackle, yoke; *ligament*,
tendon, muscle, abdominals, abs, pectorals,
pecs, biceps, triceps; *junction*, knot, ligature,
suture, seam, hinge, pivot.

adj., vb., adv. *See* 40 (union).

43 ADHESION
See also 40 (union); 539 (resolution);
540 (perseverance); 633 (cooperation).

n. *adhesion*, accretion, agglomeration,
consolidation; *cohesiveness*, stickiness,
tackiness, viscosity, density, solidity;
association, adherence, affiliation,
membership, enrolment, matriculation;
solidarity, esprit de corps, team spirit, serried
ranks, united front, phalanx; *mass*, cluster,
clump, clot, clod, cake; *adhesive*, gum, glue,
paste, fixative, cement, mortar, solder, seal,
sticky tape, flypaper; *grasp*, clutch, grip, hug,
foothold, toehold, stranglehold; *limpet*,
barnacle, leech, bur, clinging vine; *tenacity*,
perseverance, resolution, stamina, staying
power; *commitment*, dedication, zeal,
militancy.

adj. *adhesive*, sticky, gummy, tacky, gluey,
viscous, gooey (*colloq.*); *cohesive*, dense, close,
solid, compact; *adhering*, clinging, tight-
fitting, skintight; *united*, associated,

inseparable, indivisible, inextricable; *tenacious*, firm, unshakable, unwavering, persistent, resolute; *committed*, dedicated, engagé, card-carrying, true-blue, zealous, militant.

vb. *adhere*, stick, cling, cleave; *cohere*, bunch, mass, congeal, cluster, cake, coagulate, set, solidify; *associate*, affiliate, join, enrol, matriculate, subscribe to, adopt, wed, espouse; *glue*, gum, paste, plaster, cement, solder, weld; *grasp*, grip, clutch, clasp, hug, intertwine, interlace, interlock; *persevere*, hold out, stand firm, stay the course; *commit oneself*, take sides, take the plunge (*colloq.*), nail one's colours to the mast, come down on the side of.

adv. *side by side*, shoulder to shoulder, cheek by jowl.

44 NON-ADHESION

See also 41 (separation); 541 (vacillation).

n. *non-adhesion*, smoothness, slipperiness, runniness, wateriness, looseness, slackness, separateness, detachedness; *independence*, individualism, aloofness, self-sufficiency, non-alignment, separatism, maverick, free spirit, renegade; *irresolution*, vacillation, fickleness, inconstancy, defection; *apathy*, indifference, floating vote, don't knows.

adj. *non-adhesive*, smooth, slippery, runny, watery; *separate*, loose, free, free-floating, flyaway, floppy, slack, baggy; *independent*, aloof, self-sufficient, individualist, non-aligned, separatist; *irresolute*, vacillating, fickle, volatile, inconstant; *uncommitted*, apathetic, indifferent, lukewarm, wishy-washy (*colloq.*).

vb. *not adhere*, slide, slip, flow, thaw, melt, hang, dangle, flap; *unstick*, free, loosen, slacken, release; *be independent*, go it alone, do one's own thing (*colloq.*), stand on one's own two feet, paddle one's own canoe (*colloq.*); *be irresolute*, waver, vacillate, fluctuate, be in two minds, have second thoughts; *be uncommitted*, sit on the fence (*colloq.*), face both ways, hedge one's bets.

adv. *apart*, asunder.

45 COMBINATION

See also 38 (mixture); 633 (cooperation).

n. *combination*, fusion, blend, alloy, amalgam, mixture, merger, synthesis; *union*, marriage, alliance, association, league, confederation, corporation, combine, cartel, cabal, clique, unholy alliance, conspiracy; *cooperation*, partnership, teamwork, joint

effort, job-sharing, collective, cooperative; *compilation*, anthology, compendium, miscellany; *composition*, collage, jigsaw, mosaic, patchwork; *unification*, integration, incorporation, absorption, assimilation.

adj. *combined*, corporate, joint, allied, united; *cooperative*, communal, collaborative, symbiotic.

vb. *combine*, mix, fuse, alloy, blend, amalgamate, merge; *unify*, lump together, incorporate, synthesize, assemble, marry up, integrate, homogenize; *unite*, ally, associate, band together, join forces, pool one's resources, team up, get together, pair off.

adv. *in addition*, plus, moreover, on top of that; *in league*, in tandem, in cahoots (*colloq.*), in partnership, in the same boat (*colloq.*).

46 DISINTEGRATION

See also 41 (separation); 593 (deterioration).

n. *disintegration*, fragmentation, fission, breakup, collapse; *decomposition*, decay, dilapidation, erosion, corrosion; *dissection*, analysis, breakdown, anatomization; *dispersal*, disbandment, dissolution, atomization, pulverization.

adj. *disintegrated*, fragmented, shattered, broken, brittle, fissile; *soluble*, biodegradable, disposable, recyclable; *decomposed*, decaying, dilapidated, crumbling.

vb. *disintegrate*, fragment, break up, collapse, fall apart, go to pieces (*colloq.*), crack up (*colloq.*); *split*, fracture, crack, splinter, shatter, shiver, smash, explode; *decompose*, decay, erode, corrode, crumble, degenerate; *dissect*, analyse, break down, dismantle, dismember, anatomize, put under the microscope; *disperse*, disband, dissolve, scatter, atomize, pulverize.

adv. *apart*, asunder, into pieces, into smithereens (*colloq.*).

47 WHOLE

See also 29 (greatness); 49 (completeness); 51 (inclusion).

n. *whole*, entity, unit, ensemble, complex, total, sum, aggregate, corpus; *wholeness*, unity, integrity, entirety, completeness, totality, universality, fullness, comprehensiveness; *universe*, world, cosmos, globe, microcosm; *panorama*, survey, overview, bird's eye view, synopsis; *everything*, the lot (*colloq.*), the works (*colloq.*), the whole thing, the whole shooting match (*colloq.*), the whole kit and caboodle (*colloq.*), the whole nine yards (*colloq.*), the full monty

(*colloq.*); *everyone*, Tom, Dick and Harry, all
the world and his wife.

adj. *whole*, entire, complete, full, total,
aggregate, gross; *integral*, organic, intact,
virgin, pristine, flawless, seamless,
unadulterated, undiluted, unabridged,
unedited; *universal*, all-embracing, cosmic,
global, holistic, panoramic, omnibus;
comprehensive, catch-all, sweeping, blanket,
exhaustive, wholesale, outright.

vb. *See* 49 (completeness).

adv. *wholly*, entirely, totally, fully,
unreservedly, body and soul, one hundred
per cent; *outright*, lock, stock and barrel,
hook, line and sinker, in one fell swoop, at a
stroke; *altogether*, all told, in all, as a whole,
en masse.

48 **PART**

See also 50 (incompleteness);
53 (component); 78 (fraction).

n. *part*, bit, portion, segment, section,
sector; *share*, cut, whack (*colloq.*), slice of the
cake, lion's share; *subdivision*, category, class,
branch, offshoot, tributary, feeder,
department, compartment; *component*,
element, ingredient, constituent, factor,
item, detail; *proportion*, percentage, fraction,
minority, majority; *instalment*, issue,
number, volume, partwork, part-payment,
deposit, down payment; *body part*, member,
limb, organ, appendage, trunk, torso; *piece*,
wedge, chunk, slab, hunk, wodge (*colloq.*);
passage, extract, snippet, gobbet, excerpt,
clip; *small piece*, scrap, morsel, shred, crumb,
drop, bite; *fragment*, sliver, shard, splinter,
flake, chip, granule.

adj. *partial*, incomplete, unfinished,
fragmentary, piecemeal; *scrappy*, bitty,
patchy, uneven; *divided*, segmented,
fractional, sectional, departmental,
compartmentalized.

vb. *part*, split, divide, bisect, section,
segment, partition; *subdivide*, branch, ramify,
fork, radiate; *disintegrate*, fragment, disband,
dissolve, break up; *dissect*, take apart,
dismember, dismantle, anatomize,
cannibalize.

adv. *partly*, in part; *partially*, incompletely,
in some degree; *bit by bit*, piecemeal, in dribs
and drabs (*colloq.*), in fits and starts, in
snatches.

49 **COMPLETENESS**

See also 29 (greatness); 47 (whole);
653 (completion).

n. *completeness*, wholeness, entirety,
totality; *fullness*, plenitude, repleteness,
satiety, bellyful (*colloq.*), skinful (*colloq.*);
refill, top-up, finishing/last touch, second
helping; *maximum*, upper limit, ceiling,
summit, acme, crowning glory, ne plus ultra,
culmination, apotheosis, saturation point,
the last straw, clincher (*colloq.*);
comprehensiveness, exhaustiveness,
thoroughness, inclusiveness, A to Z, alpha
and omega, gamut, everything but the
kitchen sink (*colloq.*); *all-rounder*, polymath,
Renaissance man, jack of all trades,
superman, superwoman.

adj. *whole*, entire, total, full-length, full-
time, full-scale, full-blown; *replete*, full, sated,
brim-full, bursting at the seams, jam-packed,
crammed, stuffed, bulging, chock-a-block
(*colloq.*); *comprehensive*, exhaustive, inclusive,
all-embracing, in-depth, encyclopedic, all-
round, wide-ranging; *absolute*, utter,
thoroughgoing, radical, wholesale,
unmitigated, unqualified, unstinting, wholehearted, unreserved, downright, out-and-out;
sheer, pure, arrant, rank, gross, regular, arch,
dyed-in-the-wool.

vb. *complete*, finish off, follow up/through,
round off, put the finishing touches to,
perfect, clinch (*colloq.*), set the seal on,
dispatch, polish off, mop up; *sate*, satisfy,
gorge, stuff, cram, pack, fill; *replenish*, refill,
top up; *saturate*, swamp, drown, overrun,
overwhelm; *do* one's *utmost*, go all out, go
the whole hog (*colloq.*), go for broke (*colloq.*),
pull out all the stops, leave no stone
unturned.

adv. *completely*, fully, thoroughly, to the
hilt, to the top of one's bent, body and soul,
down to the ground; *entirely*, root and
branch, hook, line and sinker, lock, stock
and barrel; *absolutely*, unreservedly,
wholeheartedly, head and shoulders; *utterly*,
wholly, downright, thoroughly, plain, clean,
stark, to the core, through and through; *all
over*, high and low, far and wide, from top to
toe.

50 **INCOMPLETENESS**

See also 48 (part); 65 (discontinuity);
585 (imperfection); 655 (non-completion).

n. *incompleteness*, inadequacy, deficiency,
defectiveness, scantiness, meagreness;
insufficiency, deficit, shortage, shortfall, short
measure, lack, want, need; *superficiality*,
perfunctoriness, cursoriness, half measures;
immaturity, rawness, callowness, greenness,

crudity; *unevenness*, scrappiness, patchiness, bittiness, sketchiness, loose ends, curate's egg; *outline*, rough copy, rough draft, sketch, jottings, notes; *gap*, break, breach, hiatus, hole, flaw, omission, lacuna, missing link.

adj. *incomplete*, insufficient, scanty, meagre, underweight, under strength; *inadequate*, deficient, defective, wanting, lacking, missing; *superficial*, perfunctory, cursory, cosmetic; *immature*, raw, green, callow, ill-digested, half-baked (*colloq.*); *uneven*, patchy, scrappy, bitty, sketchy, fragmentary; *provisional*, temporary, makeshift, crude, rough and ready; *unfinished*, half-finished, unpolished, ragged, rough-hewn, uncut, unrefined, coarse.

vb. *be incomplete*, lack, need, want, miss, fall short, leave something to be desired, not come up to scratch, not make the grade; *not complete*, skimp, scamp, bodge, patch up, paper over the cracks; *interrupt*, leave off, break off, leave hanging; *omit*, skip, jump, miss out, skate over.

adv. *incompletely*, partially, nearly, almost, all but, virtually; *in preparation*, under way, nearing completion, on the stocks.

51 INCLUSION
See also 47 (whole); 69 (generality).

n. *inclusion*, incorporation, integration, assimilation, absorption; *inclusiveness*, comprehensiveness, encyclopedicity, blanket coverage, catch-all, package deal; *universality*, catholicity, eclecticness, ecumenism, broad church, something for everyone; *admission*, membership, admissibility, eligibility.

adj. *including*, comprising, containing, consisting of; *inclusive*, all-in, all-embracing, comprehensive, overall; *universal*, catholic, eclectic, broad-based.

vb. *include*, comprise, subsume, contain, comprehend; *incorporate*, encapsulate, cover, assimilate, encompass, embrace; *admit*, accommodate, receive, number among, count in.

adv. *inclusive*, across the board, from A to Z.

52 EXCLUSION
See also 790 (unsociability).

n. *exclusion*, expulsion, eviction, rejection, banishment, exile, extradition, deportation, excommunication; *prohibition*, ban, embargo, boycott, blockade; *segregation*, colour bar, apartheid, quarantine, ostracism; *barrier*, barricade, closed door, lockout, partition,

peace wall, the Iron Curtain, the Bamboo Curtain, the Berlin Wall, no-man's-land, demilitarized zone, exclusion zone, no-go area; *exclusiveness*, cliquishness, clannishness, freemasonry; *clique*, coterie, in-group, clan, inner circle, elect; *monopoly*, cartel, closed shop, restrictive practices.

adj. *excluding*, debarring, prohibitive, restrictive, monopolistic, protectionist; *exclusive*, clannish, cliquey, snobbish, up-market; *excluded*, inadmissible, struck off, disallowed, debarred.

vb. *exclude*, evict, expel, deport, reject, banish, exile, extradite, outlaw, excommunicate; *prohibit*, ban, boycott, blockade, black, blacklist, blackball; *segregate*, quarantine, demarcate, cordon off, lock out, ostracize, send to Coventry, cold-shoulder (*colloq.*); *except*, omit, pass over, count out, leave out, rule out of court; *prevent*, preclude, forestall, obviate; *monopolize*, corner, hog (*colloq.*), bag (*colloq.*).

adv. *excluding*, barring, excepting, save; *out of the running*, out of the reckoning.

53 COMPONENT
See also 48 (part).

n. *component*, part, piece, element, ingredient, constituent; *unit*, module, building block, Lego (*tdmk*), Meccano (*tdmk*); *attachment*, fixture, accessory, spare part; *member*, associate, colleague, cog in the wheel, organization man, party hack, apparatchik; *machinery*, works, innards, insides, guts.

adj. *component*, constituent, essential, intrinsic, inherent; *integral*, fitted, built-in, modular; *associate*.

vb. *compose*, comprise, make up, constitute; *belong to*, inhere, reside in, consist in, be part and parcel of; *construct*, assemble, compile, fashion, knock together (*colloq.*).

54 FOREIGN BODY
See also 6 (extraneousness); 331 (nationality).

n. *foreign body*, extraneous element, reject, discard, spanner in the works; *foreignness*, ethnicity, alienness, extraneousness, undesirability, superfluousness, irrelevance; *foreigner*, barbarian, alien, refugee, (illegal) immigrant, asylum-seeker, economic migrant, stranger, incomer, new face, expatriate, colonial, guest worker; *intruder*, interloper, trespasser, squatter, gatecrasher, cuckoo in the nest; *misfit*, outsider, black sheep, fish out of water, pariah, leper;

extraterrestrial, alien, Martian, little green men; *abroad*, overseas, foreign parts, exotica.

adj. *foreign*, alien, extraneous, superfluous, irrelevant, unwanted, undesirable; *strange*, exotic, outlandish, imported, borrowed, ethnic; *extraterrestrial*, alien, space-age, futuristic.

vb. *be foreign*, be out of one's element, stick out like a sore thumb (*colloq.*); *introduce*, borrow, import, naturalize, assimilate; *intrude*, trespass, squat, gatecrash.

adv. *abroad*, overseas.

55 ORDER
See also 57 (arrangement);
64 (consecutiveness); 68 (class).

n. *order*, arrangement, array, disposition, layout; *orderliness*, tidiness, neatness, apple-pie order, alignment; *system*, method, organization, routine, pattern, coordination, regularity, uniformity, coherence; *harmony*, quiet, peace, calm, law and order, rule of law, discipline, stability; *rank*, series, hierarchy, gradation, ascending/descending order, pecking order.

adj. *orderly*, tidy, neat, (all) shipshape and Bristol fashion, spruce, trim, groomed, dapper, smart, not a hair out of place; *disciplined*, law-abiding, peaceable, docile, well-behaved, obedient; *harmonious*, quiet, peaceful, calm, stable; *serial*, hierarchical, gradational, ordinal; *systematic*, methodical, organized.

vb. *order*, arrange, dispose, deploy, align; *organize*, sort, sift, classify, systematize, rationalize; *tidy*, neaten, smarten up, spruce up, groom, put to rights, lick/knock into shape (*colloq.*), declutter; *restore order*, pacify, discipline, control, police, tighten up on, take in hand; *be in order*, function, work, go like clockwork.

adv. *in order*, OK, all present and correct, under control; *methodically*, systematically, step by step.

56 DISORDER
See also 58 (disturbance).

n. *disorder*, disarray, untidiness, unkemptness, scruffiness, neglect; *confusion*, muddle, welter, jumble, mix-up, mess, cock-up (*colloq.*), balls-up (*vulg.*); *litter*, clutter, shambles, pigsty, midden, dump (*colloq.*), tip (*colloq.*); *tangle*, snarl, web, warren, jungle, maze, labyrinth; *commotion*, uproar, to-do, trouble, hubbub, hullabaloo, bedlam, babel, pandemonium; *tumult*, turmoil, turbulence,

chaos, upheaval, ferment, free-for-all, fracas, melee, rumpus, roughhouse, brawl, punch-up (*colloq.*), dust-up (*colloq.*), aggro (*colloq.*), breach of the peace, affray, disturbance, riot, anarchy, mob rule.

adj. *disordered*, untidy, unkempt, scruffy, dishevelled, bedraggled, tousled, windswept; *confused*, muddle-headed, incoherent, featherbrained, scatterbrained, disorganized; *careless*, slipshod, neglectful, messy, sloppy, shambolic (*colloq.*); *intricate*, complex, involved, tangled, convoluted, labyrinthine; *random*, desultory, haphazard, rambling, wandering; *turbulent*, tumultuous, chaotic, hell-raising, riotous, disorderly, wild, unruly, undisciplined, harum-scarum, lawless, anarchic.

vb. *make disordered*, untidy, rumple, ruffle, dishevel, bedraggle, tousle; *disorganize*, upset, disperse, throw into disarray, randomize, shuffle, scatter; *confuse*, muddle, botch, mess up, foul up, cock up (*colloq.*), balls up (*vulg.*); *complicate*, entangle, embroil, ensnare; *be disorderly*, riot, rampage, storm, mob, run wild/amuck, get out of hand.

adv. *in disorder*, in disarray, pell-mell, haywire, higgledy-piggledy (*colloq.*), all anyhow, upside down, topsy turvy, arsy versy (*colloq.*); *confusedly*, at sixes and sevens, at cross-purposes; *out of order*, off the rails, kaput, on the blink (*colloq.*).

57 ARRANGEMENT
See also 55 (order); 60 (sequence); 76 (list);
559 (preparation).

n. *arrangement*, order, disposition, layout, line-up (*colloq.*), distribution, composition, organization, structure; *classification*, categorization, listing, hierarchy, taxonomy, paradigm, pattern, system; *catalogue*, directory, list, table, index, inventory, checklist, register, file, slot, niche, pigeonhole; *chart*, diagram, schema, programme, agenda, timetable, schedule, graph, flow chart, critical path.

adj. *arranged*, ordered, classified, graded, sorted; *schematic*, diagrammatic, tabular, paradigmatic; *systematic*, methodical, organizational.

vb. *arrange*, order, dispose, array, marshal, group, deploy, distribute, sort, label, rank, range, grade, size, alphabetize; *catalogue*, tabulate, programme, index, timetable, schedule, cross-refer, file, pigeonhole, compartmentalize.

adv. *in place*, in line, in order.

58 DISTURBANCE

See also 56 (disorder); 161 (displacement);
447 (insanity).

n. *disturbance*, displacement, dislocation,
dislodgement, derailment, disorientation,
dispersion; *upset*, upheaval, convulsion,
perturbation, agitation; *interference*,
interruption, perversion, subversion,
agitprop, sabotage; *derangement*, madness,
insanity, a screw loose (*colloq.*).

adj. *disturbed*, displaced, dislocated,
disorientated, dispersed; *upset*, perturbed,
agitated, confused, disconcerted; *deranged*,
mad, unhinged, unbalanced, insane.

vb. *disturb*, displace, dislocate, dislodge,
derail, unseat, disorientate, throw off course;
upset, agitate, discompose, disconcert,
perturb, ruffle, fluster, put off one's stride/
stroke; *disperse*, scatter, shuffle, jumble,
randomize; *interfere*, interrupt, pervert,
subvert, sabotage, throw out of joint, throw a
spanner in the works; *derange*, unhinge,
unbalance, drive insane, drive round the
bend/up the wall (*colloq.*).

adv. *on the wrong track*, off the rails, off
course; *out of gear*, out of joint, out of place.

59 PRECEDENCE

See also 61 (beginning); 99 (priority).

n. *precedence*, antecedence, ancestry,
pedigree, primogeniture; *priority*, pride of
place, head start, initiative, first come, first
served, front of the queue, forefront, avant-
garde, vanguard; *forerunner*, eldest, firstborn,
ancestor, precursor, senior, predecessor;
guide, scout, outrider, pilot, beacon,
harbinger, messenger, pioneer, trail-blazer,
pathfinder, trendsetter; *precedent*, antecedent,
example, sample, preview, foretaste, forecast,
prognosis, trailer, prequel; *introduction*,
initiation, inauguration, baptism of fire,
christening; *preliminary*, preface, prologue,
foreword, frontispiece, prelude, preamble,
overture, curtain-raiser, aperitif, starter,
appetizer.

adj. *preceding*, antecedent, anterior, prior,
former, previous, foregoing, aforementioned;
leading, foremost, avant-garde, pioneering,
innovative, exploratory; *introductory*, initial,
preliminary, prefatory, initiatory, inaugural,
baptismal; *elder*, senior, superior.

vb. *precede*, antedate, predate, anticipate,
preempt, preclude, forestall; *lead*, go before,
front, head, spearhead, pioneer, explore,
blaze a trail; *announce*, herald, forecast,
presage, foretell, usher in, advertise, trail

(*colloq.*); *introduce*, preface, initiate, baptize,
christen, inaugurate, blood.

adv. *first*, above all, first and foremost;
ahead, in front, up-front (*colloq.*); *in advance*,
previously, beforehand.

60 SEQUENCE

See also 37 (remainder); 64 (consecutiveness);
100 (succession).

n. *sequence*, series, succession, chain,
string, progression; *programme*, agenda,
timetable, schedule, flow chart, critical path,
timeline; *posterity*, line, lineage, issue,
progeny, offspring; *consequence*, effect, end
result, outcome, upshot, legacy, by-product,
spin-off, aftereffect, aftermath, sequel,
hangover (*colloq.*), fallout; *appendage*, follow-
up, tailpiece, epilogue, afterword, postscript,
coda, afterthought, supplement, post
mortem, dessert, afters (*colloq.*); *rear*,
posterior, train, trail, wake, tail; *rearguard*,
runner-up, straggler, sweeper, tail-end
Charlie (*colloq.*), last man in, booby prize,
wooden spoon.

adj. *sequential*, successive, consecutive,
serial; *succeeding*, following, subsequent,
next, later, resulting, ensuing; *rear*, posterior,
hindmost.

vb. *succeed*, come after, follow, come in
the wake of, follow in the footsteps of, step
into sb's shoes, tread on sb's heels, supplant,
supersede; *pursue*, tail, trail, shadow, dog sb's
footsteps; *result*, ensue, turn out, come to
pass; *come last*, bring up the rear, lag, dawdle.

adv. *in succession*, in turn, one after the
other, back to back (*colloq.*); *in sequence*, in
order; *next*, then, afterwards, subsequently; *in
consequence*, as a result, therefore; *behind*, in
sb's wake/train.

61 BEGINNING

See also 59 (precedence); 132 (cause).

n. *beginning*, start, commencement, onset;
foundation, inception, inauguration,
instigation, institution; *initiation*,
christening, baptism, honeymoon, debut,
first night, premiere, maiden speech, maiden
voyage, launch, housewarming, send-off;
starting-point, outset, first base, first lap, first
round, qualifier, square one, zero, alpha,
kick-off (*colloq.*); *introduction*, opening
gambit, preliminaries, lead-in, foreword,
preface; *preparation*, rudiments, first
principles, groundwork, spadework (*colloq.*),
trial run, teething troubles, growing pains,
birth pangs; *origin*, birth, infancy, dawn,

morning, cradle, genesis, the Big Bang; *germ*, seed, bud, embryo, nucleus, primordial soup; *beginner*, apprentice, learner, novice, tyro, probationer, new boy.

adj. *beginning*, primary, initial, first; *primal*, primordial, primeval, aboriginal; *introductory*, preliminary, prefatory, initiatory, preparatory, inaugural, baptismal; *fundamental*, rudimentary, elementary, basic; *infant*, embryonic, budding, incipient, nascent.

vb. *begin*, start, commence, make a start, set about, get under way, set in motion, tackle, broach; *set out*, kick off (*colloq.*), set the ball rolling, blast off, fire away, take the plunge, break the ice, pull one's finger out (*colloq.*), get weaving/cracking (*colloq.*), clock in; *initiate*, inaugurate, instigate, found, institute, launch, christen, baptize, be in on the ground floor; *originate*, generate, provoke, prompt, sow the seeds of, trigger off, spark off; *pioneer*, explore, embark on, break new ground, blaze a trail; *arise*, appear, emerge, see the light of day, spring up, crop up; *recommence*, resume, make a fresh start, go back to square one, go back to the drawing board.

adv. *from the beginning*, ab ovo, from scratch (*colloq.*), from the word go (*colloq.*); *in the beginning*, at first, at the outset, initially, early on, to begin with; *in the first place*, firstly, for a start, for a kick-off (*colloq.*).

62 **END**

See also 60 (sequence); 133 (effect); 323 (death).

n. *end*, cessation, termination, completion, conclusion, end result, payoff, expiry; *ending*, final, finale, death, demise, last words, last gasp, swansong; *end point*, terminus, goal, omega, last lap, last round, home stretch, end of the road; *extremity*, boundary, limit, peak, summit; *finality*, final offer, ultimatum, deadline, last orders, time up, closing time, close of play, closedown, adjournment, dissolution, the Big Crunch; *climax*, resolution, denouement, death blow, coup de grâce, clincher (*colloq.*); *the last judgement*, the last trump, doomsday, apocalypse, the twilight of the gods, holocaust.

adj. *final*, last, terminal, ultimate, concluding; *rear*, back, hindmost, posterior; *finished*, ended, over and done with, played out, kaput (*colloq.*), clapped out (*colloq.*), washed up (*colloq.*); *apocalyptic*, eschatological.

vb. *end*, finish, cease, stop, terminate, conclude, close down, ring down the curtain, shut up shop, sign off, clock off, call it a day; *come to an end*, die, expire, run one's course, run out of time, fade out, peter out, fizzle out (*colloq.*), tail off; *bring to an end*, conclude, terminate, discontinue, dispose of, drop, write off, wash one's hands of, wind up (*colloq.*), wrap up (*colloq.*); *complete*, finish off, round off.

adv. *in the end*, finally, at last, at the end of the day, in the final analysis, in the long run, when the chips are down (*colloq.*); *once and for all*, for good, forever, conclusively, definitively.

63 **MIDDLE**

See also 27 (average).

n. *middle*, midst, centre, thick, heart, core, kernel, marrow, focus, hub, nucleus, pivot, fulcrum; *midpoint*, midway, midweek, midsummer, midwinter, midstream, middle distance, equator, midriff, middle age, midlife crisis, halfway house; *average*, mean, median, happy medium; *mediation*, intervention, arbitration, compromise, no-man's-land, middle ground, grey area, borderline case; *intermediary*, middleman, agent, broker, mediator, go-between, buffer, arbitrator, third force, pig-in-the-middle (*colloq.*).

adj. *middle*, central, mid, medial, median, interim, equidistant; *mean*, average, middle-of-the-road; *intermediate*, neutral, halfway, grey, indeterminate.

vb. *straddle*, lie betwixt and between, hold the centre, occupy the middle ground; *compromise*, meet sb halfway, steer a middle course, fall between two stools, be neither fish nor fowl; *intervene*, mediate, come between; *split down the middle*, halve, divide fifty-fifty, bisect.

adv. *midway*, halfway; *amidst*, among; *in between*, between Scylla and Charybdis, between the devil and the deep blue sea.

64 **CONSECUTIVENESS**

See also 55 (order); 60 (sequence).

n. *consecutiveness*, sequence, succession, causality, cause and effect, domino theory, knock-on effect, repercussion; *continuity*, stability, routine, flow, trend, run; *series*, string, chain, ladder, suite, scale, arpeggio, spectrum, hierarchy, colonnade, dynasty, line, family tree; *one of a series*, instalment, row, tier, storey, echelon, rank, course;

continuum, assembly line, conveyor belt, treadmill, endless band, Mobius strip, vicious circle; *procession*, column, cortege, train, caravan, queue, crocodile, tailback.

adj. *consecutive*, successive, following, serial; *continuous*, perpetual, endless, non-stop, unbroken, seamless, running, ongoing; *progressive*, linear, gradual.

vb. *be consecutive*, succeed, run on, follow on, overlap; *continue*, extend, run, flow, persist, endure; *arrange in succession*, range, rank, line up, stagger.

adv. *consecutively*, successively, one after another, back to back (*colloq.*), in succession, in turn; *continuously*, non-stop, day in, day out, round the clock, twenty-four hours a day, 24/7, on the trot (*colloq.*); *end to end*, nose to tail, bumper to bumper.

65 **DISCONTINUITY**

See also 50 (incompleteness).

n. *discontinuity*, disconnectedness, disjointedness, alternation, unevenness, sporadicness, jerkiness; *disruption*, break, gap, breach, interval, caesura, hiatus, pause, stopover, time lag, time warp, missing link, non sequitur, anacoluthon; *interruption*, digression, parenthesis, interjection, interpolation; *irregularity*, collage, patchwork, crazy paving.

adj. *discontinuous*, discrete, broken, uneven, distinct; *disconnected*, disjointed, fitful, jerky, spasmodic, sporadic, episodic; *intermittent*, desultory, irregular, alternate, periodic, stop-go, on-off; *digressive*, parenthetical, interjectional.

vb. *discontinue*, suspend, terminate, interrupt; *break off*, leave off, stop off/over, digress, pause, take time out (*colloq.*); *interject*, interpose, intervene, cut in, butt in, chip in, put one's oar in; *omit*, miss out, jump, skip, leapfrog (*colloq.*); *alternate*, oscillate, fluctuate, blow hot and cold (*colloq.*).

adv. *discontinuously*, periodically, now and then, occasionally, off and on, at intervals; *by degrees*, by fits and starts, in dribs and drabs (*colloq.*); *off-line*.

66 **ASSEMBLY**

See also 40 (union).

n. *assembly*, meeting, rally, convention, conference, company, congregation, caucus, party, rendezvous, tryst, get-together (*colloq.*); *collection*, compilation, compendium, anthology, roundup (*colloq.*); *group*, band, troupe, collective, syndicate, union, guild, team, stable, string, squad, crew, posse, force, regiment; *social group*, circle, family, clan, tribe, peer group, age group, generation, clique, coterie, mafia; *crowd*, throng, mob, press, huddle, scrum, crush, swarm, bevy, gang; *multitude*, host, galaxy, constellation, storm, shower, hail, volley, deluge, spate, flood, slew (*colloq.*), raft (*colloq.*); *bunch*, bouquet, spray, knot, clump, cluster, bundle, parcel, bale, roll, bolt, skein, hank, truss, sheaf, conglomeration, heap, pile, mass; *flock*, herd, shoal, pack, drove, brood, school, clutch, litter, covey (partridges), flight/gaggle/skein (geese), pride (lions), leap (leopards), kindle (kittens), skulk (foxes), charm (goldfinches), exaltation (larks).

adj. *assembled*, gathered, congregated; *crowded*, congested, packed, teeming, milling, seething, crawling (*colloq.*); *converging*, centripetal.

vb. *assemble*, collect, forgather, meet, unite, congregate, get together, rendezvous, fall in, join forces, team up, band together, gang up; *crowd*, flock, mass, mill, seethe, swarm, teem, pack, huddle, throng; *bring together*, summon, convoke, convene, rally, mobilize, herd, muster, shepherd, round up; *bunch*, bundle, parcel, package, clump, knot, cluster, bind, truss; *accumulate*, amass, agglomerate, stack, heap, pile; *compress*, cram, crush, squash, stuff, squeeze.

adv. *collectively*, all together, as one, in a body, en masse.

67 **DISPERSION**

See also 41 (separation).

n. *dispersion*, diffusion, dissemination, propagation, distribution, spread; *disbandment*, dissolution, breakup, demobilization, decentralization; *divergence*, branching, radiation, ramification; *emigration*, exodus, diaspora, population drift, overspill, new town, suburbia, urban sprawl, ribbon development.

adj. *dispersed*, scattered, far-flung, widespread; *sparse*, strung out, dotted about, sporadic, few and far between, thin on the ground; *loose*, stray, straggling, wandering, sprawling; *divergent*, branching, radiating, centrifugal.

vb. *disperse*, diffuse, spread, disseminate, propagate, broadcast, distribute; *disband*, disintegrate, dissolve, break up, fall out, demobilize, decentralize; *scatter*, strew, sprinkle, litter, spatter; *emigrate*, wander, drift, stray, straggle, sprawl; *diverge*, branch, radiate, ramify, fan out, hive off.

adv. *here and there*, round and about; *in all directions*, to the four winds, to the four corners of the earth.

68 CLASS
See also 55 (order).

n. *class*, category, variety, kind, sort, strain, brand, make, marque; *division*, group, species, genus, order, phylum; *type*, manner, stamp, mould, stripe, breed, race, tribe, ilk, kidney, cast, colour, complexion, hue; *classification*, rank, order, system, hierarchy, taxonomy.

adj. *classificatory*, hierarchical, taxonomic; *typical*, representative, generic, stereotypical.

vb. *class*, group, divide, sort, grade, range, rank; *classify*, typify, categorize, identify, label, brand, stamp.

69 GENERALITY
See also 27 (average); 51 (inclusion).

n. *generality*, universality, comprehensiveness, inclusiveness, catholicity, ecumenicalism, broad church, eclecticism, cosmopolitanism; *non-specificness*, broad canvas, broad spectrum, blanket coverage, catch-all, dragnet, grapeshot, panacea, cure-all, open house, open meeting, open letter, circular, something for everyone; *average*, ordinariness, common run, lowest common denominator; *everyman*, the man in the street, the man on the Clapham omnibus, Joe Bloggs, Tom, Dick and Harry, every man Jack; *common people*, the general public, the masses, admass, grassroots, vox populi.

adj. *general*, non-specific, generic, representative, typical, standard; *universal*, comprehensive, all-inclusive, blanket, across-the-board; *common*, ordinary, popular, middlebrow, vernacular, vulgar, down-market; *prevalent*, widespread, ubiquitous, worldwide, global, endemic; *multipurpose*, versatile, adaptable.

vb. *generalize*, spread, broaden, widen, popularize, vulgarize, broadcast, disseminate; *prevail*, obtain, predominate.

adv. *generally*, in general, as a rule, by and large, in the main, broadly speaking, typically.

70 SPECIALITY
See also 22 (originality); 79 (one).

n. *speciality*, individuality, originality,

uniqueness, particularity, singularity, distinctiveness, specificity; *feature*, attribute, trait, peculiarity, characteristic, quirk, idiosyncrasy, hallmark, trademark; *particulars*, specifications, details, minutiae, ins and outs (*colloq.*); *exception*, special case, one-off, nonce word, rara avis; *subjectivity*, individualism, egoism, self, number one, numero uno (*colloq.*), ego-trip (*colloq.*), solipsism, me generation.

adj. *special*, particular, peculiar, specific, unique, singular, distinctive, original, individual; *characteristic*, idiomatic, peculiar, typical, personal, idiosyncratic, quirky, eccentric; *exceptional*, one-off, unique, sui generis, inimitable, esoteric, way-out (*colloq.*); *exclusive*, bespoke, made-to-order, made-to-measure, custom-made, personalized, own-brand; *subjective*, individualistic, self-centred, egotistical, solipsistic.

vb. *specify*, enumerate, list, detail, itemize, spell out; *particularize*, cite, mention, quote, name names; *isolate*, distinguish, individuate, pick out, single out, highlight, pinpoint, put one's finger on (*colloq.*); *stand out*, shine, excel, be in a class of one's own, be out of the ordinary, be off the beaten track.

adv. *especially*, in particular, above all; *specifically*, namely, respectively; *personally*, ad hominem.

71 RULE
See also 549 (habit); 657 (authority); 852 (legality).

n. *rule*, regulation, ruling, standing order, injunction, law, degree, edict, statute, by-law; *code*, canon, rulebook, charter, statute book, constitution; *precept*, guideline, criterion, standard, benchmark, litmus test, principle, tenet, prescription, precedent; *procedure*, system, method, practice, drill, routine, form.

adj. *regulatory*, normative, prescriptive; *legal*, compulsory, obligatory, de rigueur, statutory, mandatory; *standard*, normal, conventional, orthodox, canonical; *procedural*, routine, formulaic, copybook.

vb. *rule*, prescribe, ordain, decree, lay down the law; *regulate*, standardize, normalize, bring into line, regularize; *obey orders*, stick to the rules, keep to the straight and narrow, keep one's nose clean (*colloq.*), toe the line (*colloq.*), work to rule, mind one's Ps and Qs.

adv. *according to the rules*, by the book.

72 **CONFORMITY**

See also 15 (uniformity); 549 (habit).

n. *conformity*, agreement, harmony, consistency, compatibility; *usage*, convention, orthodoxy, conservatism, traditionalism, Babbitry, conventional wisdom, the done thing, the order of the day, received idea, party line; *assimilation*, absorption, levelling, acclimatization, adaptation, indoctrination, re-education, rehabilitation; *pattern*, mould, stereotype, matrix; *conformist*, traditionalist, silent majority, herd, sheep, copycat, running dog, yes-man, company man, timeserver, party hack, apparatchik.

adj. *conformist*, conventional, orthodox, conservative, law-abiding, traditionalist, bourgeois; *consistent*, compatible, harmonious, consonant; *typical*, stock, standard, identikit, average, common or garden, unexceptional; *adaptable*, flexible, malleable, compliant, pliable.

vb. *conform*, accord, agree, correspond, match, tally, run true to form; *make conform*, standardize, stereotype, process, assimilate, bring into line, adapt, adjust, mould; *indoctrinate*, brainwash, re-educate, rehabilitate; *follow suit*, fall into line, follow the crowd, keep up appearances, keep up with the Joneses, climb/jump on the bandwagon, swim with the tide.

adv. *in place*, in keeping, in line.

73 **NONCONFORMITY**

See also 20 (disparity).

n. *nonconformity*, disparity, disagreement, inconsistency, incompatibility, incongruity, contrast; *nonconformism*, unorthodoxy, heresy, schism, iconoclasm, revolt, dissent, protest, deviationism; *unconventionality*, eccentricity, oddity, rarity, singularity; *nonconformist*, maverick, renegade, lone wolf, outsider, outlaw, outcast, pariah, blackleg, scab, marginal, lunatic fringe; *rebel*, Bohemian, hippie, dropout, angry young man, dissident, young Turk, radical, freethinker, iconoclast, heretic; *exception*, anomaly, aberration, abnormality, special case, odd man out; *eccentric*, character, card (*colloq.*), weirdo (*colloq.*), oddball, freak, misfit, deviant; *homosexual*, gay, lesbian, dyke (*colloq.*), queer (*colloq.*), poof (*colloq.*), poofter (*colloq.*), woofter (*colloq.*), pansy (*colloq.*), fairy (*colloq.*), bisexual, transvestite, crossdresser, transsexual, hermaphrodite.

adj. *nonconformist*, inconsistent, incompatible, incongruous, contrasting; *unorthodox*, independent, freethinking, radical, iconoclastic, heretical; *rebellious*, Bohemian, boho (*colloq.*), dissident, deviationist; *eccentric*, unconventional, odd, rare, unusual, exotic, out-of-the-ordinary, fringe, outlandish, offbeat (*colloq.*), wayout (*colloq.*), weird; *exceptional*, anomalous, aberrant, abnormal, deviant; *homosexual*, gay, lesbian, queer (*colloq.*), bent (*colloq.*), bisexual, LGBT, AC/DC (*colloq.*).

vb. *not conform*, diverge, dissent, protest, rebel, kick over the traces, rock the boat (*colloq.*); *be independent*, deviate, break ranks, step out of line, go one's own way, do one's own thing (*colloq.*), break the mould, drop out (*colloq.*).

adv. *out of step*, out of keeping, out of line, out on a limb; *out of the way*, out of the common run, off the beaten track.

74 **NUMBER**

See also 75 (calculation).

n. *number*, numeral, digit, figure, integer, character, cipher, decimal; *sum*, total, aggregate, remainder; *factor*, multiple, quotient, product, function, variable, expression, coefficient, formula; *fraction*, numerator, denominator, vulgar fraction, common fraction; *power*, exponent, root, square, logarithm, mantissa.

adj. *numerical*, digital, prime, whole, real, even, odd, cardinal, ordinal, binary, decimal.

vb. *number*, enumerate, count, tell, reckon, tick off (*colloq.*); *amount to*, total, come to, make, notch up (*colloq.*).

75 **CALCULATION**

See also 74 (number); 570 (store).

n. *calculation*, estimation, computation, numeration, addition, subtraction, multiplication, division; *count*, score, tally, census, poll, head-count, stocktaking, roll call; *mathematics*, arithmetic, calculus, algebra, geometry, trigonometry, statistics; *data processing*, computing, number-crunching (*colloq.*), information retrieval, informatics, information technology, IT, software engineering; *cybernetics*, artificial intelligence, AI, robotics; *computer*, mainframe, microcomputer, minicomputer, personal/desktop computer, laptop, palmtop, notebook, notepad, microprocessor, chip, circuit, hardware, visual display unit, printout, core, memory, floppy disk, software, program, machine code, machine language, computer language, programming language; *abacus*, ready reckoner, slide rule, calculator; *numerator*, mathematician, accountant, actuary, teller, statistician, programmer, systems analyst, liveware.

adj. *computational*, actuarial, mathematical, arithmetical, statistical, geometric, algebraic.

vb. *calculate*, estimate, compute, add, subtract, multiply, divide, square, cube; *automate*, computerize, process, input, throughput, program.

76 **LIST**

See also 57 (arrangement).

n. *list*, record, register, table, file, listing; *index*, catalogue, directory, inventory, checklist, bibliography, filmography, discography; *agenda*, programme, timetable, schedule, bill of fare, table of contents, prospectus; *vocabulary*, glossary, lexicon, dictionary, thesaurus, gazetteer, almanac, yearbook; *roll*, roster, rota, short list, waiting list, blacklist, dramatis personae, credits.

vb. *list*, enter, log, register, record, table, file; *catalogue*, index, inventorize, schedule, timetable, minute; *enrol*, inscribe, enlist, matriculate, sign on.

77 **ZERO**

See also 2 (non-existence).

n. *zero*, nothing, none, naught, nix, nada, zilch (*colloq.*), sweet f.a. (*colloq.*); *nought*, nil, null, love, duck; *nullity*, nothingness, blank, cipher, void.

adj. *zero*, no, nil.

78 **FRACTION**

See also 30 (smallness); 48 (part).

n. *fraction*, part, piece, portion, section, segment, percentage, proportion; *fragment*, particle, atom, iota, scrap, shred, whit, jot; *less than one*, quarter, half, three quarters.

adj. *fractional*, small, tiny, slight, infinitesimal; *partial*, fragmentary, incomplete.

adv. *fractionally*, slightly, marginally, partially.

79 **ONE**

See also 40 (union); 70 (speciality).

n. *one*, ace, unit, entity, individual, atom, monad; *item*, detail, bit, isolated instance; *oneness*, unity, wholeness, integrity, indivisibility, indissolubility; *individualism*,

separatism, isolationism, unilateralism; *solitariness*, isolation, aloneness, solitude, loneliness; *soloist*, one-man band, one-man show, solo effort, monologue, soliloquy; *single person*, spinster, bachelor, bachelor girl, single parent, widow, widower, celibacy, monogamy; *monopoly*, cartel, multinational.

adj. *one*, solo, single, mono, whole, indivisible, indissoluble; *individual*, separatist, isolationist, unilateralist, insular; *solo*, single-handed, alone, isolated, solitary; *single*, unmarried, celibate, monogamous; *unified*, integrated, joined up, linked.

vb. *be one*, stand alone, plough a lonely furrow, stand on one's own two feet, do one's own thing (*colloq.*), paddle one's own canoe (*colloq.*); *become one*, unite, cohere, combine, merge, fuse; *isolate*, single out, specify, prick out.

adv. *one by one*, singly, one at a time; *on one's own*, by oneself, on one's tod (*colloq.*); *solely*, only, merely, simply; *in unison*, as one.

80 **PLURALITY**

See also 86 (multitude).

n. *plurality*, majority, multiple; *variety*, multiplicity, multifariousness, multilateralism, polygamy, polysemy, pluralism; *all-rounder*, polymath, Renaissance man, pluralist.

adj. *plural*, many, numerous, multiple; *various*, divers, sundry, several; *versatile*, multifarious, multipurpose, pluralist, multilateralist, polygamous, polysemous, polytheist.

81 **TWO**

n. *two*, deuce, pair, couple, duo, brace, span, twosome, twins, conjoined/Siamese twins; *double*, couplet, doublet, duet, two-hander, diptych, double-decker, tandem, two-seater, two-wheeler, bicycle, biplane; *duality*, dichotomy, polarity, dualism, bilingualism, bisexuality, ambidexterity, ambiguity, ambivalence, duplicity, double-dealing; *duplication*, doubling, repetition, reproduction; *bisection*, bifurcation, fork, branch, swallowtail; *half*, moiety, hemisphere, semicircle, semitone, semibreve.

adj. *dual*, double, binary, duple, duplex, twofold, double-barrelled, biennial, biannual; *both*, amphibious, ambidextrous, bilingual, bisexual, ambiguous, ambivalent, double-edged, duplicitous, double-dealing, two-faced; *two-way*, dual-purpose, reciprocal, bilateral, bipartite, binaural, split, cloven; *duplicate*, second, repeat, twin.

vb. *double*, duplicate, repeat, copy, mirror, echo, second; *pair*, twin, match, mate; *bisect*, halve, bifurcate, split, cleave; *go halves*, go fifty-fifty; *have it both ways*, have the best of both worlds, have one's cake and eat it (*colloq.*).

adv. *twice*, twofold, as much again, doubly.

82 **THREE**

n. *three*, triad, trio, trinity, triune, threesome, troika, triumvirate; *treble*, triplet, tercet, trilogy, three-decker, three-hander, triangle, triptych, three-wheeler, tricycle, trident, tripod, trimester, hat trick; *third*, tierce, third party, the Third World.

adj. *triple*, ternary, triplex, threefold, triplicate, three-ply, three-dimensional; *three-way*, triangular, trilateral, tripartite; *third*, tertiary.

vb. *triple*, treble, cube, triplicate.

adv. *thrice*, trebly, threefold, in triplicate.

83 **FOUR**

n. *four*, quartet, tetrad, foursome, quaternity, quadriga, four-in-hand, quad bike, four-poster; *quadruplicate*, quadrangle, square, tetrahedron, quadruped, quadruplet, quad, tetralogy, quatrain, tetrameter, four-letter word; *quarter*, fourth, quarterly, quarto, tetrarch.

adj. *quadruple*, quaternary, fourfold; *square*, foursquare, quadrate, quadrilateral, tetrahedral; *quarterly*, quadraphonic, quadrennial.

vb. *quadruple*, quadruplicate, square, quadrate; *quarter*.

adv. *fourfold*; *squarely*, foursquare.

84 **FIVE AND OVER**

n. *five*, quintet, quintuplet, quin, fiver (*colloq.*), pentad, pentagon, pentangle, quincunx, pentameter, Pentateuch, pentathlon; *six*, half a dozen, sextet, sextuplet, sixer, hexad, hexagon, hexameter, sestina, Hexateuch; *seven*, heptad, septet, heptagon, Sabbath, sabbatical, Heptateuch; *eight*, octet, octad, octagon, octave, octoroon, octopus, octavo; *nine*, nonet, nonagon, novena; *ten*, tenner (*colloq.*), decade, decalogue, decagon, decathlon, tenth, decimal, tithe; *eleven*, double figures; *twelve*, dozen, dodecahedron, alexandrine; *thirteen*, baker's dozen, long dozen, teens; *twenty and*

over, score, fifty, quinquagenarian, sixty, sexagenarian, seventy, septuagenarian, eighty, octogenarian, ninety, nonagenarian; *hundred*, centenarian, century, three figures, gross, bicentenary, tercentenary, quadricentennial, quincentenary; *thousand*, K, millennium, grand (*colloq.*); *million*, billion, trillion.

adj. *fifth*, fivefold etc, quintuple, sixth, sextuple, seventh, septuple, eighth, octuple, ninth, nonary, tenth, decimal, twelfth, duodecimal, centennial, millionth, billionth.

vb. *quintuple etc*, multiply; *decimate*, decimalize.

adv. *fivefold* etc, hundredfold.

85 **ACCOMPANIMENT**

See also 35 (addition); 789 (sociability); 793 (friendship).

n. *accompaniment*, coexistence, symbiosis, conjunction, cohabitation, company, society, fellowship, companionship, friendship, togetherness, mateyness (*colloq.*); *companion*, friend, comrade, mate, buddy (*colloq.*), colleague, partner, cohabitee, consort; *escort*, guide, convoy, outrider, attendant, chaperon, bodyguard, minder (*colloq.*); *follower*, dependant, satellite, hanger-on, camp follower; *shadow*, tail, stalker; *concomitant*, attribute, feature, symptom, accessory, appurtenance, appendage, corollary, sine qua non, prerequisite.

adj. *accompanying*, attendant, associated, concomitant, accessory, incidental; *parallel*, simultaneous, contemporaneous, coexistent; *inseparable*, thick as thieves, symbiotic.

vb. *accompany*, escort, guide, convoy, attend, partner, chaperon, squire, mind (*colloq.*); *attach oneself to*, dance attendance on, tag along, string along, dog sb's footsteps, shadow, tail, stalk, track; *belong with*, complement, go together, go hand in hand; *associate*, consort, frequent, hobnob (*colloq.*), socialize, club together, team up, gang up.

adv. *together*, in a body; *in convoy*, in tow, in sb's wake/train, on sb's coat-tails.

86 **MULTITUDE**

See also 29 (greatness); 80 (plurality).

n. *multitude*, multiplicity, infinity, myriad, millions, billions, etc (see 29 Greatness); *host*, army, legion, horde, fleet, swarm, brood, sea, forest, galaxy; *throng*, crowd, masses, mob, press, crush.

adj. *multitudinous*, countless, numberless, innumerable, myriad; *endless*, infinite, boundless, vast, untold, inexhaustible; *numerous*, many, manifold, ample, abundant, profuse, plenty, bumper, umpteen (*colloq.*), galore (*colloq.*); *crowded*, packed, overcrowded, overmanned, overpopulated, high-density, thick on the ground.

vb. *crowd*, throng, flock, troop, pour, flood, stream; *swarm*, crawl, infest, mill, seethe, teem, pullulate, multiply; *overrun*, outnumber, swamp, snow under.

adv. *in droves*, en masse, thick and fast.

87 FEW
See also 30 (smallness).

n. *few*, handful, trickle, sprinkling, minority, low turnout; *scarcity*, paucity, shortage, scantiness; *sparseness*, rarity, infrequency.

adj. *few*, scant, scarce, straggly, wispy, few and far between; *sparse*, infrequent, intermittent, dotted about, strung out, scattered; *underpopulated*, low-density, thin on the ground, understaffed, undermanned.

vb. *scatter*, sprinkle, dot; *thin*, reduce, rarefy, weed out, eliminate, decimate.

adv. *thinly*, in ones and twos, in dribs and drabs (*colloq.*); *seldom*, rarely, infrequently, occasionally.

88 REPETITION
See also 119 (regularity).

n. *repetition*, recapitulation, reiteration, tautology, reproduction, duplication; *renewal*, resumption, reprise, rehearsal, repeat, rerun, (action) replay, Groundhog Day (*colloq.*), reprint, remake, reissue, rehash; *recurrence*, reappearance, renaissance, rebirth, return, cycle, revival, relapse, reversion; *regularity*, rhythm, beat, pulse, rhyme, alliteration, assonance; *refrain*, chorus, encore, repeat performance, second helping; *repetitiveness*, routine, monotony, familiarity, cliché, chestnut (*colloq.*), mantra (*colloq.*), same old story, mixture as before, same song, second verse.

adj. *repetitive*, reiterative, tautological, repetitious; *recurrent*, regular, rhythmical, periodic, cyclical; *monotonous*, routine, familiar, stale, hackneyed, trite.

vb. *repeat*, recapitulate, reiterate, restate, re-emphasize, hammer into, din into, harp, nag; *reproduce*, copy, mirror, duplicate, echo, chorus, parrot; *renew*, resume, revive, reprise, rehearse, rerun, replay, remake, reissue,

reprint, rehash, recycle; *recur*, reappear, return, crop up; *relapse*, regress, revert, retrace one's steps, go back over old ground.

adv. *repeatedly*, again and again, time after time, over and over, ad nauseam; *once more*, da capo.

89 INFINITY
See also 95 (eternity).

n. *infinity*, infinitude, immensity, boundlessness, limitlessness, vastness, abyss; *eternity*, perpetuity, immortality, everlastingness.

adj. *infinite*, boundless, limitless, bottomless, immeasurable, vast, unfathomable, ineffable; *countless*, innumerable, incalculable, numberless, untold; *endless*, indefinite, open-ended, never-ending, interminable, inexhaustible; *eternal*, immortal, perpetual, everlasting.

vb. *be infinite*, know no bounds, go on and on, last forever.

adv. *infinitely*, immeasurably, incalculably, vastly, ineffably; *ad infinitum*, to the nth degree, forever, eternally, perpetually; *indefinitely*, sine die.

90 TIME
See also 92 (period); 97 (timekeeping).

n. *time*, spacetime, duration, continuity; *age*, epoch, aeon, century, lifetime, time immemorial, time out of mind; *period*, span, course, season, spell, phase; *interim*, meanwhile, meantime, interval, interlude, time lag, timewarp; *hour*, zero hour, moment, point in time, local time, time zone, standard time, summertime, man hour, flexitime, overtime.

adj. *temporal*, periodical, seasonal; *continual*, ongoing, present, current, pending.

vb. *pass*, elapse, continue, run, roll, glide; *pause*, take time out, mark time, bide one's time, stand still, tick over, vegetate; *spend*, while away, kill (*colloq.*), waste, idle, fritter, squander.

adv. *meanwhile*, in the meantime, in the interim, for the time being; *at present*, now, currently; *soon*, in time, one fine day; *sometimes*, from time to time, at times; *once*, once upon a time, at one time.

91 TIMELESSNESS
See also 95 (eternity).

n. *timelessness*, eternity, perpetuity,

unchangingness, immutability; *immortality*, agelessness, datelessness, everlastingness.

adj. *timeless*, eternal, perpetual, unchanging, unchangeable, immutable; *immortal*, ageless, dateless, classic, evergreen.

adv. *never*, at no time, not in a month of Sundays, over one's dead body; *indefinitely*, sine die, till the cows come home (*colloq.*).

92 **PERIOD**

See also 90 (time); 120 (irregularity).

n. *period*, season, cycle, span, spell, phase, stint, watch, stretch, bout, round, innings; *time*, breakfast-time, lunchtime, teatime, drive-time; *term*, quarter, trimester, semester; *hour*, lunch hour, witching hour, rush hour, small hours; *day*, weekday, rest day, red-letter day; *week*, fortnight, month, calendar month, lunar month; *year*, twelvemonth, leap year, light-year, solar year; *decade*, century, millennium; *anniversary*, birthday, saint's day, jubilee, centenary, bicentenary, tercentenary; *age*, epoch, generation, aeon.

adj. *periodic*, seasonal, cyclical; *daily*, quotidian, weekly, hebdomadal, fortnightly, monthly, menstrual, quarterly, biannual, yearly, annual, biennial, centennial, perennial.

vb. *be periodic*, recur, come round, go in phases; *alternate*, take one's turn.

adv. *periodically*, from time to time, sometimes, now and then, at times.

93 **DURATION**

See also 95 (eternity); 124 (continuity).

n. duration, continuance, permanence; *long time*, lifetime, ages, month of Sundays (*colloq.*), donkey's years (*colloq.*), yonks (*colloq.*), long haul, marathon; *protraction*, prolongation, filibustering, stonewalling; *durability*, toughness, endurance, stamina, staying power, persistence, survival instinct.

adj. *lasting*, abiding, enduring, continuing, ongoing, permanent, surviving; *long-term*, long-haul, long-standing, lifelong; *protracted*, long-drawn-out, time-consuming, longwinded, interminable; *durable*, tough, long-lasting, imperishable, evergreen, perennial.

vb. *last*, abide, endure, continue, remain, persist; *survive*, outlast, outstay, outlive, have nine lives; *protract*, prolong, spin out, linger, dawdle, take forever, play for time, temporize, filibuster, stonewall.

adv. *for a long time*, at length, for ages; *in the long run*, in the end, at the end of the day.

94 **TRANSIENCE**

See also 130 (changeableness).

n. *transience*, impermanence, evanescence, brevity, instantaneity; *changeability*, volatility, instability, precariousness, fragility, brittleness, perishability; *shooting star*, bubble, spindrift, flare, flicker, shifting sand, nomad, bird of passage, ship that passes in the night, nine days' wonder, flash in the pan (*colloq.*).

adj. *transient*, ephemeral, shortlived, evanescent, passing, fleeting, brief, cursory, momentary, transitory; *temporary*, makeshift, provisional, ad hoc, short-term, impermanent, disposable, throwaway; *changeable*, volatile, mutable, perishable, fragile, brittle; *precarious*, unstable, unsettled, drifting, rootless, nomadic.

vb. *pass*, fade, die, expire, disappear, vanish, melt, evaporate; *flare*, flicker, flash, spurt, explode.

adv. *briefly*, momentarily; *temporarily*, provisionally, for the time being.

95 **ETERNITY**

See also 89 (infinity); 91 (timelessness); 93 (duration).

n. *eternity*, perpetuity, infinity, forever; *timelessness*, agelessness, immortality, imperishability, indestructibility, permanence, endurance.

adj. *eternal*, perpetual, sempiternal, everlasting; *immortal*, deathless, undying, imperishable, indestructible, self-perpetuating; *timeless*, ageless, classic, evergreen; *endless*, ceaseless, never-ending, unremitting, relentless.

vb. *perpetuate*, immortalize; *preserve*, conserve, freeze, embalm, mummify.

adv. *eternally*, for ever, for ever and a day, for good, for keeps (*colloq.*), till doomsday, for good and all; *endlessly*, incessantly, non-stop, relentlessly, around the clock.

96 **IMMEDIACY**

See also 94 (transience); 245 (speed).

n. *immediacy*, instantaneousness, simultaneity, suddenness, abruptness; *promptness*, speediness, alacrity, spontaneity, impulsiveness.

adj. *immediate*, instant, instantaneous, simultaneous; *sudden*, abrupt, spontaneous, impulsive, unpremeditated; *prompt*, punctual, speedy, rapid-fire, staccato.

vb. *act on impulse*, improvise, extemporize, ad lib; *start*, dart, flit, bolt, pelt, flash, dash.

adv. *immediately*, forthwith, pronto (*colloq.*), overnight; *suddenly*, in a flash, on the spur of the moment, at the drop of a hat, off the cuff; *at once*, at a stroke, in one fell swoop; *punctually*, on time, to the second, on the dot (*colloq.*), on the nail.

97 **TIMEKEEPING**
See also 90 (time).

n. *timekeeping*, horology, chronometry, timing, clockwatching; *dateline*, time zone, meridian, daylight saving, local time, standard time; *chronology*, calendar, almanac, agenda, timetable, schedule, timesheet, journal, diary, log(book), chronicle, annals; *timepiece*, chronometer, sundial, waterclock, hourglass, siren, hooter, time signal, gong, chimes, speaking clock, metronome; *clock*, grandfather clock, alarm, repeater, fobwatch, hunter, turnip, wristwatch, digital watch, stopwatch, dial, face, hand, pendulum, escapement, mainspring.

adj. *timekeeping*, chronometrical, horological; *chronological*, temporal, historical.

vb. *record*, chronicle, log, clock up, time, timetable, schedule.

adv. *clockwise*; *around the clock*, twenty-four hours a day; *anticlockwise*, against the clock, out of time.

98 **WRONG TIME**
n. *wrong time*, mistiming, bad timing, untimeliness, wrong moment; *anachronism*, precocity, prematurity, outdatedness, unfashionableness.

adj. *mistimed*, untimely, unseasonable, inopportune; *unpunctual*, late, tardy, dilatory, behindhand, early, previous; *anachronistic*, precocious, premature, overdue, outdated, posthumous, old-fashioned.

vb. *mistime*, bring forward, antedate, jump the gun (*colloq.*); *delay*, retard, postdate, hold up, tarry, be slow off the mark, be behind the times, put the clock back, regress.

adv. *in advance*, prematurely, ahead of time; *belatedly*, tardily, late in the day.

99 **PRIORITY**
See also 59 (precedence).

n. *priority*, anteriority, preexistence, prehistory; *precedence*, primogeniture, antecedence, right of way, early bird, first come, first served; *firstborn*, eldest, antecedent, forbear, precursor; *premonition*,

presentiment, forewarning, briefing, prior notice, foresight.

adj. *prior*, previous, preexisting, anterior, antecedent, earlier, first; *former*, onetime, erstwhile, sometime; *preemptive*, preventive, preventative, anticipatory.

vb. *precede*, predate, preexist, predecease; *foreshadow*, presage, anticipate, forestall, obviate, prevent; *preempt*, preclude, steal a march on, jump the queue, present with a fait accompli.

adv. *before*, beforehand, in advance, previously.

100 **SUCCESSION**
See also 60 (sequence).

n. *succession*, posterity, issue, inheritance, legacy; *aftereffect*, aftermath, fallout, upshot, outcome; *youngest*, junior, benjamin, latecomer; *successor*, heir, descendant, inheritor; *afterthought*, hindsight, second thoughts, post mortem, debriefing.

adj. *successive*, subsequent, following, last, posterior, next, rear; *future*, budding, would-be, elect, designate; *posthumous*.

vb. *succeed*, follow, take over from, inherit the mantle of, step into sb's shoes; *defer*, put off, postpone, postdate.

adv. *after*, afterwards, subsequently, thereafter, thereupon.

101 **PRESENT TIME**
See also 96 (immediacy); 103 (same time); 106 (newness).

n. *present time*, present, simultaneity, contemporaneousness, present day, the here and now, modern times; *contemporary*, one's generation, age group, peer group; *topicality*, currency, current affairs, news; *present event*, happening, occurrence, incident, episode, development, affair, matter, concern, transaction; *crisis*, turn of events, emergency, chapter of accidents, vicissitudes, ups and downs (*colloq.*).

adj. *present*, existing, extant, ongoing, actual, current, contemporaneous, simultaneous, live; *present-day*, contemporary, modern, up-to-date, topical, latest, up-to-the-minute, now (*colloq.*), du jour; *temporary*, provisional, ad hoc, makeshift, stopgap.

vb. *be present*, be in the air, be in the wind; *exist*, live from hand to mouth, live for the present; *attend*, show up, put in an appearance, turn up; *take place*, happen, occur, come about, coincide, arise, spring up, crop up (*colloq.*), transpire, supervene; *experience*, encounter, undergo, go through.

adv. *at present*, at the moment, today, nowadays, these days, in this day and age; *now*, now or never, immediately, instantly, on the spot; *until now*, hitherto, to date; *for the present*, for the time being, temporarily, provisionally.

102 DIFFERENT TIME
See also 98 (wrong time).

n. *different time*, another time, alternative date; *past*, days gone by, better days; *future*, days to come, distant future.

adj. *out-of-date*, anachronistic, behind the times, overdue, advanced, futuristic.

adv. *not now*, later, some time, one of these days, one fine day, sooner or later; *then*, earlier, previously, at one time; *out of step*, out of phase, out of sync.

103 SAME TIME
See also 101 (present time).

n. *same time*, synchronism, coexistence, coincidence, simultaneity, clash, concurrence, contemporaneousness, unison, chorus; *same age*, vintage, generation, peer group, age group, contemporary, coeval; *synchronization*, sync, meridian, time zone, dead heat, photo finish.

adj. *synchronous*, synchronic, simultaneous, contemporaneous, concurrent, coexistent, coincidental; *contemporary*, coeval, isochronous.

vb. *synchronize*, tune, phase, align; *coincide*, come together, clash, double-book; *chorus*, chime, chant; *keep up*, keep abreast, keep in step.

adv. *at the same time*, simultaneously, concurrently, in the same breath; *in step*, in phase, in sync, in concert, in unison.

104 FUTURE TIME
See also 100 (succession); 450 (expectation).

n. *future time*, futurity, tomorrow, morrow, time to come; *future*, prospect, outlook, expectation, lookout (*colloq.*); *potential*, promise, raw material; *imminence*, proximity, approach, advent; *fate*, destiny, karma, predestination, inevitability; *horoscope*, stars, forecast, prediction, divination, futurology, crystal-gazing; *afterlife*, the hereafter, the next world, millennium, doomsday.

adj. *future*, -to-be, coming, approaching, impending, imminent, due, ahead; *potential*, promising, budding, aspiring, would-be,

prospective; *predestined*, fated, doomed, inevitable, inescapable.

vb. *lie ahead*, threaten, loom, draw nigh, be just around the corner; *anticipate*, foresee, foreshadow, predict, divine.

adv. *in future*, henceforth, from now on; *eventually*, in due course, in the fullness of time, in the long run; *at hand*, in view, in the offing, on the horizon, on the cards, on the agenda.

105 PAST TIME
See also 107 (oldness).

n. *past time*, bygone days, yesteryear, days of yore, good old days, auld lang syne; *souvenir*, memento, retrospective, golden oldie (*colloq.*), blast from the past (*colloq.*); *recollection*, memory, remembrance, nostalgia, hindsight; *regression*, atavism, reversion, relapse, throwback; *obsoleteness*, antiquity, time immemorial, prehistory, the Dark Ages, the Stone Age; *relic*, archaism, antique, fossil, dinosaur, ruin, ancient monument, museum, archive; *archaeology*, palaeology, palaeography, antiquarianism; *thing of the past*, dead letter, ancient history, old news, has-been (*colloq.*), yesterday's man; *revival*, resurrection, resuscitation, exhumation.

adj. *past*, bygone, archaic, antiquated, obsolete, extinct; *retrospective*, nostalgic, retroactive, regressive, atavistic; *ancient*, prehistoric, Stone-Age, antediluvian; *lapsed*, date-expired, finished with, over and done with, irrevocable, irreversible; *former*, late, erstwhile, onetime, sometime, previous.

vb. *be past*, have run its course, have had its day, have seen better days; *pass*, elapse, expire, run out, die out, fade away, blow over (*colloq.*); *recollect*, remember, recall, look back, hark back, put the clock back, go over old ground, regress, revert; *revive*, exhume, resurrect, resuscitate.

adv. *in the past*, formerly, previously, before, at one time, time was; *long ago*, once upon a time, in the dim and distant past.

106 NEWNESS
See also 101 (present time); 111 (youth).

n. *newness*, recentness, freshness, bloom; *novelty*, innovation, neologism, scoop, exclusive; *modernity*, up-to-dateness, topicality, currency, trendiness, the latest thing, the last word, dernier cri, flavour of the month (*colloq.*); *avant-garde*, modernism, new wave, futurism; *modernization*,

revolution, renovation, restoration, facelift,
overhaul, update, new edition, new look,
revision; *immaturity*, greenness, rawness,
callowness, inexperience; *novice*, raw recruit,
tyro, fledgling, apprentice, greenhorn
(*colloq.*), new boy, newcomer, newbie
(*colloq.*), new broom, new blood; *rising
generation*, bright young thing (*colloq.*),
trendy (*colloq.*), upstart, parvenu, nouveaux
riches.

adj. *new*, brand-new, born-again, fresh,
virgin, pristine, evergreen; *novel*, innovative,
new-minted, hot off the press; *modern*, up-to-
date, current, topical, up-to-the-minute,
fashionable, trendy (*colloq.*), in (*colloq.*), with
it (*colloq.*), happening (*colloq.*), now (*colloq.*);
immature, green, callow, raw, inexperienced,
untried, new to the game, budding.

vb. *make new*, modernize, renew, renovate,
refurbish, rejuvenate, freshen up, give a new
lease of life, update, revise, overhaul;
innovate, introduce, invent, patent, coin,
mint.

adv. *newly*, recently, lately, of late; *as new*,
in mint condition; *anew*, afresh.

107 **OLDNESS**
See also 105 (past time); 112 (age).

n. *oldness*, age, antiquity, archaism,
obsolescence, obsoleteness; *antique*,
heirloom, collector's piece, museum piece,
relic, fossil; *tradition*, custom, folklore,
legend, mythology, oral history, urban
myth/legend; *maturity*, ripeness, experience,
seniority, wisdom; *veteran*, old hand, old-
timer (*colloq.*), doyen, father figure; *old age*,
longevity, senility, senescence; *decay*,
decline, dilapidation, erosion, ruin.

adj. *old*, age-old, ancient, olden, bygone,
antique, vintage, old-world, archaic,
obsolescent, obsolete, antediluvian;
traditional, time-honoured, long-standing,
historical, old as the hills, mythological,
primordial; *outdated*, outmoded, antiquated,
superannuated, passé, disused, discontinued,
old hat (*colloq.*), out of the ark (*colloq.*);
dilapidated, mouldering, crumbling,
motheaten, threadbare, clapped out (*colloq.*),
rusty, musty, distressed; *aged*, venerable,
hoary, geriatric, past it (*colloq.*), senile, gaga
(*colloq.*).

vb. *grow old*, age, wither, fade, crumble,
moulder, decay, rust.

adv. *for ages* (*colloq.*), since the year dot,
since Adam was a boy.

108 **SEASON**
n. *season*, high/low season, close season;
spring, springtime, seedtime, youth, vernal
equinox; *summer*, summertime, midsummer,
high summer, dog days, summer solstice;
autumn, fall (*US*), back end, Indian summer,
autumn equinox; *winter*, wintertime,
Christmas, yuletide, the festive season,
midwinter, hibernation, decline, decay,
winter solstice.

adj. *seasonal*, springlike, vernal,
burgeoning, summery, aestival, autumnal,
equinoctial, wintry, hibernal, bleak.

109 **MORNING**
n. *morning*, morn, daybreak, dawn, sunrise,
Aurora, cockcrow, sunup; *forenoon*, morning,
noon, midday, high noon; *dawn chorus*, early
bird, early riser, reveille, matins.

adj. *morning*, matutinal, daytime, diurnal.

adv. *a.m.*, ante meridiem; *at first light*, at
the crack of dawn, with the lark.

110 **EVENING**
n. *evening*, eventide, eve, sunset, sundown,
twilight, half-light, dusk, gloaming,
cockshut; *night*, nightfall, nighttime,
darkness, moonrise, dead of night, midnight,
witching hour, small hours; *afternoon*,
matinée, soirée, cocktail, sundowner,
evensong, vespers, lights out, curfew,
lighting-up time, the last post, bedtime,
night hawk, night owl, moonlight flit.

adj. *nightly*, nocturnal, dark, twilight,
crepuscular, overnight.

adv. *p.m.*, post meridiem; *by night*,
overnight, under cover of darkness.

111 **YOUTH**
See also 106 (newness).

n. *youth*, springtime, heyday, salad days;
youthfulness, freshness, immaturity,
callowness; *babyhood*, infancy, childhood,
tender years, formative years; *adolescence*,
teens, puberty, awkward age, pubescence,
growing pains; *cradle*, nursery, kindergarten,
playschool; *pupillage*, nonage, tutelage,
wardship; *youngster*, infant, babe in arms,
suckling, toddler, tot, mite, ankle-biter
(*colloq.*), rug rat (*colloq.*); *child*, kid (*colloq.*),
brat (*colloq.*), urchin, nipper (*colloq.*), minx,
madam, moppet; *adolescent*, juvenile,
teenager, tweenager, tweeny, sub-teen,
delinquent, whippersnapper (*colloq.*),
stripling, tearaway, skinhead, yob (*colloq.*),
chav (*colloq.*), lass, nymphet, Lolita,

teenybopper, tomboy, ladette, wild child; *pupil*, ward, minor.

adj. *young*, youthful, fresh, young-at-heart, ageless; *immature*, green, callow, wet behind the ears (*colloq.*); *newborn*, babyish, infantile, preschool, childish, puerile, adolescent, pubescent, virginal, coltish, junior, teenage.

112 AGE
See also 107 (oldness).

n. *age*, older generation, adulthood, manhood, legal age, majority, seniority; *middle age*, prime, maturity, menopause, male menopause, climacteric, change of life, midlife crisis, mutton dressed as lamb, no spring chicken (*colloq.*); *old age*, longevity, a ripe old age, declining years, the evening of one's life, second childhood, senility, dotage; *adult*, grown-up, matron; *old person*, matriarch, patriarch, oldster (*colloq.*), old-age pensioner, OAP, senior citizen, golden ager (*colloq.*), coffin-dodger (*colloq.*), grandfather, grandad (*colloq.*), old boy (*colloq.*), old fogy, old buffer (*colloq.*), greybeard, grandmother, granny (*colloq.*), old dear (*colloq.*), crone, hag, Darby and Joan; *old hand*, veteran, expert, old-timer, elder, elder statesman, grand old man, doyen, grande dame, doyenne; *gerontocracy*, gerontology, geriatrics, old folks' home, granny flat.

adj. *old*, adult, grown-up, mature; *middle-aged*, menopausal, matronly, of a certain age, ageing, getting on (*colloq.*), long in the tooth (*colloq.*); *aged*, elderly, sprightly, geriatric, doddering, failing, senile, gaga (*colloq.*), white-haired, with one foot in the grave (*colloq.*).

113 EARLINESS
See also 99 (priority).

n. *earliness*, promptness, dispatch, timeliness, immediacy, punctuality; *prematurity*, precocity, forwardness; *immaturity*, unreadiness, unpreparedness, unripeness; *foresight*, anticipation, preparedness, forward planning, prior warning, head start.

adj. *early*, prompt, immediate, punctual, timely; *premature*, precocious, previous, forward, advanced; *immature*, unripe, unready, unprepared; *preliminary*, preparatory, anticipatory.

vb. *be early*, reserve, book, get in first, jump the queue, jump the gun (*colloq.*); *preempt*, take the initiative, forestall, nip in the bud; *dispatch*, expedite, lose no time, take time by the forelock.

adv. *early on*, first thing; *beforehand*, in advance, before one's time, out of turn.

114 LATENESS
See also 100 (succession).

n. *lateness*, late hour, small hours, eleventh hour, last minute, high time, brinksmanship; *tardiness*, slowness, delayed reaction, time lag, afterthought; *dilatoriness*, unpunctuality, delay, holdup, latecomer; *backwardness*, retardation, slow starter, late developer; *postponement*, adjournment, deferment, procrastination, suspension, reprieve, moratorium.

adj. *late*, late in the day, last-minute, deathbed, posthumous; *belated*, overdue, behindhand, tardy, dilatory, unpunctual; *backward*, retarded, slow; *postponed*, deferred, suspended.

vb. *be late*, oversleep, keep late hours, burn the midnight oil; *be slow*, linger, dawdle, tarry, loiter, dilly-dally (*colloq.*); *postpone*, put off, defer, adjourn, shelve, mothball, put on ice/in cold storage, procrastinate; *delay*, stall, stonewall, filibuster, play for time, suspend, hang fire, sleep on it, take one's time, cool one's heels, wait and see.

adv. *late*, till all hours; *at last*, ultimately, in the end; *tardily*, belatedly, at the last minute, in the nick of time.

115 TIMELINESS
See also 580 (convenience).

n. *timeliness*, opportuneness, convenience, expediency, right moment; *opportunity*, golden opportunity, chance, break (*colloq.*), piece of luck, opening; *key moment*, psychological moment, the moment of truth, pinch (*colloq.*), push (*colloq.*), crunch (*colloq.*); *critical point*, point of no return, critical mass, crux, turning point, crisis, emergency, narrow escape, close shave.

adj. *timely*, welcome, seasonable, fortuitous, well-timed, auspicious, opportune, providential, propitious, heaven-sent; *convenient*, handy, expedient, advantageous.

vb. *seize* one's *opportunity*, profit by, take advantage of, exploit, turn to good account, capitalize on, strike while the iron is hot, make hay while the sun shines.

adv. *at the right moment*, conveniently, not before time, in the nick of time, at the last minute, at the eleventh hour.

116 **UNTIMELINESS**

See also 581 (inconvenience).

n. *untimeliness*, inconvenience, inopportuneness, wrong moment, evil hour, off-day, one of those days; *mistiming*, intrusion, interruption, misjudgement, blunder, clanger (*colloq.*).

adj. *untimely*, inopportune, inauspicious, untoward, disadvantageous, unlucky, ill-starred; *mistimed*, intrusive, misjudged, malapropos, awkward, inconvenient.

vb. *mistime*, misjudge, miss one's opportunity, miss the boat (*colloq.*), blow it (*colloq.*); *intrude*, break in on, talk out of turn, put one's foot in it (*colloq.*), drop a brick (*colloq.*).

adv. *at a bad time*, at the wrong moment, inopportunely, inconveniently.

117 **FREQUENCY**

See also 88 (repetition); 119 (regularity).

n. *frequency*, recurrence, regularity, repetition, rhythm; *predictability*, familiarity, commonness, monotony, banality.

adj. *frequent*, numerous, recurrent, periodic, regular, repeated, rhythmic; *continual*, sustained, constant, monotonous, relentless, remorseless; *predictable*, familiar, common, prevalent, banal, two a penny.

vb. *be frequent*, recur, keep on, continue.

adv. *frequently*, often, many a time; *repeatedly*, constantly, again and again, time and time again, regularly, continually; *commonly*, generally, more often than not.

118 **INFREQUENCY**

See also 87 (few); 120 (irregularity).

n. *infrequency*, rarity, scarcity, scantness, sparseness; *intermittence*, irregularity, unpredictability.

adj. *infrequent*, rare, few and far between, spaced out, occasional, scarce, sparse; *intermittent*, irregular, unpredictable, uncommon, unusual.

adv. *infrequently*, rarely, seldom; *occasionally*, once in a while, every now and then, once in a blue moon (*colloq.*); *intermittently*, off and on, now and then.

119 **REGULARITY**

See also 88 (repetition); 92 (period); 117 (frequency).

n. *regularity*, rhythm, recurrence, repetition, periodicity; *reliability*, steadiness, constancy, predictability, uniformity; *beat*, throb, tick, pulse, measure, refrain, chorus;

alternation, ebb and flow, to and fro, shuttle service, swing, pendulum, piston; *rotation*, rota, roster, revolution, circuit, cycle, menstruation, biorhythms; *routine*, daily round, nine to five, treadmill; *anniversary*, birthday, leap year, immovable feast.

adj. *regular*, rhythmic, repeated, recurring, periodic; *reliable*, predictable, steady, constant, uniform, even, measured; *alternating*, seasonal, cyclical, rotational.

vb. *recur*, come round again, revolve, rotate, alternate, reciprocate, take turn about; *be rhythmic*, beat, throb, tick, chime, swing; *go to and fro*, ply, commute.

adv. *regularly*, at regular intervals, seasonally, cyclically; *periodically*, at intervals, now and again; *alternately*, in rotation, in turn; *to and fro*, back and forwards.

120 **IRREGULARITY**

See also 118 (infrequency).

n. *irregularity*, variability, unpredictability, randomness, inconstancy, capriciousness; *unevenness*, unsteadiness, fitfulness, jerkiness, sporadicness, spasmodicness, fluctuation; *caprice*, whim, variable, unknown quantity, movable feast.

adj. *irregular*, variable, unpredictable, random, changeable, capricious, erratic; *uneven*, unsteady, fitful, jerky, sporadic, spasmodic, intermittent, arhythmic, stop-go.

vb. *be irregular*, vary, change, waver, flicker, fluctuate, come and go.

adv. *irregularly*, off and on, spasmodically, in fits and starts.

121 **CHANGE**

See also 125 (conversion); 127 (revolution); 130 (changeableness).

n. *change*, alteration, modification, version, adjustment, modulation, inflection, mutation; *transformation*, transfiguration, transmogrification, metamorphosis, conversion; *adaptation*, variation, permutation, shift; *transition*, changeover, switch, substitution, transposition, transference; *flux*, flow, mobility, impermanence, instability, vicissitudes, ups and downs (*colloq.*); *change for the better/ worse*, improvement, reformation, revision, upturn, deterioration, degeneration, downturn; *fluctuation*, seesaw, change of mind, vacillation, change of direction, deviation, diversion, U-turn, volte-face, about-turn; *revolution*, overthrow, upheaval, sea change, step change, wind of change, innovation, reform, reconstruction, reorganization; *adapter*, alterant, transformer, catalyst, metabolism, alchemy, enzyme, leaven, yeast; *reformer*, radical, revolutionary, agitator, new broom.

adj. *changing*, fluid, plastic, mobile, unstable, protean, impermanent, volatile; *transitional*, provisional, temporary, interim, ad hoc; *revolutionary*, radical, progressive, innovative, reformist.

vb. *change*, alter, modify, adjust, temper, modulate, inflect, mutate; *transform*, transfigure, transmogrify, transmute, metamorphose, convert, metabolize; *vary*, diversify, adapt, ring the changes; *improve*, reform, turn over a new leaf, change for the better; *deteriorate*, degenerate, fall away, change for the worse; *fluctuate*, vacillate, change one's tune, shift, veer, chop and change, blow hot and cold (*colloq*.); *interchange*, swap (*colloq*.), switch, change round, substitute, transpose, transfer; *revolutionize*, revamp, remodel, reconstruct, refurbish, reorganize, revise; *process*, treat, adulterate, denature, doctor, massage.

adv. *mutatis mutandis*, vice versa.

122 **PERMANENCE**
See also 131 (stability); 549 (habit).

n. *permanence*, unchangingness, immutability, fixity, immobility, stasis; *endurance*, continuity, persistence, subsistence, survival; *stability*, steadiness, constancy, firmness, bedrock, solidity; *tradition*, custom, habit, routine, status quo, conservatism, laissez-faire; *conservative*, neo-conservative, neo-liberal, right-winger, reactionary, hawk, diehard, stick-in-the-mud (*colloq*.); *invariability*, inflexibility, rigidity, immovableness, stubbornness, obstinacy.

adj. *permanent*, unchanging, unchangeable, immutable, fixed, set in stone, stationary, immobile, static; *enduring*, persistent, continuing, lasting, surviving; *stable*, steady, constant, firm, solid, unbudgeable, unwavering, steadfast; *invariable*, inflexible, rigid, immovable, stubborn, obstinate, dyed-in-the-wool, unreconstructed; *conservative*, right-wing, reactionary.

vb. *be permanent*, endure, last, abide, subsist, persist, survive; *remain*, stay, tarry, stay put, stand still, dig in one's toes, tread water, mark time; *settle*, establish, fix,

entrench, put down roots; *maintain*, sustain, uphold, persevere, conserve.

adv. *permanently*, for good, for ever.

123 **CESSATION**
See also 235 (motionlessness).

n. *cessation*, discontinuation, termination, closure, shutdown, closedown, collapse, failure, crash; *stop*, halt, standstill, deadlock, stasis, stalemate, checkmate; *hitch*, check, holdup, snag, hiccup, blockage, bottleneck, jam; *stoppage*, walkout, strike, work-to-rule, go-slow, lockout, sit-in; *pause*, lull, break, interruption, letup, rest, breather (*colloq*.), respite, cooling-off period; *suspension*, freeze, abeyance, moratorium, truce, cease-fire, armistice, amnesty; *end*, conclusion, expiry, end-date, terminus, end of the road.

vb. *cease*, stop, desist, refrain, hold off; *halt*, stop short, stop in one's tracks, pull up, baulk, stall, seize up; *discontinue*, pause, break, break off, leave off, ring off, knock off (*colloq*.); *strike*, walk out, down tools, come out, work to rule, go slow, occupy; *check*, arrest, stem, block, veto, thwart, foil, parry, checkmate; *suspend*, drop, hold over, put on ice, freeze, shelve, mothball; *end*, terminate, finish, conclude, expire, run out, peter out, fizzle out (*colloq*.); *collapse*, fail, fold, go into liquidation, wind up, go belly-up (*colloq*.), shut up shop, ring down the curtain; *retire*, resign, stand down, pull out, withdraw, scratch.

124 **CONTINUITY**
See also 64 (consecutiveness); 93 (duration).

n. *continuity*, continuation, perpetuation, maintenance, prolongation; *flow*, run, course, progress, current; *regularity*, constancy, uniformity, steadiness, smoothness, monotony; *link*, bridge, stopgap, potboiler (*colloq*.), filler, padding.

adj. *continuous*, uninterrupted, unbroken, non-stop, ongoing, flowing, seamless; *perpetual*, unceasing, incessant, never-ending, inexhaustible, undying; *continual*, steady, constant, uniform, regular, recurrent, monotonous, unremitting, relentless.

vb. *continue*, proceed, progress, advance, carry on, keep on; *maintain*, uphold, sustain, preserve, conserve, perpetuate; *endure*, persist, persevere, hang on, plod on, peg away (*colloq*.), stick; *prolong*, protract, extend, spin out, drag out.

adv. *continuously*, forever, round the clock, twenty-four hours a day, 24/7, on and on, to the bitter end; *continually*, constantly, repeatedly.

125 **CONVERSION**
See also 121 (change).

n. *conversion*, mutation, switch, changeover, transformation, metamorphosis; *processing*, treatment, chemistry, alchemy, evaporation, liquefaction, crystallization, solidification; *convertibility*, adaptability, versatility, flexibility; *laboratory*, melting pot, crucible, test tube; *convert*, proselyte, neophyte, apostate, turncoat, deserter.

adj. *convertible*, mutable, adaptable, versatile, flexible, recyclable, biodegradable; *converted*, reborn, born-again, reformed; *proselytizing*, evangelical, crusading, missionary, revivalist.

vb. *convert*, adapt, change, assimilate, mutate, metamorphose, transform; *process*, treat, liquefy, evaporate, solidify, crystallize, recycle, break down; *proselytize*, evangelize, win over, persuade; *be converted*, change one's mind, defect, go over to the other side, desert.

126 **REVERSION**
See also 254 (backward motion).

n. *reversion*, return, regression, atavism, throwback; *relapse*, recidivism, backsliding, recurrence, recrudescence; *reaction*, response, feedback, backlash, whiplash, recoil, retaliation, repercussion, reverberation; *reversal*, overthrow, overturn, upset, about-turn, U-turn, volte-face, swing of the pendulum; *restoration*, recovery, retrieval, restitution, reinstatement; *retreat*, withdrawal, retraction, retrogression, retrenchment, recession.

adj. *reverted*, reflexive, retrogressive, retroactive; *retrograde*, reactionary, unreconstructed, backward-looking, retrospective, regressive; *reacting*, responsive, reflex, repercussive, reverberative; *reversible*, convertible, inverted, two-way.

vb. *revert*, return, relapse, regress, retrace one's steps, retreat, recede, withdraw; *undo*, unmake, overthrow, overturn, upset; *react*, respond, retort, counter, recoil, rebound; *restore*, reinstate, redress, recover, retrieve.

adv. *inside out*, back to front, upside down; *as you were*, back to square one, back to the drawing board.

127 **REVOLUTION**
See also 121 (change); 662 (disobedience).

n. *revolution*, unpheaval, upset,

convulsion, shakeup, coup d'état, overthrow, regime change; *rotation*, full circle, circuit, lap, turn; *revolt*, uprising, insurrection, rebellion, insurgency, mutiny; *extremism*, militancy, radicalism, agitprop, entryism, subversion, sedition; *complete change*, clean sweep, clean slate, tabula rasa, new dawn; *revolutionary*, militant, radical, extremist, fanatic, rebel, insurgent, guerrilla, freedom fighter, fifth column.

adj. *revolutionary*, radical, extreme, far-reaching, sweeping, thoroughgoing, draconian, root and branch; *rebellious*, mutinous, bolshie (*colloq.*), militant, extremist, insurgent, underground, seditious, subversive, entryist, anarchistic.

vb. *revolutionize*, shake up, change the face of, remodel, reconstruct; *overturn*, overthrow, subvert, undermine, infiltrate; *revolt*, rebel, rise up, mutiny, kick over the traces.

128 **SUBSTITUTION**
See also 129 (exchange).

n. *substitution*, exchange, switch, swap (*colloq.*), changeround, shuffle, musical chairs; *substitute*, agent, deputy, proxy, replacement, stand-in, surrogate, understudy, relief, reserve, locum, whipping boy, scapegoat; *equivalent*, approximation, imitation, second best, makeshift, expedient, stopgap.

adj. *substitutable*, surrogate, alternative, equivalent, interchangeable, vicarious; *substitute*, imitation, fake, ersatz, faux, mock.

vb. *substitute*, exchange, switch, swap (*colloq.*), change round, shuffle; *replace*, supplant, oust, supersede, take over from; *deputize*, stand in for, understudy, cover up for, impersonate.

adv. *instead*, in lieu; *in one's place/stead*, in one's shoes, by proxy.

129 **EXCHANGE**
See also 11 (reciprocity); 128 (substitution).

n. *exchange*, barter, trade, handover, transfer, swap (*colloq.*); *reciprocity*, give and take, mutuality, quid pro quo, retort, rejoinder, riposte, repartee, dialogue; *interaction*, interplay, interchange, cooperation; *substitution*, transposition, transliteration, transcription; *retaliation*, requittal, reprisals, tit for tat (*colloq.*).

adj. *exchanged*, mutual, reciprocal, cooperative, two-way; *interchangeable*, substitutable, equivalent, convertible.

vb. *exchange*, barter, trade, swap (*colloq.*),

hand over, transfer; *reciprocate*, retaliate, retort, bandy words; *interchange*, switch, transpose, transcribe, shuffle, substitute.

adv. *in exchange*, instead, in kind, in return.

130 **CHANGEABLENESS**
See also 94 (transience); 121 (change).

n. *changeableness*, changeability, mutability, variability; *fluidity*, plasticity, malleability, flexibility, versatility, adaptability; *inconstancy*, impermanence, instability, volatility, unreliability, unpredictability, waywardness, fickleness, capriciousness; *fluctuation*, vacillation, hesitation, indecision, irresolution; *mobility*, restlessness, unease, fidgetiness; *changeable thing*, kaleidoscope, prism, chameleon, mercury, quicksilver, shot silk.

adj. *changeable*, mutable, variable, unstable, impermanent; *fluid*, plastic, malleable, flexible, versatile, adaptable, quick-change, protean, mercurial; *inconstant*, volatile, fickle, flighty, unreliable, wayward, capricious, erratic, unpredictable; *vacillating*, hesitant, indecisive, irresolute, uncertain; *mobile*, restless, shifty, fidgety, uneasy; *desultory*, fitful, spasmodic, sporadic.

vb. *vary*, change, shift, fluctuate, waver, vacillate, hesitate, blow hot and cold (*colloq.*); *move*, dart, dance, flit, flicker, twinkle, gutter, shimmer.

adv. *spasmodically*, off and on.

131 **STABILITY**
See also 122 (permanence).

n. *stability*, steadiness, firmness, fixity, permanence, solidity, immobility; *balance*, equilibrium, homoeostasis, self-regulation, self-control, composure, even-temperedness, even keel; *reliability*, predictability, invariability, constancy, regularity, sureness; *stabilizer*, ballast, counterweight, prop, buttress, foundation, pillar, bedrock, anchor, mooring; *confirmation*, ratification, validation, corroboration.

adj. *stable*, steady, firm, fixed, permanent, immobile; *balanced*, homoeostatic, self-regulating, self-controlled, calm, composed, even-tempered; *immovable*, entrenched, solid, unwavering, inalterable, unshakable, unassailable; *reliable*, predictable, invariable, constant, regular, perennial; *indelible*, fast, ingrained, deep-rooted, deep-seated, ineradicable.

vb. *be stable*, stand firm/fast, stay put, dig in, settle down, put down roots; *stabilize*, support, buttress, shore up, prop up, anchor, embed, entrench, fix; *confirm*, establish, validate, ratify, corroborate.

132 **CAUSE**
See also 61 (beginning); 134 (motive).

n. *cause*, motive, reason, casus belli, ground, explanation, rationale, factor, influence, determinant; *causality*, instrumentality, aetiology, necessity, determinism; *motivation*, mainspring, provocation, stimulus, impetus, encouragement, inducement; *creator*, prime mover, author, inventor, originator, founder, architect; *creation*, evolution, natural selection, intelligent design; *source*, fount, fountainhead, cradle, womb, nursery, seed bed, breeding ground, hotbed; *genesis*, origin, ancestry, roots, derivation, etymology; *instrument*, means, motor, pivot, lever, hinge, dynamo; *germ*, seed, fetus, embryo, raw material.

adj. *causal*, instrumental, determinant, pivotal, influential, formative; *basic*, original, primary, fundamental, elemental, embryonic; *creative*, dynamic, innovative, inventive, productive, generative, fertile, seminal.

vb. *cause*, give rise to, create, generate, produce, originate; *found*, establish, institute, launch, initiate; *bring about*, occasion, unleash, precipitate, trigger; *organize*, arrange, set up, engineer, stage-manage; *provoke*, elicit, evoke, release; *stimulate*, kindle, inspire, encourage, foster, promote; *determine*, decide, entail, require, necessitate.

prep. *because of*, owing to, due to, as a result of.

133 **EFFECT**
See also 62 (end).

n. *effect*, consequence, result, end result, development, outcome, upshot; *aftereffect*, sequel, aftermath, fallout, reaction, backlash, ripple effect, knock-on effect, chain reaction; *product*, produce, crop, harvest, fruit, output; *derivative*, by-product, side effect, spin-off, legacy.

adj. *resultant*, consequent, subsequent, secondary, ensuing; *dependent*, contingent, concomitant; *derivative*, inherited, hereditary, genetic.

vb. *result*, develop, arise, unfold, evolve, spring up, issue, emerge; *derive from*, emanate from, go back to, originate in, have one's roots in; *depend on*, hinge, pivot, turn, hang.

adv. *consequently*, hence, as a result, in consequence.

134 MOTIVE
See also 132 (cause); 551 (persuasion).

n. *motive*, reason, hypothesis, theory, inference, assumption, grounds, basis; *explanation*, occasion, pretext, excuse, justification, rationale; *motivation*, impetus, driving force, impulsion, mainspring, trigger, inspiration, inducement, carrot, incentive; *attribution*, imputation, responsibility, accountability, credit, blame.

adj. *motivated*, caused, inspired, occasioned; *attributable*, assignable, ascribable, accountable, responsible, culpable; *inferred*, assumed, hypothetical, putative.

vb. *motivate*, cause, occasion, instigate, inspire; *attribute*, ascribe, assign, put down to, lay at the door of, blame, implicate; *explain*, account for, justify, interpret; *assume*, infer, derive, hypothesize.

adv. *hence*, for this reason; *therefore*, consequently.

prep. *owing to*, on account of, because of.

135 LACK OF MOTIVE
See also 554 (chance).

n. *lack of motive*, fortuitousness, gratuitousness, arbitrariness, randomness; *chance*, luck, fortune, pot luck, hazard, accident, fluke; *unaccountability*, unpredictability, coincidence, haphazardness, indeterminacy.

adj. *motiveless*, groundless, causeless, gratuitous, uncalled for, arbitrary, random; *unmotivated*, unintentional, accidental, coincidental, fortuitous, lucky; *unpredictable*, unaccountable, inexplicable, unexpected, chance, haphazard.

vb. *chance*, light upon, stumble upon, hit upon.

adv. *by chance*, accidentally, coincidentally; *unpredictably*, unexpectedly, out of the blue.

136 OPERATION
See also 138 (instrumentality); 567 (means).

n. *operation*, action, agency, influence, power, stress, pressure; *execution*, implementation, performance, application, effect, force; *process*, function, working, running, handling, administration.

adj. *operative*, effective, conducive, influential; *operational*, functional, working, active, live, on-stream; *practical*, feasible, applicable, manageable; *executive*, administrative, managerial.

vb. *operate*, work, function, run, tick over, idle; *execute*, perform, carry out, put into effect/practice; *affect*, influence, work on, act on, take effect; *activate*, power, drive, run, switch on, plug in, wind up.

adv. *into action*, into operation, into force, into play.

137 COUNTERACTION
See also 28 (compensation); 632 (opposition).

n. *counteraction*, opposition, retaliation, reprisals, counterattack, counterblast, counterrevolution; *reaction*, response, retort, riposte, repercussion, backlash; *recoil*, resistance, friction, drag; *compensation*, counterbalance, counterweight, foil, corrective, checks and balances, antidote, remedy, cure.

adj. *counteractive*, counter, contrary, counterproductive, opposing, retaliatory; *reactionary*, counterrevolutionary, resistant, recalcitrant; *compensatory*, countervailing, makeweight; *restorative*, corrective, remedial, curative.

vb. *counteract*, counter, oppose, combat, militate against; *react*, retaliate, respond, answer, riposte, retort; *compensate*, offset, make up for, counterbalance, neutralize, defuse, cancel out; *check*, prevent, foil, thwart, cross, obviate; *remedy*, cure, restore, correct.

138 INSTRUMENTALITY
See also 136 (operation); 568 (tool); 631 (help).

n. *instrumentality*, agency, means, services, action, aid, assistance; *intervention*, intercession, mediation, intermediary; *mechanism*, device, contrivance, deus ex machina, means to an end; *utility*, usefulness, helpfulness, serviceability, convenience, handiness.

adj. *instrumental*, effective, influential, conducive; *useful*, serviceable, practicable, convenient, handy; *helpful*, contributory, favourable, supportive.

vb. *be instrumental*, work, act, influence, affect; *serve*, help, encourage, support, promote, foster, advance, champion; *intervene*, intercede, interpose, mediate, have a hand in.

prep. *by means of*, through, via, per; *thanks to*, courtesy of; *on behalf of*, for the sake of.

139 INFLUENCE
See also 551 (persuasion).

n. *influence*, dominance, sway, ascendancy, power, hegemony; *leverage*, pull, weight, clout (*colloq.*), whip hand, upper hand, casting vote; *persuasion*, suggestion, manipulation, string-pulling, lobbying, pester power, propaganda, soft sell, brainwashing; *charm*, magnetism, charisma, hypnotism, mesmerism, sorcery, magic, seduction, fascination; *patronage*, nepotism, freemasonry, old-boy network, friend at court, the powers that be, the Establishment; *moving force*, lobby, pressure group, ginger group, the power behind the throne, grey eminence, agent provocateur, mole; *infiltration*, subversion, entryism.

adj. *influential*, important, dominant, prevailing, powerful, pervasive; *persuasive*, suggestive, convincing, manipulative, subversive; *charming*, charismatic, magnetic, hypnotic, mesmeric, bewitching, fascinating.

vb. *influence*, dominate, override, outweigh, master, subdue, have under one's thumb. *have influence*, count, tell, weigh, matter, carry weight, wear the trousers, call the tune; *persuade*, convince, manipulate, sway, have the ear of, work on, lean on, prevail on, pressurize, lobby; *charm*, mesmerize, hypnotize, bewitch, fascinate, captivate; *permeate*, infiltrate, penetrate, subvert, undermine.

140 TENDENCY
See also 430 (misjudgement).

n. *tendency*, trend, tenor, course, direction, mainstream, current; *inclination*, leaning, penchant, proclivity, propensity, predilection, soft spot; *predisposition*, cast, bent, bias, prejudice; *proneness*, liability, susceptibility, likelihood, vulnerability; *aptitude*, instinct, flair, gift.

adj. *tending*, conducive, leading, tendentious, biased, partisan, partial; *predisposed*, inclined, prone, apt, liable, susceptible, likely.

vb. *tend*, incline, lean, gravitate, verge; *predispose*, bias, prejudice, influence.

141 POWER
See also 143 (strength); 145 (vigour).

n. *power*, might, omnipotence, rule, authority, dominance, ascendancy,

hegemony, influence, sway; *strength*, forcefulness, cogency, impact, effectiveness, teeth, muscle; *vigour*, life, energy, dynamism, drive, overdrive; *ability*, capability, potential, competence, reach, grasp, aptitude; *powerful person*, chief, mandarin, mogul, magnate, tycoon, big battalions, the power behind the throne, linchpin, moving spirit, driving force; *energy*, impetus, momentum, propulsion, drive, thrust, pressure, horsepower, locomotion; *energy source*, fuel (see 341 *fuel*); *motor*, engine, generator, turbine, dynamo, battery, reactor, power station.

adj. *powerful*, mighty, all-powerful, omnipotent, dominant, influential, authoritative; *strong*, forceful, cogent, telling, hard-hitting, effective; *able*, capable, competent, efficacious, adequate; *powered*, locomotive, automated, self-propelled, souped-up; *active*, live, operative, on-stream, working.

vb. *power*, drive, charge, propel, electrify, automate, mechanize; *activate*, plug in, switch on, wire up; *strengthen*, invigorate, energize, galvanize, boost; *dominate*, rule, govern, hold sway, prevail, pull rank, rule the roost, wear the trousers (*colloq.*).

adv. *in power*, in force, in operation.

142 POWERLESSNESS
See also 144 (weakness); 593 (deterioration).

n. *powerlessness*, impotence, helplessness, defencelessness, vulnerability; *weakness*, frailness, feebleness, debility, disablement, handicap, senility; *inability*, incapacity, incompetence, unfitness, ineffectiveness, inadequacy; *prostration*, exhaustion, paralysis, lifelessness, torpor, inertia, atrophy; *broken reed*, sitting duck, lame duck, paper tiger, man of straw.

adj. *powerless*, impotent, helpless, defenceless, vulnerable; *weak*, frail, feeble, disabled, handicapped, differently abled, physically challenged, hamstrung, senile, debilitated, incapacitated; *prostrate*, inert, paralysed, lifeless, torpid, comatose, exhausted, all in, laid up, invalid, bedridden; *unable*, incompetent, ineffectual, unfit, inadequate, spineless, toothless.

vb. *make powerless*, disarm, disable, put out of action, neutralize, invalidate; *weaken*, undermine, sap, cripple, handicap, cramp sb's style, put a spoke in sb's wheel; *prostrate*, exhaust, paralyse, atrophy, drain.

adv. *out of commission*, hors de combat, in dock (*colloq.*).

143 **STRENGTH**

See also 141 (power); 664 (compulsion).

n. *strength*, might, brute force, muscle, brawn, toughness, hardness, steel, iron; *potency*, virility, manliness, ruggedness, fitness, health, soundness; *endurance*, resistance, durability, stamina, staying power, grit, backbone, guts, bottle (*colloq.*), pluck; *vigour*, force, energy, assertiveness, strength of character, resolution; *invulnerability*, impregnability, impermeability, indomitability, resilience; *athleticism*, gymnastics, weightlifting, body building, pumping iron (*colloq.*); *strong man*, weightlifter, muscleman, iron man, he-man (*colloq.*), Samson, Tarzan, Hercules, beefcake (*colloq.*), amazon; *support*, reinforcement, rampant, buttress, mainstay, pillar, tower of strength.

adj. *strong*, powerful, mighty, well-armed, tough, hard, steely; *potent*, virile, manly, rugged, robust, fit, healthy, sound; *vigorous*, energetic, dynamic, forceful, assertive, resolute; *invulnerable*, impregnable, impermeable, indestructible, durable; *resilient*, plucky, indomitable, unflagging, staunch, stalwart, doughty; *athletic*, able-bodied, muscular, brawny, burly, hefty, strapping, amazonian.

vb. *strengthen*, reinforce, fortify, buttress, brace, steel, nerve, gird one's loins; *assert*, affirm, stress, underline, emphasize; *invigorate*, energize, hearten, enliven, animate.

adv. *strongly*, with might and main, forcefully.

144 **WEAKNESS**

See also 142 (powerlessness).

n. *weakness*, feebleness, puniness, slightness, frailty; *flimsiness*, fragility, brittleness, delicacy, fineness; *ineffectiveness*, impotence, powerlessness, helplessness, vulnerability, uselessness; *softness*, tenderness, womanliness, effeminacy, effeteness; *limpness*, flaccidity, flabbiness, slackness, sponginess; *debility*, infirmity, weakliness, decrepitude, sickliness, invalidism, valetudinarianism; *prostration*, fatigue, languor, listlessness, lethargy, lassitude; *insipidness*, tastelessness, wateriness, thinness, pallor, bloodlessness, anaemia; *instability*, insecurity, shakiness,

unsteadiness, precariousness, house of cards, matchwood; *weak point*, soft spot, foible, Achilles' heel, inadequacy, defect, flaw, weak link, the weakest link (*colloq.*), chink in sb's armour; *weakling*, milksop, sissy, lame duck, invalid, jellyfish, doormat, wet (*colloq.*), wimp (*colloq.*), drip (*colloq.*), weed (*colloq.*).

adj. *weak*, feeble, puny, slight, frail, fragile, brittle, delicate, flimsy; *ineffectual*, impotent, powerless, helpless, unarmed, unaided, vulnerable; *soft*, tender, womanly, effeminate, babyish, effete; *weak-willed*, irresolute, gutless, weak-kneed, spineless, wet (*colloq.*), drippy (*colloq.*), wimpish (*colloq.*); *limp*, flaccid, flabby, slack, spongy; *infirm*, sickly, weakly, decrepit, invalid, disabled, lame, halt; *prostrate*, weary, languid, spent, listless, lethargic, burnt-out; *insipid*, tasteless, watery, thin, pale, anaemic, dilute, wishy-washy (*colloq.*), washed-out; *unstable*, insecure, shaky, wobbly, rocky, rickety, precarious, ramshackle, gimcrack.

vb. *weaken*, sap, undermine, disarm; *disable*, maim, lame, cripple, enfeeble, debilitate, enervate; *decline*, dwindle, fade, wither, wilt, languish, flag, sag, slacken; *mitigate*, extenuate, lessen, soften, cushion, muffle, blunt; *dilute*, thin, water down, adulterate, tone down, moderate; *shake*, waver, quaver, tremble, totter, teeter, dodder.

145 **VIGOUR**

See also 141 (power); 507 (emphasis).

n. *vigour*, energy, life, vitality, dynamism, dash, elan, liveliness, impetus, vim, pep (*colloq.*), zap (*colloq.*), oomph (*colloq.*), va-va-voom (*colloq.*), pizzazz or pzazz (*colloq.*); *enthusiasm*, fervour, zest, joie de vivre, gusto, relish; *enterprise*, initiative, drive, dynamism, aggressiveness, thrust, punch, attack, verve, get-up-and-go (*colloq.*); *spirit*, mettle, fire, guts (*colloq.*), pluck, spunk (*colloq.*), bottle (*colloq.*); *stimulus*, boost, shot in the arm, fillip, tonic, stimulant, pick-me-up (*colloq.*), upper (*colloq.*), Viagra (*tdmk*), pep talk (*colloq.*); *whiz kid*, livewire (*colloq.*), bright spark (*colloq.*), self-starter, go-getter (*colloq.*).

adj. *vigorous*, energetic, lively, animated, racy, spirited, zappy (*colloq.*); *enthusiastic*, keen, go-ahead, enterprising, high-powered; *forceful*, aggressive, thrusting, punchy (*colloq.*); *stimulating*, invigorating, bracing, tonic, brisk, no-nonsense (*colloq.*).

vb. *invigorate*, enliven, animate, energize, vitalize, galvanize, electrify, ginger up, put a bomb under (*colloq.*); *stimulate*, rouse, encourage, boost, kindle, inflame, intoxicate; *drive*, thrust, push, attack, go at, pull out all the stops; *be vigorous*, thrive, blossom, bloom, flourish, be in fine fettle.

adv. *vigorously*, hard, full steam ahead.

146 INERTNESS

See also 144 (weakness); 608 (inaction); 610 (inactivity).

n. *inertness*, inactivity, languor, sluggishness, lethargy, inertia, torpor, lifelessness; *immobility*, stillness, stagnation, hibernation, dormancy; *dullness*, apathy, passivity, sloth, indolence, laziness, stolidity, impassivity, nonchalance.

adj. *inert*, inactive, languid, lethargic, sluggish, torpid; *immobile*, still, stagnant, dormant, fallow; *lifeless*, heavy, sleepy, numb, paralysed; *dull*, apathetic, lazy, idle, slothful, indolent, passive, indifferent, nonchalant, stolid.

vb. *be inert*, stagnate, vegetate, tick over, idle; *sleep*, doze, slumber, hibernate.

147 VIOLENCE

See also 639 (attack).

n. *violence*, vehemence, intensity, force, power; *outbreak*, outburst, spasm, paroxysm, convulsion, eruption, earthquake, upheaval, explosion, cataclysm; *onrush*, torrent, tidal wave, hurricane, storm, tempest; *turbulence*, turmoil, uproar, furore; *ferocity*, savagery, brutality, frenzy, rage, passion; *assault*, hammering (*colloq.*), thrashing, grievous bodily harm, rape, drug rape, gangbang (*colloq.*), battering, mugging; *fight*, punch-up (*colloq.*), dust-up (*colloq.*), brawl, melee, aggro (*colloq.*), bovver (*colloq.*), hooliganism, thuggery, riot, mayhem, mob rule; *killing*, murder, homicide, massacre, slaughter, carnage; *brute*, beast, savage, barbarian, thug, hooligan, ruffian, bully, yob (*colloq.*); *killer*, assassin, murderer, butcher, axeman, hatchetman, death squad; *fury*, spitfire, termagant, virago, hothead, firebrand.

adj. *violent*, vehement, intense, forceful, powerful; *turbulent*, tumultuous, cataclysmic, explosive, convulsive, volcanic; *wild*, frenzied, frantic, hysterical, unrestrained, unbridled, sweeping, overwhelming; *rampant*, raging, rabid, fuming, tempestuous, stormy; *fierce*, ferocious, vicious, brutal, savage, murderous, bloodthirsty; *aggressive*, belligerent, tough, rowdy, boisterous, riotous.

vb. *be violent*, convulse, erupt, explode,

burst, let fly, lash out; *rage*, storm, fume, rant, see red, see (the) red mist, go berserk; *charge*, stampede, rampage, riot, run amuck; *surge*, gush, flood, inundate, overwhelm; *dash*, hurtle, rush, fling, pelt, hurl; *smash*, crash, break, shatter, demolish, pulverize, crush; *assault*, rape, violate, strike, punch, mug, lay into, beat up, thrash, hammer (*colloq.*), batter, work over, dust up (*colloq.*); *make violent*, rouse, goad, lash, whip up, exasperate, infuriate, enrage, madden.

adv. *violently*, tooth and nail, hammer and tongs; *precipitately*, headlong, headfirst, at full tilt.

148 MODERATION

See also 63 (middle); 733 (impassivity).

n. *moderation*, reasonableness, rationality, sanity, sobriety, common sense; *calmness*, composure, cool-headedness, impassivity, restraint, self-control, anger management; *middle way*, golden mean, happy medium, the middle of the road; *mildness*, harmlessness, innocuousness, gentleness, blandness; *alleviation*, mitigation, abatement, relief, easing, relaxation; *pacification*, mollification, appeasement; *palliative*, balm, emollient, lubricant, salve, sedative, tranquillizer, opiate, downer (*colloq.*), analgesic; *mediator*, peacemaker, arbitrator, conciliator; *brake*, check, curb, rein, damper, cushion, wet blanket (*colloq.*); *moderate*, centrist, reformist, pinko (*colloq.*), woolly liberal (*colloq.*).

adj. *moderate*, reasonable, rational, sensible, sane, sober; *calm*, composed, cool-headed, impassive, restrained, low-key, subdued, tame; *mild*, gentle, soothing, bland, anodyne, insipid; *average*, middlebrow, middle-of-the-road.

vb. *moderate*, temper, mitigate, lessen, tone down, dampen, muffle, blunt, take the edge off; *curb*, check, quell, subdue, tame, bring to heel; *alleviate*, allay, assuage, relieve, deaden, numb, dull; *pacify*, calm, appease, lull, soothe, pour oil on troubled waters.

adv. *in moderation*, within reason, within bounds; *gradually*, softly softly (*colloq.*).

149 PRODUCTION

See also 152 (fertility); 611 (work).

n. *production*, creation, origination, generation, invention; *manufacture*, fabrication, concoction, preparation, formation, construction; *industrialization*, mass production, factory farming, assembly line, automation, new technology; *industry*, trade, craft, skill, cottage industry, homeworking, telecommuting; *product*, end-product, output, throughput, yield, productivity, produce, crop, harvest, by-product, waste, extract; *artefact*, handiwork, ware, goods, merchandise, finished article; *composition*, piece, opus, oeuvre, work of art, chef d'oeuvre, masterpiece, brainchild; *handicrafts*, ceramics, pottery, metalworking, silversmithing, weaving, tapestry, embroidery, patchwork, crochet, knitting, macramé; *producer*, creator, maker, originator, inventor, founder, author, architect, engineer, composer, designer; *manufacturer*, industrialist, workman, labourer, craftsman, artisan; *farmer*, grower, breeder, market gardener.

adj. *productive*, creative, generative, inventive, constructive; *fruitful*, rich, prolific, fertile, profitable; *synthetic*, artificial, man-made, ready-made.

vb. *produce*, create, originate, generate, invent, devise, conceive, design; *make*, fabricate, concoct, frame, fashion, forge, cast, coin, mint, cobble together; *craft*, sew, knit, spin, weave, embroider; *manufacture*, machine, synthesize, process, treat, mass-produce, assemble, turn out; *accomplish*, achieve, contrive, engineer, develop, exploit; *farm*, grow, breed, cultivate, propagate.

150 DESTRUCTION

See also 147 (violence); 324 (killing); 593 (deterioration); 838 (wickedness).

n. *destruction*, obliteration, nullification, abolition, deterioration, erosion, eradication, extirpation; *extinction*, annihilation, extermination, liquidation, decimation, assassination, murder, slaughter, massacre, genocide; *demolition*, bombardment, blitz, scorched-earth policy, defoliation; *disaster*, catastrophe, cataclysm, holocaust, earthquake, flood, disaster area; *devastation*, chaos, ruin, wreckage, damage, harm, ravages, shambles; *collapse*, smash-up, crash, collision, wreck; *destructiveness*, vandalism, sabotage, arson, character assassination, smear campaign; *destroyer*, vandal, wrecker, arsonist, saboteur, killer, assassin, butcher, hitman (*colloq.*); *blight*, bane, cancer, canker, poison, toxin, corrosive; *battering ram*, bulldozer, steamroller, juggernaut.

adj. *destructive*, disastrous, catastrophic, cataclysmic, ruinous, fatal, terminal; *harmful*, injurious, pernicious, corrosive; *murderous*,

homicidal, suicidal, deadly, lethal, self-destructive; *destroyed*, ruined, undone, washed-up, burnt-out, kaput (*colloq.*), done for (*colloq.*).

vb. *destroy*, harm, damage, injure, erode; *obliterate*, nullify, delete, expunge, erase, cancel out, undo, unmake; *abolish*, extinguish, eradicate, extirpate, stamp out, wipe out, annihilate; *exterminate*, liquidate, assassinate, decimate, murder, massacre, slaughter, butcher, do in (*colloq.*); *engulf*, consume, devour, swallow up, swamp, drown; *devastate*, ravage, despoil, ransack, pillage, lay waste; *flatten*, blitz, raze, level, bulldoze, demolish; *ruin*, wreck, vandalize, sabotage, torpedo, sink, scuttle, scupper (*colloq.*), put the mockers/kibosh on (*colloq.*); *dismantle*, scrap, shred, pulp, break up, make mincemeat of (*colloq.*); *crash*, collide, write off, smash up, shatter; *suppress*, quell, quash, smother, stifle, strangle, suffocate, nip in the bud; *be destroyed*, go under/down, go to rack and ruin, go to the wall, succumb, go to the dogs (*colloq.*), be done for, be toast (*colloq.*).

adv. *on the scrapheap*, on the rocks (*colloq.*).

151 REPRODUCTION

See also 21 (imitation); 88 (repetition).

n. *reproduction*, procreation, regeneration, reincarnation; *reduplication*, repetition, multiplication, mass production; *remake*, reprint, reissue, repeat, copy; *renewal*, revitalization, resurgence, renaissance, rebirth, resuscitation, revival.

adj. *reproductive*, regenerative, procreative, prolific; *resurgent*, born-again, rejuvenated.

vb. *reproduce*, procreate, breed, multiply; *repeat*, duplicate, copy, mass-produce, churn out; *remake*, rebuild, reprint, reissue; *renew*, revive, resurrect, resuscitate.

152 FERTILITY

See also 149 (production).

n. *fertility*, fecundity, virility, potency; *procreation*, propagation, proliferation, multiplication, reproduction, the facts of life, the birds and the bees (*colloq.*); *productiveness*, abundance, richness, glut, cornucopia, horn of plenty, baby boom, population explosion; *motherhood*, maternity, childbearing, midwifery, obstetrics; *fertilization*, insemination, pollination, irrigation, artificial insemination, conception, gestation, pregnancy, test-tube baby; *childbirth*, birthing, parturition, confinement, delivery, happy event, stillbirth, miscarriage;

womb, uterus, ovary, cervix, loins; *ovum*, seed, pollen, sperm, semen, cum (*vulg.*); *genitals*, private parts, vagina, cunt (*vulg.*), twat (*vulg.*), fanny (*colloq.*), pudenda, penis, phallus, pizzle, cock (*vulg.*), prick (*vulg.*), dick (*colloq.*), testicles, balls (*vulg.*), bollocks (*vulg.*), goolies (*vulg.*), nads (*vulg.*), crown jewels (*colloq.*).

adj. *fertile*, fecund, procreative, potent, virile, productive, seminal; *pregnant*, gravid, expecting, broody, with child, antenatal, obstetric; *abundant*, copious, rich, plentiful, fruitful.

vb. *fertilize*, impregnate, inseminate, pollinate, irrigate, manure; *procreate*, propagate, breed, spawn, cultivate, rear, multiply, increase; *conceive*, fall, beget, engender, sire; *give birth*, bring forth, drop, lamb, farrow, whelp, pup, litter, hatch; *proliferate*, sprout, mushroom, blossom, burgeon, bloom, flourish.

adv. *with child*, in the family way, up the spout (*colloq.*), in the club (*colloq.*).

153 **INFERTILITY**
See also 579 (uselessness).

n. *infertility*, sterility, impotence, barrenness, unproductiveness, aridity; *fruitlessness*, futility, unprofitability, zero growth, stagnation; *desolation*, desert, tundra, wasteland, dustbowl, famine, dearth; *contraception*, family planning, birth control, abortion, sterilization, vasectomy, menopause, castration; *eunuch*, castrato, gelding, neuter, freemartin, hermaphrodite.

adj. *infertile*, sterile, impotent, barren, childless, subfertile; *unproductive*, fruitless, arid, unprofitable, fallow, stillborn.

vb. *be unproductive*, lie fallow, stagnate, wither on the vine, abort, miscarry, die aborning; *sterilize*, castrate, emasculate, geld, neuter, spay.

154 **PARENT**
See also 12 (family relations); 668 (restraint).

n. *parent*, parenthood, parenting, single parent, one-parent family, donor, biological mother/father, godparent, adoptive parent, foster parent, guardian; *family*, blood, stock, strain, line, pedigree, extraction, ancestry; *motherhood*, maternity, mother-to-be, earth mother, surrogate mother, mum (*colloq.*), mater, mamma, matron, matriarch; *fatherhood*, paternity, sire, progenitor, dad (*colloq.*), pater, papa, paterfamilias, patriarch.

adj. *parental*, familial, ancestral; *maternal*,

motherly, matronly, matriarchal; *paternal*, fatherly, patriarchal.

vb. *father*, sire, beget.

adv. in loco parentis.

155 **OFFSPRING**
See also 111 (youth).

n. *offspring*, progeny, issue, young, spawn, litter, brood; *heir*, heiress, successor, descendant, posterity, offshoot, branch, scion, love child, bastard; *descent*, lineage, succession, dynasty, illegitimacy; *pup*, puppy, cub, kitten, foal, colt, piglet, lamb, calf, kid; *fawn*, joey, leveret, chick, chicken, pullet; *duckling*, gosling, cygnet, fledgling, nestling.

adj. *familial*, lineal, filial, hereditary, genetic.

156 **SPACE**
See also 157 (region).

n. *space*, space-time, extension, outer space; *dimensions*, proportions, size, extent, area, volume, capacity, circumference; *range*, span, compass, coverage, radius, sweep, scope, spread; *region*, expanse, tract, reach, stretch; *room*, latitude, margin, clearance, leeway, legroom, headroom, accommodation.

adj. *spatial*, three-dimensional, spatio-temporal; *extensive*, widespread, far-reaching, global, worldwide; *spacious*, roomy, capacious, voluminous, commodious, expansive.

vb. *extend*, range, spread, stretch, sweep; *span*, straddle, cover, enclose, encompass, contain, accommodate.

adv. *extensively*, far and wide, all over, high and low.

157 **REGION**
See also 156 (space).

n. *region*, locality, area, zone, belt, heartland, parallel, latitudes, climes, parts, neck of the woods (*colloq.*); *sphere*, field, domain, arena, theatre; *territory*, enclave, ghetto, exclusion zone, precinct; *state*, realm, kingdom, dominion, protectorate, colony, dependency, republic, superstate; *district*, county, province, shire, parish, ward, borough, hamlet, village; *city*, town, built-up area, new town, conurbation, inner city, city centre, quarter; *suburb*, dormitory town, green belt, stockbroker belt; *environs*, neighbourhood, vicinity, outskirts, hinterland.

adj. *regional*, zonal, provincial; *local*, municipal, parochial, urban, suburban.

158 **LOCATION**

See also 165 (habitat).

n. *location*, situation, site, whereabouts, seat; *haunt*, habitat, patch, pitch, beat, territory, stamping ground; *abode*, residence, quarters, address, premises; *place*, spot, corner, nook, niche, hole, slot, groove; *enclosure*, stockade, compound, pen, paddock, field, quadrangle, courtyard; *compartment*, recess, alcove, cubicle, locker, pigeonhole.

vb. *locate*, site, situate, place; *quarter*, billet, station, post; *reside in*, inhabit, frequent, haunt; *pinpoint*, track, home in, zero in.

adv. *locally*, on the spot.

159 **SITUATION**

See also 160 (placement).

n. *situation*, position, setting, locale, scene, venue; *orientation*, direction, bearings, standpoint, viewpoint; *geography*, topography, orienteering, mapreading.

adj. *situated*, orientated, positioned, located; *geographical*, topographical, directional.

vb. *situate*, site, position, station, post, locate; *orientate*, direct, head.

adv. *in place*, in situ, on site; *on course*, on the right track.

160 **PLACEMENT**

See also 159 (situation).

n. *placement*, emplacement, installation, settlement, establishment; *post*, position, station, base, depot, camp, encampment; *niche*, resting-place, berth, anchorage, garage, storehouse, repository.

adj. *placed*, lodged, installed, ensconced, entrenched, dug in.

vb. *place*, position, install, station, post; *lodge*, establish, embed, fix, house; *anchor*, moor, tether, berth, dock, park; *settle*, colonize, encamp, camp, dig in, pitch, squat.

adv. *in position*, in place; *at rest*, at anchor.

161 **DISPLACEMENT**

See also 58 (disturbance); 266 (expulsion).

n. *displacement*, dislocation, dislodgement, disturbance; *transfer*, transposition, removal, relocation, evacuation; *deposition*, overthrow, coup, takeover, palace revolution; *relegation*, demotion, expulsion, banishment, exile, eviction, homelessness; *dismissal*, sacking,

redundancy, layoff, decruitment, constructive dismissal; *displaced person*, waif, stray, evacuee, refugee, alien, (illegal) immigrant, asylum-seeker, economic migrant, guest worker.

adj. *displaced*, dislocated, disturbed; *disorientated*, uprooted, rootless, homeless; *misplaced*, mislaid, lost, gone astray.

vb. *displace*, dislocate, dislodge, disturb; *transfer*, transpose, shunt, remove, relocate, evacuate; *depose*, unseat, dethrone, usurp, oust, supersede; *relegate*, demote, dismiss, lay off, sack, fire, kick upstairs (*colloq.*), banish, exile, expel; *misplace*, mislay, lose.

adv. *out of place*, out of joint; *out of the running*, out of the picture, out in the cold (*colloq.*), in limbo.

162 **PRESENCE**

See also 85 (accompaniment).

n. *presence*, existence, pervasiveness, omnipresence, ubiquitousness; *situation*, location, position, whereabouts; *availability*, readiness, handiness, convenience; *attendance*, appearance, participation, accompaniment; *residence*, occupancy, habitation; *conspicuousness*, obviousness, visibility; *spectator*, onlooker, audience, bystander, eye-witness, participant, the usual suspects (*colloq.*).

adj. *present*, existent, pervasive, omnipresent, ubiquitous; *available*, ready, handy, convenient; *attendant*, participant, concomitant, accompanying; *resident*, live-in, in-house, residential; *conspicuous*, obvious, visible, eye-catching.

vb. *be present*, pervade, permeate, imbue; *reside*, occupy, inhabit, live in; *participate*, take part, watch, witness, assist at, spectate; *attend*, turn up, present oneself, show up, put in an appearance, look in; *be conspicuous*, stand out, stick out like a sore thumb (*colloq.*), make one's presence felt.

adv. *at hand*, on the spot, on the ground; *to hand*, within reach, on call, on tap; *close to*, under one's nose, to one's face, before one's very eyes; *in person*, live; *at home*, in town, on the premises.

163 **ABSENCE**

See also 2 (non-existence).

n. *absence*, non-existence, disappearance, loss; *non-appearance*, non-attendance, absenteeism, truancy, desertion, defection, French leave; *emptiness*, vacuum, blankness, void, vacancy, gap, omission; *lack*, shortage, want, scarcity, deficiency; *absentee*, non-person, missing person, defector, deserter; *leave of absence*, furlough, holiday, vacation.

adj. *absent*, non-existent, gone, lost, flown, fled; *away*, out, unavailable, off (*colloq.*); *empty*, vacant, void, blank, vacuous, hollow; *lacking*, missing, minus, devoid, deficient, short; *unoccupied*, deserted, abandoned, depopulated, godforsaken.

vb. *be absent*, stay away, be conspicuous by one's absence, vote with one's feet; *depart*, withdraw, retreat, absent oneself, make oneself scarce (*colloq.*); *abandon*, desert, defect, forsake, walk out on; *miss*, skip, go AWOL, play hooky (*colloq.*).

adv. *in one's absence*, in absentia, behind one's back; *off the premises*, out of house; *on leave*, on vacation, on holiday, out of town.

164 **INHABITANT**
See also 165 (habitat).

n. *inhabitant*, dweller, citizen, denizen; *occupant*, resident, householder, owner-occupier; *tenant*, lodger, boarder, paying guest, au pair; *inmate*, incumbent, in-patient; *native*, aborigine, local, villager, parishioner, townee, suburbanite, commuter, city slicker (*colloq.*); *cottager*, crofter, smallholder, peasant, rustic, yokel, country bumpkin; *incomer*, immigrant, settler, colonist, squatter; *household*, ménage; *community*, commune, colony, population, demographic.

adj. *inhabited*, occupied, rented, leased; *native*, indigenous, aboriginal, ethnic, vernacular; *domestic*, local, household, home.

165 **HABITAT**
See also 158 (location); 164 (inhabitant); 762 (recreation).

n. *habitat*, abode, dwelling, domicile, residence, haunt, hang-out (*colloq.*); *base*, headquarters, seat, camp, bivouac, pad (*colloq.*), gaff (*colloq.*); *accommodation*, quarters, billet, lodgings, digs (*colloq.*), squat, hostel, dormitory, dosshouse (*colloq.*); *home*, hearth, fireside, homestead, cradle, home town, birthplace, stamping ground, motherland, fatherland; *lair*, den, burrow, warren, earth, sett, holt, nest, drey, aviary, apiary; *house*, villa, bungalow, chalet, prefab, townhouse, houseboat, caravan, mobile home; *cottage*, cabin, shack, hovel, lean-to, outhouse; *flat*, maisonette, studio, apartment, mews, penthouse, pied-à-terre, bedsitter, granny flat; *mansion*, seat, hall,

grange, manor, chateau, stately home; *housing*, conurbation, housing estate/scheme, tower block, slum, shanty town; *stable*, byre, cowshed, sty, kennel, fold, stall, coop, hutch; *hotel*, boutique hotel, bed and breakfast, b and b, motel, roadhouse, inn, tavern, public house, pub, bar, hostelry, local (*colloq.*), boozer (*colloq.*); *restaurant*, wine bar, bistro, brasserie, trattoria, gastropub; *café*, cafeteria, caff (*colloq.*), transport café, snack bar, juice bar, tearoom, canteen, buffet, takeaway, diner, fish-and-chip shop, pizzeria, kebab shop, Internet café, cybercafé, cannabis café; *retreat*, haven, refuge, sanctuary, halfway house, hospice; *park*, gardens, allotment, arbour, pergola, gazebo, folly, conservatory, glasshouse.

adj. *residential*, built-up, metropolitan, urban, surburban; *detached*, semidetached, terraced, purpose-built, multistorey, high/low rise; *rural*, rustic, countrified; *local*, parochial, municipal.

vb. *inhabit*, occupy, people, settle, colonize, populate; *reside*, dwell, sojourn, lodge, put up at, doss down (*colloq.*), crash (*colloq.*), camp; *frequent*, haunt, visit, hang out at (*colloq.*).

166 **CONTENTS**
See also 53 (component).

n. *contents*, ingredients, components, stuffing, filling, centre; *insides*, guts, entrails, bowels, pith, marrow; *containment*, load, cargo, shipment, freight.

vb. *contain*, hold, enclose, conceal; *insert*, stuff, pack, cram; *take in*, absorb, assimilate, ingest; *containerize*, load, freight, ship, transport.

167 **CONTAINER**
n. *container*, receptacle, holder, frame; *cover*, case, envelope, wrapper, packaging, sheath, cocoon; *depository*, reservoir, store, warehouse, treasury; *boxroom*, cloakroom, strongroom, cellar, bunker, attic; *compartment*, locker, cupboard, cabinet, closet; *box*, chest, casket, coffer, crate, hamper, basket, punnet; *suitcase*, overnight bag, holdall, grip, trunk, baggage; *capsule*, pillbox, canister, carton, caddy, tin, can, tub; *bag*, knapsack, rucksack, haversack, backpack, kitbag, duffel bag; *satchel*, pannier, creel, saddlebag; *purse*, wallet, money-belt, briefcase, attaché case, file, portfolio; *vessel*, barrel, cask, vat, tun, tank, keg, cistern; *vase*, jug, pitcher, carafe, decanter, vial, phial,

flagon, carboy; *bucket*, pail, bin, hopper, silo; *basin*, ewer, pan, pot, urn, kettle, cauldron; *cup*, chalice, goblet, wineglass, schooner, beaker, tumbler, tankard, mug; *bottle*, demijohn, magnum, jeroboam, rehoboam, methuselah; *bowl*, porringer, ramekin, tureen; *plate*, platter, charger, salver.

168 **SIZE**
See also 23 (quantity); 29 (greatness).

n. *size*, proportions, dimensions, amplitude, girth, bulk, magnitude; *extent*, area, volume, mass, weight; *largeness*, bigness, hugeness, vastness, immensity, enormity; *colossus*, mountain, skyscraper, pyramid, mausoleum; *giant*, monster, leviathan, whale, whopper (*colloq.*); *fatness*, obesity, corpulence, portliness, fleshiness, corporation, beer belly/gut, midriff bulge, spare tyre (*colloq.*), flab (*colloq.*); *fat person*, fattie (*colloq.*), hulk, Falstaff, Billy Bunter, slimmer, weight watcher.

adj. *large*, big, sizable, considerable, hefty (*colloq.*); *large-scale*, life-size, full-grown, king-size, economy-size, mammoth, jumbo, outsize, giant, industrial (*colloq.*); *massive*, bulky, huge, enormous, hulking, whopping (*colloq.*); *gigantic*, colossal, monumental, immense, vast, astronomical, gargantuan, Brobdingnagian; *fat*, stout, corpulent, obese, overweight, portly, rotund, plump, chubby, podgy, roly-poly, tubby, buxom, pot-bellied, Falstaffian.

169 **LITTLENESS**
See also 30 (smallness); 179 (shortness).

n. *littleness*, diminutiveness, minuteness, smallness; *scantiness*, meagreness, paucity, skimpiness; *miniature*, mini, baby, microcosm, pinhead, atom, particle, molecule; *dwarf*, midget, manikin, pygmy, Tom Thumb, homunculus; *gnat*, flea, sprat, tiddler, minnow, shrimp, runt, small fry; *microorganism*, microbe, germ, virus, bacterium; *microelectronics*, microcomputer, microprocessor, integrated circuit; *spot*, fleck, dot, speck, mote, crumb, grain, granule, drop, shred.

adj. *little*, small, diminutive, minute, tiny, petite, dainty, dinky (*colloq.*); *small-scale*, toy, baby, mini, miniaturized, pint-sized, wee, titchy (*colloq.*), Lilliputian; *dwarfish*, puny, runty, stunted, undersized; *scanty*, meagre, insufficient, skimpy.

170 **EXPANSION**
See also 33 (increase); 180 (breadth).

n. *expansion*, increase, enlargement, augmentation, amplification, aggrandizement, globalization; *development*, spread, deployment, sweep, sprawl; *inflation*, distension, swollenness, inflammation, tumescence, puffiness, turgidity, dilation; *extensibility*, elasticity, stretchiness, give; *padding*, stuffing, wadding, waffle (*colloq.*), bombast.

adj. *expanded*, inflated, bloated, distended, dilated, taut; *expandable*, stretchy, elastic, extensible; *swollen*, turgid, overblown, tumescent, tumid, bulbous, distended, pot-bellied; *wide*, gaping, flared, bell-bottomed, splayed, spreadeagled, outstretched.

vb. *expand*, broaden, widen, flare, splay; *increase*, augment, enlarge, magnify, wax, amplify; *spread*, develop, fan out, deploy, sprawl, mushroom; *inflate*, balloon, belly, dilate, distend, puff up, swell, inflame; *pad*, stuff, bulk up, beef up (*colloq.*).

171 **CONTRACTION**
See also 34 (decrease); 179 (shortness).

n. *contraction*, shrinkage, reduction, abatement, diminution, decrease, attenuation; *curtailment*, abbreviation, abridgement, constriction, compaction, compression; *decline*, falling-off, slump, recession, squeeze; *compressor*, constrictor, tourniquet, straitjacket, corset.

adj. *contracted*, shrunk, compacted, condensed, abridged, compressed; *constricted*, pinched, drawn, wizened, shrivelled, stunted; *astringent*, tight, constricting, binding.

vb. *contract*, diminish, lessen, decrease, reduce, curtail; *compress*, condense, abridge, abbreviate, boil down; *constrict*, nip, pinch, tighten, clench; *compact*, pack, squeeze, bind, cramp, squash, flatten; *narrow*, taper, attenuate, thin, slim, extrude; *shrivel*, wrinkle, wizen, pucker, crease; *dwarf*, stunt, shorten.

172 **DISTANCE**
See also 178 (length).

n. *distance*, farness, remoteness, inaccessibility; *extent*, range, reach, span, sweep, coverage; *long distance*, long haul, trek, marathon; *outskirts*, purlieus, periphery, frontier, outback, back of beyond; *horizon*, skyline, background, middle distance;

aloofness, detachedness, reserve, stand-offishness.

adj. *distant*, far, far-away, far-off, far-flung, farthest; *remote*, outlying, off-shore, peripheral, inaccessible, out-of-the-way, godforsaken; *foreign*, antipodean, overseas, exotic; *long-distance*, long-range, long-haul; *aloof*, stand-offish, unapproachable, reserved.

vb. *distance*, outdistance, outstrip, outrun, outdo; *carry*, extend, stretch, reach; *keep one's distance*, keep clear of, give a wide berth to, not touch with a bargepole (*colloq.*).

adv. *afar*, far afield, far off, far and wide, to the ends of the earth; *off the beaten track*, in the middle of nowhere, out in the sticks (*colloq.*); *at a distance*, at arm's length; *out of range*, out of sight, out of earshot.

173 **NEARNESS**
See also 176 (juxtaposition).

n. *nearness*, proximity, propinquity, juxtaposition, closeness; *locality*, vicinity, neighbourhood, environs; *close range*, close quarters, pointblank range, foreground, ringside seat; *edge*, brink, verge, border, bank; *short distance*, shortcut, beeline, walking distance, hop, step and jump, stone's throw, spitting distance, hair's breadth; *closeness*, intimacy, understanding, rapport, affection.

adj. *near*, close, approximate, rough; *nearby*, adjoining, local, neighbouring, accessible, handy; *short-distance*, short-range, short-haul; *close*, affectionate, intimate, inseparable; *crowded*, packed, serried.

vb. *be near*, hug, skirt, brush, graze, skim; *approximate*, approach, be in the right ballpark (*colloq.*); *adjoin*, abut, border, verge, touch; *close up*, close ranks, huddle, press, crowd, jostle, elbow, rub shoulders; *follow*, shadow, tail, dog sb's footsteps, tread on sb's heels.

adv. *nearly*, almost, approximately, circa, thereabouts; *nearby*, close to, face to face, eyeball to eyeball, in view; *nigh*, at hand; *practically*, virtually, to all intents and purposes.

174 **INTERVAL**
See also 65 (discontinuity).

n. *interval*, space, gap, interstice, hole, lacuna; *breach*, break, fissure, rupture, crevice, crack, rift, chasm, gulf; *network*, lattice, mesh, trellis, reticulation; *margin*, clearance, leeway, headroom.

adj. *spaced out*, intermittent, sporadic, periodic; *latticed*, criss-cross, gap-toothed, crenellated, filigree, lacy.

vb. *space out*, stagger, intersperse; *gape*, yawn, split, tear, rend, crack; *lattice*, mesh, criss-cross, reticulate, interweave.

adv. *at intervals*, now and then, off and on, here and there.

175 **LAYER**
See also 202 (covering).

n. *layer*, stratum, bed, course, string, vein, seam, band; *level*, floor, storey, tier; *thickness*, ply, coat, overlay, top-coat, veneer; *lamina*, sheet, strip, foil, leaf; *flake*, scale, wafer, slice, lamella, shavings, peelings, parings; *sandwich*, double-decker, onion, Chinese boxes, nest of tables.

adj. *layered*, laminated, lamellate; *flaky*, peeling, scaly, squamose; *overlaid*, overlapping, shingled, clinker-built.

vb. *layer*, laminate, stratify, deck; *overlay*, plate, veneer, coat; *flake*, peel, pare, shave; *overlap*, tile, flag, shingle.

176 **JUXTAPOSITION**
see also 173 (nearness); 207 (interface).

n. *juxtaposition*, contiguity, contact, tangency, proximity; *border*, dividing line, demarcation, watershed, interface, meeting, junction.

adj. *juxtaposed*, adjacent, coterminous, contiguous, adjoining, interconnecting.

vb. *juxtapose*, bring together, butt, dovetail, overlap; *adjoin*, border, abut, skirt, fringe, hem.

adv. *side by side*, cheek by jowl, arm in arm, abreast; *end to end*, bumper to bumper.

177 **MEASUREMENT**
See also 23 (quantity).

n. *measurement*, mensuration, triangulation, calculation, computation, quantification; *valuation*, estimation, assessment, appreciation, appraisal; *geometry*, trigonometry, surveying, sounding; *measure*, gauge, scales, balance, ruler, yardstick, footrule, tape measure; *compass*, callipers, protractor, sextant, quadrant, theodolite; *meter*, thermometer, barometer, speedometer, tacheograph, metronome, Geiger counter; *reference point*, grid, water line, tidemark, Plimsoll line, bench mark.

adj. *metric*, imperial, avoirdupois, troy, SI.

vb. *measure*, mensurate, compute,

calculate, quantify; *estimate*, sound, reckon, weigh up, pace out, valuate, assess, gauge; *rule*, graduate, calibrate, mark off.

178 **LENGTH**
See also 172 (distance).

n. *length*, extent, expanse, reach, stretch, span; *lengthening*, elongation, extension, extrusion; *protraction*, prolongation, slowness, longueur, tedium; *line*, queue, file, string, crocodile; *longitude*, parallel, wavelength, waveband, frequency.

adj. *long*, longitudinal, extended, elongated, extruded; *lengthy*, protracted, prolonged, long-drawn-out, long-winded, tedious; *full-length*, uncut, unabridged.

vb. *lengthen*, elongate, extend, extrude, stretch, expand; *protract*, prolong, draw out, spin out, drag out.

adv. *lengthways*, from stem to stern, from top to toe; *at length*, lengthily, long.

179 **SHORTNESS**
See also 169 (littleness); 171 (contraction).

n. *shortness*, scarcity, scantiness, skimpiness; *abridgement*, condensation, summary, precis, résumé; *conciseness*, compression, succinctness, terseness, ellipsis, thumbnail sketch; *brevity*, transience, fleetingness; *squatness*, dumpiness, stockiness, stubbiness.

adj. *short*, scanty, scarce, insufficient, skimpy; *abridged*, condensed, potted, cut; *concise*, terse, succinct, elliptical, laconic, curt; *brief*, transient, fleeting, short-lived; *curtailed*, foreshortened, truncated, headless, retroussé, blunt; *squat*, dumpy, stocky, petite, stubby, stunted.

vb. *shorten*, cut, curtail, reduce, contract; *abridge*, abbreviate, condense, summarize, precis, telescope, compress; *cut short*, interrupt, truncate, guillotine, behead, foreshorten, dock, prune, lop.

adv. *in short*, briefly, in sum, to cut a long story short, in a nutshell.

180 **BREADTH**
See also 170 (expansion).

n. *breadth*, width, girth, latitude, span, diameter; *amplitude*, scope, range, extent; *expanse*, panorama, vista, sweep; *broad-mindedness*, tolerance, permissiveness, liberalness.

adj. *broad*, wide, wide-angle, wide-bodied, broad in the beam, broad-shouldered, flared, bell-bottomed; *wide-ranging*, extensive,

sweeping, far-reaching; *expansive*, roomy, spacious, ample; *broad-minded*, liberal, tolerant, permissive.

vb. *broaden*, widen, extend, stretch, spread one's wings; *splay*, sprawl, spreadeagle, flare, bell.

adv. *widthways*, across; *broadly*, loosely, roughly.

181 **NARROWNESS**
See also 171 (contraction); 183 (thinness).

n. *narrowness*, tightness, constriction, compression, contraction; *confinement*, restrictedness, crampedness, overcrowding, tight fit, tight squeeze, no room to swing a cat; *narrow space*, corner, cranny, nook, crack, cleft, chink, crevice; *strait*, gully, gorge, ravine, pass, defile; *neck*, isthmus, chimney, funnel, bottleneck, hourglass; *line*, path, strip, vein, streak, stripe, bar, belt, band, ribbon, knife-edge, pinhead; *narrow-mindedness*, intolerance, prejudice, bigotry.

adj. *narrow*, tight, constricted, compressed, pinched; *skin-tight*, figure-hugging, clinging, slinky; *confined*, overcrowded, cramped, restricted, straitened; *narrow-minded*, intolerant, prejudiced, bigoted.

vb. *narrow*, converge, streamline, taper, funnel; *tighten*, contract, pinch, squeeze, constrict; *confine*, cramp, restrict, tether, hobble, fetter; *cling*, hug, cleave, adhere, stick like glue.

182 **THICKNESS**
See also 168 (size); 317 (semiliquid).

n. *thickness*, solidity, massiveness, bulk, body, density, consistency; *breadth*, ampleness, generosity, fullness, abundance; *viscosity*, tackiness, lumpiness, stodginess, clottedness, pulpiness, soupiness; *sediment*, mud, silt, jelly, curd, soup, pulp; *thickener*, padding, wadding, stuffing, bulk, starch, emulsifier; *thick-headedness*, dullness, stolidness, crassness, stupidity.

adj. *thick*, solid, massive, bulky, dense; *ample*, generous, lavish, full, plentiful, abundant, thick on the ground; *clotted*, lumpy, stodgy, starchy, soupy, pulpy, viscous, tacky; *thick-headed*, dull, stolid, obtuse, crass, stupid, blockheaded.

vb. *thicken*, fatten, pad, wad, stuff, bulk up; *solidify*, coagulate, clot, curdle, congeal, gel.

183 **THINNESS**
See also 171 (contraction); 181 (narrowness).

n. *thinness*, slimness, slenderness, leanness,

skinniness, emaciation, anorexia; *thin person*, beanpole, rake, scarecrow, anorexic; *filament*, stalk, tendril, antenna, wire, thread, fibre, capillary; *streak*, strand, splinter, sliver, wafer, shavings; *fineness*, delicacy, transparency, translucency, sheerness; *gauze*, tulle, chiffon, gossamer, cobweb, eggshell; *sparseness*, rarity, infrequency.

adj. *thin*, slim, slender, svelte, willowy, lissom, lithe, leggy, lean, wiry, sinewy, spare; *underweight*, skinny, skeletal, emaciated, anorexic, spindly, lanky, scraggy, scrawny, gaunt, haggard, raw-boned; *threadlike*, filamentous, fine-spun, stringy, fibrous, streaky; *flimsy*, fragile, delicate, transparent, translucent, sheer, diaphanous; *fluid*, runny, watery, dilute, weak; *sparse*, infrequent, thin on the ground.

vb. *thin*, reduce, slim down, streamline, prune, weed out; *rarefy*, attenuate, dilute, water down, liquefy, melt; *contract*, narrow, taper, shrink.

184 **HEIGHT**

See also 188 (summit); 190 (verticality); 274 (ascent); 276 (raising).

n. *height*, altitude, elevation, stature, tallness, loftiness, verticality, steepness; *high point*, summit, climax, zenith, ceiling, heavens, sky; *vantage point*, bird's eye view, overview, watchtower, lookout, crow's nest, platform, dais, rostrum; *heights*, highland, upland, mountain, alp, peak, crest, Everest; *cliff*, precipice, bluff, escarpment, slope, gradient, incline; *tower*, spire, steeple, mast, telemast, skyscraper, tower block, penthouse, attic, rooftop, the Empire State Building; *ascent*, climb, rise, takeoff.

adj. *high*, sky-high, aerial, elevated, lofty; *steep*, vertical, vertiginous, precipitous; *mountainous*, alpine, towering, soaring, multistorey, high-rise; *tall*, lanky, rangy, gangly.

vb. *heighten*, raise, elevate, uplift; *tower*, soar, hover, overlook, overhang; *ascend*, rise, climb, scale, mount.

adv. *above*, overhead, upstairs, on high, aloft.

185 **LOWNESS**

See also 189 (base); 275 (descent); 277 (lowering).

n. *lowness*, smallness, squatness, dwarfishness; *flatness*, floor, sea level, plain, foothills, depression, flats, lowland, valley; *low point*, nadir, base, rock bottom, plinth,

foot, ground; *underneath*, underside, underbelly, worm's-eye view; *descent*, dip, fall, drop, decline.

adj. *low*, supine, prostrate, laid low, flat out; *bent*, hunched, bowed, stooping, crouched; *small*, squat, petite, stunted, dwarfish; *low-lying*, flat, level, sunken, depressed, subterranean, underground.

vb. *lower*, depress, flatten, level, raze, lay low; *bend*, stoop, hunch, crouch, cower, duck, crawl, kneel, knuckle under, bow; *descend*, fall, tumble, dip, plunge.

adv. *below*, underfoot, underneath, underground, downstairs.

186 **DEPTH**

See also 277 (lowering).

n. *depth*, the deep end, depression, hollow, crater, pit, shaft, well, mine, excavation; *depths*, the deep, abyss, chasm, bowels, underworld; *plunge*, dive, immersion, submersion; *cellar*, basement, vault, crypt, dungeon; *profundity*, deep thought, searching, thoroughness.

adj. *deep*, profound, thorough, probing, in-depth; *cavernous*, yawning, gaping, bottomless, fathomless, unplumbed; *entrenched*, embedded, deep-seated, deep-rooted; *buried*, underground, subterranean, deep-sea, underwater.

vb. *deepen*, darken, worsen, intensify; *excavate*, dig, hollow, gouge out; *sound*, probe, fathom, plumb the depths; *bury*, entrench, embed, entomb; *sink*, submerge, plummet, dive, plunge.

adv. *deeply*, profoundly, intensely; *at bottom*, deep down; *out of* one's *depth*, over one's head, in deep water.

187 **SHALLOWNESS**

See also 577 (unimportance).

n. *shallowness*, slightness, cursoriness, superficiality, triviality; *shallows*, shoals, ford, puddle; *surface*, façade, overlay, topcoat, veneer, gloss; *surface wound*, scratch, pinprick, graze, scrape.

adj. *shallow*, slight, perfunctory, cursory, trivial, lightweight, superficial, -light *or* -lite; *surface*, skin-deep, cosmetic; *thin*, light, sparse, meagre.

vb. *be shallow*, skim, graze, scrape, brush, tickle; *dabble*, paddle, tinker, scratch the surface, make no impression on; *face*, coat, gloss, veneer, touch up.

188 **SUMMIT**

See also 184 (height).

n. *summit*, brow, top, peak, crest, pinnacle, tip, crown, apex, vertex; *high point*, zenith, acme, apogee, apotheosis, culmination, climax; *maximum*, high-water mark, ceiling, upper limit; *roof*, coping, capstone, steeple, spire; *head*, pate, poll, noddle (*colloq.*), bonce (*colloq.*), block (*colloq.*), nut (*colloq.*), loaf (*colloq.*).

adj. *topmost*, top, highest, uppermost, maximal; *crowning*, climactic, supreme.

vb. *top*, cap, crown, tip, crest; *climax*, peak, go through the roof.

adv. *at the top of the tree*, on the top rung of the ladder.

189 **BASE**

See also 185 (lowness); 193 (support).

n. *base*, foot, bottom, root, underneath; *foundation*, basis, infrastructure, underlay, substratum, bedrock; *support*, plinth, pedestal, stand; *ground*, ground floor, basement, mezzanine, entresol; *minimum*, floor, lower limit, rock bottom, nadir; *starting point*, first base, square one; *foot*, plates of meat (*colloq.*), toe, tootsie (*colloq.*).

adj. *base*, bottom, lowest, underlying, nethermost; *basic*, fundamental, elemental, rudimentary, elementary, entry-level.

vb. *base*, ground, set, establish, found; *support*, underpin, underlie, maintain, uphold; *bottom out*, go through the floor, hit bedrock.

adv. *basically*, at bottom, when you get down to it.

190 **VERTICALITY**

See also 184 (height).

n. *verticality*, perpendicularity, uprightness, erectness; *steepness*, precipitousness, sheerness, plumbness; *vertical*, upright, pillar, column, ramrod, obelisk, stalagmite, standing-stone, menhir; *wall*, cliff, precipice, bluff, escarpment, sheer drop.

adj. *vertical*, upright, erect, perpendicular, standing, rampant; *steep*, precipitous, sheer, abrupt, plumb, vertiginous.

vb. *be vertical*, rear, stand, be upstanding; *erect*, pitch, raise, upend, cock, stick up; prick up; *plunge*, plummet, drop like a stone.

adv. *vertically*, on end, bolt upright; *from north to south*, from top to toe.

191 **HORIZONTALITY**

See also 292 (smoothness).

n. *horizontality*, flatness, breadth, levelness, proneness, supineness; *sweep*, vista, panorama, horizon, skyline; *plane*, level, plateau, tableland, steppe, flats, fens; *ledge*, shelf, terrace, tier, balcony; *iron*, bulldozer, steamroller, juggernaut.

adj. *horizontal*, level, plane, even, flush, flat; *prone*, prostrate, reclining, recumbent, supine, couchant.

vb. *be horizontal*, stretch, sweep, sprawl, extend; *recline*, repose, loll, lie back; *flatten*, level, even, roll, iron out, tread, trample, stamp; *raze*, floor, ground, bring down, topple.

adv. *horizontally*, widthways, from side to side, from east to west.

192 **SUSPENSION**

n. *suspension*, hanging, pendency, fall; *droopiness*, pendulousness, bagginess, looseness; *droop*, sag, hang, swing; *pendulum*, bob, plumbline, pendant, tassel, earring, icicle, stalactite, chandelier, hammock; *curtain*, hanging, drapery, train, skirt; *dewlap*, jowls, lobe, wattle, double chin; *hanger*, suspender, hook, spar, boom, gallows, gibbet, crane, jib.

adj. *suspended*, hanging, pendent; *pendulous*, saggy, droopy, baggy, slack; *loose*, dangling, trailing, weeping; *free-hanging*, floating, flyaway, free-floating.

vb. *suspend*, hang, drape, hitch, hook; *fall*, droop, sag, bag; *dangle*, swing, flap, trail, weep, straggle, stream, float.

193 **SUPPORT**

See also 189 (base).

n. *support*, underpinning, chassis, undercarriage, mounting; *reinforcement*, back-up, encouragement, sponsorship; *foundation*, base, cornerstone, mainstay, bedrock, backbone; *prop*, shore, strut, stay, buttress, pier, beam, joist, rafter, girder; *cane*, stick, rod, pole, staff, walking stick, crutch, shooting stick; *stand*, tripod, trivet, easel, trestle, pedestal, plinth; *bolster*, cushion, mattress, pillow, headrest, footstool; *brace*, truss, corset, foundation garment, splint, surgical collar; *floor*, ground, pavement, terra firma, dry land; *banister*, balustrade, handrail, parapet; *bracket*, shelf, ledge, sill, platform, counter; *pivot*, fulcrum, lever, axle, spine; *supporter*, backer, sponsor, patron, ally, helpmate, tower of strength.

adj. *supporting*, structural, sustaining.

vb. *support*, sustain, maintain, carry, bear, shoulder, uphold; *prop*, shore up, underpin, buttress, brace, bolster, stay; *reinforce*, back, stand by, stick up for, sponsor, champion, buoy up, encourage; *frame*, mount, cradle, pillow, cushion.

194 **PARALLELISM**

n. *parallelism*, equidistance, coextension; *correspondence*, similarity, analogy, comparison; *parallelogram*, trapezium, rectangle, tramlines, railway lines.

adj. *parallel*, equidistant, coextensive; *similar*, corresponding, analogous, comparable.

vb. *be parallel*, correspond, match, tally; *compare*, liken, equate, draw a parallel.

adv. *in parallel*, side by side, alongside, abreast.

195 **OBLIQUENESS**

See also 220 (angle).

n. *obliqueness*, indirectness, implicitness, ellipsis; *diagonal*, tangent, zigzag, chevron, herringbone; *deviation*, divergence, bias, slant; *slope*, incline, gradient, ramp, bank; *angle*, batter, bevel, rake, cant, list.

adj. *oblique*, indirect, implicit, elliptical, circuitous, roundabout; *angled*, squint, aslant, diagonal, transverse, sideways, sidelong.

vb. *be oblique*, lean, list, tilt, pitch, tip; *slope*, incline, shelve, bank, slant, cant, careen; *diverge*, sidestep, jink, dodge, zigzag, edge, sidle; *angle*, bevel, warp, camber, chamfer, mitre.

adv. *obliquely*, at an angle, edgeways, crabwise; *to one side*, out of true, out of plumb.

196 **INVERSION**

See also 126 (reversion); 129 (exchange).

n. *inversion*, transposition, substitution, swap (*colloq.*), changeover, retroversion, eversion; *anagram*, metathesis, palindrome, spoonerism; *upset*, capsizal, somersault, cartwheel, revolution; *reversal*, about-turn, U-turn, volte-face.

adj. *inverted*, inverse, topsy-turvy, upside-down.

vb. *invert*, transpose, interchange, change round, put the cart before the horse, reverse, turn the tables; *capsize*, overturn, upset, upend, stand on its head; *revolve*, somersault, turn turtle, come full circle; *tip*, tilt, keel over, topple.

adv. *inversely*, vice versa; *back to front*, inside out, upside down, head over heels, topsy turvy.

197 **INTERWEAVING**

See also 174 (interval); 299 (texture); 569 (materials).

n. *interweaving*, criss-crossing, network, complex, figure of eight, wickerwork, basketry; *grid*, grille, lattice, trellis, reticulation, netting, webbing; *tracery*, fretwork, filigree, honeycomb, mesh, openwork, yarn, fabric, textile; *braid*, wreath, plait, skein, knot, bow, cat's cradle, tangle, snarl; *cross*, intersection, crossroads, crucifix, ankh, saltire, swastika.

adj. *interwoven*, interlocking, pleached, criss-cross, cruciform; *complex*, intricate, involved, tangled, ravelled, matted.

vb. *interweave*, interlace, interlock, intertwine; *plait*, braid, wreathe, pleach, twist, spin, weave, darn; *cross*, intersect, cut across, criss-cross; *enmesh*, entangle, ravel, snarl, embroil, implicate, involve.

198 **EXTERIOR**

See also 6 (extraneousness); 52 (exclusion).

n. *exterior*, periphery, circumference, perimeter, sidelines; *surface*, appearance, face, façade, shell, mask; *externalization*, extroversion, embodiment, concretization, materialization; *exclusion*, eviction, expulsion, ejection; *outside*, out of doors, open air, the great outdoors; *outdoor type*, fresh-air fiend; *outside world*, parole, day release, day boy/girl, outsider, ex-prisoner.

adj. *exterior*, external, outlying, peripheral, extraneous; *outer*, surface, superficial, prima facie, skin-deep, cosmetic, facial; *extrovert*, outward-looking, outgoing; *outside*, outdoor, out-of-house, extramural, public.

vb. *externalize*, embody, body forth, project, materialize; *expel*, eject, exclude, evict, banish; *cover*, surround, circumscribe, enclose.

adv. *on the outside*, out in the cold, in limbo; *on the face of it*, to all appearances, at first sight; *outside*, in the open, al fresco, out and about.

199 **INTERIOR**

See also 5 (essence); 166 (contents).

n. *interior*, inside, centre, heartland, core, hub, nub, heart, nerve centre; *pith*, marrow, quick, kernel, heartwood; *insides*, innards, inner man, vitals, viscera, entrails, guts, bowels; *introversion*, introspection, self-

absorption, egotism; *insider*, inmate,
internee, boarder, stay-at-home, homebody;
insertion, injection, introduction,
intromission; *absorption*, assimilation,
incorporation, ingestion.

adj. *interior*, internal, inner, innermost,
central; *inside*, private, intimate, domestic,
home, indoor, in-house; *endemic*, deep-
seated, ingrained, ingrown; *introverted*,
inward-looking, introspective.

vb. *internalize*, incorporate, assimilate,
absorb, ingest, inhale; *enclose*, enfold,
embrace, encapsulate; *confine*, intern,
imprison, shut in.

adv. *inside*, indoors, at home, en famille;
inwardly, deep down, at heart.

200 CENTRE
See also 63 (middle).

n. *centre*, heart, nucleus, hub, epicentre,
bull's eye; *middle*, waistline, midriff,
diameter, watershed, parting; *pivot*, fulcrum,
hinge, axis; *focus*, centre of attraction,
cynosure, centrepiece; *meeting point*,
junction, rallying point, node; *centrality*,
importance, relevance.

adj. *central*, focal, key, crucial, vital,
pivotal; *centripetal*, convergent.

vb. *centralize*, converge, concentrate, focus,
home in on, zero in on; *centre on*, hinge on,
turn on, pivot on.

adv. *at the heart*, at the core.

201 LINING
See also 202 (covering).

n. *lining*, liner, facing, interlining, inlay;
filling, wadding, padding, quilting, stuffing;
insulation, soundproofing, backing,
panelling, cladding; *coating*, furring,
encrustation, scale.

vb. *line*, face, interline, inlay; *fill*, stuff,
wad, pad, quilt, pack; *coat*, fur, encrust.

202 COVERING
See also 175 (layer); 201 (lining); 378 (screen).

n. *covering*, surface, overlay, overlap,
superimposition; *cover*, coating, topping,
wrapping, packaging, lagging; *lid*, flap,
shutter, trapdoor, cap, stopper, plug, bung;
envelope, sheath, scabbard, ferule, holster;
tarpaulin, loose cover, dustsheet, pillowcase,
tea cosy; *case*, wrapper, dustjacket, boards,
record sleeve, folder; *roof*, thatch, canopy,
awning, tent, marquee; *hood*, umbrella,
sunshade, blind, screen, curtain; *cocoon*,
shroud, winding sheet, swaddling clothes,

bandage; *skin*, epidermis, integument, bark,
peel, rind, husk, pod, jacket; *shell*, armour,
carapace, shield, crust, scab; *fur*, pelt, fleece,
hair, hide, plumage; *blanket*, sheet, mantle,
robe, cloak, veil, pall, mask, disguise; *veneer*,
varnish, lacquer, enamel, glaze, paint,
whitewash; *flooring*, linoleum, vinyl,
matting, paving, cobblestones, screed,
asphalt, tarmac.

adj. *covered*, overlaid, surfaced, paved,
metalled; *wrapped*, veiled, cloaked, clad,
enveloped.

vb. *cover*, overlay, superimpose, layer; *coat*,
spread, smear, smother; *envelop*, cloak,
blanket, shroud; *wrap*, bandage, swathe,
cocoon; *encase*, encapsulate, enclose,
sheathe, box, pack; *roof*, thatch, tile, slate,
cap, top; *surface*, floor, pave, metal, tarmac;
paint, render, whitewash, varnish, veneer,
lacquer, enamel, glaze; *mask*, hood, conceal,
disguise, draw a veil over.

203 UNCOVERING
See also 205 (undress); 469 (disclosure).

n. *uncovering*, stripping, denudation,
defoliation, shedding, moulting; *bareness*,
undress, nakedness, baldness, alopecia;
disclosure, unveiling, revelation, exposure;
paint-remover, stripper, solvent, depilatory,
hair-remover, defoliant; *detective*, private eye,
sleuth, investigator.

adj. *uncovered*, bare, naked, stripped,
denuded, threadbare; *hairless*, bald, leafless,
plucked, skinned, clean-shaven, thin on top.

vb. *uncover*, divest, disrobe, strip; *skin*, flay,
scalp, pluck, peel, husk, pod, shell; *shed*, cast,
moult, slough; *denude*, lay bare, defoliate,
devastate; *unpack*, unwrap, unfold, expose;
disclose, divulge, reveal, unmask, unveil, take
the lid off *(colloq.)*.

204 DRESS
See also 202 (covering).

n. *dress*, cover, clothing, apparel, attire,
garb, costume, raiment; *wardrobe*, outfit,
ensemble, rig-out *(colloq.)*, wear, gear, togs
(colloq.), clobber *(colloq.)*, duds *(colloq.)*;
garment, coordinates, separates, underwear,
lingerie, outerwear, headgear, footwear;
dressing-up, evening dress, white tie, finery,
toilette, Sunday best, one's best bib and
tucker, glad rags *(colloq.)*, fancy dress;
uniform, regalia, livery, subfusc, weeds,
mourning, khaki, fatigues; *old clothes*, rags,
hand-me-downs, cast-offs; *clothier*, tailor,
costumier, outfitter, designer, couturier;

fashion, rag trade, haute couture, high fashion.

adj. *dressed*, clad, decent, got up, overdressed, dressed up to the nines (*colloq.*), tarted up (*colloq.*), dolled up (*colloq.*); *well-dressed*, soigné, groomed, fashionable, well turned-out, smart; *tailored*, bespoke, made-to-measure, custom-made, off-the-peg, ready-to-wear.

vb. *dress*, clothe, array, robe, garb, deck out; *wear*, don, sport, try on, slip on, throw on; *dress up*, spruce up, titivate, prink, smarten up.

205 UNDRESS
See also 203 (uncovering).

n. *undress*, casual wear, civvies, plain clothes, mufti, dishabille; *nakedness*, nudity, indecent exposure, naturism, striptease, exotic dancing, birthday suit (*colloq.*), the full monty (*colloq.*); *stripper*, ecdysiast, flasher (*colloq.*), streaker (*colloq.*), exhibitionist, nudist, naturist.

adj. *undressed*, bare, half-dressed, underdressed, barelegged, barefooted, naked, nude, starkers (*colloq.*); *décolleté*, plunging, low-necked, revealing, skimpy, mini.

vb. *undress*, strip, peel off (*colloq.*), disrobe, divest oneself, get naked (*colloq.*); *undo*, untie, unbutton, unzip; *take off*, throw off, slip out of.

adv. *in the nude*, in the altogether (*colloq.*), in the buff (*colloq.*), in the raw (*colloq.*), without a stitch on.

206 SURROUNDINGS
See also 210 (enclosure).

n. *surroundings*, milieu, environment, background, setting, frame; *circumference*, perimeter, periphery, outskirts, boundary, environs, purlieus; *neighbourhood*, vicinity, precincts, region; *ambience*, atmosphere, mood, climate.

adj. *surrounding*, peripheral, environmental, climatic, ambient, atmospheric.

vb. *surround*, encompass, encircle, envelop, enclose, embrace; *ring*, circumscribe, contain, cordon off, hem, circle.

adv. *on all sides*, all around, to right and to left.

207 INTERFACE
See also 176 (juxtaposition); 269 (insertion).

n. *interface*, meeting point, junction, crossroads, intersection; *boundary*, frontier,

divide, watershed, parting; *midpoint*, median, midriff, diaphragm; *partition*, curtain, screen, party wall, buffer, bulkhead; *intervention*, intercession, interception, interference.

adj. *intervening*, interjacent, juxtaposed; *intermediate*, coterminous, contiguous; *interfering*, intrusive, obtrusive.

vb. *put between*, layer, sandwich, wedge, bracket; *interpose*, intercalate, introduce, interleave, interlard; *interfere*, intercede, intercept, intervene; *divide*, come between, separate, demarcate.

208 OUTLINE
See also 223 (circularity).

n. *outline*, profile, silhouette, relief, contour, shape; *frame*, border, surround, rim, edge, periphery, circumference; *sketch*, diagram, figure, delineation; *broad/rough outline*, skeleton, germ, gist, embryo.

vb. *outline*, delineate, trace, frame, silhouette, profile; *sketch*, jot, rough out, map out, block out.

209 EDGE
See also 211 (limit).

n. *edge*, verge, brink, fringe, margin, tip, corner; *lip*, rim, brim, flange, welt; *boundary*, extremity, outer limit, perimeter, confines; *coastline*, seaboard, littoral, shoreline, beach; *roadside*, kerb, verge, gutter, hard shoulder; *threshold*, sill, doorstep, porch; *edging*, frame, mounting, hem, border, frill, trim, piping.

adj. *marginal*, peripheral, borderline, fringe; *riverside*, riparian, wayside, roadside; *scalloped*, bevelled, deckle-edged.

vb. *edge*, trim, hem, fringe, border; *rim*, skirt, verge.

210 ENCLOSURE
See also 206 (surroundings).

n. *enclosure*, fold, pen, compound, paddock, stockade, corral; *arena*, pitch, ring, court, yard, rink, ground, stadium, amphitheatre; *fence*, railing, cordon, paling, barrier, palisade, hedge; *ditch*, trench, moat, ha-ha; *case*, envelope, wrapper, jacket, cover.

vb. *enclose*, pen, cage, hem in, fence in, wall up, immure, confine, corral; *encircle*, encompass, surround, besiege, picket, seal off, cordon off; *encase*, enfold, wrap, envelop.

211 LIMIT
See also 209 (edge).

n. *limit*, threshold, edge, boundary; *upper/lower limit*, ceiling, cut-off point, sticking point, saturation point; *extremity*, end, terminus, finishing line, winning post, destination; *frontier*, border, no-man's land, borderline; *dateline*, horizon, equator, skyline; *deadline*, time limit, ultimatum, final offer; *delimitation*, definition, circumscription, demarcation, restriction.

adj. *limited*, defined, demarcated, set; *bordering*, coterminous, edging.

vb. *limit*, bound, border, edge, mark out, demarcate; *delimit*, define, outline, circumscribe; *curb*, confine, restrict, contain.

212 **FRONT**
See also 59 (precedence).

n. *front*, fore, forefront, foreground, prominence, high profile; *anteroom*, forecourt, threshold, entrance; *frontage*, façade, fascia, facing, veneer; *vanguard*, spearhead, avant-garde, front line, firing line; *bow*, prow, nose, beak, brow, forehead; *right side*, topside, recto, heads; *face*, countenance, physiognomy, kisser (*colloq.*), mush (*colloq.*), dial (*colloq.*), mug (*colloq.*); *front man*, presenter, spokesman/-person/-woman, figurehead, cover, decoy.

adj. *frontal*, forward, anterior, full-frontal; *facing*, opposite, oncoming, head-on; *frontline*, in the firing line, at the coalface; *advance*, leading, head, foremost, prominent, up-front (*colloq.*).

vb. *front*, lead, head up, spearhead; *come to the fore*, step forward, advance, forge ahead, be out in front; *face*, confront, brave, breast.

adv. *in front*, forward, downstage; *ahead*, in advance, in the forefront.

213 **REAR**
See also 60 (sequence).

n. *rear*, tail, stern, back end, wake, train; *rearguard*, sweeper, back, backstop; *background*, back seat, low profile, back-room boy; *backdrop*, backstage, back door, hinterland; *reverse*, verso, flipside, tails; *hindquarters*, buttocks, backside (*colloq.*), behind (*colloq.*), posterior, bum (*colloq.*), arse (*vulg.*).

adj. *rear*, back, hind, hindmost, rearmost; *reverse*, backward, back-to-front; *dorsal*, vertebral, lumbar.

vb. *back*, reverse, retrace one's steps, double back, turn tail; *bring up the rear*, lag, trail, straggle.

adv. *in the rear*, behind, upstage, aft, astern, backwards.

214 **SIDE**
See also 252 (deviation).

n. *side*, flank, broadside, wing, profile; *sidelines*, siding, edge, margin, fringe; *diversion*, deflection, sidestep, bypass, digression, tangent; *right*, right hand, off side, starboard; *left*, left hand, near side, on side, port, larboard, southpaw.

adj. *lateral*, side, sidelong; *oblique*, tangential, indirect, roundabout, circuitous; *right*, clockwise, ambidextrous, dextral; *left*, anticlockwise, sinistral.

vb. *flank*, edge, sidle, skirt, border; *divert*, sidetrack, deflect; *deviate*, digress, sidestep, bypass.

adv. *sideways*, crabwise; *side by side*, abreast, alongside.

215 **CONTRAPOSITION**
See also 14 (oppositeness).

n. *contraposition*, polarity, contrariety; *opposite*, antithesis, reverse, inverse; *polarization*, confrontation, opposition.

adj. *opposite*, contrary, counter, antithetical, opposed, adverse; *polar*, antipodean, arctic, antarctic.

vb. *be opposite*, face, confront, oppose, run counter to, challenge.

adv. *against*, contrariwise.

216 **FORM**
See also 149 (production); 298 (structure).

n. *form*, shape, figure, configuration; *outline*, silhouette, contour, profile; *design*, style, appearance, look, lines, format; *structure*, build, architecture, skeleton, framework, infrastructure; *layout*, arrangement, feng shui; *pattern*, mould, template, die, stamp, prototype; *formation*, production, creation, formulation, expression.

adj. *formative*, architectural, structural; *plastic*, fictile, malleable, pliable, impressionable; *shaped*, defined, solid, three-dimensional.

vb. *form*, make, create, produce, shape, fashion, style; *outline*, sketch, design, draft; *pattern*, mould, die, stamp, coin; *model*, carve, turn, throw, sculpt, chisel, hew, cast, forge; *formulate*, express, devise, work up, lick/knock into shape (*colloq.*); *take shape*, materialize, develop, come into being.

217 **SHAPELESSNESS**
See also 219 (distortion).

n. *shapelessness*, amorphousness,

formlessness, chaos; *indefiniteness*, indistinctness, vagueness, fuzziness, woolliness, blur; *fluidity*, liquidity, volatility, mobility, changeability; *raw material*, rough diamond, embryo, amoeba; *scribble*, scrawl, doodle, squiggle.

adj. *shapeless*, amorphous, formless, featureless, unformed, inchoate; *indefinite*, indeterminate, vague, indistinct, nebulous, blurred, fuzzy, woolly, messy, chaotic; *fluid*, liquid, volatile, mobile, unstable, protean; *raw*, rough, crude, brute, embryonic; *unfinished*, unprocessed, rough-hewn, uncut, unpolished.

vb. *deform*, warp, twist, distort, knock out of shape; *blur*, smudge, confuse, jumble, mess up; *dissolve*, melt, thaw, liquefy.

218 **SYMMETRY**
See also 25 (equality).

n. *symmetry*, proportion, balance, equilibrium; *correspondence*, equivalence, analogy, parallelism; *harmony*, regularity, evenness, rhythm.

adj. *symmetrical*, proportional, balanced, equal; *corresponding*, parallel, analogous, similar; *harmonious*, regular, even, classical.

219 **DISTORTION**
See also 217 (shapelessness).

n. *distortion*, contortion, twistedness, convolution, tortuousness; *asymmetry*, inequality, imbalance, irregularity, disproportion, lopsidedness, squintness; *deformity*, malformation, abnormality, disfigurement, mutilation; *misrepresentation*, bias, skew, exaggeration, perversion.

adj. *distorted*, contorted, convoluted, tortuous, twisted, gnarled; *asymmetrical*, unequal, disproportionate, uneven, irregular; *askew*, awry, crooked, squint, lopsided, skew-whiff (*colloq.*); *bent*, buckled, bowed, bandy, hunch-backed, knock-kneed; *deformed*, misshapen, abnormal, stunted, crippled; *biased*, loaded, skewed, perverted.

vb. *distort*, contort, twist, screw, knot; *bend*, buckle, bow, warp, crumple, give; *grimace*, scowl, pucker, frown, pull a face; *deform*, disfigure, mangle, mutilate, cripple, stunt; *misrepresent*, misconstrue, pervert, fudge, bias, weight, skew.

220 **ANGLE**
See also 195 (obliqueness).

n. *angle*, crook, bend, hook, elbow, dog-leg, branch, fork, crutch; *corner*, nook, recess,

niche, cranny; *triangle*, wedge, arrowhead, chevron, prism, pyramid; *square*, cube, rectangle, oblong, diamond, lozenge, rhombus, parallelogram; *polygon*, pentangle, Star of David, hexagon, octagon.

adj. *angular*, aquiline, hooked, right-angled, L-shaped; *bent*, akimbo, forked, pointed, jagged, zigzag; *triangular*, cuneiform, pyramidal, wedge-shaped; *square*, cuboid, rectangular, rhomboid; *polygonal*, hexagonal, octagonal.

vb. *angle*, point, corner, hook, bend, crook, fold, zigzag; *fork*, branch, ramify, deviate, go off at a tangent.

221 **CURVE**
See also 224 (convolution); 226 (convexity).

n. *curve*, flexion, arc, trajectory, parabola, sweep; *curvature*, sinuosity, concavity, convexity; *deflection*, swerve, deviation, detour; *bend*, turn, hairpin, U-turn, horseshoe, oxbow, bay, bight, cove; *loop*, endless belt, Möbius strip, oval, scallop, festoon, swag; *bow*, arch, arcade, vault, ogive, crescent, sickle, half-moon; *hump-back*, wave, undulation, S-bend, figure of eight, switchback, roller coaster.

adj. *curved*, arched, bent, ovoid, rounded, curvilinear; *semicircular*, convex, concave, domed, hemispherical; *curvy*, shapely, curvaceous, voluptuous, pear-shaped; *wavy*, undulating, rolling, sinuous; *heart-shaped*, bow-legged, bandy-legged, swan-necked; *turned-up*, retroussé, tip-tilted.

vb. *curve*, swerve, turn, bend, sweep; *bow*, flex, round, arch, vault, dome; *loop*, coil, scallop, festoon, swag; *roll*, undulate, unfold, unfurl.

222 **STRAIGHTNESS**
See also 190 (verticality); 191 (horizontality).

n. *straightness*, alignment, linearity, directness, verticality, horizontality, perpendicularity; *rigidity*, stiffness, tautness, inflexibility; *straight line*, beeline, direct route, short cut; *vertical*, horizontal, upright, poker, plumb, ramrod.

adj. *straight*, linear, rectilinear, true, level, horizontal; *vertical*, perpendicular, upright; *direct*, undeviating, unswerving, unbending, rigid, inflexible, stiff.

vb. *straighten*, align, level, even out, flatten, smooth, iron out; *stretch*, extend, unfold, unroll, uncurl, uncoil, unbend.

adv. *straight*, plumb, in true; *direct*, as the crow flies.

223 **CIRCULARITY**

See also 208 (outline); 225 (roundness);
251 (circuit); 279 (rotation).

n. *circularity*, roundness, rotundity,
curvedness; *circumference*, equator, orbit,
circuit, cycle; *circulation*, rotation, revolution,
gyration, spin, pirouette; *circle*, ring, torus,
round, disc, wheel, loop, saucer; *sphere*, orb,
globe, bulb, ball; *dome*, hemisphere, boss,
knob, stud; *crown*, circlet, coronet, halo,
nimbus, corona, aureole; *collar*, necklace,
garland, wreath, bracelet, anklet, belt, girdle.

adj. *circular*, round, discoid, toroid,
annular; *spherical*, globular, tubular,
cylindrical; *cyclic*, circulatory, rotatory,
gyratory.

vb. *circle*, orbit, lap, wheel; *rotate*, revolve,
circulate, gyrate, spin, spiral, pirouette;
encircle, surround, loop, girdle, circumscribe.

224 **CONVOLUTION**

See also 221 (curve); 279 (rotation).

n. *convolution*, twist, torsion, contortion;
roll, coil, winding, spring, spiral, screw, helix,
worm, corkscrew; *curl*, wave, lock, kink,
ringlet, frizz, tendril; *ripple*, swirl, whorl,
vortex, whirlpool; *scroll*, flourish, curlicue,
squiggle; *maze*, network, labyrinth, warren;
convolutedness, intricacy, complexity,
tortuousness, sinuousness.

adj. *convoluted*, twisted, contorted,
knotted; *tortuous*, sinuous, intricate,
involved, complex, labyrinthine; *spiral*,
helical, loopy, coiled, serpentine, snaky,
squiggly; *wavy*, corrugated, rippling, crinkly,
curly, kinky, frizzy, crimped.

vb. *twist*, contort, corkscrew, writhe,
squirm, wriggle, worm; *roll*, undulate,
meander, loop, coil, snake; *entwine*, wreathe,
enmesh, embroil; *curl*, wave, perm, crimp,
crinkle, corrugate.

225 **ROUNDNESS**

See also 223 (circularity); 226 (convexity).

n. *roundness*, curvedness, circularity,
rotundity, convexity; *sphere*, globe, balloon,
bubble, ball, orb, bulb, bullet, pea, globule,
bead, drop; *cylinder*, cone, tube, pipe, roller,
rung, bole, trunk, drum, barrel; *paunch*, pot-
belly, corporation, beer belly/gut; *bulge*,
swelling, hump, dome, hemisphere.

adj. *round*, curved, circular, beady, convex;
spherical, globular, globose, bulbous, swollen;
cylindrical, tubular, columnar, conical; *rotund*,
rounded, paunchy, pot-bellied, barrel-
chested.

vb. *round*, arch, curve, bend; *bulge*, swell,
balloon, distend, inflate; *ball*, roll, coil, furl.

226 **CONVEXITY**

See also 221 (curve); 225 (roundness);
228 (prominence).

n. *convexity*, curvature, roundedness,
tumescence, swollenness; *hemisphere*, dome,
cupola, beehive, cup; *bulge*, hump, bow,
arch, curve, ridge, hog's back, camber;
swelling, excrescence, growth, tumour,
nodule, lump; *pimple*, blister, boil, carbuncle,
bunion; *knob*, boss, bump, nubble, bud,
button; *breast*, bosom, pap, udder, dug,
nipple, teat, bust, boobs (*colloq.*), bristols
(*colloq.*), tits (*colloq.*), knockers (*colloq.*), rack
(*colloq.*).

adj. *convex*, round, curved, arched, domed,
hemispherical, bouffant; *swollen*, puffy,
tumescent, tumid, distended, bloated; *raised*,
embossed, bumpy, lumpy, nubbly, pimply;
curvaceous, busty, buxom, bosomy, well-
stacked (*colloq.*).

vb. *be convex*, arch, curve, rise, bow; *bulge*,
swell, belly, billow.

227 **CONCAVITY**

See also 221 (curve); 231 (furrow).

n. *concavity*, hollow, depression, dip,
indentation, impression; *cavity*, hole, recess,
nook, alcove, burrow, cave, grotto, cavern,
pothole; *basin*, pan, saucer, bowl, dish, cup;
dent, dimple, pockmark, perforation; *pit*,
crater, well, shaft, borehole, tunnel; *valley*,
gorge, gully, ravine, crevasse; *groove*, socket,
channel, furrow, trench; *spoon*, scoop, ladle,
trowel, bucket.

adj. *concave*, hollow, cavernous, gaping,
yawning; *pitted*, dented, dimpled,
pockmarked, perforated; *recessed*, indented,
sunken, excavated; *grooved*, channelled,
furrowed, corrugated.

vb. *make concave*, buckle, dent, stave in,
cave in; *hollow*, indent, recess, depress; *gouge*,
groove, channel, bore, burrow, excavate;
hole, pit, pockmark, perforate.

228 **PROMINENCE**

See also 226 (convexity).

n. *prominence*, eminence, height,
conspicuousness, high profile; *projection*,
tongue, salient, promontory, headland, spur,
point, spit; *overhang*, shelf, ledge, outcrop,
crag, ridge, buttress; *protuberance*,
excrescence, outgrowth, lump, bump, hump;
beak, bill, nose, conk (*colloq.*), snout,

proboscis, antenna, feeler, horn; *relief*, convexity, embossing, cameo, high relief.

adj. *prominent*, high, conspicuous, noticeable; *projecting*, salient, jutting, overhanging, beetle-browed, craggy, buck-toothed; *protuberant*, raised, convex, bulging, lumpy, humped, pop-eyed.

vb. *project*, jut, stick out, stand out, protrude, bulge; *rise*, bristle, cock, prick up, erect.

229 **NOTCH**
See also 296 (sharpness).

n. *notch*, serration, indentation, crenellation, scallop, zigzag, deckle edge; *nick*, V-shape, wick, cut, gash, incision; *tooth*, sprocket, ratchet, comb, saw.

adj. *notched*, serrated, jagged, ragged, saw-toothed; *stepped*, crenellated, indented, scalloped.

vb. *notch*, serrate, tooth, mill; *indent*, crimp, pink, scallop; *nick*, snick, cut, snip, clip.

230 **FOLD**
See also 231 (furrow).

n. *fold*, pleat, tuck, gather; *frill*, flounce, ruffle, ruche; *lapel*, cuff, turn-up, crease; *ridge*, furrow, groove, corrugation; *wrinkle*, crinkle, pucker, frown, crow's feet.

adj. *folded*, plicate, ridged, gathered, pleated, frilly; *crumpled*, creased, crushed, crinkled, dog-eared, puckered, corrugated, lined.

vb. *fold*, furl, drape, swathe, festoon; *furrow*, groove, corrugate, wrinkle, pucker, crinkle, purse, concertina; *frill*, ruffle, ruche, pleat, gather, tuck.

231 **FURROW**
See also 227 (concavity); 230 (fold).

n. *furrow*, groove, chase, channel, track, slot, rut; *slit*, chink, cranny, crack, crevice; *hollow*, trough, gutter, gully, ditch, trench, moat; *wave*, ripple, fluting, ribbing, corduroy; *wrinkle*, frown, corrugation, rifling, etching, incision, gash, slash.

adj. *furrowed*, wrinkled, puckered, lined, etched, incised; *grooved*, fluted, ribbed, ridged, rutted, striated.

vb. *furrow*, groove, chase, channel, chamfer, flute, rifle; *plough*, rut, rib, corrugate, wrinkle; *line*, etch, incise, score, gash, slash.

232 **OPENING**
See also 174 (interval).

n. *opening*, aperture, gap, hole, breach, lacuna, hiatus, break; *space*, crack, chink, interstice, cavity, pocket, orifice; *perforation*, pore, puncture, indentation, bore, pinhole, eyelet; *sieve*, strainer, colander, riddle; *mesh*, netting, fretwork, openwork, lace, filigree, broderie anglaise; *outlet*, nozzle, vent, spout, gullet, nostril, mouth, maw, gob (*colloq.*), trap (*colloq.*), cakehole (*colloq.*); *compartment*, slot, keyhole, pigeonhole, letterbox; *window*, grille, fanlight, skylight, porthole, loophole, peephole; *door*, gate, portal, entrance, hatch, trapdoor, manhole, flap; *tunnel*, shaft, bolthole, burrow, foxhole; *funnel*, chimney, flue, duct, tube, pipe; *open space*, clearing, glade, bomb site, waste ground, vista, panorama; *opener*, aperient, purgative, open sesame, password; *tin-opener*, corkscrew, key, handle, knob; *punch*, bodkin, skewer, gimlet, drill, auger, bradawl; *openness*, accessibility, penetrability, permeability, porosity.

adj. *open*, ajar, agape, yawning, open-mouthed; *perforated*, riddled, honeycombed, shot through; *holey*, lacy, leaky, porous, permeable, absorbent; *accessible*, clear, unobstructed, uncluttered.

vb. *open*, unlock, unfasten, uncork, unwrap, unpack, undo; *gape*, yawn, split, rend, part, burst, explode, leak; *pierce*, puncture, perforate, gore, hole, bore, drill, punch, tattoo, riddle, pepper; *stab*, prick, skewer, nail, spear, transfix, impale; *enter*, penetrate, permeate, pervade.

adv. *openly*, out in the open, open to the four winds, al fresco.

233 **CLOSURE**
See also 202 (covering).

n. *closure*, occlusion, strangulation, obstruction, blockage, stoppage; *clot*, blood clot, thrombosis, deep vein thrombosis, economy-class syndrome; *impasse*, dead end, cul de sac, roadblock, barricade; *impermeability*, imperviousness, staunchness, impenetrability; *stopper*, cork, bung, spigot, plug, wad, tampon; *valve*, tap, stopcock, ballcock, choke, damper; *gag*, muzzle, tourniquet, compress; *cover*, top, lid, cap, seal, shutter; *lock*, bolt, bar, latch, deadlock.

adj. *closed*, shut, barred, bolted, shuttered; *impermeable*, impenetrable, impervious, staunch, watertight, airtight, hermetically sealed; *impassable*, inaccessible, blocked, barricaded.

vb. *close*, shut, occlude, strangulate, obstruct, clog (up); *lock*, bar, bolt, fasten; *stop*, plug, bung, caulk, cork, seal; *block*, dam, choke, throttle, gag, muzzle.

234 **MOTION**
See also 236 (land travel); 239 (transfer).

n. *motion*, movement, mobility, locomotion, perambulation; *momentum*, impetus, propulsion, impulsion; *advance*, progress, headway, ascent; *retreat*, regression, withdrawal, descent; *oscillation*, fluctuation, vibration, agitation, tremor; *activity*, unrest, stir, bustle, traffic; *passage*, transit, transfer, shift, transport, conveyance; *flow*, flux, drift, current, course, run; *gait*, walk, carriage, bearing, tread, stride.

adj. *moving*, mobile, motile, locomotive, automotive, self-propelled; *transitional*, passing, shifting, fleeting; *wandering*, ambulant, peripatetic, nomadic, restless, drifting; *kinetic*, dynamic, cinematographic.

vb. *move*, go, walk, proceed, make one's way, advance, progress; *march*, tramp, stride, lope, jog, amble, saunter, stroll, waddle, shuffle; *stalk*, strut, swagger, mince; *run*, race, gallop, hare, fly, dash; *roll*, taxi, trundle, chug, wheel, coast, cruise, freewheel; *travel*, roam, wander, drift, stray; *transfer*, transport, shift, convey, dispatch; *push*, shove, budge, drive, hustle; *draw*, pull, drag, tug, haul.

adv. *in motion*, on the move, on the go, up and about; *under way*, on the road, en route, in transit.

235 **MOTIONLESSNESS**
See also 123 (cessation).

n. *motionlessness*, stillness, rest, immobility; *stability*, equilibrium, poise, balance, stasis; *suspension*, cessation, stagnation, inertia, deadlock, stalemate; *standstill*, stop, halt, pause, truce, lull; *stoppage*, embargo, freeze, strike; *calm*, still, quiet, hush.

adj. *motionless*, still, immobile, becalmed; *static*, stationary, stagnant, inactive, idle; *immovable*, stuck, rigid, paralysed, unbudgeable; *transfixed*, spellbound, rooted to the spot, stock-still; *sedentary*, stay-at-home, home-loving, housebound, bedridden, disabled.

vb. *be motionless*, stand still, stay put, sit tight, mark time, stagnate; *cease*, stop, come to a halt, settle, subside, die down; *pause*, rest, tarry, take a breather (*colloq.*), rest on one's oars; *immobilize*, lock, jam, stick, lodge,

catch; *halt*, stop short, stop in one's tracks, brake, check, pull up.

236 **LAND TRAVEL**
See also 234 (motion); 242 (vehicle); 762 (recreation).

n. *land travel*, tourism, globe-trotting, sightseeing, exploration, peregrination, health/medical tourism; *journey*, voyage, odyssey, expedition, trek, safari, scalpel safari (*colloq.*); *trip*, jaunt, outing, excursion, spin, ride; *walk*, constitutional, stroll, ramble, hike, tramp, march, walkabout, Shank's pony; *run*, jog, race, sprint, cross-country, marathon; *route*, itinerary, stopover, terminus, destination, journey's end; *traveller*, voyager, passenger, commuter, tourist, wayfarer, sightseer, tripper; *walker*, pedestrian, hiker, rambler, jogger, runner, sprinter; *wanderer*, rover, globe-trotter, migrant, nomad, drifter, rolling stone, vagabond, vagrant, gypsy, Roma, tramp, gentleman of the road.

adj. *travelling*, itinerant, peripatetic, globe-trotting, ambulant; *wandering*, migratory, nomadic, restless, vagrant, vagabond, errant.

vb. *travel*, journey, voyage, explore, tour, shuttle, commute, knock about (*colloq.*); *walk*, pace, saunter, stroll, amble; *hike*, trek, tramp, march, ramble; *trudge*, plod, slog, stump, hoof it, foot it, leg it; *run*, race, jog, sprint; *wander*, rove, roam, migrate, traipse.

adv. *by road*, overland, on foot; *on the road*, on the trail, on the beat.

237 **WATER TRAVEL**
See also 243 (ship); 762 (recreation).

n. *water travel*, sailing, navigation, cruising, yachting, boating; *voyage*, circumnavigation, cruise, crossing, sail; *seamanship*, seafaring, sea legs, weather eye; *navy*, fleet, merchant navy, shipping, flotilla; *water sport*, aquatics, surfing, swimming, natation, diving, windsurfing, canoeing, sculling, rowing; *seaman*, mariner, sailor, submariner, seafarer, sea dog, old salt; *captain*, crew, complement, boatswain, master, mate, pilot, navigator; *coastguard*, lifeboatman, boatman, ferryman, Charon.

adj. *seafaring*, maritime, marine, naval, nautical, navigational, aquatic, deep-sea, ocean-going, longshore, seaworthy, waterborne.

vb. *put to sea*, set sail, embark, cast off, launch, weigh anchor; *voyage*, sail, cruise, ply, steam, ferry, run, circumnavigate;

navigate, steer, pilot, captain; *disembark*, land, dock, berth, tie up, moor, drop anchor; *row*, scull, canoe, punt, paddle; *swim*, float, tread water, bathe, surf, windsurf, wade, paddle.

adv. *at sea*, aboard, afloat, on the high seas.

238 AIR TRAVEL
See also 244 (aircraft).

n. *air travel*, aeronautics, aerospace, aerodynamics; *flying*, aviation, gliding, hang-gliding, ballooning, parachuting, sky-diving, aerobatics; *flight*, scheduled flight, charter (flight), redeye (flight), shuttle (service), airlift, airline, low-cost/budget airline, Air Miles (tdmk); *airlane*, airway, airspace, flight path; *airport*, (air) terminal, airfield, airbase, aerodrome, landing strip, runway, airstrip, heliport, helipad; *takeoff*, touchdown, landing, crash-landing, nosedive, prang (*colloq.*); *pilot*, aeronaut, aviator, aviatrix, airman/-woman, flier, balloonist, parachutist, paratrooper; *flight attendant*, air hostess, steward/-ess, cabin crew; *jetlag*, deep vein thrombosis, economy-class syndrome; *space travel*, space flight, countdown, liftoff, blastoff, orbit, docking, space station, re-entry, splashdown; *astronaut*, cosmonaut, spaceman/-woman, space traveller.

adj. *flying*, aeronautic, aerodynamic, aerobatic; *aerial*, airborne, in-flight, airworthy.

vb. *fly*, pilot, aviate, glide, balloon, parachute, jet; *take off*, taxi, fly, overfly, hover, drift, cruise; *come down*, touch down, land, crash, nosedive, crashland, ditch, bail out, eject; *lift off*, blast off, orbit, dock, splash down.

adv. *in flight*, in the air, in orbit, on the wing.

239 TRANSFER
See also 234 (motion); 697 (transfer of property).

n. *transfer*, relocation, shift, removal, transferral, transplantation, deportation; *transmission*, conduction, convection, transfusion, contagion; *transportation*, conveyance, dispatch, transshipment, exportation, importation, delivery; *carriage*, transport, haulage, cartage; *freight*, consignment, shipment, cargo, container.

adj. *transferable*, movable, portable; *transmissible*, communicable, contagious, infectious.

vb. *transfer*, shift, move, convey, transmit;

dispatch, transport, ship, transship, export, import; *send*, consign, post, mail, forward.

adv. *in transit*, on the way, en route, under way.

240 WAY
See also 271 (passage); 315 (channel).

n. *way*, manner, method, procedure, modus operandi, measures, steps; *course*, route, direction, line, tack, short cut, detour; *approach*, access, entrance, passage, right of way; *path*, track, orbit, trajectory, channel; *trail*, footpath, bridlepath, towpath; *walk*, drive, avenue, boulevard, promenade; *road*, highway, thoroughfare, artery, trunk road, ring road, bypass, dual carriageway, motorway; *street*, terrace, crescent, circus; *sidestreet*, lane, alley, close, wynd; *railway*, railroad, main line, branch line, siding, marshalling yard; *underground*, subway, tube, funicular, monorail; *bridge*, footbridge, drawbridge, viaduct, aqueduct, flyover, cloverleaf; *causeway*, gangway, catwalk, aisle, underpass.

241 CARRIER
n. *carrier*, bearer, porter, coolie, messenger, courier, runner, postman; *common carrier*, transporter, shipper, haulier, carter, importer, exporter; *beast of burden*, packhorse, draught horse, mule, donkey; *carrier bag*, tote bag, trolley, stretcher, litter, conveyor belt.

vb. *carry*, bear, shoulder, hump, cart, heave, haul, lug, tote (*colloq.*), schlepp (*colloq.*); *convey*, post, send, forward, transport, ship, ferry.

242 VEHICLE
See also 236 (land travel).

n. *vehicle*, conveyance, transport, wheels (*colloq.*); *wagon*, dray, cart, tumbril; *carriage*, landau, brougham, hansom, buggy, gig, fly, trap; *bicycle*, tandem, pushbike, tricycle, trike, moped, scooter, motorcycle, motorbike; *car*, motor car, automobile, saloon, hatchback, convertible, coupé, shooting brake, station wagon, runabout, limousine, stretch limo; *van*, camper, pickup, float, pantechnicon, hearse, Black Maria, ambulance, lorry, truck, juggernaut; *bus*, coach, charabanc, doubledecker, tram, trolleybus, streetcar (*US*); *stagecoach*, post chaise, hackney carriage, cab, taxi, minicab, rickshaw, trishaw; *train*, express, high-speed

train, locomotive, tender, tanker, goods
train, underground, subway.

adj. *vehicular*, wheeled, motorized,
automotive, locomotive.

243 **SHIP**
See also 237 (water travel).

n. *ship*, vessel, boat, craft, tub (*colloq.*);
passenger ship, ferry, packet, steamer,
steamboat, steamship, paddleboat, paddle
steamer, riverboat, hovercraft, hydrofoil;
liner; *freighter*, barge, tramp, tanker, collier,
dredger, tug, supertanker; *launch*, lighter,
painter, dinghy, wherry, lifeboat, longboat;
sailing ship, tall ship, galleon, sloop,
schooner, ketch, yawl, clipper,
merchantman, Indiaman; *fishing boat*,
trawler, drifter, smack, whaler, factory ship;
yacht, skiff, catamaran, trimaran, multihull,
junk, sampan, dhow, caique, felucca; *rowing
boat*, scull, canoe, punt, coracle, kayak,
pirogue, gondola, galley, trireme, longship;
warship, man o' war, battleship, frigate,
corvette, cruiser, destroyer, aircraft carrier,
submarine, U-boat.

adj. *nautical*, maritime, marine, seagoing,
oceangoing, transatlantic.

244 **AIRCRAFT**
See also 238 (air travel).

n. *aircraft*, aeroplane, plane, flying
machine, monoplane, biplane, seaplane,
crate (*colloq.*); *airliner*, jet, jumbo jet, airbus,
shuttle, Concorde; *helicopter*, whirlybird
(*colloq.*), chopper (*colloq.*); *warplane*, fighter,
bomber; *airship*, dirigible, balloon, blimp,
glider, hang-glider; *spaceship*, spacecraft,
space shuttle, rocket, capsule, module
satellite, space station.

adj. *aviational*, aeronautical, wide-bodied,
heavier-than-air, supersonic.

245 **SPEED**
See also 96 (immediacy); 615 (haste).

n. *speed*, velocity, rapidity, swiftness;
quickness, alacrity, promptness, suddenness,
instantaneity; *pace*, rate, tempo, momentum,
rate of knots (*colloq.*), lick (*colloq.*); *haste*,
hurry, rush, dispatch; *acceleration*, flying
start, spurt, sprint, full throttle; *run*, race,
dash, charge, gallop, stampede, bolt; *runner*,
harrier, sprinter, racer, speed merchant
(*colloq.*), boy racer (*colloq.*); *racehorse*,
greyhound, hare, cheetah, gazelle.

adj. *speedy*, fast, swift, rapid, meteoric;
quick, lively, snappy, quick-fire, brisk, smart;

prompt, immediate, sudden, double-quick,
alacritous, hasty, expeditious; *light-footed*,
nimble, agile, fleet-footed, mercurial; *high-
speed*, breakneck, headlong, precipitous,
runaway.

vb. *speed*, race, flash, streak, shoot, fly; *dart*,
flit, whisk, zoom, whiz (*colloq.*), zip, rush, tear,
dash; *run*, gallop, hare, sprint, hotfoot it, belt,
pelt, hurtle, career, stampede; *dive*, pounce,
spring, swoop, lunge; *run away*, bolt, scoot,
take to one's heels, scamper, scuttle, scarper
(*colloq.*), skedaddle (*colloq.*); *accelerate*, hurry,
hasten, quicken, hustle, step on it (*colloq.*), get
a move on (*colloq.*), get weaving/cracking
(*colloq.*), get one's skates on (*colloq.*), jump to
it.

adv. *at full speed*, swiftly, flat out, hell for
leather, like a bat out of hell, in haste,
hotfoot, post haste, helter skelter, apace;
promptly, pronto (*colloq.*), smartish (*colloq.*),
quick-smart (*colloq.*), at the double, in a trice,
before you can say Jack Robinson, like snow
off a dyke, like hot cakes, like a bomb, like
gangbusters (*colloq.*).

246 **SLOWNESS**
See also 616 (lack of haste).

n. *slowness*, sluggishness, lethargy,
languor, inertia, slackness; *lack of haste*,
patience, methodicalness, deliberation,
unhurriedness, leisureliness; *hesitation*,
tardiness, reluctance, unwillingness; *delay*,
holdup, slowdown, work-to-rule, go-slow;
deceleration, brake, curb, restraint,
retardation; *slow motion*, snail's pace, amble,
stroll, saunter, dawdle; *slow creature*,
slowcoach (*colloq.*), sloth, tortoise, snail.

adj. *slow*, sluggish, lethargic, listless,
languid, slack; *deliberate*, patient,
painstaking, methodical, unhurried,
leisurely; *hesitant*, reluctant, unwilling, tardy,
dilatory, slow off the mark.

vb. *move slowly*, amble, saunter, dawdle,
stroll, linger, loaf; *creep*, crawl, inch, trickle,
drip, ooze; *plod*, trudge, limp, hobble, shuffle,
shamble, mooch (*colloq.*); *lag*, delay, dilly-
dally (*colloq.*), drag one's feet, take one's
time, run out of steam, falter; *slow down*,
decelerate, slacken, retard, brake, backpedal,
ease off, let up.

adv. *slowly*, adagio, largo, little by little,
softly softly (*colloq.*).

247 **IMPULSION**
See also 255 (propulsion).

n. *impulsion*, impetus, momentum, thrust,

drive, propulsion, force, charge; *impact*, brunt, shock, jolt, nudge, bump, cannon, collision, crash, smash; *blow*, bang, thud, knock, rap, punch, thwack, thump; *stroke*, hit, smack, cuff, slap, clap, lash, flick, tap; *hammer*, club, cudgel, cosh, truncheon, knocker, ram, bulldozer.

vb. *impel*, thrust, drive, kick, charge; *throw*, fling, propel, launch, hurl, toss; *push*, shove, force, press, ram, bulldoze; *jerk*, jog, jolt, jar, nudge, butt, wrench, tug; *collide*, smash, crash, bang, cannon, bump, careen; *hit*, strike, clout, cuff, spank, smack, slap, rap, tap, knock; *punch*, slug, pummel, pound, bludgeon, hammer; *beat*, bash, thrash, wallop (*colloq.*), clobber (*colloq.*), belt (*colloq.*), slosh (*colloq.*), whack (*colloq.*).

248 **RECOIL**
See also 137 (counteraction).

n. *recoil*, rebound, bounce, spring, swing of the pendulum; *reflex*, kickback, ricochet, boomerang, cannon; *echo*, reflection, repercussion, reverberation, backlash; *reflector*, mirror, sounding board, echo chamber; *response*, reply, retort, riposte, rebuff; *reaction*, double take, wince, start.

adj. *reactive*, responsive, reflexive, knee-jerk (*colloq.*); *echoey*, resonant, reverberative, repercussive; *springy*, bouncy, elastic.

vb. *recoil*, rebound, cannon, boomerang, ricochet; *spring*, bounce back, kick back, backfire; *echo*, reflect, mirror, reverberate; *react*, respond, reply, retort, rebuff.

249 **DIRECTION**
See also 159 (situation).

n. *direction*, bearings, situation, orientation, location, compass point, cardinal point; *trend*, tendency, drift, thrust, tack, line; *course*, route, short cut, beeline; *destination*, goal, aim, target, objective; *compass*, direction finder, signpost, map, street/road map, road atlas, A–Z, tracking device.

adj. *directed*, headed, bound for, set.

vb. *direct*, indicate, signpost, guide, steer, level, point, aim; *orientate*, situate, take one's bearings, pinpoint, locate, track; *head for*, make for, aim for, make tracks for.

adv. *direct*, straight, point blank; *on course*, on the right track, on the right lines.

250 **MIDDLE WAY**
See also 63 (middle); 148 (moderation).

n. *middle way*, short cut, beeline, diameter, centre; *middle course*, median, average, happy medium, the golden mean; *midpoint*, central reservation, traffic island; *the middle of the road*, halfway house, compromise, moderation.

adj. *middle*, central, equidistant, direct, straight; *midway*, halfway, intermediate, medial; *neutral*, moderate, middle-of-the-road, unextreme.

251 **CIRCUIT**
See also 223 (circularity).

n. *circuit*, detour, bypass, loop, ring road; *digression*, deviation, way round, circumlocution.

adj. *circuitous*, roundabout, out-of-the-way; *circumlocutory*, long-winded, indirect.

vb. *circuit*, lap, loop, ring; *deviate*, digress, go out of one's way; *bypass*, skirt, avoid, give a wide berth.

252 **DEVIATION**
See also 214 (side); 260 (divergence).

n. *deviation*, aberration, wrong turning, disorientation; *detour*, sidestep, zigzag, swerve, veer; *diversion*, shift, deflection, divergence; *digression*, aside, tangent, parenthesis.

adj. *deviant*, aberrant, off-course, off-beam, stray, wide of the mark; *digressive*, wandering, rambling, off the point, discursive.

vb. *deviate*, wander, stray, lose one's bearings, be on the wrong track; *sidestep*, diverge, veer, slew, zigzag; *digress*, go off at a tangent, get side-tracked.

253 **FORWARD MOTION**
n. *forward motion*, progress, advance, headway; *course*, march, tide, current, flood; *step*, stride, leap, jump, spurt; *advancement*, preferment, promotion, leg-up; *development*, growth, evolution, furtherance; *improvement*, betterment, perfectibility.

adj. *forward*, progressive, advanced, up-to-date, forward-looking; *go-ahead*, enterprising, go-getting (*colloq.*); *ongoing*, continuing, inexorable, irreversible.

vb. *go forward*, proceed, progress, advance, make headway, get the go-ahead (*colloq.*); *keep on*, press on, push on, make strides, gain ground, forge ahead, get somewhere (*colloq.*); *develop*, evolve, further, bring on; *promote*, upgrade, better, improve.

adv. *forward*, onward, ahead; *progressively*, by leaps and bounds.

254 **BACKWARD MOTION**

See also 126 (reversion).

n. *backward motion*, recession, retraction, retreat, withdrawal, retirement, flight; *retroaction*, retrospection, regression, nostalgia; *reversion*, backward step, relapse, backsliding; *decline*, fall off, slump, ebb; *about-turn*, volte-face, U-turn.

adj. *backward*, retrograde, retrogressive; *receding*, recessive, retreating, retractile; *retroactive*, retrospective, nostalgic.

vb. *recede*, retire, withdraw, back off, fall back; *regress*, return, revert, hark back, relapse, backslide; *reverse*, back, backtrack, backpedal, retrace one's steps, double back; *turn tail*, about-face, wheel, turn on one's heel.

adv. *backwards*, in reverse, anticlockwise, widdershins (*dial.*).

255 **PROPULSION**

See also 247 (impulsion).

n. *propulsion*, impulsion, drive, momentum, impetus, kick; *throw*, cast, toss, pitch, bowl; *discharge*, volley, salvo, bombardment, cannonade; *archery*, toxophily, ballistics, gunnery, artillery; *missile*, projectile, arrow, dart, bullet, shot, pellet, shell, cannonball, torpedo, rocket; *propellant*, charge, explosive, dynamite; *propeller*, pedal, oar, turbine, booster, thruster; *firearm*, shotgun, rifle, catapult, sling, bow, peashooter; *shooter*, marksman, crack shot, gunner, sniper, archer, bowler, pitcher.

adj. *propulsive*, propellent, expulsive, ballistic.

vb. *propel*, launch, project, impel, drive, thrust, kick; *throw*, cast, toss, pitch, bowl, chuck, fling, hurl, lob, bung; *fire*, catapult, pitchfork, send flying; *shoot*, discharge, loose off, volley, bombard.

256 **TRACTION**

See also 257 (attraction).

n. *traction*, haulage, draught, pulling, tug of war; *pull*, tug, heave, tow, trawl, haul, drag, friction; *magnetism*, attraction, charisma, drawing power; *tractor*, towrope, tugboat, windlass, dragnet, magnet.

adj. *retractive*, retractable, ductile; *magnetic*, attractive, charismatic.

vb. *draw*, pull, haul, heave, tow; *drag*, trawl, dredge, winch, reel in; *pull at*, tug, jerk, tweak, pluck, yank; *draw in*, withdraw, retract, sheathe; *attract*, magnetize, spellbind.

257 **ATTRACTION**

See also 256 (traction).

n. *attraction*, pull, draw, influence, gravity, magnetism; *allure*, fascination, seductiveness, charm; *lure*, bait, decoy, snare, siren, temptress; *focal point*, cynosure, centre of attraction, magnet, lodestone.

adj. *attractive*, seductive, charming, irresistible; *magnetic*, gravitational, focal, centripetal, convergent.

vb. *attract*, pull, draw, influence; *lure*, bait, ensnare, seduce; *tempt*, captivate, enthral, magnetize, mesmerize.

258 **REPULSION**

See also 266 (expulsion).

n. *repulsion*, rejection, rebuff, dismissal, snub, brush-off (*colloq.*); *deflection*, defence, counterstroke, parry, foil, counterattack, resistance.

adj. *repulsive*, repellent, antipathetic, offensive, off-putting; *defensive*, resistant, hostile, dismissive.

vb. *repel*, drive away, chase, dismiss; *deflect*, ward off, fend off, keep at bay, head off, parry; *reject*, rebuff, snub, cold-shoulder; *eject*, throw out, show the door, send packing (*colloq.*).

259 **CONVERGENCE**

n. *convergence*, confluence, concurrence, concourse, concentration; *approach*, advance, confrontation, collision course; *union*, meeting, congress, assembly, congregation; *focus*, centre, pivot, hub.

adj. *convergent*, centripetal, confluent, advancing, oncoming.

vb. *converge*, close in, approach, draw near; *come together*, assemble, congregate, concentrate, gather, cluster; *focus*, centre, home in, zero in.

260 **DIVERGENCE**

See also 252 (deviation).

n. *divergence*, difference, deviation, contradiction, contrariety; *radiation*, branching, ramification, bifurcation; *crossroads*, fork, intersection, parting of the ways.

adj. *divergent*, radial, centrifugal; *branching*, forked, splayed, spreadeagled.

vb. *diverge*, radiate, fan out, diffuse, go one's separate ways; *branch*, ramify, fork, splay, spreadeagle.

261 **ARRIVAL**

n. *arrival*, advent, approach, coming, onset, advance; *entrance*, appearance, emergence, debut; *attainment*, accession, achievement, fulfilment; *landing*, disembarkation, landfall, touchdown; *destination*, goal, journey's end, terminus; *reception*, welcome, greeting, handshake, hospitality.

adj. *arriving*, incoming, immigrant; *approaching*, impending, imminent, oncoming, advancing; *attainable*, approachable, accessible, get-at-able (*colloq.*); *welcoming*, inviting, hospitable.

vb. *arrive*, reach, approach, draw up, gain, attain, get to, end up in, fetch up in; *land*, dismount, alight, set foot in, touch down, disembark, dock, moor; *appear*, turn up, show up, roll up (*colloq.*), drop in (*colloq.*), blow in (*colloq.*), make an entrance; *receive*, greet, welcome, kill the fatted calf.

262 **DEPARTURE**

n. *departure*, going, leaving, setting out; *embarkation*, takeoff, liftoff, blastoff; *emigration*, exodus, evacuation, exit, walkout; *flight*, retreat, escape, getaway, decampment, elopement, moonlight flit; *parting*, farewell, leavetaking, separation, send-off; *goodbye*, adieu, parting shot, valediction, obituary; *point of departure*, starting point, outset, springboard, jumping-off point.

adj. *departing*, farewell, valedictory; *outgoing*, outward bound, emigratory.

vb. *depart*, leave, quit, turn one's back on, vote with one's feet; *move out*, emigrate, pull out, evacuate, strike camp; *set out*, embark, set sail, take off, get under way; *escape*, flee, decamp, elope, abscond, bolt; *retire*, withdraw, retreat, bow out, sign off; *separate*, bid farewell, part company, take one's leave; *be off*, make tracks, up sticks, clear off (*colloq.*), push off (*colloq.*), slope off (*colloq.*), buzz off (*colloq.*); *rush off*, make oneself scarce (*colloq.*), beetle off (*colloq.*), vamoose (*colloq.*), skedaddle (*colloq.*), scarper (*colloq.*), beat it (*colloq.*), scram (*colloq.*).

263 **ENTRY**

See also 265 (admittance); 269 (insertion).

n. *entry*, admission, access, ingress; *influx*, incursion, invasion, intrusion; *inroad*, encroachment, penetration, infiltration; *enrolment*, enlistment, initiation, induction; *intake*, immigration, importation, open door, free trade; *entrance*, way in, door, gate, mouth, orifice, inlet; *entrant*, incomer,

immigrant, settler, colonist; *intruder*, invader, gatecrasher, housebreaker, burglar.

adj. *incoming*, immigrant, imported; *invasive*, incursive, intrusive.

vb. *enter*, gain admittance, set foot in, cross the threshold, drop in (*colloq.*), pop in (*colloq.*); *enrol*, enlist, inscribe, induct, sign on, initiate, admit; *invade*, irrupt, trespass, encroach, gatecrash, break and enter, burgle; *penetrate*, infiltrate, permeate, percolate; *rush in*, breeze in, barge in, butt in, muscle in (*colloq.*).

264 **EXIT**

See also 266 (expulsion); 270 (extraction).

n. *exit*, egress, way out, fire escape, exit strategy; *outflow*, effluent, issue, outpouring, discharge, leak; *emanation*, emission, seepage, exudation, secretion; *eruption*, outburst, breakout, sortie, sally; *emigration*, exodus, walkout, departure; *vent*, outlet, outfall, spout, drain, overflow; *escape route*, loophole, back door, let-out.

adj. *outgoing*, emigrant, departing; *leaky*, oozy, weeping, escaping.

vb. *exit*, emerge, issue, debouch; *erupt*, sally forth, break out, escape; *emigrate*, evacuate, clear out, bale out; *emit*, discharge, exude, secrete; *ooze*, weep, bleed, leak, seep; *pour*, overflow, gush, jet, spout.

265 **ADMITTANCE**

See also 263 (entry).

n. *admittance*, access, admission, reception, acceptance; *receptivity*, openness, accessibility, open arms, hospitality; *acceptability*, admissibility, suitability; *introduction*, initiation, rite of passage, baptism, enrolment, registration; *intake*, incorporation, absorption, ingestion.

adj. *admissible*, acceptable, suitable; *receptive*, open, accessible, welcoming, inviting, hospitable; *initiatory*, introductory, baptismal; *absorbent*, assimilative, digestive.

vb. *admit*, receive, take in, shelter; *welcome*, embrace, adopt, accept; *register*, enrol, enlist, inscribe, include; *initiate*, baptize, introduce, show the ropes (*colloq.*); *incorporate*, assimilate, internalize, absorb, digest.

266 **EXPULSION**

See also 161 (displacement); 258 (repulsion); 264 (exit); 270 (extraction).

n. *expulsion*, ejection, eviction, dislodgement; *dismissal*, discharge, rustication, excommunication, disbarment, constructive dismissal, the sack, the push (*colloq.*), the boot (*colloq.*), the bum's rush (*colloq.*); *deportation*, extradition, banishment, exile, repatriation, relegation; *removal*, elimination, evacuation, clearance, voidance; *ejector*, bouncer (*colloq.*), chucker-out, heavy (*colloq.*); *nausea*, vomiting, sickness, expectoration.

adj. *expulsive*, expellant, emetic, purgative, cathartic, excretory.

vb. *expel*, eject, evict, dislodge, turn out; *dismiss*, discharge, excommunicate, rusticate, send down, strike off, disbar, sack, fire; *throw out*, turf out, chuck out, drum out, root out, eradicate; *deport*, repatriate, extradite, banish, exile, relegate; *eliminate*, evacuate, void, empty, clear, purge; *emit*, disgorge, spit out, vomit, spew, retch, throw up (*colloq.*), puke (*colloq.*).

267 **INGESTION**

n. *ingestion*, digestion, consumption, imbibing, mastication, chewing; *nutrition*, sustenance, alimentation, dietetics, domestic science, home economics; *gluttony*, gourmandise, overeating, voraciousness; *gastronomy*, epicureanism, haute cuisine, cookery; *eater*, diner, gourmet, gastronome, connoisseur, epicure, trencherman; *provisions*, provender, foodstuffs, victuals, comestibles, rations; *food*, the staff of life, ambrosia, tuck (*colloq.*), grub (*colloq.*), nosh (*colloq.*), chow (*colloq.*); *convenience food*, fast food, junk food, TV dinner, health food, wholefood; *meal*, fare, snack, titbit, morsel, bite, brunch, elevenses, tiffin; *feast*, banquet, junket, beanfeast (*colloq.*), bunfight (*colloq.*), beano (*colloq.*), slap-up meal (*colloq.*), blowout (*colloq.*); *dish*, hors d'oeuvres, starter, appetizer, entrée, pudding, sweet, dessert, afters (*colloq.*); *beverage*, infusion, cocktail, brew, tipple, poison (*colloq.*); *alcohol*, spirits, hard stuff (*colloq.*), booze (*colloq.*), hooch (*colloq.*), vino (*colloq.*), plonk (*colloq.*), rotgut (*colloq.*); *drink*, draught, sip, gulp, swig (*colloq.*), dram, snort (*colloq.*), nightcap.

adj. *edible*, digestible, nutritious, drinkable, potable; *appetizing*, wholesome, tasty, palatable, moreish (*colloq.*); *scrumptious* (*colloq.*); *culinary*, dietary, gastronomic, cordon bleu, underdone, oven-ready, rare; *carnivorous*, herbivorous, vegetarian, omnivorous, gluttonous.

vb. *ingest*, digest, chew, masticate, munch, crunch, chomp, gnaw, consume; *eat*, feed,

feast, dine, sup, put away (*colloq.*), tuck into (*colloq.*), polish off; *devour*, bolt, wolf, gorge, gobble, guzzle, browse, graze; *taste*, nibble, peck at, sample; *drink*, imbibe, sip, quaff, down, gulp, knock back, tipple, booze (*colloq.*); *cook*, prepare, fix (*US*), boil, simmer, poach, stew, braise, grill, roast, bake, serve up, dish up.

268 **EXCRETION**

n. *excretion*, secretion, exudation, discharge, expulsion, ejection, expectoration; *defecation*, evacuation, voidance, bowel movement, number two (*colloq.*), constipation, dysentery, diarrhoea, the runs (*colloq.*), the trots (*colloq.*), holiday tummy, Montezuma's revenge (*colloq.*), the Aztec two-step (*colloq.*), Delhi belly (*colloq.*); *urination*, micturation, call of nature, number one (*colloq.*), incontinence, weak bladder, enuresis; *excreta*, excrement, faeces, stool, turd (*vulg.*), dung, muck, shit (*vulg.*), crap (*vulg.*), manure, droppings, guano, coprolite; *urine*, water, pee (*colloq.*), piddle (*colloq.*), wee (*colloq.*), piss (*vulg.*); *saliva*, mucus, catarrh, spittle, sweat, perspiration.

adj. *excretory*, diuretic, laxative, purgative, cathartic; *faecal*, urinary, excremental, shitty (*vulg.*), crappy (*vulg.*); *continent*, toilet-trained, housetrained.

vb. *excrete*, evacuate, discharge, expel, eject, pass; *defecate*, foul, soil, be caught short, shit (*vulg.*), crap (*vulg.*); *urinate*, relieve oneself, micturate, spend a penny (*colloq.*), pee (*colloq.*), piddle (*colloq.*), widdle (*colloq.*), piss (*vulg.*); *secrete*, exude, perspire, sweat; *expectorate*, spit, salivate, drool, slobber, hawk.

269 **INSERTION**

See also 207 (interface); 263 (entry).

n. *insertion*, introduction, interjection, interpolation, intercalation; *injection*, inoculation, vaccination, transfusion, implantation, impregnation; *insert*, inlay, inclusion, filling, stuffing.

adj. *inserted*, included, interjectional, parenthetical, by-the-by (*colloq.*).

vb. *insert*, introduce, interject, interpolate, intercalate, include, drag in (*colloq.*); *infuse*, instil, imbue, impregnate; *inject*, inoculate, vaccinate, transfuse, implant; *inset*, inlay, embed, encapsulate, sheathe, encase; *immerse*, plunge, bury, steep, souse, dunk.

270 **EXTRACTION**
See also 264 (exit); 266 (expulsion).

n. *extraction*, removal, withdrawal, excision; *displacement*, dislodgement, excavation, extrication, suction, aspiration; *extortion*, squeezing, expression, wringing out; *distillation*, separation, refinement, condensation; *extract*, essence, distillate, sublimate; *extractor*, excavator, dredger, digger, scoop; *forceps*, tweezers, pliers, wrench, syringe, siphon, pump.

vb. *extract*, remove, withdraw, excise; *displace*, dislodge, extricate, winkle out; *extort*, elicit, squeeze, force, express, wring out, get blood out of a stone; *excavate*, mine, quarry, dredge, dig up; *pump*, suck, vacuum, aspirate, siphon off, tap, milk; *distil*, refine, separate, condense, cream off.

271 **PASSAGE**
See also 240 (way).

n. *passage*, movement, transit, crossing, journey, voyage; *access*, right of way, thoroughfare, traffic, circulation; *entrance*, infiltration, penetration, permeation, percolation, osmosis; *crossing point*, bridge, ford, zebra crossing, frontier post, checkpoint; *passport*, visa, safe-conduct, laissez-passer, ID.

vb. *pass*, proceed, move through, circulate, journey, voyage, patrol, do the rounds (*colloq.*); *cross*, traverse, negotiate, transit, overfly; *enter*, penetrate, permeate, osmose, percolate, infiltrate; *bridge*, ford, straddle, span.

272 **OVERSTEPPING**
See also 575 (excess); 820 (lack of entitlement).

n. *overstepping*, trespass, entrenchment, encroachment, intrusion, invasion; *going too far*, a bridge too far (*colloq.*); *transgression*, violation, infringement, infraction, breach; *excessiveness*, exaggeration, overestimation, hyperbole.

adj. *excessive*, undue, unwarranted, uncalled-for; *intrusive*, invasive, encroaching; *exaggerated*, overdone, far-fetched, over the top (*colloq.*).

vb. *overstep*, go too far, overshoot, overrun, overreach; *trespass*, entrench, encroach, impinge, intrude, invade, poach, muscle in on; *transgress*, violate, infringe, usurp, breach; *exceed*, surpass, outdo, transcend, excel; *exaggerate*, overdo, overrate, overestimate.

273 **SHORTFALL**
See also 574 (insufficiency).

n. *shortfall*, insufficiency, short measure, shortage, deficit; *lack*, want, dearth, scarcity, famine; *shortcoming*, inadequacy, imperfection, defect, deficiency; *incompleteness*, half measures, perfunctoriness, cursoriness.

adj. *short*, deficient, minus, wanting, lacking, missing; *defective*, imperfect, inadequate, substandard; *incomplete*, half-done, perfunctory, cursory.

vb. *fall short*, miss, lack, want, need, require, cry out for; *fail*, fall through, disappoint, leave something to be desired, not come up to scratch (*colloq.*).

274 **ASCENT**
See also 184 (height); 276 (raising).

n. *ascent*, climb, rise, ascension, levitation, liftoff, takeoff; *upturn*, upsurge, upswing, increase, spiral, quantum jump; *jump*, leap, vault, spring, bound, hop, skip, high jump; *mountaineering*, climbing, alpinism; *gradient*, incline, slope, hill, ramp; *stairway*, ladder, steps, escalator, lift; *climber*, mountaineer, alpinist, steeplejack, high-jumper, hurdler, steeplechaser.

adj. *ascending*, upward, uphill; *rising*, mounting, buoyant, bullish.

vb. *ascend*, climb, rise, mount, soar, spiral; *take off*, lift off, rocket, surge; *jump*, spring, leap, vault, bound, hop, skip; *scale*, top, breast, clear, hurdle, shin up.

adv. *upwards*, in the ascendant, on the up and up (*colloq.*).

275 **DESCENT**
See also 185 (lowness); 277 (lowering).

n. *descent*, plunge, dive, swoop, slide, dip, landing, touchdown; *decline*, fall, drop, slump, downturn, tumble, spill; *collapse*, failure, comedown, demotion, downfall, débâcle; *avalanche*, subsidence, cascade, waterfall, chute, precipice; *caving*, potholing, mining, speleology; *diver*, submariner, caver, potholer, speleologist.

adj. *descending*, downward, downhill; *falling*, sinking, declining, bearish; *sagging*, droopy, depressed, down-in-the-mouth (*colloq.*).

vb. *descend*, plunge, dive, swoop, settle, subside, dip; *land*, touch down, alight, dismount, get down; *decline*, fall, drop, plummet, crash, slump, tumble, spill; *cascade*, overflow, pour, shower; *sink*,

submerge, drown, go under; *trip*, stumble,
lurch, totter, stagger, collapse, nosedive, bite
the dust (*colloq.*).

276 **RAISING**
See also 184 (height); 274 (ascent).

n. *raising*, erection, elevation, uplift,
levitation; *boost*, promotion, upgrading, leg-
up (*colloq.*); *height*, eminence, loftiness,
sublimity; *raising agent*, leaven, yeast,
fermentation; *lifter*, crane, derrick, lever,
hoist, jack, lift, escalator, dumb waiter,
springboard.

adj. *raised*, erect, upstanding, vertical;
elevated, sky-high, lofty, eminent, high-
flown, sublime.

vb. *raise*, erect, build, put up; *lift*, uplift,
hoist, lever, jack up, prop up, shoulder; *send
up*, lob, loft, flight; *elevate*, enhance, exalt,
put on a pedestal; *arise*, rear, jump up, be
upstanding, jump to one's feet.

277 **LOWERING**
See also 185 (lowness); 186 (depth);
275 (descent).

n. *lowering*, depression, deflation, levelling,
demolition; *debasement*, demotion,
downgrading, humiliation; *overthrow*,
overturn, upset, toppling; *crouch*, hunch,
duck, bend, stoop, bob, curtsy, genuflection.

adj. *lowered*, depressed, deflated, flattened;
lowering, humiliating, debasing, demeaning.

vb. *lower*, depress, deflate, squash; *flatten*,
level, raze, demolish, fell, ground; *bring
down*, topple, floor, overthrow, undermine,
torpedo, scuttle; *demote*, downgrade, debase,
humble, cashier; *crouch*, stoop, bend, hunch,
duck, curtsy, bob, kneel, genuflect.

278 **ORBITAL MOTION**
See also 279 (rotation).

n. *orbital motion*, rotation, revolution,
circulation, circumnavigation; *orbit*, lap,
circuit, tour, round trip; *circle*, wheel, spiral,
gyre; *satellite*, moon, planet, spaceship,
sputnik; *ring road*, orbital, bypass.

adj. *orbital*, roundabout, circular,
circuitous.

vb. *orbit*, turn, lap, circuit, revolve, rotate,
spiral, wheel; *ring*, circle, circumscribe, gird,
loop.

279 **ROTATION**
See also 223 (circularity); 224 (convolution);
278 (orbital motion).

n. *rotation*, revolution, orbit, cycle; *turn*,

roll, spiral, gyration, twirl, corkscrew,
pirouette, whirl; *swirl*, eddy, whirlpool,
vortex, maelstrom, whirlwind, cyclone,
tornado; *roundabout*, merry-go-round,
carousel, turntable, gyratory; *rotor*, propeller,
screw, turbine, windmill; *spindle*, axle, lathe,
shaft, pivot.

adj. *rotary*, gyratory, spinning, revolving,
cyclic.

vb. *rotate*, revolve, orbit, circuit; *turn*,
spiral, corkscrew, pirouette, twirl, whirl,
swirl; *roll*, wind, reel, spin; *pivot*, swivel,
hinge.

280 **OSCILLATION**
See also 119 (regularity); 281 (agitation).

n. *oscillation*, fluctuation, alternation,
reciprocation, undulation, ebb and flow;
vibration, flutter, tremor, agitation, shake,
quiver; *palpitation*, pulse, throb, beat;
pendulum, bob, oscillator, vibrator,
metronome; *rocker*, seesaw, cradle, shuttle,
swing; *vacillation*, wavering, indecision,
hesitation.

adj. *oscillating*, fluctuating, alternating,
reciprocating; *vibrating*, pulsating, throbbing,
rhythmical; *vacillating*, hesitant, indecisive,
irresolute.

vb. *oscillate*, swing, alternate, fluctuate,
reciprocate, undulate; *vibrate*, quake, tremble,
quiver, flutter, palpitate; *pulsate*, throb, beat,
pound, tick; *rock*, sway, seesaw, zigzag, teeter,
reel, stagger; *vacillate*, waver, hesitate, falter.

adv. *to and fro*, from side to side, back and
forth.

281 **AGITATION**
See also 280 (oscillation).

n. *agitation*, vibration, jerkiness,
unsteadiness, tremulousness, palpitation;
tumult, turmoil, commotion, confusion, stir,
bustle; *fuss*, bother, song and dance (*colloq.*),
fluster, flap (*colloq.*), tizz (*colloq.*); *turbulence*,
ferment, effervescence, seethe, swell, squall;
disturbance, perturbation, nervousness,
jumpiness, edginess, butterflies (*colloq.*), the
jitters (*colloq.*), the heebie-jeebies (*colloq.*),
collywobbles (*colloq.*); *restlessness*,
feverishness, itchiness, fidgetiness,
twitchiness; *hyperactivity*, ADHD (attention-
deficit hyperactive disorder); *tremor*, quiver,
shiver, shudder, judder, throb; *convulsion*,
paroxysm, spasm, fit, throes, seizure; *jolt*, jar,
shock, start, jerk, twitch.

adj. *agitated*, troubled, disturbed, confused,
shaken, shocked; *restless*, feverish, fidgety,

itchy, twitchy; *nervous*, anxious, perturbed,
jumpy, edgy, jittery (*colloq.*), nervy, like a cat
on hot bricks (*colloq.*); *flustered*, fussing,
fluttery, hot and bothered (*colloq.*); *overactive*,
hyperactive; *convulsive*, jerky, fitful,
spasmodic, paroxysmic; *turbulent*, stormy,
tempestuous, seething, effervescent;
tremulous, shaky, wobbly, quaking,
quivering, trembling.

vb. *be agitated*, boil, churn, heave, seethe,
ferment, bubble, effervesce; *convulse*, writhe,
squirm, thresh, toss and turn; *vibrate*, quake,
throb, palpitate, tremble, flutter, quiver,
shiver, shake; *shudder*, judder, jolt, jar, jerk,
twitch; *disturb*, rumple, ruffle, muddy, stir,
whisk, beat; *flicker*, twinkle, sparkle, glimmer,
gutter, sputter.

282 **MATERIAL WORLD**
See also 3 (reality).

n. *material world*, matter, mass, substance,
stuff, body, material, fabric; *embodiment*,
incarnation, materialization, solid object,
flesh and blood; *concreteness*, corporeality,
solidity, tangibility, palpability; *thing*, object,
article, gadget, thingamajig (*colloq.*),
thingamabob (*colloq.*), thingie (*colloq.*),
thingummy (*colloq.*); *ingredient*, element,
constituent, component, particle, atom,
molecule.

adj. *material*, real, physical, actual,
objective; *concrete*, solid, palpable, tangible,
sensible; *corporeal*, bodily, fleshly, carnal,
worldly, materialistic.

vb. *materialize*, embody, body forth,
objectify, incarnate.

283 **NON-MATERIAL WORLD**
See also 396 (intellect).

n. *non-material world*, unreality,
insubstantiality, incorporeality, intangibility,
impalpability; *spirituality*, otherworldliness,
idealism, transcendence, unearthliness;
occultism, spiritualism, mysticism,
paranormal, extra-sensory perception; *psyche*,
mind, intellect, soul, spirit, subjectivity, self,
inner child.

adj. *immaterial*, incorporeal, intangible,
ideal, abstract, non-physical, insubstantial;
disembodied, shadowy, ghostly, ethereal,
unreal; *spiritual*, otherworldly, transcendent,
unearthly; *occult*, mystical, psychic,
spiritualist.

vb. *dematerialize*, disembody, disintegrate;
idealize, intellectualize, conceptualize,
spiritualize.

284 **UNIVERSE**
n. *universe*, world, creation, cosmos,
macrocosm, space, outer space, galaxy; *earth*,
globe, sphere, planet earth, spaceship earth;
heavens, firmament, empyrean, primum
mobile, ether, atmosphere; *celestial body*,
planet, star, constellation, comet, meteor,
Near Earth Object, asteroid, satellite, quasar,
pulsar, black hole, nova, nebula, falling/
shooting star, meteorite; *zodiac*, horoscope,
house, ascendant, astrological sign; *sun*, solar
system, eye of heaven, daystar, midnight
sun; *astronomy*, stargazing, astrophysics,
cosmology, cosmography; *earth sciences*,
geology, geography, orography,
hydrography, cartography.

adj. *universal*, cosmic, macrocosmic,
galactic, interstellar; *earthly*, global, worldly,
terrestrial, earthbound, tellurian; *celestial*,
heavenly, extraterrestrial, ethereal, empyreal,
alien; *starry*, stellar, astral, sidereal; *solar*,
lunar, nebular, planetary, asteroidal;
astronomical, cosmological, astrophysical;
geological, geographical, orographic,
cartographic.

285 **HEAVINESS**
See also 287 (density).

n. *heaviness*, gravity, weight, bulk; *mass*,
force, pressure, density; *load*, burden,
encumbrance, cargo, freight, ballast,
counterweight, counterpoise; *heavy object*,
paperweight, sandbag, millstone, lead, stone,
plumb, sinker, a lead balloon, a ton of bricks
(*colloq.*); *weighing machine*, scales, balance,
weighbridge; *weightiness*, ponderousness,
gravitas, seriousness.

adj. *heavy*, bulky, massive, solid, dense;
overweight, top-heavy, laden, charged;
burdensome, onerous, cumbersome,
unwieldy, clumsy, awkward; *leaden*,
oppressive, crushing, insupportable; *weighty*,
ponderous, grave, serious, heavyweight
(*colloq.*).

vb. *weigh*, balance, outweigh, tip the
scales; *pressurize*, lean on, weigh on,
encumber, oppress; *burden*, saddle, weigh
down, load, overload, weight.

286 **LIGHTNESS**
See also 306 (air).

n. *lightness*, weightlessness, buoyancy,
portability; *airiness*, thinness, transparency,
translucence, flimsiness, delicacy, fluffiness;
light object, cork, float, bob, buoy, inflatable;
air, foam, froth, bubble, fluff, gauze,

gossamer, feather, thistledown; *raising agent*, leaven, yeast, aerator, lightener, thinner.

adj. *light*, buoyant, weightless, portable; *lightweight*, underweight, flyweight, bantamweight; *insubstantial*, flimsy, floaty, feathery, fluffy, frothy; *thin*, gauzy, diaphanous, transparent, translucent.

vb. *be light*, levitate, rise, surface, float, hover, waft, soar; *lighten*, leaven, thin, reduce; *unload*, disencumber, throw overboard, jettison, discard.

287 DENSITY
See also 182 (thickness); 285 (heaviness).

n. *density*, solidity, compactness, concreteness; *mass*, bulk, body, thickness, consistency; *consolidation*, concretization, crystallization, solidification, coagulation; *condensation*, concentration, congestion, saturation; *impenetrability*, impermeability, imperviousness, incompressibility; *solid*, block, bar, brick, lump, chunk, cake, slab, nugget, clot, clod, dod.

adj. *dense*, solid, compact, concrete, hard, stiff; *bulky*, massive, substantial, thick; *clotted*, curdled, caked, matted; *condensed*, packed, serried, concentrated, thick on the ground; *impenetrable*, impermeable, non-porous, incompressible.

vb. *become dense*, crystallize, harden, stiffen, set, freeze; *solidify*, congeal, coagulate, thicken, clot, curdle, cake; *make dense*, pack, compress, condense, concentrate; *crowd*, mass, throng, accumulate.

288 SPARSENESS
See also 183 (thinness).

n. *sparseness*, thinness, fineness, wispiness; *rarefaction*, dilution, attenuation, adulteration; *rarity*, infrequency, smattering, sprinkling.

adj. *sparse*, thin, fine, wispy, straggly; *rare*, infrequent, intermittent; *scattered*, dotted, strung out, thin on the ground.

vb. *rarefy*, thin, reduce, adulterate, attenuate, dilute; *scatter*, dot, sprinkle, strew.

289 HARDNESS
See also 294 (toughness).

n. *hardness*, toughness, resilience, resistance, firmness, resoluteness; *stiffness*, rigidity, inflexibility, intractability; *petrification*, ossification, fossilization, sclerosis; *hard-heartedness*, unyieldingness, harshness, callousness, insensitivity; *hard*

substance, stone, grit, flint, rock, granite, cement, brick, marble, diamond, steel, iron; *hardwood*, oak, teak, board, bone, horn, shell, armour, carapace.

adj. *hard*, tough, resilient, resistant, firm, unyielding; *rock-hard*, unbreakable, shatterproof, adamantine; *stiff*, rigid, inflexible, intractable, unbending; *stony*, gritty, flinty, steely, rocky; *bony*, horny, woody, crystalline, glassy, vitreous; *hardened*, reinforced, tempered, case-hardened, vitrified; *hard-hearted*, callous, harsh, insensitive.

vb. *harden*, toughen, reinforce, temper; *stiffen*, starch, freeze, solidify; *petrify*, ossify, fossilize, crystallize, vitrify.

290 SOFTNESS
See also 293 (elasticity); 317 (semiliquid).

n. *softness*, suppleness, springiness, elasticity, give; *pliancy*, flexibility, plasticity, malleability, tractability, ductility; *flaccidity*, limpness, flabbiness, floppiness, slackness, sponginess, doughiness; *tenderness*, gentleness, mildness, mellowness; *pulp*, mud, clay, dough, putty, butter, wax; *down*, velvet, cushion, pillow, feather bed, padding, wadding.

adj. *soft*, yielding, springy, supple, elastic; *pliant*, flexible, plastic, malleable, tractable, ductile; *flaccid*, limp, flabby, floppy, slack; *spongy*, doughy, soggy, pulpy, mushy; *downy*, velvety, cushiony, feathery; *tender*, gentle, mellow, mild.

vb. *soften*, tenderize, mash, pulp, squash, dissolve, melt; *yield*, give, bend, flex; *relax*, ease, sag, flop, slacken; *cushion*, pillow, pad, buffer; *mellow*, relent, temper, sweeten.

291 ROUGHNESS
See also 301 (friction).

n. *roughness*, asperity, harshness, coarseness, crudity; *hairiness*, shagginess, scaliness, scratchiness; *ruggedness*, cragginess, unevenness, jaggedness, knobbliness, brokenness; *rough object*, file, sandpaper, emery board; *bristle*, prickle, tweed, sackcloth, scab, scale, encrustation.

adj. *rough*, harsh, grating, coarse, grainy, gravelly; *uneven*, rutted, pitted, ridged, bumpy, knobbly; *crude*, unfinished, roughcast, rough-hewn; *rugged*, gnarled, craggy, jagged, serrated; *hairy*, hirsute, shaggy, unshaven, dishevelled, unkempt, tousled; *bristly*, scratchy, prickly, tweedy, scaly, scabby, encrusted.

vb. *roughen*, coarsen, harshen; *ridge*, corrugate, serrate, notch; *ruffle*, ripple, dishevel, tousle; *bristle*, prickle, chafe, grate, abrade.

292 SMOOTHNESS
See also 191 (horizontality); 302 (lubrication).

n. *smoothness*, evenness, flatness, levelness; *continuity*, unbrokenness, uninterruptedness; *softness*, silkiness, shininess, glassiness; *slipperiness*, slitheriness, oiliness, greasiness; *suavity*, urbanity, polish, sleekness; *finish*, glaze, lustre, sheen, gloss, shine, varnish; *velvet*, satin, glass, marble, mirror, millpond; *roller*, iron, sandpaper, file.

adj. *smooth*, even, flat, level; *continuous*, uninterrupted, unbroken, smooth-running, streamlined; *soft*, silky, satiny, velvety, clean-shaven; *shiny*, glassy, glossy, lustrous; *sleek*, suave, urbane, polished; *slippery*, slithery, greasy, oily.

vb. *smooth*, even, plane, level, flatten, roll, iron out; *shine*, gloss, polish, buff, glaze, finish; *oil*, grease, slick, lubricate; *slide*, slip, glide, skate, coast.

293 ELASTICITY
See also 290 (softness).

n. *elasticity*, pliability, flexibility, ductility; *expandibility*, extensibility, stretch, give; *spring*, bounce, recoil; *rubberiness*, resilience, buoyancy; *elastic band*, indiarubber, spring, coil.

adj. *elastic*, pliable, flexible, ductile, tensile; *expandable*, extensible, stretchy; *springy*, bouncy, rubbery, resilient, buoyant.

vb. *be elastic*, stretch, expand, give, extend, flex; *bounce*, recoil, spring, rebound.

294 TOUGHNESS
See also 289 (hardness).

n. *toughness*, hardness, strength, durability; *resistance*, tenacity, resilience, stamina; *leatheriness*, chewiness, rubberiness, elasticity; *fibre*, sinew, cartilage, gristle.

adj. *tough*, hard, strong, unbreakable; *durable*, hard-wearing, long-lasting, imperishable; *resistant*, tenacious, unflagging, indefatigable; *leathery*, chewy, rubbery, gristly, cartilaginous; *fibrous*, woody, stringy, sinewy.

vb. *be tough*, wear, outlast, survive, stay the course; *toughen*, harden, strengthen, temper.

295 BRITTLENESS
n. *brittleness*, breakability, frangibility, fragility; *frailty*, flimsiness, delicateness, fineness; *sharpness*, crispness, crunchiness, flakiness, crumbliness, friability; *brittle substance*, glass, eggshell, matchwood, thin ice.

adj. *brittle*, breakable, frangible, fragile; *frail*, flimsy, insubstantial, delicate, papery, wafer-thin; *sharp*, crisp, crunchy, crispy, flaky, crumbly, friable, powdery.

vb. *be brittle*, snap, crack, split, chip, break; *fragment*, fracture, splinter, disintegrate, flake, crumble.

296 SHARPNESS
See also 229 (notch).

n. *sharpness*, pointedness, jaggedness, prickliness, serratedness; *incisiveness*, acuteness, keenness, acuity, mordancy, trenchancy; *sting*, bite, prick, cut, stab; *needle*, pin, nail, barb, point, prong, spur, spike, tine; *spine*, prickle, thorn, tooth, fang, tusk, incisor; *cutting edge*, blade, razor, knife, scissors, shears, secateurs, scalpel, cleaver, guillotine; *sharpener*, file, whetstone, grindstone, carborundum, steel.

adj. *sharp*, pointed, jagged, toothed, serrated, notched; *prickly*, spiny, thorny, barbed, spiky; *razor-sharp*, cutting, keen, biting, acute, incisive, trenchant, mordant.

vb. *sharpen*, grind, hone, file, whet, edge; *point*, taper, barb, spur; *prick*, sting, bite, pierce, stab, lance.

297 BLUNTNESS
n. *bluntness*, smoothness, roundedness, stubbiness, flatness; *dullness*, obtuseness, insensitivity; *outspokenness*, frankness, directness, straightforwardness.

adj. *blunt*, smooth, rounded, stubby, snub, flat; *dull*, obtuse, insensitive; *outspoken*, frank, direct, straightforward.

vb. *blunt*, dull, bate, take the edge off, flatten, round.

298 STRUCTURE
See also 216 (form).

n. *structure*, organization, arrangement, pattern, plan; *form*, shape, architecture, make-up, composition, constitution; *framework*, fabric, bodywork, skeleton, anatomy, infrastructure; *construction*, building, edifice, erection, superstructure, elevation.

adj. *structural*, organizational, constructional, architectural, tectonic; *organic*, anatomical, formal, skeletal.

vb. *structure*, organize, plan, pattern, arrange; *shape*, form, construct, build, erect, raise, assemble.

299 **TEXTURE**
See also 197 (interweaving).

n. *texture*, structure, tissue, web, network; *finish*, surface, feel, touch, sensation; *weave*, grain, warp, weft, woof, nap, pile; *fibre*, filament, yarn, thread, string, tow; *textile*, cloth, material, fabric.

adj. *textural*, textile, woven, spun; *rough*, ribbed, hairy, woolly, tweedy, fibrous, coarse-grained, granulated; *smooth*, finespun, delicate, silky, satiny, cottony.

300 **POWDERINESS**
n. *powderiness*, dustiness, frosting, efflorescence, bloom; *crumbliness*, flakiness, friability, looseness; *pulverization*, grinding, pounding, erosion, abrasion, attrition; *powder*, dust, sand, pollen, flour, grit, talc, ash, chalk; *granule*, grain, speck, mote, particle, flake, crumb; *grinder*, crusher, mill, hammer, pestle.

adj. *powdery*, dusty, sandy, floury, farinaceous, chalky; *crumbly*, flaky, friable, loose; *ground*, granulated, pulverized, gritty, grainy.

vb. *powder*, dust, sand, flour, sprinkle; *pulverize*, pound, grind, bruise, crush, mill; *crumble*, flake, granulate, chip.

301 **FRICTION**
See also 291 (roughness).

n. *friction*, drag, resistance, roughness; *rubbing*, abrasion, erosion, corrosion, attrition; *rub*, scrape, graze, polish, elbow grease; *irritation*, grating, tension, irascibility, prickliness; *rubber*, eraser, scraper, sander, emery paper, pumice, sandpaper, file, rasp.

adj. *frictional*, abrasive, irritant; *rough*, rasping, grating.

vb. *rub*, smooth, burnish, scour, polish, buff; *abrade*, scrape, scuff, bark, graze, scratch; *erode*, corrode, wear away, fray; *grind*, rasp, file, plane; *irritate*, chafe, grate, fret, rub up the wrong way.

302 **LUBRICATION**
See also 292 (smoothness); 319 (oiliness).

n. *lubrication*, non-friction, smoothness, slipperiness; *oiliness*, greasiness,

unctuousness, waxiness; *lubricant*, oil, wax, grease, tallow; *ointment*, salve, balm, cream, lotion, emollient.

adj. *lubricated*, oiled, smooth-running; *oily*, greasy, waxy, slippery.

vb. *lubricate*, oil, grease, wax; *smear*, anoint, cream, daub; *ease*, smooth over, oil the wheels, pour oil on troubled waters.

303 **FLUID**
n. *fluid*, liquid, gas, condensation, water; *juice*, sap, liquor, gravy, stock, whey; *body fluid*, blood, rheum, pus, saliva, lymph, mucus, plasma, serum; *solution*, infusion, suspension, decoction; *fluidity*, liquidity, juiciness, wateriness, runniness; *liquefaction*, liquidization, dissolution, deliquescence, thaw; *flow*, flux, haemorrhage, suppuration, secretion; *solvent*, liquidizer, blender, liquefier.

adj. *fluid*, liquid, gaseous, soluble; *watery*, runny, juicy, sappy, moist; *molten*, liquefied, dissolved, deliquescent; *rheumy*, weeping, bleeding, pussy, suppurating.

vb. *make fluid*, liquefy, dissolve, deliquesce, condense; *liquidize*, melt, thaw, defrost, render, melt down, smelt; *flow*, run, pour, stream, well up.

304 **GAS**
n. *gas*, air, ether, atmosphere, exhalation; *smoke*, steam, fumes, reek, cloud, miasma; *vaporization*, distillation, evaporation, atomization; *vaporizer*, atomizer, spray, aerosol, condenser; *gaseousness*, volatility, effervescence, fermentation, fizziness.

adj. *gaseous*, vaporous, volatile, airy, atmospheric, ethereal; *smoky*, steamy, cloudy, misty; *gassy*, fizzy, effervescent, carbonated, sparkling, bubbly.

vb. *gasify*, evaporate, vaporize, volatilize, atomize, distil; *aerate*, fumigate, oxygenate, carbonate; *smoke*, steam, fume, reek, exhale, give off.

305 **WATER**
See also 308 (moisture).

n. *water*, H_2O, fluid, liquid, wet; *moisture*, steam, vapour, condensation; *sweat*, perspiration, exudate, tears, saliva, spittle; *wateriness*, wetness, dampness, runniness; *dilution*, solution, saturation, hydration; *rainwater*, sea water, fresh water, meltwater, ice, salt water, brine; *shower*, douche, bath, dip, wash, hydrotherapy, irrigation; *irrigator*, well, oasis, hydrant, tap, standpipe, sprinkler.

adj. *watery*, fluid, aqueous, liquid, aquatic; *dilute*, hydrated, saturated, watered down; *wet*, soaked, drenched, streaming, dripping, wringing, sopping, waterlogged, awash.

vb. *water*, moisten, sprinkle, irrigate, hydrate; *water down*, dilute, thin, adulterate, dissolve; *wet*, soak, souse, douse, steep, immerse, wash, bathe, rinse, sluice, hose down; *drench*, flood, inundate, saturate, waterlog, deluge, swamp.

306 **AIR**
See also 286 (lightness); 316 (wind).

n. *air*, gas, ether, atmosphere, oxygen, ozone; *wind*, breeze, blast, gust; *open air*, open, fresh air, the great outdoors; *ventilation*, air-conditioning, airing, exposure; *airiness*, lightness, buoyancy, weightlessness; *air bubble*, froth, foam, suds, lather, spray, spindrift, mousse, soufflé, meringue; *aeration*, fermentation, leavening, yeast, raising agent.

adj. *airy*, gaseous, ethereal, weightless; *aerial*, buoyant, inflated, lighter-than-air, pneumatic; *bubbly*, foamy, frothy, aerated, yeasty, fizzy; *breezy*, windy, blowy, fresh, gusty; *open-air*, outdoor, al fresco.

vb. *aerate*, inflate, oxygenate, air, ventilate, expose; *blow*, blast, gust, puff, huff; *bubble*, froth, foam, sparkle, fizz, gurgle, simmer, ferment.

307 **WEATHER**
See also 308 (moisture); 316 (wind).

n. *weather*, elements, weather conditions, climate; *high*, anticyclone, blue skies, heatwave, scorcher (*colloq.*), dry spell, drought; *low*, depression, cyclone, precipitation; *rainfall*, rain, drizzle, shower, downpour, cloudburst, deluge, monsoon, rainy season, rains; *fog*, mist, haze, smog, pea-souper (*colloq.*); *snow*, sleet, hail, snowfall, snowstorm, blizzard, black ice, frost, cold snap; *storm*, high wind, squall, gale, hurricane, typhoon, whirlwind, tornado; *cloud*, cloud cover, cumulus, cirrus, nimbus, stratus, mackerel sky; *barometer*, glass, weather vane, weathercock, windsock, weather forecast, weatherman, meteorologist, climatologist.

adj. *meteorological*, climatic, atmospheric, barometric; *windy*, stormy, squally, blustery, unsettled; *rainy*, showery, drizzly; *freezing*, snowy, wintry, baltic (*colloq.*); *cloudy*, overcast, misty, hazy, foggy; *fair*, clear, sunny, bright, hot, baking, scorching, boiling, sweltering.

vb. *rain*, pour, bucket down, sleet, hail, snow, freeze; *clear up*, change, brighten up, shine, break through; *blow*, gust, blow up, brew.

308 **MOISTURE**
See also 305 (water); 307 (weather).

n. *moisture*, dampness, humidity, dankness, wetness; *vapour*, steam, condensation, rising damp, seepage; *perspiration*, sweat, dew, drizzle, spray, precipitation, mist; *mud*, wet, slime, mire, ooze, sludge; *marsh*, swamp, bog, quicksand, quagmire, wetlands, fen, floodplain.

adj. *moist*, humid, damp, dank, clammy, muggy, close; *wet*, tear-stained, dewy, sweaty, misty, drizzly; *marshy*, swampy, boggy, oozy, soggy, squelchy, muddy, sodden, sludgy, waterlogged, splashy, slushy.

vb. *moisten*, dampen, humidify; *sprinkle*, spatter, spray, dabble, splash, slosh (*colloq.*); *be moist*, perspire, sweat, ooze, leak, seep, trickle, dribble.

309 **DRYNESS**
n. *dryness*, aridity, parchedness, thirst, drought; *dehydration*, drainage, evaporation, desiccation; *desert*, sand dune, dustbowl, wasteland, Sahara; *dryer*, absorbent, blotter, sponge, mop, towel, wringer, spin-dryer, tumble-dryer.

adj. *dry*, bone-dry, parched, thirsty; *desert*, arid, rainless, sandy, dusty, barren; *dehydrated*, desiccated, sun-dried, baked; *waterproof*, dampproof, rainproof, showerproof, watertight; *dried-up*, withered, shrivelled, sere.

vb. *dry*, freeze-dry, drain, dehydrate, evaporate, desiccate; *absorb*, blot, mop up, wipe, sponge, towel; *dry up*, parch, wither, shrivel, bake, toast; *drip-dry*, spin-dry, tumble-dry, wring.

310 **OCEAN**
See also 314 (running water).

n. *ocean*, sea, briny, the deep, the blue, drink (*colloq.*); *high seas*, open sea, the seven seas, main, waters; *seaboard*, coastline, littoral, inshore waters; *channel*, sound, strait, fiord, sea loch, inlet; *estuary*, mouth, delta, firth; *gulf*, bay, bight, cove, lagoon, creek; *wave*, billow, breaker, roller, surf, white horses; *oceanography*, hydrography, hydrology.

adj. *oceanic*, pelagic, deep-sea, marine, maritime, underwater, submarine; *coastal*, littoral, inshore, offshore, seagoing, oceangoing.

311 **LAND**

See also 313 (plain); 321 (mineral).

   n. *land*, ground, terrain, dry land, terra firma; *mainland*, continent, inland, interior, hinterland; *island*, isle, islet, atoll, reef, sandbank, archipelago; *peninsula*, promontory, headland, isthmus, spit; *plain*, desert, steppe, tundra, polder, highland, lowland; *shore*, strand, beach, seaside, riverbank, floodplain; *earth*, soil, topsoil, alluvium, clay, loam, gravel; *rock*, stone, boulder, pebble, scree; *crag*, outcrop, cliff, escarpment; *limestone*, sandstone, granite, shale, schist, chalk.

   adj. *terrestrial*, mainland, inland, continental, overland; *coastal*, onshore, riparian, riverine; *rocky*, stony, pebbly, gritty, gravelly, sandy; *clayey*, alluvial, loamy, chalky, flinty, slaty; *insular*, peninsular, sea-girt, marooned, high and dry, cast away.

312 **LAKE**

   n. *lake*, loch, lough, lagoon, inland sea, sea loch, fiord; *creek*, basin, mudflat, wash, fen, marsh; *pool*, pond, tarn, mere, millpond, reservoir, dam; *waterhole*, oasis, puddle, wallow, well.

313 **PLAIN**

See also 311 (land).

   n. *plain*, expanse, open country, downs, wold, champaign, plateau, tableland; *lowland*, flats, valley, basin, delta; *desert*, tundra, heath, moorland; *grassland*, prairie, steppe, savannah, pampas, veld; *pasture*, field, meadow, lea, park, grounds, green belt, greensward, common.

314 **RUNNING WATER**

See also 310 (ocean); 315 (channel).

   n. *running water*, flow, tide, bore, current, undertow; *river*, waterway, watercourse, canal; *stream*, tributary, feeder, rivulet, brook, burn, beck, rill, runnel; *torrent*, freshet, rapids, white water; *waterfall*, cataract, cascade, falls, weir, Niagara; *flood*, spate, flash flood, tidal wave, tsunami; *spring*, fountain, jet, geyser, waterspout; *wash*, backwash, wake, eddy, swirl, millrace, whirlpool.

   adj. *running*, flowing, tidal, fluvial; *choppy*, broken, rough, gurgling, babbling; *smooth*, calm, glassy, meandering, sluggish.

   vb. *run*, flow, pour, stream, course, race,

rush; *tumble*, surge, roll, dash, swirl, eddy; *gush*, spout, squirt, well up, bubble up; *splash*, lap, swash, wash, slosh (*colloq.*), plash; *trickle*, dribble, ooze, leak, seep; *flow gently*, murmur, babble, gurgle, meander, wind, glide, slide; *flood*, cascade, overflow, spill, inundate, deluge.

315 **CHANNEL**

See also 240 (way); 314 (running water).

   n. *channel*, conduit, course, canal, waterway; *ditch*, trench, moat, riverbed, gutter, pipeline, aqueduct; *lock*, sluice, floodgate, watergate, weir, barrier; *drain*, gully, overflow, culvert, outfall, waterspout, sewer, downpipe, drainpipe.

316 **WIND**

See also 306 (air); 307 (weather).

   n. *wind*, air, draught, downdraught, current, thermal; *blast*, headwind, crosswind, airstream, slipstream, jetstream, tailwind; *trade wind*, sirocco, chinook, föhn, mistral, harmattan; *breeze*, zephyr, whiff, waft, puff, breath; *squall*, flurry, storm, tempest, hurricane, typhoon, whirlwind, tornado; *bellows*, windbag, air pipe, airway, lung, gill, nostril, blowhole; *respiration*, breathing, inhalation, exhalation, expiration, flatulence, belch, burp (*colloq.*), hiccup, fart (*vulg.*); *pant*, gasp, sigh, sniff, wheeze, cough, sneeze, asthma.

   adj. *windy*, airy, draughty, exposed, windswept; *breezy*, blowy, gusty, squally, blustery, stormy; *panting*, out of breath, snuffly, wheezy, chesty, asthmatic.

   vb. *blow*, waft, sigh, sough, stir; *blast*, gust, buffet, bluster, blow up, freshen, storm, rage; *air*, fan, ventilate, air-condition; *breathe*, inhale, exhale, expire; *pant*, gasp, puff, wheeze, sniff, snuffle, snort; *belch*, burp (*colloq.*), hiccup, break wind, fart (*vulg.*).

317 **SEMILIQUID**

See also 182 (thickness); 290 (softness).

   n. *semiliquid*, semifluid, emulsion, paste, colloid; *soup*, stew, gruel, porridge, slops; *mud*, slush, ooze, slime, silt, sludge, lava; *pulp*, puree, pap, mush, stodge, curd, batter; *pulpiness*, sponginess, squelchiness, sogginess, squashiness, runniness; *juiciness*, succulence, sappiness, overripeness.

   adj. *semiliquid*, semifluid, runny, watery; *juicy*, sappy, succulent, overripe; *thick*, clotted, curdled, coagulated; *pulpy*, soupy, mushy, squashy, spongy, squelchy, soggy, sloppy, sludgy.

vb. *pulp*, puree, mash, liquidize, stew; *thicken*, curdle, clot, congeal, emulsify.

318 **VISCOSITY**

n. *viscosity*, viscidity, stickiness, clamminess, glutinousness, adhesiveness, tackiness; *adhesive*, glue, gum, resin, paste, size, birdlime, tar; *mucus*, phlegm, albumen, pus, matter; *glaze*, gelatine, syrup, honey, treacle, jelly, slime, goo (*colloq.*), gunge (*colloq.*).

adj. *viscous*, viscid, sticky, tacky, clammy; *adhesive*, gluey, gummy, resinous, tarry; *slimy*, mucous, syrupy, treacly, gooey (*colloq.*), gungy (*colloq.*).

319 **OILINESS**

See also 302 (lubrication).

n. *oiliness*, unctuousness, greasiness, fattiness, soapiness; *oil*, lubricant, petroleum, paraffin, kerosene; *fat*, grease, soap, tallow, lanolin, blubber, suet, lard, dripping, butter, cream; *ointment*, unguent, salve, liniment, embrocation, pomade, brilliantine.

adj. *oily*, unctuous, oleaginous, slippery, lubricated; *fatty*, soapy, greasy, adipose, pinguid, blubbery, waxy, buttery, creamy.

vb. *oil*, lubricate, grease, wax, soap; *smear*, spread, anoint, baste, butter, cream.

320 **ORGANISM**

See also 322 (life).

n. *organism*, micro-organism, bacterium, bacillus, virus, germ, pathogen; *cell*, protoplasm, enzyme, protein, gene, chromosome, DNA; *animal*, plant, flora, fauna, creature, being; *life sciences*, biology, biochemistry, ecology, botany, zoology, cryptozoology; *evolution*, development, natural selection, Darwinism; *creationism*, creation science; *genetics*, genetic engineering, gene technology, genetic modification, biotechnology, cloning, clone, GMO.

adj. *organic*, bacterial, viral, microscopic; *cellular*, single-celled, chromosomal, genetic; *biological*, ecological, zoological, biochemical, botanical; *genetically-modified*, GM.

321 **MINERAL**

See also 311 (land).

n. *mineral*, rock, ore, gemstone, metal, precious metal, alloy; *petrification*, fossil, ammonite, trilobite, coprolite; *fossil fuel*, coal, lignite; *deposit*, vein, stratum, layer, coal measures; *quartz*, topaz, beryl, corundum, feldspar, basalt, obsidian; *mineralogy*, geology, metallurgy.

adj. *mineral*, inorganic, inanimate; *fossilized*, crystalline, glassy, hard, metallic; *mineralogical*, geological, metallurgical.

322 **LIFE**

See also 1 (existence); 152 (fertility); 320 (organism).

n. *life*, living, being, animation, growth, vital force; *creation*, propagation, birth, nativity, procreation; *existence*, lifetime, one's born days, life history, life cycle, longevity; *soul*, spirit, heart, lifeblood, breath, wind; *creature*, being, mortal, individual, human, organism; *mortality*, the way of all flesh, the human condition, man's estate, life expectancy, quality of life; *resuscitation*, survival, artificial respiration, the kiss of life, lifesaver, life-support system; *vitality*, vigour, vivaciousness, liveliness, verve, energy.

adj. *living*, live, alive and kicking, breathing, quick, viable; *vital*, lively, animated, vivacious, spirited, vigorous; *human*, mortal, finite, ephemeral; *existing*, surviving, long-lived.

vb. *live*, exist, breathe, draw breath; *survive*, outlive, be spared, keep body and soul together, have nine lives, be in the land of the living; *be born*, hatch, come into the world, arrive, see the light of day; *revitalize*, revive, resuscitate, breathe new life into, give a new lease of life; *animate*, enliven, liven up, invigorate, energize.

323 **DEATH**

See also 2 (non-existence); 62 (end); 324 (killing); 325 (burial).

n. *death*, mortality, fatality, casualty, losses, death toll; *extinction*, decease, departure, exit, demise, release; *natural death*, accidental death, cot death, stillbirth, miscarriage, brain death, abortion; *unnatural death*, murder, foul play, suicide, mercy killing, assisted suicide, euthanasia; *deathbed*, death knell, dying day, last hour, dying breath, death rattle, death throes, last words, the last rites, last will and testament; *afterlife*, eternity, the other side, the next world, heaven, hell, the happy hunting grounds (*colloq.*), the underworld, Hades, Valhalla; *the dead*, ancestors, forefathers, spirits, shades; *death notice*, death certificate, obituary, post mortem, autopsy, inquest; *bereavement*, loss, mourning, widowhood, orphanage.

adj. *dying*, moribund, half-dead, not long for this world, done for, slipping away, in extremis; *dead*, deceased, departed, stone dead, dead and gone, dead as a doornail, extinct, defunct, kaput (*colloq.*); *lifeless*, inert, inanimate, stillborn; *deathly*, fatal, mortal, lethal, deadly; *surviving*, bereaved, widowed, orphaned; *late*, lamented, sainted, posthumous.

vb. *die*, perish, expire, pass over/away, fall asleep, give up the ghost, depart this life, croak (*colloq.*), snuff it (*colloq.*), peg out (*colloq.*), pop one's clogs (*colloq.*), kick the bucket (*colloq.*), push up daisies (*colloq.*); *die out*, wither, fade, go west, go the way of all flesh, go for a burton (*colloq.*); *be dying*, have one foot in the grave (*colloq.*), be on one's last legs (*colloq.*), be at death's door, be a goner (*colloq.*); *drop dead*, die in harness, fall, lay down one's life, be slain.

324 KILLING
See also 150 (destruction); 323 (death); 860 (punishment); 861 (means of punishment).

n. *killing*, destruction, bloodshed, bloodletting, blood sport, cull; *murder*, homicide, manslaughter, suicide, self-slaughter, hara kiri, felo de se; *execution*, capital punishment, decapitation, hanging, the rope, the gallows, electrocution, garrotte, the stake, auto-da-fé; *assassination*, liquidation, extermination, annihilation, genocide; *carnage*, massacre, bloodbath, butchery, slaughter, holocaust, pogrom, night of the long knives; *killer*, murderer, mass murderer, serial killer, butcher, assassin, hitman (*colloq.*), cutthroat, axeman, executioner, hangman, lynch mob, death squad; *corpse*, body, remains, cadaver, stiff (*colloq.*), mummy, carcass.

adj. *deadly*, destructive, lethal, fatal, toxic, malignant; *murderous*, homicidal, bloodthirsty, psychopathic; *suicidal*, self-destructive, kamikaze; *cadaverous*, corpselike, deathly.

vb. *kill*, slaughter, destroy, put down, butcher, massacre, exterminate, liquidate, annihilate, decimate; *murder*, assassinate, do in (*colloq.*), lynch, bump off (*colloq.*), rub out (*colloq.*); *slay*, dispatch, bring down, shoot, stab, run through, string up, strangle, smother, suffocate; *execute*, hang, decapitate, behead, guillotine, electrocute, gas, garrotte; *kill oneself*, take one's life, commit suicide, do oneself in (*colloq.*).

325 BURIAL
See also 323 (death).

n. *burial*, interment, entombment, cremation; *funeral*, obsequies, the last rites, lying-in-state, mourning, wake, cortege; *cemetery*, graveyard, crematorium, churchyard, Calvary, golgotha, catacombs; *grave*, tomb, shrine, sepulchre, mausoleum, vault, crypt; *funeral parlour*, mortuary, morgue; *coffin*, sarcophagus, catafalque, bier, pyre, hearse, pall, shroud, winding sheet; *requiem*, dead march, dirge, lament, elegy, epitaph, obituary.

adj. *buried*, interred, dead and buried, six feet under; *funeral*, funerary, mortuary, elegiac, sepulchral.

vb. *bury*, inter, lay to rest, entomb, enshrine, cremate, embalm, mummify; *mourn*, lament, regret, keen, pay one's last respects; *disinter*, exhume, dig up, unearth.

326 ANIMAL
See also 155 (offspring); 328 (agriculture).

n. *animal*, beast, dumb animal, creature, wildlife, fauna; *quadruped*, biped, invertebrate, vertebrate, omnivore, herbivore, carnivore; *mammal*, amphibian, reptile, marsupial, ruminant, rodent, crustacean, fish; *domestic animal*, livestock, pet, vermin; *wild animal*, game, endangered species; *bird*, fowl, poultry, bird of prey, hen, cock, chick, fledgling; *cow*, cattle, heifer, bull, calf, bullock, ox, milch cow; *horse*, mare, stallion, foal, filly, colt, pony, nag (*colloq.*), hack, hunter, gee-gee (*colloq.*); *sheep*, ewe, ram, lamb, wether; *pig*, swine, sow, boar, piglet, hog; *dog*, bitch, pup, mongrel, cur, hound, tyke (*colloq.*), mutt (*colloq.*), pooch (*colloq.*), bow-wow (*colloq.*), man's best friend; *cat*, tabby, tom, kitten, pussy (*colloq.*), moggy (*colloq.*), big cat, wildcat; *insect*, larva, grub, pupa, imago, creepy-crawly (*colloq.*); *zoo*, menagerie, safari park, game reserve, aviary, apiary, aquarium.

adj. *animal*, bestial, brutish, feral, wild; *domestic*, tame, house-trained, broken in; *mammalian*, reptilian, amphibian, bovine, equine, ovine, porcine, canine, feline; *omnivorous*, herbivorous, carnivorous, insectivorous.

327 PLANT
See also 329 (horticulture).

n. *plant*, flower, vegetable, weed, herb, shrub, bush, tree; *annual*, hardy annual, biennial, perennial; *sapling*, seedling, plug plant; *plant life*, flora, vegetation, biomass, greenery, verdure; *wood*, greenwood, woodland, forest, jungle, rainforest, cloud forest, heath, scrub, undergrowth; *copse*, thicket, spinney, plantation, orchard, grove; *branch*, bough, twig, shoot, leaf, foliation, stem, stalk, trunk, bole; *root*, tuber, bulb, corm, rhizome, seed; *flowerhead*, bloom, floret, bud, petal, inflorescence, raceme, panicle; *grass*, pasture, sward, lawn, turf, sod, divot.

adj. *vegetal*, floral, botanical, horticultural; *evergreen*, deciduous, coniferous, hardy, annual, biennial, perennial; *verdant*, leafy, grassy, herbaceous, lush, overgrown, rank; *woody*, sylvan, arboreal, bosky, scrubby, shrubby, jungly.

vb. *plant*, afforest, cultivate, garden, botanize; *grow*, germinate, sprout, shoot, take root, strike.

328 **AGRICULTURE**
See also 326 (animal).

n. *agriculture*, farming, stockbreeding, factory farming, animal husbandry, agronomy, veterinary science; *farm*, ranch, hatchery, stud farm, battery, piggery; *stable*, byre, cowshed, sheepfold, pen, coop, sty, hutch; *farmstead*, collective farm, kolkhoz, kibbutz, estate, smallholding, croft; *farmer*, agronomist, tenant farmer, peasant, yeoman, smallholder, crofter, shepherd, farmhand, serf; *crop*, produce, yield, harvest, glut.

adj. *agricultural*, agronomic, agrarian; *arable*, pastoral, bucolic, rustic, rural; *purebred*, thoroughbred, crossbred, hybrid, domesticated.

vb. *farm*, ranch, raise, rear, breed, grow; *dig*, till, plough, cultivate, rotivate, drain, reclaim; *irrigate*, fertilize, manure, rake, harrow, hoe; *sow*, broadcast, drill, mow, reap, harvest, gather in, thresh, winnow.

329 **HORTICULTURE**
See also 327 (plant).

n. *horticulture*, arboriculture, viticulture, market gardening, landscape gardening, topiary; *nursery*, garden centre, orchard, plantation, vineyard; *garden*, allotment, kitchen garden, cabbage patch, herbaceous border, shrubbery, rockery; *park*, arboretum, botanical gardens, herbarium; *hothouse*, greenhouse, glasshouse, orangery, conservatory, cold frame, cloche; *gardener*, horticulturalist, nurseryman, seedsman, market gardener, planter.

adj. *horticultural*, floral, herbal, herbaceous, alpine, hardy, exotic.

vb. *cultivate*, garden, grow, propagate, force, graft; *sow*, plant out, harden off, prick out, transplant; *fertilize*, manure, topdress, mulch.

330 **HUMANKIND**
n. *humankind*, humanity, human race, mankind, womankind; *human being*, creature, homo sapiens, *hominid*, apeman, Neanderthal man, troglodyte, savage, barbarian; *humanoid*, alien, extraterrestrial, Martian, little green men; *android*, robot, automaton, cyborg; *person*, individual, mortal, soul, body, personage, figure; *fellow*, character (*colloq.*), customer (*colloq.*), card (*colloq.*), cove (*colloq.*); *family*, house, tribe, clan, sept, line, dynasty; *community*, public, society, the masses, tribalism, herd instinct; *population*, populace, people, nation, civilization, culture.

adj. *human*, humanoid, anthropoid, hominoid; *anthropological*, sociological, cultural, ethnological; *interpersonal*, familial, tribal, social, communal, collective, public, civic.

331 **NATIONALITY**
See also 157 (region).

n. *nationality*, ethnicity, nationhood, statehood; *nationalism*, patriotism, chauvinism, jingoism, racism, antisemitism; *nation*, state, superstate, commonwealth, republic, people, ethnic minority; *native*, Brit (*colloq.*), Pommie (*colloq.*), Sassenach (*derog.*), Jock (*colloq.*), Paddy (*colloq.*), Mick (*offens.*), Taffy (*colloq.*); *foreigner*, outsider, immigrant, wop (*offens.*), wog (*offens.*), black, coloured, darkie (*offens.*), coon (*offens.*), nigger (*offens.*), Asian, Paki (*offens.*); *Continental*, Latin, Frog (*offens.*), Kraut (*offens.*), Eyetie (*offens.*), dago (*offens.*), Polack (*offens.*), Yid (*offens.*), Argie (*offens.*), Yank (*colloq.*).

adj. *national*, racial, ethnic; *nationalistic*, patriotic, jingoistic, chauvinist, racist.

332 **MALE**
n. *male*, he, man, boy, youth, lad, stripling, Adam, spear side; *masculinity*, manliness, virility, manhood, mannishness, patriarchy, machismo; *gentleman*, lord, master, sir, mister; *fellow*, chap (*colloq.*), bloke (*colloq.*), geezer (*colloq.*), codger (*colloq.*), buffer (*colloq.*), guy (*colloq.*), mate (*colloq.*), buddy (*colloq.*), squire (*colloq.*), governor (*colloq.*);

he-man, hunk (*colloq.*),, beefcake (*colloq.*), stud, male chauvinist (pig), MCP, misogynist; *bachelor*, homosexual, boyfriend, escort, husband, bridegroom, family man, househusband, pater familias, widower, patriarch; *male animal*, cock, drake, gander, capon, jack, buck, stag, dog, stallion, bull, ox, colt, boar, ram, billy, tom.

adj. *male*, masculine, manly, virile, mannish, butch (*colloq.*), macho; *unmanly*, womanish, effeminate, androgynous.

333 **FEMALE**

n. *female*, she, woman, Eve, the fair sex, the weaker sex, the distaff side; *femininity*, womanhood, womanliness, motherliness; *feminism*, sisterhood, Women's Movement, Women's Lib/Liberation, matriarchy, misandry, lesbianism; *girl*, lass, wench, damsel, maiden, colleen, nymphet, dolly bird; *bachelor girl*, career woman, spinster, old maid, girlfriend, bride, wife, housewife, homemaker, domestic goddess, widow, dowager; *lady*, madam, ma'am, dame (*colloq.*), chick (*colloq.*), doll (*colloq.*), bird (*colloq.*), bint (*colloq.*), broad (*colloq.*), skirt (*colloq.*), crumpet (*colloq.*), cheesecake (*colloq.*); *female animal*, hen, goose, duck, bitch, vixen, heifer, mare, ewe, filly, nanny, doe, hind.

adj. *female*, feminine, gynaecological, obstetric; *womanly*, ladylike, matronly, maternal; *feminist*, liberated, sisterly, lesbian.

334 **SENSATION**
See also 729 (feeling); 730 (sensitivity).

n. *sensation*, feeling, sensitivity, sensibility; *hypersensitivity*, allergy, soreness, tenderness, rawness; *sense*, feel, touch, perception, awareness; *response*, reaction, reflex, impression; *physicality*, sensuality, body language.

adj. *sentient*, sensible, sensory; *sensitive*, responsive, perceptive, aware, impressionable, susceptible; *sore*, tender, raw, exposed, hypersensitive, allergic; *physical*, bodily, sensuous.

vb. *sense*, feel, see, hear, touch, taste, smell; *respond*, react, register, realize; *awaken*, arouse, sensitize, impress.

335 **INSENSIBILITY**
See also 731 (insensitivity).

n. *insensibility*, deadness, numbness, dullness, anaesthesia; *insensitivity*, indifference, callousness; *inertness*, paralysis,

catalepsy, catatonia, stupor; *unconsciousness*, coma, trance, faint, swoon, blackout; *anaesthetic*, analgesic, painkiller, sedative, tranquillizer, narcotic.

adj. *insensible*, numb, dead, dull, anaesthetized; *inert*, paralysed, catatonic, cataleptic; *unconscious*, comatose, stupefied, punch-drunk; *insensitive*, unfeeling, callous, thick-skinned.

adj. *desensitize*, deaden, numb, dull, anaesthetize; *drug*, dope, put under, knock out, sedate, tranquillize; *lose consciousness*, swoon, faint, pass out, black out.

336 **PHYSICAL PLEASURE**
See also 734 (joy).

n. *physical pleasure*, enjoyment, satisfaction, gratification; *pleasure-seeking*, sensuality, debauchery, dissipation, hedonism; *excitement*, arousal, kick (*colloq.*), thrill, turn-on (*colloq.*), orgasm, ecstasy; *ease*, comfort, contentment, well-being, euphoria, creature comforts, a bed of roses, the lap of luxury.

adj. *pleasurable*, agreeable, enjoyable, gratifying, titillating; *comfortable*, easy, luxurious, cosseted, pampered, cushy (*colloq.*); *sensual*, voluptuous, rakish, debauched, hedonistic, dissipated.

vb. *enjoy*, relish, savour, revel, wallow, bask, luxuriate; *excite*, titillate, arouse, thrill, turn on (*colloq.*); *thrive*, prosper, be in clover, live the life of Riley (*colloq.*).

337 **PHYSICAL PAIN**
See also 735 (sorrow).

n. *physical pain*, illness, suffering, distress, discomfort; *hurt*, injury, wound, trauma, shock, anguish, agony; *wound*, cut, gash, abrasion, bruise, contusion, sprain, fracture; *pang*, twinge, stab, sting, cramp, stitch, gripe, colic.

adj. *painful*, sore, aching, tender, raw, uncomfortable; *distressing*, agonizing, excruciating, exquisite; *injured*, wounded, hurt, traumatized; *stinging*, itchy, smarting, throbbing, stabbing, shooting.

vb. *cause pain*, distress, agonize, torment; *injure*, wound, cut, gash, lacerate, sprain, wrench; *hurt*, ache, smart, burn, gnaw, sting, throb; *wince*, flinch, writhe, squirm.

338 **TOUCH**

n. *touch*, feel, contact, friction, pressure, squeeze; *handling*, manipulation, massage, reflexology; *light touch*, graze, brush, stroke, caress, pat, flick, tap; *sensation*, itch, scratch, tickle, tingle, prickly heat, pins and needles.

adj. *tactile*, touchable, tangible, palpable; *deft*, delicate, gentle, nimble, feathery; *firm*, tight, clumsy, heavy-handed, rough.

vb. *touch*, feel, finger, sense, fumble, grope, scrabble; *brush*, graze, skim, stroke, caress, pat, dab, paw, nuzzle; *handle*, manhandle, manipulate, massage, knead.

339 HEAT

n. *heat*, warmth, tepidness, lukewarmness, white-heat, incandescence; *fever*, flush, glow, sweat, lather; *temperature*, boiling point, flashpoint, overheating, fever pitch, global warming; *fire*, flame, spark, blaze, bonfire, conflagration, inferno, holocaust; *heating*, burning, cauterization, combustion, ignition, incineration, cremation; *burn*, scald, scorch, brand, sunburn; *heater*, radiator, solar panel, space heater, geyser, boiler; *cooker*, stove, oven, hob, range, grate, fireplace, hearth; *furnace*, kiln, forge, incinerator, oasthouse.

adj. *hot*, red-hot, white-hot, incandescent, glowing; *feverish*, boiling, sweltering, baking, scorching, torrid, tropical, sultry; *warm*, tepid, lukewarm, temperate, mild, balmy; *burning*, fiery, flaming, ablaze, aflame, afire, alight; *flammable*, inflammable, combustible, incendiary.

vb. *heat*, warm, boil, bake, scald, toast, scorch, fry, roast, grill; *burn*, kindle, flame, catch fire, flare up, blaze.

340 COLD

n. *cold*, coolness, chilliness, coldness, frostiness, iciness; *chill*, hypothermia, chilblains, frostbite; *wintriness*, snow, sleet, hail, frost, ice, black ice, hoarfrost, rime, icicle; *refrigeration*, glaciation, congelation, freezing; *refrigerator*, cooler, icebox, fridge, deep-freeze, freezer, cold storage.

adj. *cold*, stone-cold, ice-cold, frigid, chilly, parky (*colloq.*); *wintry*, icy, frosty, arctic, Siberian; *keen*, biting, piercing, raw, bitter, cutting; *frozen*, glacé, frappé, on the rocks.

vb. *chill*, cool, freeze, refrigerate, deep-freeze; *frost*, ice, ice up, sleet, hail, snow.

341 FUEL

See also 141 (power).

n. *fuel*, kindling, firewood, tinder, faggot, log; *fossil fuel*, coal, charcoal, coke, lignite, anthracite, peat, petroleum, petrol, diesel, biodiesel, biofuel, kerosene, paraffin, gas, natural gas; *nuclear power*, atomic power,

solar energy, electricity, hydroelectricity, wave power, wind power, wind farm; *lighter*, flint, firelighter, taper, spill, match, fuse, touchpaper.

adj. *combustible*, flammable, inflammable, incendiary, explosive.

vb. *fuel*, feed, stoke, power, add fuel to the flames; *light*, kindle, fire, catch.

342 TASTE

n. *taste*, flavour, savour, tang, bite, aftertaste, body, richness, tastiness; *sharpness*, sweetness, bitterness, saltiness, brackishness, piquancy, tanginess, spiciness; *appetite*, gusto, relish, zest, heartiness; *palate*, tongue, taste buds, sweet tooth; *delicacy*, titbit, ambrosia, nectar, caviar.

adj. *tasty*, savoury, wholesome, flavourful, flavoursome; *sharp*, tangy, piquant, bitter, salty, peppery, spicy, sweet; *rich*, full-bodied, mellow, fruity. *delicious*, tempting, appetizing, mouthwatering, delectable, palatable, moreish (*colloq.*), scrumptious (*colloq.*), yummy (*colloq.*).

vb. *taste*, sample, try, sip, lick; *savour*, relish, smack one's lips, come back for more, enjoy; *taste of*, savour of, smack of.

343 TASTELESSNESS

n. *tastelessness*, insipidness, blandness, staleness, flatness; *unwholesomeness*, unsavouriness, rankness, rottenness, rancidness; *gruel*, porridge, bread and water, slops, sawdust, dishwater, junk food.

adj. *tasteless*, flavourless, insipid, bland, thin, watery, wishy-washy, diluted; *unappetizing*, unwholesome, unpalatable, stale, overcooked, underdone, inedible; *unsavoury*, bitter, sour, rancid, bad, addled, putrid, rank, off, rotten, sickly, cloying, yukky (*colloq.*).

vb. *pall*, cloy, sicken, nauseate, repel, disgust, turn one's stomach.

344 PIQUANCY

n. *piquancy*, pungency, tastiness, bite, zest, tang, nip; *savouriness*, sharpness, tartness, sourness, saltiness, pepperiness, spiciness; *seasoning*, condiment, flavouring, additive, aromatic, herb, relish, spice, dressing; *ginger*, pepper, chilli, cayenne, curry, marinade.

adj. *piquant*, pungent, tasty, hot, tangy; *savoury*, salty, peppery, gingery, spicy, bitter, sour, tart, bittersweet, sweet-and-sour.

vb. *flavour*, season, spice, curry, ginger up, marinade.

345 SWEETNESS

n. *sweetness*, sugariness, saccharinity, sickliness; *sweetener*, sugar, brown/white/demerara/granulated/caster/icing sugar, cane/beet sugar; *sucrose*, glucose, fructose, lactose; *artificial sweetener*; saccharin, aspartame, acesulfame K; *honey*, honeycomb, nectar, mead, syrup, maple syrup, treacle, molasses; *confectionery*, candy, fudge, bonbon, sweetmeat, fondant, icing, frosting.

adj. *sweet*, sugary, sticky, saccharine, sickly, cloying, syrupy, treacly; *sugared*, honeyed, candied, crystallized, iced, glacé, frosted.

vb. *sweeten*, sugar, sugar-coat, candy, crystallize, ice, frost.

346 SOURNESS

n. *sourness*, tartness, astringency, acidity, acerbity, bitterness, sharpness; *acid*, vinegar, lemon, bitters, gall, alum, wormwood, acid drop.

adj. *sour*, sourish, unsweetened, tart, acid, astringent, acerbic, bitter; *green*, unripe, vinegary, sharp, unsweetened, dry.

vb. *sour*, turn, curdle, acidulate, set one's teeth on edge.

347 ODOUR

See also 349 (fragrance); 350 (stench).

n. *odour*, smell, aroma, scent, fragrance, bouquet, perfume; *stink*, stench, pong (*colloq.*), pollution; *exhalation*, breath, whiff, fumes, reek, vapour, effluvium; *redolence*, headiness, pungency, acridness.

adj. *odorous*, odoriferous, redolent, smelly; *scented*, perfumed, fragrant, heady, sweet-smelling; *foul*, stale, noxious, polluted, pungent, rank; *olfactory*, nasal.

vb. *smell*, exhale, give off, emit, stink, reek; *inhale*, sniff, nose, breathe in.

348 ODOURLESSNESS

n. *odourlessness*, lack of smell, freshness, sweetness, fresh air, unpollutedness, smokeless zone; *deodorization*, purification, fumigation, ventilation; *deodorant*, fumigant, disinfectant, air freshener.

adj. *odourless*, unscented, unperfumed, scentless; *deodorized*, pure, fresh, unpolluted, sweet-smelling.

vb. *deodorize*, freshen, clean, purify, ventilate, air, fumigate.

349 FRAGRANCE

See also 347 (odour).

n. *fragrance*, sweet smell, scent, bouquet, odour, aroma; *perfume*, toilet water, eau de cologne, aftershave, pomade; *pomander*, pot pourri, joss stick, air freshener; *essential oil*, fixative, civet, musk, ambergris, attar; *balm*, spice, incense, sandalwood, camphor, honeysuckle, lavender, rose.

adj. *fragrant*, odorous, aromatic, redolent; *sweet-smelling*, perfumed, musky, flowery, spicy, fruity.

vb. *scent*, perfume, spice, sweeten.

350 STENCH

See also 347 (odour).

n. *stench*, stink, pong (*colloq.*), niff (*colloq.*), fetor, bad breath, halitosis, BO; *foulness*, rankness, putrefaction, rancidness, staleness, mustiness, fustiness; *atmospheric pollution*, fumes, smog, reek, miasma, fug, frowst, global warming, global dimming; *stinker*, stinkbomb, skunk, bad egg, ammonia, sulphur.

adj. *smelly*, stinking, fetid, foul, offensive, noxious, pongy (*colloq.*), niffy (*colloq.*); *high*, gamy, off, putrid, rancid, rank, pungent, foxy; *stale*, stuffy, fuggy, frowsty, polluted, acrid, smoky.

vb. *stink*, reek, fume, smell, pong (*colloq.*), hum (*colloq.*), stink to high heaven.

351 HEARING

See also 353 (sound).

n. *hearing*, audition, auscultation, acoustics; *audibility*, distinctness, loudness, earshot, hearing distance; *overhearing*, eavesdropping, bugging, wire-tapping; *listener*, auditor, hearer, audience; *headphones*, stethoscope, earpiece, hearing aid.

adj. *aural*, audiovisual, auditory, acoustic; *audible*, loud, distinct, clear.

vb. *hear*, listen, catch, be all ears (*colloq.*), hearken, heed, lend an ear, prick up one's ears; *overhear*, eavesdrop, listen in on, bug, wire-tap.

352 DEAFNESS

n. *deafness*, hardness of hearing, tone-deafness, deaf-mutism; *inaudibility*, indistinctness, faintness, softness; *lip-reading*, sign language, deaf aid, ear trumpet.

adj. *deaf*, hard of hearing, deaf-mute, deaf and dumb, stone-deaf, deaf as a post; *inaudible*, indistinct, faint, muted; *tone-deaf*, tin-eared (*colloq.*), cloth-eared (*colloq.*); *deafening*, earsplitting, earshattering.

vb. *deafen*, make one's ears ring; *go unheard*, fall on deaf ears, go unheeded; *not listen*, turn a deaf ear, ignore.

353 SOUND

See also 351 (hearing); 355 (loudness); 526 (voice).

n. *sound*, noise, utterance, speech-sound; *resonance*, reverberation, sonority, loudness; *sound effect*, soundtrack, sound wave, voiceover; *tone*, pitch, level, timbre, intonation, cadence, lilt; *audibility*, distinctness, clarity; *record-player*, gramophone, hi-fi, stereo, sound system, music centre; *acoustics*, dynamics, phonetics.

adj. *sounding*, sonic, acoustic, dynamic, radiophonic; *audio*, mono, stereophonic, binaural, quadraphonic; *audible*, distinct, loud, clear, noisy, sonorous.

vb. *sound*, resound, ring out, reverberate, carry; *utter*, emit, speak, vocalize, voice.

354 SILENCE

See also 527 (voicelessness).

n. *silence*, noiselessness, soundlessness, stillness, hush, lull, peace and quiet; *muteness*, voicelessness, speechlessness, taciturnity; *silencer*, gag, muzzle, blackout.

adj. *silent*, noiseless, soundless, soundproof, hushed, still, quiet, peaceful; *mute*, unspoken, voiceless, speechless, tongue-tied, lost for words, monosyllabic, taciturn.

vb. *silence*, still, hush, quieten, lull; *mute*, tone down, subdue, quell; *muffle*, gag, muzzle, drown out.

355 LOUDNESS

See also 353 (sound); 357 (sudden sound); 359 (resonance).

n. *loudness*, distinctness, clarity, audibility; *volume*, crescendo, decibels, sonority; *noise*, report, bang, roar, crash, boom, reverberation; *stridency*, shrillness, vociferousness, noisiness, clamorousness; *shout*, yell, bellow, guffaw, cry, shriek, scream, screech, blare, bray, catcall, boo; *din*, row, racket, clamour, outcry, hullabaloo, hubbub, caterwauling; *amplifier*, loud pedal, megaphone, loudhailer, loudspeaker, microphone, public-address system; *siren*, alarm, klaxon, foghorn, gong, trumpet.

adj. *loud*, audible, distinct, clear; *noisy*, clamorous, lusty, strident, vociferous,

stentorian, loud-mouthed; *resonant*, sonorous, ringing, plangent; *shrill*, high-pitched, piercing, earsplitting, deafening.

vb. *be loud*, reverberate, resound, peal, swell, ring out, clang, blare, crash, thunder; *shout*, yell, bellow, roar, guffaw, cry out, screech, scream, shriek; *be noisy*, clamour, deafen, raise Cain, raise the roof (*colloq.*), make the rafters ring.

adv. *loudly*, at the top of one's voice, fortissimo.

356 FAINTNESS

See also 360 (muteness).

n. *faintness*, softness, lowness, mutedness, indistinctness, inaudibility; *low sound*, whisper, undertone, sigh, murmur, mutter, mumble, hum, moan, groan, squeak; *tinkle*, rustle, swish, whirr, purr, lap, pad, patter.

adj. *faint*, soft, low, muted, murmured, soft-spoken, indistinct, inaudible; *quiet*, hushed, subdued, muffled, distant, far-off.

vb. *be faint*, die away, fade, weaken; *whisper*, murmur, croon, mutter, moan, groan, sigh; *tinkle*, chirr, whirr, purr, lap, swish, rustle, sough.

adv. *faintly*, under one's breath, sotto voce, piano, out of earshot.

357 SUDDEN SOUND

See also 355 (loudness).

n. *sudden sound*, report, pistol shot, gunfire, backfire, explosion, sonic boom, thunderclap; *bang*, crash, crack, peal, blast, burst, volley, salvo; *knock*, rap, tap, clap, rat-a-tat; *shout*, yell, whoop, hoot, screech, scream, shriek.

vb. *bang*, crash, thunder, crack, burst out; *explode*, backfire, erupt, go off, ring out, peal; *cry out*, shout, scream, yelp, whoop, hoot.

358 REPEATED SOUND

n. *repeated sound*, reverberation, echo, roll, rumble; *rattle*, clatter, racket, chatter, babble, rhubarb, background noise; *drumming*, tattoo, thrumming, strumming, throbbing, pulse; *trill*, tremolo, vibrato, quaver; *buzz*, whirr, chirr, hum, drone.

vb. *roll*, rumble, grumble, reverberate, echo; *drum*, thrum, strum, beat, tick, throb; *trill*, vibrate, tremble, quaver; *rattle*, clatter, chatter, drone, hum, whirr.

359 RESONANCE

See also 355 (loudness).

n. *resonance*, reverberation, plangency,

sonorousness, hollowness; *echo*, overtone; *ring*, ping, clang, twang, peal, chime, ringtone; *tinkle*, clink, chink, clank, jangle, jingle; *bell*, gong, chimes, cymbals, tubular bells, glockenspiel, echo chamber.

adj. *resonant*, reverberant, plangent, sonorous, hollow, echoey, lingering, vibrant; *metallic*, tinkly, jingling, ringing, clanking.

vb. *resonate*, vibrate, carry, reverberate, echo; *peal*, chime, ring, ting, ping, twang, jingle, jangle; *clink*, clank, chink, tinkle.

360 **MUTEDNESS**
See also 356 (faintness).

n. *mutedness*, non-resonance, deadness, dullness, muffledness, indistinctness; *thud*, thump, thwack, clump, plonk, clonk, plop; *mute*, silencer, damper, soft pedal.

adj. *muted*, dead, dull, muffled, subdued, indistinct.

vb. *mute*, deaden, dull, soften; *subdue*, damp, stifle, muffle, tone down, lower; *thud*, thump, pound, clump, clonk, plonk, plop.

361 **HISSING SOUND**
adj. *hissing*, sibilant, fizzy, wheezy, splashy, sploshy.

vb. *hiss*, whisper, splash, swish, swash, sigh, sough; *rustle*, rasp, whistle, wheeze; *buzz*, fizz, sizzle, spit, sputter.

362 **HARSH SOUND**
See also 366 (dissonance).

n. *harsh sound*, screech, squawk, croak, caw, skirl, shriek; *rasp*, cough, hawk, grate, scrape, scratch; *roughness*, hoarseness, huskiness, gruffness; *stridency*, shrillness, raucousness, braying; *discord*, dissonance, cacophony, jangle, clash.

adj. *harsh*, strident, shrill, raucous, brassy, tinny; *hoarse*, husky, gruff, throaty, growly, guttural; *rough*, rasping, grating, scratchy, rusty, creaky; *discordant*, jarring, cacophonous, dissonant, jangly, clashing.

vb. *shriek*, screech, squawk, croak, caw, bray, skirl, blare, clang; *scrape*, scratch, grate, rasp, saw, grind, creak; *jar*, clash, jangle, set one's teeth on edge.

363 **HUMAN CRY**
See also 355 (loudness).

n. *human cry*, shout, call, exclamation, ejaculation; *outcry*, clamour, raised voices, noise, din, hubbub; *yell*, yelp, whoop, hoot, halloo; *cheer*, hurrah, boo, catcall; *howl*, wail,

roar, guffaw, bellow; *shriek*, scream, screech, squeal; *moan*, groan, grunt, whimper, gasp.

adj. *loud*, high-pitched, clamorous, noisy, vocal, vociferous, lusty, full-throated.

vb. *cry out*, call out, exclaim, ejaculate; *shout*, clamour, yell, bawl, holler (*colloq.*), howl, yowl, wail, caterwaul; *shriek*, screech, squeal, yelp; *chant*, chorus, cheer, whoop, boo, yodel; *roar*, rant, bellow, guffaw, hoot; *moan*, groan, whinge (*colloq.*), whimper, sob, gasp, grunt.

364 **ANIMAL CRY**
n. *animal cry*, call, birdcall, note, song.

vb. *cry*, call, caw, coo, quack, cluck, crow, cackle, honk, croak, gobble; *cheep*, peep, chirrup, tweet, whistle, warble, twitter, chatter; *squawk*, screech, squeal, scream; *bark*, yap, yelp, bay, bell, howl, whine; *grunt*, growl, snarl, roar; *neigh*, bray, whinny, whicker, snort, snicker; *miaow*, mew, purr, hiss, spit; *bleat*, baa, moo, low, bellow; *hum*, drone, buzz, chirr.

365 **MELODY**
See also 367 (music).

n. *melody*, harmony, euphony, concord, tonality, consonance; *melodiousness*, tunefulness, musicality, mellifluousness, sweetness; *tune*, air, song, strain, refrain, ditty, signature tune/song, theme tune/song; *pitch*, intonation, register, key.

adj. *melodic*, tuneful, musical, true, in tune; *melodious*, harmonious, euphonious, sweet, mellifluous, dulcet, silvery, bell-like; *catchy*, lilting, memorable, singable, hummable.

vb. *be melodious*, harmonize, blend, chime in, chorus.

366 **DISSONANCE**
See also 362 (harsh sound).

n. *dissonance*, discord, disharmony, tone-deafness, atonality; *harshness*, raucousness, tonelessness, monotony; *cacophony*, caterwauling, Babel, row, racket, din.

adj. *dissonant*, discordant, atonal, out-of-tune, off-key, tone-deaf, flat, sharp; *inharmonious*, untuneful, unmusical, toneless, monotonous, singsong; *cacophonous*, raucous, harsh, jarring, jangling, grating.

vb. *be dissonant*, jangle, jar, grate, clash.

367 **MUSIC**

See also 365 (melody); 368 (musician); 524 (dance).

n. *music*, harmony, melody, music-making, musicianship; *classical music*, chamber music; *light music*, Muzak (*tdmk*); *pop music*, skiffle, jive, rock, soft rock, glam rock, progressive rock, hard rock, heavy metal, blues, soul, northern soul, folk, world music, roots music, country and western, punk, new wave, hip-hop, rap, drum 'n' base, house, acid house, garage, disco, electronic music, techno, trance, reggae, bhangra *or* bangra; *jazz*, swing, ragtime, trad, bop, boogie(-woogie), jazz-rock; *performance*, recital, concert, gig (*colloq.*), jam session, recording session, remixing, sampling, scratching; *tune*, theme, signature tune, backing, incidental music; *score*, libretto, lyrics, songbook, sheet music; *piece*, composition, work, opus, arrangement, setting, orchestration, improvisation; *song*, ballad, hymn, carol, psalm, spiritual, aria, madrigal; *opera*, operetta, oratorio, chorale, mass, musical; *overture*, sonata, fugue, suite, concerto, symphony; *dance music*, jig, minuet, gavotte, mazurka, polka, waltz, foxtrot; *prelude*, intermezzo, impromptu, nocturne, scherzo, serenade, requiem, rondo.

adj. *musical*, tuneful, melodic, polyphonic, contrapuntal; *classical*, highbrow, straight, romantic, baroque; *popular*, lowbrow, middlebrow, bluesy, jazzy, hot (*colloq.*), cool (*colloq.*), funky (*colloq.*); *vocal*, operatic, choral, unaccompanied; *instrumental*, orchestral, symphonic, solo.

368 **MUSICIAN**

See also 367 (music).

n. *musician*, player, performer, soloist, accompanist, instrumentalist, artiste, virtuoso; *minstrel*, bard, troubadour, busker, one-man band; *singer*, vocalist, songster, chorister, prima donna, diva; *soprano*, mezzosoprano, contralto, treble, alto, countertenor, tenor, baritone, bass; *composer*, arranger, librettist, songwriter; *conductor*, maestro, leader, bandmaster, bandleader; *orchestra*, chamber orchestra, symphony orchestra, ensemble, group, band, steel band, pop group, rock group, boy/girl band, tribute group; *duo*, trio, quartet, quintet, sextet, septet, octet; *disc jockey*, DJ, scratch DJ, turntablist.

vb. *play*, perform, execute, interpret, play by ear, sight-read, accompany; *sound*, pluck,

bow, blow, beat, finger, tickle the ivories (*colloq.*); *sing*, vocalize, intone, carol, trill, chant, chorus; *arrange*, score, orchestrate, compose, set to music, transpose.

369 **MUSICAL INSTRUMENT**

n. *musical instrument*, synthesizer, record-player, tape-recorder, cassette deck, music centre, sound system; *record*, disc, album, cassette, tape, LP, EP, single, compact disc, digital record; *wind instrument*, brass, trumpet, trombone, bugle, flugelhorn, saxophone, French horn, tuba, euphonium, bagpipes; *woodwind*, oboe, bassoon, flute, clarinet; *stringed instrument*, double bass, cello, violin, fiddle (*colloq.*), viola, harp; *guitar*, mandolin, lute, banjo, ukulele, cithar, zither, dulcimer; *keyboard instrument*, piano, grand, baby grand, upright, harpsichord, virginals, spinet, harmonium, organ, accordion; *percussion*, timpani, kettledrum, cymbal, triangle, tambourine, drum, vibraphone, marimba, xylophone, gong, chimes, glockenspiel, maracas, castanets.

370 **VISION**

See also 371 (blindness); 372 (visibility).

n. *vision*, seeing, sight, eyesight; *perception*, recognition, insight, imagination, mind's eye; *visual defect*, short-sightedness, myopia, long-sightedness, presbyopia, astigmatism, squint, strabismus, cast, colour-blindness, cataract; *eye*, naked eye, peepers (*colloq.*), orbs (*colloq.*), glad eye (*colloq.*), sheep's eyes, evil eye; *look*, gaze, stare, glance, eye contact, glimpse, peek, peep, butcher's (*colloq.*), dekko (*colloq.*), once-over (*colloq.*), look-see (*colloq.*); *inspection*, scrutiny, reconnaissance, surveillance, watch, observation, look-out; *view*, sight, spectacle, eyesore, eyeful (*colloq.*), sight for sore eyes (*colloq.*); *survey*, perspective, overview, bird's eye view, outlook; *viewer*, spectator, observer, watcher, eye witness, onlooker, bystander, audience; *optical device*, telescope, binoculars, field glasses, spotting scope, microscope, magnifying glass; *spectacles*, glasses, specs (*colloq.*), goggles, contact lens, pince-nez, monocle, bifocals; *optical illusion*, mirage, will-o'-the-wisp, ignus fatuus, trick photography, trompe l'oeil, phantom.

adj. *visual*, ocular, optical, ophthalmic; *perceptive*, observant, clear-sighted, perspicacious; *sharp-eyed*, watchful, eagle-eyed, hawk-eyed, lynx-eyed; *short-sighted*, myopic, purblind, long-sighted, presbyopic, colour-blind, cross-eyed, wall-eyed, astigmatic.

vb. *see*, behold, perceive, discern, make out, recognize; *glimpse*, catch sight of, spot, espy, clap eyes on; *look*, gaze, stare, gape, glare, peer, focus, fix, eye; *glance*, peek, peep, peer, wink, blink, squint, leer, ogle; *inspect*, scrutinize, scan, peruse, browse, look up and down, pore over; *watch*, observe, look out for, keep a weather eye open, keep one's eyes skinned/peeled (*colloq.*).

371 **BLINDNESS**

n. *blindness*, sightlessness, night-blindness, snow-blindness, colour-blindness, word-blindness, dyslexia; *blind spot*, blind side, tunnel vision; *blinkers*, blindfold, eye patch.

adj. *blind*, visually handicapped, visually challenged, blind as a bat, sightless, eyeless, unseeing; *blinded*, blindfold, blinkered, benighted; *blinding*, dazzling, flashing.

vb. *blind*, dazzle, blinker, blindfold, hoodwink; *go blind*, lose one's sight, be in the dark, not see the wood for the trees.

372 **VISIBILITY**
See also 370 (vision).

n. *visibility*, conspicuousness, obviousness, prominence; *distinctness*, clarity, plainness, discernibility, perceptibility; *seeing distance*, field of vision, eyeshot, view.

adj. *visible*, discernible, perceptible, observable, detectable; *noticeable*, conspicuous, eye-catching, prominent; *apparent*, evident, obvious, plain, clear, crystal-clear, distinct, definite, clear-cut; *unmistakable*, glaring, blatant, flagrant, egregious.

vb. *be visible*, stand out, show up, leap to the eye, stick out like a sore thumb (*colloq.*); *appear*, come into view, loom, materialize.

adv. *visibly*, in full view, before one's very eyes, under one's nose.

373 **INVISIBILITY**
See also 376 (dimness); 469 (concealment).

n. *invisibility*, imperceptibility, indistinctness, vagueness, dimness; *poor visibility*, mistiness, haziness, fogginess; *concealment*, disguise, smokescreen, veil, curtain.

adj. *invisible*, unseen, imperceptible, indiscernible, unrecognizable; *inconspicuous*, microscopic, minute, faint; *indistinct*, unclear, vague, blurred, hazy, misty, foggy; *hidden*, obscured, submerged, latent.

vb. *be invisible*, hide, lurk, escape notice, be lost to view; *disappear*, fade, vanish, submerge; *conceal*, veil, screen, curtain.

adv. *out of sight*, out of focus.

374 **LIGHT**
See also 377 (light source).

n. *light*, first light, dawn, broad daylight, sunlight, twilight, dusk, half-light, moonlight, starlight; *illumination*, lamplight, candlelight, artificial light; *brightness*, radiance, brilliance, luminosity; *shine*, lustre, gloss, sheen, iridescence, highlight; *ray*, beam, shaft, pencil, streak, chink; *flash*, glint, glitter, twinkle, sparkle, flicker; *gleam*, glimmer, shimmer, glow, nimbus, halo; *dazzle*, glare, blaze, flare; *luminescence*, fluorescence, phosphorescence, northern lights, aurora borealis; *play of light*, light and shade, dappling, chiaroscuro; *radiation*, X-ray, laser, hologram; *reflection*, refraction, diffraction.

adj. *light*, lit, floodlit, spotlit; *bright*, radiant, brilliant, effulgent; *gleaming*, lambent, flickering, shimmery; *sparkly*, glittery, glinting, twinkly, flashing, coruscating; *shiny*, lustrous, glossy, wet-look; *incandescent*, glowing, luminescent, phosphorescent, fluorescent, Day-glo (*tdmk*).

vb. *shine*, blaze, dazzle, flash, sparkle, glitter, glint; *gleam*, glow, shimmer, flicker, twinkle; *radiate*, beam, reflect, refract, emit; *illuminate*, irradiate, light up, brighten.

375 **DARKNESS**
See also 376 (dimness); 384 (black).

n. *darkness*, blackness, murkiness, gloominess, night, nightfall; *dusk*, gloom, murk, shadow, silhouette; *blackout*, eclipse, fade-out, lights out.

adj. *dark*, black, inky, pitch-black, coal-black; *gloomy*, sombre, murky, shadowy, dingy; *nocturnal*, night-time, benighted, unlit, starless, moonless.

vb. *darken*, blacken, dim, fade out; *extinguish*, douse, switch off, snuff out; *befog*, obscure, obfuscate, eclipse, overshadow.

376 **DIMNESS**
See also 373 (invisibility); 380 (opaqueness).

n. *dimness*, faintness, indistinctness, vagueness, fuzziness; *cloudiness*, mistiness, smokiness, haziness, opacity; *twilight*, half-light, gloaming, dusk, bad light; *murk*, gloom, shade, penumbra, shadow; *mist*, fog, haze, blur, film, cloud; *global dimming*.

adj. *dim*, faint, indistinct, bleary, blurred, fuzzy; *vague*, nebulous, confused, grey; *filmy*, cloudy, opaque, obscured; *hazy*, misty, foggy, smoky; *shadowy*, twilit, gloomy, murky, dingy.

vb. *dim*, fade, wane, die away; *obscure*, bedim, befog, mist up, cloud, muddy; *blur*, smear, dirty, besmirch.

377 **LIGHT SOURCE**
See also 374 (light).

n. *light source*, naked light, flare, torch, bonfire; *fire*, coal, ember, brand, flame; *match*, lighter, taper, spill, candle; *lamp*, flashlight, lantern, headlamp, searchlight, floodlight; *light bulb*, fluorescent tube, strip lighting, strobe light, neon light, spotlight; *warning light*, sidelight, indicator, tail light, traffic light, lighthouse, beacon; *light fitting*, chandelier, pendant, standard lamp, uplighter, downlighter.

adj. *luminous*, flaming, glowing, incandescent, dazzling, well-lit.

378 **SCREEN**
See also 202 (covering).

n. *screen*, shield, shelter, covering, shade; *awning*, canopy, windbreak, safety curtain; *sunscreen*, visor, sunglasses, eyeshade, parasol, umbrella; *blind*, shutter, jalousie, curtain, netting; *veil*, hood, mask, cloak, blindfold, blinkers.

adj. *screened*, shaded, protected, shuttered, blinkered; *shady*, sheltered, secluded.

vb. *screen*, shield, protect, shelter, shade; *conceal*, curtain, veil, cloak, blanket, hood, mask, shroud.

379 **TRANSPARENCY**
n. *transparency*, clearness, limpidity, pellucidity; *translucence*, thinness, fineness, gauziness, diaphanousness; *glass*, ice, water, crystal, Cellophane (*tdmk*), Perspex (*tdmk*); *gauze*, lace, chiffon, gossamer.

adj. *transparent*, clear, limpid, pellucid, sheer, see-through; *translucent*, thin, fine, filmy, gauzy, lacy, diaphanous, revealing; *glassy*, crystalline, vitreous, crystal-clear.

380 **OPAQUENESS**
See also 376 (dimness).

n. *opaqueness*, opacity, filminess, cloudiness, muddiness, turbidity, murkiness; *opalescence*, milkiness, pearliness, frosting; *fog*, mist, film, smokescreen, smoked glass; *mattness*, thickness, density.

adj. *opaque*, filmy, cloudy, muddy, turbid, unclear, murky; *opalescent*, milky, pearly, matt, frosted; *foggy*, misty, smoky, hazy.

vb. *make opaque*, cloud, film, frost, smoke, darken, muddy, dim.

381 **COLOUR**
See also 490 (painting).

n. *colour*, hue, saturation, tone, brilliance, intensity; *chromaticism*, primary/secondary/complementary colour; *shade*, tint, tincture, dash, touch, tinge; *coloration*, colouring, pigmentation, colour scheme; *spectrum*, prism, rainbow, palette; *pigment*, paint, dye, stain, watercolour, wash, distemper; *colourfulness*, vividness, gaudiness, garishness.

adj. *coloured*, chromatic, tinted, dyed, colourfast; *colourful*, multicoloured, polychrome, variegated, technicoloured, psychedelic; *gaudy*, bright, vivid, garish, harsh, shocking, clashing, lurid, loud; *pale*, subdued, soft, subtle, pastel, muted; *deep*, rich, glowing, intense, brilliant.

vb. *colour*, tint, shade, tinge; *dye*, stain, wash, distemper, rouge; *paint*, pigment, enamel, crayon, daub.

382 **COLOURLESSNESS**
See also 383 (white).

n. *colourlessness*, achromatism, neutrality, monochrome; *discoloration*, fading, bleaching, whitening; *pallor*, paleness, whiteness, bloodlessness, pastiness, sallowness, anaemia; *greyness*, drabness, insipidness, dullness, dinginess; *decolorant*, bleach, peroxide, whitener.

adj. *colourless*, achromatic, neutral, monochromatic; *natural*, undyed, bleached, faded, discoloured; *pale*, pallid, wan, pasty, sallow, washed-out, anaemic, etiolated, livid, ashen; *fair*, ash-blonde, mousy, albino; *grey*, dull, drab, dingy, insipid, lacklustre.

vb. *lose colour*, fade, run, discolour, pale; *decolorize*, bleach, whiten, blanch, etiolate.

383 **WHITE**
See also 382 (colourlessness).

n. *white*, ivory, magnolia, off white, broken white, ecru, cream; *whiteness*, paleness, creaminess, blondness, fairness; *milkiness*, pearliness, silverness, snowiness; *white heat*, incandescence, white light, white water, white horses, spume; *snow*, alabaster, milk, moonstone, hoarfrost, rime; *whitener*, whitewash, blanco, pipeclay, chalk; *white metal*, white gold, platinum, nickel.

   adj. *white*, light, bright, dazzling; *pure white*, snow-white, lily-white, milk-white; *fair*, blond, ash-blond, flaxen, platinum-blond, albino; *white-haired*, hoary, silvery, snowy, grizzled; *whitish*, creamy, milky, pearly, chalky, floury, mealy, frosted; *white-skinned*, Caucasian, pale, ashen, waxen.

   vb. *whiten*, lighten, fade, pale; *silver*, frost, rime, grizzle; *blanch*, bleach, whitewash.

384 **BLACK**
See also 375 (darkness).

   n. *black*, ebony, sable, jet, ink, soot, carbon, coal, pitch; *blackness*, swarthiness, inkiness, sootiness; *Negro*, coloured, nigger (*derog.*), blackamoor.

   adj. *black*, blackish, dirty, inky, sooty, fuliginous; *jet-black*, blue-black, pitch-black, coal-black, black as the ace of spades; *black-haired*, raven-haired, dark-haired, brunette; *dark-skinned*, swarthy, dusky, Negroid, coloured, of colour; *dark*, sombre, murky, gloomy, Stygian.

   vb. *blacken*, darken, singe, char; *dirty*, smudge, tarnish, besmirch.

385 **GREY**
   n. *grey*, taupe, pewter, lead, slate, gunmetal; *greyness*, dullness, drabness, colourlessness.

   adj. *grey*, pearl-grey, dapple-grey, silver-grey, dove-grey, oyster; *dark grey*, blue-grey, slaty, steely, leaden; *opalescent*, pearly, silvery, frosted; *grey-haired*, greying, grizzled, pepper-and-salt, hoary; *greyish*, neutral, drab, smoky, hazy.

386 **BROWN**
   n. *brown*, ochre, sepia, raw sienna, burnt umber, bistre; *bronze*, amber, copper, cinnamon, coffee, caramel, mocha, chocolate, mahogany; *brunette*, redhead, bay, roan, sorrel.

   adj. *brown*, brownish, hazel, dun, nut-brown, tan, tawny, khaki; *light brown*, fawn, biscuit, beige, buff, oatmeal, café-au-lait; *reddish-brown*, coppery, chestnut, russet, liverish, auburn, peaty; *dark brown*, swarthy, bronzed, tanned, sunburnt.

   vb. *brown*, burn, scorch, toast, tan, bronze.

387 **RED**
   n. *red*, carmine, vermilion, crimson lake, cochineal, rouge, henna; *redness*, rosiness, floridness, ruddiness, blush, flush, glow, high

colour; *ruby*, garnet, coral, flame, blood, gore; *rose*, poppy, cherry, lobster, beetroot; *wine*, port, burgundy, claret.

   adj. *red*, reddish, ruddy, rosy, apple-cheeked, rubicund, florid, sanguine; *blood-red*, bloody, gory, bloodshot; *red-hot*, glowing, flaming, warm; *bright red*, scarlet, crimson, pillarbox-red, brick-red, terracotta; *reddish-brown*, russet, rufous, oxblood; *red-gold*, titian, redheaded, strawberry blond; *light red*, pink, salmon-pink, shell pink, peachy, flesh-coloured, old rose; *dark red*, purplish, cerise, magenta, rose.

   vb. *redden*, rouge, henna, raddle; *blush*, flush, glow, crimson, mantle, colour.

388 **ORANGE**
   n. *orange*, amber, burnt orange, gamboge; *copper*, rust, bronze, ginger, henna; *tangerine*, apricot, peach, marmalade, marigold.

   adj. *orange*, orangey, tan, russet, *coppery*, auburn, gingery, carroty.

389 **YELLOW**
   n. *yellow*, chrome yellow, ochre, saffron, turmeric; *yellowness*, sallowness, biliousness, jaundice; *yellow metal*, gold, brass, ormolu; *lemon*, mustard, egg yolk, cream, butter; *primrose*, jonquil, daffodil, jasmine, mimosa, buttercup.

   adj. *yellow*, yellowy, golden, blonde, flaxen; *pale yellow*, creamy, honey-coloured, corn-coloured; *bright yellow*, lemon-yellow, primrose-yellow, canary-yellow, sulphur-yellow; *dark yellow*, old gold, mustardy, tawny, sandy, sallow.

390 **GREEN**
   n. *green*, viridian, bice, verdigris, chlorophyll; *greenness*, greenery, verdure, leafiness, green belt, grass, turf; *emerald*, jade, aquamarine, beryl; *lime*, greengage, avocado, olive.

   adj. *green*, greenish, glaucous, viridescent; *grassy*, leafy, mossy, verdant; *bright green*, grass-green, apple-green, pea-green, chartreuse, lime-green; *dark green*, sage-green, sea-green, celadon, moss-green, bottle-green, olive-green, khaki; *greenish-blue*, eau-de-Nil, turquoise.

391 **BLUE**
   n. *blue*, cyan, cobalt blue, Prussian blue, ultramarine, indigo, woad; *sapphire*, lapis lazuli, turquoise, aquamarine; *forget-me-not*, cornflower, harebell, gentian, delphinium.

   adj. *blue*, bluish, cerulean, sky-blue, azure;

light blue, powder blue, duck-egg blue, Cambridge blue, Wedgwood blue; *bluey-green*, turquoise, kingfisher blue, peacock blue, electric blue; *bluey-grey*, slaty, steely, gunmetal; *dark blue*, Oxford blue, royal blue, midnight blue, blue-black, navy.

392 **PURPLE**

n. *purple*, amethyst, gentian violet, Tyrian purple; *plum*, aubergine, mulberry, damson, cherry; *lilac*, heather, violet, lavender, heliotrope, fuchsia; *wine*, burgundy, claret, grape.

adj. *purple*, purplish, mauve, maroon, puce, magenta, cerise.

393 **VARIEGATION**

n. *variegation*, diversity, variety, non-uniformity, colourfulness; *patchwork*, motley, tartan, mosaic, chequerboard, marquetry; *kaleidoscope*, spectrum, rainbow, prism, coat of many colours; *iridescence*, shot silk, mother of pearl, tiger's eye, watered silk; *jasper*, agate, tortoiseshell, marble; *patch*, blotch, splotch, spot, dot, fleck, speck, freckle, speckle.

adj. *variegated*, multicoloured, polychromatic, colourful; *iridescent*, chatoyant, opalescent, pearly, nacreous, moiré; *patchy*, mottled, chequered, particoloured; *striped*, barred, marbled, veined, streaky; *pied*, grizzled, brindled, pepper-and-salt, piebald, skewbald; *spotted*, speckled, stippled, dotted, studded.

vb. *variegate*, diversify, chequer, patch, counterchange; *sprinkle*, pepper, dot, spangle, speckle, dapple; *stripe*, bar, vein, marble, streak, striate; *stain*, splash, blotch, mottle.

394 **APPEARANCE**
See also 464 (display).

n. *appearance*, phenomenon, manifestation, realization, materialization, embodiment; *aspect*, exterior, outside, externals, appearances; *front*, veneer, image, façade, pose, semblance, guise, first impressions; *look*, expression, countenance, mien, demeanour, air, bearing; *sight*, spectacle, panorama, display, exhibition; *apparition*, vision, mirage, hallucination, phantom, will-o'-the-wisp.

adj. *apparent*, outward, external, superficial, visible, manifest; *seeming*, ostensible, specious, plausible, deceptive, meretricious.

vb. *appear*, seem, look, come over as; *show*, exhibit, display, manifest; *arise*, materialize, come into being, emerge, come to light, surface; *arrive*, turn up, show up, put in an appearance, pop up (*colloq.*), crop up.

adv. *apparently*, ostensibly, on the face of it, to all appearances; *superficially*, at face value, at first sight, prima facie; *on view*, on show, on display.

395 **DISAPPEARANCE**
See also 373 (invisibility).

n. *disappearance*, departure, flight, escape, elopement; *loss*, shrinkage, diminution, evaporation, dissolution; *extinction*, obliteration, erasure, cancellation, dispersal; *eclipse*, fade-out, blackout, disappearing trick; *evanescence*, transience, transitoriness, elusiveness.

adj. *disappearing*, vanishing, evanescent, transient, fleeting; *vanished*, missing, absentee, gone, lost to view, invisible.

vb. *disappear*, vanish, dematerialize, melt into thin air, sink without trace; *evaporate*, dissolve, dispel, disperse, scatter; *fade*, pale, shrink, dwindle; *depart*, escape, flee, elope, decamp, absent oneself, do a bunk (*colloq.*), play truant, go AWOL; *hide*, lurk, lie low, hide out; *obliterate*, erase, expunge, wipe out; *withdraw*, remove from the scene, carry off, kidnap, spirit away.

396 **INTELLECT**
See also 283 (non-material world); 398 (thought).

n. *intellect*, mind, psyche, consciousness, awareness, self; *perception*, cognition, intuition, imagination, insight; *rationality*, reason, sense, understanding, comprehension, judgement, discernment, acumen; *intelligence*, IQ, wits, senses, brains, grey matter, head, loaf (*colloq.*); *common sense*, nous (*colloq.*), savvy (*colloq.*), gumption, horse sense; *cleverness*, brilliance, braininess, high IQ, genius; *intellectual*, egghead (*colloq.*), blue stocking, highbrow, genius, brainbox (*colloq.*), brains (*colloq.*), brainiac (*colloq.*), Einstein (*colloq.*), rocket scientist (*colloq.*); *psychologist*, psychiatrist, psychoanalyst, psychotherapist, shrink (*colloq.*), trick cyclist (*colloq.*).

adj. *intellectual*, mental, conceptual, abstract, cerebral, theoretical; *cognitive*, perceptual, conscious, aware, intuitive, imaginative; *intelligent*, clever, brilliant, bright, gifted, forward, quick-witted, brainy (*colloq.*); *sensible*, rational, commonsensical, logical, reasoned; *psychic*, psychological, psychosomatic, subliminal, subconscious.

vb. *think*, conceive, imagine, reason, intellectualize, theorize, conceptualize; *perceive*, realize, understand, comprehend, discern, sense; *be intelligent*, use one's head, have one's wits about one, know a thing or two (*colloq.*).

397 **LACK OF INTELLECT**

See also 399 (lack of thought).

n. *lack of intellect*, instinct, intuition, unreason, unintellectuality; *unintelligence*, brainlessness, mindlessness, inanity, vacuity; *stupidity*, dullness, slowness, obtuseness, low IQ; *backwardness*, retardation, arrested development, mental deficiency, cretinism, imbecility, feeblemindedness; *stupid person*, dullard, dunderhead, dunce, blockhead (*colloq.*), thicko (*colloq.*); *mental defective*, cretin, moron, idiot, half-wit, cabbage.

adj. *unintellectual*, intuitive, instinctive, animal, brute; *irrational*, unreasoning, illogical; *mindless*, brainless, vacuous, empty-headed, inane, scatterbrained; *unintelligent*, stupid, slow-witted, dim (*colloq.*), dull, obtuse, thick (*colloq.*), dense, boneheaded (*colloq.*), slow on the uptake; *mentally deficient*, backward, retarded, subnormal, feebleminded, wanting, not all there, cretinous, moronic.

398 **THOUGHT**

See also 396 (intellect); 400 (reason).

n. *thought*, thinking, cogitation, concentration, cerebration, speculation, brainwork, intellectual exercise; *thoughtfulness*, pensiveness, abstractedness, preoccupation, absorption, daydreaming, brown study; *consideration*, contemplation, deliberation, rumination, introspection, meditation, soul-searching; *reflection*, hindsight, afterthought, second thoughts; *forethought*, prudence, foresight, forward planning.

adj. *thinking*, deliberative, speculative, imaginative, cerebral, intellectual; *thoughtful*, pensive, studious, abstracted, preoccupied, engrossed, dreamy; *reflective*, meditative, introspective, contemplative.

vb. *think*, conceive, imagine, fancy; *cogitate*, ruminate, cerebrate, deliberate, rack one's brains; *consider*, contemplate, reflect, meditate, muse, brood, introspect, mull over, chew over; *think of*, invent, devise, dream up, think up; *speculate*, theorize, hypothesize,

fantasize; *reconsider*, review, think again, have second thoughts; *preoccupy*, engross, absorb, obsess; *strike one*, come to mind, occur, cross one's mind.

adv. *on reflection*, on consideration, on second thoughts, with hindsight; *in mind*, on one's mind, on the brain.

399 **LACK OF THOUGHT**

See also 397 (lack of intellect); 401 (intuition).

n. *lack of thought*, intuition, spontaneity, instinct, flair, gut reaction, reflex, knee-jerk reaction/response; *thoughtlessness*, mindlessness, senselessness, irrationality, illogicality; *ignorance*, stupidity, empty-headedness, fatuousness, inanity.

adj. *unthinking*, unreflective, unimaginative, unoriginal; *intuitive*, spontaneous, instinctive, automatic, reflexive; *mindless*, thoughtless, ill-considered, senseless, irrational, illogical, half-baked (*colloq.*); *ignorant*, stupid, empty-headed, fatuous, inane, vacuous, blank.

vb. *not think about*, ignore, disregard, put out of one's mind, dismiss, laugh off, not give a second thought; *intuit*, sense, feel in one's bones.

400 **REASON**

See also 398 (thought).

n. *reason*, rationality, logic, ratiocination; *argumentation*, disputation, analysis, speculation, abstraction, rationalization; *induction*, deduction, lateral thinking, implication, inference, conclusion; *premise*, hypothesis, postulate, assumption, supposition, thesis, theorem.

adj. *rational*, logical, conceptual, abstract, academic; *reasonable*, sensible, cogent, coherent, objective; *hypothetical*, theoretical, suppositional, putative, speculative; *analytical*, deductive, a priori, inductive, a posteriori.

vb. *reason*, argue, dispute, rationalize, intellectualize, philosophize; *theorize*, speculate, hypothesize, assume, presuppose; *infer*, deduce, conclude, imply, work out, put two and two together; *be logical*, follow, cohere, hang together, stand to reason, add up (*colloq.*), hold water, make sense.

401 **INTUITION**

See also 397 (lack of intellect); 455 (prediction).

n. *intuition*, instinct, feeling, insight, spontaneity, gut reaction; *irrationality*, illogicality, incoherence, unreason; *hypersensitivity*, sixth sense, extra-sensory perception, telepathy, second sight, clairvoyance; *presentiment*, hunch, guess, foreboding, premonition.

adj. *intuitive*, instinctive, visceral, spontaneous, impulsive; *irrational*, illogical, incoherent, subjective, impressionistic; *involuntary*, subconscious, subliminal, reflex, automatic, Pavlovian, mechanical, knee-jerk; *psychic*, clairvoyant, telepathic.

vb. *intuit*, guess, divine, sense, feel in one's bones; *use guesswork*, feel one's way, play it by ear (*colloq.*), follow one's nose (*colloq.*).

402 **CURIOSITY**
See also 414 (question).

n. *curiosity*, interest, concern, eagerness, inquiring mind; *inquisitiveness*, prying, officiousness, nosiness (*colloq.*); *morbid curiosity*, prurience, salaciousness, voyeurism, ghoulishness; *interrogation*, cross-examination, detection, quizzing, grilling, third degree (*colloq.*); *spy*, eavesdropper, voyeur, peeping Tom, ghoul, snooper (*colloq.*), rubberneck (*colloq.*), nosy parker (*colloq.*); *gossip*, scandalmonger, newsmonger, newshound, busybody.

adj. *curious*, interested, inquisitive, eager, agog; *prurient*, salacious, voyeuristic, ghoulish; *meddlesome*, interfering, officious, nosy (*colloq.*); *inquisitorial*, questioning, interrogatory.

vb. *be curious*, eavesdrop, listen in on, spy, snoop (*colloq.*); *question*, interrogate, cross-examine, quiz; *enquire*, ask, seek to know; *meddle*, interfere, pry, poke/stick one's nose in.

403 **LACK OF CURIOSITY**
See also 405 (inattention); 756 (indifference).

n. *lack of curiosity*, unconcern, detachment, aloofness; *indifference*, nonchalance, insouciance, impassivity; *apathy*, inertia, boredom, listlessness.

adj. *incurious*, uninterested, unconcerned, detached, aloof; *indifferent*, nonchalant, insouciant, phlegmatic, impassive; *apathetic*, unenthusiastic, bored, blasé, listless, past caring.

404 **ATTENTION**
See also 406 (carefulness).

n. *attention*, notice, regard, heed; *mindfulness*, thoughtfulness, solicitude, consideration; *attentiveness*, concentration,

alertness, watchfulness, vigilance; *observation*, inspection, scrutiny, surveillance; *preoccupation*, absorption, raptness, intentness, undivided attention; *studiousness*, application, diligence, assiduousness; *attention to detail*, meticulousness, scrupulousness, punctiliousness, conscientiousness.

adj. *attentive*, mindful, solicitous, considerate, thoughtful; *diligent*, studious, sedulous, assiduous; *meticulous*, scrupulous, punctilious, painstaking; *alert*, aware, conscious, watchful, observant, vigilant; *preoccupied*, absorbed, intent, rapt, engrossed, wrapped up in, riveted; *fixated*, obsessed, single-minded, brooding.

vb. *pay attention*, attend, heed, be on the ball (*colloq.*); *notice*, register, spot, take note, sit up and take notice, prick up one's ears; *observe*, watch, scrutinize, inspect, peruse; *concentrate*, drink in, lap up, hang on sb's words, be all ears (*colloq.*); *preoccupy*, engross, absorb, captivate; *draw attention to*, point out, mention, alert to.

405 **INATTENTION**
See also 403 (lack of curiosity); 407 (negligence).

n. *inattention*, negligence, carelessness, unawareness; *forgetfulness*, obliviousness, oversight, lapse, senior moment; *thoughtlessness*, heedlessness, inconsiderateness, unconcern; *casualness*, offhandedness, desultoriness, cursoriness, disregard, vagueness; *absentmindedness*, distractedness, abstraction, daydreaming, wool-gathering; *dreamer*, scatterbrain, butterfly mind.

adj. *inattentive*, negligent, careless, unmindful; *forgetful*, oblivious, absentminded, unaware, unobservant; *thoughtless*, heedless, inconsiderate, cavalier; *casual*, offhand, desultory, cursory, superficial; *abstracted*, vague, pensive, dreamy, lost in thought, distracted; *flighty*, dizzy, mercurial, featherbrained, scatty (*colloq.*), ditzy (*colloq.*).

vb. *be inattentive*, overlook, neglect, disregard, miss, let slip; *forget*, lose track of, digress, lose the thread, wander; *daydream*, muse, moon, build castles in Spain; *distract*, disconcert, bewilder, put off.

406 **CAREFULNESS**
See also 404 (attention); 754 (caution).

n. *carefulness*, mindfulness, solicitude,

consideration, attentiveness; *prudence*, circumspection, judiciousness, caution, vigilance; *care*, heed, concern, regard; *conscientiousness*, thoroughness, meticulousness, trouble, pains; *methodicalness*, orderliness, tidiness, neatness, fastidiousness; *accuracy*, precision, exactitude, rigour, perfectionism.

adj. *careful*, mindful, thoughtful, considerate, attentive, solicitous; *prudent*, cautious, circumspect, judicious, wary; *conscientious*, thorough, meticulous, scrupulous, painstaking; *methodical*, orderly, neat, tidy, fastidious, fussy; *exacting*, accurate, rigorous, perfectionist, pedantic.

vb. *be careful*, mind, heed, take into consideration; *watch out*, tread warily, mind one's step, mind one's Ps and Qs; *beware of*, look out for, give a wide berth, steer clear of; *check up on*, keep tabs on, keep under surveillance.

407 **NEGLIGENCE**
See also 405 (inattention).

n. *negligence*, carelessness, forgetfulness, inattentiveness; *neglect*, oversight, dereliction, omission, lapse; *imprudence*, recklessness, impetuosity, indiscretion; *inexactitude*, inaccuracy, looseness, loose ends; *laxity*, slackness, sloppiness, untidiness, slovenliness.

adj. *negligent*, careless, forgetful, inattentive, remiss, neglectful; *casual*, lax, lackadaisical, slack, sloppy, slovenly, slipshod; *neglected*, untidy, unkempt, uncared-for; *reckless*, imprudent, indiscreet, off one's guard, impetuous.

vb. *neglect*, omit, miss, forget; *disregard*, ignore, overlook, turn a blind eye to; *discount*, dismiss, pooh-pooh (*colloq.*), laugh off; *avoid*, dodge, shirk, let slide, leave in the lurch; *gloss over*, scamp, skate over, skip; *procrastinate*, drift, freewheel, let the grass grow under one's feet.

408 **IDEA**
n. *idea*, notion, concept, abstraction, thought; *imagination*, fancy, invention, brainchild, wheeze (*colloq.*), wrinkle (*colloq.*); *theory*, hypothesis, conjecture, supposition, conception; *attitude*, opinion, viewpoint, point of view, stance, angle; *fixed idea*, idée fixe, obsession, fixation, one-track mind.

adj. *ideal*, abstract, notional, conceptual; *theoretical*, hypothetical, conjectural,

suppositional; *fanciful*, whimsical, imaginary, all in the mind.

409 **TOPIC**
n. *topic*, subject, concern, matter, food for thought; *theme*, message, burden, gist, content, thread; *question*, problem, issue, thesis, point, argument, case; *proposal*, suggestion, motion, resolution; *news*, rumour, gossip, current events, current affairs.

adj. *topical*, current, actual, up-to-the-minute; *newsworthy*, thought-provoking, controversial, debatable.

adv. *on the agenda*, under discussion; *in the air*, on everyone's lips.

410 **ARGUMENT**
See also 635 (disagreement).

n. *argument*, discussion, dialogue, debate, exchange of views; *dispute*, quarrel, altercation, war of words, slanging match (*colloq.*); *controversy*, disputation, polemics, argumentation, dissension; *case*, thesis, grounds, premise, point at issue, pros and cons; *argumentativeness*, contentiousness, quarrelsomeness, combativeness.

adj. *argumentative*, disputatious, quarrelsome, litigious; *controversial*, contentious, polemical, provocative; *arguable*, debatable, questionable, controvertible, moot; *heated*, stormy, violent, ding-dong (*colloq.*); *well-argued*, cogent, coherent, logical, analytical, rational.

vb. *argue*, debate, discuss, bandy words; *quibble*, split hairs, chop logic, nit-pick, argue the toss; *quarrel*, dispute, wrangle, bicker, cross swords, have words; *attack*, pick holes in, outargue, shoot down in flames, demolish; *defend*, plead for, support, make out a case for, champion.

411 **SOPHISTRY**
n. *sophistry*, false logic, illogicality, circularity; *casuistry*, speciousness, rationalization, doublethink; *ambiguity*, equivocation, mystification, obscurantism, woolliness; *quibbling*, hair-splitting, chicanery, choplogic; *fallacy*, contradiction in terms, non sequitur, inconsistency; *distortion*, perversion, newspeak, double talk.

adj. *sophistical*, casuistical, Jesuitical; *illogical*, unsound, circular, specious; *ambiguous*, equivocal, woolly, flimsy, waffly (*colloq.*); *fallacious*, contradictory, inconsistent, misleading; *captious*, hair-splitting, pettifogging, nit-picking.

vb. *reason falsely*, equivocate, quibble, cavil, split hairs; *mislead*, pervert, distort, mystify, bamboozle (*colloq.*), blind sb with science; *avoid the issue*, beat about the bush, miss the point, digress.

412 DEMONSTRATION
See also 417 (verification); 420 (evidence).

n. *demonstration*, proof, justification, validation, vindication, affirmation; *argument*, exposition, explanation, elucidation, illustration, clarification.

adj. *demonstrable*, arguable, justifiable, verifiable; *expository*, explanatory, elucidatory, illustrative; *affirmative*, conclusive, corroborative, irrefutable, incontrovertible, unanswerable.

vb. *demonstrate*, show, prove, establish, make out a case for, prove one's point; *affirm*, justify, vindicate, validate, substantiate, corroborate; *explain*, expound, illustrate, elucidate.

413 REFUTATION
See also 415 (answer); 421 (counterevidence).

n. *refutation*, confutation, disproof, rebuttal; *challenge*, disputation, contention, calling in question; *contradiction*, negation, denial, repudiation; *exposure*, invalidation, denunciation, criticism, hatchet job (*colloq.*).

adj. *refuted*, disproved, invalidated, demolished; *negatory*, contradictory, condemnatory, denunciatory.

vb. *refute*, rebut, invalidate, prove wrong, disprove; *contradict*, negate, deny, repudiate, gainsay, give the lie to; *challenge*, pick sb up on, take issue with, contend, disagree with; *expose*, show up, explode, denounce, condemn; *outargue*, puncture, deflate, squash, crush, shoot down in flames.

414 QUESTION
See also 402 (curiosity).

n. *question*, enquiry, query, request, petition; *interrogation*, examination, investigation, inquisition, quiz; *exploration*, quest, probe, search, inquest, survey, fact-finding mission; *questionnaire*, poll, interview, canvass, vox pop; *review*, scrutiny, study, inspection, cross-examination, analysis; *riddle*, enigma, problem, brainteaser (*colloq.*), poser, 64 000 dollar question.

adj. *questioning*, enquiring, inquisitive, searching, quizzical, interrogative;

exploratory, preliminary, investigative, detective, forensic; *problematical*, knotty, enigmatic, baffling, puzzling.

vb. *question*, ask, enquire, request; *probe*, look into, investigate, delve into, leave no stone unturned; *explore*, try out, test, put out feelers, take the temperature of; *survey*, scrutinize, inspect, screen, canvass, poll; *challenge*, badger, pester, heckle, lobby.

415 ANSWER
See also 413 (refutation).

n. *answer*, reply, reaction, response, acknowledgement, feedback; *retort*, rejoinder, riposte, comeback; *repartee*, backchat, lip (*colloq.*), badinage; *rebuttal*, countercharge, right of reply, counterblast, retaliation.

adj. *answering*, responsive, affirmative, positive; *negative*, contradictory, defensive, retaliatory.

vb. *answer*, reply, respond, take one's cue, acknowledge; *retort*, riposte, rebut, come back on; *react*, counter, parry, retaliate; *contradict*, negate, deny, disclaim.

416 EXPERIMENT
n. *experiment*, attempt, try-out, test, trial, dry run, practice shot, pilot scheme, rehearsal, audition, run-through; *experimentation*, research, verification, proving; *speculation*, guesswork, trial and error, gamble, long shot, shot in the dark; *testing agent*, litmus test, benchmark, yardstick, criterion, touchstone; *subject*, guinea pig, control sample, sounding board.

adj. *experimental*, empirical, practical; *provisional*, tentative, probationary, unproven; *speculative*, hypothetical, exploratory, open-ended, hit-or-miss, random.

vb. *experiment*, test, sample, try out, research; *practise*, rehearse, audition, run through; *speculate*, hypothesize, gamble, fly a kite; *improvise*, feel one's way, play it by ear (*colloq.*), muddle through.

417 VERIFICATION
See also 412 (demonstration); 427 (certainty).

n. *verification*, demonstration, affirmation, validation, substantiation, authentication; *confirmation*, attestation, certification, corroboration, justification, vindication, proof; *check*, audit, inquest, post mortem, autopsy.

adj. *verified*, certified, attested, proven, tried and tested, authentic, genuine;

verifiable, demonstrable, ascertainable, provable.

vb. *verify*, establish, prove, demonstrate, affirm, substantiate; *validate*, authenticate, attest, certify; *vindicate*, justify, confirm, corroborate, bear out; *check*, go over, cross-check, double check.

418 **DISCRIMINATION**

See also 18 (dissimilarity); 429 (judgement).

n. *discrimination*, discernment, circumspection, judgement, acumen; *distinction*, differentiation, nuance, nicety, shade of meaning; *perspicacity*, penetration, astuteness, shrewdness, insight, sensitivity; *appreciation*, refinement, connoisseurship, taste, flair, subtlety; *selectivity*, choosiness (*colloq.*), fussiness, fastidiousness.

adj. *discriminating*, perspicacious, judicious, circumspect, discerning; *fastidious*, selective, fussy, choosy (*colloq.*), picky (*colloq.*), difficult; *subtle*, delicate, fine, nice, nuanced; *critical*, exacting, rigorous, careful.

vb. *discriminate*, distinguish, differentiate, discern; *sort*, sift, tell apart, separate the sheep from the goats; *appraise*, judge, evaluate; *select*, choose, pick out, single out.

419 **LACK OF DISCRIMINATION**

n. *lack of discrimination*, unperceptiveness, insensitivity, coarseness; *crudeness*, randomness, inexactness, haphazardness; *confusion*, jumble, hotchpotch, muddle, mixed bag, grist to the mill.

adj. *undiscriminating*, unselective, uncritical, unperceptive, insensitive; *unrefined*, crude, rough and ready, coarse, unpolished, unsubtle; *indiscriminate*, random, haphazard, hit-or-miss; *broad*, generalized, wholesale, blanket.

vb. *not discriminate*, lump together, roll into one, jumble, muddle, confuse, blur.

420 **EVIDENCE**

See also 412 (demonstration).

n. *evidence*, indication, sign, symptom, clue, forensics; *data*, facts, information, dossier, documentation, file; *proof*, corroboration, verification, support, foundation, backing, incriminating evidence, smoking gun (*colloq.*); *testimony*, witness, exhibit, statement, affidavit, attestation, deposition, allegation; *recommendation*, endorsement, reference, testimonial, credentials, warranty, seal of approval.

adj. *evidential*, indicative, symptomatic,

suggestive, telling; *factual*, documentary, first-hand, straight from the horse's mouth; *corroborative*, reliable, affirmative, conclusive, irrefutable.

vb. *evidence*, show, indicate, reveal, suggest, betoken, evince; *give evidence*, attest, testify, bear witness; *recommend*, vouch for, guarantee, endorse; *support*, ratify, corroborate, confirm, bear out, verify.

421 **COUNTEREVIDENCE**

See also 413 (refutation).

n. *counterevidence*, contradiction, counterclaim; *rebuttal*, refutation, negation, denial; *conflicting evidence*, disproof, hostile witness, discrepancy.

adj. *contradictory*, negatory, conflicting, damaging.

vb. *contraindicate*, run counter to, point in the other direction, give the lie to, disprove; *refute*, rebut, contradict, negate, go against; *weaken*, damage, undermine, expose.

422 **QUALIFICATION**

n. *qualification*, reservation, proviso, condition, stipulation, prerequisite; *limitation*, specification, exception, restriction, modification; *exemption*, concession, allowance, mitigation, extenuation; *loophole*, escape clause, let-out, get-out.

adj. *qualifying*, restrictive, conditional, provisional, contingent, dependent; *mitigating*, extenuating, concessionary.

vb. *qualify*, modify, limit, restrict; *stipulate*, specify, lay down, insist on; *concede*, exempt, make allowance for, take into account; *mitigate*, moderate, extenuate, play down.

423 **POSSIBILITY**

See also 425 (probability).

n. *possibility*, eventuality, contingency, chance, off-chance, opportunity, likelihood; *potentiality*, virtuality, makings, possibilities, promise; *feasibility*, practicability, viability, capability.

adj. *possible*, potential, virtual, hypothetical; *attainable*, realizable, doable, achievable, obtainable; *practicable*, workable, viable, feasible; *credible*, reasonable, plausible, conceivable, likely, arguable.

vb. *make possible*, enable, facilitate, bring about; *have possibilities*, show promise, have the makings of, have potential, have legs (*colloq.*).

adv. *possibly*, perhaps, maybe; *arguably*, potentially.

424 **IMPOSSIBILITY**
See also 426 (improbability).

n. *impossibility*, impracticability, hopelessness, absurdity; *impasse*, deadlock, dead end, blank wall, hopeless case, no-no (*colloq.*).

adj. *impossible*, impracticable, unworkable, not on (*colloq.*); *inconceivable*, unthinkable, unimaginable, implausible, unlikely, unreasonable; *insuperable*, insurmountable, insoluble, incurable, incorrigible; *unobtainable*, unavailable, unattainable, inaccessible.

vb. *be impossible*, be out of the question, be beyond the bounds of possibility; *make impossible*, rule out, prohibit, disallow, exclude; *attempt the impossible*, wish for the moon, find a needle in a haystack, get blood out of a stone, square the circle.

425 **PROBABILITY**
See also 423 (possibility).

n. *probability*, likelihood, expectation, prospect, promise; *predictability*, reliability, liability, fair chance, sporting chance; *conjecture*, assumption, educated guess, safe bet.

adj. *probable*, likely, foreseeable, predictable, liable, expected; *plausible*, reasonable, convincing, credible; *prospective*, hopeful, promising, rising.

vb. *be probable*, be on the cards, be in the offing; *foresee*, expect, predict, look forward to; *assume*, conjecture, guess, suppose.

adv. *probably*, in all likelihood, ten to one.

426 **IMPROBABILITY**
See also 424 (impossibility).

n. *improbability*, unlikelihood, doubtfulness, remote/outside/slim chance, long odds; *implausibility*, inconceivability, absurdity, ludicrousness; *forlorn hope*, pious hope, long shot, shot in the dark.

adj. *improbable*, unlikely, doubtful, dubious, uncertain; *implausible*, unconvincing, unbelievable, far-fetched, absurd.

427 **CERTAINTY**
See also 417 (verification); 434 (belief).

n. *certainty*, certitude, likelihood, inevitability, inexorability; *reliability*, dependability, infallibility, trustworthiness, unimpeachability; *assurance*, conviction,

confidence, blind faith; *predictability*, definiteness, foregone conclusion, safe bet, dead cert (*colloq.*), sure thing (*colloq.*).

adj. *certain*, definite, sure, categorical; *unmistakable*, unequivocal, unambiguous, conclusive; *inevitable*, unavoidable, inexorable, ineluctable; *uncontrovertible*, undeniable, unquestionable, unimpeachable, bulletproof (*colloq.*); *assured*, confident, convinced, unshakable; *reliable*, trustworthy, dependable, rock-solid; *infallible*, foolproof, failsafe, low-risk, gilt-edged; *certain to*, sure to, bound to.

vb. *know for certain*, feel sure of, put one's shirt on, put money on, bet one's bottom dollar; *rely on*, depend on, bank on, trust in; *make certain*, ensure, guarantee, confirm, check, double check; *finalize*, settle, firm up (*colloq.*), decide, clinch, wrap up (*colloq.*); *be certain to*, be sure to, be bound to.

adv. *certainly*, doubtless, definitely, come rain or shine, no matter what, come hell or high water.

428 **UNCERTAINTY**
See also 435 (disbelief).

n. *uncertainty*, indefiniteness, doubtfulness, dubiousness; *ambiguity*, ambivalence, vagueness, borderline case, grey area; *indecision*, diffidence, hesitation, vacillation, irresolution; *unreliability*, fallibility, untrustworthiness, unpredictability, volatility, capriciousness; *doubt*, query, question mark, misgivings; *conjecture*, gamble, guess, toss-up (*colloq.*), unknown quantity, pig in a poke.

adj. *uncertain*, unsure, doubtful, dubious; *precarious*, chancy, risky, dodgy (*colloq.*), touch and go; *unpredictable*, unforeseeable, unknowable, fickle, volatile, capricious; *fallible*, untrustworthy, unreliable; *indefinite*, vague, ambivalent, ambiguous, undecided; *hesitant*, indecisive, diffident, unconfident, irresolute; *questionable*, arguable, debatable, moot.

vb. *be uncertain*, be in two minds, hesitate, waver, vacillate, shilly-shally (*colloq.*), dither (*colloq.*); *doubt*, disbelieve, wonder, suspect, challenge, query; *grope*, fumble, flounder, not know which way to turn; *hinge*, depend, hang in the balance, be in the lap of the gods, go to the wire (*colloq.*).

429 **JUDGEMENT**
See also 418 (discrimination).

n. *judgement*, discretion, discernment,

discrimination, acumen; *adjudication*, arbitration, umpirage, refereeing; *estimation*, evaluation, appraisal, assessment, conclusion; *criticism*, opinion, comment, review, critique; *verdict*, ruling, decree, award, decision, settlement; *impartiality*, objectivity, fairness, justice; *judge*, umpire, referee,. arbitrator, adjudicator, assessor.

adj. *judicial*, discretionary, judicatory; *judicious*, discerning, circumspect, shrewd; *judgemental*, critical, censorious, condemnatory; *approving*, appreciative, favourable, lenient; *impartial*, unbiased, objective, fair, just, broad-minded.

vb. *judge*, referee, umpire, adjudicate, arbitrate, decide, settle; *estimate*, appraise, assess, evaluate, size up, weigh up; *criticize*, review, pass judgement on, rule on; *pronounce*, decree, conclude, sum up.

430 **MISJUDGEMENT**
See also 140 (tendency); 441 (error).

n. *misjudgement*, miscalculation, error, mistake, misconception; *wrong-headedness*, obstinacy, foolishness, fallibility; *partiality*, bias, partisanship, favouritism, one-sidedness, prejudice, bigotry; *injustice*, unfairness, discrimination, intolerance; *narrow-mindedness*, racism, chauvinism, sexism, colour prejudice, apartheid, segregation; *insularity*, parochialism, provincialism, closed mind.

adj. *mistaken*, misguided, wrong-headed, fallible; *partial*, biased, partisan, one-sided, unfair, unjust; *prejudiced*, bigoted, opinionated, dogmatic; *discriminatory*, sexist, racist, chauvinist; *insular*, parochial, provincial, narrow-minded, intolerant, hidebound, petty.

vb. *misjudge*, miscalculate, mistake, misconceive; *prejudice*, preconceive, presuppose, jump to conclusions; *bias*, predispose, warp, load, slant, skew, distort; *favour*, take sides, discriminate.

431 **OVERESTIMATION**
See also 482 (exaggeration).

n. *overestimation*, overvaluation, excessiveness, exorbitancy; *overstatement*, exaggeration, hyperbole, puff (*colloq.*), hype (*colloq.*), ballyhoo (*colloq.*); *overconfidence*, overoptimism, presumption, arrogance.

adj. *overrated*, overpraised, disappointing, not up to expectation; *overvalued*, overpriced, exorbitant, excessive; *overstated*, overdone, overemphasized, hyperbolic, over the top

(*colloq.*); *overconfident*, overoptimistic, overenthusiastic, overambitious.

vb. *overestimate*, overshoot, overrate, overvalue; *overemphasize*, overpraise, exaggerate, hype (*colloq.*), lay it on with a shovel/trowel (*colloq.*); *maximize*, make much of, make a mountain out of a molehill.

432 **UNDERESTIMATION**
See also 483 (understatement).

n. *underestimation*, undervaluation, understatement, conservative estimate; *self-deprecation*, modesty, reticence, humility; *pessimism*, defeatism, despondency; *depreciation*, disparagement, belittlement.

adj. *underrated*, undervalued, neglected, overlooked, unsung; *modest*, self-effacing, self-deprecating, retiring; *pessimistic*, defeatist, despondent, gloomy; *disparaging*, derogatory, depreciative.

vb. *underestimate*, undervalue, underrate, underprice; *neglect*, overlook, do less than justice to, pass over; *minimize*, understate, play down, soft-pedal (*colloq.*); *disparage*, belittle, slight, pooh-pooh (*colloq.*), run down.

433 **DISCOVERY**
n. *discovery*, exploration, research, experimentation, excavation, prospecting; *encounter*, close encounter, meeting, brush; *happening*, coincidence; *realization*, revelation, inspiration, flash of insight, eureka moment, the penny drops; *invention*, find, results, findings, strike; *location*, identification, sighting, detection.

adj. *exploratory*, experimental, fact-finding; *probing*, investigative, detective.

vb. *discover*, invent, come up with, find out, learn; *happen on*, come across, hit upon, light upon, stumble across, encounter; *realize*, tumble to, see the light, catch on (*colloq.*), twig (*colloq.*); *unearth*, uncover, disinter, dig up, bring to light, ferret/nose out, detect; *find*, track down, locate, spot, sight, identify; *explore*, excavate, probe, investigate.

434 **BELIEF**
See also 427 (certainty); 868 (religion).

n. *belief*, credence, acceptance, conviction, assurance, certainty; *confidence*, faith, trust, reliance, expectation; *opinion*, persuasion, view, sentiment; *credo*, tenet, principle, creed, dogma, profession, ideology, doctrine, article of faith; *attitude*, position, viewpoint, point of view, standpoint, outlook, angle, aspect, side, world-view, culture; *prejudice*, dogmatism, bigotry, fanaticism; *credulity*, blind faith, superstition, naïvety, gullibility; *credibility*, plausibility, likelihood.

adj. *believable*, credible, plausible, convincing, persuasive; *trustworthy*, dependable, reliable, trusty; *confident*, certain, sure, positive, convinced, assured; *opinionated*, dogmatic, doctrinaire, bigoted, fanatical; *credulous*, naïve, gullible, superstitious, trusting, confiding.

vb. *believe*, maintain, hold, profess, avow; *trust*, rely, depend, count, bank, swear by, give credence; *adopt*, embrace, espouse, believe in; *think*, deem, allow, grant, be of the opinion; *be credulous*, fall for, take on trust, swallow (*colloq.*), buy (*colloq.*); *convince*, persuade, assure, win over, convert.

435 **DISBELIEF**
See also 428 (uncertainty); 869 (unbelief).

n. *disbelief*, incredulity, scepticism, cynicism; *doubt*, uncertainty, dubiety, unsureness; *unbelief*, agnosticism, atheism, heresy; *distrust*, mistrust, suspicion, wariness, misgiving, doubts, qualms, scruples; *recantation*, retraction, renunciation, disclaimer, apostasy; *derision*, scorn, mockery, ridicule.

adj. *disbelieving*, incredulous, sceptical, cynical, unconvinced; *doubtful*, dubious, unsure, uncertain; *unbelieving*, agnostic, atheistic, heretical, lapsed; *distrustful*, mistrustful, suspicious, wary, hesitant; *incredible*, unbelievable, inconceivable, implausible, unlikely; *untrustworthy*, unreliable, suspect, questionable; *derisive*, mocking, scornful.

vb. *disbelieve*, reject, call in question, challenge, discredit; *mock*, deride, scorn, laugh in the face of, laugh out of court; *mistrust*, distrust, suspect, have one's doubts about, hesitate; *recant*, retract, disclaim, renounce, change one's mind.

436 **ASSENT**
See also 19 (accord).

n. *assent*, agreement, concurrence, consent; *acceptance*, acknowledgement, acquiescence, submission, compliance; *sanction*, ratification, green light, go-ahead (*colloq.*); *approval*, approbation, thumbs-up (*colloq.*), endorsement, backing, support;

cooperation, collaboration, unanimity, harmony, unison.

adj. *assenting*, consenting, agreeable, favourable, sympathetic; *accepting*, acquiescent, compliant, submissive; *cooperative*, collaborative, unanimous, like minded; *approved*, unopposed, signed, carried.

vb. *assent*, consent, concur, agree, see eye to eye; *accept*, abide by, acquiesce, submit, comply, accede; *cooperate*, collaborate, meet sb halfway, fall in with; *admit*, concede, grant, allow, acknowledge; *sanction*, ratify, approve, welcome, applaud, okay (*colloq.*); *endorse*, support, champion, back, second, go along with, sympathize with.

437 **DISSENT**
n. *dissent*, disagreement, discord, dissension; *dispute*, argument, quarrel, wrangle, controversy, difference of opinion; *negation*, contradiction, denial, repudiation, opposition, defiance; *disapproval*, dissatisfaction, discontent, disaffection, secession; *protest*, remonstration, objection, demurral, rejection, refusal; *disinclination*, reluctance, unwillingness, recalcitrance, disobedience.

adj. *dissenting*, dissident, off-message (*colloq.*), recusant, disaffected, dissatisfied, discontented; *disinclined*, reluctant, unwilling, opposed, defiant, disobedient, bolshie (*colloq.*).

vb. *dissent*, disagree, agree to differ; *quarrel*, argue, fall out, wrangle, bicker; *dispute*, challenge, resist, oppose, defy, disobey; *refuse*, negate, reject, repudiate, deny; *object*, protest, demur, cavil, expostulate, remonstrate; *disapprove*, look askance at, frown on, hold no brief for.

438 **KNOWLEDGE**
See also 444 (wisdom); 624 (skill).

n. *knowledge*, wisdom, learning, erudition, scholarliness, pedantry; *awareness*, cognizance, understanding, comprehension, grasp, ken; *familiarity*, acquaintance, experience, dealings; *education*, schooling, instruction, enlightenment, information, illumination; *literacy*, numeracy, the three Rs, rote-learning, book-learning; *skill*, accomplishment, expertise, proficiency, mastery, savvy (*colloq.*), know-how (*colloq.*); *scholar*, student, intellectual, pedant, bookworm, polymath, Renaissance man, know-all (*colloq.*).

adj. *knowing*, wise, all-knowing, omniscient; *knowledgeable*, informed, well up on, au courant, au fait; *educated*, literate, numerate, well-read, lettered, enlightened, cultivated; *scholarly*, learned, bookish, erudite, donnish, academic, pedantic; *aware*, cognizant, conscious, familiar with, conversant, versed; *proficient*, skilful, accomplished, experienced.

vb. *know*, understand, comprehend, grasp; *get to know*, familiarize oneself with, acquaint oneself with, experience; *learn*, study, memorize, master; *know thoroughly*, know off pat, have at one's fingertips, know inside out, know backwards; *educate*, instruct, inform, enlighten.

439 **IGNORANCE**
See also 625 (unskilfulness).

n. *ignorance*, unknowingness, unawareness, incomprehension; *unfamiliarity*, inexperience, greenness, rawness; *inexpertness*, amateurishness, clumsiness, awkwardness, unskilfulness; *benightedness*, superstition, philistinism, illiteracy, stupidity, folly; *ignoramus*, dunce, booby, philistine, moron.

adj. *ignorant*, unknowing, uncomprehending, unwitting, unaware, unconscious; *unfamiliar*, inexperienced, raw, green, uninitiated; *uneducated*, uninformed, unenlightened, illiterate, philistine, crass, stupid; *inexpert*, unskilful, amateurish, clumsy, clueless (*colloq.*); *unknown*, uncharted, undiscovered, mysterious, enigmatic.

vb. *be ignorant*, not know, not have the foggiest idea, not have a clue (*colloq.*), not have an inkling; *mystify*, keep in the dark, baffle, perplex.

440 **ACCURACY**
See also 478 (truth).

n. *accuracy*, exactness, precision, exactitude; *correctness*, rightness, aptness, appropriateness; *meticulousness*, punctiliousness, rigour, pedantry, perfectionism; *fidelity*, truth, realism, authenticity, verisimilitude.

adj. *accurate*, precise, exact, spot on (*colloq.*), dead on (*colloq.*), bang on (*colloq.*); *correct*, right, apt, appropriate; *meticulous*, punctilious, rigorous, pedantic, perfectionist; *faithful*, true-to-life, factual, documentary, historical.

vb. *be accurate*, ring true, hit the nail on the head (*colloq.*); *prove accurate*, corroborate, substantiate, validate, bear out.

adv. *literally*, to the letter, verbatim, word for word.

441 **ERROR**
See also 430 (misjudgement); 479 (untruth).

n. *error*, mistake, miscalculation, misjudgement; *misunderstanding*, misconception, fallacy, misconstruction, misrepresentation, delusion; *inaccuracy*, imprecision, inexactness, carelessness, sloppiness; *wrongness*, unsoundness, falseness, misguidedness; *blunder*, oversight, gaffe, faux pas, lapse, howler (*colloq.*), bloomer (*colloq.*), clanger (*colloq.*); *misprint*, literal, erratum, corrigendum.

adj. *erroneous*, wrong, false, fallacious, delusory; *inaccurate*, incorrect, imprecise, inexact, wide of the mark; *misleading*, untrue, apocryphal, unfounded; *mistaken*, misguided, misinformed, misled; *erring*, fallible, wrong-headed, gone astray, off the rails (*colloq.*).

vb. *err*, be in the wrong, misjudge, miscalculate, blot one's copybook; *misunderstand*, misconceive, misinterpret, be at cross-purposes, bark up the wrong tree (*colloq.*); *blunder*, slip up, put one's foot in it (*colloq.*), boob (*colloq.*), make a balls-up/cock-up (*vulg.*); *mislead*, misinform, deceive, delude, lead astray.

442 **MAXIM**
n. *maxim*, proverb, saying, adage, byword, saw, dictum; *epigram*, aphorism, apophthegm, witticism; *watchword*, slogan, catch phrase, motto; *moral*, golden rule, object lesson, cautionary tale; *truism*, cliché, platitude, bromide, chestnut (*colloq.*).

adj. *proverbial*, gnomic, aphoristic, epigrammatic; *pithy*, terse, witty, cryptic; *trite*, banal, hackneyed, commonplace, platitudinous, corny (*colloq.*).

443 **NONSENSE**
See also 445 (folly); 459 (lack of meaning); 772 (ridiculousness).

n. *nonsense*, silliness, foolishness, ridiculousness, absurdity; *senselessness*, meaninglessness, fatuousness, inanity; *rubbish*, drivel, gibberish, twaddle (*colloq.*), crap (*vulg.*), bullshit (*vulg.*), codswallop (*colloq.*).

adj. *nonsensical*, ridiculous, silly, foolish, laughable, ludicrous, absurd; *senseless*, meaningless, fatuous, asinine, inane; *crazy*, mad, preposterous, harebrained, crackpot (*colloq.*).

vb. *be absurd*, fool about/around, make a fool of oneself, act the fool; *rant*, rave, talk rot (*colloq.*), talk through a hole in one's head (*colloq.*).

444 **WISDOM**
See also 396 (intellect); 438 (knowledge).

n. *wisdom*, sagacity, sapience, profundity; *discernment*, perspicacity, penetration, acumen, insight; *understanding*, awareness, enlightenment, far-sightedness; *knowledge*, experience, learning, erudition, scholarliness; *common sense*, horse sense, level-headedness, sanity, realism, shrewdness, astuteness; *wise man*, sage, guru, mentor, pundit, thinker, Solomon.

adj. *wise*, sagacious, sapient, profound, deep; *perspicacious*, discerning, insightful, penetrating; *enlightened*, aware, understanding, far-sighted, long-headed; *knowledgeable*, experienced, learned, erudite, scholarly; *commonsensical*, realistic, level-headed, shrewd, astute.

vb. *be wise*, know the ways of the world, know what's what, have one's feet on the ground, have one's head screwed on (*colloq.*).

445 **FOLLY**
See also 397 (lack of intellect); 443 (nonsense); 447 (insanity).

n. *folly*, foolishness, silliness, stupidity; *futility*, pointlessness, fatuousness, meaninglessness, senselessness, absurdity; *imprudence*, indiscretion, recklessness, wildness; *lunacy*, madness, craziness, insanity, infatuation; *shallowness*, frivolity, levity, light-headedness, giddiness; *fool*, dolt, clot, idiot, imbecile, moron, cretin, donkey, ass, goose (*colloq.*); *clown*, buffoon, simpleton, ninny, booby, sap, twit (*colloq.*), twerp (*colloq.*), berk (*colloq.*), prat (*colloq.*), eejit (*colloq.*).

adj. *foolish*, stupid, silly, idiotic, asinine; *futile*, pointless, senseless, meaningless, absurd; *lunatic*, mad, crazy, insane; *unwise*, imprudent, indiscreet, irresponsible, reckless, wild; *shallow*, frivolous, light-headed, scatterbrained, giddy, scatty (*colloq.*); *puerile*, infantile, brainless, moronic, soft in the head.

vb. *be foolish*, look an idiot, make a fool of oneself, get one's fingers burned, never learn; *ramble*, burble, drivel, gibber, maunder,

rabbit (*colloq.*); *go mad*, take leave of one's senses, be out of one's mind.

446 **SANITY**
n. *sanity*, saneness, rationality, coherence, reasonableness, *normality*, balance, stability, equilibrium; *common sense*, sobriety, lucidity, composure, clear-headedness, level-headedness.

adj. *sane*, rational, reasonable, coherent, sound; *normal*, balanced, stable, on an even keel; *lucid*, compos mentis, clear-headed, sober, calm, level-headed.

vb. *be sane*, be in one's right mind, be in possession of one's faculties; *see reason*, come to one's senses, calm down, compose oneself.

447 **INSANITY**
See also 58 (disturbance); 445 (folly).

n. *insanity*, mental illness, madness, lunacy, derangement; *maladjustment*, psychosis, neurosis, psychopathy, senility; *schizophrenia*, paranoia, hysteria, senile dementia, catatonia; *mania*, compulsion, obsession, phobia, fixation, complex, hang-up (*colloq.*), emotional baggage; *delusion*, hallucination, split personality, delirium, frenzy; *nervous breakdown*, neurasthenia, depression, baby blues (*colloq.*), melancholy, melancholia, SAD, seasonal affective disorder, winter blues; *eccentricity*, oddness, queerness, crankiness, weirdness; *lunatic*, madman, psychopath, schizophrenic, paranoiac, obsessive, maniac, nutcase (*colloq.*), nut (*colloq.*), loony (*colloq.*), bunny boiler (*colloq.*); *eccentric*, crank, freak (*colloq.*), nutter (*colloq.*), oddball (*colloq.*), weirdo (*colloq.*).

adj. *insane*, mentally ill, mad, lunatic, disturbed, deranged, unbalanced, unhinged, senile, gaga (*colloq.*); *maladjusted*, autistic, neurotic, psychotic, schizoid, paranoid, hysterical, neurasthenic; *maniacal*, obsessive, fixated, compulsive, phobic, depressive, melancholic, manic-depressive; *crazed*, frenzied, possessed, wild, berserk, delirious, raving, incoherent, demented, non compos mentis; *frantic*, distraught, at the end of one's tether, stir-crazy (*colloq.*); *crazy* (*colloq.*), screwy (*colloq.*), loony (*colloq.*), nuts (*colloq.*), bonkers (*colloq.*), crackers (*colloq.*), bananas (*colloq.*), cuckoo (*colloq.*); *touched*, wanting, barmy (*colloq.*), batty (*colloq.*), daft (*colloq.*), potty (*colloq.*), dotty (*colloq.*), not all there, not right in the head, certifiable; *eccentric*, odd, queer, weird, cranky; *perverted*, twisted, warped, sick, kinky (*colloq.*).

vb. *be insane*, rave, ramble, wander, see things, have a screw loose (*colloq.*); *go mad*, go out of one's mind, break down (*colloq.*), crack up (*colloq.*), flip one's lid (*colloq.*), lose one's marbles (*colloq.*), go off one's rocker (*colloq.*); *madden*, craze, unhinge, unbalance, drive up the wall/round the bend (*colloq.*).

448 **MEMORY**
See also 486 (record).

n. *memory*, recollection, reminiscence, remembrance, recall, evocation; *good memory*, retention, total recall, photographic memory; *nostalgia*, retrospection, hindsight, flashback, blast from the past (*colloq.*), golden oldie (*colloq.*); *souvenir*, memento, keepsake, reminder, memorial, monument, relic; *memorandum*, memo, aide-memoire, mnemonic, cue.

adj. *remembered*, fresh, vivid, distinct; *memorable*, unforgettable, indelible, haunting; *reminiscent*, evocative, redolent, nostalgic, retrospective, commemorative.

vb. *remember*, recollect, recall, bring to mind, evoke; *retain*, not forget, stamp on/fix in one's memory; *reminisce*, recapture, relive, go down memory lane, hark back, cast one's mind back, dredge up, dig up; *remind*, prompt, jog the memory, refresh one's memory, call up, bring back, ring a bell; *memorize*, commit to memory, learn by heart, get off pat.

449 **OBLIVION**
See also 405 (inattention).

n. *oblivion*, unconsciousness, unawareness, blankness, limbo; *forgetfulness*, absentmindedness, inattention, abstractedness; *loss of memory*, amnesia, mental block, blank; *obliteration*, effacement, erasure.

adj. *oblivious*, unconscious, unaware, heedless, unmindful; *forgetful*, absentminded, abstracted, inattentive, amnesiac; *forgotten*, half-remembered, dim, hazy, indistinct.

vb. *forget*, misremember, clean forget, have a memory like a sieve; *be forgotten*, slip one's mind, go in one ear and out the other; *half-remember*, have on the tip of one's tongue, have at the back of one's mind; *efface*, obliterate, wipe out, erase; *forgive*, amnesty, bury the hatchet, let bygones be bygones.

450 **EXPECTATION**
See also 104 (future time); 453 (foresight).

n. *expectation*, expectancy, anticipation, suspense, curiosity; *optimism*, confidence, hope, trust, certainty; *pessimism*, apprehension, dread, anxiety, angst; *forecast*, outlook, prospect, lookout.

adj. *expectant*, waiting, ready, prepared, forewarned; *eager*, curious, agog, itching; *optimistic*, hopeful, confident, sanguine; *pessimistic*, apprehensive, gloomy, anxious; *expected*, foreseen, hoped for, longed for; *prospective*, future, impending.

vb. *expect*, contemplate, foresee, forecast, predict, see coming, bargain for; *await*, stand by, be at the ready, be on the edge of one's seat, be on tenterhooks; *anticipate*, look forward to, hope for, long for; *rely on*, count on, bank on, have confidence in; *dread*, fear, have qualms/misgivings; *be expected*, be in store, loom, be on the cards.

adv. *expectantly*, with bated breath, in suspense.

451 **SURPRISE**
See also 454 (lack of foresight); 759 (wonder).

n. *surprise*, shock, astonishment, amazement, wonderment; *revelation*, eye-opener (*colloq.*), bombshell, bolt from the blue, windfall, stunner (*colloq.*); *unexpectedness*, suddenness, unpredictability, uncertainty.

adj. *surprised*, astonished, astounded, startled, stunned, thunderstruck, dumbfounded; *off-guard*, taken aback, caught unawares/off one's guard, caught napping/on the hop (*colloq.*), caught with one's pants/trousers down (*colloq.*); *unexpected*, unforeseen, unannounced, sudden, abrupt; *surprising*, amazing, shocking, staggering (*colloq.*).

vb. *not expect*, not suspect, be caught out, be wrong-footed; *ambush*, spring, pounce, trap; *amaze*, astound, astonish, startle, bowl over (*colloq.*), stun; *jolt*, electrify, galvanize, shock.

adv. *unexpectedly*, all of a sudden, out of the blue.

452 **DISAPPOINTMENT**
n. *disappointment*, disillusionment, disenchantment, false dawn, anticlimax, letdown, comedown (*colloq.*); *failure*, flash in the pan, damp squib, washout (*colloq.*); *setback*, blow, hitch, snag, hiccup (*colloq.*); *frustration*, dissatisfaction, disgruntlement,

discontent; *discouragement*, despondency, gloom, chagrin, regret.

adj. *disappointed*, dissatisfied, disgruntled, discontented; *disillusioned*, disenchanted, disabused, jaundiced, embittered, soured; *foiled*, thwarted, baffled, frustrated; *discouraged*, despondent, regretful, let down, crestfallen, sick as a parrot (*colloq.*); *disappointing*, unsatisfactory, anticlimactic, not up to expectation, overrated.

vb. *disappoint*, fall short, leave something to be desired; *frustrate*, thwart, foil, get the better of; *disillusion*, disenchant, disabuse, bring down to earth with a bang; *betray*, let down (*colloq.*), jilt, leave in the lurch (*colloq.*); *be disappointed*, learn one's lesson, learn the hard way, find out to one's cost, have one's fingers burned.

453 **FORESIGHT**
See also 450 (expectation); 455 (prediction).

n. *foresight*, anticipation, forethought, premeditation, far-sightedness, vision; *preparedness*, readiness, provision, contingency plan; *foreknowledge*, forewarning, presentiment, foreboding, prediction; *prescience*, second sight, clairvoyance, precognition.

adj. *foresighted*, prescient, clairvoyant, prophetic, visionary; *far-sighted*, provident, prudent, prepared, ready; *anticipatory*, preemptive, premeditated.

vb. *foresee*, forecast, predict, prophesy, forewarn; *anticipate*, expect, preempt, forestall; *make provision*, prepare, premeditate, provide for, take precautions, plan ahead.

454 **LACK OF FORESIGHT**
See also 451 (surprise).

n. *lack of foresight*, unpreparedness, unreadiness, improvidence; *short-sightedness*, blindness, thoughtlessness, imprudence; *improvisation*, spontaneity, extemporization.

adj. *unprepared*, unready, unsuspecting, caught unawares/off one's guard, caught napping/on the hop (*colloq.*), caught with one's pants/trousers down (*colloq.*); *improvident*, shiftless, thoughtless, imprudent, prodigal, happy-go-lucky; *improvised*, makeshift, extempore, unpremeditated, off-the-cuff.

vb. *lack foresight*, muddle through, live from day to day, live from hand to mouth; *improvise*, extemporize, think on one's feet.

455 **PREDICTION**
See also 453 (foresight); 877 (occultism).

n. *prediction*, prophecy, forecast, prognosis; *omen*, warning, sign, presage, portent; *ominousness*, portentousness, auspiciousness; *clairvoyance*, extra-sensory perception, prescience, precognition, foreknowledge; *astrology*, palmistry, divination, augury, fortune-telling; *horoscope*, I Ching, tarot, crystal ball; *prophet*, oracle, soothsayer, seer, astrologer, medium, clairvoyant, palmist; *forecaster*, futurologist, Cassandra, doom merchant.

adj. *predictive*, prophetic, apocalyptic, revelatory; *ominous*, portentous, oracular, auspicious; *clairvoyant*, prescient, psychic.

vb. *predict*, foresee, prophesy, foretell, forewarn; *forecast*, read the future, prognosticate; *foreshadow*, presage, prefigure, augur, spell, portend.

456 **SUPPOSITION**
See also 408 (idea).

n. *supposition*, assumption, premise, postulate; *idea*, suggestion, proposition, notion, fancy, conception; *theory*, hypothesis, conjecture, surmise, guess, inkling, hunch; *speculation*, guesswork, long shot, gamble.

adj. *suppositional*, hypothetical, conjectural, notional; *theoretical*, speculative, academic, armchair; *supposed*, alleged, so-called, putative.

vb. *suppose*, assume, presume, postulate, posit; *conjecture*, surmise, guess, divine, hazard a guess; *theorize*, hypothesize, speculate, imagine; *suggest*, propose, moot, put forward.

457 **IMAGINATION**
See also 4 (unreality); 22 (originality); 479 (untruth).

n. *imagination*, creativity, inventiveness, originality, ingenuity, thinking out of the box (*colloq.*); *mental image*, conception, visualization, projection, figment; *vision*, mind's eye, insight, empathy; *notion*, idea, whim, vagary, flight of fancy; *delusion*, hallucination, mirage, phantom; *fantasy*, fiction, escapism, make-believe, romance, daydreaming, wishful thinking, pipe dream, cloud-cuckoo-land.

adj. *imaginative*, creative, inventive, original, ingenious; *imaginary*, unreal, fictitious, make-believe, fabulous, legendary, mythological; *fanciful*, whimsical, fantastical, escapist, romantic, quixotic, idealistic.

vb. *imagine*, invent, create, devise, dream up, make up; *conceive*, think of, conjure up, visualize; *fantasize*, idealize, romanticize; *pretend*, make believe, daydream, build castles in Spain.

458 **MEANING**

See also 460 (intelligibility); 503 (clarity).

n. *meaning*, substance, essence, content, pith, matter; *sense*, import, force, tenor, drift, gist; *significance*, meaningfulness, point; *hidden meaning*, connotation, association, implication, suggestion, allusion; *figure of speech*, metaphor, simile, hyperbole; *symbolism*, allegory, parable, double meaning, ambiguity.

adj. *meaningful*, significant, pithy, meaty; *pointed*, telling, pregnant, revealing; *suggestive*, allusive, elliptical, implicit; *figurative*, metaphorical, allegorical, symbolic, connotative; *equivocal*, ambiguous, nebulous; *literal*, unambiguous, unequivocal, denotative; *synonymous*, equivalent, tautologous, tantamount; *semantic*, linguistic, philological.

vb. *mean*, denote, signify, designate; *symbolize*, stand for, connote, imply, suggest; *refer*, allude, mention, drive at, get at (*colloq.*); *convey*, express, communicate.

adv. *in a sense*, so to speak, as it were, that is to say.

459 **LACK OF MEANING**

See also 443 (nonsense); 461 (unintelligibility).

n. *lack of meaning*, meaninglessness, senselessness; *irrelevance*, insignificance, unimportance; *hollowness*, emptiness, triteness, banality, flatness; *unintelligibility*, illegibility, indecipherability, opaqueness; *nonsense*, gibberish, jargon, doubletalk, double Dutch (*colloq.*), gobbledygook (*colloq.*), bafflegab (*colloq.*); *rubbish*, verbiage, twaddle (*colloq.*), claptrap (*colloq.*), piffle (*colloq.*), bunk (*colloq.*), flannel, hot air, eyewash (*colloq.*), guff (*colloq.*), waffle (*colloq.*).

adj. *meaningless*, senseless, expressionless, inscrutable, blank; *incomprehensible*, incoherent, unintelligible, opaque; *irrelevant*, insignificant, unimportant; *hollow*, empty, trivial, banal, trite; *nonsensical*, absurd, inane, fatuous; *verbose*, long-winded, waffly (*colloq.*).

vb. *mean nothing*, make no sense, not add

up (*colloq.*); *talk nonsense*, prattle, babble, prate, rattle on, rabbit on (*colloq.*), blather; *jabber*, gibber, gabble, drivel, rant, rave.

460 **INTELLIGIBILITY**

See also 458 (meaning); 503 (clarity).

n. *intelligibility*, comprehensibility, legibility, readability, audibility; *clarity*, lucidity, limpidity, coherence; *simplicity*, straightforwardness, unambiguousness, explicitness; *simplification*, translation, explanation, demystification, popularization, vulgarization.

adj. *intelligible*, comprehensible, understandable, not rocket science (*colloq.*), legible, readable, audible, decipherable; *clear*, lucid, limpid, coherent, transparent; *recognizable*, discernible, distinguishable, visible; *simple*, straightforward, plain, explicit, unambiguous, forthright; *self-evident*, self-explanatory, obvious.

vb. *be intelligible*, make sense, add up (*colloq.*), speak for itself; *understand*, comprehend, penetrate, fathom; *take in*, take on board, cotton on, tumble to, twig (*colloq.*); *recognize*, discern, distinguish, make out; *clarify*, simplify, elucidate, decode, decipher, translate.

461 **UNINTELLIGIBILITY**

See also 459 (lack of meaning); 504 (obscurity).

n. *unintelligibility*, incomprehensibility, meaninglessness, incoherence; *difficulty*, obscurity, impenetrability, opaqueness; *illegibility*, indecipherability, unreadability, inaudibility, indistinctness; *jargon*, gibberish, mumbo-jumbo (*colloq.*), hocus-pocus (*colloq.*), double Dutch (*colloq.*); *equivocation*, pun, double entendre, weasel word, newspeak; *puzzlement*, perplexity, bafflement.

adj. *unintelligible*, incomprehensible, meaningless, incoherent; *impenetrable*, unfathomable, inscrutable, opaque; *obscure*, abstruse, esoteric, recondite, obfuscatory; *illegible*, indecipherable, unreadable, inaudible; *puzzling*, mysterious, enigmatic, cryptic; *ambiguous*, equivocal, paradoxical, evasive; *puzzled*, baffled, perplexed, nonplussed, flummoxed (*colloq.*), stumped (*colloq.*).

vb. *not understand*, make nothing of, not make head or tail of (*colloq.*), be at sea (*colloq.*); *be unintelligible*, baffle, perplex, puzzle, go over one's head, be beyond one;

equivocate, prevaricate, fudge, obscure, obfuscate, complicate.

462 **INTERPRETATION**

n. *interpretation*, explanation, elucidation, clarification, illustration, exemplification; *account*, commentary, exposition, exegis, explication, critique; *rendition*, version, paraphrase, adaptation; *annotation*, gloss, crib, translation, transcription; *application*, reading, construction, diagnosis, analysis.

adj. *interpretative*, explanatory, explicatory, elucidatory, illustrative; *critical*, analytical, diagnostic, evaluative.

vb. *interpret*, explain, expound, elucidate; *illuminate*, clarify, throw light on, account for; *read*, construe, understand, analyse, diagnose; *render*, reword, paraphrase, translate, transcribe, adapt; *comment on*, criticize, annotate, edit, gloss; *decipher*, decode, explain, solve, puzzle out, read between the lines.

adv. *namely*, to wit, that is, viz.

463 **MISINTERPRETATION**

n. *misinterpretation*, misunderstanding, misreading, misconstruction; *mistake*, misconception, misapprehension, error, delusion; *misrepresentation*, distortion, perversion, falsification; *travesty*, parody, caricature, mockery.

vb. *misinterpret*, misunderstand, misread, misconstrue, read into; *mistake*, confuse, get hold of the wrong end of the stick, get one's wires crossed; *falsify*, distort, twist, colour, spin, pervert, garble, scramble; *misrepresent*, travesty, parody, caricature.

464 **DISPLAY**

See also 394 (appearance); 785 (showiness).

n. *display*, presentation, demonstration, exhibition; *manifestation*, appearance, materialization, realization; *revelation*, disclosure, publication, exposure; *visibility*, prominence, conspicuousness, obviousness; *exhibit*, specimen, evidence, showpiece, collector's item; *show*, fair, exposition, market, parade, pageant; *showroom*, showcase, shop window, market place.

adj. *displayed*, conspicuous, prominent, noticeable, striking; *visible*, apparent, manifest, plain; *marked*, pronounced, evident, obvious, patent; *glaring*, flagrant, overt, eye-catching, blatant, public; *open*, candid, frank, above board, up-front (*colloq.*).

vb. *display*, present, demonstrate, exhibit;

manifest, show, evince, give signs of; *unfold*, reveal, unveil, divulge, disclose; *expose*, lay bare, unearth, unfurl, unsheathe; *emphasize*, highlight, spotlight, feature, throw into prominence/relief, foreground; *advertise*, publicize, proclaim, announce; *flaunt*, parade, show off, brandish, flourish.

adv. *on display*, on view, on show; *in public*, openly, for all to see.

465 **LATENCY**

See also 373 (invisibility); 467 (secret); 469 (concealment).

n. *latency*, dormancy, imperceptibility, invisibility; *concealment*, secrecy, hiddenness, obscurity; *insidiousness*, treacherousness, stealthiness, underhandedness; *undercurrent*, undertone, insinuation, hint, innuendo; *enigma*, unknown quantity, snake in the grass, nigger in the woodpile, mole (*colloq.*), secret agent.

adj. *latent*, dormant, quiescent, hidden, imperceptible; *invisible*, concealed, submerged, subterranean, underground; *inconspicuous*, unseen, obscure, unsung, backroom; *unspoken*, unsaid, tacit, implicit; *secret*, clandestine, covert, undercover; *insidious*, treacherous, underhand, stealthy; *indirect*, veiled, suggestive, allusive.

vb. *be latent*, hide, keep a low profile, lie low, lie doggo (*colloq.*); *steal*, creep, slink, lurk; *hint*, imply, suggest, insinuate.

466 **INFORMATION**

See also 470 (publication); 471 (news).

n. *information*, knowledge, intelligence, news, facts, data, statistics, info (*colloq.*), gen (*colloq.*), dope (*colloq.*), lowdown (*colloq.*); *interest*, colour; *communication*, report, message, statement, bulletin, communiqué, dispatch, press release, handout, update; *dissemination*, diffusion, transmission, broadcast, distribution, circulation; *announcement*, notification, intimation, warning, instruction, briefing; *hint*, clue, advice, tip-off (*colloq.*), word in one's ear; *informant*, reporter, messenger, spokesman/-person/-woman, courier; *informer*, source, channel, the grapevine (*colloq.*), a little bird (*colloq.*), supergrass, mole (*colloq.*), nark (*colloq.*), stool pigeon, sneak, telltale.

adj. *informative*, instructive, helpful, enlightening; *communicative*, forthcoming, chatty, newsy, gossipy; *informed*, briefed, posted, apprised, primed, clued up (*colloq.*), genned up (*colloq.*), au courant.

vb. *inform*, apprise, acquaint, enlighten, fill sb in, put in the picture, wise up (*colloq.*); *instruct*, brief, notify, warn, advise, tip off (*colloq.*); *communicate*, convey, put across/over, transmit, diffuse, broadcast, circulate, put about; *be informed*, know the score (*colloq.*), be in the know (*colloq.*), be in the loop (*colloq.*), know the state of play; *impart*, reveal, tell, leak, blab (*colloq.*), blow the gaff (*colloq.*), let the cat out of the bag (*colloq.*); *inform on*, betray, denounce, tell tales on, squeal (*colloq.*), rat (*colloq.*), shop (*colloq.*).

467 **SECRET**
See also 465 (latency).

n. *secret*, mystery, riddle, puzzle, enigma, code, cipher; *suppression*, concealment, censorship, misinformation, blackout, cover-up; *secrecy*, privacy, confidence, discretion, reticence; *secretiveness*, furtiveness, shiftiness, stealth.

adj. *secret*, top-secret, hush-hush (*colloq.*), confidential, classified; *covert*, clandestine, undercover, behind-the-scenes, anonymous, incognito; *underhand*, hole-and-corner, furtive, shifty, stealthy; *secretive*, unforthcoming, uncommunicative, buttoned-up, tight-lipped, close; *private*, discreet, reticent, cagey (*colloq.*).

vb. *keep secret*, keep under wraps, not let on, not breathe a word, hold one's tongue, clam up, keep one's counsel; *suppress*, gag, censor, whitewash; *conceal*, cover up, hush up, sweep under the carpet; *be uninformed*, be out of the loop (*colloq.*).

adv. *in secret*, in private, in camera, behind closed doors; *confidentially*, privately, between ourselves; *secretly*, on the sly, on the quiet.

468 **DISCLOSURE**
See also 203 (uncovering); 470 (publication).

n. *disclosure*, exposure, revelation, discovery, exposé; *publication*, announcement, proclamation, promulgation; *betrayal*, indiscretion, leak, give-away (*colloq.*); *confession*, admission, avowal, acknowledgement.

adj. *disclosed*, revealed, exposed, out, public; *revealing*, indiscreet, tell-tale, informative; *candid*, frank, open, up-front. (*colloq.*), forthcoming.

vb. *disclose*, divulge, reveal, uncover; *expose*, unveil, lay bare, unmask, blow sb's cover; *publish*, air, ventilate, take the lid off

(*colloq.*); *announce*, declare, proclaim, promulgate; *confess*, admit, own up, come clean (*colloq.*), make a clean breast of it, hold one's hands up (*colloq.*), put one's hand up to (*colloq.*); *confide*, open up, bare one's soul, unburden oneself, tell all; *betray*, let slip, leak, give the game away, spill the beans (*colloq.*), let the cat out of the bag (*colloq.*).

469 **CONCEALMENT**
See also 465 (latency).

n. *concealment*, hiding, dissimulation, pretence, masquerade; *conspiracy*, intrigue, machinations, plotting; *disguise*, camouflage, subterfuge, smokescreen, anonymity, pseudonym; *mask*, cloak, veil, cover; *hiding-place*, hideout, hidey-hole (*colloq.*), cache, den, lair, retreat, refuge.

adj. *concealed*, latent, hidden, buried, gone to ground/earth; *disguised*, masked, anonymous, incognito; *clandestine*, secret, furtive, hole-and-corner; *conspiratorial*, cloak-and-dagger, backdoor, surreptitious, Machiavellian.

vb. *conceal*, hide, stow away, secrete, stash (*colloq.*), bury; *disguise*, dissimulate, camouflage, mask, cloak, veil, cover up; *hide*, lurk, skulk, lie low, steal, slink, creep; *ambush*, creep up on, lie in wait, waylay; *conspire*, intrigue, plot, contrive.

470 **PUBLICATION**
See also 466 (information); 468 (disclosure); 471 (news).

n. *publication*, proclamation, announcement, disclosure; *circulation*, dissemination, diffusion, broadcasting; *publicity*, promotion, advertising, hype (*colloq.*), ballyhoo (*colloq.*), media coverage; *public relations*, PR, image-making, soft sell, showmanship; *public place*, forum, arena, theatre, platform, rostrum, pulpit, soapbox; *public*, audience, readership, market, admass; *notice*, advertisement, placard, poster, mailshot, puff (*colloq.*), blurb (*colloq.*); *slogan*, commercial, plug (*colloq.*), trailer; *publicist*, promoter, advertiser, adman, PR man; *herald*, announcer, messenger, town crier, barker, tout; *common knowledge*, open secret, public property, household name.

adj. *published*, broadcast, current, circulating, available; *public*, notorious, infamous, celebrated.

vb. *publish*, announce, proclaim, disclose; *distribute*, circulate, put about, disseminate, diffuse; *broadcast*, relay, pass on, spread the word, noise abroad, shout from the rooftops; *herald*, trumpet, blaze aboard, beat the drum; *publicize*, promote, sell, advertise, hype (*colloq.*), plug (*colloq.*), trail.

471 NEWS

See also 466 (information); 470 (publication).

n. *news*, current affairs, tidings, intelligence, word; *report*, story, newsflash, headlines, stop press, scoop, exclusive, soundbite; *press*, the fourth estate, journalism, Fleet Street; *newspaper*, daily, broadsheet, quality, heavy (*colloq.*), tabloid, red-top (*colloq.*), rag (*colloq.*), gutter press, yellow press, underground press; *organ*, journal, periodical, weekly, gazette, magazine, glossy; *rumour*, hearsay, buzz, canard, gossip, tittle-tattle, scandal, muckraking, sensationalism; *reporter*, journalist, correspondent, newsman, newshound, stringer, gossip, scandalmonger, muckraker, the grapevine, the bush telegraph; *electronic publishing*, electronic book, e-book, e-magazine, e-mag, e-zine.

adj. *newsworthy*, scandalous, sensational; *current*, abroad, topical, going round, rumoured, rife; *newsy*, chatty, gossipy, informative.

vb. *report*, publish, spread, noise abroad; *be newsworthy*, make news, hit the headlines, cause a sensation, make a splash.

472 COMMUNICATIONS

See also 471 (news); 515 (correspondence); 570 (store)

n. *communications*, signalling, semaphore, Morse code, telegraphy, telephony; *telecommunications*, telegram, telemessage, cable, wire, text, text-message; *telephone*, phone, blower (*colloq.*), cellphone, car phone, cordless telephone, mobile phone, mobile, camera phone, videophone, walkie-talkie, intercom, pager, bleeper (*colloq.*), answering machine, voice mail, party line, telephone exchange, switchboard, operator, call centre; *texting*, text-messaging, predictive texting, multimedia messaging, photo-messaging, picture messaging, teleconferencing, videoconferencing; *post*, mail, pigeon post, parcel post, recorded delivery, registered post, snail mail (*colloq.*), *hate mail*, poison-pen letter, letter bomb, parcel bomb; *media*, broadcasting, television, TV, small screen, telly (*colloq.*), gogglebox (*colloq.*), cable/satellite/digital/terrestrial/pay TV, free-to-air broadcasting, free-to-view

programmes, set-top box, plasma screen; *video*, videocassette, videorecorder, videocassette recorder, VCR, videotape, video nasty, video game; *radio*, wireless, transmitter, crystal set, steam radio, transistor; *station*, channel, network, wavelength, frequency, airwaves; *broadcast*, transmission, relay, telecast, simulcast, outside broadcast; *programme*, recording, repeat, sitcom, docudrama, period/costume drama, soap opera, chat show, quiz, phone-in, telethon, reality TV, infotainment; *broadcaster*, newsreader, presenter, announcer, commentator, anchorman/-woman, talking head; *Internet*, the Net, the World Wide Web, the Web, information highway/superhighway, cyberspace, virtual reality; *website*, web page, home page, weblog, blog, webcast, webcam, email, domain name, search engine, browser, chatroom, thread, emoticon, smiley, broadband; *hacker*, spam, virus, flame (mail), firewall; *telecommuter*, Internet café, cybercafé; *e-business/commerce*, dot com company; *computer crime/fraud*, cybercrime, e-stalking.

vb. *telephone*, phone, call, ring, give sb a call/ring/buzz/tinkle, text, (send a) text-message; *email*, post; *write*, send a letter, drop sb a line/note; *record*, video, download, upload, burn; *broadcast*, transmit, telecast.

473 AFFIRMATION

See also 436 (assent).

n. *affirmation*, declaration, assertion, pronouncement, statement; *profession*, admission, confession, avowal; *allegation*, claim, accusation, charge; *assurance*, confirmation, corroboration, support, endorsement, backing; *pledge*, promise, commitment, guarantee; *insistence*, emphasis, stress, vehemence.

adj. *affirmative*, positive, declarative; *definite*, categorical, unequivocal, express; *assertive*, peremptory, emphatic, insistent; *pledged*, committed, sworn, fully paid-up; *plain*, blunt, round, outspoken.

vb. *affirm*, state, express, declare, assert, pronounce; *profess*, admit, hold one's hands up (*colloq.*), put one's hand up to (*colloq.*), avow, own up to; *allege*, claim, maintain, hold; *confirm*, assure, corroborate, second, endorse, support, back; *emphasize*, stress, reiterate, insist on, urge; *promise*, pledge, swear, engage, commit.

474 **NEGATION**

See also 437 (dissent).

n. *negation*, nay, negative, veto, refusal, rejection; *denial*, disavowal, repudiation, disclaimer, dissociation; *rebuttal*, refutation, challenge, contradiction; *renunciation*, abnegation, abjuration, retraction; *revocation*, repeal, cancellation, abrogation, annulment.

adj. *negative*, negatory, contrary, contradictory; *opposed*, antagonistic, dissident, recusant.

vb. *negate*, negative, veto, deny, refuse; *refute*, rebut, gainsay, contradict, reject; *repudiate*, disavow, disown, disclaim, dissociate oneself; *renounce*, forswear, abjure, abnegate; *revoke*, abrogate, cancel, annul, repeal.

475 **TEACHING**

See also 477 (school).

n. *teaching*, pedagogy, schooling, education, edification, enlightenment; *guidance*, instruction, tuition, coaching; *induction*, initiation, training, preparation; *inculcation*, indoctrination, brainwashing, propaganda; *lesson*, class, seminar, tutorial, clinic, workshop; *course*, curriculum, syllabus, timetable; *adult education*, night school, evening classes, day release, sandwich course, block release; *teacher*, instructor, coach, trainer, tutor, educationalist, pedagogue, master, mistress, mentor, guru.

adj. *educational*, pedagogic, scholastic, academic; *educative*, didactic, instructive; *extramural*, extracurricular, recreational; *vocational*, liberal, technical, practical.

vb. *teach*, instruct, tutor, lecture; *coach*, train, school, drill, exercise; *educate*, guide, cultivate, edify, enlighten; *initiate*, induct, prepare, break in, show the ropes (*colloq.*); *instil*, inculcate, indoctrinate, din in, hammer in.

476 **LEARNING**

See also 438 (knowledge).

n. *learning*, lore, knowledge, skill; *wisdom*, erudition, scholarliness, learnedness; *apprenticeship*, tutelage, pupillage, novitiate, training; *self-improvement*, study, application, industry; *lesson*, assignment, project, homework, prep (*colloq.*), revision; *learner*, apprentice, disciple, beginner, recruit, tyro, novice, probationer; *scholar*, pupil, tutee, undergraduate, swot (*colloq.*), bookworm.

adj. *studious*, industrious, diligent,

motivated; *learned*, scholarly, lettered, academic, erudite, knowledgeable, wise.

vb. *learn*, find out, study, apply oneself; *train*, practise, get the hang of (*colloq.*), acquire the knack; *revise*, learn up, swot (*colloq.*), brush up (*colloq.*), burn the midnight oil, mug up (*colloq.*), bone up (*colloq.*).

477 **SCHOOL**

See also 475 (teaching); 476 (learning).

n. *school*, beacon school, the blackboard jungle, the chalkface; *primary school*, infant school, nursery, creche, kindergarten; *secondary school*, high school, comprehensive (school), grammar/public/state/prep/ boarding/faith school, crammer, finishing school, sixth-form college, city academy, city technology college; *further education*, tertiary education, college, campus, university, varsity (*colloq.*), Oxbridge, redbrick/plate-glass university, university college, polytechnic, poly (*colloq.*), institute of technology, academy, institute, seminary, conservatoire, groves of academe, alma mater; *schoolroom*, classroom, lecture hall, amphitheatre, auditorium.

478 **TRUTH**

See also 440 (accuracy).

n. *truth*, the plain/honest truth, the facts of life, home truths; *truthfulness*, veracity, honesty, integrity, probity; *candour*, sincerity, openness, frankness; *straightforwardness*, forthrightness, downrightness, bluntness; *ingenuousness*, naïvety, artlessness, guilelessness.

adj. *truthful*, veracious, honest, upright; *reliable*, trustworthy, bona fide, honest-to-goodness, genuine; *candid*, sincere, open, frank, above board, up-front (*colloq.*); *straightforward*, forthright, blunt, direct, bald, downright; *ingenuous*, naïve, artless, guileless.

vb. *be truthful*, tell the truth, stick to the facts, give the true story; *speak* one's *mind*, speak up, make no bones about, call a spade a spade; *confess*, own up, open one's heart, make a clean breast of it, hold one's hands up (*colloq.*), put one's hand up to (*colloq.*).

479 **UNTRUTH**

See also 441 (error); 457 (imagination).

n. *untruth*, inaccuracy, falsehood, exaggeration, misrepresentation, distortion, perversion; *invention*, fabrication, fiction, romance, faction; *half-truth*, evasion, equivocation, ambiguity, white lie; *dishonesty*, disingenuousness, insincerity, falseness, duplicity, mendaciousness; *lie*, fib, whopper (*colloq.*), porky *or* porky pie (*colloq.*); *hoax*, tall story, yarn (*colloq.*), cock and bull story, fairy story/tale, old wives' tale, superstition, fantasy.

adj. *untrue*, false, fictitious, unreal, imaginary; *fictional*, made-up, make-believe, fairy-tale, fabulous, legendary; *dishonest*, disingenuous, insincere, duplicitous, mendacious, lying; *evasive*, equivocal, ambiguous, hypocritical, two-faced; *spurious*, bogus, phoney, so-called.

vb. *lie*, pretend, dissemble, make believe; *invent*, fabricate, spin, weave, cook up; *exaggerate*, embellish, embroider, dress up, sex up.

480 DECEPTION

n. *deception*, dishonesty, duplicity, double-dealing, fraudulence; *deceitfulness*, artfulness, guile, craftiness, cunning; *treachery*, betrayal, perfidy, treason; *deceptiveness*, illusoriness, speciousness, meretriciousness; *trickery*, chicanery, sharp practice, sleight of hand, skulduggery (*colloq.*), hanky-panky (*colloq.*), jiggery-pokery (*colloq.*); *fraud*, racket, dodge, swindle, fiddle (*colloq.*), cheat, swiz (*colloq.*), rip-off (*colloq.*), con (*colloq.*); *trick*, ruse, stratagem, contrivance, wheeze (*colloq.*); *deceiver*, hypocrite, liar, impostor, traitor; *trickster*, cheat, fake, charlatan, quack, mountebank, rogue, swindler, conman (*colloq.*), shyster, wide boy (*colloq.*), spiv (*colloq.*), cowboy; *dupe*, fool, gull, soft touch, patsy (*colloq.*), mug (*colloq.*), fall guy (*colloq.*), sucker (*colloq.*).

adj. *deceitful*, dishonest, lying, duplicitous, treacherous, perfidious; *tricky*, artful, crafty, sly, wily, cunning; *fraudulent*, underhand, shifty, furtive; *deceptive*, illusory, specious, meretricious; *duped*, taken in, gulled, hoodwinked, taken for a ride (*colloq.*).

vb. *deceive*, defraud, cheat, fiddle (*colloq.*), wangle (*colloq.*), con (*colloq.*), swindle, fleece, diddle (*colloq.*), rip off (*colloq.*); *beguile*, delude, mislead, dupe, hoodwink, gull, bamboozle (*colloq.*), double-cross, put one over on (*colloq.*), lead sb up the garden path (*colloq.*); *be deceived*, be had (*colloq.*), fall for, get taken for a ride (*colloq.*).

481 FALSEHOOD
See also 479 (untruth).

n. *falsehood*, dishonesty, disingenuousness,

insincerity, bad faith, mendaciousness; *hypocrisy*, cant, lip-service, cupboard love, crocodile tears; *deceitfulness*, duplicity, fraudulence, perjury, treason; *pretence*, dissimulation, play-acting, trickery; *front*, façade, show, semblance, sham, bluff, simulation; *falsification*, counterfeiting, forgery, faking.

adj. *false*, dishonest, untrue, mendacious, lying; *hypocritical*, insincere, two-faced, disingenuous, mealy-mouthed; *deceitful*, shifty, sly, double-dealing, duplicitous, treacherous, perfidious; *falsified*, unfounded, trumped-up, rigged, framed, fixed; *seeming*, feigned, put on, assumed, pretended; *fake*, bogus, sham, phoney, counterfeit, simulated, fraudulent.

vb. *be false*, lie, fib, lie through one's teeth, perjure oneself, bear false witness; *falsify*, doctor, fiddle (*colloq.*), cook (*colloq.*), fix, rig, frame, nobble (*colloq.*); *fake*, forge, counterfeit, simulate; *pretend*, feign, dissimulate, dissemble, play-act, pass oneself off as.

482 EXAGGERATION
See also 431 (overestimation).

n. *exaggeration*, overemphasis, overstatement, overkill, overexposure; *extravagance*, excessiveness, exorbitance, outrageousness, flamboyance; *inflatedness*, bombast, pomposity, hyperbole, hot air (*colloq.*); *fuss*, to-do, ballyhoo (*colloq.*), storm in a teacup; *melodrama*, purple patch, sensationalism, hype (*colloq.*); *yarn* (*colloq.*), tall story (*colloq.*), fisherman's tale, flight of fancy.

adj. *exaggerated*, overstated, overdone, over the top (*colloq.*); *extravagant*, outrageous, flamboyant, preposterous; *excessive*, exorbitant, inordinate, disproportionate, astronomical; *inflated*, bombastic, pompous, high-flown, overblown; *melodramatic*, histrionic, sensational, highly coloured, overwritten, hyperbolic.

vb. *exaggerate*, overemphasize, overstate, overexpose, overdo, go too far, go to extremes; *inflate*, magnify, talk up, blow up, make mountains out of molehills; *dramatize*, embroider, play up, hype (*colloq.*), pile on the agony, lay it on thick (*colloq.*).

483 UNDERSTATEMENT
See also 432 (underestimation).

n. *understatement*, underemphasis, minimization, underestimation; *subtlety*, delicacy, restraint, refinement; *simplicity*, plainness, bareness, austereness; *reserve*, reticence, diffidence, modesty; *suggestion*, trace, suspicion, soupçon; *insipidness*, pallidness, tastelessness, wishy-washiness (*colloq.*).

adj. *understated*, underemphasized, underestimated, underrated; *simple*, plain, bare, stark, unadorned, basic, bog-standard (*colloq.*), entry-level; *delicate*, subtle, restrained, pastel, watercolour; *insipid*, pallid, diluted, wishy-washy (*colloq.*); *reserved*, reticent, diffident, modest, unassuming; *imperceptible*, inconspicuous, unimpressive, underwhelming (*colloq.*).

vb. *understate*, underemphasize, underplay, underestimate, underrate; *moderate*, tone down, play down, water down, dilute; *deflate*, puncture, cut down to size, bring down to earth.

484 SIGN

n. *sign*, indication, mark, evidence, symptom; *image*, symbol, emblem, token, emoticon, smiley; *hint*, pointer, clue, indicator, signpost, omen; *marker*, milestone, landmark, monument, memorial; *signal*, semaphore, tick-tack, warning sign, siren, alarm, beacon; *sign language*, mime, dumb show, charades, body language; *gesture*, nod, wink, shrug, nudge, wave; *applause*, clap, cheer, big hand (*colloq.*); *hiss*, boo, catcall, V-sign, raspberry, slow handclap; *badge*, insignia, coat of arms, crest, bearings, blazon; *uniform*, livery, dress, colours, tartan, old school tie; *flag*, ensign, standard, banner, pennant, tricolour, Union Jack/Flag, Blue Peter, skull and crossbones, the Stars and Stripes.

adj. *indicative*, symptomatic, revealing, telling, significant; *symbolic*, token, emblematic, representational; *expressive*, suggestive, redolent.

vb. *indicate*, show, point to, signal, signpost; *reveal*, manifest, betoken, betray, attest to, evince; *symbolize*, stand for, represent, signify; *mark out*, designate, delimit, demarcate; *gesticulate*, mimic, act out, mime, copy; *gesture*, motion, wave, beckon, nod, shrug, point; *frown*, scowl, grimace, pout, smile.

485 IDENTIFICATION

n. *identification*, classification, designation, naming; *identity*, individuality, selfhood, particularity, idiosyncrasy; *identifying sign*, name, signature, autograph, fingerprint,

initials, monogram, brand, earmark, ring; *proof of identity*, passport, (biometric) ID card, entitlement card, visiting card; *trademark*, hallmark, brand name, imprint, logo, colophon, signature tune/song/dish etc; theme tune/song; *marking*, track, spoor, footprint; *password*, watchword, shibboleth; *label*, nameplate, ticket, tag, docket, sticker; *seal*, stamp, counterfoil, stub, duplicate.

adj. *identifying*, classificatory, designatory; *characteristic*, typical, individual, idiosyncratic, quirky; *identifiable*, recognizable, distinguishable, discernible; *identified*, named, known, branded, earmarked.

vb. *identify*, name, classify, categorize, pin down, pigeonhole; *label*, ticket, tag, docket, stamp, number, letter; *sign*, seal, autograph, countersign, initial, brand, tattoo, earmark, ring.

486 RECORD
See also 448 (memory).

n. *record*, register, roll, catalogue, inventory; *documentation*, file, dossier, case history, curriculum vitae; *account*, report, minutes, notes, jottings, memo; *diary*, journal, scrapbook, album, log(book), chronicle, archive, annals; *notebook*, notepad, memo pad; *index card*, filing system, microfiche, tape-recording, videotape, data bank, data base; *monument*, statue, memorial, cairn, obelisk; *trace*, vestige, relic, remains; trail, track, path, swath, wake, wash, tidemark; *recorder*, registrar, clerk, amanuensis, scribe, secretary; *chronicler*, historian, diarist, archivist.

vb. *record*, register, document, catalogue, index, list, file; *report*, document, chronicle, set down, film, tape-record, photograph, video, download, upload, burn; *note*, minute, jot down, table, log; *score*, chalk up, mark up, notch up, tick off.

adv. *on record*, in black and white, on tape, in the can (*colloq.*).

487 OBLITERATION
See also 449 (oblivion).

n. *obliteration*, erasure, effacement, deletion; *cancellation*, annulment, revocation, repeal; *suppression*, censorship, blackout; *abolition*, elimination, liquidation, annihilation; *blank*, void, tabula rasa, clean slate; *rubber*, eraser, sponge, Snopake (*tdmk*).

vb. *obliterate*, erase, efface, rub out, wipe out, blot out, snopake; *delete*, cross out, score out, strike out, scrub (*colloq.*); *cancel*, annul, revoke, repeal; *suppress*, quash, censor, blue-pencil, black out; *expunge*, eliminate, liquidate, annihilate; *bury*, submerge, cover up.

488 **REPRESENTATION**

n. *representation*, depiction, description, delineation; *enactment*, performance, rendering; *personification*, imitation, characterization, impersonation, identity theft; *illustration*, exemplification, typification, symbolization, figuration; *impression*, likeness, portrayal, image; *portrait*, icon, effigy, statue, waxwork, dummy, photograph, painting, hologram; *reproduction*, facsimile, duplicate, copy; *design*, blueprint, sketch, outline, diagram; *plan*, map, chart, projection; *ornamental art*, fine arts, performing arts, photography, cinematography.

adj. *representative*, typical, exemplary, symbolic, emblematic, figurative; *descriptive*, graphic, vivid, evocative, Impressionistic; *representational*, illustrative, pictorial, realistic, naturalistic, true-to-life.

vb. *represent*, stand for, symbolize, connote, mean, signify; *typify*, characterize, illustrate, exemplify; *personify*, epitomize, embody, incarnate; *enact*, perform, mimic, impersonate, imitate; *depict*, describe, delineate, draw; *portray*, picture, figure, image, capture, evoke; *design*, sketch, draft, block out, map, chart, outline.

489 **MISREPRESENTATION**

n. *misrepresentation*, distortion, exaggeration, perversion, falsification; *travesty*, caricature, parody, mockery; *poor likeness*, daub, scrawl, botch, pale imitation, mere shadow; *misinterpretation*, misconstruction, misreading.

adj. *misrepresented*, falsified, distorted, inaccurate, misleading; *flat*, cardboard, unrealistic, infelicitous, inept.

vb. *misrepresent*, distort, exaggerate, pervert, falsify, mislead; *travesty*, caricature, parody, make a mockery of.

490 **PAINTING**

n. *painting*, art, fine art, graphics, illustration; *artistry*, composition, technique, draughtsmanship, brushwork, palette; *representation*, treatment, handling, rendering, depiction, portrayal; *artistic medium*, watercolour, oil, pastel, crayon,

charcoal, tempera, gouache, acrylic; *picture*, mural, fresco, poster, canvas; *sketch*, line drawing, model, cartoon, maquette; *work of art*, old master, chef d'oeuvre, masterpiece; *studio*, atelier, gallery, museum; *portrait*, still life, collage, miniature, landscape, seascape, interior; *artist*, painter, draughtsman, designer, colourist.

adj. *artistic*, painterly, pictorial, picturesque, scenic, graphic; *representational*, realistic, figurative, Impressionist; *abstract*, non-representational, non-objective, Expressionist, Cubist, minimalist.

vb. *paint*, portray, depict, illustrate, limn, daub; *draw*, sketch, crayon, pencil; *colour*, shade, tint, wash, ink.

491 **PHOTOGRAPHY**

See also 525 (cinema).

n. *photography*, photojournalism, cinematography, radiography, holography; *photograph*, photo, X-ray, hologram, snapshot, snap, still, frame; *slide*, diapositive, transparency, print; *negative*, exposure, enlargement, blow-up, shot; *film*, filmstrip, microfilm, spool, reel, cassette, cartridge; *camera*, lens, viewfinder, flash, enlarger, projector, viewer, epidiascope, carousel, digital camera, webcam, camera phone.

adj. *photographic*, cinematographic, radiographic, holographic; *photogenic*, camera-shy, snap-happy (*colloq.*); *overexposed*, underexposed, fuzzy, grainy.

vb. *photograph*, take, snap, photostat, X-ray; *expose*, develop, print, process, enlarge, reproduce.

492 **SCULPTURE**

n. *sculpture*, plastic arts, modelling, carving, origami; *relief*, cameo, embossing, bas-relief, low relief, mezzo-relievo, high relief; *statue*, statuary, figurine, statuette, bust, head, torso, construction, mobile, stabile; *model*, maquette, death mask, cast, mould; *bronze*, stone, marble, clay, papier-mâché.

adj. *sculptured*, sculpted, graven, moulded, glyptic; *plastic*, mouldable, fictile, malleable; *embossed*, raised, repoussé.

vb. *sculpt*, sculpture, carve, hew, cut, chisel; *model*, fashion, mould, shape, cast; *raise*, emboss, undercut.

493 **ENGRAVING**

n. *engraving*, etching, intaglio, drypoint, line engraving, photogravure; *mezzotint*, aquatint, woodcut, linocut; *chasing*, fluting, chamfering, groove, line, channel, incision, glyph; *chisel*, burin, graver, needle.

adj. *engraved*, graven, etched; *incised*, carved, grooved, chased, sunk, recessed, fluted, chamfered.

vb. *engrave*, etch, chase, chamfer, chisel, incise; *impress*, stamp, recess.

494 **LANGUAGE**

See also 496 (word); 500 (grammar).

n. *language*, speech, tongue, talk, communication, body language, sign language; *style*, diction, parlance, vocabulary, idiom, phraseology, terminology, lingo (*colloq.*), patter, jargon; *natural language*, mother tongue, lingua franca, pidgin, creole, franglais; *classical language*, Latin, Greek; *artificial language*, Esperanto, Ido, Volapük; *computer language*, machine language, machine code, programming language, Ada, Algol, BASIC, FORTRAN, COBOL, PASCAL, Perl; *usage*, Standard English, Queen's English, Received Pronunciation; *dialect*, regionalism, vernacular, patois, Scouse, Brummie, Geordie, Mummerset; *accent*, brogue, burr, twang; *slang*, colloquialism, argot, cant, back slang, pig Latin, rhyming slang; *linguistics*, philology, grammar, syntax, morphology, semantics, phonetics.

adj. *linguistic*, philological, grammatical, syntactic, morphological, semantic, phonetic; *idiomatic*, colloquial, slangy, racy, vulgar, demotic, common; *dialectal*, regional, local, broad, thick; *bilingual*, fluent, polyglot, multilingual.

495 **LETTER**

See also 513 (writing).

n. *letter*, character, sign, symbol, alphabet, ABC, syllabary; *picture writing*, ideogram, pictogram, hieroglyphic, cuneiform, rune, emoticon, smiley; *lettering*, italic, copperplate, cursive, minuscule, capital, majuscule, uncial; *initial*, monogram, abbreviation, contraction, acronym, acrostic; *speech sound*, vowel, consonant, phoneme, syllable; *spelling*, orthography, transliteration, misspelling, cacography, dyslexia.

adj. *alphabetical*, hieroglyphic, runic, Cyrillic; *syllabic*, consonantal, vocalic; *capital*, upper-case, small, lower-case, italic, roman.

vb. *alphabetize*, syllabify, transliterate, spell; *initial*, letter, sign.

496 **WORD**

See also 494 (language).

n. *word*, expression, term, name, locution, phrase; *synonym*, antonym, homonym, homophone; *abbreviation*, contraction, acronym, portmanteau word, blend; *word origin*, etymology, root, derivative, folk etymology; *word-play*, pun, spoonerism, anagram, nonce word, neologism, coinage, weasel word; *slogan*, catch phrase, watchword, vogue word, buzzword, cliché; *swearword*, four-letter word, obscenity, oath, billingsgate, bad language; *long word*, polysyllable, mouthful, tongue twister; *barbarism*, corruption, malapropism, solecism; *word list*, glossary, vocabulary, lexicon, dictionary, thesaurus, index, concordance.

adj. *verbal*, lexical, terminological; *literal*, verbatim, word-for-word; *articulate*, fluent, expressive; *wordy*, verbose, sesquipedalian.

vb. *word*, state, formulate, phrase; *articulate*, express, put into words, verbalize.

497 **NAME**

n. *name*, designation, appellation, denomination; *epithet*, handle (*colloq.*), moniker (*colloq.*), nickname, pet name, sobriquet, pseudonym, pen name; *forename*, first/Christian/given name, middle name, surname, maiden name, last/family name, patronymic, metronymic; *place name*, toponym, eponym, namesake; *nomenclature*, terminology, classification, identification; *naming*, roll call, dubbing ceremony, christening, baptism; *title*, style, form of address, signature, label.

adj. *named*, titled, nee, alias, a.k.a., so-called; *nominal*, titular, in name only, named after, eponymous.

vb. *name*, call, term, designate, denominate; *title*, style, christen, baptize, dub, nickname; *classify*, identify, label, tag.

498 **MISNOMER**

n. *misnomer*, wrong name, pseudonym, pen name, nom de plume, alias, false name, nom de guerre; *nickname*, pet name, sobriquet, assumed name, stage name; *false identity*, impersonation, imposture, mistaken identity; *misnaming*, miscalling, malapropism, solecism; *anonymity*, namelessness, facelessness, no name, anon, so-and-so, A.N. Other, Mr X; *unnamed thing*, what's-its-name, thingummy (*colloq.*), thingamajig (*colloq.*), thingamabob (*colloq.*), thingie (*colloq.*).

adj. *misnamed*, pseudonymous, professed, so-called, self-styled, would-be; *anonymous*, nameless, faceless, unknown, unidentified, unnamed, incognito.

vb. *misname*, miscall, mistake; *impersonate*, pass oneself off as, go under the name of.

499 PHRASE

n. *phrase*, expression, turn of phrase, locution, construction, collocation, idiom; *set phrase*, saying, formula, proverb, catch phrase, cliché, motto; *inscription*, phrasing, wording, diction, parlance; *rephrasing*, rewording, restatement, paraphase, circumlocution.

vb. *phrase*, word, express, state, formulate, put into words; *rephrase*, reword, restate, paraphrase.

500 GRAMMAR

n. *grammar*, usage, syntax, word order, morphology, word formation; *declension*, inflection, conjugation, case, person, number, tense, voice, mood, agreement; *word class*, part of speech, noun, pronoun, adjective, modifier, verb, adverb, conjunction, article, determiner, preposition, interjection; *subject*, predicate, object, complement, apposition; *affix*, prefix, suffix, infix.

adj. *grammatical*, syntactic, morphological, correct, well-formed, standard, acceptable; *nominal*, adjectival, verbal, adverbial, prepositional, interjectional; *comparative*, superlative, absolute; *active*, passive, subjunctive.

vb. *parse*, analyse, construe, conjugate, inflect, decline; *qualify*, modify, govern, take, agree.

501 GRAMMATICAL ERROR

n. *grammatical error*, solecism, misusage, barbarism; *mistake*, slip of the tongue/pen, split infinitive, double negative, dangling participle; *ungrammaticality*, misconstruction, hypercorrection.

adj. *ungrammatical*, incorrect, hypercorrect, unacceptable; *non-standard*, substandard, loose, sloppy, careless.

502 STYLE

n. *style*, mode, fashion, manner, idiom, vein, strain; *phraseology*, vocabulary, wording, diction, register, level, tone; *fluency*, mastery,

articulacy, eloquence, word power, command, rhetoric, oratory; *elegance*, power, vigour, raciness, pizzazz or pzazz (*colloq.*); *inelegance*, awkwardness, clumsiness, stiltedness.

adj. *stylistic*, literary, rhetorical, oratorical; *mannered*, stylized, idiosyncratic, quirky; *elegant*, well turned, well crafted, fluent, articulate, eloquent; *inelegant*, infelicitous, stilted, clumsy, awkward, ponderous, flat, prosaic.

503 CLARITY
See also 460 (intelligibility).

n. *clarity*, clearness, lucidity, limpidity, transparency; *intelligibility*, perspicuity, straightforwardness, unambiguousness; *exactness*, preciseness, explicitness, directness; *simplicity*, plainness, unadornedness, baldness.

adj. *clear*, lucid, limpid, transparent; *intelligible*, perspicuous, understandable, straightforward, uncomplicated, unambiguous; *simple*, plain, uncluttered, unadorned; *exact*, precise, clear-cut, explicit, direct, spelt out, in words of one syllable.

504 OBSCURITY
See also 461 (unintelligibility).

n. *obscurity*, unintelligibility, abstruseness, opaqueness; *complexity*, convolutedness, denseness, overcompression; *vagueness*, indefiniteness, ambiguity, obfuscation, obscurantism; *inexactness*, impreciseness, looseness, diffuseness, sloppiness; *wordiness*, verbosity, bombast, waffle (*colloq.*).

adj. *obscure*, unclear, unintelligible, opaque; *abstruse*, esoteric, recondite, recherché; *vague*, indefinite, ambiguous, obscurantist, obfuscatory; *complex*, involved, intricate, dense, compressed; *inexact*, imprecise, loose, woolly, sloppy, diffuse; *wordy*, verbose, overwritten, bombastic.

505 CONCISENESS
See also 179 (shortness); 520 (summary).

n. *conciseness*, concision, succinctness, brevity, pithiness; *terseness*, curtness, compression, economy, laconicism; *shorthand*, telegraphese, ellipsis; *condensation*, abridgement, summary, résumé.

adj. *concise*, succinct, brief, economical, short and sweet; *terse*, curt, monosyllabic, laconic, lapidary; *pithy*, epigrammatic, aphoristic, sententious; *compressed*, dense, compact, condensed, summarized; *crisp*, clipped, trenchant, incisive.

vb. *be concise*, come straight to the point, cut a long story short, not beat about the bush, cut the cackle (*colloq.*); *abbreviate*, contract, abridge, summarize; *compress*, condense, boil down, telescope.

adv. *in brief*, in a word, in a nutshell.

506 **DIFFUSENESS**
See also 530 (talkativeness).

n. *diffuseness*, wordiness, verbosity, long-windedness, prolixity; *discursiveness*, repetitiveness, filibustering, padding, waffle (*colloq.*); *digression*, excursus, disquisition, peroration, harangue, tirade; *pleonasm*, tautology, redundancy, circumlocution.

adj. *diffuse*, verbose, wordy, long-winded, prosy, prolix; *repetitive*, redundant, tautologous, pleonastic, circumlocutory, roundabout; *protracted*, lengthy, tedious, long-drawn-out; *discursive*, digressive, rambling, off the point.

vb. *be diffuse*, enlarge, expand, dilate, amplify, elaborate, expatiate; *draw out*, spin out, pad, protract, filibuster; *discourse*, hold forth, harangue, perorate; *digress*, wander, ramble, rabbit (*colloq.*), blather (*colloq.*), gush, waffle (*colloq.*).

adv. *at length*, ad nauseam, on and on.

507 **EMPHASIS**
n. *emphasis*, stress, reiteration, insistence, vehemence; *force*, strength, power, vigour, punch (*colloq.*); *vividness*, raciness, verve, sparkle; *incisiveness*, trenchancy, pointedness, bite, edge, mordancy; *conviction*, fervour, passion, eloquence, cogency; *grandiloquence*, solemnity, weight, gravitas.

adj. *emphatic*, reiterative, insistent, vehement; *forceful*, powerful, cogent, vigorous, strongly worded, hard-hitting, punchy (*colloq.*); *vivid*, lively, sparkling, graphic, racy; *incisive*, trenchant, pointed, biting, cutting, mordant; *passionate*, fervent, convincing, persuasive, eloquent, effective; *serious*, weighty, measured, solemn, grave; *grandiloquent*, inspired, lofty, sublime.

vb. *emphasize*, stress, insist on, reiterate, underline, underscore, spell out, ram home, say in no uncertain terms; *persuade*, convince, carry weight, hit home.

508 **LACK OF EMPHASIS**
n. *lack of emphasis*, insipidness, vapidness, flatness; *prosiness*, turgidity, stiltedness,

ponderousness; *dullness*, dryness, tediousness, jejuneness; *ineffectiveness*, feebleness, limpness, understatedness; *sentimentality*, mawkishness, schmaltz (*colloq.*).

adj. *unemphatic*, weak, insipid, colourless, flat; *prosy*, turgid, stilted, ponderous; *dull*, dry, thin, impoverished; *ineffective*, feeble, limp, understated; *prosaic*, pedestrian, clichéd, hackneyed, trite; *sentimental*, mawkish, novelettish, schmaltzy (*colloq.*), corny (*colloq.*).

509 **SIMPLICITY**
n. *simplicity*, straightforwardness, clarity, directness; *plainness*, naturalness, restraint, no frills, austerity, starkness, baldness; *unaffectedness*, unpretentiousness, homeliness, unsophistication, artlessness, naïvety; *frankness*, candour, matter-of-factness, downrightness, bluntness.

adj. *simple*, straightforward, direct, uncomplicated, easy; *plain*, unadorned, unvarnished, uncluttered, natural, homespun; *austere*, restrained, stark, bare, bald; *unpretentious*, unaffected, unassuming, down-to-earth, no-nonsense, matter-of-fact; *unsophisticated*, artless, naïve, innocent; *everyday*, workaday, homely, commonplace, humdrum.

vb. *speak plainly*, not mince one's words, spell it out, call a spade a spade, get down to brass tacks.

adv. *simply*, in plain English, in words of one syllable, not to put too fine a point on it.

510 **ORNAMENT**
See also 766 (decoration).

n. *ornament*, adornment, embellishment, enhancement; *ornamentation*, decoration, embroidery, frills, fuss, clutter; *ornateness*, preciousness, tweeness, floweriness, floridness, purple passage; *rhetoric*, bombast, fustian, pomposity, turgidity; *extravagance*, flamboyance, showiness, flashiness; *pretentiousness*, affectation, sententiousness, grandioseness.

adj. *ornate*, elaborate, rich, lavish; *decorative*, ornamental, architectural; *fussy*, frilly, cluttered, busy; *precious*, twee, flowery, florid; *extravagant*, flamboyant, showy, flashy; *rhetorical*, orotund, resonant, high-flown, grandiloquent; *inflated*, pompous, turgid, bombastic, pretentious, sententious.

vb. *decorate*, embellish, enhance,

embroider, sex up, lay it on with a shovel/ trowel (*colloq*.).

511 ELEGANCE

n. *elegance*, taste, style, refinement, beauty, gracefulness; *restraint*, simplicity, classicism, proportion; *symmetry*, balance, flow, rhythm, harmony, smoothness, ease; *poise*, decorum, distinction, stateliness, dignity; *correctness*, propriety, appropriateness, felicity; *stylishness*, sophistication, smartness, polish, flair.

adj. *elegant*, tasteful, stylish, beautiful, graceful, refined; *restrained*, simple, understated, classical, symmetrical; *harmonious*, balanced, well-proportioned, flowing, rhythmic, smooth; *felicitous*, appropriate, well-put, correct, proper; *distinguished*, stately, dignified, poised, decorous; *sophisticated*, smart, polished, soigné, well-groomed.

vb. *make elegant*, beautify, refine, polish, finish, smarten up.

512 INELEGANCE

n. *inelegance*, gracelessness, ugliness, unsightliness, unshapeliness, lumpishness; *gaucheness*, awkwardness, clumsiness, ungainliness, unwieldiness; *artificiality*, stiffness, stiltedness, woodenness; *tastelessness*, vulgarity, impropriety, incorrectness, inappropriateness; *crudeness*, boorishness, uncouthness, coarseness, yob culture.

adj. *inelegant*, graceless, gauche, awkward, clumsy, ungainly; *ugly*, unsightly, unshapely, lumpy; *artificial*, forced, contrived, laboured, stiff, stilted, wooden; *inappropriate*, infelicitous, jarring, grating, incorrect, improper; *tasteless*, vulgar, unrefined, common; *crude*, coarse, boorish, uncouth.

513 WRITING

See also 495 (letter); 515 (correspondence).

n. *writing*, composition, authorship, journalism, hackwork, Grub Street; *correspondence*, paperwork, documentation, bumf (*colloq*.), notes; *written matter*, script, copy, manuscript, typescript, transcript, minutes; *caption*, heading, legend, epigraph, inscription, rubric; *handwriting*, longhand, scribble, scrawl, cacography; *shorthand*, stenography, speedwriting, typewriting; *calligraphy*, penmanship, copperplate, pothook, flourish; *alphabet*, braille, code, cipher, hieroglyphics, pictogram, ideogram,

cryptogram; *stationery*, vellum, parchment, papyrus, scroll.

adj. *written*, graphic, handwritten, manuscript, autograph, holograph; *italic*, roman, cursive, uncial; *bold*, round, flowing, spidery, cramped, crabbed.

vb. *write*, pen, trace, print, type, scribble, scrawl; *compose*, draft, put into writing, set down in black and white, put pen to paper; *copy*, transcribe, take down, jot, note, minute.

514 PRINT

n. *print*, type, newsprint, copy, text, printout; *publication*, impression, edition, offprint, reprint, print run; *printing*, lithography, offset, letterpress; *typesetting*, filmsetting, photocomposition, cold type, Monotype (*tdmk*), Linotype (*tdmk*), hot metal; *typography*, typeface, fount, upper/lower case, boldface, lightface, serif, sanserif; *page*, folio, proof, galley (proof), page proof, revise, bromide; *printer's error*, correction, literal, typo; *printer*, typesetter, compositor, proofreader, copy editor, subeditor.

adj. *printed*, typographic, typeset, in/out of print.

vb. *print*, print off, run off, publish; *typeset*, photocompose, filmset.

515 CORRESPONDENCE

See also 513 (writing).

n. *correspondence*, communication, exchange, acknowledgement, reply, answer; *post*, mail, letters, mailbag, postbag, delivery, dispatch, mailing list, mailshot; *letter*, epistle, missive, circular, chain letter, round robin, junk mail (*colloq*.); *greetings card*, postcard, love letter, Valentine, billet doux, hate mail, poison-pen letter; *correspondent*, addressee, sender, recipient, penfriend, penpal; *envelope*, s.a.e., cover, stamp, seal, postcode.

adj. *epistolary*, postal, air-mail.

vb. *correspond*, write, communicate, acknowledge, reply, drop sb *a* line/note (*colloq*.); *post*, forward, mail, send; *address*, stamp, frank, seal.

516 BOOK

See also 518 (literature).

n. *book*, volume, tome, manuscript, MS, title; *bestseller*, blockbuster (*colloq*.), page-turner (*colloq*.), classic, magnum opus, potboiler, remainder; *publication*, edition, impression, reprint, reissue; *text*, libretto, screenplay, scenario, lyrics; *library*, set, collection, anthology, series, compendium, annual; *booklet*, pamphlet, leaflet, tract, brochure, prospectus; *bibliography*, catalogue, reading list, index; *cover*, dust jacket, binding, spine, boards; *page*, recto, verso, flyleaf, endpaper, frontispiece, appendix; *reader*, bookworm, bibliophile, librarian, bookseller, publisher; publishing, desktop publishing, electronic publishing, e-book.

adj. *hardback*, cased, softback, bound, looseleaf, paperback.

517 **DESCRIPTION**
See also 488 (representation).

n. *description*, account, exposition, delineation, portrayal, profile; *narration*, report, recital, tale, anecdote; *non-fiction*, reportage, documentary, biography, travelogue; *story*, narrative, plot, subplot, scenario, storyline; *history*, chronicle, annals, memoirs, case history, life story; *summary*, thumbnail sketch, cameo, vignette; *narrator*, story-teller, raconteur, historian, chronicler.

adj. *descriptive*, expository, narrative, graphic; *colourful*, vivid, scenic, picturesque; *true-to-life*, naturalistic, realistic, photographic; *expressive*, evocative, suggestive, impressionistic.

vb. *describe*, depict, delineate, characterize, represent; *draw*, paint, sketch, outline; *narrate*, recount, relate, tell, report, chronicle.

518 **LITERATURE**
See also 472 (communications); 516 (book); 521 (poetry); 522 (prose).

n. *literature*, prose, poetry, drama; *criticism*, lit crit; *novel*, classic, short story, novella, novelization; *non-fiction*, autobiography, diary, biography, memoirs; *fiction*, romance, love story, science fiction, sci-fi, detective story, thriller, whodunnit (*colloq.*), western, historical novel, bodice-ripper (*colloq.*), family saga, gothic novel, ghost story, chick lit, lad lit; *pulp fiction*, trash, pap, novelette, penny dreadful; *bestseller*, blockbuster (*colloq.*), page-turner (*colloq.*), classic, potboiler, instant book; *writer*, author, dramatist, poet, novelist, litterateur, ghostwriter, wordsmith.

adj. *literary*, poetic, epic, heroic, mock-heroic, picaresque; *fictional*, romantic, cloak-and-dagger.

vb. *write*, author, compose, ghostwrite, compile, edit; *fictionalize*, dramatize, novelize, adapt.

519 **DISSERTATION**
n. *dissertation*, discourse, essay, treatise, thesis, monograph, paper; *exposition*, disquisition, examination, enquiry, survey, study, commentary, analysis, critique; *review*, notice, article, piece, write-up, editorial, leader.

adj. *discursive*, expository, critical, analytical.

vb. *dissertate*, treat, handle, discuss, examine; *develop*, amplify, go into, expatiate on, discourse on; *criticize*, comment, review, survey, write up.

520 **SUMMARY**
See also 505 (conciseness).

n. *summary*, résumé, précis, abstract, synopsis; *contents*, substance, gist, the long and short of it; *outline*, sketch, rundown, digest; *selection*, condensation, anthology, compilation, miscellany.

adj. *summarized*, abridged, condensed, potted; *concise*, brief, succinct, sketchy.

vb. *summarize*, sum up, précis, abstract; *condense*, conflate, abridge, boil down.

521 **POETRY**
See also 518 (literature).

n. *poetry*, poesy, verse, rhyme, alliteration, assonance; *poem*, verses, lines, epic, ode, hymn, elegy, lay; *light verse*, ballad, jingle, doggerel, limerick, clerihew, ditty; *verse form*, sonnet, haiku, couplet, triplet, quatrain, sestina, stanza, blank verse; *prosody*, versification, scansion, metrics; *metre*, foot, accent, beat, stress, rhythm, cadence; *poet*, bard, poet laureate, versifier, poetaster, rhymester, troubadour, minstrel.

adj. *poetic*, lyric, rhapsodic, epic, bardic, heroic, elegiac; *metrical*, prosodic, rhythmical, accented.

vb. *versify*, compose, scan, rhyme, elegize.

522 **PROSE**
See also 518 (literature).

n. *prose*, writing, running text, chapter, paragraph; *non-fiction*, history, biography, memoirs, reportage; *fiction*, novel, short story, essay, prose poem, stream of consciousness; *prosaicness*, plainness, prosiness, dullness, matter-of-factness; *speech*, address, talk, discourse, anecdote.

adj. *prosaic*, prosy, pedestrian, dull; *unaccented*, flat, unrelieved, uninspired; *historical*, factual, biographical.

523 **DRAMA**

n. *drama*, play, production, revival, spectacle, vehicle; *tragedy*, comedy, farce, melodrama, pantomime, revue, skit; *vaudeville*, music hall, variety, musical comedy, cabaret, floor show; *theatre*, stage, footlights, the West End, Broadway, theatreland, show business; *premiere*, opening night, preview, first night, sell-out, smash hit; *performance*, act, turn, role, part, bit/walk-on part, cameo, audition, rehearsal; *theatricals*, mime, charade, masque, dumb show; *stage directions*, exit, entrance, cue, prompt; *prologue*, epilogue, finale, final curtain, encore; *scenery*, set, props, costume, wardrobe, grease paint, make-up; *auditorium*, front of house, proscenium, apron, wings, flies, theatre-in-the-round; *balcony*, stalls, circle, the gods (*colloq.*), stage door; *actor*, actress, leading lady/man, understudy, extra, trouper, thespian, entertainer, performer; *theatricality*, histrionics, staginess, ham (*colloq.*); *cast*, dramatis personae, company, troupe, chorus line.

adj. *dramatic*, theatrical, histrionic, stagy; *tragic*, straight, legitimate, melodramatic, blood-and-thunder, kitchen-sink; *comic*, farcical, burlesque, slapstick, knockabout (*colloq.*).

vb. *dramatize*, stage, present, put on, produce, direct; *perform*, play, act, enact, mime, tread the boards, go on stage, audition, rehearse; *overact*, play to the gallery, ham it up (*colloq.*), upstage, steal the limelight; *underact*, miss one's cue, fluff one's lines, dry (*colloq.*), corpse (*colloq.*), ad-lib.

524 **DANCE**

n. *dance*, ballet, tap dance, modern dance, folk dance, morris dance, barn dance, square dance, war dance; *choreography*, solo, pirouette, pas de deux, set; *minuet*, gavotte, mazurka, polka, polonaise; *ballroom dancing*, old-time dancing, waltz, foxtrot, quickstep, tango, bossa nova, rumba, cha-cha, samba, conga, lambada, macarena, salsa, cerok, flamenco, bolero, fandango, cancan; *country dance*, jig, reel, hornpipe, strathspey, sword dance, Highland dancing, Highland fling, Irish dancing; *rock 'n' roll*, twist, jive, disco, Charleston, black bottom, boogie (*colloq.*); *line dancing*, belly dancing, break-dancing, gogo dancing, lap dancing, pole dancing, exotic dancing; *ball*, hop, thé dansant, knees-up (*colloq.*); *dancer*, chorus girl, hoofer (*colloq.*), (prima) ballerina, corps de ballet.

adj. *balletic*, graceful, stately, rhythmic, lively.

vb. *dance*, take the floor, shuffle, trip the light fantastic; *leap*, skip, spin, pirouette, cavort, cut a caper; *twist*, jive, bop (*colloq.*), disco, stomp (*colloq.*), jitterbug (*colloq.*), boogie (*colloq.*).

525 **CINEMA**

See also 491 (photography).

n. *cinema*, motion pictures, celluloid, silver/big screen, Hollywood, Bollywood; *cinematography*, montage, soundtrack, sound effects, Technicolor (*tdmk*), Cinerama (*tdmk*), CinemaScope (*tdmk*), Panavision (*tdmk*), IMAX (*tdmk*); *credits*, titles; *camerawork*, shot, still, tracking shot, special effects, close-up, fade-out, freeze-frame; *script*, screenplay, scenario, shooting script, continuity; *film*, movie, remake, silent, talkie, newsreel, trailer, short, feature film, epic, blockbuster (*colloq.*), B-movie, western, horse opera, spaghetti western, musical, biopic, horror film, video nasty, road movie, buddy movie, chick flick, blue film/movie, skinflick (*colloq.*), weepie (*colloq.*), tearjerker (*colloq.*); *cartoon*, animation, computer animation, anime, hentai; *studio*, set; *picture house*, picture palace, multiplex, arthouse, fleapit (*colloq.*), box office; *director*, star, co-star, screen idol, starlet, stand-in, body double, stunt double, stuntman/-woman.

adj. *cinematic*, cinematographic, photogenic, star-studded, bankable.

vb. *film*, shoot, roll, pan, track; *show*, project, screen, release; *script*, edit, produce, direct, cast, bankroll (*colloq.*).

526 **VOICE**

See also 353 (sound); 528 (speech).

n. *voice*, speech, utterance, tongue, exclamation, ejaculation; *articulation*, enunciation, delivery, pronunciation, elocution; *intonation*, modulation, inflection, pitch, tone, timbre; *accent*, burr, twang, drawl, lisp; *loud voice*, roar, shout, bellow, yell; *soft voice*, murmur, whisper, hiss.

adj. *vocal*, oral, phonetic, vocalic; *distinct*, aloud, clear, bell-like, fluting, sing-song; *loud*, shrill, strident, booming.

vb. *voice*, speak, utter, verbalize, vocalize, give voice/tongue, exclaim, ejaculate; *articulate*, enunciate, pronounce, elocute; *modulate*, inflect, intone, drone, drawl; *flute*, carol, warble, trill; *raise one's voice*, speak up, shout, boom, roar, bellow; *lower* one's *voice*, pipe down (*colloq.*), whisper, breathe, hiss.

527 **VOICELESSNESS**

See also 354 (silence); 531 (taciturnity).

n. *voicelessness*, silence, muteness, dumbness, speechlessness, inarticulacy; *hoarseness*, huskiness, gruffness, croakiness, breathiness, wheeziness.

adj. *voiceless*, speechless, silent, mute, dumb; *inarticulate*, tongue-tied, dumbstruck, taciturn, mum; *hoarse*, husky, cracked, croaky, breathy, wheezy.

vb. *lose* one's *voice*, be mute, be struck dumb, be at a loss for words; *say nothing*, hold one's tongue (*colloq.*), shut up (*colloq.*), stick in one's throat, choke on; *silence*, gag, muffle, stifle, cut short, break in on.

528 **SPEECH**

See also 526 (voice); 532 (address).

n. *speech*, language, utterance, tongue, word of mouth; *articulacy*, fluency, eloquence, a way with words, the gift of the gab (*colloq.*); *discourse*, talk, conversation, dialogue, monologue, spiel, patter (*colloq.*); *rhetoric*, public speaking, oration, peroration, declamation, earful (*colloq.*); *comment*, remark, observation, aside, a word in edgeways; *speaker*, talker, lecturer, orator, spokesman/-person/-woman, mouthpiece.

adj. *spoken*, oral, verbal, vocal; *articulate*, fluent, eloquent, bilingual, polyglot; *rhetorical*, oratorical, declamatory, tub-thumping.

vb. *speak*, vocalize, voice, utter, say, articulate, verbalize; *speak up*, break one's silence, pipe up, find one's tongue, open one's mouth; *declare*, declaim, speak out, sound off, say one's piece, have one's say; *lecture*, orate, sermonize, pontificate, speechify, spout; *dictate*, trot out, reel off, recite.

529 **SPEECH DEFECT**

n. *speech defect*, aphasia, speech impediment, stammer, stutter, lisp, cleft palate; *inarticulacy*, indistinctness, mumbling, slur, drawl, twang; elocution, speech therapy.

adj. *inarticulate*, indistinct, thick, slurred; *nasal*, adenoidal, twangy, sibilant.

vb. *speak badly*, stammer, stutter, falter, hem and haw, hesitate; *mutter*, mumble, swallow one's words, gabble; *slur*, drawl, lisp, nasalize, speak with a plum in one's mouth.

530 **TALKATIVENESS**

See also 506 (diffuseness).

n. *talkativeness*, loquacity, garrulity, chattiness, fluency, volubility; *verbosity*, wordiness, prolixity, logorrhoea, verbal diarrhoea; *chatter*, prattle, jaw (*colloq.*), gossip, tittle-tattle, blather, gush, waffle (*colloq.*), gas (*colloq.*), hot air (*colloq.*); *chatterer*, chatterbox (*colloq.*), blatherskite (*colloq.*), windbag (*colloq.*), gasbag (*colloq.*).

adj. *talkative*, loquacious, voluble, garrulous; *verbose*, prolix, wordy, long-winded; *fluent*, glib, effusive, gushing, fulsome; *chatty*, gossipy, gabby (*colloq.*), gassy (*colloq.*).

vb. *be talkative*, chatter, prattle, run on, talk nineteen to the dozen, talk the hind leg(s) off a donkey, rabbit on (*colloq.*), yak (*colloq.*); *jabber*, gabble, prate, blather, yap (*colloq.*); *digress*, ramble, wander, maunder, go on and on, drone on, harp on, bang on, monopolize/hog the conversation; *expatiate*, sound off, spout (*colloq.*), outtalk, filibuster.

531 **TACITURNITY**

n. *taciturnity*, muteness, speechlessness, silence, quietness; *reserve*, reticence, uncommunicativeness, discretion; *curtness*, brusqueness, gruffness, terseness, laconism.

adj. *taciturn*, silent, mum, mute, speechless, tongue-tied; *reserved*, reticent, unforthcoming, uncommunicative, discreet, tight-lipped, close; *curt*, gruff, brusque, terse, laconic, monosyllabic.

vb. *be taciturn*, give nothing away, keep one's counsel, hold one's peace, hold one's tongue (*colloq.*), keep one's mouth shut, save one's breath, dry up, shut up (*colloq.*).

532 **ADDRESS**

See also 528 (speech).

n. *address*, apostrophe, aside, salutation, greeting; *speech*, public address, lecture, talk, oration, peroration, toast; *invocation*, appeal, interpellation, exhortation, pep talk (*colloq.*); *sermon*, homily, harangue, tirade; *addressee*, audience, captive audience, listener.

vb. *address*, apostrophize, greet, hail, salute, accost, buttonhole (*colloq.*); *orate*, perorate, speechify, pontificate; *invoke*, appeal, exhort, interpellate; *preach*, sermonize, harangue, lecture.

533 **CONVERSATION**

n. *conversation*, talk, dialogue, communication; *exchange*, banter, badinage, repartee, slanging match (*colloq.*); *chat*, tête à tête, heart-to-heart, natter (*colloq.*), confab (*colloq.*), chinwag (*colloq.*); *gossip*, chitchat, tittle-tattle, small talk; *conference*, parley, colloquy, symposium, summit, convention, pow-wow (*colloq.*), chatroom; *consultation*, interview, audience; *discussion*, debate, talking shop (*colloq.*).

adj. *conversational*, chatty, newsy, forthcoming, communicative; *animated*, heated, quick-fire, ding-dong (*colloq.*).

vb. *converse*, talk, chat, pass the time of day, bandy words; *gossip*, tittle-tattle, natter (*colloq.*), chew the fat (*colloq.*); *confer*, parley, talk over, discuss, debate, go into a huddle.

534 **SOLILOQUY**

n. *soliloquy*, monologue, monody, aside, apostrophe; *solo*, one-man show, one-man band, one-hander.

vb. *soliloquize*, talk to oneself, think aloud, talk to a brick wall (*colloq.*), waste one's breath.

535 **WILL**

See also 537 (willingness); 539 (resolution).

n. *will*, volition, intention, purpose; *wish*, desire, inclination, preference, mind, disposition; *resolution*, determination, wilfulness, obstinacy; *will power*, assertiveness, self-control, self-determination, autonomy; *free will*, choice, option, discretion, free hand.

adj. *willing*, desirous, inclined, disposed, agreeable; *spontaneous*, unasked, unprompted, ready; *voluntary*, optional, discretionary, arbitrary; *autonomous*, independent, unconstrained, assertive, autocratic; *wilful*, self-willed, single-minded, determined; *intentional*, volitional, deliberate, willed, designed.

vb. *will*, wish, desire, want; *intend*, determine, purpose, plan; *be independent*, know one's own mind, be one's own man, go one's own way; *assert oneself*, impose one's will, have one's own way; *choose*, opt for, plump for, favour.

adv. *at will*, ad libitum, as one pleases; *willingly*, voluntarily, of one's own accord, off one's own bat.

536 **NECESSITY**

See also 547 (predetermination).

n. *necessity*, compulsion, obligation, Hobson's choice, no choice, no option, the only game/show in town (*colloq.*); *last resort*,

nuclear option; *determinism*, fatalism, force of circumstances, act of God; *inevitability*, unavoidability, destiny, fate, karma, lot; *prerequisite*, precondition, requirement, imperative, must, must-do (*colloq.*), must-have (*colloq.*), must-see (*colloq.*); *instinct*, compulsion, reflex, Pavlovian reaction, knee-jerk reaction/response.

adj. *necessary*, required, requisite, imperative, indispensable; *compulsory*, obligatory, binding, mandatory, unavoidable, inescapable; *inevitable*, inexorable, ineluctable, preordained, fateful; *involuntary*, automatic, instinctive, mechanical.

vb. *necessitate*, oblige, dictate, compel; *require*, demand, insist, stipulate; *have no alternative/option*, bow to fate, take it or leave it, make a virtue of necessity; *preordain*, destine, doom, predetermine.

537 **WILLINGNESS**

See also 535 (will).

n. *willingness*, readiness, promptness, alacrity, zeal, eagerness; *inclination*, disposition, tendency, propensity, penchant; *goodwill*, cooperation, collaboration, helpfulness, spontaneity; *consent*, compliance, acquiescence, receptiveness; *obedience*, docility, tractability, pliability.

adj. *willing*, agreeable, acquiescent, compliant; *cooperative*, helpful, spontaneous, voluntary, unprompted; *prompt*, ready, eager, keen, zealous, enthusiastic; *inclined*, favourable, amenable, receptive, game; *obedient*, submissive, tractable, docile, manageable.

vb. *be willing*, feel like, have a mind to, desire to, want to, like to, care to; *agree*, acquiesce, comply, consent; *cooperate*, collaborate, show willing, go along with, bend over backwards; *volunteer*, jump at, leap at, not hesitate.

adv. *willingly*, readily, gladly, voluntarily, with good grace, at the drop of a hat, like a shot.

538 **UNWILLINGNESS**

See also 542 (obstinacy); 630 (hindrance).

n. *unwillingness*, reluctance, disinclination, hesitation; *doubt*, scruple, qualm, reservation; *disagreement*, disfavour, objection, demurral; *aversion*, repugnance, dislike, avoidance; *recalcitrance*, refractoriness, obstinacy, sullenness, obstructiveness, bloody-mindedness, awkward squad; *indifference*, apathy, abstention, dissociation.

adj. *unwilling*, reluctant, disinclined, loath; *half-hearted*, begrudging, forced, lukewarm; *averse*, opposed, unfavourable, hostile; *uncooperative*, unhelpful, obstructive, sullen, bloody-minded, bolshie (*colloq*.); *recalcitrant*, refractory, obstinate, awkward, disaffected; *hesitant*, tentative, cautious, unenthusiastic; *indifferent*, apathetic, uninterested, past caring, negligent.

vb. *be unwilling*, force oneself, not have the heart to, not like to, stick at, jib, balk, dig in one's heels; *object*, demur, cavil, protest; *hesitate*, scruple, hold off, hang back, drag one's feet; *recoil*, fight shy of, duck, shirk, slack, not pull one's weight.

adv. *unwillingly*, with bad grace, with heavy heart, under protest.

539 **RESOLUTION**
See also 43 (adhesion); 535 (will).

n. *resolution*, determination, resolve, firmness; *tenacity*, perseverance, staunchness, constancy; *will power*, relentlessness, ruthlessness, iron will; *drive*, energy, vigour, forcefulness; *commitment*, single-mindedness, devotion, dedication; *fortitude*, character, backbone, moral fibre; *spirit*, mettle, pluck, guts (*colloq*.).

adj. *resolute*, resolved, determined, single-minded, intent, set, bent on; *tenacious*, persevering, staunch, firm; *forceful*, energetic, driving, strong-willed; *uncompromising*, committed, wholehearted, diehard; *ruthless*, grim, steely, implacable, indomitable; *intransigent*, inflexible, unbending, immovable, unshakable.

vb. *be resolute*, stand firm, stand one's ground, not budge, not give an inch; *resolve*, determine, make up one's mind, decide, will; *commit oneself*, set one's heart on, go all out for, not take no for an answer, put one's foot down (*colloq*.).

540 **PERSEVERANCE**
See also 43 (adhesion); 542 (obstinacy).

n. *perseverance*, persistence, tenacity, firmness; *steadfastness*, staunchness, constancy, dedication, devotion; *stamina*, staying power, patience, endurance; *tirelessness*, indefatigability, stalwartness, doggedness; *application*, assiduousness, sedulousness, diligence.

adj. *persevering*, persistent, tenacious, stubborn; *steadfast*, staunch, firm, stalwart,

doughty; *constant*, devoted, dedicated, unwavering; *patient*, long-suffering, dogged, plodding; *undaunted*, unflagging, unfailing, tireless, indefatigable; *assiduous*, sedulous, industrious, diligent.

vb. *persevere*, persist, keep on, keep at it, never say die; *hold out*, hang on, stick it out, stay the course; *plod*, slog, beaver (*colloq*.), plug away (*colloq*.), peg away (*colloq*.).

adv. *to the bitter end*, come hell or high water, through thick and thin, come what may.

541 **VACILLATION**
See also 44 (non-adhesion); 544 (caprice).

n. *vacillation*, irresolution, indecision, uncertainty; *hesitation*, doubt, half-heartedness, apathy; *weakness*, faint-heartedness, gutlessness, spinelessness; *capriciousness*, fickleness, inconstancy, unpredictability; *suggestibility*, impressionability, malleability, pliancy.

adj. *vacillating*, indecisive, hesitant, wavering, changeable; *irresolute*, unresolved, uncertain, undecided; *capricious*, unstable, unpredictable, inconstant, fickle; *weak*, spineless, weak-kneed, faint-hearted, pusillanimous; *suggestible*, impressionable, malleable, pliable; *apathetic*, lukewarm, tepid, unenthusiastic.

vb. *vacillate*, fluctuate, waver, seesaw, blow hot and cold, shilly-shally (*colloq*.), dither; *hesitate*, falter, be in two minds, have second thoughts, hem and haw.

542 **OBSTINACY**
See also 538 (unwillingness); 540 (perseverance).

n. *obstinacy*, determination, perseverance, doggedness; *stubbornness*, obduracy, mulishness, pig-headedness; *intransigence*, inflexibility, toughness, hard line; *intractability*, incorrigibility, sullenness, dourness; *perverseness*, contrariness, bloody-mindedness, cussedness (*colloq*.).

adj. *obstinate*, tenacious, persevering, dogged; *stubborn*, obdurate, self-willed, stiff-necked, pig-headed, mulish, dour; *intransigent*, tough, adamant, unyielding, inflexible, hard-line, immovable, unshakable; *dogmatic*, diehard, hidebound, opinionated, set in one's ways; *perverse*, contrary, cussed (*colloq*.), bloody-minded; *intractable*, incorrigible, headstrong, wilful, unmanageable.

vb. *be obstinate*, persevere, persist, stick to

one's guns; *resist*, hold out, dig in one's heels, put one's foot down, play hardball with (*US*).

adv. *over one's dead body* (*colloq.*), no way (*colloq.*), not on your life (*colloq.*).

543 EQUIVOCATION

n. *equivocation*, evasiveness, ambiguity, slipperiness, shiftiness; *uncertainty*, unpredictability, unreliability, untrustworthiness; *opportunism*, timeserving, hypocrisy, double-dealing; *infidelity*, disloyalty, treachery, perfidy; *defection*, desertion, apostasy, recantation; *reversal*, about-turn, U-turn, second thoughts, volte-face.

adj. *equivocal*, evasive, ambiguous, deceptive; *untrustworthy*, unreliable, shifty, slippery; *duplicitous*, hyocritical, two-faced, timeserving; *capricious*, fickle, changeable, mercurial; *disloyal*, disaffected, apostate.

vb. *equivocate*, face both ways, say one thing and mean another, run with the hare and hunt with the hounds, have it both ways; *change* one's *mind/tune*, get cold feet, back out; *recant*, retract, go back on one's word, backtrack, backpedal; *desert*, defect, cross the floor, change sides.

544 CAPRICE

See also 541 (vacillation).

n. *caprice*, whim, fancy, impulse, notion; *humour*, mood, fad, craze, nine days' wonder; *capriciousness*, whimsicality, changeability, inconstancy, instability; *unreliability*, unpredictability, inconsistency, arbitrariness.

adj. *capricious*, whimsical, fanciful, irrational; *temperamental*, moody, changeable, mercurial; *fickle*, unpredictable, inconstant, volatile; *erratic*, wayward, irresponsible, feckless.

vb. *be capricious*, chop and change, blow hot and cold, act on impulse, take it into one's head.

545 SELECTION

n. *selection*, choice, option, alternative, pick 'n' mix (*colloq.*); *selectiveness*, eclecticism, choosiness, discrimination; *preference*, predilection, fancy, pick, favourite; *discretion*, first refusal, casting vote, veto; *vote*, ballot, poll, election, plebiscite, referendum.

adj. *selective*, eclectic, discriminating, fastidious, choosy (*colloq.*), particular; *optional*, discretionary, preferential, à la carte,

pick 'n' mix (*colloq.*); *select*, choice, hand-picked, recherché.

vb. *select*, choose, pick, opt for, plump, settle on; *prefer*, fancy, favour, earmark, single out, reserve, pre-select; *discriminate*, shop around, pick and choose, pick 'n' mix (*colloq.*), make up one's mind; *cull*, glean, sift, winnow, cream off.

546 REJECTION

n. *rejection*, dismissal, exclusion, veto; *disapproval*, dissatisfaction, fault-finding, captiousness; *refusal*, rebuff, disclaimer, denial, repudiation; *reject*, discard, seconds, cast-off; *undesirability*, unsuitability, ineligibility, inadmissibility.

adj. *rejected*, unwanted, discarded, excluded; *undesirable*, unsuitable, ineligible, inadmissible.

vb. *reject*, turn down, decline, pass over; *refuse*, spurn, disdain, look a gift horse in the mouth; *discard*, scrap, ditch, junk (*colloq.*), throw out; *deny*, rebuff, repudiate, disown, disclaim; *dismiss*, rule out of court, give short shrift to, show sb the door; *exclude*, veto, blackball, cold-shoulder, give sb the brush-off (*colloq.*).

547 PREDETERMINATION

See also 536 (necessity); 559 (preparation).

n. *predetermination*, preordination, predestination, necessity; *preparation*, premeditation, prearrangement, rehearsal, forward planning; *agenda*, plan, order of the day, timetable, schedule; *foregone conclusion*, fix (*colloq.*), dead cert (*colloq.*), put-up job, frame-up (*colloq.*).

adj. *predetermined*, foreordained, premeditated, prearranged; *planned*, deliberate, preconceived, intentional, appointed.

vb. *predetermine*, predestine, foreordain, appoint; *premeditate*, preconceive, prepare, prearrange; *plan*, rehearse, schedule, timetable; *rig*, engineer, stage-manage, fix (*colloq.*).

548 IMPROVISATION

See also 560 (lack of preparation).

n. *improvisation*, extemporization, ad-libbing, makeshift; *spontaneity*, impetuosity, impulsiveness, instinctiveness; *reflex*, impulse, snap decision, flash of inspiration, brainwave (*colloq.*).

adj. *improvised*, extempore, impromptu, makeshift, ad hoc; *spontaneous*, impulsive,

impetuous, instinctive; *sudden*,
unpremeditated, involuntary, automatic,
unthinking, knee-jerk.

vb. *improvise*, act on impulse, extemporize,
ad-lib, vamp, think on one's feet, play it by
ear, wing it (*colloq.*).

adv. *on the spur of the moment*, offhand, off
the cuff (*colloq.*), off the top of one's head
(*colloq.*).

549 **HABIT**
See also 71 (rule); 72 (conformity).

n. *habit*, disposition, custom, wont,
tendency, second nature; *familiarity*, force of
habit, routine, regularity, daily round,
groove, rut; *tradition*, precedent, orthodoxy,
convention, mores, practice, usage; *protocol*,
ritual, the done thing, received wisdom;
habituation, acclimatization, adjustment,
conditioning; *creature of habit*.

adj. *habitual*, customary, regular, wonted,
usual; *familiar*, conversant, known,
accustomed, commonplace; *traditional*,
orthodox, conventional, accepted; *long-
standing*, time-honoured, hallowed,
venerable; *ingrained*, deep-seated, deep-
rooted, dyed-in-the-wool, unreconstructed;
seasoned, practised, inured, hardened, set in
one's ways.

vb. *be in the habit of*, make a habit of, tend
to; *adjust to*, accustom oneself to, get used to,
get the hang/feel of; *habituate*, acclimatize,
naturalize, condition.

550 **UNACCUSTOMEDNESS**
n. *unaccustomedness*, unwontedness,
unfamiliarity, strangeness, novelty;
unconventionality, unorthodoxy,
nonconformity, irregularity; *neglect*, decay,
rustiness, disuse.

adj. *unaccustomed*, unused, unfamiliar,
novel, new; *unusual*, strange, odd, peculiar,
funny, funny peculiar; *irregular*, unwonted,
unprecedented; *unconventional*, unorthodox,
nonconformist, radical; *neglected*, disused,
rusty, decaying.

vb. *discontinue*, leave off, break with
tradition, break the mould, turn over a new
leaf; *wean*, cure, break the habit.

551 **PERSUASION**
See also 134 (motive); 139 (influence);
434 (belief).

n. *persuasion*, advertising, salesmanship,
spiel (*colloq.*), honeyed words; *inducement*,
incitement, pressure, pester power (*colloq.*),

carrot (*colloq.*); *persuadability*, credulity,
credulousness, gullibility, susceptibility;
temptation, bribery, enticement,
encouragement; *persuader*, salesman,
tempter; *pretext*, justification, plea, defence,
pretence, allegation; *conviction*, conversion;
submission, compliance; *concession*,
agreement.

adj. *persuasive*, convincing, seductive,
honey-tongued, plausible; *tempting*, enticing,
seductive; *persuadable*, credulous, gullible,
susceptible, easily swayed, submissive,
compliant.

vb. *persuade*, advertise, get sb to do sth;
goad, cajole, wheedle, bully into, egg on
(*colloq.*); *coerce*, push into, induce, brainwash,
twist round one's little finger (*colloq.*); *incite*,
stimulate, prick, prompt; *tempt*, bribe, entice,
encourage; *plead*, claim, pretend, allege;
convince, convert; *be persuaded*, succumb,
yield, submit, comply; *concede*, agree.

552 **DISSUASION**
n. *dissuasion*, discouragement, no
encouragement; *deterrence*, disincentive,
intimidation; *deterrent*, killjoy, wet blanket
(*colloq.*).

adj. *dissuasive*, discouraging; *deterrent*,
intimidating, daunting; *cautionary*.

vb. *dissuade*, discourage, talk out of, advise
against, put off, pour cold water on; *deter*,
deflect, intimidate, daunt; *caution/warn
against*.

553 **INTENTION**
See also 539 (resolution); 557 (plan);
755 (desire).

n. *intention*, intent, resolve, resolution,
determination, threat; *project*, plan, design,
calculation, meaning; *aim*, goal, objective,
target, end, mission statement; *destination*,
terminus, station, port, airport.

adj. *intent/hell-bent on*; intentional,
deliberate, voluntary, conscious.

vb. *intend*, resolve, decide, determine,
threaten, look; *plan*, project, purpose,
propose, undertake, mean, earmark; *aim*, go
for; *hope*, expect, aspire, reckon on, calculate;
consider, contemplate.

554 **CHANCE**
See also 135 (lack of motive).

n. *chance*, accident, fluke, coincidence,
luck, luck of the draw, fate, the way the
cookie crumbles (*colloq.*), toss-up (*colloq.*);

good luck, bad luck, fortune, misfortune; *risk*, hazard, speculation, flutter, pig in a poke; *gambling*, gamble, bet, wager, stake; *horse-/ greyhound-racing*, tote, football pools, fantasy football; *casino*, bingo, roulette, one-armed bandit; *lottery*, raffle, tombola, draw, premium bond; *stock exchange*, bear, bull, stag; *gambler*, speculator, punter, backer; *bookmaker*, bookie, turf accountant.

adj. *chance*, accidental, coincidental, lucky, fortuitous; *unintentional*, inadvertent, involuntary, unconscious; haphazard, random, happy-go-lucky; *risky*, hazardous, speculative, chancy.

vb. *gamble*, bet, wager, stake, game, punt, back; *risk*, hazard, speculate, have a flutter, run a risk, take risks, venture; *draw straws*, pick the short straw, spin a coin, toss for it.

adv. *by chance*, accidentally, coincidentally, as it happens, oddly enough; *on the off chance*.

555 **PURSUIT**
See also 414 (question); 761 (recreation).

n. *pursuit*, chase, hue and cry; *hunt*, stalk, trap, snare; *hunting*, fishing, hawking, falconry, ferreting, rabbiting, mousing; *steeplechase*, paper chase, hare and hounds, treasure hunt, geocaching, metal detecting; *search*, close search, fingertip search, frisking, prosecution; *enquiry*, investigation, research, *exploration*, excavation, dig, quest; *pursuer*, posse, tail; *searcher*, seeker, search party, explorer, researcher, investigator; *hunter*, huntsman, poacher, trapper, beater, stalker, tracker, fisherman, angler; *ratter*, rabbiter, mouser; *trawler*, drifter, whaler; *quarry*, prey; *fugitive*, escapee.

adj. *pursuant*, in pursuit, on one's tail; *searching*, exploratory, investigative.

vb. *pursue*, follow, chase, seek, search, quest, look for, be after; *enquire*, investigate, browse, surf (the Net); *forage*, rummage, ferret, leave no stone unturned, sniff out (*colloq.*); *explore*, excavate, dig; *hunt*, stalk, beat, trail, track, poach, shoot, fish, angle, trawl; *harry*, dog, shadow, tail, stalk.

556 **AVOIDANCE**
See also 605 (escape).

n. *avoidance*, sidestep, evasive action, dodge; *escape*, evasion; *forbearance*, moderation, abstinence; *refusal*, rejection, boycott; *non-participation*, non-involvement, non-cooperation; *avoider*, dodger, abstainer; *shirker*, idler, deserter, truant, coward. -

adj. *avoiding*, evasive, shy, reluctant, elusive; *forbearing*, abstemious; *uncooperative*, reluctant, unwilling, reticent, unforthcoming; *avoidable*, unavoidable, inescapable.

vb. *avoid*, sidestep, dodge; *escape*, evade; *prevent*, avert; *eschew*, shun, fight shy of, give a miss, not go near, leave, let alone; *steer clear of*, give a wide berth to, not touch with a barge pole (*colloq.*), not go there (*colloq.*); *refuse*, reject, black (*colloq.*); *forbear*, refrain, abstain, forswear, hold back, do without; *shirk*, duck, cop out (*colloq.*), chicken out (*colloq.*).

557 **PLAN**
See also 488 (representation).

n. *plan*, project, proposal, suggestion, scheme, intention; *programme*, layout, design, blueprint, outline, recipe, organization; *diagram*, pattern, model, map, sketch, cartography; *strategy*, approach, course of action, road map, agenda, schedule; *plot*, intrigue, conspiracy, (little) game (*colloq.*); *planner*, proposer, originator; *designer*, layout artist, map-maker, cartographer; *strategist*, plotter, conspirator.

adj. *planned*, projected, proposed; *schematic*, strategic; *plotting*, conspiratorial, scheming.

vb. *plan*, project, propose, suggest; *lay out*, draft, design, model, draw up, set out; *conceive*, hatch, dream up (*colloq.*); *organize*, schedule, approach, think ahead, orchestrate, engineer; *map*, sketch; *plot*, scheme, conspire, intrigue.

558 **REQUIREMENT**
See also 536 (necessity).

n. *requirement*, need, must, necessary, requisite; *necessity*, prerequisite, essential, sine qua non, stipulation; *want*, lack, demand, call for, shortage; *compulsion*, obligation.

adj. *required*, necessary, needed, indispensable; *essential*, vital; *wanted*, lacking, called for, in demand; *needy*, in need, deprived, destitute; *compulsory*, obligatory.

vb. *require*, need, stand in need of, necessitate, stipulate; *want*, lack, call for, feel the lack of; *compel*, oblige, must.

adv. *in need*, in want; *of necessity*, necessarily.

559 **PREPARATION**

See also 57 (arrangement);
547 (predetermination).

n. *preparation*, making ready, getting
ready, groundwork; *preliminaries*, tuning,
priming, loading, approach, run-up;
acclimatization, seasoning, hardening (off);
trial, trial run, pilot (scheme), practice,
rehearsal, dress rehearsal; *study*, prep,
homework; *arrangement*, prearrangement,
premeditation; *precaution*, provision,
allowance, nest egg; *provisioning*, provisions,
equipment; *preparedness*, readiness, fitness;
preparer, trainer, pioneer, trail-blazer,
répétiteur, coach.

adj. *preparatory*, precautionary,
preliminary, in preparation; *prepared*, ready
(and waiting), standing by, fit, rehearsed,
keyed up, primed, tuned, equipped, in
readiness; *acclimatized*, seasoned, weathered,
hardened (off); *ready-made*, off-the-peg,
cooked, processed, oven-ready, ready to eat,
instant.

vb. *prepare*, make ready, pave the way, lay
the foundations, blaze a trail, prepare the
ground, clear the decks, stand by, arrange
(for); *prime*, load, tune, warm up, soften
up, dig (over); *provide*, provision, equip, fit
out; *acclimatize*, season, weather, harden
(off); *rehearse*, practise, coach, train,
groom, do one's homework, study;
allow for, make provision for, put by (for a
rainy day).

560 **LACK OF PREPARATION**

See also 111 (youth); 451 (surprise);
548 (improvisation).

n. *lack of preparation*, unpreparedness,
unreadiness; *lack of rehearsal/training/practice*;
rush, haste; *improvisation*; *surprise*.

adj. *unprepared*, unready, caught unawares/
off one's guard, caught napping/on the hop
(*colloq.*), caught with one's pants/trousers
down (*colloq.*); *unrehearsed*, untrained,
unpractised; *rushed*, ill-equipped,
disorganized, half-baked; *improvised*,
impromptu, snap, extempore, extemporized,
ad hoc; *unseasoned*, not weathered, not
hardened (off); *raw*, uncooked.

vb. *be unprepared*, unready etc, not prepare,
plan, etc, live from day to day, cross that
bridge when one comes to it, make no
provision for; *improvise*, extemporize.

adv. *extempore*, off the cuff, off the top of
one's head (*colloq.*).

561 **ATTEMPT**

n. *attempt*, try, essay, bid; *endeavour*, effort; *go*
(*colloq.*), shot (*colloq.*), stab (*colloq.*), bash
(*colloq.*), jab (*colloq.*), crack (*colloq.*).

adj. *game*, venturesome, tenacious,
obstinate; *successful*, futile, desperate.

vb. *attempt*, try, essay, bid, seek; *endeavour*,
make an/the effort, lift a finger; *strain*,
struggle, strive, go all out, do one's best; *give
it/have a go/shot/stab/bash/jab/crack* (*colloq.*),
give it a whirl (*colloq.*).

562 **UNDERTAKING**

See also 61 (beginning); 683 (promise).

n. *undertaking*, enterprise, business, task,
job; *exercise*, operation, project, matter in
hand, concern, cause; *adventure*, quest, cause;
promise, contract, agreement, obligation,
commitment.

adj. *enterprising*, daring, adventurous,
venturesome; *contracted*, obliged, committed.

vb. *undertake*, go in for, tackle, address
oneself to; *take part in*, participate in, engage
in, busy oneself with; *embark on*, launch into,
take up, assume, take on (oneself), get
involved in, let oneself in for, get to grips
with, get one's teeth into (*colloq.*); *promise*,
contract, agree, commit oneself.

563 **RELINQUISHMENT**

See also 543 (equivocation); 696 (disposal).

n. *relinquishment*, giving up, abdication,
renunciation, abandonment, castaway;
departure, leaving, defection, desertion, walkout, secession, retirement; *surrender*, handing
over, ceding, cession, waiver.

adj. *relinquished*, abandoned, marooned,
cast off.

vb. *relinquish*, give up, abdicate, renounce,
forswear; *abandon*, maroon, cast away,
forsake, ditch (*colloq.*); *depart*, leave, quit,
defect, desert, withdraw, walk out, secede,
retire, drop out, unsubscribe; *surrender*, hand
over, cede, waive, forgo; *resign*, give in, drop,
chuck (*colloq.*).

564 **USE**

See also 566 (misuse); 578 (usefulness).

n. *use*, employment, utilization,
exploitation; *application*, appliance, exercise,
adoption, practice, usage; *consumption*, wear,
wear and tear; *usefulness*, applicability,
benefit, practicality, purpose, point,
pragmatism.

adj. *used*, in use, employed, utilized,
applied, accepted, adopted; *worn*, used up,

worn out, second-hand, 'nearly new'
(*colloq.*); *useful*, practical, pragmatic; *usable*,
available, disposable.

vb. *use*, employ, put to use, put into
service, utilize, make use of, avail oneself of,
resort to; *exploit*, harness, capitalize on, take
advantage of, cash in on (*colloq.*); *apply*,
exercise, practise, put into practice, adopt;
consume, expend, use up, wear, wear away/
down/out; *reuse*, recycle; *requisition*,
commandeer, deploy.

565 **NON-USE**
See also 62 (end); 563 (relinquishment);
579 (uselessness).

n. *non-use*, abeyance, unemployment;
discontinuance, disuse, withdrawal,
suspension, abolition; *rejection*,
abandonment, scrapping; *abstinence*,
avoidance; *store*, storage; *uselessness*.

adj. *unused*, unutilized, in abeyance, not in
use, out of order; *new*, brand new, pristine;
unemployed, resting, idle; *discontinued*,
withdrawn, suspended, abolished; *disused*,
derelict, neglected, laid up, left to rot, in
mothballs, mothballed; *extra*, spare, in hand,
in reserve, surplus, superfluous; *useless*,
impractical, pointless, senseless; *unusable*,
unavailable.

vb. *not use*, etc, avoid, do without;
discontinue, withdraw, suspend, abolish,
dispense with; *reject*, abandon, scrap, ditch,
drop, dump; *shelve*, lay/put aside, put in
mothballs, mothball, put on a back burner.

566 **MISUSE**
See also 564 (use); 572 (waste).

n. *misuse*, abuse, maltreatment,
mishandling, rough handling, malpractice,
misapplication; *perversion*, prostitution,
desecration; *wrong*, hurt; *overuse*,
extravagance; *waste*.

vb. *misuse*, abuse, maltreat, mishandle,
handle roughly, force, misapply; *pervert*,
prostitute, desecrate; *wrong*, hurt;
misappropriate, embezzle; *overuse*, overwork;
waste, squander.

567 **MEANS**
See also 136 (operation); 568 (tool);
569 (materials).

n. *means*, method, way, device, medium;
ability, knowledge, skill; *equipment*,
wherewithal, materiel, provisions, facilities,
tools, resources, channel; *money*, capital,
necessary, credit; *manpower*.

vb. *enable*, provide the means, equip,
resource; *finance*, back, raise the money; *be
able*, manage, find a way.

568 **TOOL**
See also 138 (instrumentality); 567 (means).

n. *tool*, implement, utensil, gadget,
instrument; *knife*, fork, spoon, tin-opener,
bottle-opener, corkscrew, nutcracker; *nail*,
hammer, screw, screwdriver; *drill*, bit, auger,
brace, punch; *pliers*, pincers, tweezers,
wrench, spanner, jemmy, crowbar, lever;
cutter, chisel, plane, spokeshave, saw, router;
machine, machinery, device, apparatus,
mechanism, appliance; *wheel*, pulley, handle,
block and tackle, clockwork, gears; *motor*,
engine, petrol/diesel engine, internal
combustion engine, steam engine, jet
engine, rocket motor; *generator*, dynamo,
turbine; *computer*, robot, calculator; *press*,
mill.

adj. *mechanical*, mechanized, automatic.

569 **MATERIALS**
See also 197 (interweaving); 202 (covering);
567 (means).

n. *materials*, raw materials, building
blocks; *mineral*, ore, sand, asbestos, clay,
stone, marble, flint, masonry; *metal*, iron,
gold, silver, copper, tin, nickel, lead, zinc;
alloy, (stainless) steel, brass, bronze,
gunmetal; *brick*, breeze block, glass, plaster,
plasterboard, cement, (reinforced) concrete,
mortar; *paving*, tarmac, asphalt, chippings,
gravel, cobbles, flagstones; *tile*, slate, thatch,
roofing felt; *wood*, timber, board, plank,
rafter, joist, lath, plywood, chipboard,
hardboard; *leather*, skin, hide; *paper*, rag,
esparto grass, pulp, (card)board, millboard,
pasteboard, strawboard, papier mâché; *bank*,
bond, wove, laid; *cartridge paper*, art paper,
(super)calendered paper, notepaper, carbon
paper; *tissue paper*, tracing paper, crepe paper,
newsprint; *plastic*, polythene, polystyrene,
Perspex, PVC (polyvinyl chloride), Celluloid,
Cellophane, fibreglass; *textile*, cloth, material,
fabric, stuff; *cotton*, calico, poplin, shirting,
towelling, terry, denim, gingham; *wool*,
jersey, cashmere, angora; *suiting*, tweed,
worsted, serge, mohair, felt, baize; *linen*,
lawn, cambric, holland; *silk*, satin, taffeta,
cheesecloth, chiffon, crêpe de chine, muslin,
voile; *velvet*, corduroy, cord, velour, twill,
flannelette; *nylon*, rayon, polyester,
polycotton, Crimplene, Terylene, Dacron;
chintz, damask, candlewick; *jute*, hessian,

sacking, ticking, sailcloth, canvas, tapestry, mull.

570 **STORE**
See also 66 (assembly); 75 (calculation); 472 (communication); 603 (preservation).

n. *store*, provision, stock, stock-in-trade, stockpile, backlog; *supply*, source, fount; *heap*, pile, load, mass, mound, collection, abundance, profusion, wine lake (*colloq.*), butter mountain (*colloq.*); *collection*, file, dictionary, thesaurus; *quarry*, mine, deposit, field, lode, vein, seam; *funds*, assets, reserves, nest egg, investment, holding; *horde*, treasure, cache; *bank*, account, deposit, savings, balance, credit, PEP, ISA; *dowry*, trousseau, bottom drawer; *storage*, warehousing, safekeeping; *warehouse*, stockroom, depot, garage, depository, repository, vault, magazine, arsenal; *battery*, accumulator; *cellar*, pantry, larder, storeroom, cupboard, loft, attic; *barn*, silo, granary, haystack, hayrick; *reservoir*, water tower, gasholder, gasometer, septic tank, cesspit; *refrigerator*, fridge, freezer; *trunk*, chest, safe; *computer*, microcomputer, microprocessor, word processor, desktop (computer), laptop, palmtop, notebook, notepad; *computing*, electronic data processing, EDP, information retrieval; *hardware*, keyboard, terminal, VDU (visual display unit), disk drive, tape-reader, CPU (central processing unit), printer, mouse; *software*, program, computer language, machine code/language, programming language, data, bit, byte, input, output, interface; *memory*, data base, data bank, punched cards, magnetic tape, (floppy) disk, disk pack, printout.

adj. *stored*, etc, in store; *in hand*, in reserve, in stock; *spare*.

vb. *store*, pile up, heap up, load up, stack (up); *store away*, put away, file (away), stash away (*colloq.*); *stock up*, stockpile, amass, accumulate, buy in, buy up, lay in, fuel (up); *save*, bank, invest, deposit; *save up*, hoard, squirrel away, put by for a rainy day; *garage*, warehouse, put in store; *lay up*, cocoon, put in mothballs, mothball; *preserve*, pickle, bottle, preserve, salt, dry, refrigerate, freeze; *keep in reserve/hand*, lay/put aside.

571 **PROVISION**
See also 453 (foresight); 559 (preparation); 685 (negotiation).

n. *provision*, supply, furnishing, delivery,

purveying, fitting out, provisioning, catering; *provisions*, food, rations, supplies, stores, reserves, equipment; *budget*, management; *maintenance*, alimony, assistance; *provider*, supplier, purveyor, caterer; *storekeeper*, butler, quartermaster, housekeeper, cook; *shopkeeper*, merchant, grocer; *lender*, manager, purser, bursar, steward.

adj. *provided*, supplied, furnished, catered, all found, available, well-equipped.

vb. *provide*, supply, furnish, deliver, procure, purvey, fit out, arm, provision, cater; *feed*, serve, afford, give; *maintain*, board, put up (*colloq.*); *budget*, make provision, stock up, manage.

572 **WASTE**
See also 566 (misuse); 727 (extravagance).

n. *waste*, profligacy, wastefulness; *extravagance*, overspending, unnecessary expense; *consumption*, wear, attrition, erosion, atrophy, exhaustion, depletion; *leakage*, loss, escape, pollution; *overproduction*, superfluity, excess, misuse; *rubbish*, scrap, waste product, effluent.

adj. *wasteful*, profligate, extravagant, unnecessary; *superfluous*, disposable; *wasted*, lost, exhausted, misspent, futile, down the drain (*colloq.*).

vb. *waste*, squander, throw away, blow (*colloq.*); *misuse*, overwork; *consume*, wear, erode, deplete, exhaust; *leak*, escape, dissipate, pollute; *come to nothing*, go down the drain (*colloq.*).

573 **SUFFICIENCY**
See also 29 (greatness); 49 (completeness); 738 (satisfaction).

n. *sufficiency*, adequacy, acceptability, competence; *enough*, (bare) minimum, right amount, pass mark, quorum, what is acceptable, breadline, subsistence; *plenty*, abundance, copiousness; *a lot*, lashings (*colloq.*), bags (*colloq.*), oodles (*colloq.*); *profusion*, riot, feast; *lushness*, luxuriance.

adj. *sufficient*, adequate, enough, minimal, quorate; *satisfactory*, acceptable, competent, just right; *plentiful*, plenteous, abundant, copious; *wealthy*, affluent, generous, liberal; *profuse*, lush, luxuriant.

vb. *suffice*, be sufficient/enough; *satisfy*, fill the bill, do, pass muster, qualify; *be plentiful*, abound, swarm, proliferate; *teem/bristle with*, crawl with (*colloq.*).

574 **INSUFFICIENCY**

See also 50 (incompleteness); 273 (shortfall); 739 (dissatisfaction).

n. *insufficiency*, inadequacy, incompetence; failure; *not enough*, too little, too few, lack; *deficit*, shortfall, insufficient funds; *poverty*, need, starvation diet; *famine*, starvation, drought; *scarcity*, dearth, shortfall.

adj. *insufficient*, inadequate, not enough, too little, too few; *unsatisfactory*, unacceptable, incompetent; *poor*, disadvantaged, underprivileged, on supplementary benefit; *scarce*, in short supply, rare; *lacking*, deficient, light on (*colloq.*), thin, scant; *miserly*, mingy.

vb. *not suffice* etc, be insufficient etc, fall short, not come up to; *fail*, lack, want, require.

575 **EXCESS**

See also 272 (overstepping); 727 (extravagance); 844 (self-indulgence).

n. *excess*, too many, too much, overabundance, enough and to spare, mountain; *redundance*, redundancy, superfluity, glut, plethora, duplication, overkill; *flood*, inundation, saturation, congestion; *extra*, add-on, bonus, spare, surplus, balance; *overdoing it*, officiousness, ostentation, extravagance, obtrusiveness; *overindulgence*, too much of a good thing, overdose, overeating, binge-eating, binge-drinking; *fat*, obesity, flab (*colloq.*), cellulite; *satiety*, engorgement, surfeit.

adj. *excessive*, too many, too much, overmuch, inordinate; *redundant*, superfluous, unnecessary; *flooded*, overflowing, saturated, stuffed, overloaded; *extra*, spare, surplus; *officious*, ostentatious, extravagant, exorbitant, over the top (*colloq.*); *fat*, obese; *satiated*, sated, jaded, gorged.

vb. *be excessive* etc, overstep, overdo it, go over the top (*colloq.*); *flood*, saturate, overflow; *overindulge*, overeat; *duplicate*, go begging; *satiate*, sate, jade, pall, gorge.

576 **IMPORTANCE**

See also 5 (essence); 31 (superiority); 774 (repute).

n. *importance*, significance, consequence; *substance*, matter, consideration, weight, value, moment, import, big deal (*colloq.*); *seriousness*, solemnity, gravity, no laughing matter; *prominence*, eminence; *the heart of the matter*, cornerstone, linchpin, the be-all and end-all; *urgency*, priority, emergency, matter of life and death; *VIP*, notable, personality, personage, magnate, tycoon, big gun (*colloq.*), bigwig (*colloq.*), big noise (*colloq.*).

adj. *important*, significant, big; *substantial*, considerable, weighty, urgent, momentous, eventful, earth-shattering; *serious*, solemn, grave; *leading*, notable, foremost, conspicuous; *central*, chief, basic, essential, major, main, fundamental, primary, principal; *influential*, formidable, illustrious, powerful; *exceptional*, imposing, outstanding, eminent, august, distinguished; *famous*, prominent, well-known.

vb. *be important* etc, matter, count, carry weight, deserve attention; *make important*, promote, put on a pedestal; *stress*, underline, highlight, emphasize; *glorify*, honour, value, think a lot of, celebrate.

577 **UNIMPORTANCE**

See also 32 (inferiority); 187 (shallowness); 780 (humility).

n. *unimportance*, insignificance, triviality, frivolity, pettiness; *irrelevance*, immateriality, red herring; *the little man*, nonentity, figurehead, pawn, second fiddle; *trifle*, storm in a teacup, nothing to speak/write home about, technicality, small beer, pinprick.

adj. *unimportant*, ordinary, insignificant, inconsequential; *little*, negligible, wretched, paltry, measly (*colloq.*); *irrelevant*, immaterial, obscure, contemptible; *inessential*, unnecessary, fringe, peripheral.

vb. *be unimportant* etc, not matter, not count, cut no ice, play second fiddle; *make light of*, think unimportant, play down.

578 **USEFULNESS**

See also 152 (fertility); 564 (use); 580 (convenience).

n. *usefulness*, utility, handiness, practicality; *adaptability*, suitability, applicability, efficacy; *convenience*, serviceability, availability, helpfulness; *value*, worth, advantage, profitability, productivity, mileage (*colloq.*).

adj. *useful*, handy, practical, functional; *adaptable*, suitable, applicable, efficacious, effective; *convenient*, multi-purpose, versatile, serviceable, available, helpful; *valuable*, invaluable, worthwhile, profitable, productive, economic; *pragmatic*.

vb. *be useful* etc, be of use, come in handy (*colloq.*); *function*, work, serve, help.

579 USELESSNESS

See also 153 (infertility); 565 (non-use); 581 (inconvenience).

n. *uselessness*, inutility; *unsuitability*, inefficacy, inadequacy, inconvenience, unavailability; *pointlessness*, futility, disadvantage, waste of time, wild-goose chase; *worthlessness*, waste, rubbish, dead duck.

adj. *useless*, unusable, unpractical; *unadaptable*, unsuitable, unemployable; *inconvenient*, unserviceable, unavailable, unhelpful, out of order, broken down; *pointless*, futile, vain; *worthless*, good-for-nothing, unprofitable, unrewarding; *ineffectual*, feckless.

vb. *be useless* etc, not work, not function, not help, come to nothing; *flog a dead horse*, tilt at windmills; *make useless* etc, sabotage, cripple, disable, spike.

580 CONVENIENCE

See also 115 (timeliness); 578 (usefulness); 629 (easiness).

n. *convenience*, ease, ease of use, easiness, facilitation, straightforwardness; *accessibility*, ease of access, closeness; *suitability*, pragmatism, expediency; *opportunism*, timeserving, utilitarianism, profit, advantage; *opportunity*, spare time, leisure; *freedom*, comfort, service, speed.

adj. *convenient*, easy to use, user-friendly; *accessible*, close, nearby, easy to reach, get-at-able (*colloq.*); *practical*, suitable, workable, pragmatic; *auspicious*, opportune, profitable, advantageous; *opportunist*, timeserving, utilitarian; *comfortable*, fast.

vb. *be convenient* etc, not clash, suit, do work, fit; *benefit*, help, pay; *fit in with*, accommodate, oblige.

581 INCONVENIENCE

See also 116 (untimeliness); 579 (uselessness); 628 (difficulty).

n. *inconvenience*, difficulty, hindrance, drawback, handicap; *unsuitability*, previous engagement, awkwardness, unpleasantness; *discomfort*, disadvantage, inadvisability.

adj. *inconvenient*, difficult to use, cumbersome, unwieldy; *unsuitable*, unsatisfactory, inappropriate, awkward, unhappy; *inopportune*, untimely; *inadvisable*, disadvantageous, inexpedient.

vb. *be inconvenient* etc, not do, not work, not help, not benefit; *inconvenience*, put out, incommode, bother, disrupt.

582 WORTH

See also 721 (price); 584 (perfection); 837 (virtue).

n. *worth*, goodness, excellence, greatness, quality, merit, virtue; *good quality*, redeeming feature, good point, saving grace; *value*, price; *pick*, elite, elect, chosen few, cream, crème de la crème; *superman*, superwoman, genius, ace, champion, paragon, the cat's pyjamas/whiskers (*colloq.*), the bee's knees (*colloq.*); *masterpiece*, plum, pièce de résistance, flagship; *hit*, knockout, blockbuster, the best thing since sliced bread (*colloq.*); *classic*, all-time great.

adj. *good*, excellent, outstanding, fine, great, mean (*colloq.*), quality; *worthy*, commendable, creditable, admirable, praiseworthy; *choice*, handpicked, select; *superb*, wonderful, magnificent, fantastic, fabulous, glorious, marvellous, splendid, terrific, top-notch (*colloq.*); *super*, brill (*colloq.*), magic (*colloq.*), ace (*colloq.*), out of this world; *best*, prime, premium, A-1, first-class, blue-chip, supreme; *classic*, vintage; *wholesome*, healthy, sound; *valuable*, priceless, good value; *not bad*, passable, tolerable, satisfactory, decent, acceptable, OK.

vb. *have value*, be worth it, rate, count; *do good*, improve, enhance, benefit.

583 WORTHLESSNESS

See also 32 (inferiority); 604 (harm).

n. *worthlessness*, poor/low quality, shoddiness, mediocrity; *unworthiness*, wickedness, baseness, vileness, nastiness; *corruption*, depravity, obscenity, indecency, vulgarity.

adj. *worthless*, poor-/low-quality, second-rate, mediocre, indifferent, poor man's; *shoddy*, low-grade, cheap, tacky, cheap and nasty, trashy; *lousy* (*colloq.*), rotten (*colloq.*), crummy (*colloq.*), ropy (*colloq.*); *awful*, dreadful, ghastly, wretched, horrid, horrible, terrible, beastly, grotty (*colloq.*); *wicked*, evil, base, vile, nasty, mean, shabby, vicious, villainous; *corrupt*, depraved, obscene, indecent, vulgar, sordid; *unworthy*, despicable, disgraceful, shameful, deplorable.

vb. *make worthless*, devalue, debase, cheapen, degrade; *do no good*, make things worse, be of no value.

584 PERFECTION

See also 49 (completeness); 188 (summit); 582 (worth); 653 (completion).

n. *perfection*, faultlessness, flawlessness,

impeccability; *correctness*, irreproachability, infallibility, integrity; *ideal*, sanspareil, paragon, model; *summit*, height, acme, peak; *example*, standard, pattern, showpiece.

adj. *perfect*, picture perfect, ideal, faultless, flawless, impeccable; *unbeatable*, unrivalled, beyond compare, matchless, peerless, supreme; *correct*, irreproachable, infallible; *immaculate*, pristine, spotless, stainless; *unsullied*, lilywhite; *pure*, unadulterated, -free, whole, entire, complete, one hundred per cent, sound.

vb. *perfect*, hone, polish, refine; *consummate*, crown, cap, seal, round off.

585 IMPERFECTION
See also 50 (incompleteness); 767 (blemish).

n. *imperfection*, faultiness, unsoundness; *immaturity*, underdevelopment, incompleteness, inadequacy, deficiency; *deformity*, disfigurement, discoloration, distortion, damage; *unevenness*, patchiness; *flaw*, fault, mistake, failing, defect, shortfall; *catch*, snag, drawback; *blemish*, mark, chip, crack, scratch, impurity.

adj. *imperfect*, faulty, unsound, flawed, defective; *immature*, underdeveloped, incomplete, inadequate, deficient, missing; *deformed*, disfigured, discoloured, distorted, damaged; *uneven*, patchy; *fair*, middling, could do better (*colloq.*); *blemished*, impure, marked, chipped, cracked, scratched, shop-soiled.

vb. *fall short*, not make the grade, be found wanting; *flaw*, mar, spoil.

586 CLEANNESS
See also 39 (purity); 590 (hygiene); 850 (morality).

n. *cleanness*, spotlessness, whiteness, shine, polish; *cleaning* (up), cleansing, washing (down/off/out/up), wiping (down/off/up), mopping up, scouring, scrubbing; *a clean*, brush, sweep, dust, wipe, wash, polish, scrub; *purge*, flush, dialysis, purification, filtration; *decontamination*, sterilization, delousing; *hygiene*, sanitation; *bath* (tub), public baths, shower, sauna, Turkish bath, Jacuzzi (*tdmk*), (wash)basin, bidet; *washing machine*, launderette, laundry, dishwasher; *soap* (flakes), shampoo, toothpaste, pumice (stone); *washing powder*, detergent, biological powder; *disinfectant*, bleach, antiseptic, cleanser; *polish*, shoe polish, wax, whitewash, blacking, blanco; *brush*, scrubbing brush, toothbrush, nailbrush, broom, mop, sponge,

duster; *vacuum cleaner*, Hoover (*tdmk*), filter, mat; *cleaner*, washerwoman, launderer, char(lady), roadsweeper, dustman.

adj. *clean*, spotless, fresh, shiny, polished, neat, tidy; *sterile*, aseptic, antiseptic; *hygienic*, sanitary, disinfectant, detergent.

vb. *clean*, freshen, whiten, shine, polish; *cleanse*, wash (down/off/out/up), wipe (down/off/up), rinse, sluice, mop up, scour, scrub, sponge; *flush*, purify, dialyse, filter; *launder*, bleach, dry-clean; *bath*, bathe, shower; *sweep* (up), brush, dust, vacuum, hoover, spring-clean; *sanitize*, sterilize, disinfect, deodorize.

587 DIRTINESS
See also 591 (lack of hygiene); 851 (immorality).

n. *dirtiness*, uncleanness, uncleanliness, squalor; *contamination*, adulteration, pollution; *dirt*, filth, muck, mess; *mud*, slime, grease, dust, grime, oil, gunge (*colloq.*); *stain*, smear, patch, ring, mark, smudge, tarnish; *pigsty*, tip, slum, gutter, sewer; *slut*, pig (*colloq.*), mucky pup (*colloq.*).

adj. *dirty*, unclean, foul, squalid, filthy, mucky, messy, grotty (*colloq.*); *muddy*, slimy, greasy, dusty, grimy, oily, gungy (*colloq.*); *stained*, smeared, marked, smudged, tarnished; *contaminated*, adulterated, polluted.

vb. *dirty*, mess up, begrime, soil, muddy; *stain*, smear, mark, smudge, tarnish; *contaminate*, adulterate, pollute, foul.

588 HEALTH
See also 145 (vigour); 590 (hygiene).

n. *health*, healthiness, good condition, good health, convalescence, recovery; *fitness*, wellbeing, vitality, soundness; *salubrity*, wholesomeness, health food, fresh air, non-smoker, health freak (*colloq.*).

adj. *healthy*, in good health, well; *convalescent*, on the mend, up and about, fully recovered; *fit* (as a fiddle), sound, robust, strapping, hale and hearty; *health-giving*, wholesome, nutritious, salubrious, non-smoking, invigorating, beneficial, good for, therapeutic.

vb. *enjoy good health*, keep well, have a clean bill of health, feel fit, be in the pink (*colloq.*).

589 ILL HEALTH
See also 146 (inertness); 591 (lack of hygiene).

n. *ill health*, poor health, infirmity,

indisposition; *illness*, sickness, disease, disorder, ailment, complaint, affliction, condition; *lack of fitness*, weakness, debility; *attack*, seizure, fit, stroke, breakdown; *infection*, epidemic, contagion, inflammation, fever, virus, bug (*colloq.*), superbug (*colloq.*), MRSA; *cold*, influenza, flu, fever, sore throat, headache, cough; *measles*, German measles, chickenpox, smallpox; *polio(myelitis)*, multiple sclerosis, muscular dystrophy, rheumatism, arthritis, ulcer, gangrene; *whooping cough*, pneumonia, tuberculosis, bronchitis, tonsillitis; *malaria*, typhoid, cholera, scarlet fever, hepatitis, leprosy; *diarrhoea*, dysentery, gastroenteritis, stomach upset; *heart disease*, allergy, anaemia; *cancer*, tumour, leukaemia; *diphtheria*, tetanus, rabies; *venereal disease*, VD, sexually transmitted disease, STD, chlamydia, gonorrhoea, herpes, syphilis, pox (*colloq.*), Aids, HIV; *food-poisoning*, botulism, salmonella, E coli.

adj. *unhealthy*, in poor health, poorly, sickly, infirm, off colour (*colloq.*), under the weather (*colloq.*); *ill*, sick, diseased, ailing, indisposed, down with, laid up; *unfit*, weak, out of condition; *unwholesome*, poisonous, toxic, bad for, debilitating; *infectious*, contagious, catching, endemic, epidemic.

vb. *be unhealthy* etc, not feel well, etc; *suffer from*, ail, complain of; *sicken*, fall ill, catch, contract, go down with.

590 **HYGIENE**
See also 586 (cleanness); 588 (health).

n. *hygiene*, sanitation, cleanliness, public health, preventive medicine; *quarantine*, biosecurity, vaccination, inoculation, immunization; *disinfection*, sterilization, purification, pasteurization, chlorination, antisepsis; *hygienist*, sanitary inspector, sanitary engineer.

adj. *hygienic*, sanitary, germ-free; *disinfected*, sterilized, sterile, purified, pasteurized, chlorinated, antiseptic.

vb. *sanitize*, disinfect, sterilize, purify, boil, pasteurize, chlorinate; *vaccinate*, inoculate, immunize.

591 **LACK OF HYGIENE**
See also 587 (dirtiness); 589 (ill health).

n. *lack of hygiene*, lack of sanitation, no proper drainage, dirtiness; *epidemic*, outbreak, infestation, pollution, miasma.

adj. *unhygienic*, insanitary, dirty, germ-

ridden, infected; *infested*, polluted, unfit for human habitation, condemned.

vb. *infect*, infest, pollute, condemn.

592 **IMPROVEMENT**
See also 253 (forward motion); 594 (repair).

n. *improvement*, amelioration, betterment; *development*, progress, advance; *reform*, modernization, new broom; *refinement*, enrichment, polish, enhancement; *advancement*, promotion; *upturn*, recovery, boom; *correction*, amendment, revision, editing, proofreading; *improver*, reformer, refiner, reviser, editor, proofreader.

adj. *improved*, better, reformed, amended, revised, edited; *developed*, advanced; *reforming*, reformatory, progressive.

vb. *improve*, get better, raise one's game; *better oneself*, rise in/go up in the world, prosper; *reform*, turn over a new leaf, mend one's ways, go straight, pull one's socks up (*colloq.*); *develop*, progress, make progress, make advances; *improve upon*, elaborate on, go one better; *modernize*, streamline, upgrade; *refine*, enrich, polish, enhance; *advance*, promote; *correct*, amend, revise, edit, proofread, rewrite.

593 **DETERIORATION**
See also 46 (disintegration); 142 (powerlessness); 150 (destruction); 254 (backward motion); 597 (blight).

n. *deterioration*, detriment, impairment, impoverishment, degeneration, tabloidization; *decline*, retrogression, slide, downturn, slump; *dilapidation*, disrepair, ruin; *decay*, rot, rotting, rust, erosion, corrosion, decomposition; *damage*, injury, wound, blemish, mark.

adj. *deteriorated*, impaired, impoverished, degenerate; *in decline*, retrogressive, failing; *dilapidated*, tumbledown, ruined; *decayed*, rotten, rusty, eroded, corroded, decomposed; *damaged*, injured, wounded, blemished, marked.

vb. *deteriorate*, worsen, get worse, degenerate, go downhill, go to the dogs (*colloq.*), go to pot (*colloq.*), decline, fall off, retrogress, slump, fail; *decay*, rot, rust, erode, eat away, corrode, decompose; *impair*, degrade, lower, coarsen, spoil; *damage*, injure, wound, blemish, mark.

594 **REPAIR**
See also 592 (improvement); 596 (remedy).

n. *repair*, mend, mending, remedy;

restoration, renovation, refurbishment, reconditioning, refit, overhaul; *darn*, patch; *recuperation*, convalescence, recovery, healing; *cure*, refreshment, tonic, pick-me-up; *repairer*, mender, restorer, refurbisher, renovator, healer.

adj. *repaired*, mended, remedied, rectified; *restored*, renovated, refurbished, reconditioned, overhauled; *healed*, cured; *reparable*, mendable, restorable; *restorative*, curative, therapeutic, remedial, corrective.

vb. *repair*, mend, put right, fix, remedy, rectify; *restore*, renovate, refurbish, recondition, refit, overhaul; *heel*, sole, darn, patch; *heal*, cure; *recuperate*, convalesce, recover, get better.

595 **DAMAGE**
See also 604 (harm); 828 (disparagement).

n. *damage*, disrepair, injury, impairment, hurt, harm; *stain*, blemish, mark, foxing, discoloration, smudge; *tear*, dent, rip, scratch, disfigurement, scar, cicatrix; *corrosion*, rust, tarnish, rot, decay; *erosion*, weathering, wear and tear, battering; *wound*, cut, gash, bruise, sprain, strain, lesion.

adj. *damaged*, injured, impaired; *stained*, blemished, marked, foxed, discoloured, smudged; *torn*, scratched, scarred, disfigured, ravaged; *corroded*, rusty, tarnished, rotten, decayed; *eroded*, weathered, worn, frayed, battered; *wounded*, hurt, bruised, sprained, strained.

vb. *damage*, injure, impair, harm, spoil; *stain*, blemish, mark, discolour, smudge; *tear*, scratch, dent, rip, disfigure, deface; *corrode*, rust, tarnish, rot, decay; *erode*, eat away, weather, wear, batter; *wound*, hurt, cut, gash, bruise, sprain, strain.

596 **REMEDY**
See also 137 (counteraction); 594 (repair).

n. *remedy*, correction, corrective measure, cure, therapy; *help*, aid, first aid, relief; *atonement*, amends, redress; *medicine*, surgery, dentistry, health/medical tourism, scalpel safari (*colloq.*), homeopathy, alternative/ complementary medicine, TCM (traditional Chinese medicine); *medicament*, medication, treatment, drug; *placebo*, panacea, quack remedy, patent medicine; *pill*, tablet, suppository, lozenge, capsule; *mixture*, linctus, ointment, balm; *antidote*, antacid, antibiotic, emetic, laxative; *plaster*, splint, dressing, bandage, poultice; *injection*, inoculation, vaccination, vaccine, jab

(*colloq.*); *doctor*, physician, dentist, surgeon, nurse, therapist, healer; *hospital*, foundation hospital, NHS trust, infirmary, hospice, sick bay, surgery, clinic, dispensary.

adj. *remedial*, corrective, curative, healing, therapeutic; *soothing*, calming, emollient, anaesthetic; *medicinal*, medical, homeopathic, surgical.

vb. *remedy*, correct, cure, put right, fix, heal; *help*, aid, relieve, treat, tend, nurse; *soothe*, calm, drug, anaesthetize; *atone*, make amends, redress; *dress*, bathe, operate, set, inject.

597 **BLIGHT**
See also 593 (deterioration).

n. *blight*, rot, mould, mildew, fungus, rust; *infestation*, plague, pest, vermin, woodworm; *cancer*, canker, gangrene, necrosis; *bane*, curse, scourge, bugbear, cross, affliction; *nuisance*, annoyance, irritant, thorn in the flesh, pain (*colloq.*), pest (*colloq.*), pain in the arse/neck (*colloq.*); *poison*, toxin, carcinogen.

adj. *blighted*, rotten, bad, mouldy, mildewed, addled, putrid, worm-eaten; *accursed*, afflicted, wretched; *pestilential*, infuriating, pesky (*colloq.*); *cancerous*, gangrenous, diseased; *poisonous*, toxic, carcinogenic.

598 **SAFETY**
See also 600 (refuge); 687 (security).

n. *safety*, preservation, security; *guarantee*, surety, warranty, insurance, assurance, failsafe; *protection*, shelter, harbour, sanctuary, asylum, defence, firewall; *immunity*, safe conduct, invulnerability, impregnability; *safekeeping*, custody, quarantine; *safety net*, lifebelt, lifeline, lifesaver; *precaution*, preventive measure, prophylaxis, immunization; *protector*, guardian, defender, security forces, police, air/sky marshal, vigilante; *guard*, gaoler, warder, patrol, watchman, bodyguard, minder, lifeguard; *warden*, curator, custodian, keeper, gamekeeper.

adj. *safe*, secure, sure; *guaranteed*, under warranty, insured; *immune*, invulnerable, impregnable, bombproof; *hygienic*, non-toxic, childproof, unbreakable; *prophylactic*, preventive, preventative, protective; *unharmed*, safe and sound, in one piece, unscathed; *guarded*, locked up, under lock and key, behind bars, in quarantine.

vb. *be safe*, keep out of harm's way, keep a safe distance, give a wide berth, take precautions, be prepared; *safeguard*, immunize, protect, preserve; *defend*, shelter, shield, harbour, guard; *patrol*, police, watch over, have charge of, keep under surveillance.

599 **DANGER**
See also 425 (probability); 601 (trap).

n. *danger*, peril, hazard, black spot; *crisis*, flashpoint, trouble spot; *menace*, threat, the sword of Damocles; *danger signal*, warning, red light, alarm, wake-up call; *danger zone*, no-go area, firing line, no man's land; *insecurity*, jeopardy, risk, precariousness; *severity*, acuteness, extremeness, virulence.

adj. *dangerous*, perilous, hazardous, risky; *menacing*, threatening; *unsafe*, insecure, in jeopardy, precarious, dodgy (*colloq.*); *critical*, delicate; treacherous, slippery; *severe*, acute, extreme, virulent.

vb. *endanger*, put at risk, imperil, jeopardize; *menace*, threaten, loom; *hazard*, risk, expose, play with fire, tempt fate; *court danger*, skate on thin ice, sail too near the wind, enter the lions' den, run the gauntlet.

600 **REFUGE**
See also 469 (concealment); 598 (safety); 640 (defence).

n. *refuge*, retreat, asylum, sanctuary, haven, shelter, safe house; *air-raid shelter*, fallout shelter, bunker, dugout, trench, foxhole, bolthole; *central refuge*, central reservation, traffic island, emergency lane; *earth*, lair, den, burrow, nest; *fort*, castle, fortress, stockade, keep, stronghold, bastion; *screen*, cover, shield, windbreak; *refugee*, evacuee, displaced person, (illegal) immigrant, asylum-seeker, economic migrant.

vb. *seek refuge*, run for cover, take shelter, make port.

601 **TRAP**
See also 242 (vehicle); 599 (danger); 668 (restraint).

n. *trap*, pitfall, snare, ambush; *mantrap*, gin, pit, noose, booby trap, mine; *decoy*, bait, blind, lure, diversion; *reef*, bar, sandbank, shoal, submerged rock, undertow, crevasse, quicksand.

vb. *trap*, ensnare, ambush, lie in wait.

602 **WARNING**
See also 484 (sign); 623 (advice); 678 (veto).

n. *warning*, caution, notice, lesson;

information, nod, wink, word; *early warning*, advance notice, clue, hint, deterrent, warning shot; *admonishment*, rebuke, reprimand, telling-off, yellow card; *premonition*, presage, foreboding; *omen*, writing on the wall, harbinger of doom; *danger signal*, red flag, red light, fire alarm, foghorn; *horn*, hooter, klaxon, siren, tocsin; *alarm clock*, warning light, alarm bell, beacon; *SOS*, mayday, flare, distress signal.

adj. *cautionary*, warning, deterrent; *ominous*, symptomatic.

vb. *warn*, caution, give notice; *inform*, advise, notify, tip off, tip the wink (*colloq.*); *admonish*, reprove, rebuke, reprimand, tell off; *give/raise/sound the alarm*, dial 999, alert; *look out!*, watch your step!

603 **PRESERVATION**
See also 570 (store).

n. *preservation*, saving, safekeeping, maintenance; *conservation*, conservancy, protection; *game reserve*, bird sanctuary, nature reserve; *conservation area*, ancient monument, listed building; *refrigeration*, freezing, cold storage, drying, freeze-drying, canning, preserving, bottling; *embalming*, mummification, taxidermy; *preservative*, sugar, salt, brine, spice, pickle, water glass, ice, dry ice, formaldehyde.

adj. *preservative*, protective, preserving; *preserved*, salted, pickled, iced, frozen, dried, smoked, canned, tinned, potted, bottled; *well-preserved*, fresh, intact.

vb. *preserve*, save, maintain; *conserve*, protect, list; *paint*, varnish, creosote; *cure*, smoke, refrigerate, freeze, dry, can, bottle; *embalm*, mummify, stuff.

604 **HARM**
See also 583 (worthlessness); 595 (damage); 737 (unpleasantness).

n. *harm*, ill, hurt, damage, injury, detriment; *bad luck*, misfortune, disaster, destruction, ruin; *cruelty*, malevolence, viciousness, wrong, evil, persecution; *hurtfulness*, malice, spite, scandal, libel, slander, defamation; *unwholesomeness*, noxiousness, poison, toxin, pollution, radioactivity.

adj. *harmful*, damaging, injurious, pernicious, insidious, deleterious, detrimental; *disastrous*, destructive, ruinous, harsh, savage, fierce; *cruel*, malevolent, vicious, wrong, hurtful; *malicious*, spiteful, bitchy, libellous, slanderous, defamatory;

fatal, lethal, deadly, poisonous, malignant, terminal; *toxic*, noxious, polluting, radioactive; *unwholesome*, infectious, unhygienic.

vb. *harm*, hurt, damage, injure, impair; *destroy*, ruin, wreck, undermine, play havoc with; *abuse*, ill-treat, wrong, persecute, victimize; *libel*, slander, defamate; *poison*, intoxicate, pollute, irradiate.

605 ESCAPE

See also 556 (avoidance); 606 (deliverance); 822 (exemption).

n. *escape*, flight, getaway, breakout, departure; *evasion*, avoidance, truancy, desertion, (moonlight) flit (*colloq.*); *rescue*, deliverance, freeing, letting off, reprieve; *withdrawal*, retreat, decampment, elopement; *get-out*, let-out, escape clause, loophole; *leak*, discharge, burst, seepage; *narrow escape*, close/near thing, close shave (*colloq.*); *way out*, (emergency) exit, egress, escape hatch, bolthole, fire escape, ejector seat, exit strategy; *escapee*, fugitive, runaway, deserter, truant.

adj. *escaped*, free, at large, truant, flown, AWOL.

vb. *escape*, flee, depart, take flight, break out; *evade*, elude, avoid, give the slip; *desert*, abscond, play truant, do a (moonlight) flit (*colloq.*); *rescue*, deliver, save, free, reprieve; *withdraw*, retreat, decamp, elope; *leak*, discharge, burst forth.

606 DELIVERANCE

See also 598 (safety); 605 (escape).

n. *deliverance*, rescue, saving, salvage; *extrication*, salvation, redemption, cure; *reprieve*, discharge, acquittal, pardon, liberation; *respite*, cease-fire, truce, stay of execution, remission, breather (*colloq.*); *rescuer*, deliverer, saviour, redeemer, liberator.

vb. *deliver*, rescue, free, save; *be the saving of*, salvage, retrieve, extricate, redeem, cure; *reprieve*, discharge, acquit, let off, pardon, liberate.

607 ACTION

See also 523 (drama); 609 (activity); 645 (war); 856 (litigation).

n. *action*, doing, commission, perpetration, execution, performance; *step*, move, manoeuvre, initiative, measure, act, deed; *feat*, exploit, achievement, accomplishment; *activity*, work, job, task, occupation;

perpetrator, executor, performer, doer, worker, activist.

adj. *acting*, active, in operation, operational, at work, employed, in the act, occupational.

vb. *do*, act, commit, conduct, perpetrate, execute, prosecute, perform, ply; *undertake*, put into effect, implement, enact, carry out; *accomplish*, achieve, bring about/off; *work*, function, be in operation, occupy oneself.

608 INACTION

See also 146 (inertness); 610 (inactivity).

n. *inaction*, inertness, passivity, failure/inability to act, abstention; *immobility*, paralysis, stasis; *rest*, idleness, unemployment, leisure; *suspension*, abeyance.

adj. *out of action*, inoperative, inert, passive; *immobile*, paralysed, static; *resting*, idle, unemployed; *suspended*, in abeyance.

vb. *do nothing*, fail to act, refrain, abstain, stay neutral, opt out, pass the buck; *shelve*, put on ice, mothball; *not act*, let sleeping dogs lie, wait and see, bide one's time, mark time, tick over, stand (idly) by, not lift a finger; *twiddle* one's *thumbs*, kick one's heels, be at a loose end.

609 ACTIVITY

See also 607 (action).

n. *activity*, movement; *nimbleness*, agility, liveliness, briskness; *life*, energy, vigour, get-up-and-go (*colloq.*); *business*, dealing, trading; *stir*, burst, fit, flurry; *bustle*, fuss, agitation, ado, bother, to-do, commotion; *readiness*, keenness, willingness, eagerness, alacrity; *enterprise*, enthusiasm, dynamism; *concentration*, diligence, industry; *determination*, tirelessness, perseverance; *hard worker*, workaholic, slogger, busy bee (*colloq.*), eager beaver (*colloq.*); *enthusiast*, fanatic, militant, zealot.

adj. *active*, on the go, moving, in motion, working; *nimble*, agile, lively, brisk, busy; *keen*, willing, eager, enterprising, enthusiastic; *diligent*, industrious, energetic, vigorous, dynamic; *determined*, tireless, dogged, unflagging.

vb. *be active* etc; *rouse oneself*, make an/the effort, exert oneself, gird one's loins; *bustle*, hurry, get a move on, not hang about (*colloq.*), go for it (*colloq.*).

610 INACTIVITY

See also 146 (inertness); 608 (inaction); 619 (fatigue).

n. *inactivity*, inertia, torpor, listlessness; *quiet*, peace, calm, stillness; *laziness*, sloth, lethargy, apathy, indolence; *sleep*, rest, repose, nap, siesta, snooze, shut-eye (*colloq.*), kip (*colloq.*); *hibernation*, aestivation; *unconsciousness*, trance, coma, stupor; *strike*, lockout, shutdown; *laggard*, lazy-bones, slacker, loafer, passenger, sleeping partner; *layabout*, scrounger, good-for-nothing; *idle rich*, leisured classes.

adj. *inactive*, still, motionless, peaceful, calm; *slow-moving*, listless, sluggish, torpid; *idle*, slothful, indolent, lazy, leisured; *unenterprising*, apathetic, indifferent; *unconscious*, comatose, asleep; *tired*, weary, dopey, groggy, sleepy, somnolent.

vb. *be inactive* etc, stagnate, drift, let things slide; *delay*, stall, drag one's feet, loiter, dawdle; *laze about*, lounge, loaf, idle, shirk, skive; *sleep*, doze, nap, slumber, rest; *hibernate*, aestivate.

611 **WORK**
See also 149 (production).

n. *work*, task, job, assignment, mission, undertaking, venture, cause; *employment*, gainful employment, service; *post*, position, function, situation; *appointment*, vacancy, opening, headhunting; *profession*, occupation, line of work, career, trade, craft; *industry*, commerce, business, dealings, trade, affairs; *worker*, breadwinner, wage-earner, white-/blue-collar worker, professional (person), artisan, labourer.

adj. *working*, workaday, employed, self-employed, freelance, busy (with); *professional*, businesslike, efficient; *occupational*, industrial, commercial.

vb. *work*, do a job, work for, be engaged on, engage in, earn one's living; *apply for*, take a job; *employ*, take on, hire, appoint, engage, recruit, select, headhunt; *trade*, do/conduct/transact business, deal, negotiate.

612 **LEISURE**
See also 618 (ease); 761 (recreation).

n. *leisure*, free time, spare time, one's own time, time off, break, recess, retirement; *leisure activities*, recreation, relaxation, rest, sport, leisure centre; *holiday*, vacation, furlough, leave, leave of absence, garden(ing) leave, R & R, sabbatical, gap year.

adj. *leisured*, unoccupied, retired, resting; *sabbatical*, on holiday.

vb. *take time off*, take a break, holiday, go on holiday; *relax*, take one's time, have all the time in the world; *retire*, give up work, drop out.

adv. *in* one's *own time*, at one's own pace, at one's leisure, at one's convenience.

613 **WORKER**
See also 149 (production).

n. *worker*, employee, self-employed person, freelance(r); *slave*, bondsman, menial, fag, coolie, bearer; *dogsbody*, skivvy, drudge, hewer of wood and drawer of water, chief cook and bottle-washer, factotum; *servant*, domestic (servant), maid, valet, tweeny, cook, chambermaid, housekeeper, butler, footman, groom, ostler; *dustman*, cleaner, char(lady), daily, help; *farmer*, farmhand, farm labourer, dairyman, shepherd; *forester*, nurseryman, gardener; *workman*, artisan, blue-collar worker, tradesman, craftsman, handyman, odd-job man, apprentice, (casual) labourer; *mechanic*, repairman, fitter; *factory worker*, steelworker, docker; *builder*, bricklayer, mason, plasterer, decorator, painter, electrician, glazier, tiler, slater, plumber; *carpenter*, cabinetmaker, joiner; *smith*, blacksmith, welder; *miner*, coalminer, collier; *jeweller*, goldsmith, silversmith, watchmaker, clockmaker; *tailor*, dressmaker; *author*, writer, journalist, photographer, editor, printer, proofreader, bookbinder; *businessman*, businesswoman, dealer, trader, merchant, middleman, wholesaler; *retailer*, shopkeeper, shop assistant, check-out girl; *employer*, industrialist, manufacturer; *manager*, supervisor, director, executive; *staff*, personnel, workforce, labour force, manpower, payroll, human resources; *office worker*, white-collar worker, clerk, secretary, shorthand typist, personal assistant, girl Friday, tealady, teaboy; *banker*, stockbroker, jobber; *lawyer*, solicitor, barrister, legal eagle (*colloq.*), brief (*colloq.*); *engineer*, electrical/mechanical/civil engineer, architect, draughtsman, designer, town planner; *functionary*, operative, officer, executant, practitioner.

614 **WORKSHOP**

n. *workshop*, workplace, place of work; *workroom*, study, library, studio, atelier; *office*, bureau, shop, establishment, laboratory; *factory*, works, plant, installation; *yard*, site, industrial estate, depot, station, branch, dock; *shop floor*, production/assembly line; *mine*, quarry, foundry, refinery, laundry, kitchen, farm.

615 **HASTE**
See also 245 (speed); 753 (rashness).

n. *haste*, hurry, rush, bustle, scurry, scramble; *urgency*, pressure, deadline, rush job; *acceleration*, hastening, precipitation, recklessness, impatience; *dash*, burst of speed, push, spurt, sprint, race (against time).

adj. *hasty*, hurried, in a rush, fast, hustling; *urgent*, top-priority, hot off the press; *pressurized*, hard-pressed, hard-pushed; *rushed*, eleventh-hour, last-minute, skimped; *rash*, reckless, precipitate, impatient.

vb. *hurry*, rush, hustle, scurry, scramble, not waste time, lose no time; *throw together*, cobble together, whip up, hack out; *speed up*, hasten, dispatch, precipitate, expedite, railroad (*colloq.*); *hurry up*, goad, put a bomb under; *dash*, push, spurt, sprint, race, tear, zoom, whizz, bomb along (*colloq.*).

616 **LACK OF HASTE**
See also 246 (slowness); 406 (carefulness).

n. *lack of haste*, slowness, steadiness, deliberation; *leisure*, time to spare, no hurry; *dilatoriness*, hesitation, lack of enthusiasm, caution; *laziness*, procrastination, no sense of time, unpunctuality, mañana; *dawdle*, amble, saunter, stroll, trot, jog; *crawl*, snail's pace; *conscientiousness*, attention (to detail), thoroughness, accuracy; *consideration*, thoughtfulness; *dawdler*, crawler, plodder, slowcoach, Sunday-afternoon driver, late riser, lie-abed.

adj. *unhurried*, slow, steady, deliberate; *dilatory*, unenthusiastic, hesitant, cautious; *leisurely*, easygoing, phlegmatic, plodding; *lazy*, sluggish, slothful, languid; *late*, tardy, unpunctual; *painstaking*, conscientious, thorough, accurate; *considered*, thoughtout.

vb. *have all the time in the world*, take no note of time; *hesitate*, drawl, spin out, drag out; *not be hurried*, think over, weigh up, ponder, not rush into things, sleep on it; *dawdle*, amble, saunter, shamble, stroll, trot, jog; *crawl*, creep, inch; *linger*, loiter, dilly-dally.

617 **EXERTION**
n. *exertion*, effort, strain, muscle, elbow grease (*colloq.*); *force*, pressure, thrust, pull, tug, tension; *labour*, work, toil, hard graft, application; *hard work*, slog, fag (*colloq.*), grind; *trouble*, pains, sweat, bother, pain (*colloq.*); *exercise*, physical education, PE, physical training, PT, drill; *keep-fit*, jogging, aerobics, sport, games.

adj. *laborious*, gruelling, backbreaking, exhausting, arduous, uphill, killing; *industrious*, hard-working, workaholic, dogged; *strenuous*, demanding, energetic.

vb. *exert oneself*, strive, try, make an/the effort, endeavour, strain; *labour*, toil, sweat, work, hump; *grind*, plod, slog away, make heavy weather of; *apply oneself*, buckle down, knuckle down, set to, pull one's finger out; *go to great trouble*, bend over backwards, put oneself to a lot of bother, put oneself out, bust a gut (*colloq.*); *spare no effort*, do one's utmost, pull out all the stops.

adv. *laboriously*, with brute force, by the sweat of one's brow, the hard way; *with a vengeance*, all out, flat out, hammer and tongs (*colloq.*), tooth and nail (*colloq.*).

618 **EASE**
See also 612 (leisure); 629 (easiness); 740 (relief).

n. *ease*, repose, rest, relaxation; *comfort*, restfulness, peace and quiet, calm, tranquillity; *pause*, break, coffee/tea/lunch-break, lunch hour, recreation period, gap year; *holiday*, vacation, leave, furlough, day off, weekend, bank holiday.

adj. *at ease*, relaxed, casual, laid back (*colloq.*); *restful*, relaxing, comfortable, peaceful, quiet, calm, tranquil.

vb. *be at ease* etc, take one's ease, rest, take it easy, relax, put one's feet up, lounge; *stop*, take a break, slow down, take time off; *take a holiday*, get away from it all, go on leave.

619 **FATIGUE**
See also 144 (weakness); 610 (inactivity).

n. *fatigue*, tiredness, weariness, jetlag; *sleepiness*, somnolence, drowsiness, doziness; *weakness*, faintness, feebleness; *exhaustion*, prostration, collapse.

adj. *fatigued*, tired, weary; *sleepy*, somnolent, drowsy, dozy; *weak*, faint, feeble, drained; *exhausted*, worn out, all in, dead beat, dropping (*colloq.*), pooped (*colloq.*), whacked (*colloq.*), fagged out (*colloq.*), knackered (*colloq.*), shattered (*colloq.*); *fatiguing*, tiring, punishing, knackering (*colloq.*), shattering (*colloq.*).

vb. *be tired* etc; *tire*, flag, wilt, droop; *fall asleep*, nod off, drop off, conk out (*colloq.*), flake out (*colloq.*), crash out (*colloq.*), go out like a light (*colloq.*); *collapse*, drop; *fatigue*, tire, weary, exhaust, wear out, tax, flog.

620 **REFRESHMENT**
See also 145 (vigour); 267 (ingestion); 740 (relief).

n. *refreshment*, recreation, renewal, recuperation, revival, recovery, restoration, relief; *invigoration*, stimulation, fillip; *food*, drink, stimulant, tonic.

adj. *refreshing*, reviving, restoring, restorative, recuperative; *cool*, invigorating, stimulating, bracing; *refreshed*, recovered.

vb. *refresh*, freshen, revive, restore; *reinvigorate*, stimulate, perk up, enliven; *be refreshed*, recover, recuperate, get one's second wind, get one's breath back; *take a breather*, cool off, stretch one's legs, freshen up, recharge one's batteries.

621 **CONDUCT**
See also 607 (action); 622 (management).

n. *conduct*, behaviour, comportment, actions, moves; *customs*, way of life, lifestyle; *style*, manner, air, attitude, demeanour; *way of speaking*, tone of voice, presentation; *good behaviour*, (good) manners, (good) breeding; *bad behaviour*, misbehaviour, misconduct, misdemeanours, rudeness; *past* (behaviour/history), background, (track) record; *practice*, methods, system, procedure, common practice, organization; *control*, guidance, supervision; *strategy*, plan, tactics, policy, programme.

adj. *behavioural*; *strategic*, tactical, planned.

vb. *behave*, conduct oneself/one's affairs, act, acquit oneself; *behave well*, be on one's best behaviour, behave oneself, set an example, mind one's Ps and Qs; *behave badly*, misbehave, play up; *carry on*, run, manage, control, supervise.

622 **MANAGEMENT**
See also 57 (arrangement); 621 (conduct); 651 (success); 657 (authority); 665 (master).

n. *management*, direction, handling, running, administration, bureaucracy; organization, order; *authority*, command, charge, control, supervision, leadership; *government*, legislation, jurisdiction, power, regulation, politics, dictatorship, tyranny; *manager*, administrator, controller, coordinator, organizer, tsar, official, bureaucrat, executive, suit (*colloq.*), boss; *chairman*, speaker, presiding officer; *housekeeper*, steward, agent, deputy; *director*, inspector, chief, overseer, foreman/-woman, supervisor, board of directors; *legislator*, leader, politician, (prime) minister, premier, secretary of state, governor, statesman; prefect; *officer*, commander, captain; *chancellor*, vice-chancellor, governing body, warden, master, dean; *thought police*.

adj. *administrative*, organizational, bureaucratic, political; *managerial*, directorial, governmental, supervisory, legislative, governing, guiding; *authoritative*, in charge, commanding, leading, statesmanlike; *dictatorial*, tyrannical, despotic.

vb. *manage*, direct, handle, run, administer, organize, coordinate, order; *command*, be in charge of, head up, control, steer, supervise, lead, guide, be in the driving seat; *govern*, legislate, regulate, police; *take control of*, take ownership of.

623 **ADVICE**
See also 442 (maxim); 602 (warning).

n. *advice*, counsel, counselling, guidance; *recommendation*, tip, suggestion, hint, intimation, word in one's ear; *persuasion*, dissuasion, support, encouragement; *precept*, tenet, (golden) rule, guidelines; *instruction*, direction, brief, ordinance, injunction, regulation, ruling, prescription; *warning*, caution, notice, criticism, admonition, admonishment; *adviser*, counsellor, guide, tutor, confidant/-e, mentor, life coach, focus group, think tank; *consultant*, lawyer, counsel, steering committee; *busybody*, back-seat driver, fashion police.

adj. *advisory*, consultative, guiding, steering; *persuasive*, dissuasive, encouraging, supportive, cautionary; *prescriptive*, mandatory, statutory, binding.

vb. *advise*, counsel, advocate, recommend; *suggest*, submit, propose, hint, intimate; *persuade*, dissuade, encourage, enjoin, warn, guide; *consult*, call in, seek/take advice, consult counsel, see one's solicitor; *instruct*, prescribe, lay down.

624 **SKILL**
See also 141 (power); 438 (knowledge).

n. *skill*, facility, mastery, adeptness, adroitness, deftness; *ability*, competence, capability, capacity; *talent*, gift, genius, forte, flair, bent; *training*, experience, accomplishment, know-how; *expertise*, knack, touch, grip, technique; *skilled person*, man of many parts, master, veteran, old hand; *specialist*, professional, authority, expert, anorak (*colloq.*), wonk (*colloq.*); *genius*, talent; *craftsman*, artist, technician.

adj. *skilful*, skilled, apt, adept, adroit, deft,

good at; *able*, competent, capable, talented, gifted; *professional*, authoritative, expert, businesslike; *trained*, experienced, accomplished, practised.

vb. *be skilful* etc, shine, play one's cards well, have a gift/talent, know the ropes, know one's way around; excel, exceed expectations, do better than expected, surpass oneself, punch above one's weight (*colloq.*).

625 UNSKILFULNESS

See also 142 (powerlessness); 439 (ignorance).

n. *unskilfulness*, clumsiness, awkwardness; *inexperience*, lack of experience/practice, rustiness; *inability*, incapacity, ineptitude, incompetence, inefficiency; *mismanagement*, mishandling, bungling, tactlessness, thoughtlessness; *mess*, hash, shambles, faux pas, pig's ear (*colloq.*), cockup (*colloq.*); *bungler*, bodger, amateur, jack of all trades and master of none, butterfingers.

adj. *unskilful*, clumsy, awkward, ham-fisted, bumbling; *inexperienced*, unqualified, unpractised, rusty; *inept*, incapable, incompetent, ineffectual, failed; *inefficient*, impractical, inexpert, unprofessional, unbusinesslike; *amateurish*, scratch, home-made, Heath-Robinson, slapdash; *thoughtless*, tactless, ill-considered, foolish.

vb. *be unskilful* etc, not have the knack, be no good at, bumble, fumble, flounder; *botch*, spoil, fluff, make a mess/hash of, bungle, mess up (*colloq.*), cock up (*colloq.*), make a pig's ear of (*colloq.*), fuck up (*vulg.*); *mismanage*, mishandle, blunder, blow it (*colloq.*).

626 CUNNING

See also 444 (wisdom); 480 (deception).

n. *cunning*, craft, craftiness, guile, slyness, artfulness, dishonesty, deceit, stealth, sleight of hand; *ingenuity*, resourcefulness, wisdom, shrewdness, cleverness; *ruse*, plot, intrigue, scheme, trick, deception, dodge, wiles, wrinkle, chicanery; *artful dodger*, snake in the grass, slyboots, plotter, schemer, cheat, trickster, conman (*colloq.*), wide boy.

adj. *cunning*, crafty, sly, artful, wily, disingenuous, deceitful, scheming, shady; *ingenious*, resourceful, shrewd, clever, canny, sharp, smart (*colloq.*), not born yesterday (*colloq.*).

vb. *be cunning* etc, plot, intrigue, scheme; *trick*, deceive, cheat, hoax, con (*colloq.*), put

one over on (*colloq.*); *outwit*, outsmart, get the better of.

627 NAIVETY

See also 434 (belief); 439 (ignorance).

n. *naïvety*, artlessness, innocence, simplicity, ingenuousness; *naturalness*, unsophistication, unaffectedness; *sincerity*, straightforwardness, frankness, candour, openness; *innocent*, child, ingénue, greenhorn, beginner, yokel, simpleton.

adj. *naïve*, artless, green, innocent, wide-eyed, simple, ingenuous, unstudied; *natural*, unsophisticated, unaffected, childlike, unlearned; *sincere*, straightforward, frank, candid, open, up-front (*colloq.*).

vb. *be naïve* etc, rush in where angels fear to tread, say what one thinks, speak one's mind, not mince one's words.

628 DIFFICULTY

See also 581 (inconvenience); 630 (hindrance).

n. *difficulty*, arduousness, laboriousness, awkwardness, inconvenience; *ordeal*, tall order, handful, uphill struggle, hard going, the labours of Hercules, no picnic (*colloq.*); *trouble*, bother, hole (*colloq.*), scrape (*colloq.*), pickle (*colloq.*); *predicament*, dilemma, problem, fix; *puzzle*, teaser, poser, headache (*colloq.*); *obstacle*, impediment, stumbling block, complication, handicap.

adj. *difficult*, hard, arduous, laborious, tough, uphill, demanding; *awkward*, inconvenient, unmanageable, unwieldy; *troublesome*, bothersome; *problematic*, complex, complicated, involved, puzzling; *stubborn*, cussed, hard to shift, obstinate; *delicate*, ticklish, tricky, knotty; *fussy*, high maintenance (*colloq.*).

vb. *be difficult* etc, make things difficult, make difficulties for, plague; *trouble*, put to trouble/inconvenience, inconvenience, put out, perplex, bother, irk; *puzzle*, perplex, give one a headache, complicate matters; *hinder*, hamper, obstruct; *be in difficulty*, get into difficulties, run into trouble, flounder, get out of one's depth, come unstuck.

adv. *with difficulty*, uphill, the hard way, against the stream.

629 EASINESS

See also 580 (convenience); 631 (help).

n. *easiness*, ease, facility; *straightforwardness*, simplicity, convenience, feasibility; *facilitation*, simplification, deregulation; *sinecure*, cushy number (*colloq.*), soft option, easy way out, line of least resistance; *easy target*, easy meat, sitting duck; *no problem*, open-and-shut case, plain sailing, doddle (*colloq.*), picnic (*colloq.*), a piece of cake (*colloq.*), money for jam/old rope (*colloq.*), child's play (*colloq.*), kid's stuff (*colloq.*), cinch (*colloq.*), pushover (*colloq.*), walkover (*colloq.*), no-brainer (*colloq.*).

adj. *easy*, effortless, undemanding, painless, downhill, cushy (*colloq.*), nothing to it (*colloq.*); *straightforward*, simple, uncomplicated, convenient; *obvious*, clear, readable; *feasible*, manageable; *pleasant*, short, light; *helpful*, easy-going, willing.

vb. *be easy* etc, present no difficulties, give no trouble, require no effort, make no demands; *go well*, go like clockwork, run smoothly; *have no trouble*, make short work of, sail through, cruise; *ease*, facilitate, smooth, oil the wheels, not stand in the way; *free*, unharness, unfetter; *simplify*, clarify, facilitate, deregulate.

adv. *easily*, readily, standing on one's head (*colloq.*), like falling off a log, with one hand tied behind one's back, blindfold (*colloq.*); *smoothly*, like clockwork, like a dream (*colloq.*).

630 **HINDRANCE**
See also 114 (lateness); 628 (difficulty); 668 (restraint).

n. *hindrance*, impedance, impediment, nuisance, handicap, encumbrance; *obstructiveness*, picketing, boycott, blacking, filibustering, Nimby (Not In My Back Yard); *restraint*, check, curb, resistance; *retardation*, drag, friction, headwind, tide; *prohibition*, bar, ban, embargo; *restriction*, limitation, control; *obstacle*, barrier, hurdle, hazard, bunker; *interruption*, intervention, interference; *hitch*, hold-up, setback, spanner in the works (*colloq.*); *obstruction*, blockage, constriction, jam, traffic jam, tailback, snarl-up (*colloq.*), bed-blocking; *dam*, barrage, lock, weir; *bandage*, tourniquet, compress; *defence*, moat, wall, portcullis, drawbridge, fence, barricade, stockade; *gate*, tollgate, checkpoint, roadblock, stile, cattle-grid.

adj. *hindering*, obstructive; *unfavourable*, unhelpful; *restrictive*, limiting, controlling; *prohibitive*, preventive, preventative.

vb. *hinder*, impede, obstruct, hamper, handicap, encumber; *restrain*, check, resist, retard, brake; *prohibit*, bar, ban; *restrict*, limit, curb, control, clamp down on; *repress*, quell,

dam (up), cramp one's style; *constrict*, bandage, bind, cramp, hem in, hedge in; *interrupt*, intervene, interfere, meddle; *thwart*, frustrate, snooker, hamstring, stymie; *block/clog/jam (up)*, filibuster, stonewall, throw a spanner in the works (*colloq.*); *cripple*, paralyse, hobble, fetter; *picket*, boycott, black.

631 **HELP**
See also 138 (instrumentality);
578 (usefulness); 629 (easiness).

n. *help*, aid, assistance, succour, helping hand, charity; *relief*, easing, alleviation; *advice*, guidance, comfort, feedback; *encouragement*, moral support, backing; *medical assistance*, health care, first aid, treatment, nursing; *financial help/aid/assistance*, foreign aid, loan, sponsorship; *grant*, bursary, scholarship, exhibition, allowance, honorarium; *subsidy*, maintenance, benefit, social security, subsistence, hand-out; *helper*, help, assistant, aide; *right-hand man*, henchman, sidekick (*colloq.*), girl/man Friday, aide-de-camp, lieutenant, tower of strength; *adviser*, counsellor, think-tank, focus group; *good Samaritan*, neighbour, fairy godmother; *sponsor*, supporter, champion, promoter.

adj. *helpful*, of assistance, auxiliary; *supportive*, encouraging, obliging.

vb. *help (out)*, aid, assist, succour, render assistance, do sb a good turn, lend a hand (*colloq.*), give sb a leg-up (*colloq.*), put in a word for; *relieve*, ease, alleviate, comfort; *advise*, guide, show the ropes; *encourage*, support, endorse, back, champion, sustain; *treat*, minister to, nurse; *pay for*, finance, sponsor, subsidize, maintain, promote, patronize.

632 **OPPOSITION**
See also 14 (oppositeness);
137 (counteraction); 637 (defiance);
638 (resistance); 682 (protest).

n. *opposition*, antagonism, hostility; *non-cooperation*, contrariness, recalcitrance, obstinacy; *denial*, counterargument, contradiction, objection; *disagreement*, dissension, dispute, conflict, clash; *defiance*, resistance, challenge; *competition*, struggle, rivalry; *opposite*, polarity, contrast, antithesis, dichotomy; *opponent*, adversary, antagonist, enemy; *contender*, contestant, rival, competitor, challenger, candidate.

adj. *opposing*, conflicting, antagonistic, adversarial, hostile, unfriendly, defiant;

uncooperative, contrary, negative, bloody-minded, recalcitrant, obstinate, dissenting; *opposed to*, against, out of sympathy with.

vb. *oppose*, be dead against, disagree, dissent; *dispute*, deny, object, protest, argue against, contradict; *challenge*, resist, defy, fly in the face of, conflict with; *counter*, withstand, confront, hinder, obstruct; *compete against/with*, rival, contend, take up the cudgels.

633 **COOPERATION**
See also 40 (union); 43 (adhesion); 45 (combination).

n. *cooperation*, mutual assistance, fellowship, support; *working together*, joint/concerted effort, collaboration, teamwork, synergy, combined effort/operation; *merger*, amalgamation, union, coalition; *common aim*, solidarity, fellow feeling, sympathy; *league*, partnership, compact, treaty, alliance, détente; *concurrence*, unanimity, agreement, harmony, concert; *conspiracy*, collusion, connivance, complicity.

adj. *cooperative*, helpful, positive, constructive; *joint*, combined, mutual, bilateral; *sympathetic*, well-disposed, favourable, in sympathy with, concurrent; *in league*, synergic; *unanimous*, solid, united.

vb. *cooperate*, help one another, settle one's differences; *collaborate*, work together, combine/join forces, work in tandem, pull together; *help*, play ball, go along with, join in, muck in; *join together*, club together, team up, merge, amalgamate, unite, coalesce, combine; *agree*, concur, harmonize, see eye to eye; *conspire*, collude, connive, go into a huddle.

634 **PARTY**
See also 66 (assembly).

n. *party*, group, body, band; *member*, partner, adherent, follower, activist, supporter; *organization*, movement, political party, federation, association, society, circle, club; *council*, congress, parliament, legislature; *confederation*, alliance, Axis, coalition, league; *community*, fellowship, brotherhood, sisterhood, order; *confession*, church, religion, denomination, sect; *concern*, establishment, company, firm, business, corporation, partnership, syndicate, dot com company; *subsidiary*, offshoot; *committee*, board of directors/governors, cabinet, junta, executive, administration; *faction*, splinter group, clique, in-group.

adj. *cooperative*, social, communal; *federal*, confederate, affiliated, associated; *corporate*, joint; *factional*, sectional, denominational, sectarian; *committed*, card-carrying, fully paid-up, militant, true-blue.

vb. *join*, subscribe, enrol, sign on/up; *associate*, ally, federate, affiliate; *take sides*, side with, throw in one's lot with.

635 **DISAGREEMENT**
See also 18 (dissimilarity); 20 (disparity); 410 (argument); 437 (dissent); 643 (contention).

n. *disagreement*, non-agreement, difference of opinion; *dispute*, strife, contention, controversy, dissidence, dissent, dissension; *fight*, quarrel, squabble, wrangle, clash, row, tiff, feud, vendetta; *defiance*, rebellion, mutiny; *division*, split, breach, rift, schism, infighting; *disunity*, disharmony, discord, dissonance; *litigation*, legal battle, lawsuit, court action; *argument*, words, set-to, bickering, barney (*colloq.*); *bone of contention*, sore point, point at issue, talking point, hot potato (*colloq.*); *polemicist*, young Turk, rebel, firebrand, hothead.

adj. *disagreeing*, in disagreement, dissenting, nonconformist, at odds, at variance, at sixes and sevens, at loggerheads, off-message (*colloq.*); *quarrelling*, warring, feuding, antagonistic, hostile; *contentious*, polemical, controversial, provocative, litigious, in dispute; *divided*, split, internecine; *rebellious*, mutinous, quarrelsome; *discordant*, disunited, dissonant; *conflicting*, clashing, divisive.

vb. *disagree*, differ, agree to differ, not go along with (*colloq.*), stick one's neck out; *dispute*, reject, contend, dissent, object, have a bone to pick with (*colloq.*), take issue with, clash; *fight*, quarrel, squabble, wrangle, row, feud; *divide*, split, go one's separate ways; *sue*, lodge a complaint, take to court; *argue*, bicker, fall out, have words.

636 **AGREEMENT**
See also 17 (similarity); 19 (accord); 436 (assent); 684 (contract).

n. *agreement*, concurrence, consent; *contract*, compact, treaty, concordat, entente (cordiale), pact, convention, settlement, a (done) deal; *approval*, acceptance, assent; *unanimity*, unity, solidarity, consensus, general agreement; *détente*, reconciliation; *peace*, harmony, accord, mutual understanding, rapport, sweetness and light; *consistency*, symmetry, match, coincidence, correspondence.

adj. *in agreement*, agreed, undisputed, concurring, of one mind, like-minded; *agreeable*, acquiescent, favourable, consenting; *unanimous*, united, allied, solid; *peaceful*, peaceable, harmonious, reconciled; *consistent*, symmetrical, matching, compatible, corresponding.

vb. *agree*, concur, accord, go along with (*colloq.*); *see eye to eye*, get along, hit it off (*colloq.*); *be reconciled*, bury the hatchet, make it up, mend one's fences; *consent*, acquiesce, accept; *assent*, approve, condone, give one's blessing; *correspond*, match, coincide, harmonize.

637 **DEFIANCE**

See also 632 (opposition); 662 (disobedience).

n. *defiance*, provocation, disobedience; *challenge*, dare, gauntlet, clenched fist; *revolt*, rebellion, mutiny, insubordination.

adj. *defiant*, provocative, challenging; *rebellious*, mutinous, insubordinate, disobedient.

vb. *defy*, disobey, challenge, stand up to; *throw down the gauntlet*, provoke, dare; *scorn*, toss aside, snap one's fingers at; *revolt*, rebel, mutiny.

638 **RESISTANCE**

See also 137 (counteraction); 301 (friction); 632 (opposition).

n. *resistance*, stand, withstanding, retaliation; *objection*, opposition, protest, civil disobedience; *obstinacy*, reluctance, recalcitrance, unwillingness; *friction*, load, resistor.

adj. *resistant*, unyielding, proof; *obstinate*, reluctant, recalcitrant, unwilling.

vb. *resist*, withstand, stand up to, repel, hold off; *challenge*, not take lying down, put up a fight, not submit, hold out, stand one's ground, dig in one's heels, refuse to budge; *object*, protest, oppose, kick against; *frustrate*, stem, thwart, foil.

639 **ATTACK**

See also 147 (violence); 828 (disparagement).

n. *attack*, aggression, assault, first strike, offensive, onslaught; *push*, strike, charge, thrust, advance, storming, invasion, blitzkrieg, counterattack; *storming*, siege, blockade, bombardment, investment; *foray*, skirmish, sortie, sally; *raid*, air raid, blitz,

barrage, broadside, volley, salvo; *mugging*, robbery with violence, grievous bodily harm, rape, gangbang (*colloq.*); *attacker*, aggressor, assailant; *besieger*, invader, raider, bomber; *terrorist*, gunman, mugger, rapist.

adj. *attacking*, aggressive, offensive.

vb. *attack*, assault, assail; *set upon*, go for, let fly at, fall upon, lay into (*colloq.*); *besiege*, lay siege to, blockade, invest; *bombard*, shell, bomb, strafe; *invade*, advance on, board, storm; *raid*, skirmish, foray, sortie, sally; *mug*, rape, beat up, jump on.

640 **DEFENCE**

See also 598 (safety); 600 (refuge); 649 (weapon).

n. *defence*, protection, safekeeping, guard, preservation; *defensive measure*, safety precaution; *rampart*, bulwark, earthworks, wall, moat, bunker, trenches; *barbed wire*, minefield, tripwire, barrage balloon; *fort*, fortification, strongpoint, fortress, castle, keep, donjon, citadel, acropolis, barbican; *armour*, protective clothing, flak jacket, gas mask, helmet; *defender*, protector, champion; *armed forces*, security forces, civil defence, Home Guard; *guard*, sentry, patrol, watch, escort, convoy.

adj. *defensive*, protective, anti-aircraft; *defended*, armed, armoured, dug in; *fortified*, barricaded, walled, bombproof, reinforced, bulletproof.

vb. *defend*, protect, keep, safeguard, guard, preserve, shelter, screen; *garrison*, arm, munition, mobilize; *fortify*, reinforce, wall, fence; *fend off*, ward off, withstand, resist.

641 **RETALIATION**

n. *retaliation*, self-defence, counterattack, second strike, reprisal, backlash, boomerang; *revenge*, retribution, vengeance, recrimination; *punishment*, comeuppance, just deserts, a dose of one's own medicine; *vindictiveness*, revengefulness, spite; *tit for tat*, an eye for an eye and a tooth for a tooth, feud, vendetta, gangland killing; *rejoinder*, retort, riposte, repartee, counter, counterargument; *avenger*.

adj. *retaliatory*, second-strike; *recriminatory*, retributive, punitive; *vindictive*, revengeful, vengeful, spiteful.

vb. *retaliate*, counterattack, fight back, give as good as one gets; *take one's revenge*, get one's own back, avenge, get even with, pay back; *exact retribution/compensation*, punish, repay; *rejoin*, retort, riposte, counter; *get one's* *just deserts/comeuppance*, have had it coming to one, get what one deserved.

642 **SUBMISSION**
See also 72 (conformity); 663 (obedience); 782 (servility).

n. *submission*, compliance, acquiescence, acceptance; *surrender*, capitulation, yielding; *subservience*, slavishness, deference, submissiveness; *fatalism*, resignation, defeatism; *docility*, humility, passivity, meekness.

adj. *submissive*, compliant, acquiescent, obedient; *amenable*, pliant, tractable; *subservient*, deferential, slavish, crawling; *fatalistic*, resigned, defeatist; *docile*, tame, humble, passive, meek.

vb. *submit*, comply, acquiesce, accept; *knuckle under*, bend, kow-tow, take it lying down (*colloq.*); *surrender*, capitulate, yield, give in, cave in, show the white flag, throw in the towel (*colloq.*); *admit defeat*, swallow one's pride, back down, eat humble pie; *defer to*, crawl, lick sb's boots (*colloq.*), lick sb's arse (*vulg.*).

643 **CONTENTION**
See also 635 (disagreement); 645 (war).

n. *contention*, conflict, clash, strife, dispute; *fighting*, force, combat, war, warfare, battle, hostilities; *(pitched) battle*, action, encounter, incident; *fracas*, affray, mêlée, fisticuffs, brawl, scuffle, scrap, punch-up (*colloq.*), dust-up (*colloq.*), aggro (*colloq.*); *argument*, war of words, altercation, debate; *duel*, sparring match, joust, fencing; *boxing*, wrestling, judo, ju-jitsu, kung fu, karate, aikido; *contest*, competition, event, tournament, race; *game*, set, match, bout, round, rubber; *contender*, contestant, challenger, rival, competitor, candidate, nominee.

adj. *contending*, warring, competing, rival; *competitive*, sporting; *contentious*, aggressive, combative, pugnacious, bellicose, belligerent.

vb. *contend*, contest, confront, challenge, dispute, struggle, strive, tussle; *fight*, combat, battle, take on, do battle with, engage; *brawl*, spar, scrap, scuffle, come to blows; *compete*, rival, race.

644 **PEACE**
See also 235 (motionlessness); 354 (silence); 646 (pacification).

n. *peace*, freedom from war, absence of hostilities, peacetime, peace process; *truce*, armistice, amnesty, cease-fire, lull; *cold war*,

balance of power, peaceful, coexistence; *neutrality*, non-alignment, armed neutrality; *peace treaty/agreement*, non-aggression pact, nuclear freeze; *agreement*, friendship, cordiality; *pacifism*, non-violence, non-aggression, appeasement, disarmament, non-intervention; *pacifist*, dove, conscientious objector, peacemaker, disarmer, neutral.

adj. *peaceful*, at peace, peacetime; *non-violent*, bloodless; *neutral*, non-aligned, non-interventionist, peace-loving, peaceable; *friendly*, cordial.

vb. *keep the peace*, observe neutrality, call a truce, cease hostilities, make peace, disarm.

645 **WAR**
See also 643 (contention).

n. *war*, warfare, fighting, hostilities, armed conflict, combat, mobilization, call-up, conscription; *battle*, campaign, offensive, attack, strategy, tactics; *operation*, mission, invasion, raid, action; *world war*, global war, nuclear war, civil war, war of independence; *crusade*, holy war, jihad; *war of attrition*, trench/jungle/desert/guerrilla warfare, naval/submarine warfare, germ/chemical warfare; *psychological warfare*, war of nerves, propaganda war, cold war; *terrorism*, bioterrorism; *theatre of war*, battlefield, battleground, front (line), battle zone, no-man's land, arena; *belligerence*, hostility, aggressiveness, warmongering, sabre-rattling, aggression, militancy, militarism; *warmonger*, hawk, aggressor, belligerent.

adj. *warring*, hostile, at war, belligerent; *martial*, military, strategic, tactical; *armed*, under arms, on active service, mobilized; *bellicose*, militant, aggressive, hawkish, militaristic, warmongering.

vb. *wage war*, war, fight, battle, campaign; *attack*, raid, invade, engage; *declare war*, go to war, use force; *arm*, mobilize, call up, conscript, put on a war footing.

646 **PACIFICATION**
n. *pacification*, mollification, appeasement, peacemaking, détente, rapprochement, conciliation, mediation, conflict resolution; *agreement*, understanding, satisfaction, reparation, reconciliation; *truce*, armistice, cease-fire, amnesty; *treaty*, pact, convention; *disarmament*, decommissioning, demobilization, arms freeze, SALT (Strategic Arms Limitation Talks); *white flag*, peace offering, olive branch, overture, hand of friendship, pipe of peace.

adj. *pacificatory*, placatory, conciliatory, propitiatory.

vb. *pacify*, mollify, appease, placate; *conciliate*, mediate, propitiate, reconcile; *force to negotiate*, bomb to the conference table; *agree*, settle one's differences; *disarm*, demobilize, decommission; *make peace*, lay down one's arms, bury the hatchet, shake hands, forgive and forget, let bygones be bygones; *sue for peace*, offer the hand of friendship, hold out the olive branch.

647 **MEDIATION**
See also 148 (moderation).

n. *mediation*, arbitration, good offices, shuttle diplomacy, interposition, intervention, intercession; *broking*, computer dating, matchmaking; *mediator*, intermediary, middleman, peacemaker, negotiator, broker, matchmaker, go-between; *arbiter*, arbitrator, umpire, referee, adjudicator, assessor, third party, neutral; *press officer/secretary*, public relations officer, spokesman/-person/-woman, intercessor, advocate, ombudsman.

adj. *mediatory*, intercessory.

vb. *mediate*, intercede, intervene, interpose; *arbitrate*, umpire, referee, adjudicate.

648 **COMBATANT**
n. *combatant*, soldier, conscript, volunteer, fighter, warrior, legionnaire, centurion; *gunner*, rifleman, sniper, bombardier, grenadier, artilleryman, infantryman; *seaman*, sailor, marine, submariner; *pilot*, navigator, bomb-aimer; *paratrooper*, commando; *guerrilla*, underground, freedom fighter, resistance fighter; *swordsman*, man-at-arms, knight, archer, lancer, hussar, cavalry; *reservist*, territorial, militiaman, irregular; *mercenary*, soldier of fortune, adventurer, freebooter, pirate; *private*, corporal, lance corporal, sergeant, sergeant major, second lieutenant, lieutenant, captain, major, lieutenant colonel, colonel, brigadier, major general, lieutenant general, general, field marshal; *able seaman*, leading seaman, petty office, sublieutenant, lieutenant, lieutenant commander, commander, captain, rear admiral, vice admiral, admiral; *flight sergeant*, pilot officer, flying officer, flight lieutenant, squadron leader, wing commander, group captain, air commodore, air vice marshal, air marshal; *platoon*, company, battalion, brigade,

division, corps, regiment, unit, troop, squadron, flight, group, wing; *armed forces*, services, army, navy, air force, marines.

649 **WEAPON**
See also 640 (defence).

n. *weapon*, arms, armaments, weaponry, arsenal, armoury, WMD (weapon of mass destruction), weapon of mass effect; *club*, truncheon, cosh, mace, cudgel, shillelagh; *bow and arrow*, longbow, crossbow, bolt, javelin; *spear*, pike, lance, axe, sword, rapier, cutlass, sabre, scimitar, kukri, dagger, stiletto, bayonet, cold steel (*colloq.*); *explosive*, high explosive, TNT (trinitrotoluene), nitroglycerine, gunpowder, dynamite, cordite, Semtex (*tdmk*), gelignite, jelly (*colloq.*); *bomb*, atomic bomb, A-bomb, hydrogen bomb, H-bomb, nuclear bomb, neutron bomb, dirty bomb, flying bomb, smart bomb, cluster bomb, incendiary bomb, napalm bomb, fuel-air bomb, blast bomb, nail bomb, pipe bomb, car bomb, time bomb, letter bomb, parcel bomb, (hand) grenade, rocket-propelled grenade, RPG, Molotov cocktail, petrol bomb, acid bomb, depth charge, torpedo, mine; *gun*, firearm, small arms, handgun, pistol, revolver, rifle, machine gun, sub-machine gun, shotgun, musket, shooter (*colloq.*), stun gun, Taser (*tdmk*) or tazer; *field gun*, cannon, mortar, howitzer; *ammunition*, munitions, round, cartridge; *projectile*, rocket, shell, bullet, shot, slug, pellet, cannonball, grapeshot, shrapnel, flak, tracer; *guided missile*, cruise missile, ICBM (intercontinental ballistic missile), MIRV (multiple independently targeted re-entry vehicle).

vb. *weaponize*.

650 **TROPHY**
See also 448 (memory); 774 (repute); 859 (reward).

n. *trophy*, prize, award, reward, kudos; *status symbol*, trophy wife; *cup*, plate, shield, badge, blue rosette, palm, laurels; *decoration*, medal, cross, star, ribbon, gong (*colloq.*); *mention* (in dispatches), honourable mention, citation; *honour(s)*, title, order; *spoils*, plunder, loot, booty; *consolation prize*, booby prize, wooden spoon.

651 **SUCCESS**
See also 31 (superiority); 653 (completion); 655 (prosperity).

n. *success*, happy/favourable outcome,

happy ending, good fortune; *feat*, achievement, attainment, accomplishment, pass, graduation, good shot, (smash) hit (*colloq*.); *progress*, advance, lead; *good luck*, run of luck, lucky break, beginner's luck, fluke (*colloq*.); *flash in the pan*, nine days' wonder; *triumph*, victory, win, result, defeat, conquest, checkmate, game, set and match, walkover, beating, thrashing (*colloq*.); *winner*, victor, conqueror, champion, prizewinner, roaring/runaway success, successful candidate, bestseller, blockbuster.

adj. *successful*, lucky, happy, fortunate; *profitable*, fruitful, beneficial, advantageous; *prosperous*, thriving, flourishing; *winning*, victorious, prizewinning, record-breaking, bestselling, conquering, triumphant, unbeaten, undisputed.

vb. *succeed*, achieve, accomplish, attain, fulfil; *pass*, graduate, make a success of, make a go of, pull off (*colloq*.), bring off (*colloq*.); *bear fruit*, do well, pay off, work out, come off (*colloq*.); *prosper*, profit, progress, advance, thrive, flourish, be/score a hit, make it big (*colloq*.), arrive (*colloq*.); *win*, be victorious, conquer, triumph, prevail, beat, defeat, trounce, crush, get the better of, thrash (*colloq*.), come out on top (*colloq*.).

652 **FAILURE**

See also 32 (inferiority); 654 (non-completion).

n. *failure*, lack of success, disaster, débâcle, fiasco, bankruptcy, collapse, insolvency, flop (*colloq*.), washout (*colloq*.), damp squib (*colloq*.), early bath (*colloq*.); *inefficacy*, ineffectiveness, breakdown, engine failure, fault; *negligence*, omission, neglect, oversight, faux pas, slip; *futility*, wasted effort, Pyrrhic victory, wild-goose chase; *defeat*, downfall, rout, overthrow, checkmate, beating, thrashing (*colloq*.); *loser*, no-hoper, unsuccessful candidate/competitor, underdog; *failure*, dud, lame duck, also-ran (*colloq*.), has-been (*colloq*.), bankrupt.

adj. *unsuccessful*, disastrous, abortive, miscarried, misfired, failed, would-be, manqué, insolvent, bankrupt; *unfortunate*, unlucky; *ineffectual*, ineffective, dud, defunct, kaput; *unprofitable*, futile, fruitless, bootless, (in) vain; *defeated*, beaten, overthrown, foiled, done for, hoist with one's own petard.

vb. *fail*, be unsuccessful, have no success; *not make the grade*, fall down, fall short, miss, flunk (*colloq*.), come a cropper (*colloq*.); *stop working*, malfunction, seize up, break down,

falter, stall, get stuck, pack up (*colloq*.), conk out (*colloq*.); *fall flat*, come to nothing, come unstuck, fizzle out, fall through, flop (*colloq*.), bomb (*colloq*.); *go down*, go under, go to the wall, go bankrupt, crash, go bust (*colloq*.); *lose*, be defeated, suffer defeat, come last, come second, be pipped at the post.

653 **COMPLETION**

See also 49 (completeness); 584 (perfection); 651 (success).

n. *completion*, finishing off, rounding off; *perfection*, realization, fulfilment, consummation, culmination; *end*, finish, ending, conclusion, termination; *achievement*, accomplishment; *readiness*, ripeness, maturity, fruition; *final stroke*, coup de grâce, finishing touch; *the last straw*, breaking point, the bitter end.

adj. *completed*, finished, fulfilled, done, done and dusted (*colloq*.), sewn up (*colloq*.); *finishing*, concluding, conclusive, final, culminating, crowning.

vb. *complete*, finish off, round off, finalize; *perfect*, fulfil, consummate, put the finishing touches to, polish off, wrap up (*colloq*.), see through, wind up; *end*, finish, conclude, culminate, terminate, come to a head; *achieve*, accomplish, realize, work out; *mature*, ripen.

654 **NON-COMPLETION**

See also 50 (incompleteness); 652 (failure).

n. *non-completion*, non-fulfilment, a job half-done, the labour of Sisyphus, wild goose chase; *imperfection*, fault, blemish; *deficiency*, deficit, arrears, shortfall; *immaturity*, rawness, unripeness; *circular argument*, vicious circle; *stalemate*, draw; *postponement*, deferment, cold storage.

adj. *uncompleted*, unfinished, half-finished, half-done; *imperfect*, deficient, unrealized, not finalized, in the air, half-baked (*colloq*.); *immature*, unripe, underdone, parboiled; *never-ending*, endless, Sisyphean.

vb. *not complete*, leave undone, skimp, not follow through; *give up*, not stay the course, skip, drop out; *postpone*, defer, hold over, shelve, put on ice, put off.

655 **PROSPERITY**

See also 651 (success); 712 (wealth).

n. *prosperity*, success, welfare, wellbeing, happiness, good fortune; *milk and honey*, the fat of the land, blessings, high life, the life of Riley; *wealth*, riches, affluence, Easy Street, luxury, boom; *prime*, halcyon days, salad days, summer, golden age, heyday; *place in the sun*, bed of roses, clover.

adj. *prosperous*, successful, thriving, flourishing, booming, in clover; *wealthy*, affluent, fat, well-to-do, well off, comfortable; *rising*, up and coming, on the up and up; *golden*, halcyon, sunny, rosy, blissful; *promising*, auspicious, cloudless, fair.

vb. *prosper*, do well, fare well, thrive, flourish, boom, do a roaring trade; *make a fortune*, make one's pile, grow fat, win the jackpot; *be on the up and up*, work one's way up, make it, blossom; *have it made*, never have had it so good, live like a lord, be rolling in money.

656 **ADVERSITY**
See also 628 (difficulty); 735 (sorrow).

n. *adversity*, trouble, difficulty, struggle; *trial*, ordeal, adverse conditions, burden, pressure, opposition; *hardship*, hard/lean times, hard life, school of hard knocks, slings and arrows, tough time, dark age, winter, cold wind, bad patch, bad time, bad day, bad hair day, annus horribilis, mauvais quart d'heure, long dark night of the soul; *misfortune*, bad luck, sod's law, hard lines; *misadventure*, disaster, accident, catastrophe; *evil influence*, curse, unlucky star, jinx.

adj. *adverse*, unfavourable, inauspicious; *opposed*, hostile, unfriendly, cold, malign; *unfortunate*, unlucky, wretched; *troubled*, afflicted, burdened, plagued, beleaguered, bedevilled, stricken, fraught, hard pressed, up against it; *disastrous*, catastrophic, ruinous; *bleak*, cold, hard, lean.

vb. *be in trouble*, have a hard/thin time (of it), have been in the wars, go through it, be put through it, hit a bad patch, fall on hard times, feel the pinch, tighten one's belt.

657 **AUTHORITY**
See also 71 (rule); 622 (management); 661 (command); 672 (commission); 854 (jurisdiction).

n. *authority*, prestige, influence, sway, leadership; *power*, rule, jurisdiction, command, control, patronage, mandate, sovereignty; *right*, seniority, priority, prerogative; *supremacy*, ascendancy, hegemony, upper hand, dominion; *council*, panel, board, committee, cabinet, convocation, congress, convention, county/borough/town/parish council; *legislature*, legislative assembly, parliament, house,

senate, administration, government, regime; *democracy*, majority/minority rule, pluralism; *republicanism*, constitutional monarchy; *communism*, socialism; *dictatorship*, autocracy, tyranny, totalitarianism, police state, big brother; *officialdom*, bureaucracy, the powers that be, they, them, the Establishment, civil service; *councillor*, member of parliament, minister, statesman, parliamentarian, senator, representative, delegate, congressman/-woman; *symbol of authority*, badge of office, insignia, regalia, crown jewels, crown, sceptre, standard, staff, wand, baton, crosier, mitre, bat; *uniform*, epaulette, tab, stripe, star, crown, gold braid, scrambled egg (*colloq.*).

adj. *authoritative*, influential, prestigious, commanding, leading, dominant; *empowered*, ruling, governing, constitutional, in command, in control, reigning, on the throne, sovereign, in power, in office; *democratic*, pluralist, republican, monarchical, communist, socialist; *governmental*, gubernatorial, bureaucratic, administrative, official.

vb. *rule*, have power over, hold sway, reign, have control, govern, control; *tyrannize*, dictate, oppress, lord it over, domineer, have the whip hand, call the tune; *take command*, assume control/command, accede to the throne, gain power, (be asked to) form a government; *seize power*, usurp, overthrow.

658 **ANARCHY**
See also 56 (disorder); 853 (illegality).

n. *anarchy*, lawlessness, breakdown of law and order, mob rule, rioting, civil disobedience, indiscipline, disruption; *disorder*, chaos, turmoil, pandemonium; *laissez-faire*, non-interference, non-intervention, permissiveness, indulgence, tolerance, licence; *laxity*, easing, relaxation, derestriction, deregulation, legalization, free-for-all.

adj. *anarchic*, lawless, uncontrolled, disruptive, undisciplined; *disordered*, chaotic, riotous; *permissive*, tolerant, indulgent, flexible, free and easy; *lax*, relaxed, loose, soft, negligent, easy, ineffectual.

vb. *take the law into* one's *own hands*, be a law unto oneself, kick over the traces, run amuck; *misgovern*, lose control, abdicate responsibility; *tolerate*, permit, indulge, not enforce, give free rein to, waive the rules, turn a blind eye to.

659 SEVERITY

See also 745 (seriousness).

n. *severity*, strictness, rigour, rigorousness; *discipline*, firmness, rod of iron, heavy hand; *harshness*, oppression, cruelty, draconian measures, tyranny, suppression, zero tolerance; *intolerance*, bigotry, pedantry; *intransigence*, pound of flesh, no quarter, no compromise, inflexibility, full weight of the law, letter of the law; *austerity*, asceticism, self-denial, puritanism; *disciplinarian*, martinet, stickler, terror, scourge; *dictator*, despot, persecutor, oppressor; *extremist*, bigot, pedant, ascetic, puritan; *bossyboots* (*colloq.*), control freak.

adj. *severe*, strict, rigorous, extreme; *disciplined*, firm, stern, uncompromising, hard-boiled, hard-headed; *harsh*, oppressive, cruel, draconian, drastic; *tyrannical*, autocratic, dictatorial, despotic; *intolerant*, bigoted, hidebound, pedantic, censorious; *inflexible*, unbending, rigid; *austere*, ascetic, puritanical; *domineering*, bullying, bossy.

vb. *be severe* etc, tighten up on, clamp down on, crack down on; *discipline*, deal firmly with, get tough with, play hardball with (*US*), throw the book at, come down like a ton of bricks on (*colloq.*); *oppress*, tyrannize, suppress, intimidate, domineer, bully, persecute; *not tolerate*, not countenance, stand no nonsense; *insist*, put one's foot down, stand one's ground, hold out for.

660 LENIENCY

See also 813 (forgiveness).

n. *leniency*, mildness, softness, gentleness, kindness; *forgiveness*, pardon; *mercy*, clemency, quarter; *tolerance*, indulgence, sufferance, forbearance; *humanity*, compassion, sympathy, charity.

adj. *lenient*, mild, soft, gentle; *forgiving*, merciful, clement; *tolerant*, indulgent, enlightened, liberal, forbearing, easy-going, long-suffering; *humane*, compassionate, kindly, charitable, soft-hearted, sympathetic.

vb. *be lenient* etc, pull one's punches, go easy on (*colloq.*), handle with kid gloves; *show forgiveness* etc, overlook, forgive, pardon; *have mercy*, relent, take pity, spare the rod; *tolerate*, indulge, allow, put up with; *refrain*, forbear.

661 COMMAND

See also 622 (management); 657 (authority); 672 (commission); 681 (request).

n. *command*, order, direction, directive, instruction, (three-line) whip; *charge*, mandate, dictate; *decree*, proclamation, edict, papal bull, ordinance, prescription; *law*, act, injunction, writ, ruling; *summons*, subpoena, habeas corpus, order in council, sequestration; *(tax) demand*, requirement, passport.

adj. *mandatory*, compulsory, obligatory, statutory; *commanding*, imperative, peremptory, compelling.

vb. *command*, give/issue a command etc, order, direct, instruct; *charge*, mandate, dictate, make compulsory, compel; *decree*, proclaim, ordain, prescribe, lay down; *rule*, enjoin, enforce, issue a writ, lay down the law; *summon*, subpoena, sequestrate; *demand*, require.

662 DISOBEDIENCE

See also 127 (revolution); 637 (defiance); 680 (refusal); 832 (improbity).

n. *disobedience*, refusal to obey, insubordination, non-compliance; *misbehaviour*, naughtiness, mischief; *awkwardness*, contrariness, cussedness, waywardness; *crime*, breach of the peace, disturbance, trespass, contempt of court, lawlessness; *violation*, transgression, infringement, delinquency; *mutiny*, rebellion, revolt, insurrection, defection, desertion, truancy; *defiance*, intractability, recalcitrance; *insurgence*, sedition, subversion, treason; *naughty child*, mischief-maker, trouble-maker, rascal, holy terror (*colloq.*), handful (*colloq.*); *criminal*, delinquent, hooligan, tearaway; *rebel*, mutineer, deserter; *revolutionary*, radical, insurrectionist, anarchist, hothead, firebrand; *insurgent*, subversive, rioter, terrorist.

adj. *disobedient*, insubordinate; *naughty*, mischievous, unruly; *mutinous*, rebellious, riotous, dissident; *defiant*, intractable, awkward, difficult; *wayward*, contrary, bolshie, obstreperous, recalcitrant, refractory, bloody-minded; *traitorous*, treacherous, disloyal, duplicitous; *subversive*, disruptive, anarchic.

vb. *disobey*, defy, fail to obey/comply, disregard; *misbehave*, play up, cause trouble; *violate*, break, transgress, infringe, trespass; *mutiny*, rebel, revolt, defect, desert, play truant.

663 OBEDIENCE

See also 642 (submission); 670 (subjection).

n. *obedience*, compliance, good behaviour,

acquiescence; *deference*, slavishness, obsequiousness, submission, subservience, docility; *dutifulness*, devotion, loyalty, fidelity.

adj. *obedient*, compliant, acquiescent, law-abiding, well-behaved; *deferential*, slavish, obsequious, subservient; *docile*, submissive, tractable, meek, henpecked, under sb's thumb (*colloq.*); *dutiful*, devoted, loyal, faithful.

vb. *obey*, comply, observe, heed, keep, acquiesce, agree; *behave*, do as one is told, submit, do one's duty, follow the party line, toe the line; *defer*, grovel, crawl, tug one's forelock, bow and scrape.

adv. *obediently*, quietly, with good grace, unquestioningly.

664 COMPULSION

See also 143 (strength); 536 (necessity); 558 (requirement).

n. *compulsion*, constraint, obligation, no choice/option; *pressure*, force, coercion, violence, duress, arm-twisting, strong-arm tactics; *drive*, need, necessity, urgency; *threat*, blackmail, sanction, gunboat diplomacy; *conscription*, call-up, impressment, draft; *forced labour*, slavery, servitude.

adj. *compulsory*, obligatory, mandatory, binding; *compelling*, compulsive, driving, coercive, irresistible; *necessary*, imperative, unavoidable.

vb. *compel*, oblige, constrain, leave no choice; *force*, coerce, lean on, pressurize; *drive*, push, propel, urge; *require*, necessitate, dictate.

adv. *compulsorily*, bodily, under duress, under protest, of necessity.

665 MASTER

See also 31 (superiority); 622 (management).

n. *master*, mistress, lord, lady, lord of the manor, lady of the house; *director*, leader, governor, controller, overlord, superior, principal; *boss*, manager, supervisor, foreman/-woman, overseer, gangmaster, gaffer (*colloq.*), guv'nor (*colloq.*); *monarch*, sovereign, king, queen, prince, princess, regent, tsar, emperor, empress, grand duke/duchess; *president*, ruler, viceroy, potentate, chief, chieftain, margrave, elector, sheikh, sultan, proconsul, headman, maharajah, moghul, nawab; *despot*, tyrant, autocrat, Führer, Gauleiter, Duce, commissar; *official*, mayor, mayoress, provost, alderman, prefect, commissioner, civil servant, councillor,

bureaucrat; *judge*, magistrate, sheriff, justice (of the peace), beak (*colloq.*).

666 SERVANT

See also 32 (inferiority).

n. *servant*, factotum, majordomo, butler, footman, flunky, maid, parlour maid, chambermaid; *nursery nurse*, nursemaid, nanny, ayah, wet nurse, au pair; *valet*, manservant, gentleman's gentleman, scout, lady's maid, lady-in-waiting, page; *steward/-ess*, cabin crew, flight attendant, air hostess, waiter, waitress, barmaid, barman, bartender (US), barista; *housekeeper*, cook, kitchen maid, tweeny, skivvy; *daily* (woman), domestic, help, char(woman/lady), cleaning lady; *concierge*, doorman, porter, janitor, caretaker; *worker*, employee, staff, crew, complement; *menial*, drudge, fag, dogsbody, handyman, odd-job man, chief cook and bottle-washer (*colloq.*); *slave*, serf, bondsman, villein, galley slave; *assistant*, secretary, amanuensis, aide, right-hand man, bodyguard, attendant, equerry, gillie, chaplain; *subaltern*, aide-de-camp, lieutenant, batman; *underling*, henchman, lackey, minion, junior.

adj. *serving*, in service, menial, below stairs; *working*, in employment.

vb. *serve*, wait on/upon, look after, minister to, attend, make oneself useful, work for, do for (*colloq.*).

667 FREEDOM

See also 669 (liberation); 677 (permission).

n. *freedom*, liberty, independence, freedom of action/choice, free will; *free speech*, civil rights, democracy, franchise, emancipation, universal suffrage, freedom of the press; *exemption*, immunity, special dispensation; *liberalism*, libertarianism, egalitarianism; *non-intervention*, autonomy, self-government, home rule; *free enterprise*, laissez-faire, market economy, free port, free trade; *room to manoeuvre*, play, Lebensraum, elbowroom, latitude, leeway, margin, wriggle room; *free hand*, blank cheque, carte blanche, free rein, licence; *freeman*, freedman, freedwoman, ex-convict, escapee; *independent*, freethinker, freelancer; *liberal*, libertarian, egalitarian; *gratuity*, free gift, freebie (*colloq.*), freesheet.

adj. *free*, at liberty, on the loose, at large; *independent*, self-governing, autonomous, democratic; *unattached*, self-employed, freelance; *exempt*, immune, unaffected, -free; *emancipated*, enfranchised, liberated; *liberal*, libertarian, egalitarian; *unbiased*, unprejudiced, free-thinking, enlightened; *free of charge*, gratis, complimentary; *unchecked*, unrestrained, unfettered, unshackled, unbridled, unhindered, uninhibited.

vb. *be free* etc, have a free hand, be a free agent, please oneself, have the freedom/run of, make free with, feel free; *loosen up*, cut loose, let oneself go, let one's hair down (*colloq.*), let it all hang out (*colloq.*); *not interfere*, let alone, let be, live and let live, leave sb to their own devices; give sb some leeway, cut sb some slack (*colloq.*).

668 RESTRAINT

See also 148 (moderation); 601 (trap); 630 (hindrance); 695 (retention); 843 (self-restraint).

n. *restraint*, prohibition, ban, bar, veto; *suppression*, repression, constraint, control, clampdown; *slowing*, deceleration, retardation, drag, curb, brake; *rein*, leash, bit, gag, muzzle, straitjacket, bonds, ropes, handcuffs; *arrest*, detention, remand, custody, control order, house arrest, tagging, anti-social behaviour order (ASBO), acceptable behaviour contract (ABC); *imprisonment*, custodial sentence, incarceration, (solitary) confinement, internment, captivity, quarantine, care, time (*colloq.*), stretch (*colloq.*), porridge (*colloq.*); *restriction*, speed limit, curfew, roadblock; *boundary*, upper limit, ceiling, cut-off point; *economy*, freeze, cutback, credit squeeze, retrenchment, price control, prices and incomes policy; *price-fixing*, cartel, monopoly, closed shop, protectionism, tariff, restrictive practice; *gaoler*, jailer, (prison) warder/wardress, prison officer, (prison) governor, screw (*colloq.*); *keeper*, curator, custodian, attendant; *guard*, escort, bodyguard, garrison; *warden*, ranger, gamekeeper; *concierge*, porter, caretaker, housekeeper, janitor; *watchman*, coastguard, firewatcher, sentry, lookout, scout; *guardian*, foster/adoptive parent, tutor; *nanny*, nursery nurse, nursemaid, governess, childminder, baby-sitter.

adj. *restraining*, suppressive, repressive, restrictive, limiting; *restrained*, limited, controlled, disciplined; *inhibited*, straitlaced, reserved, uptight (*colloq.*); *trapped*, cornered; *custodial*, captive, imprisoned, under arrest, in detention, confined to barracks, gated; *in custody*, behind bars, in clink/jug (*colloq.*), inside (*colloq.*); *fettered*, handcuffed, manacled, in the stocks, in irons, bound, gagged; *protectionist*, monopolistic.

vb. *restrain*, limit, control, restrict; *prohibit*, ban, bar, veto; *suppress*, repress, clamp down on, inhibit; *subdue*, muzzle, silence, gag, censor; *slow*, decelerate, retard, curb, be a drag on, hold back, check; *fight back/down*, dam up, bottle up; *block*, hinder, impede, cramp, hamper; *arrest*, apprehend, detain, run in, pick up; *imprison*, remand in custody, put in prison, intern, incarcerate, confine, put behind bars (*colloq.*), put away (*colloq.*); *chain up*, fetter, manacle, handcuff, clap in irons; *economize*, freeze, cut back, control prices, tighten one's belt (*colloq.*), live within one's income/means.

669 LIBERATION

See also 606 (deliverance); 667 (freedom); 696 (disposal).

n. *liberation*, freeing, rescue, deliverance, salvation; *release*, discharge, acquittal, parole, bail; *demobilization*, disbanding; *extrication*, loosing, disengagement; *redemption*, forgiveness, absolution; *emancipation*, enfranchisement, liberalization, relaxation, easing.

vb. *liberate*, free, set free, turn loose, rescue, deliver, save; *release*, discharge, acquit, parole, bail; *demobilize*, disband, break up, demob (*colloq.*); *extricate*, disentangle, unravel, loose, disengage, unleash, let out, let off the lead; *redeem*, forgive, pardon, absolve; *emancipate*, enfranchise, give the vote, liberalize, relax, ease, deregulate.

670 SUBJECTION

See also 32 (inferiority); 663 (obedience).

n. *subjection*, subordination, subjugation, conquest, colonization, exploitation, annexation; *inferiority*, dependence; *allegiance*, nationality, subjecthood, service; *oppression*, hegemony, dominance, yoke; *enslavement*, slavery, servitude, bondage, feudalism; *slave labour*, forced labour, conscription, sweatshop.

adj. *subject*, subordinate; *inferior*, junior, subsidiary; *bound*, dependent, tied; *enslaved*, colonized, tributary, colonial; *oppressed*, downtrodden, under the yoke/jackboot, in the clutches of, under the sway of.

vb. *subjugate*, subject, conquer, subdue, reduce, subordinate, colonize, enslave, exploit; *oppress*, dominate, cow, have under one's thumb, bully, boss, push around.

671 PRISON

See also 861 (means of punishment).

n. *prison*, gaol, jail, lockup, penitentiary, maximum-security prison, open prison, clink (*colloq.*), stir (*colloq.*), jug (*colloq.*), nick (*colloq.*); *detention centre*, remand centre/home, internment camp, rehabilitation centre; *Borstal*, approved school, reformatory, reform school; *cell*, dungeon, guardroom, oubliette, cage; *condemned cell*, death row; *prisoner-of-war camp*, POW camp, concentration camp, death camp, gulag; *prisoner*, convict, inmate, jailbird/gaolbird (*colloq.*), con (*colloq.*), old lag (*colloq.*), guest of Her Majesty (*colloq.*), lifer (*colloq.*); *detainee*, accused, prisoner in the dock/at the bar; *captive*, prisoner of war, POW, enemy combatant, political prisoner; *hostage*, kidnap victim.

672 COMMISSION

See also 657 (authority); 661 (command); 675 (delegate).

n. *commission*, mandate, charge, task, errand, assignment; *delegation*, deputation, legation, embassy, representation, mission, people's bureau; *appointment*, nomination, installation, induction, enthronement, ordination, consecration, coronation, inauguration, investment, investiture; *election*, return; *sequestration*, trusteeship, power of attorney, charter, licence, proxy; *regency*, protectorate.

adj. *commissioned*, deputed, empowered, entrusted, vicarious.

vb. *commission*, delegate, depute, mandate, charge, assign; *entrust*, commit, consign; *appoint*, nominate, install, induct, enthrone, anoint, ordain, consecrate, crown, inaugurate, invest; *authorize*, empower, charter, sanction, accredit, license; *elect*, return.

673 CANCELLATION

See also 474 (negation).

n. *cancellation*, cancelling, abrogation; *annulment*, nullification, invalidation; *revoking*, revocation, repudiation, retraction, rescission; *abolition*, dissolution, repeal, countermand, reprieve, reversal; *dismissal*, removal from office, unfrocking, suspension, sacking (*colloq.*), the sack (*colloq.*), the heave (*colloq.*), the boot (*colloq.*); *discharge*, court martial, recall, relief; *demotion*, downgrading; *redundancy*, natural wastage, layoff, job

losses; *dethronement*, deposal, deposition, overthrow.

adj. *cancelled*, null and void, invalid, quashed.

vb. *cancel*, abrogate, scrub out; *annul*, nullify, invalidate, render null and void, void; *revoke*, repudiate, retract, rescind, unsubscribe; *abolish*, dissolve, repeal, countermand, reprieve, reverse, quash, overrule, set aside; *dismiss*, remove from office, defrock, unfrock, strike off, suspend, give sb notice, give sb their cards, sack (*colloq.*), fire (*colloq.*), lay off, make redundant; *discharge*, cashier, court-martial, recall, relieve; *demote*, downgrade, kick upstairs, reduce to the ranks; *dethrone*, depose, unseat, overthrow.

674 RESIGNATION

See also 563 (relinquishment).

n. *resignation*, leaving, withdrawal, retirement, abdication, desertion; *renunciation*, relinquishment, abandonment; *pension*, golden handshake, superannuation, gold watch, redundancy money.

adj. *retiring*, outgoing; *retired*, ex-, former, sometime, one-time, emeritus.

vb. *resign*, leave, withdraw, retire, take early retirement, abdicate, stand down, not stand for re-election, tender one's resignation, apply for the Chiltern Hundreds, hand in one's notice, ask for one's cards; *renounce*, relinquish, abandon, desert, give up, throw up, quit.

675 DELEGATE

See also 672 (commission).

n. *delegate*, representative, consignee, deputy, agent; *delegation*, mission, deputation, committee, working party; *broker*, middleman, stockbroker, negotiator; *nominee*, appointee, proxy, stakeholder; *trustee*, executor, licensee; *legal representative*, advocate, attorney, counsel; *diplomat*, envoy, ambassador, plenipotentiary, consul, attaché, resident, high commissioner, chargé d'affaires; *mission*, embassy, legation, consulate, high commission; *legate*, nuncio.

676 DEPUTY

See also 128 (substitution).

n. *deputy*, second-in-command, right-hand man, lieutenant, assistant, second; *representative*, proxy, substitute, stand-in, agent, understudy, double; *spokesman/-person/-woman*, mouthpiece.

adj. *deputy*, vice-, pro-, acting.

vb. *deputize*, represent, act for, speak for, stand in for, substitute for, replace.

677 PERMISSION

See also 436 (assent); 667 (freedom); 852 (legality).

n. *permission*, authority, leave, freedom, liberty, consent; *authorization*, approval, clearance, sanction, legalization, go-ahead (*colloq.*), green light (*colloq.*); *dispensation*, concession, allowance; *free hand*, blank cheque, carte blanche; *permit*, licence, royal charter, franchise, certificate, grant; *pass*, passport, visa, safe-conduct, passbook, ticket, chit.

adj. *permissive*, tolerant, indulgent, lenient; *permitted*, allowed, free, permissible, printable; *licensed*, chartered, authorized, approved.

vb. *permit*, allow, let, consent, give permission, grant leave, vouchsafe; *authorize*, clear, sanction, pass, rubber-stamp, legalize, decontrol; *license*, charter, certify, franchise; *approve*, give the go-ahead (*colloq.*), encourage; *tolerate*, brook, suffer.

678 VETO

See also 853 (illegality).

n. *veto*, prohibition, forbiddance, interdiction, (blanket) refusal, countermand, proscription, disqualification, taboo; *interference*, intervention; *ban*, bar, embargo, boycott, blacklist; *licensing laws*; *censorship*, suppression, news blackout, D-notice.

adj. *prohibitory*, prohibiting; *prohibitive*, restrictive; *prohibited*, forbidden, not allowed; *illegal*, unlawful, illicit, against the law; *banned*, barred, embargoed, blacked; *censored*, suppressed, blacked out, unprintable; *taboo*, frowned on.

vb. *veto*, prohibit, forbid, refuse, refuse permission, interdict, countermand, disqualify, restrict; *ban*, bar, boycott, embargo, proscribe, outlaw, black, blacklist; *debar*, shut out, blackball, exclude; *suppress*, censor, blue-pencil, cut.

679 OFFER

See also 537 (willingness).

n. *offer*, proffer, proffering; *bid*, tender; *proposal*, proposition, suggestion, submission, application; *approach*, advance, overture, invitation.

adj. *offered*, on offer, advertised; *for sale*,

available, for hire, to let, on the market, up for grabs (*colloq.*).

vb. *offer*, proffer, make available; *bid*, tender; *propose*, suggest, put forward, submit, apply; *approach*, make advances/overtures, invite; *advertise*, put on the market, offer for sale, put up for auction, invite tenders; *offer one's services*, come forward, stand, run for, volunteer, run.

680 REFUSAL

See also 538 (unwillingness); 662 (disobedience); 682 (protest).

n. *refusal*, failure to obey/comply, non-compliance, reluctance, recalcitrance; *rejection*, thumb's-down, non-acceptance, denial, withholding, disallowance; *ban*, veto, prohibition; *rebuff*, snub, slap in the face.

adj. *non-compliant*, negative, recalcitrant, reluctant.

vb. *refuse*, fail to obey/comply; *reject*, decline, turn down, not accept, deny, withhold, disallow, not hear of; *ban*, veto, prohibit; *rebuff*, snub, cut, scorn, not listen, turn a deaf ear, ignore; *repel*, repulse, dismiss; *harden one's heart*, have nothing to do with, turn one's back on, wash one's hands of, set one's face against; *go so far and no further*, draw a line in the sand.

681 REQUEST

See also 661 (command).

n. *request*, appeal, plea, entreaty, begging; *demand*, requisition, ultimatum, blackmail; *invitation*, invite, solicitation, canvassing; *petition*, call, application, claim, counterclaim; *prayer*, supplication, intercession, invocation; *suggestion*, proposal, motion, approach; *fund-raising*, begging letter, charity appeal, flag day, benefit game/performance; *advertising*, advertisement, circular, mailshot, small ad, personal column; *petitioner*, lobby, lobbyist, pressure group; *appellant*, plaintiff, applicant, suppliant, claimant; *advertiser*, salesman, customer, enquirer; *canvasser*, solicitor, hawker, tout, barker, pedlar; *beggar*, scrounger, tramp, bum, sponger, hitch-hiker, mendicant.

adj. *supplicatory*, imprecatory, prayerful, suppliant, on bended knee, grovelling, with cap in hand, imploring, beseeching; *begging*, mendicant, charitable, fund-raising; *urgent*, insistent.

vb. *request*, ask for, call for, invite, express a wish, ask a favour; *demand*, requisition, blackmail; *petition*, appeal, apply, claim; *appeal for funds*, pass the hat round, have a whip-round (*colloq.*); *canvass*, solicit, hawk, tout, peddle; *beg*, entreat, plead, beseech, crave; *cadge*, sponge, scrounge, hitch-hike, bum (*colloq.*), touch (*colloq.*); *pray*, supplicate, intercede, invoke, call on; *suggest*, propose, move, approach.

682 **PROTEST**
See also 538 (unwillingness); 632 (opposition); 680 (refusal); 826 (disapproval).

   n. *protest*, remonstration, deprecation, expostulation, dissent; *exception*, objection, demur, demurral; *murmur*, complaint, howl, squeal, raised voices, outcry, storm of protest, heckling; *demonstration*, protest meeting, sit-in, walkout, work-in, picket, secondary picketing, march, strike, civil disobedience, demo (*colloq.*); *disapproval*, dissatisfaction, raised eyebrows, an old-fashioned look, jeers, slow handclap; *protester*, demonstrator, objecter, dissenter, heckler.

   adj. *protesting*, dissatisfied, dissenting, protestant, deprecatory.

   vb. *protest*, lodge/register a protest, remonstrate, deprecate, ask not to; *expostulate*, take exception, raise objections, raise one's voice against; *object*, demur, kick, jib; *murmur*, complain, howl, squeal, grumble, moan, kick up a fuss, beef, heckle; *demonstrate*, march, go on strike, walk out, hold a sit in, picket; *disapprove*, raise one's eyebrows, jeer, slow-handclap.

683 **PROMISE**
See also 473 (affirmation); 562 (undertaking); 684 (contract); 821 (duty).

   n. *promise*, word (of honour), vow, pledge, credit, oath, troth, parole, assurance, signature; *profession*, declaration; *guarantee*, warranty, promissory note, banknote, bill, treasury note, IOU; *covenant*, bond, pact, contract, undertaking, agreement, commitment; *engagement*, betrothal.

   adj. *promised*, pledged, covenanted, guaranteed, promissory; *committed*, on/under oath; *engaged*, betrothed, affianced.

   vb. *promise*, give one's word, agree, engage, undertake, commit oneself, make a vow, pledge, swear; *profess*, declare, vow; *contract*, covenant, sign on the dotted line, set down in black and white; *guarantee*, assure, give an

assurance; *get engaged*, exchange vows, plight one's troth.

684 **CONTRACT**
See also 562 (undertaking); 683 (promise).

   n. *contract*, (binding) agreement, compact, conspiracy; *undertaking*, ratification, pact, covenant, arrangement, understanding; *settlement*, deal, bargain, compromise; *peace treaty*, convention, non-aggression pact, concordat, entente, charter, alliance, league.

   adj. *contractual*, binding; *contracted*, agreed (to), arranged, settled, negotiated, covenanted; *consenting*, agreeable.

   vb. *contract*, agree (terms), enter into/make/sign a contract, strike a bargain, do/clinch/make a deal, shake hands, come to an arrangement, reach a compromise, covenant, ratify.

685 **NEGOTIATION**
See also 422 (qualification); 571 (provision); 707 (trade).

   n. *negotiation*, bargaining, making terms, barter, collective bargaining, horse-trading, haggling, wheeler-dealing; *condition*, terms, small print, stipulation, frame of reference, contingency, provision, clause, proviso; *limitation*, strings, exclusion, exception, escape clause, loophole, catch, restriction, reservation, penalty.

   adj. *conditional*, contingent, provisional, dependent, subject; *limiting*, qualifying, with strings attached.

   vb. *negotiate*, bargain, haggle, barter, discuss, parley, treat; *propose conditions*, attach strings, stipulate, impose, hold out for, insist on, make demands, require.

686 **COMPROMISE**
See also 250 (middle way).

   n. *compromise*, give and take, concessions on both sides, mutual concessions, compromise solution, working arrangement, modus vivendi, middle ground, middle course.

   vb. *compromise*, give and take, make concessions, lower one's sights, meet sb halfway, back down, climb down; *split the difference*, split down the middle, go Dutch, go half and half; *steer a middle course*, make the best of a bad job, cut one's losses.

   adv. *knock for knock*, fifty-fifty.

687 SECURITY

See also 598 (safety).

n. *security*, guarantee, warranty, surety; *bond*, pledge, covenant; *collateral*, mortgage, pawn, token, indemnity, cover, hostage, forfeit; *caution money*, deposit, down payment, bail, recognizance, stake; *guarantor*, mortgagor, backer, referee.

adj. *secured*, insured, covered; *pledged*, pawned, mortgaged, deposited, in hock (*colloq.*).

vb. *secure*, insure, cover; *guarantee*, warrant, indemnify, assure, underwrite, endorse; *pledge*, pawn, mortgage, deposit, pop (*colloq.*); *give security*, go bail, bail out, stand surety.

688 OBSERVANCE

See also 72 (conformity); 549 (habit).

n. *observance*, keeping, practice, habit, carrying out, performance, execution; *adherence*, conformity, orthodoxy, heeding, regard, respect, the done thing; *conscientiousness*, diligence, pedantry, scrupulousness, punctiliousness; *fidelity*, faithfulness, devotion, loyalty, dependability, compliance, obedience.

adj. *observant*, professing, practising, religious, orthodox, conformist; *conscientious*, diligent, pedantic, scrupulous, punctilious; *faithful*, loyal, devoted, dependable, responsible, compliant, obedient.

vb. *observe*, keep, practise, carry out, perform, execute; *heed*, respect, regard, pay due attention to; *conform*, abide by, follow, adopt, adhere; *be faithful to*, do one's duty, honour one's obligations, comply, obey, fulfil, keep faith, be as good as one's word.

689 NON-OBSERVANCE

See also 73 (nonconformity); 407 (negligence).

n. *non-observance*, non-performance, non-fulfilment; *disregard*, disrespect, inattention, indifference; *nonconformity*, nonconformism; *unreliability*, negligence, neglect, laxity, omission, carelessness; *disobedience*, non-compliance, contravention, violation, transgression, infringement, sin, breach; *disloyalty*, unfaithfulness, infidelity, breach of faith.

adj. *non-observant*, non-practising; *inattentive*, indifferent; *nonconformist*, unorthodox; *unreliable*, negligent, lax, careless, irresponsible; *disobedient*, non-compliant, out of line, sinning; *disloyal*, unfaithful.

vb. *not observe*, disregard, omit, neglect; *disobey*, break, contravene, violate, transgress, infringe, sin, breach; *renege*, break faith, go back on one's word.

690 GAIN

See also 33 (increase); 35 (addition); 703 (taking); 719 (receipt).

n. *gain*, acquisition, obtaining, procurement, purchase, theft; *benefit*, yield, advantage, reward; *earnings*, income, earned income, pay, salary, wage(s), emolument, remuneration, stipend; *grant*, bursary, scholarship, exhibition, allowance, expenses, perks; *takings*, receipts, turnover, revenue, proceeds; *windfall*, jackpot, bonus, winnings, inheritance, legacy, bequest; *profit*, interest, dividend, yield, unearned income, return, Air Miles (*tdmk*); *growth*, capital gain, savings, accumulation; *realization*, encashment, redemption, recouping.

adj. *gainful*, profitable, paid, salaried, paying, money-spinning, remunerative, lucrative, worthwhile, advantageous; *acquisitive*, on the make, covetous, greedy.

vb. *gain*, acquire, get, come by; *obtain*, procure, get hold of, lay one's hands on, appropriate, take possession of, buy, steal; *store up*, hoard, save, put by; *inherit*, come into, win; *pocket*, catch, net, land, secure; *earn*, make, benefit, glean, reap, accumulate, make money; *take*, turn over, gross, bring in; *profit*, capitalize on, cash in on (*colloq.*); *realize*, encash, redeem, recoup; *show a gain/profit*, pay a dividend, yield.

691 LOSS

See also 34 (decrease); 36 (subtraction).

n. *loss*, deprivation, lack, privation, bereavement; *forfeit*, forfeiture, eviction; *wastage*, leakage, shortfall, deficit, debit.

adj. *lost*, mislaid, missing, untraced; *deprived*, bereaved, bereft, shorn, denuded, stripped; *lacking*, wanting; *forfeit*, forfeited; *wasted*, down the drain (*colloq.*), irretrievable, irrecoverable.

vb. *lose*, miss, mislay; *let slip through* one's *fingers*, throw away, fritter away, say goodbye to, forfeit, squander; *go to waste*, leak, go down the drain (*colloq.*).

692 POSSESSION

See also 694 (property).

n. *possession*, ownership, proprietorship,

custody, enjoyment; *mastery*, monopoly, domination, control, hold, grasp, clutches; *occupancy*, residence, tenancy, tenure, squatting, nine tenths of the law; *possessor*, owner, owner-occupier, proprietor, man of property, landowner, landlord, landlady, freeholder, leaseholder, lessee, householder; *occupier*, occupant, resident, tenant, squatter, lodger; *holder*, hirer.

adj. *proprietorial*, possessive, monopolistic; *propertied*, landed, to one's name.

vb. *possess*, be possessed of, own, have; *control*, monopolize, command, get one's hands on, grab, corner, hog (*colloq.*); *occupy*, fill, hold, enjoy.

693 **JOINT POSSESSION**

n. *joint possession*, joint ownership, co-ownership, partnership, participation; *public ownership*, nationalization, collectivism; *joint account*, (joint-stock) company, profit-sharing; *condominium*, time-sharing, housing association; *commune*, kibbutz, collective, kolkhoz, cooperative, coop; *common* (land), public property; *partner*, shareholder, stockholder, member, participant; *flatmate*, roommate; *communard*, kibbutznik, collectivist.

adj. *jointly owned*, joint, common, communal, participating, cooperative, collective; *public*, state-owned, nationalized.

vb. *share*, have a share in, have shares in, be in partnership with, go in with, participate, hold in common; *nationalize*, collectivize.

694 **PROPERTY**

See also 692 (possession).

n. *property*, possessions, belongings, impedimenta, trappings, accoutrements, goods and chattels, movables, effects, valuables, consumer durables, things, bits and pieces (*colloq.*), paraphernalia, clobber (*colloq.*), stuff (*colloq.*); *land*, real estate, realty, hereditament, immovables; *estate*, assets, means, capital, reserves, equity; *investment*, securities, stocks and shares, unit trusts, PEP, ISA; *rights*, interest, stake.

adj. *propertied*, landed; *proprietary*; *movable*, immovable, real, material.

695 **RETENTION**

See also 40 (union); 668 (restraint).

n. *retention*, holding, tenacity, adhesion; *hold*, grip, grasp, clasp, embrace, hug,

bearhug, clinch; *clutches*, stranglehold, half-nelson, armlock.

adj. *retentive*, tenacious, tight, vicelike, fast; *sticky*, tacky, clinging, adhesive, fusible.

vb. *retain*, hold, keep a firm hold of, grip, grasp, clench, pin, clasp, embrace, hug, clinch; *secure*, fix, lock, clamp, fasten; *cling*, stick, adhere, fuse, hang on; *detain*, confine, withhold, contain.

696 **DISPOSAL**

See also 41 (separation);
563 (relinquishment); 669 (liberation).

n. *disposal*, abandonment, relinquishment, renunciation, alienation, cession; *release*, discharge; *refuse*, flotsam and jetsam, castoffs, waste; *waste disposal*, dumping, recycling, carbon sink.

adj. *abandoned*, derelict, cast-off, on the scrapheap; *disposable*, throwaway, soluble, biodegradable; *dispensable*, expendable, transferable, saleable.

vb. *dispose of*, throw away, discard, chuck out (*colloq.*); *pass on*, bequeath, part with; *sell off*, alienate, transfer; *jettison*, ditch, dump, drop, shed; *let go*, release, free, unhand, loose; *release*, discharge, lay off, pension off; *abandon*, relinquish, renounce, yield, cede; *do without*, forgo, dispense with, spare, waive; *disown*, disinherit, cut off without a penny.

697 **TRANSFER OF PROPERTY**

See also 239 (transfer); 707 (trade);
716 (payment).

n. *transfer of property*, assignment, conveyancing, alienation, change of ownership, handover, consignment; *bequest*, inheritance, legacy, capital transfer, settlement, endowment; *purchase*, sale, lease, hire, letting, rental, exchange, barter, trade.

adj. *transferable*, alienable, exchangeable, negotiable.

vb. *transfer*, assign, convey, alienate, hand over, consign, sign over, make over, pass on; *bequeath*, will, leave, settle, endow, grant, hand down; *inherit*, succeed to, come into; *buy*, purchase, sell, lease, hire (out), let, rent, exchange, convert, barter, trade; *dispossess*, expropriate, nationalize; *change hands*, pass, revert.

698 **GIVING**

See also 725 (generosity).

n. *giving*, donation, conferral, bestowal; *charity*, alms, handout, food parcel, poor box; *gift*, present, presentation, golden handshake; *prize*, award, reward; *contribution*, subscription; *aid*, grant, subsidy, support, sponsorship; *tip*, gratuity, Christmas box; *bequest*, legacy, covenant; *largesse*, bounty, generosity; *offering*, sacrifice, church collection, offertory; *giver*, donor, contributor, subscriber, benefactor, tipper.

adj. *charitable*, votive, sacrificial; *bountiful*, generous, liberal, open-handed; *free*, gratis, complimentary.

vb. *give*, donate, confer, bestow, vouchsafe, render, afford, accord, allot, remit; *hand out*, distribute, dole out, share out; *present*, honour, award; *aid*, subsidize, support, sponsor, grant, endow; *contribute*, subscribe, help, shell out (*colloq.*), fork out (*colloq.*), put one's hand in one's pocket; *tip*; *bequeath*, leave; *offer*, sacrifice.

699 RECEIVING
See also 265 (admittance); 719 (receipt).

n. *receiving*, reception, admittance, admission, acceptance; *acquisition*, getting, gain, collection, assumption; *receipts*, winnings, proceeds, takings, income, gate; *toll*, tribute, tax, levy; *recipient*, receiver, acceptor, accepting house; *trustee*, assignee, licensee, lessee, payee; *devisee*, legatee, heir(ess), inheritor, beneficiary; *winner*, grantee; *treasurer*, bursar, tax collector, exciseman, customs officer.

adj. *receptive*, welcoming, acquisitive.

vb. *receive*, acknowledge receipt of, admit, accept, be given, attract, land; *acquire*, obtain, derive, get, gain, win, collect, assume; *take in*, pocket, gross, net, make; *inherit*, succeed to, come into; *levy*, tax, charge; *be received*, come one's way, accrue, fall into one's lap.

700 ALLOCATION
See also 48 (part).

n. *allotment*, apportionment, distribution, administration, sharing, share-out, rationing; *division*, partition, demarcation, carve-up (*colloq.*); *share*, portion, allocation, quota, allowance; *ration*, dose, dosage, measure; *serving*, helping, slice, cut, whack (*colloq.*), dollop (*colloq.*); *lot*, parcel, batch.

vb. *allocate*, appoint, assign, detail; *allot*, apportion, distribute, administer, dispense, dole out, share (out), deal, farm out, dish out (*colloq.*); *ration*, dose, measure (out), mete out; *divide up*, divvy up, lot, parcel out, zone, partition, carve up (*colloq.*); *demarcate*, delimit.

adv. *proportionately*, pro rata, per head, per capita.

701 LENDING
See also 714 (credit).

n. *lending*, hiring, letting, subletting, leasing; *loan*, advance, mortgage, overdraft, bridging loan, pawnbroking, credit; *investment*, backing, finance, (start-up) capital; *let*, sublet, lease; *lender*, moneylender, creditor, usurer, Shylock (*colloq.*), loan shark (*colloq.*); *finance house*, credit institution, bank, building society; *investor*, financier, banker, mortgagee, pawnbroker.

vb. *lend*, hire out, let, sublet, lease; *loan*, advance, extend credit, put out at interest; *invest*, finance, back, subsidize, put money up, speculate.

702 BORROWING
See also 715 (debt).

n. *borrowing*, hire, rental, leasing, chartering; *mortgage*, loan, credit card, overdraft; *hire purchase*, HP, instalment plan, easy terms (*colloq.*), the never-never (*colloq.*); *pawn*, pledge; *copying*, plagiarism, imitation; *borrower*, mortgage, debtor, sponge, leech.

vb. *borrow*, hire, rent, lease, charter; *mortgage*, have an overdraft, be creditworthy, be in the red; *sponge*, cadge, bum (*colloq.*), touch (*colloq.*); *pawn*, pledge, pop (*colloq.*); *copy*, plagiarize, lift, crib (*colloq.*).

703 TAKING
See also 690 (gain); 705 (stealing).

n. *taking*, assumption, appropriation, exploitation, extortion, blackmail; *seizure*, grab, snatch, confiscation, impounding; *requisition*, requisitioning, commandeering, compulsory purchase, nationalization; *occupation*, settlement, colonization, annexation; *expropriation*, dispossession, exaction, disinheritance, distraint, foreclosure; *capture*, apprehension, arrest; *kidnap*, kidnapping, abduction, hostage-taking, rape, drug rape, gangbang (*colloq.*), slave trade; *receipt*, acceptance; *booty*, spoils, capture, haul, prize; *kidnapper*, abductor, captor, hostage-taker, slaver, rapist; *predator*, parasite, bloodsucker, leech.

adj. *grasping*, grabbing, acquisitive, rapacious, predatory; *extortionate*, exploitative, parasitical.

vb. *take*, assume, take over, appropriate, grasp, grab, snatch, wrest, extort; *seize*, confiscate, impound; *bag*, pocket, net;

requisition, commandeer, nationalize; *occupy*, settle, colonize, annex; *expropriate*, dispossess, deprive, exact, disinherit, divest; *capture*, take by storm, lead captive, apprehend, arrest, nab (*colloq.*); *kidnap*, abduct, rape, impress, press-gang; *receive*, accept.

704 **GIVING BACK**

See also 28 (compensation).

n. *giving back*, restitution, restoration, return; *repayment*, reimbursement, indemnification, refund, rebate; *amends*, reparation, compensation, recompense, damages; *reinstatement*, rehabilitation, privatization, denationalization; *recovery*, retrieval, repossession, clawback.

adj. *restitutory*, indemnificatory, compensatory.

vb. *give back*, restitute, make restitution, restore, return; *repay*, reimburse, indemnify, refund, rebate; *make amends*, make reparations, compensate, recompense; *reinstate*, rehabilitate, privatize, denationalize; *get back*, recover, retrieve, repossess, recoup, regain, claw back.

705 **STEALING**

See also 703 (taking).

n. *stealing*, theft, robbery, grand/petty larceny, kleptomania, pilfering; *burglary*, housebreaking, breaking and entering, safe-blowing/-breaking/-cracking, raid, smash-and-grab raid (*colloq.*), heist (*colloq.*); *shoplifting*, pickpocketing, bag-snatching, hold-up (*colloq.*), stick-up (*colloq.*), mugging, robbery with violence; *looting*, pillage, plunder, rustling, poaching; *hijack*, hijacking, skyjacking, yacht-jacking, carjacking, kidnapping, dognapping, abduction, piracy, body-snatching; *embezzlement*, misappropriation, tax evasion, smuggling, moonlighting, black economy, fiddle (*colloq.*); *fraud*, swindle, con (*colloq.*), diddle (*colloq.*), rip-off (*colloq.*), identity theft; *thief*, robber, burglar, cat burglar, safe-blower/-breaker/-cracker, cracksman, raider; *shoplifter*, pickpocket, Artful Dodger, bag-snatcher, mugger; *highwayman*, bandit, brigand, footpad; *looter*, pillager, rustler, poacher; *hijacker*, skyjacker etc, kidnapper, abductor, hostage-taker, pirate, body-snatcher; *embezzler*, tax dodger/evader, smuggler; *fraud*, swindler, con, crook, rogue, shark, fiddler (*colloq.*), rip-off merchant (*colloq.*), kleptocrat.

adj. *thieving*, thievish, light-fingered, kleptomaniac, on the fiddle (*colloq.*); *marauding*, piratical, buccaneering.

vb. *steal*, thieve, rob, burgle, pilfer, filch, purloin, help oneself to, walk off with, nick (*colloq.*), pinch (*colloq.*), nobble (*colloq.*), swipe (*colloq.*), heist (*colloq.*), snaffle (*colloq.*), knock off (*colloq.*), rip off (*colloq.*); *shoplift*, pick pockets, hold up, mug; *loot*, pillage, plunder, sack, raid, rustle, poach; *hijack*, skyjack, kidnap, abduct, shanghai; *embezzle*, misappropriate, smuggle, moonlight, fiddle (*colloq.*), cook the books (*colloq.*); *defraud*, cheat, swindle, con, diddle (*colloq.*), rook (*colloq.*), fleece (*colloq.*), rip off (*colloq.*); *fall off the back of a lorry* (*colloq.*).

706 **BOOTY**

See also 650 (trophy).

n. *booty*, loot, spoils, plunder, stolen goods, contraband, swag (*colloq.*), perks (*colloq.*); *haul*, catch, find, prize, winnings, ransom, treasure trove; *kidnap victim*, hostage.

707 **TRADE**

See also 685 (negotiation); 697 (transfer of property); 708 (purchase); 709 (sale); 710 (market).

n. *trade*, commerce, business, e-business/commerce; *trading*, barter, buying and selling, traffic, trafficking, dealing; *speculation*, brokerage, jobbing, transaction; *the black market*, racketeering; *exchange*, swap, trade-in, payment in kind; *bargaining*, haggling, negotiations; *export*, import; *trader*, merchant, businessman/-woman, entrepreneur, trafficker, dealer, speculator, pedlar; *wholesaler*, middleman, retailer, shopkeeper, tradesman, chandler; *exporter*, importer; *broker*, jobber, stockbroker, estate agent; *business*, dealership, brokerage; *racketeer*, black marketeer, wheeler-dealer, slave trader, pimp, drug trafficker, fence (*colloq.*), tout (*colloq.*), cowboy (*colloq.*); *merchandise*, wares, goods, stock, supplies, stuff (*colloq.*); *article*, range, line, commodity; *durables*, consumer goods, consumer durables, perishables.

adj. *trading*, commercial, entrepreneurial, mercantile; *wholesale*, retail, marketable.

vb. *trade*, barter, merchandise, buy and sell, traffic, deal, transact; *exchange*, swap, trade in; *export*, import; *bargain*, negotiate, haggle, wheel and deal, beat down; *racketeer*, profiteer, fence (*colloq.*), tout (*colloq.*).

708 **PURCHASE**
See also 707 (trade).

n. *purchase*, buying, shopping, mail order; *hire purchase*, easy terms, tick (*colloq.*), the never-never (*colloq.*); *shopping spree*, binge-shopping, retail therapy (*colloq.*); *buy*, bargain, impulse buy; *takeover*, merger, dawn raid; *purchaser*, buyer, highest bidder, consignee; *customer*, client, shopper, clientele, patron, market, consumer; *custom*, trade, patronage, goodwill.

vb. *purchase*, make a purchase, buy, shop, go shopping, window-shop, patronize; *invest in*, put one's money into, bid for, buy up; *take over*, buy out, corner, stockpile.

709 **SALE**
See also 697 (transfer of property).

n. *sale*, auction, selling; *clearance sale*, auction, stocktaking sale, closing-down sale, end-of-season sale, January sales, special purchase; *bazaar*, jumble/rummage sale, sale of work, fête, bring-and-buy sale; *dumping*; *boom*, sell-out, high turnover; *marketing*, merchandising, sales talk/pitch, high-pressure salesmanship, hard/soft sell, spiel (*colloq.*); *seller*, vendor, tout (*colloq.*); *shopkeeper*, retailer, trader, purveyor; *sales representative*, rep, commercial traveller; *salesman*, saleswoman, shop assistant, shop walker, shop girl; *booking clerk*, travel/ticket agent.

adj. *saleable*, marketable; for/on sale, available; *in demand*, called for, sought after; *sold out*, fresh out of (*colloq.*), off (*colloq.*).

vb. *sell*, make a sale, vend, auction, knock down, flog (*colloq.*); *market*, advertise, put up for sale, put on the market; *wholesale*, retail; *peddle*, hawk, tout (*colloq.*); *dump*, unload, sell off, clear out, remainder; *be sold off*, come under the hammer; *be in demand*, sell well, sell like hot cakes, do a roaring trade.

710 **MARKET**
See also 707 (trade).

n. *market*, bazaar, arcade, covered market, flea market, farmers' market; *mart*, exchange, entrepôt, depot, warehouse; *fair*, fayre, trade fair, show; *stall*, stand, kiosk, booth, barrow; *shop*, store, department store, chain store, boutique, emporium, supermarket, hypermarket, cash-and-carry, shopping centre/precinct/mall; *free trade area*, market economy.

711 **MONEY**
See also 712 (wealth).

n. *money*, currency, Lsd, sterling, bullion, filthy lucre (*colloq.*), dough (*colloq.*), bread (*colloq.*), lolly (*colloq.*), brass (*colloq.*), shekels (*colloq.*), dosh (*colloq.*), moolah (*colloq.*); *cash*, (small) change, coin, banknote, treasury note, bill, hard cash, greenback, ready money, the ready (*colloq.*); *cheque*, postal order, money order, banker's order/draft, traveller's cheque, letter of credit, promissory note, IOU; *credit card*, cheque card, charge card, plastic card, plastic money, plastic, PIN number, chip and PIN, store card; *funds*, finances, capital, reserves, liquidity, bank account, bank balance, wherewithal (*colloq.*), the needful (*colloq.*); *pay*, salary, wages, remuneration, emolument, expenses, petty cash, pocket money, savings, nest egg; *cash flow*, turnover, profit; *forgery*, dud cheque (*colloq.*), rubber cheque (*colloq.*); *banker*, treasurer, keeper of the purse; *bursar*, purser, controller, comptroller, the purse strings; *paymaster*; *cashier*, teller, croupier; *accountant*, bookkeeper, beancounter (*colloq.*); *bank*, savings bank, building society, cash dispenser; *treasury*, strongroom, vault, coffer, safe; *till*, cash register, checkout, gate; *money box*, piggybank, kitty, purse, wallet.

adj. *monetary*, financial, fiscal, pecuniary.

vb. *mint*, issue, coin, monetize, circulate; *cash*, encash, draw out, change; *forge*, counterfeit; *withdraw*, demonetize, call in; *finance*, capitalize, fund, bankroll (*colloq.*), hold the purse strings; *save*, amass, put by.

712 **WEALTH**
See also 655 (prosperity); 694 (property); 711 (money).

n. *wealth*, affluence, prosperity, comfort, ease, creditworthiness, high income bracket; *luxury*, opulence, the fleshpots; *riches*, fortune, king's ransom, substance, assets, money, means, pile (*colloq.*), mint (*colloq.*), tidy sum (*colloq.*), packet (*colloq.*), pots of money (*colloq.*); *rich person*, millionaire/-ess, multimillionaire/-ess, billionaire/-ess, man/woman of means, Croesus, Midas, moneybags (*colloq.*), fat cat (*colloq.*), plutocrat, nouveau riche, new rich, idle rich, haves (*colloq.*).

adj. *rich*, wealthy, affluent, prosperous, well-off, comfortably off, comfortable, well-to-do, propertied, moneyed, well-heeled, of independent means, born with a silver spoon in one's mouth, in the money, flush (*colloq.*), made of money, rolling in it (*colloq.*), filthy/ stinking rich (*colloq.*), loaded (*colloq.*); *luxurious*, opulent, plush, palatial, up-market.

vb. *be rich*, have money to burn (*colloq.*), have a bob or two (*colloq.*); *afford*, make ends meet, keep the wolf from the door, do all right (*colloq.*), get by (*colloq.*); *get rich*, prosper, make money, come into money, rake it in (*colloq.*), laugh all the way to the bank (*colloq.*), make a bomb/fortune/packet/ pile (*colloq.*), strike it rich (*colloq.*), line one's pocket (*colloq.*).

713 **POVERTY**

See also 558 (requirement).

n. *poverty*, impoverishment, impecuniousness; *beggary*, mendicancy, penury, destitution, pennilessness, indigence, privation, subsistence level, breadline (*colloq.*); *insolvency*, bankruptcy, ruin, collapse, queer street; *financial difficulty*, reduced/straitened circumstances, poverty trap; *pauper*, the poor, down-and-out, slum dweller, have-nots (*colloq.*), poor whites, poor white trash (*derog.*), trailer trash (*derog.*); *beggar*, mendicant; *insolvent*, bankrupt.

adj. *poor*, impoverished, impecunious, poverty-stricken, penurious, straitened, on one's beam ends, on one's uppers, hard up (*colloq.*), short (*colloq.*); *destitute*, penniless, indigent, needy, on the breadline (*colloq.*), clean/flat/stony broke (*colloq.*), skint (*colloq.*), strapped for cash; *deprived*, underprivileged, disadvantaged, underdeveloped, low-paid, underpaid, exploited; *insolvent*, bankrupt, ruined; *down at heel*, in rags, barefoot, starving, down and out.

vb. *be poor*, live from hand to mouth, have to watch the pennies, feel the pinch, fall on hard times, go broke/bust (*colloq.*); *impoverish*, beggar, ruin.

714 **CREDIT**

See also 701 (lending).

n. *credit*, loan, mortgage, credit facilities, credit account, charge account, credit card, credit note, hire purchase, deferred payment, easy terms, tick (*colloq.*); *creditworthiness*, reputation, trust, confidence, reliability; *creditor*, mortgagee, lender, investor, depositor.

vb. *credit*, allow/give credit, charge to one's account, credit one's account, lend, defer payment, grant a loan, put on the slate (*colloq.*), be in the black (*colloq.*); *take credit*,

pay by credit card, keep an account with, borrow, mortgage.

715 **DEBT**

See also 702 (borrowing); 819 (entitlement).

n. *debt*, indebtedness, commitment, obligation, duty; *liability*, debit, mortgage, amount due/outstanding/owing, bill, arrears, back pay, bad debt; *debtor*, borrower, mortgagor, bad debtor.

adj. *indebted*, committed, obliged, bound, under an obligation; *in debt*, mortgaged, overdrawn, in the red (*colloq.*); *owed*, owing, outstanding, due, overdue, in arrears, unsettled, unpaid, payable, on credit.

vb. *owe*, be in debt, be overdrawn; *mortgage*, overdraw one's account, run up a debt/bill, get credit; *pay by credit card*, buy on hire purchase, buy on the never-never (*colloq.*), get on tick (*colloq.*).

716 **PAYMENT**

See also 697 (transfer of property).

n. *payment*, settlement, liquidation, reckoning, discharge; *remittance*, defrayment, disbursement, subsidy, subvention; *repayment*, reimbursement, recompense, restitution, refund, damages; *contribution*, subscription, donation, tribute; *deposit*, down payment, outlay, instalment; *pay*, wages, salary, emolument, honorarium, fee, remuneration, stipend, earnings, commission, pension; *payer*, paymaster, cashier, wages clerk.

vb. *pay*, settle, liquidate, reckon, discharge, honour, clear, square accounts with; *pay out*, foot the bill, pick up the tab (*colloq.*), bear the cost of, meet, stand, spend, expend, pay up, fork out (*colloq.*), shell out (*colloq.*), cough up (*colloq.*), stump up (*colloq.*); *remit*, defray, remunerate, disburse, subsidize; *repay*, reimburse, recompense, refund, pay damages; *contribute*, subscribe, donate, chip in (*colloq.*).

717 **NON-PAYMENT**

n. *non-payment*, default, failure to pay, withholding payment; *stoppage*, deduction; *tax evasion*, tax avoidance, dishonoured/dud cheque; *insolvency*, run on a bank, crash, failure, collapse, bankruptcy, liquidation; *defaulter*, bankrupt, tax dodger/evader.

adj. *defaulting*, in arrears, behind; *insolvent*, bankrupt, unable to pay, bust (*colloq.*), on the rocks (*colloq.*), washed up.

vb. *default*, fail to pay, fall into arrears;

stop, deduct, dock, refuse/withhold payment; *welsh*, fiddle one's income tax, do a (moonlight) flit (*colloq.*); *stop a cheque*, refer to drawer, bounce, freeze, dishonour, repudiate; *fail*, crash, go under, go to the wall, fold, go bankrupt, go bust (*colloq.*); *bankrupt*, ruin; *go into liquidation*, be wound up; *wind up*, liquidate, put in the hands of a receiver.

718 **EXPENDITURE**

See also 716 (payment).

n. *expenditure*, spending, payment, outlay, disbursement, outgoings, investment; *extravagance*, overspend, spending spree, blowout (*colloq.*); *costs*, overheads, (out-of-pocket) expenses.

vb. *expend*, spend, pay, lay out, invest, disburse, bear the cost, meet, foot the bill; *incur*, run up; *stand*, treat; *draw on* one's *savings*, splash out, overspend, blow, get through, use up, consume.

719 **RECEIPT**

See also 690 (gain); 699 (receiving).

n. *receipt*, acknowledgement, ticket, voucher, chit, coupon, counterfoil, stub; *receipts*, income, revenue, takings, monies, proceeds, box office receipts, gate money, returns, royalty, rent; *income*, earnings, pay, salary, wages, remuneration, emolument; *dividend*, pension, annuity, capital gain; *grant*, scholarship, exhibition, bursary, maintenance, allowance, pocket money; *winnings*, prize, legacy, inheritance, windfall, bonus.

720 **ACCOUNTS**

See also 486 (record).

n. *accounts*, accounting, accountancy, auditing, audit; *creative accounting*, fiddling; *account*, profit-and-loss account, balance sheet, budget, budget forecast; *bookkeeping*, single entry, double entry, books, journal, day book, cash book, ledger, trial balance; *statement*, bill, manifest, invoice, receipt; *accountant*, actuary, chartered accountant, certified accountant, bookkeeper, auditor.

adj. *accounting*, budgetary, actuarial; *accountable*.

vb. *account*, keep accounts, keep the books, enter, debit, credit, post, book, balance; *present*, charge, invoice, bill; *budget*, cost; *falsify the accounts*, cook the books (*colloq.*), massage the figures; *audit*, examine, inspect.

721 **PRICE**

See also 582 (worth).

n. *price*, cost/selling price, quotation, estimate, price label/tag/ticket; *list price*, recommended retail price (RRP), retail price index (RPI), price control, price freeze; *toll*, entrance/admission charge, rent, hire charge, rental, ground rent, cover charge, postage, corkage, road toll, road pricing, congestion charging; *interest rate*, commission, introduction fee, retainer; *surcharge*, supplement, currency surcharge; *tax*, taxation, duty, levy, impost, tribute, tithe, direct/indirect taxation, inland revenue; *customs duty*, excise duty, tariff, purchase tax, sales tax, value-added tax, VAT; *capital gains tax*, capital transfer tax, stamp duty, estate duty, death duties, wealth tax; *income tax*, pay-as-you-earn, PAYE, National Insurance, surtax, supertax, investment surcharge, tax credit, local income tax, corporation tax; *rates*, general rate, water rate, rating assessment, rateable value; *poll tax*, salt tax, window tax, danegeld.

adj. *taxable*, dutiable, gross.

vb. *price*, assess, cost, value, put a price on, estimate, quote, rate; *cost*, fetch, realize, go/sell for, change hands for, be priced at; *tax*, levy, impose, raise, put a tax on.

722 **DISCOUNT**

See also 36 (subtraction).

n. *discount*, reduction, rebate, deduction; *commission*, percentage, brokerage, cut, margin, mark-up, rake-off (*colloq.*); *concession*, special price/rate, bargain/cut price, special offer, bargain.

adj. *concessionary*, tax-free, duty-free, tax-deductible, net.

vb. *discount*, reduce, deduct, rebate, allow, knock off; *reduce*, cut, slash (*colloq.*).

723 **DEARNESS**

n. *dearness*, expensiveness, costliness, expense, sellers' market; *extravagance*, exorbitance, extortion, rip-off (*colloq.*), overcharging; *inflation*, inflationary spiral, rising/spiralling prices, sellers' market.

adj. *dear*, expensive, pricey, priceless, precious, up-market, extravagant, costly; *extortionate*, exorbitant, prohibitive, unreasonable, excessive, overpriced, stiff, steep; *inflationary*, rising, spiralling, soaring, climbing.

vb. *be dear*, cost a lot, cost a packet/a pretty penny/a fortune/the earth/a bomb/an arm and a leg (*colloq.*); *extort*, profiteer, overcharge, short-change, exploit, sting, fleece, bleed, rip off (*colloq.*); *pay through the nose* (*colloq.*), be done (*colloq.*), be had (*colloq.*); *go up*, rise, soar, climb, rocket, go through the roof, appreciate; *put up*, increase, revalue, mark up.

724 CHEAPNESS

See also 583 (worthlessness); 769 (vulgarity).

n. *cheapness*, inexpensiveness, reasonableness, competitiveness; *bargain*, good buy, snip (*colloq.*), good value, value for money, sale goods, rejects, seconds; *price reduction*, sale price, cheap rate, reduced rate, concessionary fare, cheap day return, package (holiday), excursion fare; *deflation*, slump, glut, buyers' market; *no charge*, free gift, labour of love, free delivery, Freepost, Freefone, reversed charges, complimentary tickets, comps (*colloq.*).

adj. *cheap*, inexpensive, reasonable, competitive, affordable, down-market; *reduced*, cut-price, cut, half-price, rock-bottom, knock-down, concessionary, marked down, to clear; *economical*, economy, budget, family-size, own-brand; *basic*, bog-standard (*colloq.*), entry-level (*colloq.*); *cheap and nasty*, shoddy, tacky (*colloq.*), cheapo (*colloq.*); *free of charge*, gratis, complimentary, for nothing, on the house, tax-free, reply-paid, toll-free, collect (*US*).

vb. *be cheap*, go cheap, go for a song; *cheapen*, reduce, cut, mark down, slash; *fall in price*, depreciate, decline, slump, drop; *flood the market*, dump, undersell, undercut; *cost nothing*, be had for the asking; *economize*, budget, shop around, bulk-buy.

725 GENEROSITY

See also 698 (giving).

n. *generosity*, munificence, liberality, lavishness, free hand; *largesse*, bounty, gifts; *hospitality*, charity, open house, kind offer.

adj. *generous*, munificent, liberal, bounteous, bountiful, free-handed, open-handed; *lavish*, right royal, handsome, fit for a king/queen, slap-up (*colloq.*); *hospitable*, charitable, kind, philanthropic, big-hearted, unselfish, unstinting.

vb. *be generous*, give generously, spare no expense, not count the cost; *lavish*, not stint, heap/shower upon, do proud, push the boat out (*colloq.*), kill the fatted calf, do things in style.

726 THRIFT

n. *thrift*, economy, frugality; *care*, prudence, husbandry, careful management, good housekeeping, conservation; *savings*, cuts, cheeseparing, economies, retrenchment.

adj. *thrifty*, economical, frugal, meagre, sparing; *careful*, prudent, canny; *money-saving*, energy-saving, labour-saving.

vb. *be thrifty*, economize, keep costs down, live within one's means/income, make ends meet; *manage*, husband, save, conserve, recycle, waste nothing; *make savings*, cut costs, cut corners, cut back, retrench, tighten one's belt (*colloq.*)

727 EXTRAVAGANCE

See also 572 (waste), 575 (excess).

n. *extravagance*, wastefulness, profligacy, dissipation, improvidence, no thought for tomorrow; *lavishness*, prodigality, profusion, conspicuous consumption, money to burn; *overspending*, permanent overdraft, deficit finance, splurge, spree; *squanderer*, wastrel, prodigal son, spendthrift, big spender.

adj. *extravagant*, wasteful, profligate, improvident, reckless, immoderate, spendthrift; *lavish*, prodigal, profuse, over-generous.

vb. *overspend*, overdraw, fritter away, dissipate, live beyond one's means; *blow/blue* one's money, splurge, lash out, not count the cost, hang the expense, spend money like water (*colloq.*), think money grows on trees (*colloq.*), spend money as if it were going out of fashion (*colloq.*); *squander*, waste, throw away, pour money down the drain, throw good money after bad.

728 MEANNESS

See also 834 (selfishness).

n. *meanness*, minginess, miserliness, stinginess, niggardliness, illiberality, cheeseparing, false economy; *skinflint*, miser, niggard, cheapskate, scrooge; *greed*, avarice, acquisitiveness, venality, voracity, avidity, covetousness, gluttony.

adj. *mean*, mingy, miserly, stingy, niggardly, illiberal, cheeseparing, penny-pinching, parsimonious, close, tight, tight-/close-fisted, grudging, sparing; *greedy*, avaricious, acquisitive, grasping, money-grubbing, mercenary, venal, voracious, avid, covetous, gluttonous, usurious, rapacious.

vb. *be mean*, begrudge; *scrimp*, scrape, skimp, do on the cheap (*colloq.*), pinch, stint, count the pennies; *be greedy*, hoard.

729 **FEELING**

See also 334 (sensation); 732 (strong emotion).

n. *feeling*, emotion, affection, sentiment, passion; *sensation*, experience, perception, sense of, consciousness, impression; *sympathy*, empathy, emotional intelligence, fellow feeling, vibes (*colloq.*), friendliness, understanding, appreciation, sensitivity, tenderness, warmth; *agitation*, commotion, trembling, tremor, tingling, quiver, flutter; *sentimentality*, emotion, lump in one's throat; *excitement*, thrill, kick (*colloq.*), buzz (*colloq.*); *enthusiasm*, vigour, ardour, zeal, fervour, fire, keenness, impatience, fanaticism, obsessiveness, mania.

adj. *feeling*, sentient, sensitive, sensible, sensuous, sensual; *sentimental*, romantic, passionate, emotional, affectionate, tender; *sympathetic*, understanding, appreciative, tender, warm; *agitated*, tense, nervous, edgy; *impressed*, influenced, affected, moved, stirred, touched, heart-felt; *enthusiastic*, vigorous, ardent, zealous, burning, keen, earnest, avid, impatient, fanatical, obsessive, manic; *excited*, worked up, keyed up, breathless, panting, exuberant, hysterical, overwrought, feverish, impassioned, dramatic.

vb. *feel*, sense, entertain, experience, endure, go through, undergo, bear, taste, enjoy; *sympathize*, empathize, suffer with, feel for, commiserate, appreciate, know the feeling; *move*, affect, impress, touch, stir, influence, fire, quicken, excite; *respond*, react, warm to, catch, thrill.

730 **SENSITIVITY**

See also 334 (sensation).

n. *sensitivity*, sensibility, sensitiveness, awareness, responsiveness, alertness, consciousness; *self-awareness*, emotional intelligence; *susceptibility*, vulnerability, hypersensitivity; *touchiness*, prickliness, irritability, soft spot, sore point; *soft touch*, easy mark, softie (*colloq.*).

adj. *sensitive*, aware, conscious, sensible, responsive, alive, awake, alert, on one's toes; *susceptible*, vulnerable, impressionable, malleable; *compassionate*, tender-hearted, soft, romantic, emotional, soppy (*colloq.*); *tender*, bruised, painful, hypersensitive, delicate; *oversensitive*, touchy, prickly, thin-skinned; *nervous*, highly-strung, irritable, impatient.

731 **INSENSITIVITY**

See also 335 (insensibility).

n. *insensitivity*, insensibility, unresponsiveness, unawareness, obliviousness, insentience, thick skin; *lethargy*, torpor, stupor, numbness, paralysis, coma, hypnosis; *calmness*, stolidness, imperturbability, impassiveness, coldness, sangfroid, detachment; *stupidity*, obtuseness, dullness; *callousness*, dourness, ruthlessness, brutality, no heart, heartlessness; *stoic*, ascetic, iceberg, robot, automaton.

adj. *insensitive*, unfeeling, insensible, unresponsive, unaware, oblivious, insentient, thick-skinned; *lethargic*, torpid, numb, paralysed, comatose, hypnotized, punchdrunk; *calm*, stolid, imperturbable, impassive, cold, unemotional, unruffled, expressionless, detached, stoical; *stupid*, obtuse, dull, bovine, unimaginative; *dead to*, blind to, deaf to, impervious; *hard-bitten*, hard-nosed, tough, inured, invulnerable; *callous*, dour, ruthless, brutal, hard-hearted, heartless, inhuman.

vb. *be unaffected*, feel no emotion, leave one cold, not turn a hair, not bat an eyelid; *harden oneself*, steel oneself, harden one's heart against, disregard, ignore, switch off (*colloq.*); *not see*, miss the point of; *benumb*, numb, deaden, toughen, harden, sear, stupefy, dull.

732 **STRONG EMOTION**

See also 729 (feeling).

n. *strong emotion*, excitement, animation, fever, frenzy, delirium; *hullabaloo*, to-do, flurry, fuss, scene, song and dance (*colloq.*); *exhilaration*, elation, euphoria, intoxication, abandon, thrill, ecstasy, ebullience, fever pitch, orgasm, high (*colloq.*); *anger*, rage, fury, temper, outburst, fit, hysterics, tantrum; *passion*, emotion, romanticism, lyricism, sensationalism, melodrama; *excitation*, agitation, stimulation, galvanization, activation, arousal; *inspiration*, invitation, incitement, appeal, provocation, encouragement; *fascination*, bewitching, interest, enchantment, captivation; *excitability*, impetuousness, impetuosity, restlessness, irritability, instability, explosiveness, hot blood, intolerance; *vehemence*, turbulence, boisterousness, recklessness, high spirits.

adj. *excited*, animated, thrilled, inspired, impassioned, stimulated, moved; *feverish*, delirious, effervescent, wound up, crazy, keyed up, a-quiver; *exhilarated*, elated, euphoric, intoxicated, ebullient, ecstatic, turned on (*colloq.*), high (*colloq.*); *angry*, furious, raging, in a temper, hysterical, on the rampage, on the warpath; *passionate*, emotional, romantic, lyrical; *exciting*, exhilarating, thrilling, stimulating, rousing; *stirring*, inspiring, moving, affecting, evocative; *gripping*, enthralling, heart-stopping, nerve-wracking, nail-biting; *interesting*, absorbing, fascinating, captivating, enchanting, bewitching, compelling; *dramatic*, momentous, sensational, melodramatic, mind-boggling; *provocative*, titillating, saucy, spicy, racy, tantalizing; *excitable*, volatile, mercurial, quicksilver, temperamental, turbulent; *highly-strung*, nervous, edgy, on edge, tense, jumpy, jittery, restless; *impetuous*, impulsive, hotheaded, headstrong; *impatient*, intolerant, irritable, quick-tempered; *enthusiastic*, keen, boisterous, high-spirited.

vb. *excite*, arouse, inflame, work up, wind up, incite, provoke, incense, impassion, fire, fuel, goad; *stimulate*, activate, awaken, animate, electrify, energize, galvanize, summon up, quicken, turn on (*colloq.*), switch on (*colloq.*); *enthuse*, inspire, stir, move, encourage, hearten, urge; *interest*, absorb, fascinate, intrigue, engage, captivate; *enthral*, enchant, bewitch, compel, delight, thrill; *anger*, enrage, make one's blood boil; *startle*, amaze, take one's breath away, arrest, impress; *get excited*, fret, fume, work oneself up, get on one's high horse, rage, explode, fly off the handle, create (*colloq.*), freak out (*colloq.*).

733 **IMPASSIVITY**
See also 148 (moderation); 335 (insensibility); 731 (insensitivity; 756 (indifference); 760 (lack of wonder).

n. *impassivity*, inexcitability, imperturbability, steadiness, level-headedness, sangfroid, phlegm; *calmness*, coolness, composure, self-control, self-restraint; *equanimity*, serenity, tranquillity, placidity; *mildness*, meekness, submissiveness, resignation, acquiescence; *detachment*, aloofness, nonchalance, dispassionateness; *apathy*, indifference, unconcern; *sobriety*, gravity, staidness, sedateness; *patience*, forbearance, stoicism, tolerance.

adj. *impassive*, inexcitable, imperturbable, phlegmatic, level-headed, unflappable

(*colloq.*); *calm*, cool, collected, composed, self-possessed; *even-tempered*, serene, tranquil, placid, cool as a cucumber (*colloq.*); *mild*, meek, submissive, uncomplaining, resigned, acquiescent; *detached*, aloof, nonchalant, dispassionate, blasé; *apathetic*, indifferent, unconcerned, uninterested, past caring; *sober*, grave, staid, sedate, reserved; *patient*, forbearing, long-suffering, stoical, tolerant, easy-going.

vb. *keep calm/cool*, keep one's temper, control oneself, master one's feelings, not excite oneself, keep a cool head, keep one's hair/shirt on (*colloq.*), keep one's cool (*colloq.*), not flap (*colloq.*), not bat an eyelid (*colloq.*); *resign oneself*, submit, swallow, take, stomach; *be patient*, tolerate, put up with, brook, abide, endure, support, suffer.

734 **JOY**
See also 336 (physical pleasure); 742 (cheerfulness); 746 (rejoicing).

n. *joy*, pleasure, delight, enjoyment, thrill, enchantment, kick (*colloq.*); *fun*, jollity, merriment, good time; *ecstasy*, rapture, elation, exhilaration, bliss, euphoria, exaltation; *glee*, relish, gusto, zest; *happiness*, gladness, felicity, satisfaction, fulfilment; *comfort*, ease, wellbeing, convenience, bed of roses, luxury, paradise; *indulgence*, self-indulgence, hedonism, self-gratification; *malice*, gloating, schadenfreude; *happy person*, happy camper (*colloq.*).

adj. *joyful*, happy, glad, delighted, pleased, satisifed, gratified, pleased as Punch; *joyous*, thrilled, excited, on top of the world; *ecstatic*, rapturous, elated, euphoric, overjoyed, enraptured, delirious, carried away, over the moon (*colloq.*), in seventh heaven; *jolly*, merry, cheery, gladsome; *pleasant*, enjoyable, comfortable, pleasurable, convenient, satisfying, cosy, welcome; *delightful*, adorable, blissful, divine (*colloq.*), heavenly (*colloq.*); *self-indulgent*, hedonistic, luxurious, palatial; *malicious*.

vb. *rejoice*, jump for joy, celebrate, congratulate oneself; *enjoy*, get pleasure from, take pleasure in, delight in, relish, have fun; *revel in*, bask in, adore, rave about, get a kick out of (*colloq.*), get off on (*colloq.*).

735 **SORROW**
See also 337 (physical pain); 447 (insanity); 656 (adversity); 743 (dejection); 747 (lamentation).

n. *sorrow*, sadness, melancholy,

unhappiness, wretchedness, misery, gloom, woe; *despair*, distress, dejection, despondency, depression, dolour, desolation; *torment*, heartache, agony, anguish, suffering; *mourning*, bereavement, grieving, grief, regret, remorse; *homesickness*, nostalgia, longing, yearning; *worry*, anxiety, care, disquiet, something on one's mind, concern, burden, angst; *problem*, headache, bother, trouble; *phobia*, neurosis, hang-up (*colloq.*), midlife crisis.

adj. *sorrowful*, sad, melancholy, unhappy, depressed, disconsolate; *gloomy*, woeful, down in the dumps (*colloq.*); *wretched*, miserable, pitiable, pathetic; *desperate*, despairing, dejected, despondent; *distressed*, upset, distraught, anguished; *troubled*, afflicted, vexed, burdened; *worried*, anxious, fretful; *sorrowing*, mournful, grief-stricken, heart-broken, cut up (*colloq.*); *homesick*, nostalgic; *distressing*, harrowing, agonizing, painful; *neurotic*, hung-up (*colloq.*), driven.

vb. *sorrow*, be unhappy, grieve, mourn, pine, yearn, eat one's heart out; *depress*, distress, upset, agonize; *worry*, bother, concern, trouble, torment, harrow.

736 PLEASANTNESS
See also 336 (physical pleasure).

n. *pleasantness*, pleasurableness, niceness, delightfulness, attractiveness, enjoyableness; *charm*, fascination, winsomeness, allure, loveliness, beauty; *amiability*, friendliness, affability; *treat*, joy, delight, fun, lark (*colloq.*); *melody*, harmony.

adj. *pleasant*, pleasurable, pleasing, genial, agreeable, nice, delightful, acceptable, welcome, enjoyable; *charming*, fascinating, winsome, ravishing, exquisite, lovely, beautiful, fetching; *good*, wonderful, marvellous, excellent; *amiable*, friendly, affable, likeable; *enchanting*, alluring, seductive, enticing, bewitching; *melodious*, harmonious, mellow, soothing; *delicious*, tasty, luscious, delectable, choice, refreshing.

vb. *please*, delight, give/afford pleasure, amuse, entertain, make happy, gladden; *comfort*, soothe, put at ease, stroke, pet; *attract*, interest, allure; *charm*, bewitch, captivate, entrance; *gratify*, satisfy, indulge, pander to, pamper, coddle; *excite*, stimulate, thrill.

737 UNPLEASANTNESS
See also 337 (physical pain); 604 (harm).

n. *unpleasantness*, disagreeableness;

hatefulness, loathsomeness, nastiness, ugliness; *disappointment*, difficulty, trouble, worry, thorn in the flesh; *persecution*, harassment, molestation; *soreness*, tenderness, inflammation; *bitterness*, unpalatability, sharpness, tastelessness, disgust; *annoyance*, nuisance, vexation, embarrassment; *curse*, pest, plague; *burden*, cross, load, affliction.

adj. *unpleasant*, disagreeable, undesirable, displeasing; *hateful*, repellent, loathsome, beastly, foul, nasty, obnoxious, disgusting, nauseating, revolting, gross (*colloq.*), offensive; *hideous*, ugly, dismal, dreary, grim, unattractive, uninviting, depressing, unappealing; *unpalatable*, tasteless; *painful*, inflamed, sore, tender; *annoying*, troublesome, bothersome, irritating, trying, tiresome, irksome, wearisome, balls-aching (*colloq.*), buttock-clenching (*colloq.*); *onerous*, burdensome, oppressive; *upsetting*, off-putting, disturbing.

vb. *displease*, dissatisfy, go against the grain, rub up the wrong way; *repel*, put one off, nauseate, disgust, sicken, gross out (*colloq.*); *shock*, horrify, scandalize, offend; *trouble*, worry, afflict, upset, disturb, distress; *bother*, incommode, inconvenience, put out, put to trouble; *torment*, harass, bait, bully, persecute, victimize; *tease*, pester, annoy, irritate, vex, obsess, haunt, molest, peeve, needle.

738 SATISFACTION
See also 573 (sufficiency); 825 (approval).

n. *satisfaction*, contentment, ease of mind, peace of mind, happiness; *comfort*, snugness, rest, ease, tranquillity, serenity; *complacency*, self-satisfaction, smugness.

adj. *satisfied*, content, contented, happy, carefree; *comfortable*, snug, relaxed, at ease, tranquil, serene, peaceful; *uncomplaining*, unenvious, easily pleased, undemanding; *complacent*, self-satisfied, smug, pleased with oneself; *satisfactory*, satisfying, acceptable, passable, unobjectionable.

vb. *be satisfied* etc, have all that one could wish for, achieve one's heart's desire, have no complaints; *satisfy*, content, gratify, please, meet with approval, go down well, meet one's needs; *appease*, mollify, pacify, propitiate, reconcile.

739 DISSATISFACTION
See also 574 (insufficiency);
747 (lamentation); 826 (disapproval).

n. *dissatisfaction*, discontent, displeasure; *irritation*, resentment, regret, pique; *depression*, sadness, unhappiness, grief, vexation; *tension*, strain, unrest, uneasiness, restlessness, restiveness; *grudge*, ill will, grievance; *criticism*, fault-finding, nit-picking; *complaint*, murmur; *critic*, fault-finder, nit-picker; *dissident*, malcontent, angry young man, protester.

adj. *dissatisfied*, discontented, displeased, disgruntled, browned/cheesed off (*colloq.*); *uneasy*, restless, tense; *cross*, piqued, sulky, tetchy, peevish, testy; *critical*, querulous, hard to please, exacting, captious, censorious; *disconsolate*, disappointed; *grudging*, jealous, envious, resentful.

vb. *be dissatisfied* etc, complain, harp, nag, grouse, grumble, moan (*colloq.*), beef (*colloq.*), bellyache (*colloq.*), mutter under one's breath; *criticize*, carp, split hairs, quibble.

740 **RELIEF**
See also 620 (refreshment).

n. *relief*, easing, alleviation, mitigation, abatement, assuagement; *help*, comfort, load off one's mind, consolation; *break in the clouds*, lull, respite, ray of sunshine; *painkiller*, sedative, analgesic, balm, anaesthetic; *remedy*, cure.

adj. *relieving*, easing, mitigating; *comforting*, consoling; *soothing*, analgesic, anodyne, anaesthetic; *remedial*, curative, restorative.

vb. *relieve*, ease, alleviate, mitigate, abate, assuage; *soften*, cushion, take the strain; *help*, comfort, console; *encourage*, buck, hearten; *lighten*, lift, unburden; *soothe*, deaden, still, lull, anaesthetize; *remedy*, cure; *be relieved*, feel relief, relieve oneself, feel better, take comfort, take heart; *breathe again*, heave a sigh of relief, thank one's lucky stars.

741 **AGGRAVATION**
See also 593 (deterioration).

n. *aggravation*, exacerbation, deterioration, worsening, degeneration; *augmentation*, intensification, strengthening, deepening, sharpening, heightening; *exasperation*, irritation, annoyance, embittering.

adj. *aggravated* etc, unmitigated, unrelieved.

vb. *aggravate*, exacerbate, deteriorate, worsen, degenerate; *augment*, intensify, strengthen, deepen, sharpen, heighten, magnify, multiply; *exasperate*, irritate, annoy, embitter, sour, inflame, fuel, make matters worse.

742 **CHEERFULNESS**
See also 734 (joy); 748 (hope).

n. *cheerfulness*, cheeriness, high spirits, blitheness, light-heartedness, levity; *happiness*, satisfaction, contentment; *optimism*, hopefulness, positive thinking; *vitality*, animation, liveliness, joie de vivre, vivacity; *mirth*, merriment, glee, laughter, mischief, gaiety, jollity, good humour, jocularity, joviality; *good nature*, geniality, amiability, affability, the life and soul of the party, conviviality.

adj. *cheerful*, cheery, high-spirited, blithe, sunny, light-hearted, chirpy, breezy, carefree, easy-going; *happy*, satisfied, content, on top of the world; *optimistic*, hopeful, sanguine, in good heart; *vital*, animated, lively, vivacious, radiant, sparkling, bouncy, ebullient, bright-eyed and bushy-tailed (*colloq.*), full of beans (*colloq.*); *merry*, mirthful, gleeful, mischievous, laughing, gay, jolly, good-humoured, jocular, jovial; *good-natured*, genial, amiable, affable, convivial; *cheering*, warming, encouraging, heartening.

vb. *be cheerful* etc, keep smiling, keep a stiff upper lip, put on a brave face, grin and bear it, keep one's chin/end/pecker up (*colloq.*); *cheer up*, perk up, take heart, pull oneself together, look on the bright side, snap out of it (*colloq.*); *cheer* (up), humour, jolly along, hearten, encourage; *console*, comfort.

743 **DEJECTION**
See also 735 (sorrow); 749 (hopelessness).

n. *dejection*, despondency, gloom, cheerlessness, low spirits, weltschmerz, the doldrums, the blues (*colloq.*); *despair*, defeatism, pessimism; *depression*, unhappiness, joylessness, misery, melancholy; *disappointment*, chagrin, disillusionment.

adj. *dejected*, despondent, sad, gloomy, cheerless, low, down, down in the mouth, morose, glum, blue (*colloq.*), down in the dumps (*colloq.*); *despairing*, defeatist, negative, pessimistic, downhearted; *depressed*, unhappy, suicidal, miserable, melancholy, dismal, world-weary, browned/cheesed off (*colloq.*); *disappointed*, dispirited, disheartened, disillusioned, crestfallen, hangdog, downcast, crushed, demoralized, broken; *upset*, put out, cut up (*colloq.*), pissed off (*colloq.*).

vb. *be dejected* etc, mope, brood, languish, pine, moan, sulk, droop, pull a long face;

despair, give up, lose heart, eat one's heart out; *depress*, dishearten, discourage, demoralize, dismay, sadden, get down; *dampen*, disappoint, put a damper on, pour cold water on.

744 HUMOUR

n. *humour*, sense of humour, wit, wittiness, jocularity; *satire*, burlesque, farce, spoof, take-off (*colloq.*); *sarcasm*, flippancy, facetiousness, irony, whimsy; *repartee*, banter, badinage, joking, buffoonery; *joke*, witticism, pun, play on words, jest, quip, wisecrack, gag, one-liner, shaggy-dog story; *dirty joke*, double entendre, innuendo, sick joke, black comedy; *practical joke*, hoax; *cartoon*, comic strip, caricature; *comedy*, slapstick, situation comedy, sit com; *limerick*, clerihew, epigram, aphorism; *laughter*, mirth, gales/roar/shriek of laughter, giggle, the giggles, snigger, titter, chuckle, chortle, guffaw, cackle; *smile*, grin, smirk, simper; *humorist*, wit, wag, card (*colloq.*), satirist, comic writer, cartoonist; *joker*, practical joker, clown, buffoon, jester, comic, (stand-up) comedian, comedienne, funnyman.

adj. *humorous*, funny, droll, amusing, comic, comical, farcical, funny ha-ha (*colloq.*); *witty*, satirical, sarcastic, ironic, sardonic; *ridiculous*, laughable, side-splitting, hilarious, uproarious, killing, killingly funny; *jocular*, jokey, joking, flippant, whimsical, facetious, tongue-in-cheek; *risqué*, near the bone, off-colour, blue.

vb. *joke*, jest, crack a joke, quip, pun, bring the house down (*colloq.*); *tease*, chaff, pull sb's leg, kid (*colloq.*); *ridicule*, make fun of, poke fun at, mock, caricature, satirize, lampoon, take off, ham up (*colloq.*), camp up (*colloq.*); *have a sense of humour*, see the funny side of, enjoy a joke; *laugh*, hoot, giggle, snigger, titter, chuckle, chortle, guffaw, cackle; *split* one's *sides*, roar with laughter, crease (*colloq.*), be in stiches, fall about, laugh like a drain, roll in the aisles (*colloq.*), nearly die (laughing) (*colloq.*); *smile*, grin, smirk, simper.

745 SERIOUSNESS

See also 659 (severity); 743 (dejection); 747 (lamentation); 762 (boredom).

n. *seriousness*, solemnity, earnestness, gravity, grimness; *sedateness*, sobriety, staidness, demureness, primness, sternness, puritanism; *dullness*, dryness, stuffiness,

colourlessness; *killjoy*, sobersides, wet blanket (*colloq.*), spoilsport, party pooper (*colloq.*).

adj. *serious*, solemn, earnest, grave, unfunny; *grim*, forbidding, frowning, stern, po-faced; *sedate*, sober, stolid, staid, demure, prim, straitlaced, stern, puritanical; *straight-faced*, deadpan, poker-faced; *dull*, dry, stuffy, colourless, dreary.

vb. *take things (too) seriously*, not get the joke, not have a sense of humour, keep a straight face, rain on sb's parade.

746 REJOICING

See also 734 (joy).

n. *rejoicing*, exultation, celebration, jubilation, triumph; *revelling*, revels, revelry, festivity, merrymaking, street party, carnival, thanksgiving; *clapping*, cheering, hallelujah, three cheers, hurrah, hooray.

adj. *rejoicing*, cock-a-hoop, over the moon (*colloq.*), exultant, jubilant; *celebratory*, triumphal, triumphant.

vb. *rejoice*, exult, celebrate, triumph; *revel*, make merry, carouse, dance/leap for joy, skip, dance in the streets, let one's hair down (*colloq.*), paint the town red (*colloq.*), push the boat out (*colloq.*); *clap*, cheer, shout, whoop, yell; *gloat*, crow, rub one's hands.

747 LAMENTATION

See also 735 (sorrow); 739 (dissatisfaction); 745 (seriousness).

n. *lamentation*, mourning, wailing, weeping, sobbing, tears, gnashing of teeth; *cry*, sob, weep, whimper, bawl; *widow's weeds*, sackcloth and ashes, black; *grief*, regret, sorrow; *lament*, threnody, elegy, dirge, requiem, funeral march, wake.

adj. *lamenting*, mourning, grief-stricken, tearful, inconsolable; *mournful*, lugubrious, plaintive; *lamentable*, pathetic, woeful, pitiable.

vb. *lament*, mourn, keen, beat one's breast; *grieve*, sorrow, go into mourning, elegize; *bemoan*, regret, deplore; *condole*, commiserate, comfort; *weep*, wail, sob, cry, burst into tears, break down; *sob*, sigh, moan, whimper, groan.

748 HOPE

See also 742 (cheerfulness); 755 (desire).

n. *hope*, aspiration, ambition, high hopes; *dream*, pipe-dream, wishful thinking, heart's desire, the promised land, utopia; *trust*, confidence, faith, reliance, optimism; *expectation*, assumption, presumption, anticipation; *promise*, good omen; *hopeful*, young hopeful, candidate, aspirant, competitor; *dreamer*, visionary, optimist.

adj. *hopeful*, aspiring, ambitious, would-be; *trusting*, confident, expectant, buoyant, optimistic, sanguine; *promising*, encouraging, favourable, auspicious, rosy.

vb. *hope*, aspire, set one's heart on, aim, long for; *trust*, rely, have faith, believe, feel confident, be in hopes of, rest assured; *expect*, assume, presume, anticipate; *look on the bright side*, live in hope, hope against hope, keep one's fingers crossed; *raise sb's hopes*, give to believe, encourage; *show promise*, have the makings of, augur well, bid fair, bode well.

749 **HOPELESSNESS**
See also 743 (dejection).

n. *hopelessness*, despondency, defeatism, despair, desperation, pessimism, cynicism, resignation, dashed hopes; *impossibility*, no chance, irrevocability; *hopeless case*, poor lookout, dead duck (*colloq.*), goner (*colloq.*); *pessimist*, Job's comforter, defeatist.

adj. *hopeless*, desperate, despondent, defeatist, pessimistic, cynical, resigned, past hoping; *vain*, futile, to no avail, impossible, irrevocable, irredeemable; *inauspicious*, unpropitious, unfavourable, ominous, bleak.

vb. *lose hope*, despair, give up, resign oneself, abandon hope, write off; *dash sb's hopes*, hold out no hope, discourage.

750 **FEAR**
See also 752 (cowardice).

n. *fear*, dread, awe, horror, fright, trepidation, terror, phobia, blue funk (*colloq.*); *panic*, alarm, scare, stampede; *intimidation*, threats, deterrence, sabre-rattling, reign of terror, hate mail, flame (mail); *timidity*, timorousness, fearfulness, nervousness; *diffidence*, shyness, hesitation; *cold feet*, misgivings, qualms, apprehension, uneasiness, disquiet; *worry*, concern, anxiety, angst, health anxiety, hypochondria; *tremor*, flutter, fear and trembling, adrenalin, cold sweat, butterflies (*colloq.*), collywobbles (*colloq.*), the heebie-jeebies (*colloq.*), the jitters (*colloq.*), the creeps (*colloq.*), the willies (*colloq.*).

adj. *afraid*, frightened, terrified, petrified, horrified, scared (stiff), alarmed, panicky, panic-stricken, white as a sheet; *timid*, timorous, fearful, nervous, jittery, jumpy, uptight (*colloq.*); *diffident*, shy, hesitant, wary;

apprehensive, uneasy; *worried*, concerned, anxious; *frightening*, frightful, alarming, awesome, horrifying, terrible, hair-raising, bloodcurdling, ghastly, grisly, gruesome, macabre; *creepy*, weird, scary, eerie.

vb. *fear*, be afraid, dread, stand in fear of; *get/have the wind up*, take fright, panic, lose one's nerve, break out in a cold sweat; *quake*, tremble, shake, quiver, shudder; *quail*, shrink, cower, funk, not be able to face, chicken out (*colloq.*); *freeze*, feel one's blood run cold/one's knees knock/one's hair stand on end; *frighten*, affright, scare, terrify, petrify, alarm; *intimidate*, menace, terrorize, put the fear of God into, browbeat, cow; *make nervous*, unnerve, put the wind up, shake, rattle, disquiet.

751 **COURAGE**
See also 539 (resolution).

n. *courage*, bravery, valour, heroism, fearlessness, intrepidity; *boldness*, audacity, daring, nerve, bottle (*colloq.*); *manliness*, prowess, chivalry, gallantry; *spirit*, dash, derring-do, pluck, mettle, backbone, guts (*colloq.*), spunk (*colloq.*); *fortitude*, resolution, morale, determination, the courage of one's convictions; *hero*, heroine, brave, Amazon, daredevil, VC, lionheart, braveheart.

adj. *courageous*, brave, valiant, heroic, ready for anything; *bold*, audacious, daring, spirited, dashing, plucky, spunky; *unafraid*, intrepid, fearless, dauntless, doughty, stout-hearted, unflinching; *manly*, chivalrous, gallant, macho.

vb. *be courageous*, have the courage/nerve to, venture, brave, beard, confront, face (the music), defy, dare to, show one's mettle, have what it takes, take it like a man, keep one's chin up (*colloq.*); *take courage*, pluck up courage, take heart, screw up one's courage, nerve oneself, brace oneself, put a brave face on; *hearten*, nerve, embolden, inspire, rally, boost, bolster, strengthen, give confidence, buck up.

752 **COWARDICE**
See also 541 (vacillation); 750 (fear).

n. *cowardice*, cowardliness, pusillanimity, faint-heartedness, timidity, weakness, spinelessness, white feather, yellow streak, funk (*colloq.*); *quitting*, defeatism; *boasting*, braggadocio, Dutch courage; *coward*, poltroon, dastard, cowardy custard (*colloq.*), rabbit (*colloq.*), chicken (*colloq.*), scaredy (colloq.), sissy (colloq.), deserter, quitter, defeatist, shirker, braggart.

adj. cowardly, craven, pusillanimous, faint-hearted, timid, lily-livered, gutless, spineless, yellow-bellied (colloq.), sissy (colloq.), yellow (colloq.), chicken (colloq.); dastardly, mean, cowering, defeatist.

vb. lack courage, not dare, have no stomach for, funk (colloq.); cringe, quail, shrink, cower, skulk; panic, desert, turn tail, slink away, cut and run; get cold feet, quit, lose one's nerve, bottle/chicken out (colloq.).

753 **RASHNESS**
See also 445 (folly); 615 (haste).

n. rashness, recklessness, carelessness, thoughtlessness, heedlessness, imprudence; indiscipline, irresponsibility, wildness, temerity, audacity; folly, indiscretion, foolhardiness, brinksmanship, gamble, a leap in the dark; impulsiveness, impetuosity, haste, hotheadedness; daredevil, hothead, tearaway, fire-eater, gambler, madcap, harum-scarum.

adj. rash, incautious, reckless, thoughtless, heedless, ill-considered, inconsiderate, unthinking; undisciplined, irresponsible, wild, buccaneering, trigger-happy; careless, slap-happy, hit-and-miss, devil-may-care; foolish, foolhardy, imprudent, indiscreet; impulsive, impetuous, overenthusiastic, hotheaded, headstrong, overhasty; precipitous, headlong, breakneck, do-or-die, suicidal.

vb. be rash etc, not care, take the plunge, throw caution to the winds, damn the consequences, stick one's neck out; rush into, tempt providence, ask for trouble; gamble, take unnecessary risks, play with fire, risk one's neck, go out on a limb, dice with danger/death, court disaster.

754 **CAUTION**
See also 406 (carefulness); 453 (foresight).

n. caution, cautiousness, heed, heedfulness, wariness, care, safety first, prudence; circumspection, reverence, respect, discretion; deliberation, planning, forethought, foresight, precaution, prophylaxis, prophylactic; vigilance, watchfulness, alertness, suspicion.

adj. cautious, wary, careful, heedful, prudent; circumspect, gingerly, respectful, suspicious, nervous; precautionary, prophylactic; vigilant, watchful, alert, canny.

vb. take care, play safe, think twice, look before one leaps; take preventive measures, keep well out of, give a wide berth, keep one's head down; look out, watch one's step,

tread warily, be on one's guard; cover oneself, see how the wind blows, feel one's way, leave nothing to chance.

755 **DESIRE**
See also 553 (intention); 681 (request); 748 (hope).

n. desire, wish, want, fancy; requirement, need; longing, yearning, hankering, yen, ambition, aspiration; curiosity, inquisitiveness, thirst for knowledge; urge, inclination, motivation, eagerness, keenness, itch, bug (colloq.); craving, covetousness, lust, mania, addiction, craze; greed, voracity, gluttony, rapacity; hunger, thirst, appetite, famine, starvation, drought; object of one's desire, desideratum, ambition, dream, fantasy.

adj. desirous, wishful; aspiring, would-be, hopeful, ambitious; eager, keen, avid, itching, bent on; curious, inquisitive; covetous, lusting, lecherous, crazy for; greedy, voracious, insatiable, rapacious; hungry, starving, ravenous, famished, empty, peckish (colloq.); thirsty, dry, parched; desirable, acceptable, welcome, enviable, appetizing, attractive.

vb. desire, wish, want, pray for; welcome, be glad of, fancy, could do with; require, need, must have; long, yearn, hanker, thirst, itch, set one's heart on, aspire, be dying for (colloq.); covet, lust after, crave, have designs on; hunger, thirst, starve, drool, could eat a horse (colloq.).

756 **INDIFFERENCE**
See also 403 (lack of curiosity); 733 (impassivity).

n. indifference, lack of interest, unconcern, apathy; insensitivity, coldness, impassivity, half-heartedness; neutrality, impartiality, disinterest; promiscuousness.

adj. indifferent, unconcerned, uninterested, apathetic, blasé, cool (colloq.); insensitive, cold, unimpressed, unmoved, uninvolved, impassive, unresponsive; half-hearted, lukewarm, not bothered, past caring, easy (colloq.); neutral, impartial, disinterested, impersonal, dispassionate; unambitious, easy-going, laid back (colloq.); promiscuous; unwanted, de trop, unwelcome, unasked, unbidden, uninvited; undesirable, unattractive.

vb. not care (less), not mind, be all the same to, can take it or leave it, not give a damn/hoot (colloq.); leave one cold, take no interest in, not care for, hold no brief for.

757 LIKING

See also 336 (physical pleasure); 795 (love).

n. *liking*, fondness, fancy, relish, weakness, partiality, sympathy, affinity, soft spot; *leaning*, inclination, penchant, propensity, proclivity; *preference*, predilection; *attraction*, fascination, appeal; *popular choice*, favourite, crowd-pleaser.

adj. *fond of*, partial to, keen on, sympathetic to; *likeable*, popular, in favour, attractive, appealing, fetching, catchy.

vb. *like*, be fond of, care for, go for, fancy, relish, be partial to, have a weakness for, take pleasure in, be into (*colloq.*); *prefer*, favour, choose, incline.

758 DISLIKE

See also 796 (hate).

n. *dislike*, disinclination, distaste; *dissatisfaction*, displeasure; *repulsion*, repugnance, disgust, abhorrence, loathing; *aversion*, allergy, antipathy, prejudice; *bête noir*, bugbear, pet hate.

adj. *displeased*, dissatisfied, disenchanted, disgusted, fed up; *averse*, allergic, antipathetic, loath, anti; *undesirable*, disagreeable, objectionable, obnoxious; *repulsive*, repugnant, abhorrent, loathsome, rebarbative; *unpopular*, out of favour, unloved.

vb. *dislike*, not care for, not find to one's taste, have no time for, have no stomach for, not go for; *take a dislike to*, turn one's nose up at, not take kindly to; *shrink from*, shudder at, detest, abhor, loathe, can't abide/bear/stand; *displease*, antagonize, go against the grain, rub up the wrong way, put off, repel, disgust, make one's gorge rise.

759 WONDER

See also 451 (surprise).

n. *wonder*, wonderment, amazement, shock, astonishment, awe, fascination, stupefaction, bewilderment, bafflement, incredulity; *sensation*, drama, miracle, marvel, prodigy, phenomenon, the seven wonders of the world; *oddity*, curiosity, rarity, freak, monster, monstrosity; *wizard*, miracle-worker, genius, child prodigy.

adj. *wondrous*, amazing, astonishing, astounding, remarkable, mind-boggling, breathtaking, stupefying, bewildering, baffling, unbelievable, out of this world; *sensational*, dramatic, miraculous, prodigious, phenomenal, extraordinary, unparalleled, monstrous, stupendous, fantastic, wonderful,

fabulous, tremendous; *odd*, curious, strange, rare, freaky, freakish, weird, mysterious; *amazed*, astonished, astounded, rapt, spellbound, dumbfounded, struck dumb, speechless, open-mouthed, bewildered, stupefied, flabbergasted, bowled over, thunderstruck, transfixed.

vb. *wonder*, marvel, gasp, whistle, not get over; *stare*, gape, gaze, goggle, gawk, gawp, not believe one's eyes, rub one's eyes; *amaze*, astonish, astound; *bowl over*, stagger, take one's breath away, flabbergast, overwhelm, dumbfound; *confound*, baffle, bewilder.

760 LACK OF WONDER

See also 733 (impassivity); 756 (indifference).

n. *lack of wonder/astonishment* etc, composure, blankness, impassivity; *expectation*, what one expected, just as one thought, nothing to speak about/write home about, nothing new under the sun, old hat (*colloq.*).

adj. *unsurprised*, unimpressed, unmoved, unperturbed; *expected*, foreseen, accustomed, common, usual.

vb. *not wonder*, not be surprised, see nothing remarkable, take in one's stride, not bat an eyelid, have seen it all before; *expect*, assume, take for granted, take as read.

761 RECREATION

See also 165 (habitat); 236 (land travel); 237 (water travel); 555 (pursuit); 612 (leisure).

n. *recreation*, amusement, pleasure, fun, leisure, spare time, diversion, relaxation, rest, (activity) holiday; *activity*, interest, pastime, hobby, pursuit, sport, game, play; *entertainment*, theatre, television, TV, video, radio, music, opera, musical; *festival*, fiesta, carnival, gala, mela; *fair*, funfair, circus; *party*, house-warming party, bottle party, picnic, barbecue, street party, dinner, banquet, feast; *outing*, trip, day trip, excursion, jaunt; *camping*, pony-trekking, hiking, orienteering, mountaineering, rock-climbing; *running*, jogging, steeplechase, paper chase, hare and hounds; *athletics*, keep-fit, aerobics; *treasure hunt*, geocaching, metal detecting; *cycling*, mountain-biking, quad-biking; *water sport*, swimming, diving, snorkelling, scuba diving, boating, rowing, sculling, canoeing, whitewater rafting, sailing, yachting, windsurfing, waterskiing, surfing; *winter sports*, skiing, ski-jumping, tobogganing, skating, ice hockey, curling; *flying*, gliding, parachuting, skydiving, parascending, hang-gliding; *equestrianism*, horseracing, showjumping, steeplechasing, dressage; *football*, soccer, the beautiful game, rugby (football), volleyball, cricket, baseball, tennis, squash (rackets), badminton, golf, hockey, lacrosse, polo, croquet, snooker, billiards; *extreme sports*, base jumping, bungee-jumping, canyoning, cliff jumping, free diving; *party game*, musical chairs, sardines, charades; *hopscotch*, leapfrog, hide-and-seek; *crossword*, jigsaw (puzzle), noughts and crosses, Rubik's cube (*tdmk*), solitaire, video game; *chess*, draughts, checkers, backgammon, mah jong, ludo, snakes and ladders, Monopoly (*tdmk*), Scrabble (*tdmk*); *card game*, bridge, rummy, canasta, patience, whist, snap, pontoon, brag, poker, old maid, happy families; *roulette*, dice, bingo, tombola; *dancing* (see 524 dance); *toy*, plaything, ball, balloon, rattle, bricks, marbles, water pistol, popgun, airgun, toy soldier; *doll*, teddy bear, golliwog, Sindy (*tdmk*) doll, Barbie (*tdmk*), Action Man (*tdmk*); *bicycle*, tricycle, fairy cycle, roller skates, skateboard, pedal car; *model railway*, train set, model, Meccano (*tdmk*), Lego (*tdmk*); *blood sports*, country sports, hunt, meet, fox-hunting, coursing, beagling, stalking, falconry, angling, fishing; *park*, gardens, playing field, recreation ground; *pitch*, ground, court, field, green, course; *theatre*, opera house, concert hall, dance hall, discotheque, night club, casino, bingo hall; *player*, sportsman, sportswoman, champion, grandmaster.

adj. *recreational*, sporting, sporty; *festive*, out to enjoy oneself, jovial, jolly; *amusing*, entertaining, diverting, pleasant, enjoyable.

vb. *amuse*, entertain, divert, delight, cheer, make one laugh, tickle; *relax*, have fun, pursue, enjoy oneself, go on holiday; *have fun*, give/throw a party, have a good time, go out, celebrate, picnic, go dancing, let off steam (*colloq.*), paint the town red (*colloq.*), have a ball (*colloq.*), large it (*colloq.*); *camp*, climb, hike, ramble; *play games*, do sport, gamble, run, jump, jog, cycle, swim, dive, sail, ski, toboggan, skate; *hunt*, shoot, ride to hounds, course, fish, go fishing.

762 **BOREDOM**
See also 745 (seriousness).

n. *boredom*, tedium, monotony, sameness; *dreariness*, drabness, deadliness, dullness, banality; *stodginess*, flatness, colourlessness, heaviness, slowness; *weariness*, world-weariness, languor, ennui, time to kill; *bore*, bind, chore, grind, treadmill, daily round, drag (*colloq.*); *pub bore*, buttonholer, pain in the arse/neck (*colloq.*).

adj. *boring*, tedious, monotonous, uneventful, repetitive, repetitious, same; *dreary*, drab, deadly, dull, unexciting, uninteresting, unfunny, unimaginative; *stodgy*, flat, colourless, heavy, ponderous, slow, turgid; *plain*, prosaic, mundane, humdrum, banal, commonplace, trite, pedestrian; *long-winded*, wordy, verbose, prolix; *wearisome*, tiresome, irksome; *bored*, at a loose end, twiddling one's thumbs; *sick of*, fed up to the back teeth; *weary*, world-weary, stale, cloyed, jaded.

vb. *bore*, bore stiff/rigid/to tears/to death, go on and on, never vary; *weary*, try, irk; *pall*, cloy, jade, lose its novelty.

adv. *in a rut.*

763 **BEAUTY**
See also 218 (symmetry); 511 (elegance); 765 (beautification).

n. *beauty*, pulchritude, loveliness, comeliness, prettiness, good looks, handsomeness, fairness, attractiveness, shapeliness; *glamour*, sex appeal, it, vital statistics, attractions; *grace*, charm, elegance, chic; *grandeur*, magnificence, splendour, resplendence, radiance, brilliance, glory; *thing of beauty*, masterpiece, work of art, showpiece; *beauty spot*, view, landscape, seascape; *idol*, vision, dream, knockout, picture, a fine figure of a man/woman, a sight for sore eyes, cheesecake (*colloq.*), beefcake (*colloq.*); *belle*, beauty queen, Venus, pin-up, It girl, stunner (*colloq.*), cracker (*colloq.*), dolly bird (*colloq.*), peach (*colloq.*), dish (*colloq.*), arm candy (*colloq.*), eye candy (*colloq.*), über-babe, supermodel, sex on a stick (*colloq.*), dreamboat (*colloq.*), heart-throb (*colloq.*).

adj. *beautiful*, lovely, attractive, comely, fair; *pretty*, bonny, sweet, pretty as a picture; *good-looking*, handsome, husky, tall, dark and handsome; *glamorous*, alluring, stunning, dishy (*colloq.*); *shapely*, well-formed, curvaceous, rounded, slim, slinky; *neat*, trim, well-kept, spruce, smart, natty, dapper; *graceful*, charming, exquisite, stylish, elegant, chic; *grand*, magnificent, splendid, resplendent, gracious, radiant, ravishing, gorgeous, brilliant, dazzling, glorious; *picturesque*, scenic, eye-catching.

764 **UGLINESS**

See also 219 (distortion); 512 (inelegance); 767 (blemish).

n. *ugliness*, hideousness, unsightliness, repulsiveness; *inelegance*, gracelessness, clumsiness; *deformity*, distortion, mutilation, defacement, disfigurement; *eyesore*, sight, fright (*colloq.*), blot on the landscape, horror, mess; *ugly duckling*, witch, scarecrow, no oil painting, plain Jane.

adj. *ugly*, hideous, unsightly, nasty, grotty (*colloq.*); *plain*, ill-favoured, frumpy, mousy; *repulsive*, horrible, ghastly, frightful, monstrous, loathsome, offensive; *deformed*, distorted, malformed, mutilated, defaced, disfigured, grotesque, misshapen; *unbecoming*, inelegant, graceless, unprepossessing, garish, gaudy; *coarse*, ungainly, cumbersome, clumsy, ill-fitting.

vb. *look a fright*, pull a face; *disfigure*, deface, mar, mutilate, distort.

765 **BEAUTIFICATION**

See also 510 (ornament); 763 (beauty); 766 (decoration).

n. *beautification*, beauty therapy, plastic surgery, cosmetic surgery, face-lift, skin graft, nose job (*colloq.*), tummy tuck, breast enlargement, breast implant, liposuction; *beauty treatment*, face mask, facial, mud pack, facial scrub, skin peel, eyebrow-plucking, waxing, bikini wax, Botox (*tdmk*), manicure, pedicure, body-piercing, tattooing; *tanning*, sun tan, sun bed, solarium; *grooming*, wash and brush-up; *hairdressing*, hair cut, trim, shave, styling, coiffure, hairdo; *short back and sides*, crewcut, pageboy, bouffant, Afro, Mohican, fringe, curls, ringlets, plait, pigtail, ponytail, bun; *shampoo and set*, perm, blow-dry, highlights, streaks; *beard*, goatee, imperial, moustache, toothbrush moustache, soup-strainer, handlebar moustache, muttonchops, sideboards, sideburns; *wig*, toupee, hairpiece, false eyelashes; *hairbrush*, comb, curlers, rollers, curling tongs, hairpin, hairgrip, kirby grip, slide, hairnet, hair dryer; *razor*, shaver, depilatory; *shampoo*, rinse, dye, henna, conditioner, hair spray, hair lacquer, hair cream; *make-up*, cosmetic, lipstick, lip gloss, eye shadow, eyeliner, mascara, rouge, blusher, foundation, moisturizer, face powder; *nail scissors*, nail clippers, nail file, nail polish; *beautician*, beauty therapist, plastic surgeon, make-up artist, visagist, manicurist; *hairdresser*, barber, coiffeur, coiffeuse, stylist; *beauty salon*, nail bar.

vb. *beautify*, prettify, improve the appearance of, dress up, primp, smarten, preen, groom, make up, titivate, doll up (*colloq.*), tart up (*colloq.*).

766 **DECORATION**

See also 510 (ornament); 765 (beautification).

n. *decoration*, adornment, ornamentation, embellishment, enrichment, finery; *interior decoration*, interior design, paint, wallpaper, furnishings; *flower arranging*, floral display, bouquet, posy, buttonhole, garland, wreath; *pattern*, design, detail, motif, tracery, scrollwork, check, pinstripe, herringbone, hound's tooth, polka dot, paisley; *needlework*, embroidery, tapestry, appliqué, smocking, broderie anglaise; *crochet*, lace, tatting, macramé, knitting; *trimming*, frill, fringe, tassel, braid, bead, bow, bobble, ribbon, sequin, diamanté; *jewellery*, bling-bling (*colloq.*), bracelet, bangle, ring, engagement/wedding ring, signet ring, necklace, pendant, locket, charm, crucifix, earring, tiara, clasp, brooch, cameo, medallion; *jewel*, gem, precious stone, diamond, ruby, pearl, opal, sapphire, turquoise, emerald, beryl, garnet, amethyst, topaz, agate, onyx, coral, jet, mother of pearl, moonstone, lapis lazuli.

adj. *decorative*, ornamental, architectural; *just for show*, cosmetic; *ornate*, fancy, elaborate, intricate; *gaudy*, garish, florid; *decorated*, adorned, ornamented, embellished, patterned, inlaid, enamelled, engraved, tooled, embossed, studded; *worked*, embroidered, trimmed; *festooned*, garlanded, wreathed, hung; *bejewelled*, decked out, dressed to kill, sporting.

vb. *decorate*, ornament, adorn, embellish, enrich, enhance, set off, pick out, smarten up; *bedeck*, deck out, hang, trim, festoon; *paint*, wallpaper, varnish, whitewash, grain, lacquer; *embroider*, work, crochet; *inlay*, enamel, engrave, tool, emboss, gild.

767 **BLEMISH**

See also 219 (distortion); 585 (imperfection); 764 (ugliness).

n. *blemish*, flaw, defect, imperfection; *smudge*, smear, blur, tarnish, rust; *mark*, spot, daub, stain, speck, blot, blotch; *crack*, chip, dent; *mole*, birthmark, strawberry mark, freckle; *wart*, carbuncle, pimple, acne.

adj. *blemished*, flawed, defective, impaired, imperfect, shop-soiled; *smudged*, blurred, tarnished, rusty; *marked*, stained, foxed, spotted; *cracked*, dented, pitted.

vb. *blemish*, flaw, spoil, impair, mar, sully, deface; *smudge*, smear, blur, tarnish, rust; *mark*, daub, stain, speck, blot; *crack*, dent, pit, chip.

768 REFINEMENT
See also 418 (discrimination); 791 (courtesy).

n. *refinement*, tastefulness, good taste, discrimination, discernment, good judgement; *connoisseurship*, epicureanism, palate, nose, flair; *tact*, tactfulness, euphemism, civility, courtesy, delicacy; *grace*, polish, sophistication, breeding, urbanity, manners, etiquette, culture, savoir faire; *decency*, propriety, decorum, respectability; *connoisseur*, epicurean, gourmet, sophisticate, cognoscente, dilettante, amateur, aesthete, critic.

adj. *refined*, discriminating, discerning, fastidious, epicurean; *tasteful*, in good taste, appreciative, aesthetic, critical; *tactful*, delicate, civil, decorous, seemly, respectable; *graceful*, dignified, polished, sophisticated, well-bred, urbane.

vb. *have good taste*, discriminate, criticize; *appreciate*, value.

769 VULGARITY
See also 419 (lack of discrimination); 785 (showiness); 792 (discourtesy).

n. *vulgarity*, tastelessness, bad/poor taste; *gaudiness*, garishness, brashness, loudness, ostentation, bling-bling (*colloq.*); *tactlessness*, uncivility, discourtesy, rudeness, crassness, boorishness, shamelessness; *artificiality*, pretension, shoddiness, kitsch; *indecency*, impropriety, indecorum, indelicacy, obscenity; *bad form*, no breeding, commonness, incorrectness; *snob*, nouveau riche, parvenu, social climber, rough diamond, cad, lout, yob (*colloq.*).

adj. *vulgar*, tasteless, in bad/poor taste, non-U, naff (*colloq.*); *gaudy*, garish, brash, loud, meretricious, ostentatious, flash (*colloq.*); *tactless*, uncivil, discourteous, rude, crass, boorish, caddish, loutish, yobbish (*colloq.*); *artificial*, pretentious, shoddy, cheap and nasty, kitschy; *indecent*, indecorous, indelicate, improper, obscene, explicit, adult; *unpolished*, gauche, unpresentable, uncultured, unsophisticated, common.

770 FASHION
See also 72 (conformity); 502 (style).

n. *fashion*, style, mode, trend, vogue; *craze*, fad, rage, cult; *the latest fashion*, latest, the last word, dernier cri; *fashionableness*,

stylishness, chic, elegance; *society*, fashionable society, high society, café society, smart set, jet set, bright young things, the beautiful people; *upper crust*, cream, crème de la crème, *man/woman about town*, jetsetter, leader of fashion, trend-setter, swinger, playboy, swell, dandy, toff, peacock, metrosexual, blood, blade, beau, debutante, deb, deb's delight (*colloq.*); *slave to fashion*, fashion victim, fashionista, fashion police.

adj. *fashionable*, modish, trendy, in vogue, all the rage, à la mode, up to the minute, with it (*colloq.*), groovy (*colloq.*), swinging (*colloq.*), in (*colloq.*), happening (*colloq.*), now (*colloq.*); *stylish*, elegant, chic, exquisite, well-dressed; *posh*, smart, classy, swish (*colloq.*); *flashy*, dashing, foppish, rakish, snazzy (*colloq.*).

vb. *become popular*, find favour, catch on; *follow the fashion*, climb/jump on the bandwagon, move with the times, follow the crowd, keep up with the Joneses, move in the right circles, get with it (*colloq.*); *lead the fashion*, set trends, push the envelope.

771 AFFECTATION
See also 480 (deception); 783 (vanity).

n. *affectation*, pretentiousness, pretension; *pose*, airs, act, image, façade, front, show, bluff; *artificiality*, mannerism, sham, humbug, insincerity, put-on (*colloq.*); *boast*, boastfulness, ostentation, bragging, swanking, self-glorification; *bravado*, bluster, bombast, hot air, grandiloquence; *charlatan*, humbug, impostor, bluffer, poser, poseur; *boaster*, braggart, big-mouth (*colloq.*), show-off.

adj. *affected*, pretentious, studied, mannered, contrived, stilted; *posing*, posturing, attitudinizing, for effect, ostentatious, camp (*colloq.*), poncy (*colloq.*); *superficial*, insincere, hypocritical, hollow, empty; *artificial*, sham, phoney, tongue in cheek; *self-righteous*, sanctimonious, mealy-mouthed, prim, stuck-up, snobbish; *boastful*, big-mouthed (*colloq.*), loud-mouthed; *bombastic*, blustering, grandiloquent.

vb. *affect*, pretend, put on; *pose*, posture, attitudinize, put on airs, ponce around (*colloq.*); *fake*, sham, feign, make a show of, bluff; *overact*, ham it up, camp it up; *boast*, brag, vaunt, show off, swank, strut; *bluster*, rant.

772 RIDICULOUSNESS
See also 443 (nonsense); 744 (humour).

n. *ridiculousness*, ludicrousness,

laughableness, risibility, absurdity;
extravagance, exaggeration, caricature;
mimicry, parody, travesty; *paradox*, catch-22
situation; *buffoonery*, fooling about/around,
tomfoolery, horseplay, clowning; *escapade*,
monkey tricks, nonsense, scrape.

adj. *ridiculous*, ludicrous, laughable, risible,
farcical, mad, daft, silly; *absurd*, grotesque,
bizarre, outlandish; *monstrous*, preposterous,
outrageous; *contemptible*, derisory;
extravagant, exaggerated, over the top
(*colloq.*); *paradoxical*; *tomfool*, asinine, idiotic.

vb. *go from the sublime to the ridiculous*; *play
the fool*, fool/lark about/around, clown, be a
laughing stock, make an exhibition of
oneself, go way over the top (*colloq.*);
caricature, mimic, parody, make a fool of.

773 **DERISION**

See also 772 (ridiculousness); 824 (disrespect).

n. *derision*, ridicule, mockery, scoffing,
scorn; *teasing*, ribbing, leg-pulling, ragging,
banter; *snigger*, titter, smirk; *irony*, sarcasm,
caricature, parody, lampoon, burlesque,
spoof, send-up, take-off; *butt*, figure of fun,
laughing stock, fair game; *stooge*, straight
man, foil.

adj. *derisive*, mocking, scoffing, scornful;
ironic, sarcastic, satirical.

vb. *deride*, ridicule, mock, scoff, scorn, jeer;
make fun of, poke fun at, tease, rib, chaff, rag,
twit; *snigger*, titter, smirk; *fool*, kid, pull sb's
leg, take the mickey out of, have on (*colloq.*);
caricature, satirize, lampoon, pillory, send up;
deflate, debunk, puncture.

774 **REPUTE**

See also 650 (trophy); 778 (title);
823 (respect); 831 (probity).

n. *repute*, reputation, good standing, good
name; *regard*, esteem, admiration,
estimation; *favour*, good odour, popularity;
prestige, glory, acclaim, honour, kudos,
cachet, dignity, illustriousness; *eminence*,
prominence, distinction, position, status;
renown, fame, celebrity; *reliability*,
respectability, trustworthiness,
dependability; *worthy*, somebody, dignitary,
pillar of society, doyen, leading light,
celebrity, star, luminary, grand old man;
legend, living legend, legend in his/her own
lifetime.

adj. *reputable*, of good repute, estimable,
worthy, meritorious, admirable; *esteemed*,
highly regarded, well thought of, highly

acclaimed, celebrated, of note; *reliable*,
trustworthy, dependable; *famous*, renowned,
celebrated, legendary; *in favour*, popular;
illustrious, eminent, prominent,
distinguished, of distinction, leading,
ranking, prestigious, august; *grand*, imposing,
dignified, majestic, royal, regal, princely,
lordly, superior, noble, aristocratic.

vb. *have a reputation*, have one's position
to consider, command respect, be looked up
to, go down in history; *gain a reputation*, do
oneself credit, win one's spurs, gain
recognition, make one's mark; *rank*, excel,
shine, star; *outshine*, overshadow, eclipse;
respect, pay respect to, regard, esteem,
honour, look up to, admire; *praise*, acclaim,
glorify, lionize, revere, put on a pedestal;
prize, value, treasure; *reward*, crown,
enthrone, ennoble, elevate to the peerage;
beatify, canonize, deify, worship.

775 **DISREPUTE**

See also 824 (disrespect); 832 (improbity).

n. *disrepute*, ill repute, bad name, discredit;
notoriety, infamy; *disfavour*, unpopularity,
bad odour; *unreliability*, untrustworthiness;
disparagement, slur, slight; *opprobrium*,
disgrace, humiliation, shame, dishonour,
ignominy, obloquy, -gate; *smear*, stain,
tarnish, blot, slur; *scandal*, calumny, gossip,
slander, defamation, libel.

adj. *disreputable*, shady, shifty; *notorious*,
infamous; *unreliable*, untrustworthy;
questionable, dubious, doubtful; *humiliating*,
degrading, infra dig; *despised*, held in
contempt; *despicable*, mean, base; *inglorious*,
shameful, dishonourable, ignominious,
disgraceful; *disgraced*, humiliated; *shabby*,
squalid, scruffy; *obscure*, unknown, unheard
of.

vb. *bring into disrepute*, take away one's
good name, disparage, tarnish, smear, cast
aspersions on, blot, sully, mar, taint,
blemish, dishonour, bring shame upon, put
to shame, disgrace, discredit, expose, cut
down to size (*colloq.*), take sb down a peg or
two (*colloq.*); *fall into disrepute*, disgrace
oneself, get a bad name, blot one's
copybook, lose one's reputation, come down
in the world, lose face; *stoop*, lower oneself,
demean oneself, degrade oneself.

776 **ARISTOCRAT**

n. *aristocrat*, nobleman, noblewoman, noble,
titled person, noble lord/lady, peer, peeress,
peer of the realm, hereditary peer, life peer;

lords temporal, duke, archduke, duchess, marquis, marquess, marchioness, earl, count, countess, viscount, viscountess, baron, baroness, baronet, dowager; *lords spiritual*, archbishop, bishop; *knight*, dame, don, squire, laird, Junker, boyar, grandee, patrician, grande dame; *king*, queen, prince, princess, monarch, sovereign, emperor, tsar, sultan, rajah, nawab, nabob, sheikh, emir, bey, khan; *aristocracy*, nobility, gentry, landed gentry, peerage, elite, privileged class, ruling class, establishment, high society, the upper classes, upper crust (*colloq.*), toff (*colloq.*), nob (*colloq.*), Sloane Ranger, hooray Henry; *royalty*, court; *nobility*, high birth, blue blood, descent, ancestry, family, house, dynasty, caste, pedigree; *rank*, distinction, position, station, majesty, prerogative, privilege.

adj. *aristocratic*, noble, titled, in Burke's Peerage, ducal, baronial; *of high birth*, well-born, blue-blooded, of good family, patrician; *royal*, regal, monarchical, majestic, kingly, queenly, princely, of royal blood; *upper-class*, respectable, top-drawer (*colloq.*), double-barrelled, posh, county, U.

777 **COMMONER**

n. *commoner*, pleb, plebeian, citizen; *ordinary person*, Joe Bloggs, John Doe, the man in the street, the man on the Clapham omnibus, common man; *worker*, housewife, blue-collar worker, white-collar worker; *nobody*, nonentity; *peasant*, yeoman, villein, serf, yokel, country bumpkin, country cousin; *tramp*, down-and-out, vagabond, bum, hobo, vagrant, outcast, untouchable; *commonality*, commons, bourgeoisie, citizenry, the people, populace, community, the general public, the masses, the rank and file, the hoi polloi, proletariat, Tom, Dick and Harry; *rabble*, herd, mob, riffraff, scum, dregs of society, the great unwashed (*colloq.*); *middle class*, bourgeoisie, salaried classes, professional classes, yuppies (*colloq.*), intelligentsia; *the lower classes*, the working class, the lower orders, have-nots, underdogs, poor whites, poor white trash (*derog.*), trailer trash (*derog.*), the underprivileged; *underworld*, demi-monde.

adj. *common*, average, ordinary; *working-class*, plebeian, proletarian; *middle-class*, (petit) bourgeois, upwardly mobile, suburban, provincial, gentrified; *lowly*, obscure, humble, mean, low, base.

778 **TITLE**

See also 774 (repute).

n. *title*, honorific, courtesy title, designation, handle (*colloq.*); *Majesty*, Royal Highness, Excellency, Grace, Lordship, Ladyship, my lord, my lady, Honourable, Right Honourable, Sir, Lady, Honour, Worship, Worshipful, Reverence; *Reverend*, Very Reverend, Right Reverend, Most Reverend, Monsignor, Holiness, padre; *Brother*, Sister, Reverend Father, Reverend Mother; *sir*, madam, ma'am, mister, Mr, mistress, Mrs, Miss, Ms; *monsieur*, madame, mademoiselle; *Herr*, Frau, Fräulein; *señor*, señora, señorita; *signore*, signora, signorina; *sahib*, memsahib, bwana, effendi; *comrade*, brother, sister, tovarisch; *academic title*, bachelor, master, doctor, professor.

779 **PRIDE**

See also 783 (vanity).

n. *pride*, self-esteem, self-respect, self-regard, dignity, reputation; *haughtiness*, condescension, disdain, arrogance, insolence; *snobbery*, conceit, vainglory, self-glorification, big-headedness; *proud person*, snob, swank, prima donna, his nibs, Lord/Lady Muck.

adj. *proud*, self-respecting, house-proud; *lofty*, dignified, commanding, stately; *haughty*, condescending, patronizing, high-and-mighty; *disdainful*, arrogant, overbearing; *conceited*, vainglorious, big-headed, swollen-headed, strutting; *snobbish*, toffee-nosed (*colloq.*), stuck-up (*colloq.*), uppity (*colloq.*).

vb. *be proud* etc, have one's pride, hold one's head high, stand erect, take pride in, pride oneself on; *be too proud*, give oneself airs, strut, be up on one's high horse; *disdain*, despise, condescend, patronize.

780 **HUMILITY**

See also 577 (unimportance); 782 (servility); 784 (modesty).

n. *humility*, humbleness, meekness, resignation; *self-abasement*, self-effacement, modesty, unpretentiousness; *lowliness*, inoffensiveness; *servility*, submissiveness, subservience, obedience.

adj. *humble*, meek, resigned; *self-abasing*, self-effacing, modest, unpretentious, unassuming; *lowly*, inoffensive, harmless; *servile*, submissive, subservient, obedient.

vb. *humble oneself*, resign oneself, turn the other cheek; *condescend*, deign, stoop, lower oneself, demean oneself; *submit*, crawl, eat humble pie, knuckle under.

781 INSOLENCE
See also 824 (disrespect).

n. *insolence*, effrontery, impudence, impertinence, rudeness, incivility; *nerve*, cheek (*colloq.*), gall, neck (*colloq.*), sauce (*colloq.*), lip (*colloq.*); *audacity*, temerity, boldness; *shamelessness*, blatancy, brazenness; *arrogance*, presumption; *disdain*, contempt; *upstart*, young pup (*colloq.*), whippersnapper, smart aleck, cheeky devil (*colloq.*).

adj. *insolent*, impudent, impertinent, rude, uncivil, impolite, offensive; *cheeky*, fresh, offhand, flippant, pert, familiar, cocky (*colloq.*), cocksure; *audacious*, bold, defiant; *shameless*, blatant, brazen; *arrogant*, presumptuous; *disdainful*, contemptuous, high-handed, imperious, snotty (*colloq.*).

vb. *get fresh*, have the cheek/nerve to, make bold to, make free with; *answer back*, cheek (*colloq.*); *get above oneself*, step out of line, presume, lord it, come the high and mighty with (*colloq.*); *express contempt*, snort, cock a snook, snap one's fingers at, give a V-sign.

782 SERVILITY
See also 642 (submission); 780 (humility).

n. *servility*, deference, compliance, subservience; *timeserving*, ingratiation, sycophancy, obsequiousness, fawning, crawling, bowing and scraping, bootlicking, arse-licking (*vulg.*), brown-nosing (*vulg.*); *sycophant*, toady, timeserver, Uriah Heep, crawler, bootlicker, arse-licker (*vulg.*), yes-man, smoothie (*colloq.*), lapdog.

adj. *servile*, deferential, compliant, subservient; under the thumb (*colloq.*); *timeserving*, ingratiating, sycophantic, obsequious, smarmy (*colloq.*); *fawning*, crawling, whining, grovelling.

vb. *toady*, ingratiate oneself, fawn, crawl, grovel, curry favour, lick sb's boots, suck up to (*colloq.*), lick sb's arse (*vulg.*), brown-nose (*vulg.*); *comply*, kowtow, defer, tug one's forelock; *fetch and carry for*, stooge, pander to.

783 VANITY
See also 431 (overestimation); 771 (affectation); 779 (pride).

n. *vanity*, immodesty, conceit, self-importance, egotism, megalomania; *self-congratulation*, self-glorification, smugness,

superciliousness, arrogance; *narcissism*, self-worship, self-love; *boastfulness*, boasting, showing off, exhibitionism; *egotist*, show-off, exhibitionist, peacock, Narcissus, God's gift to women (*colloq.*).

adj. *vain*, immodest, conceited, self-important, egotistical, megalomaniac; *self-satisfied*, complacent, smug, supercilious, arrogant, stuck-up (*colloq.*); *narcissistic*, full of oneself; *dogmatic*, opinionated; *cocky*, bumptious, pretentious, pompous, swollen-headed, bigheaded, too big for one's boots (*colloq.*).

vb. *have a high opinion of oneself*, think a lot of oneself, be puffed up, think one knows it all, fish for compliments; *get above oneself*, get too big for one's boots (*colloq.*); *show off*, strut, put on airs, talk big, blow one's own trumpet; *go to* one's *head*, turn one's head.

784 MODESTY
See also 432 (underestimation); 780 (humility).

n. *modesty*, unpretentiousness, unassuming nature, unobtrusiveness, meekness, reserve, restraint; *shyness*, diffidence, timidity, bashfulness, reticence, reluctance; *prudishness*, demureness, coyness, inhibition; *chastity*, virtue; *mouse*, shrinking violet, doormat (*colloq.*).

adj. *modest*, unpretentious, unassuming, unobtrusive; *unassertive*, low-key, unimposing, unimpressive; *meek*, reserved, restrained, self-effacing; *shy*, diffident, timid, retiring, bashful, reticent, sheepish, reluctant, backward in coming forward (*colloq.*), wet (*colloq.*); *prudish*, blushing, demure, coy, inhibited; *chaste*, virtuous.

vb. *be modest*, efface oneself, hide one's light under a bushel, take a back seat, keep a low profile, keep in the background, play second fiddle, shun the limelight; *hang back*, hesitate, shrink, crawl into one's shell; *blush*, colour, flush, go red.

785 SHOWINESS
See also 464 (display); 769 (vulgarity).

n. *showiness*, ostentation, ostentatiousness, blatancy, flagrancy, exhibitionism, showmanship; *flashiness*, gaudiness, glitter, tinsel, garishness, flamboyance; *effect*, window-dressing, show; *splendour*, grandeur, magnificence, brilliance; *pomp*, majesty, pageantry, parade, spectacle; *pomposity*, extravagance, bombast, rhetoric; *dramatics*, histrionics, theatre, theatricality, sensationalism; *heroics*, bravado, stunt; *showman*, exhibitionist.

adj. *showy*, ostentatious, blatant, flagrant, shameless; *painted*, glorified, tarted up (*colloq.*); *flashy*, gaudy, glittering, garish, loud, flamboyant, lurid, conspicuous; *pompous*, extravagant, bombastic, pretentious; *splendid*, grandiose, magnificent, brilliant, splendiferous (*colloq.*); *sumptuous*, de luxe; *dramatic*, histrionic, spectacular, theatrical, stagy, for show, done for effect, cosmetic.

vb. *do for show/effect*, put on a show, flaunt, flourish, parade; *splurge*, make a splash, pull out all the stops; *play to the gallery*, show off, take the centre of the stage, upstage, grab the limelight, make an exhibition of oneself; *give oneself airs*, swank.

786 CELEBRATION

See also 746 (rejoicing).

n. *celebration*, festivity, festivities, festive occasion, fête, ceremony, function, occasion, party, beanfeast (*colloq.*), do (*colloq.*); *honouring*, keeping, commemoration, remembrance, observance, ceremonial, solemnization, performance, ritual; *coronation*, enthronement, installation, induction, inauguration; *anniversary*, jubilee, birthday, red-letter day, centenary; *salute*, drum roll, fanfare, fireworks; *cheering*, clapping, ovation, flag-waving, tribute, appreciation; *hero's welcome*, red carpet, reception committee, ticker-tape parade; *congratulation(s)*, felicitation(s), toast, compliments, many happy returns, best wishes.

adj. *celebratory*, festive, commemorative, ceremonial; *anniversary*, centennial; *congratulatory*, welcoming, complimentary.

vb. *celebrate*, honour, keep, commemorate, remember, observe, mark; *solemnize*, perform; *crown*, enthrone, install, induct, inaugurate; *come out*, pass out, graduate; *welcome*, salute, fête, chair, lionize, garland; *cheer*, clap; *praise*, pay tribute to, sing the praises of; *throw a party*, kill the fatted calf, roll out the red carpet, hang out the flags; *congratulate*, toast, felicitate, raise one's glass to, drink to the health of.

787 FORMALITY

See also 791 (courtesy); 881 (ritual).

n. *formality*, ceremoniousness, stiffness, dignity, solemnity, etiquette, correct behaviour, the thing to do, protocol, form,

ceremony; *ceremonial*, procedure, ritual, drill, practice, routine; *dress*, formal dress, black tie, regalia, formal attire, morning dress, evening dress, dinner jacket, lounge suit, long dress, one's best bib and tucker, Sunday best.

adj. *formal*, ceremonial, ceremonious, stiff, dignified, solemn, stately; *correct*, precise, punctilious, ritual, procedural.

vb. *observe the formalities*, stand on ceremony, do things by the book.

788 INFORMALITY

n. *informality*, lack of formality, lack of ceremony; *freedom*, licence, indulgence, toleration; *non-observance*, non-adherence, breach of etiquette, bad form, gaffe; *casual dress*, shirtsleeves, mufti, civvies, dress-down Friday.

adj. *informal*, unconstrained, relaxed, unstuffy, unceremonious, casual; *unconventional*, lax, loose, tolerant, easy, free and easy.

vb. *not insist*, waive the rules, relax, show no respect for.

789 SOCIABILITY

See also 85 (accompaniment); 793 (friendship).

n. *sociability*, sociableness, gregariousness, friendliness, affability, cordiality, conviviality, geniality, heartiness, bonhomie; *compatibility*, togetherness, companionship, comradeship; *party*, social gathering, get-together, meeting, social, soirée, at-home, reception, reunion, visit, date; *dinner party*, banquet, feast, bunfight, beano (*colloq.*), barbecue, picnic; *drinks party*, cocktail party, bottle party, wine-and-cheese party, coffee morning, tea party; *dance*, ball, disco, hop, knees-up (*colloq.*); *visitor*, caller, habitué, guest; *good companion*, good neighbour, good mixer, the life and soul of the party; *host*, hostess, master of ceremonies; *gate-crasher*, unwelcome guest, freeloader.

adj. *sociable*, social, gregarious, clubbable, friendly, pally (*colloq.*), affable; *cordial*, convivial, genial, smiling, welcoming; *hospitable*, neighbourly; *compatible*, companionable, comradely; *extrovert*, outgoing, hearty.

vb. *like company*, make friends easily, mix well, get along/on well with; *invite*, entertain, host, throw a party, keep open house; *visit*, call on, drop in on; *go out*, get together, party, go nightclubbing; *gate-crash*, arrive uninvited.

790 **UNSOCIABILITY**

See also 41 (separation); 52 (exclusion).

n. *unsociability*, standoffishness, aloofness, unapproachability; *unfriendliness*, coolness; *introversion*, shyness; *uncommunicativeness*, reticence, taciturnity; *distance*, withdrawal, isolation, separation, retreat; *loneliness*, solitude, seclusion, retirement; *confinement*, quarantine, purdah; *exile*, banishment, deportation, expulsion, excommunication; *apartheid*, segregation; *ghetto*, enclave, reserve, reservation, homeland, bantustan, concentration camp, prison; *cloister*, ivory tower, desert island, den; *hermit*, loner, isolationist, recluse, stay-at-home, monk; *leper*, pariah, outsider, untouchable; *castaway*, outcast, deportee, outlaw, displaced person, alien, refugee, evacuee, illegal immigrant, asylum-seeker.

adj. *unsociable*, standoffish, distant, aloof, unapproachable, antisocial; *unfriendly*, cool, unneighbourly, unwelcoming; *uncommunicative*, reticent, taciturn, unforthcoming; *introverted*, shy, withdrawn, retiring, stay-at-home; *lonely*, friendless, desolate, solitary, unpopular; *secluded*, off the beaten track, isolated, out of the way, remote, deserted, cloistered.

vb. *keep oneself to oneself*, shun company, stay at home, shut oneself up, retire, take the veil; *cut dead*, cold-shoulder, ignore, snub, rebuff; *confine*, isolate, imprison, quarantine, segregate; *exclude*, blackball, expel, exile, outlaw, excommunicate, ostracize, send to Coventry.

791 **COURTESY**

See also 787 (formality); 823 (respect).

n. *courtesy*, politeness, good manners, civility, graciousness; *thoughtfulness*, consideration, generosity, decency, tact, discretion; *friendliness*, kindness, kindliness, amiability; *respect*, deference, obeisance; *chivalry*, gallantry, courtliness; *etiquette*, protocol, custom, convention; *culture*, breeding, gentility, correctness, refinement, urbanity, diplomacy; *condescension*, sycophancy, flattery, ingratiation; *act of courtesy*, salutation, salute, greeting, handshake, kiss, air kiss, hug, embrace, smile, wave; *bow*, nod, curtsy; *presentation*, introduction, welcome, invitation, reception,

compliment, acknowledgement, toast; *favour*, good turn.

adj. *courteous*, polite, civil, gracious, good-mannered, well-behaved, on one's best behaviour; *thoughtful*, considerate, generous, decent, tactful, discreet; *friendly*, kind, kindly, obliging, amiable; *respectful*, deferential; *chivalrous*, gallant, courtly; *cultured*, cultivated, well-bred, genteel, correct, refined, urbane, diplomatic, gentlemanly, ladylike; *condescending*, sycophantic, flattering, ingratiating.

vb. *behave oneself/well/properly*, oblige, mind one's Ps and Qs, mind one's manners, not give offence; *salute*, greet, hail, raise one's hat, touch one's cap, present arms; *shake hands*, kiss, hug, embrace, smile, wave; *show respect*, bow, nod, curtsy, kiss hands; *present*, introduce, welcome, invite, receive, compliment, acknowledge, drink to, toast.

792 **DISCOURTESY**

See also 769 (vulgarity); 824 (disrespect).

n. *discourtesy*, impoliteness, bad manners, incivility; *rudeness*, disrespect, insolence, impudence, cheek; *act of discourtesy*, rebuff, insult, snub, abuse, rude word, rude gesture, flame (mail); *vulgarity*, boorishness, lack of refinement, ill breeding, coarseness; *rude person*, boor, lout, brute, yob (*colloq*.), yahoo; *unfriendliness*, brusqueness, unpleasantness, nastiness; *thoughtlessness*, lack of consideration, inattention; *misconduct*, bad behaviour.

adj. *discourteous*, impolite, bad-mannered, uncivil, unmannerly, ungracious; *rude*, disrespectful, insolent, impudent, saucy, cheeky, impertinent, obstreperous; *insulting*, abusive, offensive, crude; *vulgar*, coarse, boorish, unrefined, ill-bred, uncouth, uncultured, ungentlemanly; *brusque*, abrupt, gruff, curt, surly, churlish; *unfriendly*, unpleasant, nasty, unkind, disagreeable; *thoughtless*, tactless, inconsiderate, insensitive, cavalier, offhand.

vb. *be rude etc*, insult, abuse, affront, outrage; *curse*, swear, damn; *snub*, ignore, cut sb dead, look right through sb, give sb the cold shoulder; *interrupt*, shout down; *frown*, scowl, pout.

793 **FRIENDSHIP**

See also 789 (sociability); 795 (love).

n. *friendship*, amity, comradeship, fraternity, fellowship, solidarity; *companionship*, togetherness, camaraderie, compatibility, intimacy, familiarity, male bonding; *friendliness*, amicability, good terms, sociability, neighbourliness; *kindness*, hospitality, warmth, cordiality, sympathy, understanding; *act of friendship*, handshake, embrace, hug, kiss; *friend*, acquaintance, companion, comrade, crony, pal, mate, chum, buddy, girlfriend, boyfriend, best friend, bosom pal, intimate, confidant/-e, classmate, roommate, playmate.

adj. *friendly*, amicable, sociable, affectionate, warm-hearted, well-meaning, kind, benevolent; *neighbourly*, brotherly, sisterly, fraternal; *intimate*, familiar, inseparable, close, pally (*colloq.*), matey (*colloq.*), up close and personal (*colloq.*); *loyal*, faithful, staunch, trustworthy, true, devoted; *cordial*, congenial, hearty.

vb. *befriend*, make friends with, strike up an acquaintance, get to know; *be friendly*, keep company with, be in with (*colloq.*), go around with, be inseparable, be as thick as thieves; *court*, date, take out, go out with, see, make advances, woo; *be hospitable*, entertain, welcome, greet, embrace, introduce, present.

794 ENMITY
See also 796 (hate).

n. *enmity*, hostility, aggression, antagonism; *antipathy*, dislike, hatred, animosity; *ill feeling*, ill will, acrimony, bitterness, rancour, dissension; *alienation*, estrangement, separation, incompatibility; *hostile act*, conflict, hostilities, state of war, vendetta, feud, hate mail, poison-pen letter, flame (mail), hate crime; *enemy*, foe, traitor, antagonist, opponent, adversary, public enemy, arch enemy, aggressor, invader.

adj. *inimical*, hostile, antagonistic, aggressive; *unfriendly*, aloof, cool, chilly, cold, ill-disposed; *estranged*, irreconcilable, alienated, incompatible; *opposed*, at daggers drawn, at loggerheads, on bad terms; *rancorous*, bitter, acrimonious, grudging, resentful; *disloyal*, unfaithful, traitorous.

vb. *be hostile*, have one's hackles up, snap, snarl, growl; *oppose*, be opposed to, conflict, differ, be at odds with, clash, collide, be incompatible, be worlds apart; *antagonize*, provoke, estrange, alienate, make enemies; *fight*, battle, feud, oppress, persecute, hound.

795 LOVE
See also 757 (liking); 800 (endearment).

n. *love*, affection, fondness, attachment, devotion, true love, Cupid; *adoration*, worship, admiration, fascination; *passion*, lust, desire, Eros, amorousness, rapture, ecstasy; *infatuation*, crush (*colloq.*), first love, calf love, puppy love, love's young dream; *Platonic love*, friendship, fellow feeling, sympathy; *predilection*, preference, fancy; *sentiment*, emotion, feeling; *romance*, love affair, relationship, amour, liaison, intrigue, flirtation; *lovableness*, charm, endearment, appeal, attractiveness, sex-appeal, coquetry; *love-making*, courtship, proposal, suit, gallantry; *lover*, flirt, philanderer, paramour, mistress, suitor, beau, escort; *boyfriend*, girlfriend, fiancé, fiancée, date, blind date, steady (*colloq.*), fella (*colloq.*), bird (*colloq.*); *admirer*, fan, aficionado, idol, hero, flame, heart-throb; *loved one*, soul mate, darling, intimate, sweetheart, valentine.

adj. *loving*, fond, affectionate, tender; loved up (*colloq.*); *romantic*, sentimental, emotional; *devoted*, adoring, admiring; *passionate*, lustful, amorous, ardent; *infatuated*, besotted, crazy about, lovesick; *enamoured*, attracted, keen on, in love; *lovable*, endearing, adorable, lovely, appealing, attractive, seductive, desirable, captivating, enchanting, to die for; *beloved*, loved, cherished, adored, darling, pet; *erotic*, sexy, erogenous, amatory.

vb. *love*, like, be fond of, fancy, care for, be partial to, delight in; *cherish*, hold dear, treasure, prize, value, esteem; *adore*, worship, admire, revere; *be in love*, dote on, be crazy about, lose one's heart, be swept off one's feet, be infatuated, have a crush on; *desire*, long, yearn; *make love*, have intercourse, have sex, have it off (*colloq.*), sleep with, sleep together; *attract*, appeal, allure, bewitch, charm, enchant, captivate, fascinate, enrapture; *seduce*, woo, set one's cap at, flirt, philander; *rouse*, stir, excite, turn on (*colloq.*).

796 HATE
See also 758 (dislike); 794 (enmity).

n. *hate*, hatred, loathing, detestation, abhorrence; *repugnance*, revulsion, repulsion, disgust; *aversion*, antipathy, dislike, disfavour, odium; *animosity*, antagonism, hostility, ill feeling; *malevolence*, malice, spite, scorn, grudge; *phobia*, prejudice, bête noire, pet hate; *anathema*, abomination, menace, pest, bugbear.

adj. *hateful*, odious, detestable, obnoxious, loathsome, abhorrent, execrable, accursed, abominable; *repugnant*, revolting, repellent, disgusting, vile, nasty, horrid, beastly; *hostile*, antagonistic, averse, set against; *malicious*, malignant, malevolent, spiteful, vicious, vindictive, rancorous.

vb. *hate*, loathe, detest, abhor, abominate, recoil at; *reject*, spurn, refuse, object to, spit upon; *condemn*, denounce, execrate; *resent*, dislike, bear a grudge, have a down on, have it in for (*colloq.*); *antagonize*, alienate, estrange, set by the ears; *embitter*, poison, exacerbate, sour.

797 **MARRIAGE**

n. *marriage*, matrimony, conjugality, wedlock, union, alliance, match; *monogamy*, bigamy, polygamy, second marriage, open marriage, marriage of convenience, shotgun wedding, arranged marriage, pre-nuptial agreement; same-sex marriage, civil partnership; *wedding*, nuptials, marriage ceremony, wedding service, civil marriage, church wedding, elopement; *reception*, wedding breakfast, marriage feast, honeymoon, anniversary; *bridal party*, best man, bridesmaid, matron of honour, page, attendant, usher; *married couple*, the happy couple, newlyweds, honeymooners, bridegroom, bride; *spouse*, partner, mate, husband, wife, trophy wife, better half (*colloq.*), trouble and strife (*colloq.*), her indoors (*colloq.*), she who must be obeyed (*colloq.*), old man, old lady, old dutch, common-law husband/wife; *matchmaker*, marriage bureau, lonely hearts column, computer dating.

adj. *matrimonial*, marital, conjugal, nuptial, connubial, premarital; *married*, wed, united, newlywed, engaged; *marriageable*, nubile, eligible, suitable.

vb. *marry*, wed, espouse, remarry, intermarry; *get married*, get spliced (*colloq.*), get hitched (*colloq.*), make an honest woman of (*colloq.*), become one, plight one's troth, say 'I do'; *join*, unite, pronounce man and wife; *give in marriage*, give away, marry off, matchmake; *honeymoon*, go away, elope, consummate; *marry well*, find a good match, marry into.

798 **DIVORCE; WIDOWHOOD**

n. *divorce*, annulment, dissolution of marriage, decree nisi, decree absolute, breakdown of marriage, broken marriage; *separation*, living apart, desertion; *divorce court*, maintenance, alimony, divorcee, co-respondent, single parent, broken home;

widowhood, widow, widower, survivor, relict, dowager, war widow, grass widow, golf widow.

adj. *divorced*, separated, on the rocks, living apart, widowed.

vb. *divorce*, get divorced, separate, split up; *leave*, walk out on, desert.

799 **CELIBACY**

n. *celibacy*, single state, bachelorhood, spinsterhood; *virginity*, maidenhood, chastity, purity; *celibate*, virgin, single person, bachelor, confirmed bachelor, not the marrying kind, misogynist, spinster, bachelor girl, old maid, maiden aunt; *monk*, nun, hermit, solitary.

adj. *celibate*, single, bachelor, unmarried, unwed, independent, free, unattached, eligible; *virginal*, chaste, pure, monastic, unconsummated.

vb. *be unmarried*, live alone, be on the shelf, take holy orders.

800 **ENDEARMENT**

See also 795 (love).

n. *endearment*, affection, fondness, attachment, love; *loving words*, blandishments, sweet nothings, flattery, compliments; *embrace*, hug, kiss, air kiss, cuddle, stroke, caress, fondling, petting, necking (*colloq.*); *courtship*, suit, lovemaking, wooing, courting, dating; *flirtation*, familiarity, pass, advances, proposition; *love-letter*, valentine, proposal, offer of marriage, engagement; *darling*, dear, love, sweetheart, beloved, dearest, angel, pet, poppet, honey (*colloq.*), precious, treasure, jewel, duck (*colloq.*), chicken (*colloq.*), lamb (*colloq.*); *favourite*, teacher's pet, blue-eyed boy, apple of one's eye.

adj. *affectionate*, loving, sentimental, soppy (*colloq.*), lovey-dovey (*colloq.*), up close and personal (*colloq.*).

vb. *cherish*, be fond of, love, coddle, cosset, pamper, pet, mother, spoil, spoonfeed, kill with kindness; *court*, woo, go out with, date, go steady, get off with (*colloq.*), pursue, chase, make overtures; *make advances*, make passes, get fresh (*colloq.*), flirt, chat up (*colloq.*), come on to (*colloq.*), ogle, make eyes, leer, proposition; *hug*, embrace, cuddle, clasp, snuggle, nuzzle, kiss, neck (*colloq.*), snog (*colloq.*), smooch (*colloq.*); *stroke*, fondle, caress, pet; *trifle*, dally, toy, play fast and loose, philander; *propose*, pop the question (*colloq.*), get engaged.

801 **CURSE**

See also 806 (malevolence).

n. *curse*, malediction, evil eye, spell; *execration*, vilification, abuse, calumny, threat, vituperation, denunciation; *profanity*, oath, obscenity, swearword, four-letter word, expletive, imprecation, invective, bad language, billingsgate; *scurrility*, vulgarity, blasphemy, sacrilege, profanation.

adj. *maledictory*, vituperative, abusive; *scurrilous*, foul-mouthed, ribald, blue, indecent, obscene, vulgar, profane, blasphemous, sacrilegious; *cursed*, accursed, damned, execrable.

vb. *curse*, damn, condemn, wish ill, confound; *execrate*, fulminate, thunder against, inveigh against; *denounce*, abuse, call names, defame, vilify, vituperate, revile; *swear*, cuss, damn, blast, eff and blind (*colloq.*), swear like a trooper, blaspheme.

802 **RESENTMENT; ANGER**

n. *resentment*, bitterness, acrimony, rancour, spleen, gall; *displeasure*, ill humour, grudge, bone to pick, malice, animosity; *offence*, umbrage, hurt, indignity, wrong, injustice, insult, affront; *anger*, rage, road/air/desk/shop rage, fury, passion, wrath, ire, (the) red mist, vexation, indignation, exasperation, annoyance, irritation, aggravation; *tantrum*, temper, tizzy (*colloq.*), paddy (*colloq.*), outburst, huff; *quarrel*, argument, tiff, fight; *frown*, scowl, glare, black look, snarl, growl.

adj. *resentful*, bitter, embittered, rancorous, acrimonious, smarting, hurt, sore; *grudging*, jealous, envious; *angry*, cross, irate, indignant, livid, furious, enraged, incensed, fuming, hopping mad (*colloq.*), beside oneself, up in arms; *irritated*, annoyed, peeved, vexed, exasperated, aggravated, infuriated; *riled*, worked up, het up (*colloq.*), shirty (*colloq.*), ratty, hot under the collar (*colloq.*), impatient.

vb. *resent*, bear malice, bear a grudge, have a bone to pick; *take umbrage*, take offence, be insulted, take exception, take amiss; *get angry*, get cross, lose one's temper, lose one's rag (*colloq.*), go mad (*colloq.*), go spare (*colloq.*), see red, see (the) red mist, throw a tantrum, blow one's top (*colloq.*), hit the roof (*colloq.*), fly off the handle (*colloq.*), explode, go up the wall (*colloq.*), go off the deep end (*colloq.*), get one's knickers in a twist (*colloq.*); *be angry*, rage, fume, rant, roar, thunder, fulminate, seethe, boil, make a scene; *frown*, scowl, glare, glower, growl, snarl, snap, bite

sb's head off (*colloq.*); *anger*, enrage, exasperate, madden, incense, infuriate, drive mad, make one's blood boil; *annoy*, irritate, upset, aggravate, needle, nettle, goad, rankle, rile, get on one's nerves, get one's dander up (*colloq.*), rub up the wrong way (*colloq.*); *vex*, bother, harass, pester, provoke, stir, ruffle; *antagonize*, offend, affront, insult.

803 **IRASCIBILITY**

n. *irascibility*, irritability, short temper, limited patience, temperament, sensitivity, touchiness; *shrew*, scold, virago, termagant, battleaxe, dragon, harridan, Tartar.

adj. *irascible*, choleric, querulous, irritable, prickly, touchy, edgy, short-tempered, tetchy, ratty (*colloq.*), shirty (*colloq.*); *peevish*, crotchety, testy, crusty, bilious, dyspeptic, cantankerous, gruff, grumpy; *sensitive*, thin-skinned, nervous, jumpy, uptight (*colloq.*); *temperamental*, moody, changeable, fractious, fretful; *snappy*, sharp, waspish, tart; *irritated*, annoyed, riled, nettled.

vb. *be irascible*, be short-tempered, be on a short fuse, snap, bark, fly at, turn on, jump down sb's throat (*colloq.*).

804 **SULLENNESS**

n. *sullenness*, ill humour, spleen, sourness, gruffness, sulkiness; *glumness*, discontent, melancholy, moroseness; *moodiness*, temperament, unsociability; *grimace*, pout, scowl, frown, glare, black look; *growl*, snarl, snap, snort.

adj. *sullen*, sulky, surly, churlish, curmudgeonly, cantankerous, unsociable; *disagreeable*, ill-humoured, sour, jaundiced, cross, crusty, crabby, grouchy, grumpy, stroppy (*colloq.*); *glum*, morose, mournful, melancholy, lugubrious, hangdog; *gloomy*, dismal, dark, sombre, cheerless; *moody*, temperamental, saturnine, dour; *gruff*, brusque, abrupt, irascible.

vb. *scowl*, glower, glare, lour, frown, grimace, pout, sulk; *snap*, snarl, growl, grunt; *grumble*, mutter, grouch, grouse, carp, complain; *mope*, be dejected, be unsociable.

adv. *sullenly*, with bad grace.

805 **BENEVOLENCE**

See also 807 (philanthropy); 809 (pity).

n. *benevolence*, kindness, kindheartedness, good will, benignity; *charity*, humanity, fellow feeling, philanthropy; *generosity*, magnanimity, altruism, selflessness; *consideration*, thoughtfulness; *pity*, sympathy, understanding, mercy, forgiveness; *good deed*, good turn, good works, service, favour, benefit; *kind person*, good Samaritan, Christian, good neighbour, philanthropist, altruist, humanitarian, reformer, well-wisher, do-gooder.

adj. *benevolent*, kind, charitable, beneficent, good, kindly, benign; *thoughtful*, considerate, well-meant, well-meaning, well-intentioned; *kindhearted*, warm-hearted, compassionate, sympathetic; *helpful*, obliging, accommodating, neighbourly; *generous*, altruistic, unselfish, philanthropic, humanitarian; *loving*, tender, affectionate, motherly, fatherly; *merciful*, tolerant, forgiving; *gallant*, chivalrous, gracious, courteous.

vb. *be kind*, have a heart of gold, be kindness itself, mean well; *do good*, philanthropize, reform; *help*, oblige, do sb a good turn, do sb a favour, render sb a service; *give one's blessing*, wish well, support, encourage; *comfort*, show concern, relieve, mother, nurse.

806 **MALEVOLENCE**

See also 808 (misanthropy); 810 (pitilessness); 836 (evil); 838 (wickedness).

n. *malevolence*, ill will, wickedness, unkindness, malignity; *malice*, spite, gall, bitterness, acrimony, rancour; *hate*, animosity, enmity, bad blood; *inhumanity*, callousness, cruelty, barbarity, ferocity, sadism, brutality, savagery, monstrousness; *severity*, harshness, ruthlessness, relentlessness, hard heartedness; *harm*, misfortune, mischief, ill turn, catastrophe, disaster; *atrocity*, foul play, outrage, act of inhumanity, violence, torture, murder; *threat*, menace, intimidation, blackmail.

adj. *malevolent*, ill-natured, wicked, bad, evil, malign, malignant, baleful, hostile; *malicious*, spiteful, catty, caustic, bitter, acrimonious, vindictive; *unkind*, nasty, mean, beastly, ungracious, unfriendly, uncharitable; *cruel*, inhuman, merciless, savage, brutal, barbarous, truculent, fierce; *harsh*, severe, ruthless, cold, callous, hard-hearted, cold-blooded, tough, intolerant; *maleficent*, venomous, treacherous; *fiendish*, devilish, diabolical, satanic, hellish, infernal; *threatening*, menacing, ominous, foreboding, impending, imminent.

vb. *be malevolent*, harm, abuse, maltreat, ill-treat, molest; *hurt*, injure, torture, torment; *victimize*, persecute, have it in for

(colloq.), hound, harry, bully, oppress, tyrannize; *bear malice*, bear a grudge, spite; *rankle*, fester, poison; *threaten*, menace, intimidate, blackmail, hold to ransom, frighten, scare; *bode ill*, spell danger.

adv. *malevolently*, with evil intent; *spitefully*, out of spite; *threateningly*, on pain of death.

807 **PHILANTHROPY**

See also 805 (benevolence).

n. *philanthropy*, humanitarianism, utilitarianism; *benevolence*, humanity, altruism, dedication; public-spiritedness, social conscience; *welfare state*, social work, social services, community service, voluntary work, charity, aid, benefit; *campaign*, crusade, worthy cause, good works; *philanthropist*, benefactor, humanitarian, do-gooder, missionary, voluntary worker; *altruist*, idealist, visionary, utopian; *patron*, founder, protector, guardian angel, supporter, fairy godmother, champion, backer; *kind person*, good neighbour, helper, good Samaritan, saint, angel.

adj. *philanthropic*, humanitarian, humane, altruistic, charitable; *enlightened*, liberal, reforming, public-spirited.

vb. *be charitable*, be public-spirited, do good, have a social conscience.

808 **MISANTHROPY**

n. *misanthropy*, hatred of mankind, misogyny, unsociability, cynicism; *selfishness*, egotism; *misanthrope*, misogynist, man-hater, woman-hater; *loner*, solitary, cynic, egotist.

adj. *misanthropic*, antisocial, unsociable, cynical.

vb. *misanthropize*, lose faith in human nature.

809 **PITY**

See also 805 (benevolence).

n. *pity*, compassion, charity, humanity, benevolence, soft-heartedness, warm-heartedness, understanding, tenderness; *sympathy*, empathy, condolence, fellow feeling, commiseration, comfort, solace, consolation, relief; *mercy*, forbearance, forgiveness, clemency, grace, favour, quarter, second chance; *remorse*, compunction, regret.

adj. *pitying*, sympathetic, comforting, sorry, consoling; *compassionate*, kind, charitable, tender, understanding, soft-hearted; *merciful*, forbearing, forgiving, lenient, clement, gracious, generous, lax; *pitiful*, piteous, pitiable, pathetic, heart-rending.

vb. *pity*, sympathize, feel for, commiserate, grieve with, weep for, console, comfort, support; *show mercy*, pardon, forgive, spare, reprieve, give a second chance, take pity on, relent, unbend, relax; *ask for mercy*, plead with, move to pity, disarm, melt, thaw.

810 **PITILESSNESS**

See also 806 (malevolence).

n. *pitilessness*, hardness of heart, callousness, mercilessness, pound of flesh, heartlessness, inhumanity, cruelty, ruthlessness, implacability, relentlessness, remorselessness.

adj. *pitiless*, unfeeling, heartless, impassive, unmoved, cold, unsympathetic, cold-blooded; *relentless*, unrelenting, unbending, inflexible, inexorable, remorseless; *severe*, harsh, hard-hearted, stony-hearted, callous, brutal; *merciless*, unforgiving, unmerciful, barbarous, vindictive, vengeful, ruthless, implacable.

vb. *be pitiless*, harden one's heart, give no quarter, turn a deaf ear to, stop at nothing, persecute, avenge.

811 **GRATITUDE**

n. *gratitude*, gratefulness, thankfulness, appreciation, indebtedness, sense of obligation; *thanks*, thank-you, thank-you letter, leaving present, reward, tip; *acknowledgement*, tribute, credit, recognition, praise, vote of thanks; *thanksgiving*, blessing, benediction, grace, prayer.

adj. *grateful*, thankful, appreciative; *indebted*, obliged, beholden; *gratified*, pleased.

vb. *be grateful*, be in sb's debt, appreciate, receive with open arms, never forget; *thank*, say thank-you, reward, tip; *requite*, repay, return a favour; *acknowledge*, pay tribute, recognize, praise, applaud; *give thanks*, say grace.

adv. *gratefully*, with thanks.

812 **INGRATITUDE**

n. *ingratitude*, ungratefulness, lack of appreciation, thanklessness; *thoughtlessness*, selfishness, rudeness, grudging thanks, thankless task, ungrateful wretch.

adj. *ungrateful*, begrudging, unappreciative; *unmindful*, forgetful, selfish, rude, discourteous; *thankless*, unrewarding, unprofitable; *unthanked*, unrewarded,

unacknowledged, without credit, unrequited.

vb. *be ungrateful*, show ingratitude, not thank, take for granted, presume upon.

813 **FORGIVENESS**

See also 660 (leniency); 809 (pity).

n. *forgiveness*, pardon, reprieve, amnesty, indemnity; *mercy*, grace, indulgence, forbearance, patience; *absolution*, remission, acquittal, release, discharge; *exoneration*, exculpation; *reconciliation*, redemption, rehabilitation, atonement.

adj. *forgiving*, merciful, lenient, forbearing, long-suffering, patient; *forgiven*, pardoned, absolved, acquitted, released, excused, let off; *reconciled*, restored, taken back, redeemed, rehabilitated, reinstated; *pardonable*, forgivable, excusable, venial.

vb. *forgive*, pardon, reprieve, grant amnesty to; *show mercy*, forbear, tolerate, bear with, relent, unbend, soften; *absolve*, remit, acquit, clear, discharge, excuse, justify; *exonerate*, exculpate; *ignore*, disregard, shut one's eyes to, wink at, overlook, condone, let pass; *be reconciled*, make it up, forgive and forget, bury the hatchet, let bygones be bygones, redeem; *ask forgiveness*, beg pardon, atone.

814 **ATONEMENT**

See also 641 (retaliation); 841 (penitence).

n. *atonement*, amends, reparation, indemnity, compensation, redress, satisfaction, repayment, restitution, requital, retribution; *propitiation*, reconciliation, appeasement, redemption, offering, sacrifice, scapegoat, substitute, representative; *expiation*, purgatory, penance, confession, shrift; *repentance*, apology, penitence.

adj. *atoning*, indemnificatory, compensatory, making amends; *propitiatory*, reconciliatory, appeasing, sacrificial, redemptive, representative, vicarious; *penitential*, penitentiary; *apologetic*, sorry, penitent, repentant.

vb. *atone*, make amends, make reparation, indemnify, compensate, redress, repay, requite, give satisfaction; *propitiate*, conciliate, reconcile, appease, apologize, beg pardon, satisfy, offer sacrifice; *expiate*, redeem, do penance, suffer purgatory.

815 **JEALOUSY**

n. *jealousy*, distrust, mistrust, suspicion, doubt, watchfulness, possessiveness; *envy*, resentment, hostility, unfaithfulness; *rivalry*, competition, competitiveness; *rival*, competitor, the eternal triangle.

adj. *jealous*, suspicious, distrustful, possessive, watchful; *envious*, resentful, jaundiced, sour.

vb. *be jealous*, mistrust, distrust, suspect, doubt; *envy*, resent.

816 **ENVY**

n. *envy*, covetousness, desire, resentment, ill-will, spite.

adj. *envious*, covetous, jealous, green with envy, grudging.

vb. *envy*, covet, desire, crave, lust after, hanker, grudge, begrudge.

817 **RIGHT**

n. *right*, rightfulness, what is right, obligation, duty; *lawfulness*, legality, legitimacy; *justice*, fairness, equity, impartiality, fair play, square deal, equality, level playing-field; *reward*, redress, retribution, just deserts, nemesis, poetic justice; *suitability*, fitness, propriety, etiquette, conformity; *morality*, virtue, decency, rectitude, integrity, probity.

adj. *right*, correct, accurate, precise, true, valid; *appropriate*, suitable, fitting, fit, apt, proper; *lawful*, legitimate, legal, rightful; *just*, fair, equitable, objective, unprejudiced, impartial, unbiased, disinterested, dispassionate, neutral, detached; *honest*, upright, straight, righteous, unimpeachable, straightforward, fair-minded, decent, sporting; *justifiable*, excusable, forgivable.

vb. *be just*, be fair, play the game, do the right thing, see fair play; *be in the right*, have grounds for, have cause to; *put right*, rectify, redress, remedy, mend, reform.

adv. *right*, rightly, equally, fairly, without distinction, without fear or favour.

818 **WRONG**

n. *wrong*, wrongness, wrongfulness, irregularity; *injustice*, inequity, unfairness; *partiality*, partisanship, prejudice, discrimination, bias, favouritism, preferential treatment, nepotism, old school tie; *grievance*, injury, mischief, foul play, raw deal; *disgrace*, shame, dishonour, slur, -gate; *sin*, vice, crime, misdeed, offence, trespass.

adj. *wrong*, wrongful, unreasonable, abnormal, irregular; *unfair*, unjust, inequitable, unsportsmanlike, not cricket (*colloq.*), below the belt; *partial*, partisan, biased, prejudiced, uneven, unbalanced,

weighted, one-sided; *incorrect*, inaccurate, erroneous, imprecise, at fault; *injurious*, harmful; *unsuitable*, inappropriate, improper, unseemly; *illegal*, illegitimate, illicit, unlawful, criminal; *wicked*, sinful, bad, vicious, immoral; *unforgivable*, unjustifiable, inexcusable, reprehensible.

vb. *wrong*, harm, hurt, injure, maltreat; *err*, be in the wrong, be at fault; *do wrong*, break the law, transgress, infringe, trespass, cheat, not play fair, hit below the belt; *discriminate*, favour, show partiality, lean towards.

819 **ENTITLEMENT**

See also 715 (debt).

n. *entitlement*, dueness, due, right, privilege, prerogative; *merits*, deserts, just deserts, comeuppance, punishment, reward, compensation; *payment*, dues, fees, levy, contribution; *duty*, obligation, responsibility, corporate social responsibility; *legal right*, claim, title, birthright, human rights; *bond*, security, title deed, patent, copyright; *warrant*, licence, charter, permit; *heir*, beneficiary, plaintiff.

adj. *entitled*, warranted, just, rightful, legitimate, lawful, legal, inviolable, inalienable; *due*, owing, payable, chargeable, unpaid, unsettled, in arrears, outstanding; *deserving*, worthy, meritorious, needy; *deserved*, merited, well-deserved; *fit*, fitting, right, proper, as it should be.

vb. *be entitled*, warrant, expect, have the right to; *claim*, lay claim to, insist on one's rights, exercise one's prerogative; *justify*, vindicate, exonerate, substantiate; *merit*, be worthy, deserve, earn, have it coming to one (*colloq.*), serve one right; *be due*, fall due, mature; *honour*, pay, discharge, meet an obligation; *assign*, attribute, give every man his due, acknowledge, credit, hand it to; *allot*, apportion, prescribe.

adv. *duly*, by right, by law.

820 **LACK OF ENTITLEMENT**

See also 272 (overstepping); 575 (excess).

n. *lack of entitlement*, absence of right, presumption, assumption, arrogation, violation; *undueness*, unfittingness, gratuitousness; *disentitlement*, dispossession, forfeiture, disqualification, disestablishment; *usurper*, pretender, impostor, squatter.

adj. *unentitled*, unqualified, unauthorized, presumptuous, without rights; *undue*, unwarranted, uncalled for, unnecessary, gratuitous; *immoderate*, excessive; *undeserved*, unmerited, unjust, unfair; *undeserving*, unworthy; *improper*, unseemly, inappropriate; *spurious*, false, would-be, fictitious, bogus; *invalid*, forfeit, illicit, illegal, illegitimate.

vb. *not be entitled to*, have no right to, presume, arrogate, overstep the mark, take liberties, go too far; *usurp*, violate, trespass, encroach, infringe; *disentitle*, disqualify, invalidate, disfranchise, disestablish, expropriate, dispossess, depose.

821 **DUTY**
See also 683 (promise).

n. *duty*, obligation, responsibility, corporate social responsibility, onus, liability, burden; *commitment*, pledge, promise, contract, engagement, debt, bond, tie, call of duty; *conscience*, sense of duty, moral obligation, moral imperative; *loyalty*, faithfulness, fealty, allegiance; *discharge of duty*, performance, acquittal, observance; *task*, commission, office, charge, station, profession; *precept*, code of duty, morality, ethics.

adj. *liable*, responsible, accountable, answerable, subject to; *obliged*, duty-bound, under obligation; *obligatory*, incumbent, mandatory, compulsory, binding, inescapable, unconditional, categorical; *dutiful*, conscientious, obedient, compliant, submissive, tractable; *ethical*, moral, honourable, decent.

vb. *be the duty of*, fall to, rest with, devolve on, be responsible for, should, ought, had better, behove; *commit oneself*, pledge oneself, engage, take/shoulder/accept responsibility for, take ownership of; *do one's duty*, discharge, fulfil, perform, acquit oneself, honour, pay; *oblige*, bind, saddle with, put under an obligation; *impose a duty*, require, detail, order, call upon, enjoin, look to, expect.

822 **EXEMPTION**
See also 605 (escape); 857 (acquittal).

n. *exemption*, immunity, non-liability, impunity; *exception*, privilege, special treatment; *freedom*, release, liberation, dispensation, absolution, acquittal, pardon; *permission*, leave, liberty, licence, charter, franchise.

adj. *exempt*, non-liable, immune, not subject to, free, -free; clear; *privileged*, unaccountable, unaffected, independent;

unrestricted, unbound, unrestrained, uncontrolled.

vb. *exempt*, free, clear, set apart, exclude; *excuse*, exonerate, exculpate, acquit, let off; *absolve*, pardon, forgive; *release*, lift restrictions, grant impunity, liberate; *be exempt*, get off scot-free, get away with it, get away with murder (*colloq.*); *shrug off*, shift the blame, pass the buck (*colloq.*), wash one's hands of.

823 **RESPECT**
See also 774 (repute); 791 (courtesy).

n. *respect*, regard, esteem, consideration, honour, high opinion, appreciation, favour; *repute*, high standing, authority; *admiration*, worship, veneration, adoration, hero-worship, awe; *praise*, reverence, homage, deference, humility, devotion; *respects*, regards, greeting, salutation, salute; *bow*, curtsy, red carpet, guard of honour.

adj. *respectful*, courteous, polite, ceremonious; *admiring*, awestruck; *reverential*, deferential, standing, kneeling, prostrate; *humble*, submissive, obsequious, servile; *respected*, well thought of, highly regarded, reputable, valued, appreciated, esteemed, venerable, time-honoured; *important*, impressive, imposing, authoritative.

vb. *respect*, think well of, regard highly, have a high opinion of, hold dear, value, appreciate, honour; *admire*, think the world of, take off one's hat to (*colloq.*), revere, look up to, hero-worship, put on a pedestal, pay homage, defer to; *praise*, extol, exalt, pay tribute, lionize; *pay one's respects*, greet, welcome, salute, drink to, toast; *show respect*, bow, curtsy, kneel, scrape, grovel, kowtow, be humble, submit; *command respect*, impress, impose, awe, overawe, overwhelm, humble.

824 **DISRESPECT**
See also 773 (derision); 781 (insolence); 792 (discourtesy).

n. *disrespect*, irreverence, discourtesy, impoliteness; *dishonour*, disrepute; *contempt*, scorn, disdain, disparagement, low opinion, low esteem, disapprobation; *insult*, affront, slight, sneer, snub, rebuff, indignity, humiliation, degradation; *ridicule*, mockery, derision, taunt, jeer, hiss, catcall, boo.

adj. *disrespectful*, irreverent, discourteous, impolite, rude; *neglectful*, negligent; *dishonourable*, humiliating, degrading; *contemptible*, disreputable, despicable, worthless, shameful, base; *contemptuous*, scornful, supercilious, haughty, disdainful; *insulting*, offensive, pejorative, slighting, cutting; *impertinent*, cheeky, saucy, insolent, insubordinate; *offhand*, airy, breezy, cavalier.

vb. *have no respect for*, hold in contempt, have no time for; *underrate*, underestimate; *scorn*, despise, look down on, disdain, look down one's nose at (*colloq.*), disparage, denigrate, belittle; *taunt*, mock, scoff, deride, jeer at, sneer at, laugh at, ridicule; *insult*, offend, affront, slight, snub, rebuff, humiliate; *dishonour*, disgrace, put to shame; *show disrespect*, lack courtesy, jostle, tread on sb's toes, brush aside, ride roughshod over; *desecrate*, profane, cheapen, lower, degrade.

825 **APPROVAL**

See also 738 (satisfaction).

n. *approval*, approbation, satisfaction; *recognition*, acknowledgement, appreciation, gratitude; *permission*, agreement, sanction, acceptance, adoption, blessing, consent, assent, seal of approval, imprimateur; *admiration*, esteem, credit, prestige, honour, favour; *commendation*, compliment, bouquet, citation, favourable review, accolade, tribute; *praise*, adulation, eulogy, panegyric; *applause*, ovation, clapping, curtain call, encore, three cheers, acclaim; *supporter*, advocate, patron, admirer, fan.

adj. *approving*, satisfied, content, appreciative; *complimentary*, commendatory, laudatory, fulsome; *approved*, favourable, satisfactory; *commendable*, praiseworthy, laudable, meritorious, estimable, creditable, admirable, unimpeachable; *approvable*, permissible, admissible, acceptable; *popular*, well thought of, in demand.

vb. *approve*, recognize, acknowledge, favour; *agree*, allow, permit, sanction, adopt; *accept*, pass, rubber-stamp, tick, endorse; *commend*, compliment, admire, take off one's hat to (*colloq.*), pay tribute, sing the praises of, speak well of, rave about, exalt, extol, boost, puff; *overrate*, exaggerate, overestimate, inflate; *applaud*, clap, cheer, stamp, whistle, hail, acclaim, welcome, drink to; *advocate*, recommend, support, back, champion; *win praise*, gain credit, find favour, meet with approval, pass muster.

826 **DISAPPROVAL**

See also 739 (dissatisfaction).

n. *disapproval*, disapprobation, non-acceptance, rejection, refusal; *dissatisfaction*, discontent, displeasure, disfavour; *disagreement*, objection, opposition, contradiction; *criticism*, hostility, fault-finding, blame culture, complaint, censure, critical review, attack, diatribe; *reprimand*, reproach, blame, rebuke, reproof, black mark, brickbat, rocket, admonition, telling-off, home truths, lecture, talking to, roasting (*colloq.*); *look of disapproval*, frown, glare, scowl, raised eyebrows, black look, old-fashioned look; *protest*, outcry, clamour, hiss, boo, catcall, raspberry; *taunt*, sneer, irony, sarcasm, dig; *blacklist*, boycott, bar, ban; *opponent*, critic, knocker (*colloq.*), anti.

adj. *disapproving*, hostile, critical, hypercritical, censorious; *reproving*, reproachful, stern, fault-finding, captious; *disparaging*, uncomplimentary, defamatory, deprecatory, unfavourable, opposed, against; *shocked*, not amused; *caustic*, trenchant, mordant, biting, venomous; *disapproved*, disreputable, insufficient, found wanting, not good enough; *reprehensible*, blameworthy, culpable, objectionable.

vb. *disapprove*, reject, not accept, object to, protest, demur; *disagree*, frown on, oppose, not hold with, take a dim view of; *regret*, deplore, lament; *disparage*, belittle, run down, denigrate, depreciate; *criticize*, complain, carp, find fault, pick holes, not think much of, censure, knock (*colloq.*), slam (*colloq.*), condemn, damn with faint praise; *reprove*, rebuke, reprimand, reprehend, upbraid, scold, chide, tell off, tick off, lecture, dress down (*colloq.*), tear sb off a strip (*colloq.*), haul sb over the coals (*colloq.*), carpet (*colloq.*), give sb a piece of one's mind; *punish*, castigate, chastise, rap sb over the knuckles; *reproach*, blame, incriminate, impeach; *boo*, hiss, whistle, heckle, lynch; *blacklist*, boycott, ban, bar; *be open to criticism*, get a bad name, get a bad press, incur blame, have a rough ride.

adv. *disapprovingly*, under protest, against one's better judgement.

827 **FLATTERY**

See also 782 (servility).

n. flattery, compliment, adulation, blandishments, blarney, soft soap (*colloq.*), flannel (*colloq.*); *insincerity*, false praise, hypocrisy, sham, eyewash (*colloq.*); *fawning*, cajolery, wheedling, obsequiousness; *flatterer*, hypocrite, toady, sycophant, yes-man, creep (*colloq.*), crawler (*colloq.*), hanger-on.

adj. *flattering*, complimentary, fulsome,

adulatory; *insincere*, plausible, bland, mealy-mouthed, honeyed, sugary, saccharine; *smooth*, unctuous, smarmy (*colloq.*), slimy; *obsequious*, servile, ingratiating, sycophantic.

vb. *flatter*, compliment, praise, puff, boost, soft-soap (*colloq.*), lay it on thick (*colloq.*), overdo it; *cajole*, wheedle, coax, inveigle, suck up to (*colloq.*), sweet-talk, butter up (*colloq.*), massage sb's ego; *fawn*, court, curry favour, be servile, ingratiate oneself.

828 DISPARAGEMENT
See also 595 (damage); 639 (attack).

n. *disparagement*, depreciation, detraction, denigration, belittling; *degradation*, debasement, vilification; *defamation*, calumny, slander, libel, mud-slinging, smear campaign, character assassination; *criticism*, bad press, attack, hatchet job (*colloq.*), brickbat, knocking copy; *aspersion*, slur, stigma, brand, smear, innuendo, insinuation; *scandal*, muckraking, backbiting, gossip; *ridicule*, caricature, skit, satire, lampoon; *detractor*, critic, knocker (*colloq.*), mud-slinger; *slanderer*, libeller, defamer; *scandalmonger*, muckraker, backbiter, gossip columnist, gutter press; *mocker*, scoffer, cynic, satirist.

adj. *disparaging*, deprecatory, derogatory, denigratory, pejorative; *defamatory*, slanderous, libellous; *contemptuous*, slighting, mocking, sarcastic, cynical, catty, snide; *caustic*, bitter, venomous, destructive.

vb. *disparage*, deprecate, detract, depreciate, belittle, play down, sell short, run down (*colloq.*); *discredit*, dishonour, defame, denigrate, blacken, vilify, malign, sully, defile, tarnish, smear, besmirch; *criticize*, slur, cast aspersions on, slight, knock (*colloq.*), pan, slate; *denounce*, decry, revile, expose, pillory; *slander*, libel, calumniate; *deride*, mock, ridicule, lampoon, satirize, guy, sneer at.

829 VINDICATION
n. *vindication*, justification, mitigation, extenuation, defence, apologia, excuse; *grounds*, right, basis, plea, alibi; *pretext*, whitewash, gloss; *exoneration*, exculpation, acquittal; *apologist*, witness, defendant, advocate, champion.

adj. *vindicating*, justifying, extenuating, mitigating, excusing; *justifiable*, arguable, defensible, plausible, allowable; *excusable*, pardonable.

vb. *vindicate*, justify, warrant, give grounds for, make excuses for; *whitewash*, varnish, gloss; *confirm*, bear out, support, show, demonstrate, prove; *uphold*, maintain, defend, plead; *exonerate*, exculpate, excuse, acquit, absolve, clear; *palliate*, mitigate, soften.

830 ACCUSATION
n. *accusation*, indictment, arraignment, prosecution, impeachment, denunciation; *charge*, allegation, complaint, imputation, incrimination, blame, censure; *insinuation*, slur, smear; *false charge*, frame-up (*colloq.*), put-up job (*colloq.*), libel, slander, calumny, perjury; *action*, suit, case, count, plaint, citation, summons; *accuser*, plaintiff, prosecutor, accused, defendant, suspect, informer, witness.

adj. *accusing*, accusatory, condemnatory; *denunciatory*, incriminating; *defamatory*, calumnious; *accused*, charged, suspect; *accusable*, chargeable, liable to prosecution, inexcusable, indefensible.

vb. *accuse*, charge, bring charges, challenge, arraign, indict, impeach; *arrest*, book, prosecute, sue; *impute*, incriminate, blame, censure, point the finger at, lay at one's door; *denounce*, expose, inform, tell, blab (*colloq.*); *implicate*, involve; *complain*, find fault with, reprove; *slander*, libel, slur, calumniate, defame; *fabricate*, trump up, concoct, invent, frame (*colloq.*), perjure oneself, bear false witness.

831 PROBITY
See also 774 (repute); 837 (virtue).

n. *probity*, rectitude, uprightness, good character; *honesty*, integrity, truthfulness, genuineness, conscientiousness, good faith; *fidelity*, faithfulness, loyalty, reliability, constancy; *morality*, moral fibre, scruples, standards; *virtue*, goodness, purity; *honour*, nobility, chivalry; *principle*, point of honour; *honourable person*, man of honour, trusty soul, good sort, brick (*colloq.*); *good sport*, sportsman, fair play, good loser.

adj. *honourable*, upright, straight, erect, right, square; *honest*, truthful, law-abiding, incorruptible; *sincere*, frank, candid, straightforward; *loyal*, faithful, dependable, reliable, trusty, sterling, trustworthy, genuine, dutiful, conscientious; *moral*, principled, ethical, scrupulous, reputable, respectable; *fair*, just, equitable, impartial; *noble*, high-minded, idealistic, chivalrous; *virtuous*, good; *immaculate*, spotless, stainless, clean, pure; *innocent*, ingenuous, artless, guileless.

vb. *be honourable*, play fair, be in good faith, keep faith, do the decent thing; *go straight* (*colloq.*), reform.

832 **IMPROBITY**
See also 662 (disobedience).

n. *improbity*, dishonesty, immorality, corruption, evil, wickedness; *guile*, cunning, artfulness, disingenuousness; *dishonour*, shame, disgrace, disrepute, -gate; *disloyalty*, infidelity, faithlessness, bad faith, double standard, duplicity, double-dealing, betrayal, sell-out; *perfidy*, treachery, treason, sedition, defection; *villainy*, roguery, foul play, skulduggery; *dishonest act*, racket, fiddle, wangle, dirty tricks.

adj. *immoral*, corrupt, evil, wicked, bad; *dishonest*, deceitful, fraudulent, criminal, bent (*colloq.*), crooked; *insincere*, two-faced, disingenuous, double-dealing; *unprincipled*, unscrupulous, unethical; *disreputable*, ignominious, ignoble; *unreliable*, faithless, unfaithful, inconstant; *perfidious*, treacherous, insidious; *sly*, underhand, crafty, devious, artful, foxy, cunning; *dubious*, shady, suspicious, questionable, fishy (*colloq.*), shifty; *base*, vile, mean, shabby, abject.

vb. *be dishonest*, deceive, lie, fib, cheat, swindle, defraud, double-cross, two-time (*colloq.*); *betray*, sell out, sell down the river.

833 **DISINTERESTEDNESS**
n. *disinterestedness*, selflessness, unselfishness, self-sacrifice, dedication, self-denial, altruism, martyrdom; *magnanimity*, generosity, liberality, nobility, philanthropy; *impartiality*, indifference; *neutrality*, objectivity, non-involvement, detachment, unconcern.

adj. *disinterested*, impartial, unbiased, unprejudiced, objective, fair, just; *indifferent*, unconcerned, dispassionate; *unselfish*, selfless, dedicated, self-sacrificing, self-effacing, humble; *magnanimous*, generous, liberal, unsparing; *noble*, high-minded, quixotic, chivalrous.

vb. *be disinterested*, put oneself last, take a back seat.

834 **SELFISHNESS**
See also 728 (meanness).

n. *selfishness*, self-interest, egoism, egotism, self-absorption, opportunism, individualism; *vanity*, narcissism, self-indulgence, self-worship; *greed*, meanness, avarice; *egoist*, egotist, narcissist, individualist, opportunist, gold-digger; *miser*, niggard.

adj. *selfish*, egocentric, self-centred, self-absorbed, self-seeking, egoistic, egotistic; *greedy*, miserly, mean, avaricious; *vain*, narcissistic, self-indulgent, conceited; *covetous*, envious, jealous, possessive, dog-in-the-manger.

vb. *be selfish*, put oneself first, look after number one; *monopolize*, hog, keep to oneself; *look out for oneself*, be on the make, have an eye for the main chance.

835 **GOOD**
See also 805 (benevolence); 837 (virtue).

n. *good*, benefit, advantage, interest; *good fortune*, providence, luck, boon, windfall, godsend, pennies from heaven, treasure trove; *gain*, profit, harvest, success, prosperity, wealth; *welfare*, wellbeing, fortune, weal; *improvement*, betterment, edification; *good turn*, help, service, favour, convenience; *common good*, public weal.

adj. *good*, beneficial, advantageous, gainful; *helpful*, useful, heaven-sent; *worthwhile*, valuable, profitable; *thriving*, successful, prosperous.

vb. *do good*, benefit, favour, bless; *be useful*, avail, serve, help; *make better*, edify, improve, do one a power of good; *do well*, flourish, thrive, prosper, succeed.

836 **EVIL**
See also 806 (malevolence); 838 (wickedness).

n. *evil*, ill; *accident*, tragedy, disaster, catastrophe, calamity, ruin; *nuisance*, trial, affliction; *misfortune*, ill luck, a crying shame, raw deal; *harm*, mischief, damage, hurt, injury, pain, anguish, distress, trouble; *wrong*, disservice, dirty trick, foul play, outrage; *wickedness*, corruption; *scourge*, pest, plague, bane; *disadvantage*, setback, hitch.

adj. *evil*, bad, ill, adverse, nefarious; *unfortunate*, catastrophic, disastrous, ruinous, calamitous; *distressing*, tragic, painful, hurtful; *wicked*, vicious, sinister, maleficent; *fatal*, fell, mortal, deadly.

vb. *do evil*, harm, damage, do mischief, do a disservice; *afflict*, ruin, trouble.

adv. *amiss*, awry, wrong.

837 **VIRTUE**

See also 582 (worth); 805 (benevolence);
831 (probity).

n. *virtue*, goodness, morality, uprightness,
rectitude, righteousness, good behaviour;
kindness, compassion, magnanimity; *honesty*,
integrity, character, honour, probity;
temperance, sanctity, saintliness, holiness;
purity, chastity, innocence; *morals*, principles,
ethics; *worth*, merit, saving grace; *good person*,
good neighbour, salt of the earth, one in a
million, good sort, brick (*colloq.*), diamond
geezer (*colloq.*), pillar of society, saint, angel;
good example, model, paragon.

adj. *virtuous*, good, upright, righteous,
proper, moral, principled; *saintly*, angelic,
holy; *kind*, kindly, generous, dutiful,
conscientious, well-intentioned; *honest*,
worthy, sterling, exemplary, unimpeachable;
perfect, irreproachable, immaculate,
impeccable, unblemished, excellent; *pure*,
chaste, innocent.

vb. *be good*, behave oneself, have a clear
conscience, set a good example, keep to the
straight and narrow; *be virtuous*, resist
temptation, go straight.

838 **WICKEDNESS**

See also 150 (destruction); 806 (malevolence);
810 (pitilessness); 836 (evil).

n. *wickedness*, vice, evil, unrighteousness,
wrongdoing; *immorality*, corruption,
depravity, wantonness, baseness; *iniquity*,
sin, wrong, perversity, sin, transgression,
trespass, offence; *outrage*, atrocity, enormity;
crime, felony, the underworld, den of vice;
malignity, malevolence, villainy, roguery;
fault, weakness, foible, bad habit, failing,
demerit, shortcoming, peccadillo; *bad person*,
wrongdoer, malefactor, evildoer, sinner,
miscreant, reprobate; *scoundrel*, wretch,
villain, vagabond, rogue, rascal, knave,
blackguard, bounder, blighter; *bad child*,
terror, imp, scamp, monkey, scallywag; *bully*,
ugly customer, nasty piece of work, ruffian,
thug, lout, hoodlum, tough, yobbo (*colloq.*),
brute, monster, beast, savage, barbarian; *idler*,
loafer, wastrel, prodigal, good-for-nothing,
ne'er-do-well, layabout, bad lot, riffraff, black
sheep, troublemaker, mischief-maker; *crook*,
liar, cheat, conman, twister, racketeer,
impostor, traitor; *criminal*, felon, lawbreaker,
offender, public enemy, thief, pickpocket,
housebreaker, burglar, delinquent, vandal,
pirate, gangster, desperado, murderer,
assassin; *rake*, profligate, pimp, wanton,
hussy; *cad*, rotter, heel (*colloq.*), bastard,
worm, rat, louse, swine.

adj. *wicked*, evil, bad, wrong; *immoral*,
corrupt, dissolute, degenerate, perverted,
depraved, indecent, wanton; *naughty*,
disobedient; *wayward*, perverse; *unscrupulous*,
unprincipled; *mean*, despicable, base, vile,
malevolent, callous, vicious, brutal, cruel;
outrageous, shocking, scandalous,
abominable, atrocious, heinous, monstrous,
unforgivable, inexcusable; *offensive*,
repugnant, distasteful; *hellish*, infernal,
diabolic, fiendish; *criminal*, lawless,
nefarious.

vb. *be wicked*, err, transgress, do wrong;
lapse, stray, fall, backslide, degenerate, go off
the rails (*colloq.*); *misbehave*, be naughty;
make wicked, corrupt, pervert, lead astray,
defile, tempt, seduce.

839 **INNOCENCE**

n. *innocence*, guiltlessness, blamelessness,
irreproachability, faultlessness; *clear
conscience*, clean hands, clean slate; *purity*,
impeccability, stainlessness, virtue;
artlessness, inexperience, unworldliness,
naïvety; *probity*, integrity, uprightness,
incorruptibility; *innocent*, child, babe, lamb,
dove; *innocent party*, injured party.

adj. *innocent*, not guilty, not responsible,
guiltless, blameless, in the clear, acquitted;
pure, clean, stainless, spotless, unsoiled,
untainted, immaculate, undefiled, -free;
perfect, impeccable, faultless, above
suspicion, sinless, unimpeachable,
incorruptible; *ignorant*, simple,
unsophisticated, inexperienced, naïve,
unworldly, green; *guileless*, artless; *harmless*,
inoffensive, innocuous; *pardonable*,
forgivable, excusable.

vb. *be innocent*, have a clear conscience,
have nothing to confess; *mean no harm*,
know no better.

840 **GUILT**

n. *guilt*, blame, culpability, charge, reproach;
responsibility, liability, accountability;
criminality, delinquency, illegality, sinfulness;
guilty conscience, bad conscience, remorse;
involvement, complicity; *guilty act*, crime,
offence, sin, transgression, trespass,
misdemeanour; *misconduct*, misbehaviour,
malpractice; *indiscretion*, peccadillo,
impropriety; *error*, fault, lapse, slip, blunder.

adj. *guilty*, found guilty, guilty as charged,
condemned, judged, convicted,

incriminated; *wrong*, at fault, to blame, culpable, reproachable; *suspected*, blamed, censured; *responsible*, liable, answerable, accountable; *red-handed*, caught in the act, caught in flagrante delicto; *sheepish*, shamefaced, embarrassed.

vb. *be guilty*, be caught in the act, plead guilty; *find guilty*, incriminate, charge, condemn.

841 **PENITENCE**

n. *penitence*, repentance, change of heart, contrition, compunction, confession; *remorse*, shame, self-reproach, regret; *self-accusation*, self-condemnation; *penance*, sackcloth and ashes, hair shirt; *apology*, atonement; *penitent*, prodigal son, reformed character, convert.

adj. *penitent*, repentant, contrite, remorseful, ashamed; *regretful*, full of regrets, sorry, apologetic; *conscience-stricken*, chastened, self-reproachful, self-accusing; *reformed*, converted.

vb. *repent*, feel shame, confess, acknowledge, own up, admit, plead guilty; *be penitent*, be contrite, regret, apologize, excuse oneself; *recant*, see the light, be converted, turn over a new leaf.

842 **IMPENITENCE**

n. *impenitence*, non-contrition, refusal to recant, obduracy, stubbornness; *hardness*, hardness of heart, heart of stone, pitilessness; *no regrets*, no apologies; *incorrigibility*, hardened sinner.

adj. *impenitent*, unrepentant, uncontrite, unashamed, unabashed, recusant; *hard*, obdurate, insensitive, callous, stubborn; *incorrigible*, irredeemable, hopeless, despaired of, lost.

vb. *be impenitent*, have no regrets, show no remorse, harden one's heart, refuse to recant, feel no compunction.

843 **SELF-RESTRAINT**

See also 668 (restraint).

n. *self-restraint*, self-control, self-discipline, restraint, asceticism, temperance, moderation, abstemiousness; *self-denial*, abstinence, continence, teetotalism, prohibitionism, vegetarianism, veganism; *abstainer*, total abstainer, teetotaller, prohibitionist, vegetarian, vegan, ascetic.

adj. *self-restrained*, self-controlled, ascetic, self-disciplined; *temperate*, moderate, restrained, measured, disciplined, careful,

continent; *sparing*, plain, frugal, spartan; *abstemious*, sober.

vb. *be self-restrained*, restrain oneself, exercise self-control, control oneself, contain oneself, deny oneself, ration oneself, be moderate, abstain, refrain; *watch oneself*, know when to stop, know when one has had enough, keep within bounds; *give up*, swear off, go on a diet; *be sober*, keep sober, go on the wagon (*colloq.*).

844 **SELF-INDULGENCE**

See also 575 (excess); 846 (gluttony)

n. *self-indulgence*, intemperance, immoderation, lack of moderation, lack of restraint; *excess*, excessiveness, extravagance, overindulgence; *incontinence*, lack of self-control, indiscipline, addiction; *wastefulness*, waste; *sensuality*, voluptuousness, carnality, the fleshpots; *gluttony*, debauchery, dissoluteness, dissipation, binge-drinking/-eating; *high living*, luxury, epicureanism, hedonism; *pleasure-seeker*, epicurean, hedonist, lotus-eater, chocaholic, bon viveur; epicure, gourmet, gourmand.

adj. *self-indulgent*, intemperate, immoderate, unrestrained; *excessive*, unlimited, overindulgent, extravagant; *incontinent*, uncontrolled, undisciplined; *wasteful*, spendthrift, uneconomical; *sensual*, sensuous, voluptuous, carnal, bodily, fleshly; *gluttonous*, debauched, dissolute, dissipated, hungover; *high-living*, pleasure-seeking, fun-loving, epicurean, hedonistic.

vb. *be self-indulgent*, indulge (oneself), be intemperate, be immoderate, luxuriate, wallow, deny oneself nothing; *have* one's *fling*, paint the town red (*colloq.*), sow one's wild oats; *overeat*, eat to excess, gorge, overindulge (oneself), binge; *drink too much*, drink to excess, go on a bender (*colloq.*); *not know when to stop*, burn the candle at both ends; *lack self-control*, lack discipline.

845 **FASTING**

n. *fasting*, abstinence from food, fast, bread and water, hunger strike; *starvation*, hunger, malnutrition, anorexia, famishment, empty stomach, snack attack (*colloq.*); *dieting*, slimming, diet, war rations; *fast day*, Lent, Ramadan, Yom Kippur.

adj. *fasting*, abstinent, abstaining, not eating; *starving*, hungry, famished; *underfed*, undernourished, poorly fed, half starved.

vb. *fast*, eat nothing, go without food; *starve*, go hungry, famish; *diet*, slim, reduce weight, lose weight, go on a diet; *go on hunger strike*, refuse food.

846 **GLUTTONY**

n. *gluttony*, greed, greediness, insatiability, voracity, intemperance, excess, overindulgence, overeating, insatiable appetite; *glutton*, gourmand, pig, hog, locust, gannet (*colloq.*), greedy pig, greedy guts (*colloq.*); *gourmet*, gastronome, epicure; *feast*, blowout (*colloq.*).

adj. *gluttonous*, greedy, insatiable, overfed; *ravenous*, voracious, omnivorous; *gastronomic*, epicurean.

vb. *overeat*, stuff oneself, make a pig of oneself, eat like a horse, eat sb out of house and home; *guzzle*, gulp down, bolt down, wolf, scoff, demolish, polish off, gobble up, devour, gorge, cram, stuff.

847 **SOBRIETY**

n. *sobriety*, soberness, temperance, teetotalism, prohibition, abstinence; *sober person*, moderate drinker, teetotaller, abstainer, total abstainer, prohibitionist; *the Band of Hope*, temperance society, Alcoholics Anonymous.

adj. *sober*, temperate, abstinent, abstemious; *teetotal*, TT, on the wagon (*colloq.*); *clear-headed*, in one's right mind, in possession of one's senses, stone-cold sober, sober as a judge; *sobered*, sobered up, dried out.

vb. *be sober*, be temperate, drink moderately, not drink, not imbibe; *become teetotal*, give up alcohol, sign the pledge, go on the wagon (*colloq.*), dry out; *hold one's drink*, have a good head for drink; *sober up*, sleep it off (*colloq.*), get rid of a hangover, clear one's head.

848 **DRUNKENNESS**

n. *drunkenness*, intoxication, inebriation, insobriety, intemperance; *drink problem*, alcoholism, binge-drinking, dipsomania, the dt's, pink elephants, drink-driving; *tipsiness*, a drop too much, one over the limit, one too many; *drunkard*, drunk, heavy drinker, hard drinker, alcoholic, boozer (*colloq.*), inebriate, old soak, tippler, wino (*colloq.*), dypso (*colloq.*), lush (*colloq.*); *drinking bout*, pub-crawl, booze-up (*colloq.*), bender (*colloq.*), blind (*colloq.*); *Dutch courage*, a hair of the dog that bit you; *hangover*, head, headache, morning-after-the-night-before feeling.

adj. *drunk*, intoxicated, inebriated, under the influence, the worse for drink, in one's cups, one over the eight, tired and emotional (*colloq.*), blind drunk, dead drunk, roaring drunk, drunk and disorderly; *tipsy*, squiffy (*colloq.*), tiddly, half-cut, merry, high, befuddled, feeling no pain, sozzled (*colloq.*), sloshed (*colloq.*), tight (*colloq.*), pickled (*colloq.*), plastered (*colloq.*), woozy, stoned (*colloq.*), blotto (*colloq.*), canned (*colloq.*), boozed up (*colloq.*), legless (*colloq.*), pissed (*colloq.*), Brahms and Liszt (*colloq.*); *seeing double*, glassy-eyed, pie-eyed.

vb. *drink*, booze (*colloq.*), tipple, swig, guzzle, drink like a fish, hit the bottle, go pub-crawling, knock back a few, bend the elbow, drown one's sorrows, wet one's whistle (*colloq.*); *be drunk*, be merry/tipsy/under the influence (of drink), have had one too many; *see double*, lurch, stagger, get stoned out of one's mind (*colloq.*), pass out, crash out; *intoxicate*, inebriate, go to one's head.

849 **DRUG-TAKING**

n. *drug-taking*, smoking; *drug dependence*, drug addiction, drug abuse, habit, narcotism, solvent/substance abuse, glue-sniffing, drug-driving; *drug*, narcotic, dope, pep pill, stimulant, upper (*colloq.*), downer (*colloq.*), hard/soft drug, designer drug, lifestyle/recreational drug; *joint*, reefer, shot, fix (*colloq.*); *tobacco*, nicotine; *cannabis*, hemp, marijuana, hash, hashish, pot (*colloq.*), grass (*colloq.*), ganja; *cocaine*, coke (*colloq.*), snow (*colloq.*), crack (*colloq.*), rock (*colloq.*), freebase (*colloq.*); *morphine*, opium, opium den; *heroin*, horse (*colloq.*), smack (*colloq.*), brown sugar (*colloq.*); *LSD*, acid, mescalin; *amphetamine*, speed (*colloq.*), bennies (*colloq.*); *Ecstasy*, E; *date-rape drug*, Rohypnol; *high* (*colloq.*), buzz (*colloq.*), rush (*colloq.*); *withdrawal symptoms*, cold turkey; *drug-dealer*, drug-pusher, pusher, drug baron, drug trafficker, cannabis café; *drug addict*, drug-user, junkie (*colloq.*).

adj. *drugged*, high (*colloq.*), stoned (*colloq.*), loved up (*colloq.*); *stimulant*, opiate, narcotic, mind-blowing (*colloq.*).

vb. *drug* (oneself), smoke, turn on (*colloq.*), inject (oneself), mainline (*colloq.*), snort, sniff, pop (*colloq.*), take a trip.

850 **MORALITY**

See also 586 (cleanness); 831 probity); 837 (virtue).

n. *morality*, morals, virtue, decency, decorum, propriety, delicacy, chastity, virginity, continence, celibacy; *purity*, cleanness, cleanliness, spotlessness, untaintedness, immaculateness; *sinlessness*, perfection; *prudery*, primness, false shame, false modesty, prudishness; *prude*, prig, old maid; *Victorian*, Puritan; *guardian of morality*, Mrs Grundy, censor; *celibate*, monk, nun.

   adj. *moral*, good, virtuous, decent, honourable, decorous, demure, abstemious, platonic, continent; *pure*, clean, spotless, untainted, immaculate, innocent, sinless, perfect; *chaste*, celibate, virgin, virginal, white; *prudish*, prim, priggish, squeamish, shockable, narrow-minded, Victorian, straitlaced, puritanical, old-maidish.

   vb. *moralize*, censor.

851 **IMMORALITY**
See also 587 (dirtiness).

   n. *immorality*, indecency, shamelessness, immodesty, unchastity, looseness of morals, easy virtue, permissive society; *impurity*, imperfection, uncleanness, filthiness, taintedness, contamination, pollution, sinfulness; *lewdness*, lasciviousness, prurience, salaciousness, dissoluteness, dissipation, debauchery, licentiousness; *ribaldry*, bawdiness; *lust*, sensuality, eroticism, libido; *obscenity*, pornography, filth, smut, soft porn, blue film/movie; *rape*, violation, indecent assault, sexual assault, incest; *promiscuity*, sleeping around (*colloq.*), dirty weekend (*colloq.*), free love, affair, extramarital relations, adultery, fornication, carnal knowledge, infidelity, unfaithfulness, the eternal triangle; *prostitution*, street-walking, whoredom; *brothel*, house of ill repute, red-light district, tolerance zone; *libertine*, lecher, womanizer, rake, playboy, stud; *whore*, prostitute, harlot, hooker (*colloq.*), tart (*colloq.*), slag (*colloq.*), slut, tramp, trollop, sex worker, rent-boy; *voyeur*, pervert, flasher (*colloq.*), dirty old man (*colloq.*).

   adj. *immoral*, amoral, indecent, wanton, shameless, immodest, unchaste, loose; *impure*, unclean, dirty, contaminated, polluted, sullied; *lewd*, lascivious, prurient, salacious, dissolute, lecherous, licentious, debauched, randy (*colloq.*); *sensual*, erotic, libidinous; *obscene*, filthy, smutty, dirty, lurid, pornographic, porno, blue, explicit, adult; *vulgar*, coarse, risqué; *adulterous*, extramarital, illicit, unfaithful, incestuous.

   vb. *be immoral*, commit adultery, have an affair, play away (from home) (*colloq.*),

fornicate, sleep around (*colloq.*), womanize; *seduce*, debauch, take advantage of; *rape*, assault, violate.

852 **LEGALITY**
See also 677 (permission).

   n. *legality*, lawfulness, permissibility, legitimacy; *legislation*, law-making, regulation, authorization, codification, sanction, enactment; *justice*, authority, right; *law*, body of law, statute book, constitution, charter, statute, legal code, code; *ordinance*, act, edict, regulation, rule, byelaw; *jurisprudence*, science of law, legal learning; *legislator*, law-maker, jurist.

   adj. *legal*, lawful, legitimate, right, just; *permissible*, permitted, allowable, sanctioned, authorized, codified, statutory, within the law, constitutional; *jurisprudential*, nomothetic.

   vb. *make legal*, enact, pass, put into effect.

   adv. *legally*, by law, by order, legitimately, in the eyes of the law.

853 **ILLEGALITY**
See also 658 (anarchy); 678 (veto).

   n. *illegality*, unlawfulness; *miscarriage* of justice, injustice, wrong verdict; *unconstitutionality*, loophole; *lawbreaking*, breach of law, trespass, offence, wrong, violation, transgression, contravention, encroachment, infringement, foul play, malpractice; *criminal offence*, crime, misdemeanour, felony; *fraud*, embezzlement, identity theft; *computer crime/fraud*, cybercrime, e-stalking; *the black market*, racketeering; *lawlessness*, breach of the peace, street violence, crime wave, anarchy, terrorism, mob rule, gang rule; *riot*, rebellion, revolt, breakdown of law and order, chaos, disorder; *illegitimacy*, bastardy; *illegitimate child*, bastard, love child.

   adj. *illegal*, unlawful, illicit, prohibited, banned, forbidden, not allowed, unauthorized, outside the law, contrary to the law, wrong; *contraband*, smuggled, hot (*colloq.*), stolen, black-market; *lawless*, anarchic, irresponsible, without law, riotous; *illegitimate*, bastard, born out of wedlock, born on the wrong side of the blanket.

   vb. *be illegal*, break the law, do wrong, disobey, violate, transgress, contravene, infringe; *take the law into one's own hands*, be a law unto oneself, stand above the law; *suspend*, annul, cancel, nullify, abrogate, void.

adv. *illegally*, illicitly, unlawfully, criminally, illegitimately, under the counter.

854 JURISDICTION
See also 657 (authority).

n. *jurisdiction*, authority, control, law and order, arm of the law, direction, supervision; *responsibility*, competence, capacity, power; *executive*, corporation, administration; *domain*, range, territory; *law officer*, judge, mayor, sheriff, legal administrator; *police*, police force, constabulary; *police officer*, policeman, policewoman, constable, cop (*colloq.*), copper (*colloq.*), bobby (*colloq.*), rozzer (*colloq.*), fuzz (*colloq.*), filth (*colloq.*); *traffic warden*, meter maid.

adj. *jurisdictional*, competent, executive, administrative, directive, judiciary, judicial.

vb. *administer*, direct, supervise; *judge*, administer/dispense justice, sit in judgement; *police*, keep order, control.

855 TRIBUNAL
n. *tribunal*, court, bench, board, judicial assembly, assizes, session, council; *throne*, woolsack, seat of justice; *dock*, witness box, bar, courthouse, lawcourt.

856 LITIGATION
n. *litigation*, going to law, judicature; *lawsuit*, case, suit, action, legal proceedings; *summons*, citation, subpoena, writ, search warrant, charge, indictment; *inquest*, inquiry, hearing, prosecution, defence, affidavit, examination, cross-examination, testimony, pleadings, arguments, reasoning, summing up; *ruling*, verdict, judgement, finding, decision; *acquittal*, favourable verdict; *condemnation*, unfavourable verdict, sentence; *appeal*, retrial, reversal of judgement; *litigant*, party, suitor, claimant, plaintiff, defendant, objector, accused, prisoner at the bar/in the dock, accuser, prosecutor; *jury*, grand jury, hung jury, twelve good men and true, juror, juryman/-woman, foreman/-woman.

adj. *litigating*, suing, accusing, litigant; *going to law*, contesting, objecting, disputing, arguing, litigious.

vb. *litigate*, go to law, appeal to law, prosecute, sue, charge, indict, bring to trial, bring to justice, bring a suit, file a suit, file a claim, petition, bring an action against; *prepare a case*, prepare a brief; *try*, hear, give a hearing to, judge, rule, arbitrate, adjudicate; *sum up*, close the pleadings, charge the jury;

pass sentence, sentence, return a verdict, rule, find, declare, pronounce, convict.

857 ACQUITTAL
n. *acquittal*, favourable verdict, verdict of not guilty, innocence; *discharge*, reprieve, release, remission, suspended sentence, pardon, clearance, case dismissed, exoneration, exculpation, let-off (*colloq.*).

adj. *acquitted*, not guilty, guiltless, innocent, in the clear, cleared, exonerated, exculpated, vindicated; *discharged*, set free, released, liberated; *reprieved*, forgiven.

vb. *acquit*, find not guilty, declare not guilty, prove innocent, vindicate, clear sb's name; *reprieve*, pardon, absolve, forgive, clear, dismiss, grant remission, discharge, let off (*colloq.*); *release*, set free.

858 CONVICTION
n. *conviction*, unfavourable verdict, condemnation, denunciation, sentence; *death sentence*, death warrant, condemned cell.

adj. *convicted*, found guilty, condemned, sentenced; *condemnatory*, damnatory.

vb. *convict*, find guilty, prove guilty, condemn, bring home the charge, judge, sentence, pass sentence on; *punish*, denounce, damn, curse; *sentence to death*, sign sb's death warrant, put on the black cap.

859 REWARD
See also 650 (trophy).

n. *reward*, award, prize, trophy, honour, decoration, accolade, bonus, premium, tribute; *recognition*, acknowledgement, thanks; *recompense*, compensation, remuneration, fee, pay, payment, guerdon, reparation, reimbursement; *profit*, return, gain; *tip*, gratuity, golden handshake, honorarium; *deserts*, just deserts; *reward for service*, pension; *bribe*, bait, kickback (*colloq.*).

adj. *rewarding*, profitable, worthwhile, advantageous, remunerative; *generous*, open-handed, charitable, unsparing, liberal.

vb. *reward*, award, honour, decorate, present, bestow a title, confer, grant; *recognize*, acknowledge, pay tribute, be grateful, thank, show one's gratitude; *recompense*, compensate, remunerate, pay, reimburse, redress, indemnify, make reparation; *bribe*, offer a bribe.

adv. *rewardingly*, profitably; *as a reward*, in compensation.

860 PUNISHMENT

See also 826 (disapproval); 861 (means of punishment).

n. *punishment*, chastisement, castigation, discipline, disciplinary action, reprimand, condemnation, sentence, reproof, correction, retribution; *penalty*, fine, damages, costs, liability; *banishment*, exile, expulsion, transportation; *prison sentence*, hard labour, solitary confinement, borstal; *control order*, house arrest, tagging, ASBO (anti-social behaviour order), community sentence, community service; *corporal punishment*, blow, clout, cane, rap, cuff, slap, smack, whip; *torture*, third degree; *capital punishment*, execution, death sentence, honour killing, the gallows, hanging, electrocution, decapitation, beheading, guillotining, garrotting, strangling, strangulation, impalement, crucifixion, drowning, burning; *mass execution*, mass murder, massacre, slaughter, genocide, pogrom, holocaust, night of the long knives, annihilation; *martyrdom*, martyrization; *punisher*, chastiser, castigator, persecutor, torturer, inquisitor; *executioner*, hangman, headsman, firing squad.

adj. *punitive*, penal, castigatory, disciplinary, corrective; *punishable*, liable.

vb. *punish*, correct, chastise, castigate, discipline, reprimand, rebuke, sentence; *penalize*, fine, deprive, confiscate, take away, endorse sb's licence; *demote*, suspend, downgrade, unfrock, cashier, reduce to the ranks; *slap*, smack, spank, wallop, cuff, clout, box sb on the ears, rap sb over the knuckles; *belt*, beat, strap, tan, cane, birch, flog, whip, whack, thrash, thrash the living daylights out of, give sb a good hiding, knock/beat six/ten bells out of; *exile*, banish, deport, transport, expel; *isolate*, ostracize, send to Coventry, outlaw; *imprison*, jail, confine; *torture*, rack, break on the wheel, tar and feather, kneecap, martyr; *execute*, put to death, kill, crucify, stone to death, hang, hang draw and quarter, behead, decapitate, guillotine, garrotte, electrocute, gas, shoot, strangle, burn alive, impale, drown, poison; *massacre*, slaughter, annihilate; *be punished*, suffer punishment, face the music (*colloq.*), take one's medicine, pay the penalty, get one's just deserts.

861 MEANS OF PUNISHMENT

See also 671 (prison)

n. *scourge*, whip, horsewhip, bullwhip,

belt, strap, cat, cat-o'-nine-tails, birch, cane, stick, rod, ruler; *pillory*, stocks, ducking stool, whipping post; *prison*, jail; *instrument of torture*, rack, wheel, thumbscrew, maiden, water torture, torture chamber; *scaffold*, gallows, gibbet, noose, rope, halter, garrotte, cross, stake, bullet, poison, guillotine, axe, electric chair, gas chamber, death chamber.

862 DIVINITY

n. *divinity*, divineness, deity, supreme deity; *God*, godhead, the Supreme Being, the Creator, Providence, the Preserver, the Prime Mover, the Eternal, the Almighty, Yahweh, Jehovah, Jah, Allah, Brahma, Siva, Vishnu, Krishna, Buddha; *the Trinity*, the Three in One; *the Father*, the Lord, the King of Kings, the Lord of Lords, the Lord of Hosts, Alpha and Omega; *Jesus Christ*, the Son of God, the Son of Man, Emmanuel, the Messiah, the Saviour, the Redeemer, the Lamb of God, the Good Shepherd, Friend, the Prince of Peace; *the Holy Spirit*, the Spirit, the Holy Ghost, the Comforter, the Paraclete, the Dove; *the gods*, Zeus, Jupiter, Apollo, Mars, Ares, Hermes, Mercury, Poseidon, Neptune, Bacchus, Dionysus, Hades, Pluto, Eros, Cupid, Venus, Aphrodite, Minerva, Athene, Pan, Baal, Isis, Ra, Ptah, Thoth, Horus, Odin, Thor; *object of worship*, god, goddess, idol, false god, golden calf, mumbo jumbo, cargo cult; *divine manifestation*, theophany, incarnation, transfiguration, glory; *divine task*, creation, preservation, judgement, mercy, grace, salvation, propitiation, atonement, redemption, mediation, intercession.

adj. *divine*, godlike; *heavenly*, celestial, sublime, ineffable; *infinite*, supreme, absolute, omnipresent, sovereign; *transcendent*, immanent, self-existent, changeless, unchanging; *eternal*, everlasting, immortal, timeless; *almighty*, omnipotent, all-powerful; *omniscient*, all-knowing, all-wise; *just*, merciful; *gracious*, loving, forgiving, providential; *holy*, godly, hallowed, sanctified, sacred; *religious*, mystical, spiritual, superhuman, supernatural, not of this world.

863 SAINT

See also 872 (holiness).

n. *saint*, believer, convert, man of prayer, man of God, holy man, patron saint; *the saints*, the children of God, the righteous, the just, the chosen people, the elect; *follower*, disciple, apostle; *saintliness*, sanctity, beatitude; *mystic*, holy person, fakir, dervish, ascetic; *good spirit*, angel, archangel, ministering spirit, guardian angel, seraph, cherub, (heavenly) host, principalities, authorities, powers, dominions.

adj. *saintly*, sanctified, beatified, blessed, holy, pious, righteous, just; *angelic*, ministering, guardian, heavenly, celestial.

864 DEVIL
see also 876 (sorcery); 877 (occultism).

n. *devil*, Satan, the Evil One, fallen angel, Mephistopheles, Beelzebub, the Prince of Darkness, the Lord of Misrule, Lucifer, serpent, the Tempter, the Accuser, the Adversary, the Antichrist, Old Harry (*colloq.*), Old Nick (*colloq.*); *evil spirit*, devil, demon, unclean spirit, succubus, incubus, fiend, powers of darkness; *devil worship*, demonism, Satanism, witchcraft, black magic, voodoo; *devil-worshipper*, Satanist.

adj. *satanic*, devilish, Mephistopholean; *wicked*, diabolical, fiendish; *infernal*, hellish.

865 FAIRY
n. *fairy*, spirit, little people, fairy godmother, fairy queen; *elf*, brownie, goblin, gnome, dwarf, pixie, sprite, hobgoblin, imp, puck, leprechaun, troll, gremlin; *genie*, centaur, satyr, faun, mermaid, Lorelei, nymph, yeti, Abominable Snowman, the Green Man; *fairy tale/story*, folklore; *ghost*, spectre, phantom, spirit, poltergeist, spook (*colloq.*), dybbuk, wraith, visitant, departed spirit, presence, zombie; *nightmare*, night terror; *apparition*, vision, appearance; *vampire*, ghoul, werewolf, ghoul, ogre, bogey (man).

adj. *fairylike*, elfish, impish; *mythical*, imaginary; *ghostly*, spooky (*colloq.*), eerie, haunted, weird, uncanny, supernatural, phantom, ghoulish, nightmarish.

vb. *haunt*, visit, walk, return from the dead.

866 HEAVEN
n. *heaven*, paradise, bliss, glory, eternal rest, celestial bliss, the presence of God, Abraham's bosom, the heavenly city, the holy city, the new Jerusalem, the kingdom of heaven, the kingdom of God, the next world, the hereafter, the world to come, kingdom come (*colloq.*), the happy hunting grounds (*colloq.*), seventh heaven, cloud nine (*colloq.*), Elysium, the Garden of Eden, nirvana; *resurrection*, afterlife, rapture, glorification,

translation, ascension, assumption, millennium.

adj. *heavenly*, celestial, eternal, blessed, blissful, glorious, glorified.

867 HELL
n. *hell*, the underworld, lower world, nether regions, abyss, bottomless pit, inferno, everlasting fire, hellfire, lake of fire and brimstone, place of departed spirits, Sheol, Gehenna, Hades, perdition, purgatory, limbo; *judgement*, punishment, darkness, separation, destruction, wrath, weeping and gnashing of teeth.

adj. *hellish*, infernal, damned.

868 RELIGION
See also 434 (belief); 879 (clergy).

n. *religion*, natural religion, revealed religion; *deism*, theism, monotheism, polytheism, pantheism, animism, gnosticism; *religious teaching*, Judaism, Christianity, Mormonism, Islam, Baha'i, Zoroastrianism, Hinduism, Brahminism, Jainism, Sikhism, Buddhism, Theravada, Hinayana, Mahayana, Zen, Confucianism, Taoism, Shintoism, Theosophy, Scientology; *revelation*, declaration, inspiration, illumination, prophecy; *sacred writings*, truth, the Word of God, Holy Writ, (Holy) Scriptures, (Holy) Bible, the Good Book (*colloq.*), canon, Old Testament, Talmud, Torah, Pentateuch, the Ten Commandments, the Law and the Prophets, Psalms, Apocrypha, New Testament, Gospel, Good News, Acts (of the Apostles), the Epistles, Revelation, the Apocalypse, Koran *or* Qur'an, Vedas, Upanishads, Bhagavad Gita, Tripitaka, Granth, Tao Te Ching, Avesta; *vision*, sign, miracle, theophany, incarnation, the Word made flesh; *belief*, faith, teaching, doctrine, creed, dogma, tenet, articles of faith, the Thirty-nine Articles, confession; *study of religion*, theology, divinity, religious education, RE, religious instruction, RI, religious knowledge, RK; *religious teacher*, apostle, prophet, rabbi, imam, caliph, ayatollah, preacher, lay preacher, interpreter, commentator, expositor, evangelist, missionary, guru; *theologian*, scholar, divine.

adj. *religious*, holy, spiritual, divine, devout, godly; *revealed*, scriptural, holy, sacred, inspired, prophetic, biblical, canonical, apostolic, authoritative, infallible, trustworthy, evangelical, evangelistic, devotional; *theological*, doctrinal, dogmatic.

869 UNBELIEF

See also 435 (disbelief)

n. *unbelief*, atheism; *irreligion*, godlessness, unholiness, nothing sacred, profaneness, ungodliness; *wickedness*, sinfulness; *false religion*, idolatry, heresy; *heathenism*, paganism; *disbelief*, scepticism, doubt, agnosticism; *lack of faith*, lapse from faith; *free-thinking*, rationalism, humanism, secularism, materialism, worldliness; *unbeliever*, dissenter, rationalist, freethinker, atheist; *agnostic*, sceptic, doubter, doubting Thomas; *idolater*, heretic; *materialist*, worldling; *heathen*, pagan; *infidel*, apostate.

adj. *unbelieving*, atheistic; *irreligious*, godless, unholy, profane, ungodly, unspiritual; *wicked*, sinful; *disbelieving*, doubting, agnostic; *heathen*, pagan, idolatrous; *heretical*, unorthodox; *freethinking*, rationalistic, humanistic, secular, materialistic, worldly; *apostate*, unfaithful, lapsed, dissenting; *non-practising*, unconverted, lost.

870 ORTHODOXY

n. *orthodoxy*, strictness, soundness, fundamentalism; *heresy-hunting*, persecution, witch hunt; *conformist*, traditionalist, fundamentalist; *believer*, true believer; *the faithful*, congregation, flock, pillar of the church, communicant.

adj. *orthodox*, sound, pure, true, right-minded, non-heretical; *loyal*, devout, obedient; *practising*, committed, conforming, card-carrying (*colloq.*), true-blue; *conventional*, traditional, conservative; *scriptural*, canonical, strict; *fundamentalist*, evangelical.

871 HETERODOXY

n. *heterodoxy*, unorthodoxy, wrong belief, modernism, liberalism; *sectarianism*, separatism, partisanship, schismatism, party spirit; *bigotry*, prejudice; *denominationalism*, nonconformism; *division*, dissociation, secession, separation, withdrawal, excommunication; *heresy*, divergence, distortion, perversion; *sect*, schism, division, split, faction, branch, offshoot; *denomination*, tradition; *separatist*, rebel, dissident, dissenter, nonconformist, heretic.

adj. *heterodox*, unorthodox, unsound, unconventional, nonconformist, unauthorized; *heretical*, divergent, perverted; *sectarian*, partisan, schismatic, breakaway, exclusive, denominational.

vb. *declare heretical*, condemn,
excommunicate; *secede*, separate, withdraw, break away.

872 HOLINESS

See also 863 (saint).

n. *holiness*, sanctity, consecration, godliness, saintliness, sacredness, goodness, spirituality, unworldliness, piety, devotion; *loyalty*, dutifulness, faithfulness, zeal, commitment, dedication, perseverance, allegiance, earnestness; *reverence*, worship, awe, fear of God, humility, prayerfulness, meditation, contemplation, communion, mysticism; *sanctimoniousness*, pietism, show of piety, religiosity, formalism; *fanaticism*, fundamentalism, bibliolatry; *the saints*, the righteous, the just, man of prayer, believer; *fanatic*, zealot, bigot, Pharisee, scribe, fundamentalist, Bible puncher (*colloq.*), hot-gospeller (*colloq.*), missionary, evangelical, revivalist, pilgrim.

adj. *holy*, pious, devout, consecrated, godly, saintly, sacred, solemn, spiritual, unworldly, otherworldly; *loyal*, faithful, zealous, committed, practising, dedicated, earnest; *reverent*, worshipful, prayerful, humble, meek, pure in heart, God-fearing; *meditative*, contemplative; *sanctimonious*, self-righteous, holier-than-thou, goody-goody (*colloq.*); *fanatical*, fundamentalist, Pharisaic, evangelical, born-again, crusading, fervent, enthusiastic.

vb. *be holy*, fear God, worship, praise, pray, say one's prayers, go to church, persevere, keep the faith, fight the good fight (*colloq.*); *become holy*, repent and believe, be converted, see the error of one's ways, see the light; *make holy*, sanctify, consecrate, dedicate, hallow; *bring to God*, convert, proselytize; *canonize*, beatify.

873 PROFANITY

n. *profanity*, impiety, godlessness, irreverence; *blasphemy*, sacrilege, desecration, violation, defilement; *scoffing*, derision; *worldliness*, materialism; *hypocrisy*, false piety, self-righteousness, cant, lip service; *profane person*, blasphemer, sinner, reprobate; *scoffer*, mocker; *worldling*, materialist; *hypocrite*; *unbeliever*, backslider, apostate.

adj. *profane*, unholy; *impious*, godless, ungodly, unrighteous, sinful, irreverent, irreligious, worldly, earthbound; *hardened*, brazen; *blasphemous*, sacrilegious, swearing; *hypocritical*, self-righteous, insincere, deceitful; *apostate*, unregenerate.

vb. *profane*, desecrate, violate, defile, commit sacrilege; *blaspheme*, swear, take the name of the Lord in vain; *backslide*, apostasize, harden one's heart.

874 **WORSHIP**

n. *worship*, honour, reverence, homage, respect, adoration, veneration, exaltation, devotion, praise; *act of worship*, service, rite, liturgy, mantra; *prayer*, prayer for the day, intercession, vigils, rogation, supplication, litany, benediction, collect, blessing, grace, petition, request, invocation, thanksgiving; *private devotion*, meditation, quiet time, prayer; *hymn*, song, song of praise, carol, worship song, psalm, chant, anthem, canticle, chorus; *worshipper*, adorer, venerator; *churchgoer*, Christian, communicant; *congregation*, church, flock, assembly; *supplicant*, intercessor, petitioner, man of prayer.

adj. *worshipping*, devoted, reverent, supplicant, devout, prayerful, religious; *worshipful*, reverential, solemn, sacred, holy, devotional, liturgical; *meditating*, praying, interceding, communicating, kneeling; *worshipped*, revered, adored.

vb. *worship*, revere, honour, adore, venerate, exalt, praise, glorify, respect, do worship to, pay homage to, homage, laud, humble oneself, prostrate oneself, kneel, genuflect; *pray*, say a prayer, say one's prayers, meditate; *give thanks*, thank, bless; *petition*, supplicate, intercede, entreat, ask, invoke, beseech; *idolize*, deify; *sing hymns*, sing psalms, chant.

875 **IDOLATRY**

n. *idolatry*, false worship, idolism, idol-worship, image-worship, iconolatry; *heathenism*, paganism, irreligion, fetishism, anthropomorphism, demonism, demonolatry, devil-worship, sun-worship, hero-worship, animal-worship, mumbo jumbo, hocus-pocus, sorcery; *idolization*, apotheosis, deification; *idol*, graven image, false god, image, icon, statue, fetish, totem; *idolater*, idol-worshipper, pagan, heathen, idolizer, fetishist, demonist, devil-worshipper; *idol-maker*, image-maker.

adj. *idolatrous*, heathen, pagan, fetishistic, idol-worshipping, devil-worshipping.

vb. *idolatrize*, worship idols, worship the golden calf; *enshrine*, deify, apotheosize; *idolize*, worship, put on a pedestal, sing the praises of, dote on, treasure.

876 **SORCERY**

See also 864 (devil).

n. *sorcery*, witchcraft, the craft, wicca, wizardry, magic, superstition, occultism, diabolism, black magic, black art; *miracle-working*, thaumaturgy; *witch-doctoring*, voodooism; *exorcism*, ghost-laying; *magic rite*, invocation, incantation, spell; *enchantment*, bewitchment, curse, hoodoo, evil eye, jinx, influence, possession, trance; *magic word*, hocus-pocus, abracadabra, open sesame, mumbo jumbo; *charm*, fetish, amulet, talisman, mascot, lucky charm; *sorcerer*, witch, wizard, enchanter, spellbinder; *magician*, conjuror, juggler, illusionist; *witch-doctor*, medicine-man, shaman, voodoo; *seer*, soothsayer, wise man, diviner, clairvoyant; *astrologer*, alchemist; *miracle-worker*, thaumaturgist; *spiritualist*, medium, spirit-raiser, occultist, necromancer, exorcist; *spiritism*, spiritualism, spirit communication; *séance*, ouija board, planchette, automatic writing, table-turning.

adj. *sorcerous*, devilish, diabolic, occult, necromantic; *magical*, spellbinding, enchanting, supernatural, uncanny, weird, eerie; *bewitched*, enchanted, spellbound, charmed; *cursed*, under the evil eye.

vb. *practise sorcery*, do magic, divine, conjure; *exorcise*, lay ghosts; *raise spirits*, call up spirits; *recite a spell*, recite an incantation, wave a wand; *bewitch*, enchant, charm, fascinate, spellbind; *possess*, curse, put under a curse; *hold a séance*.

877 **OCCULTISM**

See also 455 (prediction); 864 (devil).

n. *occultism*, mysticism, religion, occult lore; *astrology*, alchemy, divination, prediction; *hypnotism*, hypnosis; *spiritualism*, spirit communication, sitting, séance; *spirit manifestation*, ghost, automatic writing, spirit message; *psychics*, parapsychology, psychic science, ESP, clairvoyance, intuition, second sight, telepathy, psychokinesis, spoon-bending; *mystic*, yogi, esoteric; *fortune-teller*, crystal-gazer, palmist; *spiritualist*, medium; *psychic*, clairvoyant, telepathist, mind-reader; *seer*, prophet, oracle.

adj. *occult*, cabbalistic, religious, mystic, mysterious, dark, transcendental, supernatural, paranormal; *psychic*, psychical, telepathic, clairvoyant, fey.

vb. *practise occultism*, alchemize, astrologize, transform, divine; *practise spiritualism*, study spiritualism; *hold a séance*, attend a séance; *materialize*, dematerialize; *hypnotize*, mesmerize.

878 **ECCLESIASTICISM**

n. *ecclesiasticism*, churchdom, the church, ministry; *call*, vocation, mission; *holy orders*, ordination, induction, appointment, installation; *Holy Office*, priesthood, pastorship, papacy, primacy, incumbency; *parish*, diocese, bishopric, see; *preaching*, spiritual guidance, pastoral care, confession, absolution, ministration; *prayer*, fellowship, communion; *synod*, convocation, council, chapter, tribunal.

adj. *ecclesiastical*, orthodox, authoritative, apostolic, spiritual; *priestly*, sacerdotal, ministerial, pastoral, pontifical, papal, episcopal, clerical.

vb. *ordain*, order, enthrone, frock; *consecrate*, sanctify; *take holy orders*, be ordained.

879 **CLERGY**

n. *clergy*, hierarchy, clerical order; *clergyman/-woman*, servant of God, man/woman of the cloth, preacher, minister, pastor, priest, prelate, vicar, parson, rector, parish priest, curate, chaplain, cleric, padre; *archbishop*, bishop, deacon, archdeacon, dean, canon, prior, primate, patriarch, cardinal; *pope*, pontiff, the Holy Father, the Vicar of Christ; *spiritual director*, (father) confessor; *monk*, friar, prior, abbot, superior, Benedictine, Trappist, Franciscan, Augustinian, Cistercian; *nun*, sister, bride of Christ, abbess, Mother Superior; *missionary*, evangelist; *rabbi*, imam, caliph, ayatollah, lama.

adj. *clerical*, ordained, pastoral, episcopal, papal, monastic.

vb. *be ordained*, enter the ministry, take holy orders, take the veil.

880 **LAITY**

n. *laity*, layman, lay people, lay brethren; *parish*, flock, sheep, fold, community, church, congregation, assembly; *parishioner*, church member, elder, deacon, lay preacher, lay reader, novice, altar boy, chorister, beadle, verger, sexton, church officer.

adj. *lay*, laical, secular, non-clerical, unordained; *temporal*, of the world, civil; *irreligious*, unholy, profane, unsacred, unconsecrated.

vb. *laicize*, secularize, deconsecrate.

881 **RITUAL**

See also 787 (formality).

n. *ritual*, custom, institution, observance, practice; *order*, form, litany, liturgy, ordinance; *rite*, ceremony, celebration; *service*, divine worship, matins, evensong, vespers, mass, prayer meeting, Bible study, Sunday School; *sacrament*, Holy Communion, the Lord's Supper, Eucharist, baptism, christening, marriage service, nuptial mass, requiem mass; *ritual object*, cross, crucifix, altar, candle, chalice, incense, holy water, sacred relics, prayer wheel, prayer book, hymn book, psalter; *clerical dress*, canonicals, surplice, vestment, cassock, chasuble, cope, mitre, staff, crook, crosier; *holy day*, feast day, festival, the Sabbath, the Lord's Day, Advent, Christmas, Epiphany, Lent, Shrove Tuesday, Ash Wednesday, Easter, Good Friday, Whitsun, Pentecost, Passover.

adj. *ritual*, formal, solemn, ceremonial, customary, liturgical.

vb. *perform ritual*, celebrate, observe, keep; *officiate*, minister, baptize, confirm, ordain, excommunicate; *worship*, pray, take communion; *bless*, dedicate, consecrate; *kneel*, genuflect, bow, cross oneself.

882 **TEMPLE**

n. *temple*, shrine, sanctuary, pantheon, place of worship, house of prayer, holy place; *church*, house of God, kirk, chapel, tabernacle, meeting-house, mission; *cathedral*, minster, abbey; *synagogue*, mosque; *monastery*, friary, priory, nunnery, convent; *parsonage*, presbytery, rectory, manse, vicarage, deanery, the Vatican; *cemetery*, graveyard, churchyard; *altar*, font, pulpit, lectern, pew; *nave*, aisle, transept, chancel, choir, vestry, crypt; *tower*, steeple, belfry, buttress, cloister, lych-gate.

How to use this index

Almost all the words and phrases contained in the text of the *Pocket Thesaurus* are included in this index. Two categories, however, are excluded:

1 Compounds such as *duck-egg blue, kingfisher blue,* etc; *hydrogen bomb, petrol bomb,* etc; *trench warfare, naval warfare,* etc; and others of a similar type are not in the index. For items like these, you should simply look up the more general terms *blue, bomb, warfare,* etc, and then turn to the relevant sections of the thesaurus where you will find a compete list of the words you are looking for. For example, at Section 391 BLUE, you would find *sky-blue, light blue, powder blue, duck-egg blue, Cambridge blue, Wedgwood blue; kingfisher blue, peacock blue, electric blue, dark blue, Oxford blue, royal blue* and *midnight blue.* There is therefore no need for any of these to have a separate listing in the index.

2 'Difficult' words such as *cerulean, champaign, ecdysiast, limn, pirogue, quincunx, sempiternal, sesquipedalian, strabismus, threnody* and *viridian* are likewise not included in the index. While these might well be the very words you are looking for in the text of the thesaurus, they would be very unlikely starting-points for searches in the index. As a general rule, if you cannot find a particular word in the index, think of a simpler or more general word related to it and look for that word instead.

Words and phrases are listed in this index in strict alphabetical order; thus:

> go
> goad
> go against
> go against the grain
> go-ahead
> goal
> go all out, etc

Certain words, however, are ignored for the purposes of alphabetical order: i) Initial *the* and *a/an*; thus:

> apple-cheeked
> *the* apple of one's eye
> apple-pie order

bridge
a bridge too far
bridging loan

ii) *One's* and *oneself*; thus:

achieve
achieve *one's* heart's desire
achievement
acquit
acquit *oneself*
acquittal
acquitted

iii) the abbreviations *sb* (= 'somebody'), *sb's* (= 'somebody's'), and *sth* (= 'something'); thus:

cut costs
cut *sb* dead
cut down
cut *sb* down to size
cut in

bite
bite *sb's* head off
bite the dust
biting

do for
do *sth* for effect/show
dog

As can be seen from the above examples, words that are ignored in this way are printed in italics in the index.

Index

across-the-board *adj.*
69
across the board *adv.*
15, 51
acrostic *n.* 495
acrylic *n.* 490
act *n.* 523, 607, 661,
771, 852; *vb.* 138,
523, 607, 621
act for *vb.* 676
acting *adj.* 607, 676
action *n.* 136, 138,
607, 643, 645, 830,
856
Action Man *n.* 761
action replay *n.* 88
actions *n.* 621
activate *vb.* 136, 141,
732
activation *n.* 732
active *adj.* 136, 141,
500, 607, 609
activist *n.* 607, 634
activity *n.* 234, 607,
609, 761
act of courtesy *n.* 791
act of discourtesy *n.*
792
act of friendship *n.*
793
act of God *n.* 536
act of inhumanity *n.*
806
act of worship *n.* 874
act on *vb.* 136
act on impulse *vb.* 96,
544, 548
actor *n.* 523
act out *vb.* 484
actress *n.* 523
Acts *n.* 868
act the fool *vb.* 443
actual *adj.* 1, 3, 101,
282, 409
actuality *n.* 1, 3
actualization *n.* 1
actualize *vb.* 3
actually *adv.* 1
actuarial *adj.* 75, 720
actuary *n.* 75, 720
acuity *n.* 296
acumen *n.* 396, 418,
429, 444
acute *adj.* 296, 599
acuteness *n.* 296, 599
adage *n.* 442

adagio *adv.* 246
Adam *n.* 332
adamant *adj.* 542
adamantine *adj.* 289
adapt *vb.* 19, 72, 121,
125, 462, 518
adaptability *n.* 125,
130, 578
adaptable *adj.* 19, 69,
72, 125, 130, 578
adaptation *n.* 19, 72,
121, 462
adapter *n.* 121
add *vb.* 33, 35, 75
addendum *n.* 35
add fuel to the flames
vb. 341
addiction *n.* 755, 844
addition *n.* 33, 35, 75
additional *adj.* 33, 35
additive *n.* 35, 344
addled *adj.* 343, 597
add-on *n.* 35, 575
add on *vb.* 35
address *n.* 158, 522,
532; *vb.* 515, 532
addressee *n.* 515, 532
address the question
vb. 9
address *oneself* to *vb.*
562
add up *vb.* 400, 460
adenoidal *adj.* 529
adept *adj.* 624
adeptness *n.* 624
adequacy *n.* 573
adequate *adj.* 27, 141,
573
ADHD *n.* 281
adhere *vb.* 43, 181,
688, 695
adherence *n.* 43, 688
adherent *n.* 634
adhering *adj.* 43
adhesion *n.* 43, 695
adhesive *adj.* 40, 43,
318, 695; *n.* 42, 43,
318
adhesiveness *n.* 318
ad hoc *adj.* 94, 101,
121, 548, 560
ad hominem *adv.* 70
adieu *n.* 262
ad infinitum *adv.* 89
adipose *adj.* 319
adjacent *adj.* 176

adjectival *adj.* 500
adjective *n.* 500
adjoin *vb.* 173, 176
adjoining *adj.* 173,
176
adjourn *vb.* 114
adjournment *n.* 62,
114
adjudicate *vb.* 429,
647, 856
adjudication *n.* 429
adjudicator *n.* 429,
647
adjunct *n.* 35
adjust *vb.* 19, 72, 121
adjustment *n.* 19,
121, 549
adjust to *vb.* 549
ad-lib *vb.* 96, 523,
548
ad-libbing *n.* 548
ad libitum *adv.* 535
adman *n.* 470
admass *n.* 69, 470
administer *vb.* 622,
700, 854
administer justice *vb.*
854
administration *n.*
136, 622, 634, 657,
700, 854
administrative *adj.*
136, 622, 657, 854
administrator *n.* 622
admirable *adj.* 582,
774, 825
admiral *n.* 648
admiration *n.* 774,
795, 823, 825
admire *vb.* 774, 795,
823, 825
admirer *n.* 795, 825
admiring *adj.* 795,
823
admissibility *n.* 51,
265
admissible *adj.* 265,
825
admission *n.* 51, 263,
265, 468, 699, 473
admission charge *n.*
721
admit *vb.* 51, 263,
265, 436, 468, 473,
699, 841
admit defeat *vb.* 642

admittance *n.* 265,
699
admixture *n.* 35, 38
admonish *vb.* 602
admonishment *n.*
602, 623
admonition *n.* 623,
826
ad nauseam *adv.* 88,
506
ado *n.* 609
adolescence *n.* 111
adolescent *adj.* 111;
n. 111
adopt *vb.* 12, 43, 265,
434, 564, 688, 825
adopted *adj.* 12, 564
adoption *n.* 12, 564,
825
adoptive *adj.* 12
adoptive parent *n.*
154, 668
adorable *adj.* 734,
795
adoration *n.* 795,
823, 874
adore *vb.* 734, 795,
874
adored *adj.* 795, 874
adorer *n.* 874
adoring *adj.* 795
adorn *vb.* 766
adorned *adj.* 766
adornment *n.* 510,
766
adrenalin *n.* 750
adroit *adj.* 624
adroitness *n.* 624
adulation *n.* 825, 827
adulatory *adj.* 827
adult *adj.* 112, 69,
851; *n.* 112
adult education *n.*
475
adulterate *vb.* 38,
121, 144, 288, 305,
587
adulterated *adj.* 587
adulteration *n.* 288,
587
adulterous *adj.* 851
adultery *n.* 851
adulthood *n.* 112
advance *adj.* 212; *n.*
33, 234, 253, 259,
261, 592, 639, 651,

agonize *vb.* 337, 735

agonizing *adj.* 337, 735

agony *n.* 337, 735

agrarian *adj.* 328

agree *vb.* 9, 17, 19, 72, 436, 500, 537, 551, 562, 633, 636, 646, 663, 683, 684, 825

agreeable *adj.* 336, 436, 535, 537, 636, 684, 736

agreed *adj.* 636, 684

agreeing *adj.* 19

agreement *n.* 9, 11, 15, 19, 72, 436, 500, 551, 562, 633, 636, 646, 646, 683, 684, 825

agree to differ *vb.* 437, 635

agricultural *adj.* 328

agriculture *n.* 328

agronomic *adj.* 328

agronomist *n.* 328

agronomy *n.* 328

ahead *adj.* 104; *adv.* 59, 212, 253

ahead of time *adv.* 98

AI *n.* 75

aid *n.* 138, 596, 631, 698, 807; *vb.* 596, 631, 698

aide *n.* 631, 666

aide-de-camp *n.* 631, 666

aide-memoire *n.* 448

Aids *n.* 589

aikido *n.* 643

ail *vb.* 589

ailing *adj.* 589

ailment *n.* 589

aim *n.* 249, 553; *vb.* 249, 553, 748

aim for *vb.* 249

air *n.* 286, 304, 306, 316, 365, 394, 621; *vb.* 306, 316, 348, 468

airborne *adj.* 238

air bubble *n.* 306

airbus *n.* 244

air commodore *n.* 648

air-condition *vb.* 316

air-conditioning *n.* 306

aircraft *n.* 244

aircraft carrier *n.* 243

airfield *n.* 238

air force *n.* 648

air freshener *n.* 348, 349

airgun *n.* 761

air hostess *n.* 238, 666

airiness *n.* 286, 306

airing *n.* 306

air kiss *n.* 791, 800

airlane *n.* 238

airlift *n.* 238

airline *n.* 238

airliner *n.* 244

air-mail *adj.* 515

airman *n.* 238

air marshal *n.* 598, 648

Air Miles *n.* 238, 690

air pipe *n.* 316

airport *n.* 238, 553

air rage *n.* 802

air raid *n.* 639

air-raid shelter *n.* 600

airs *n.* 771

airship *n.* 244

airstream *n.* 316

airstrip *n.* 238

air terminal *n.* 238

airtight *adj.* 233

air travel *n.* 238

air vice marshal *n.* 648

airwaves *n.* 472

airway *n.* 316

airwoman *n.* 238

airworthy *adj.* 238

airy *adj.* 304, 306, 316, 824

aisle *n.* 240, 882

ajar *adj.* 232

akimbo *adj.* 220

akin *adj.* 17

à la *adv.* 17

alabaster *n.* 383

à la carte *adj.* 545

alacritous *adj.* 245

alacrity *n.* 96, 245, 537, 609

à la mode *adj.* 770

alarm *n.* 97, 355, 484, 599, 750; *vb.* 750

alarm bell *n.* 602

alarm clock *n.* 602

alarmed *adj.* 750

alarming *adj.* 750

albino *adj.* 382, 383

album *n.* 369, 486

albumen *n.* 318

alchemist *n.* 876

alchemize *vb.* 877

alchemy *n.* 121, 125, 877

alcohol *n.* 267

alcoholic *n.* 848

Alcoholics Anony-mous *n.* 847

alcoholism *n.* 848

alcove *n.* 158, 227

alderman *n.* 665

alert *adj.* 404, 730, 754; *vb.* 602

alertness *n.* 404, 730, 754

alert to *vb.* 404

al fresco *adj.* 306; *adv.* 198, 232

algebra *n.* 75

algebraic *adj.* 75

alias *adj.* 497; *n.* 498

alibi *n.* 829

alien *adj.* 6, 10, 54, 284; *n.* 54, 161, 330, 790

alienable *adj.* 697

alienate *vb.* 696, 697, 794, 796

alienated *adj.* 794

alienation *n.* 696, 697, 794

alienness *n.* 6, 54

alight *adj.* 339; *vb.* 261, 275

align *vb.* 15, 19, 55, 103, 222

alignment *n.* 19, 55, 222

alike *adj.* 15

alimentation *n.* 267

alimony *n.* 571, 798

alive *adj.* 37, 730

alive and kicking *adj.* 322

Allah *n.* 862

all anyhow *adv.* 16, 56

all around *adv.* 206

allay *vb.* 148

all but *adv.* 50

allegation *n.* 420, 473, 551, 830

allege *vb.* 473, 551

alleged *adj.* 456

allegiance *n.* 670, 821, 872

allegorical *adj.* 458

allegory *n.* 458

all-embracing *adj.* 47, 49, 51

allergic *adj.* 334, 758

allergy *n.* 334, 589, 758

alleviate *vb.* 148, 631, 740

alleviation *n.* 148, 631, 740

alley *n.* 240

all found *adj.* 571

alliance *n.* 40, 45, 633, 634, 684, 797

allied *adj.* 40, 45, 636

all-in *adj.* 51, 142, 619

all in all *adv.* 27

all-inclusive *adj.* 69

all in the mind *adj.* 408

alliteration *n.* 17, 88, 521

all-knowing *adj.* 438, 862

allocate *vb.* 700

allocation *n.* 700

all of a sudden *adv.* 451

allot *vb.* 23, 698, 700, 819

allotment *n.* 165, 329, 700

all out *adv.* 617

all over *adv.* 49, 156

allow *vb.* 434, 436, 660, 677, 722, 825

allow credit *vb.* 714

allowable *adj.* 829, 852

allowance *n.* 28, 422, 559, 631, 677, 690, 700, 719

allowed *adj.* 677

allow for *vb.* 28, 559

alloy *n.* 38, 45, 321, 569; *vb.* 45

all-powerful *adj.* 141, 862

all present and correct *adv.* 55

all-round *adj.* 16, 49

all-rounder *n.* 49, 80

all shipshape and Bristol fashion *adj.* 55

all the rage *adj.* 770

all the same *adv.* 17

all the world and his wife *n.* 47

all things being equal *adv.* 11

all things considered *adv.* 27

all-time great *n.* 582

all together *adv.* 66

all told *adv.* 47

allude *vb.* 458

allure *n.* 257, 736; *vb.* 736, 795

alluring *adj.* 736, 763

allusion *n.* 458

allusive *adj.* 458, 465

alluvial *adj.* 37, 311

alluvium *n.* 311

all-wise *adj.* 862

ally *n.* 193; *vb.* 40, 45, 634

alma mater *n.* 477

almanac *n.* 76, 97

almighty *adj.* 862

the Almighty *n.* 862

almost *adv.* 30, 50, 173

alms *n.* 698

aloft *adv.* 184

alone *adj.* 41, 79

aloneness *n.* 79

alongside *adv.* 194, 214

aloof *adj.* 41, 44, 172, 403, 733, 790, 794

aloofness *n.* 44, 172, 403, 733, 790

alopecia *n.* 203

a lot *n.* 573

aloud *adj.* 526

alp *n.* 184

alpha *n.* 61

alpha and omega *n.* 49

Alpha and Omega *n.* 862

alphabet *n.* 495, 513

alphabetical *adj.* 495

alphabetize *vb.* 57, 495

alpha male/female *n.* 31

alpine *adj.* 184, 329

alpinism *n.* 274

alpinist *n.* 274

also-ran *n.* 32, 652

altar *n.* 881, 882

altar boy *n.* 880

alter *vb.* 121

alterant *n.* 121

alteration *n.* 121

altercation *n.* 410, 643

alter ego *n.* 11, 13

alternate *adj.* 65; *vb.* 11, 65, 92, 119, 280

alternately *adv.* 119

alternating *adj.* 11, 119, 280

alternation *n.* 11, 65, 119, 280

alternative *adj.* 128; *n.* 545

alternative date *n.* 102

altitude *n.* 23, 184

alto *n.* 368

altogether *adv.* 47

altruism *n.* 805, 807, 833

altruist *n.* 805, 807

altruistic *adj.* 805, 807

alum *n.* 346

a.m. *adv.* 109

amalgam *n.* 38, 45

amalgamate *vb.* 38, 40, 45, 633

amalgamation *n.* 633

amanuensis *n.* 486, 666

amass *vb.* 66, 570, 711

amateur *n.* 625, 768

amateurish *adj.* 439, 625

amateurishness *n.* 439

amatory *adj.* 795

amaze *vb.* 451, 732, 759

amazed *adj.* 759

amazement *n.* 451, 759

amazing *adj.* 451, 759

amazon *n.* 143, 751

amazonian *adj.* 143

ambassador *n.* 675

amber *n.* 386, 388

ambergris *n.* 349

ambidexterity *n.* 81

ambidextrous *adj.* 81, 214

ambience *n.* 206

ambient *adj.* 206

ambiguity *n.* 81, 411, 428, 458, 479, 504, 543

ambiguous *adj.* 81, 411, 428, 458, 461, 479, 504, 543

ambition *n.* 748, 755, 755

ambitious *adj.* 748, 755

ambivalence *n.* 81, 428

ambivalent *adj.* 81, 428

amble *n.* 246, 616; *vb.* 234, 236, 246, 616

ambrosia *n.* 267, 342

ambulance *n.* 242

ambulant *adj.* 234, 236

ambush *n.* 601; *vb.* 451, 469, 601

amelioration *n.* 592

amenable *adj.* 537, 642

amend *vb.* 592

amended *adj.* 592

amendment *n.* 592

amends *n.* 28, 596, 704, 814

amethyst *n.* 392, 766

amiability *n.* 736, 742, 791

amiable *adj.* 736, 742, 791

amicability *n.* 793

amicable *adj.* 793

amidst *adv.* 38, 63

amiss *adv.* 836

amity *n.* 793

ammonia *n.* 350

ammonite *n.* 321

ammunition *n.* 649

amnesia *n.* 449

amnesiac *adj.* 449

amnesty *n.* 123, 644, 646, 813; *vb.* 449

amoeba *n.* 217

among *adv.* 38, 63

amoral *adj.* 851

amorous *adj.* 795

amorousness *n.* 795

amorphous *adj.* 217

amorphousness *n.* 217

amount *n.* 23

amount due/outstanding/owing *n.* 715

amount to *vb.* 74

amour *n.* 795

amphetamine *n.* 849

amphibian *n.* 326; *n.* 326

amphibious *adj.* 81

amphitheatre *n.* 210, 477

ample *adj.* 23, 29, 86, 180, 182

ampleness *n.* 182

amplification *n.* 170

amplifier *n.* 355

amplify *vb.* 170, 506, 519

amplitude *n.* 23, 29, 168, 180

amply *adv.* 29

amputate *vb.* 36

amputation *n.* 36

amulet *n.* 876

amuse *vb.* 736, 761

amusement *n.* 761

amusing *adj.* 744, 761

anachronism *n.* 98

anachronistic *adj.* 98, 102

anacoluthon *n.* 65

anaemia *n.* 144, 382, 589

anaemic *adj.* 144, 382

anaesthesia *n.* 335

anaesthetic *adj.* 596, 740; *n.* 335, 740

anaesthetize *vb.* 335, 596, 740

anaesthetized *adj.* 335

anagram *n.* 196, 496

arbitrator *n.* 63, 148, 429, 647

arboreal *adj.* 327

arboretum *n.* 329

arboriculture *n.* 329

arbour *n.* 165

arc *n.* 221

arcade *n.* 221, 710

arch *adj.* 49; *n.* 42, 221, 226; *vb.* 221, 225, 226

archaeology *n.* 105

archaic *adj.* 105, 107

archaism *n.* 105, 107

archangel *n.* 863

archbishop *n.* 776, 879

archdeacon *n.* 879

archduke *n.* 776

arched *adj.* 221, 226

archer *n.* 255, 648

archery *n.* 255

archetypal *adj.* 22

archetype *n.* 22

archipelago *n.* 311

architect *n.* 132, 149, 613

architectural *adj.* 216, 298, 510, 766

architecture *n.* 216, 298

archive *n.* 105, 486

archivist *n.* 486

arctic *adj.* 215, 340

ardent *adj.* 729, 795

ardour *n.* 729

arduous *adj.* 617, 628

arduousness *n.* 628

area *n.* 23, 156, 157, 168

arena *n.* 157, 210, 470, 645

argot *n.* 494

arguable *adj.* 410, 412, 423, 428, 829

arguably *adv.* 423

argue *vb.* 400, 410, 437, 635

argue against *vb.* 632

argue the toss *vb.* 410

arguing *adj.* 856

argument *n.* 409, 410, 412, 437, 635, 643, 802

argumentation *n.* 400, 410

argumentative *adj.* 410

argumentativeness *n.* 410

arguments *n.* 856

arhythmic *adj.* 120

aria *n.* 367

arid *adj.* 153, 309

aridity *n.* 153, 309

arise *vb.* 1, 61, 101, 133, 276, 394

aristocracy *n.* 776

aristocrat *n.* 776

aristocratic *adj.* 774, 776

arithmetic *n.* 75

arithmetical *adj.* 75

arm *n.* 35; *vb.* 571, 640, 645

armaments *n.* 649

arm candy *n.* 763

armchair *adj.* 456

armed *adj.* 640, 645

armed conflict *n.* 645

armed forces *n.* 640, 648

armed neutrality *n.* 644

armful *n.* 23

arm in arm *adv.* 40, 176

armistice *n.* 123, 644, 646

armlock *n.* 695

arm of the law *n.* 854

armour *n.* 202, 289, 640

armoured *adj.* 640

armoury *n.* 649

arms *n.* 649

arms freeze *n.* 646

arm-twisting *n.* 664

army *n.* 86, 648

aroma *n.* 347, 349

aromatic *adj.* 349; *n.* 344

around the clock *adv.* 95, 97

arousal *n.* 336, 732

arouse *vb.* 334, 336, 732

arpeggio *n.* 64

arraign *vb.* 830

arraignment *n.* 830

arrange *vb.* 55, 57, 132, 298, 368, 559

arranged *adj.* 57, 684

arranged marriage *n.* 797

arrange in succession *vb.* 64

arrangement *n.* 55, 57, 216, 298, 367, 559, 684

arranger *n.* 368

arrant *adj.* 49

array *n.* 55; *vb.* 57, 204

arrears *n.* 654, 715

arrest *n.* 668, 703; *vb.* 123, 668, 703, 732, 830

arrested development *n.* 397

arrival *n.* 261

arrive *vb.* 261, 322, 394, 651

arrive uninvited *vb.* 789

arriving *adj.* 261

arrogance *n.* 431, 779, 781, 783

arrogant *adj.* 779, 781, 783

arrogate *vb.* 820

arrogation *n.* 820

arrow *n.* 255

arrowhead *n.* 220

arse *n.* 213

arse-licker *n.* 782

arse-licking *n.* 782

arsenal *n.* 570, 649

arson *n.* 150

arsonist *n.* 150

arsy versy *adv.* 56

art *n.* 490

artefact *n.* 149

artery *n.* 240

artful *adj.* 480, 626, 832

artful dodger *n.* 626, 705

artfulness *n.* 480, 626, 832

arthouse *n.* 525

arthritis *n.* 589

article *n.* 282, 500, 519, 707

article of faith *n.* 434

articles of faith *n.* 868

articulacy *n.* 502, 528

articulate *adj.* 496,

502, 528; *vb.* 496, 526, 528

articulation *n.* 526

artificial *adj.* 17, 21, 149, 512, 769, 771

artificial insemination *n.* 12, 152

artificial intelligence *n.* 75

artificiality *n.* 512, 769, 771

artificial light *n.* 374

artificial respiration *n.* 322

artificial sweetener *n.* 345

artillery *n.* 255

artilleryman *n.* 648

artisan *n.* 149, 611, 613

artist *n.* 490, 624

artiste *n.* 368

artistic *adj.* 490

artistic medium *n.* 490

artistry *n.* 490

artless *adj.* 478, 509, 627, 831, 839

artlessness *n.* 478, 509, 627, 839

art paper *n.* 569

as a result *adv.* 60, 133

as a result of *prep.* 132

as a reward *adv.* 859

as a rule *adv.* 27, 69

as a whole *adv.* 47

asbestos *n.* 569

ASBO *n.* 668, 860

ascend *vb.* 184, 274

ascendancy *n.* 31, 139, 141, 657

ascendant *n.* 284

ascending *adj.* 274

ascending order *n.* 55

ascension *n.* 274, 866

ascent *n.* 184, 234, 274

ascertainable *adj.* 417

ascetic *adj.* 659, 843; *n.* 659, 731, 843, 863

asceticism *n.* 659, 843

ascribable *adj.* 134

ascribe *vb.* 134

aseptic *adj.* 586

bearings *n.* 159, 249, 484

bearish *adj.* 275

bear malice *vb.* 802, 806

bear out *vb.* 417, 420, 440, 829

bear the cost *vb.* 718

bear the cost of *vb.* 716

bear with *vb.* 813

bear witness *vb.* 420

be as good as *one's* word *vb.* 688

beast *n.* 147, 326, 838

be as like as two peas in a pod *vb.* 13

be as thick as thieves *vb.* 793

beastly *adj.* 583, 737, 796, 806

beast of burden *n.* 241

beat *n.* 88, 119, 158, 280, 521; *vb.* 119, 247, 280, 281, 358, 368, 555, 651, 860

beat about the bush *vb.* 411

be at a loose end *vb.* 608

be at a loss for words *vb.* 527

beat *one's* breast *vb.* 747

be at cross-purposes *vb.* 441

be at death's door *vb.* 323

beat down *vb.* 707

be at ease *vb.* 618

beaten *adj.* 652

beater *n.* 555

be at fault *vb.* 818

beat hollow *vb.* 31

beatified *adj.* 863

beatify *vb.* 774, 872

beating *n.* 651, 652

beat it *vb.* 262

beatitude *n.* 863

be at odds *vb.* 18

be at odds with *vb.* 794

be at sea *vb.* 461

beat six/ten bells out of *vb.* 860

beat the drum *vb.* 470

be at the ready *vb.* 450

beat up *vb.* 147, 639

be at variance *vb.* 18

beau *n.* 770, 795

beautician *n.* 765

beautification *n.* 765

beautiful *adj.* 511, 736, 763

the beautiful game *n.* 761

the beautiful people *n.* 770

beautify *vb.* 511, 765

beauty *n.* 511, 736, 763

beauty queen *n.* 763

beauty salon *n.* 765

beauty spot *n.* 763

beauty therapist *n.* 765

beauty therapy *n.* 765

beauty treatment *n.* 765

beaver *vb.* 540

be behind the times *vb.* 98

be below par *vb.* 26

be beyond *one vb.* 461

be beyond the bounds of possibility *vb.* 424

be born *vb.* 322

be bound to *vb.* 427

be brittle *vb.* 295

becalmed *adj.* 235

be capricious *vb.* 544

be careful *vb.* 406

be caught in the act *vb.* 840

be caught out *vb.* 451

be caught short *vb.* 268

because of *prep.* 132, 134

be certain to *vb.* 427

be charitable *vb.* 807

be cheap *vb.* 724

be cheerful *vb.* 742

beck *n.* 314

beckon *vb.* 484

become dense *vb.* 287

become holy *vb.* 872

become one *vb.* 79, 797

become popular *vb.* 770

become small *vb.* 30

become teetotal *vb.* 847

be concise *vb.* 505

be consecutive *vb.* 64

be conspicuous *vb.* 162

be conspicuous by *one's* absence *vb.* 163

be contrite *vb.* 841

be convenient *vb.* 580

be converted *vb.* 125, 841, 872

be convex *vb.* 226

be courageous *vb.* 751

be crazy about *vb.* 795

be creditworthy *vb.* 702

be credulous *vb.* 434

be cunning *vb.* 626

be curious *vb.* 402

bed *n.* 175; *vb.* 40

bed and breakfast *n.* 165

bed-blocking *n.* 630

be dead against *vb.* 632

be dear *vb.* 723

be deceived *vb.* 480

bedeck *vb.* 766

be defeated *vb.* 652

be dejected *vb.* 743, 804

be descended from *vb.* 12

be destroyed *vb.* 150

bedevilled *adj.* 656

be difficult *vb.* 628

be diffuse *vb.* 506

bedim *vb.* 376

be disappointed *vb.* 452

be dishonest *vb.* 832

be disinterested *vb.* 833

be disorderly *vb.* 56

be disparate *vb.* 20

be dissatisfied *vb.* 739

be dissimilar *vb.* 18

be dissonant *vb.* 366

bedlam *n.* 56

a bed of roses *n.* 336, 655, 734

be done *vb.* 723

be done for *vb.* 150

bedraggle *vb.* 56

bedraggled *adj.* 56

bedridden *adj.* 142, 235

bedrock *n.* 122, 131, 189, 193

be drunk *vb.* 848

bedsitter *n.* 165

bedtime *n.* 110

be due *vb.* 819

be dying *vb.* 323

be dying for *vb.* 755

be early *vb.* 113

be easy *vb.* 629

beef *vb.* 682, 739

beefcake *n.* 143, 332, 763

beef up *vb.* 33, 35, 170

beehive *n.* 226

be elastic *vb.* 293

beeline *n.* 173, 222, 249, 250

Beelzebub *n.* 864

be engaged on *vb.* 611

be enough *vb.* 573

be entitled *vb.* 819

be equal *vb.* 25

beer belly/gut *n.* 168, 225

the bee's knees *n.* 582

be essential *vb.* 5

beetle-browed *adj.* 228

beetle off *vb.* 262

beetroot *n.* 387

be excessive *vb.* 575

be exempt *vb.* 822

be expected *vb.* 450

be extraneous *vb.* 6

be faint *vb.* 356

be fair *vb.* 817

be faithful to *vb.* 688

be false *vb.* 481

befog *vb.* 375, 376

be fond of *vb.* 757, 795, 800

be foolish *vb.* 445

before *adv.* 99, 105

bulging *adj.* 49, 228
bulk *n.* 23, 29, 168, 182, 285, 287; *vb.* 29
bulk-buy *vb.* 724
bulkhead *n.* 207
bulk large *vb.* 3
bulk up *vb.* 170, 182
bulky *adj.* 23, 29, 168, 182, 285, 287
bull *n.* 326, 332, 554
bulldoze *vb.* 150, 247
bulldozer *n.* 150, 191, 247
bullet *n.* 225, 255, 649, 861
bulletin *n.* 466
bulletproof *adj.* 427, 640
bullion *n.* 711
bullish *adj.* 274
bullock *n.* 326
bull's eye *n.* 200
bullshit *n.* 4, 443
bully *n.* 147, 838; *vb.* 659, 670, 737, 806
bully into *vb.* 551
bulwark *n.* 640
bullwhip *n.* 861
bum *n.* 213, 681, 777; *vb.* 681, 702
bumble *vb.* 625
bumbling *adj.* 625
bumf *n.* 513
bump *n.* 226, 228, 247; *vb.* 247
bumper *adj.* 86
bumper to bumper *adv.* 64, 176
bump off *vb.* 324
bumptious *adj.* 783
bumpy *adj.* 226, 291
the bum's rush *n.* 266
bun *n.* 765
bunch *n.* 66; *vb.* 43, 66
bundle *n.* 23, 66; *vb.* 66
bunfight *n.* 267, 789
bung *n.* 202, 233; *vb.* 233, 255
bungalow *n.* 165
bungee jumping *n.* 761
bungle *vb.* 625
bungler *n.* 625

bungling *n.* 625
bunion *n.* 226
bunk *n.* 459
bunker *n.* 167, 600, 630, 640
buoy *n.* 286
buoyancy *n.* 286, 293, 306
buoyant *adj.* 274, 286, 293, 306, 748
buoy up *vb.* 193
bur *n.* 43
burble *vb.* 445
burden *n.* 285, 409, 656, 735, 737, 821; *vb.* 285
burdened *adj.* 656, 735
burdensome *adj.* 285, 737
bureau *n.* 614
bureaucracy *n.* 622, 657
bureaucrat *n.* 622, 665
bureaucratic *adj.* 622, 657
burgeon *vb.* 33, 152
burgeoning *adj.* 108
burglar *n.* 263, 705, 838
burglary *n.* 705
burgle *vb.* 263, 705
burgundy *n.* 387, 392
burial *n.* 325
buried *adj.* 186, 325, 469
burin *n.* 493
burlesque *adj.* 523; *n.* 21, 744, 773; *vb.* 21
burly *adj.* 143
burn *n.* 314, 339; *vb.* 337, 339, 386, 472, 486
burn alive *vb.* 860
burning *adj.* 339, 729; *n.* 339, 860
burnish *vb.* 301
burn the candle at both ends *vb.* 844
burn the midnight oil *vb.* 114, 476
burnt-out *adj.* 144, 150
burp *n.* 316; *vb.* 316

burr *n.* 494, 526
burrow *n.* 165, 227, 232, 600; *vb.* 227
bursar *n.* 571, 699, 711
bursary *n.* 631, 690, 719
burst *n.* 357, 605, 609; *vb.* 147, 232
burst forth *vb.* 605
bursting at the seams *adj.* 49
burst into tears *vb.* 747
burst of speed *n.* 615
burst out *vb.* 357
bury *vb.* 186, 269, 325, 469, 487
bury the hatchet *vb.* 449, 636, 646, 813
bus *n.* 242
bush *n.* 327
the bush telegraph *n.* 471
business *n.* 562, 609, 611, 634, 707
businesslike *adj.* 611, 624
businessman/ -woman *n.* 613, 707
busker *n.* 368
bust *adj.* 717; *n.* 226, 492
bust a gut *vb.* 617
bustle *n.* 234, 281, 609, 615; *vb.* 609
busty *adj.* 226
busy *adj.* 510, 609, 611
busy bee *n.* 609
busybody *n.* 402, 623
busy *oneself* with *vb.* 562
butch *adj.* 332
butcher *n.* 147, 150, 324; *vb.* 150, 324
butcher's *n.* 370
butchery *n.* 324
butler *n.* 571, 613, 666
butt *n.* 773; *vb.* 176, 247
butter *n.* 290, 319, 389; *vb.* 319
buttercup *n.* 389

butterfingers *n.* 625
butterflies *n.* 281, 750
butterfly mind *n.* 405
butter mountain *n.* 570
butter up *vb.* 827
buttery *adj.* 319
butt in *vb.* 65, 263
buttock-clenching *adj.* 737
buttocks *n.* 213
button *n.* 226
buttoned-up *adj.* 467
buttonhole *n.* 766; *vb.* 532
buttonholer *n.* 762
buttress *n.* 131, 143, 193, 228, 882; *vb.* 131, 143, 193
buxom *adj.* 168, 226
buy *n.* 708; *vb.* 434, 690, 697, 708
buy and sell *vb.* 707
buyer *n.* 708
buyers' market *n.* 724
buy in *vb.* 570
buying *n.* 708
buying and selling *n.* 707
buy on hire purchase/the never-never *vb.* 715
buy out *vb.* 708
buy up *vb.* 570, 708
buzz *n.* 358, 471, 729, 849; *vb.* 361, 364
buzz off *vb.* 262
buzzword *n.* 496
bwana *n.* 778
by *oneself adv.* 79
by and large *adv.* 69
by chance *adv.* 135, 554
by comparison *adv.* 9
by degrees *adv.* 24, 65
by fits and starts *adv.* 65
bygone *adj.* 105, 107
bygone days *n.* 105
bylaw *n.* 71, 852
by law *adv.* 819, 852
by leaps and bounds *adv.* 253
by means of *prep.* 138
by night *adv.* 110
by order *adv.* 852

canvasser *n.* 681

canvassing *n.* 681

canyoning *n.* 761

cap *n.* 188, 202, 233; *vb.* 188, 202, 584

capability *n.* 141, 423, 624

capable *adj.* 141, 624

capacious *adj.* 23, 29, 156

capacity *n.* 23, 156, 624, 854

capillary *n.* 183

capital *adj.* 495; *n.* 495, 567, 694, 701, 711

capital gain *n.* 690, 719

capital gains tax *n.* 721

capitalize *vb.* 711

capitalize on *vb.* 115, 564, 690

capital punishment *n.* 324, 860

capital transfer *n.* 697

capital transfer tax *n.* 721

capitulate *vb.* 642

capitulation *n.* 642

capon *n.* 332

caprice *n.* 120, 544

capricious *adj.* 120, 130, 428, 541, 543, 544

capriciousness *n.* 120, 130, 428, 541, 544

capsizal *n.* 196

capsize *vb.* 26, 196

capstone *n.* 188

capsule *n.* 167, 244, 596

captain *n.* 31, 237, 622, 648; *vb.* 31, 237

caption *n.* 513

captious *adj.* 411, 739, 826

captiousness *n.* 546

captivate *vb.* 139, 257, 404, 732, 736, 795

captivating *adj.* 732, 795

captivation *n.* 732

captive *adj.* 668; *n.* 671

captive audience *n.* 532

captivity *n.* 668

captor *n.* 703

capture *n.* 703; *vb.* 488, 703

car *n.* 242

carafe *n.* 167

caramel *n.* 386

carapace *n.* 202, 289

caravan *n.* 64, 165

carbon *n.* 384

carbonate *vb.* 304

carbonated *adj.* 304

carbon copy *n.* 13, 21

carbon paper *n.* 569

carbon sink *n.* 696

carborundum *n.* 296

carboy *n.* 167

carbuncle *n.* 226, 767

carcass *n.* 324

carcinogen *n.* 597

carcinogenic *adj.* 597

card *n.* 73, 330, 485, 744

cardboard *adj.* 489

card-carrying *adj.* 43, 634, 870

card game *n.* 761

cardinal *adj.* 3, 74; *n.* 879

cardinal point *n.* 249

care *n.* 406, 668, 726, 735, 754

careen *vb.* 195, 247

career *n.* 611; *vb.* 245

career woman *n.* 333

care for *vb.* 757, 795

carefree *adj.* 738, 742

careful *adj.* 406, 418, 726, 754, 843

careful management *n.* 726

carefulness *n.* 406

careless *adj.* 56, 405, 407, 501, 689, 753

carelessness *n.* 405, 407, 441, 689, 753

caress *n.* 338, 800; *vb.* 338, 800

caretaker *n.* 666, 668

care to *vb.* 537

cargo *n.* 166, 239, 285

cargo cult *n.* 862

caricature *n.* 21, 463, 489, 744, 772, 773, 828; *vb.* 21, 463, 489, 744, 772, 773

caricaturist *n.* 21

carjacking *n.* 705

carnage *n.* 147, 324

carnal *adj.* 282, 844

carnality *n.* 844

carnal knowledge *n.* 40, 851

carnival *n.* 746, 761

carnivore *n.* 326

carnivorous *adj.* 267, 326

carol *n.* 367, 874; *vb.* 368, 526

carouse *vb.* 746

carousel *n.* 279, 491

carp *vb.* 739, 804, 826

carpenter *n.* 613

carpet *vb.* 826

carriage *n.* 234, 239, 242

carried *adj.* 436

carried away *adj.* 734

carrier (bag) *n.* 241

carrot *n.* 134, 551

carroty *adj.* 388

carry *vb.* 172, 193, 241, 353, 359

carrying out *n.* 688

carry off *vb.* 395

carry on *vb.* 124, 621

carry out *vb.* 136, 607, 688

carry the day *vb.* 31

carry weight *vb.* 139, 507, 576

cart *n.* 242; *vb.* 241

cartage *n.* 239

carte blanche *n.* 667, 677

cartel *n.* 45, 52, 79, 668

carter *n.* 241

cartilage *n.* 294

cartilaginous *adj.* 294

cartographer *n.* 557

cartographic *adj.* 284

cartography *n.* 284, 557

carton *n.* 167

cartoon *n.* 490, 525, 744

cartoonist *n.* 744

cartridge *n.* 491, 649

cartridge paper *n.* 569

cartwheel *n.* 196

carve *vb.* 216, 492

carved *adj.* 493

carve-up *n.* 700

carve up *vb.* 700

carving *n.* 492

cascade *n.* 275, 314; *vb.* 275, 314

case *n.* 167, 202, 210, 409, 410, 500, 830, 856

cased *adj.* 516

case dismissed *n.* 857

case-hardened *adj.* 289

case history *n.* 486, 517

cash *n.* 711; *vb.* 711

cash-and-carry *n.* 710

cash book *n.* 720

cash dispenser *n.* 711

cash flow *n.* 711

cashier *n.* 711, 716; *vb.* 277, 673, 860

cash in on *vb.* 564, 690

cashmere *n.* 569

cash register *n.* 711

casino *n.* 554, 761

cask *n.* 167

casket *n.* 167

Cassandra *n.* 455

cassette *n.* 369, 491

cassette deck *n.* 369

cassock *n.* 881

cast *n.* 68, 140, 255, 370, 492, 523; *vb.* 149, 203, 216, 255, 492, 525

castanets *n.* 369

cast aspersions on *vb.* 775, 828

cast away *adj.* 311

castaway *n.* 563, 790

cast away *vb.* 563

caste *n.* 776

castigate *vb.* 826, 860

castigation *n.* 860

castigator *n.* 860

castigatory *adj.* 860

casting vote *n.* 26, 139, 545

castle *n.* 600, 640

centre of attraction *n.* 200, 257
centre on *vb.* 200
centrepiece *n.* 200
centrifugal *adj.* 67, 260
centripetal *adj.* 66, 200, 257, 259
centrist *n.* 148
centurion *n.* 648
century *n.* 84, 90, 92
ceramics *n.* 149
cerebral *adj.* 396, 398
cerebrate *vb.* 398
cerebration *n.* 398
ceremonial *adj.* 786, 787, 881; *n.* 786, 787
ceremonious *adj.* 787, 823
ceremoniousness *n.* 787
ceremony *n.* 786, 787, 881
cerise *adj.* 387, 392
cerok *n.* 524
certain *adj.* 427, 434
certainly *adv.* 427
certain to *adj.* 427
certainty *n.* 427, 434, 450
certifiable *adj.* 447
certificate *n.* 677
certification *n.* 417
certified *adj.* 417
certified accountant *n.* 720
certify *vb.* 417, 677
certitude *n.* 427
cervix *n.* 152
cessation *n.* 62, 123, 235
cession *n.* 563, 696
cesspit *n.* 570
cha-cha *n.* 524
chafe *vb.* 291, 301
chaff *n.* 37; *vb.* 744, 773
chagrin *n.* 452, 743
chain *n.* 42, 60, 64
chain letter *n.* 515
chain reaction *n.* 133
chain store *n.* 710
chain up *vb.* 668
chair *vb.* 786
chairman *n.* 622

chalet *n.* 165
chalice *n.* 167, 881
chalk *n.* 300, 311, 383
chalk and cheese *n.* 14
chalkface *n.* 477
chalk up *vb.* 486
chalky *adj.* 300, 311, 383
challenge *n.* 413, 474, 632, 637; *vb.* 14, 215, 413, 414, 428, 435, 437, 632, 637, 638, 643, 830
challenger *n.* 632, 643
challenging *adj.* 637
chambermaid *n.* 613, 666
chameleon *n.* 130
chamfer *vb.* 195, 231, 493
chamfered *adj.* 493
chamfering *n.* 493
champion *adj.* 31; *n.* 31, 582, 631, 640, 651, 761, 807, 829; *vb.* 138, 193, 410, 436, 631, 825
chance *adj.* 10, 135, 554; *n.* 115, 135, 423, 554; *vb.* 135
chancel *n.* 882
chancellor *n.* 622
chancy *adj.* 428, 554
chandelier *n.* 192, 377
chandler *n.* 707
change *n.* 121, 711; *vb.* 120, 121, 125, 130, 307, 711
changeability *n.* 16, 94, 130, 217, 544
changeable *adj.* 16, 94, 120, 130, 541, 543, 544, 803
changeableness *n.* 130
changeable thing *n.* 130
change for the better/ worse *n.* 121; *vb.* 121
change hands *vb.* 697

change hands for *vb.* 721
changeless *adj.* 862
change one's mind *vb.* 125, 435, 543
change of direction *n.* 121
change of heart *n.* 841
change of life *n.* 112
change of mind *n.* 121
change of ownership *n.* 697
changeover *n.* 121, 125, 196
changeround *n.* 128
change round *vb.* 121, 128, 196
change sides *vb.* 543
change the face of *vb.* 127
change one's tune *vb.* 121, 543
changing *adj.* 121
channel *n.* 42, 240, 227, 231, 310, 315, 466, 472, 493, 567; *vb.* 227, 231
channelled *adj.* 227
chant *n.* 874; *vb.* 103, 363, 368, 874
chaos *n.* 56, 150, 217, 658, 853
chaotic *adj.* 56, 217, 658
chap *n.* 332
chapel *n.* 882
chaperon *n.* 85; *vb.* 85
chaplain *n.* 666, 879
chapter *n.* 522, 878
chapter of accidents *n.* 101
char *n.* 586, 613, 666; *vb.* 384
charabanc *n.* 242
character *n.* 5, 73, 74, 330, 495, 539, 837
character assassination *n.* 150, 828
characteristic *adj.* 70, 485; *n.* 70
characterization *n.* 488

characterize *vb.* 5, 488, 517
charade *n.* 523
charades *n.* 484, 761
charcoal *n.* 341, 490
charge *n.* 245, 247, 255, 473, 622, 639, 661, 672, 821, 830, 840, 856; *vb.* 141, 147, 247, 661, 672, 699, 720, 830, 840, 856
chargeable *adj.* 819, 830
charge account *n.* 714
charge card *n.* 711
charged *adj.* 285, 830
chargé d'affaires *n.* 675
charger *n.* 167
charge the jury *vb.* 856
charge to one's account *vb.* 714
charisma *n.* 29, 139, 256
charismatic *adj.* 29, 139, 256
charitable *adj.* 660, 681, 698, 725, 805, 807, 809, 859
charity *n.* 631, 660, 698, 725, 805, 807, 809
charity appeal *n.* 681
charlatan *n.* 21, 480, 771
Charleston *n.* 524
charm *n.* 66, 139, 257, 736, 763, 766, 795, 876; *vb.* 139, 736, 795, 876
charmed *adj.* 876
charming *adj.* 139, 257, 736, 763
Charon *n.* 237
chart *n.* 57, 488; *vb.* 488
charter *n.* 71, 238, 672, 684, 819, 822, 852; *vb.* 672, 677, 702
chartered *adj.* 677
chartered accountant *n.* 720

chop and change *vb.*
121, 544
choplogic *n.* 411
chop logic *vb.* 410
chopper *n.* 244
choppy *adj.* 314
choral *adj.* 367
chorale *n.* 367
chore *n.* 762
choreography *n.* 524
chorister *n.* 368, 880
chortle *n.* 744; *vb.*
744
chorus *n.* 19, 88, 103,
119, 874; *vb.* 19,
21, 88, 103, 363,
365, 368
chorus girl *n.* 524
chorus line *n.* 523
the chosen few *n.* 31,
582
the chosen people *n.*
863
chow *n.* 267
christen *vb.* 59, 61,
497
christening *n.* 59, 61,
497, 881
Christian *n.* 805, 874
Christianity *n.* 868
Christian name *n.*
497
Christmas *n.* 108, 881
Christmas box *n.* 698
chromatic *adj.* 381
chromaticism *n.* 381
chromosomal *adj.*
320
chromosome *n.* 12,
320
chronicle *n.* 97, 486,
517; *vb.* 97, 486,
517
chronicler *n.* 486,
517
chronological *adj.* 97
chronology *n.* 97
chronometer *n.* 97
chronometrical *adj.*
97
chronometry *n.* 97
chubby *adj.* 168
chuck *vb.* 255, 563
chucker-out *n.* 266
chuckle *n.* 744; *vb.*
744

chuck out *vb.* 266,
696
chug *vb.* 234
chum *n.* 793
chunk *n.* 48, 287
church *n.* 634, 874,
880, 882
the church *n.* 878
church collection *n.*
698
churchdom *n.* 878
churchgoer *n.* 874
church member *n.*
880
church officer *n.* 880
churchyard *n.* 325,
882
churlish *adj.* 792,
804
churn *vb.* 281
churn out *vb.* 151
chute *n.* 275
cicatrix *n.* 595
cinch *n.* 629
cinema *n.* 525
CinemaScope *n.* 525
cinematic *adj.* 525
cinematographic *adj.*
234, 491, 525
cinematography *n.*
488, 491, 525
cinema vérité *n.* 3
Cinerama *n.* 525
cinnamon *n.* 386
cipher *n.* 74, 77, 467,
513
circa *adv.* 173
circle *n.* 66, 223, 278,
523, 634; *vb.* 206,
223, 278
circlet *n.* 223
circuit *n.* 75, 119,
127, 223, 251, 278;
vb. 251, 278, 279
circuitous *adj.* 195,
214, 251, 278
circular *adj.* 223, 225,
278, 411; *n.* 69,
515, 681
circular argument *n.*
654
circularity *n.* 223,
225, 411
circulate *vb.* 223, 271,
466, 470, 711
circulating *adj.* 470

circulation *n.* 223,
271, 278, 466, 470
circulatory *adj.* 223
circumference *n.* 6,
156, 198, 206, 208,
223
circumlocution *n.*
251, 499, 506
circumlocutory *adj.*
251, 506
circumnavigate *vb.*
237
circumnavigation *n.*
237, 278
circumscribe *vb.* 198,
206, 211, 223, 278
circumscription *n.*
211
circumspect *adj.* 406,
418, 429, 754
circumspection *n.*
406, 418, 754
circus *n.* 240, 761
cirrus *n.* 307
Cistercian *n.* 879
cistern *n.* 167
citadel *n.* 640
citation *n.* 650, 825,
830, 856
cite *vb.* 70
citizen *n.* 164, 777
citizenry *n.* 777
city *n.* 157
city academy *n.* 477
city centre *n.* 157
city slicker *n.* 164
city technology col-
lege *n.* 477
civet *n.* 349
civic *adj.* 330
civil *adj.* 768, 791,
880
civil defence *n.* 640
civil disobedience *n.*
638, 658, 682
civil engineer *n.* 613
civility *n.* 768, 791
civilization *n.* 330
civil marriage *n.* 797
civil partnership *n.*
797
civil rights *n.* 667
civil servant *n.* 665

civil service *n.* 657
civil war *n.* 645
civvies *n.* 205, 788
clad *adj.* 202, 204
cladding *n.* 201
claim *n.* 473, 681,
819; *vb.* 473, 551,
681, 819
claimant *n.* 681, 856
clairvoyance *n.* 401,
453, 455, 877
clairvoyant *adj.* 401,
453, 455, 877; *n.*
455, 876, 877
clamminess *n.* 318
clammy *adj.* 308, 318
clamorous *adj.* 355,
363
clamour *n.* 355, 363,
826; *vb.* 355, 363
clamourousness *n.*
355
clamp *vb.* 40, 695
clampdown *n.* 668
clamp down on *vb.*
630, 659, 668
clam up *vb.* 467
clan *n.* 12, 52, 66,
330
clandestine *adj.* 465,
467, 469
clang *n.* 359; *vb.* 355,
362
clanger *n.* 116, 441
clank *n.* 359; *vb.* 359
clanking *adj.* 359
clannish *adj.* 52
clannishness *n.* 52
clap *n.* 247, 357, 484;
vb. 746, 786, 825
clap eyes on *vb.* 370
clap in irons *vb.* 668
clapped out *adj.* 62,
107
clapping *n.* 746, 786,
825
claptrap *n.* 459
claret *n.* 387, 392
clarification *n.* 39,
412, 462
clarify *vb.* 39, 460,
462, 629
clarinet *n.* 369
clarity *n.* 353, 355,
372, 460, 503, 509
clash *n.* 14, 103, 362,

comic *adj.* 523, 744;
n. 744

comical *adj.* 744

comic strip *n.* 744

comic writer *n.* 744

coming *adj.* 104; *n.*
261

coming into being *n.*
1

command *n.* 502,
622, 657, 661; *vb.*
622, 661, 692

commandeer *vb.* 564,
703

commandeering *n.*
703

commander *n.* 31,
622, 648

commanding *adj.*
622, 657, 661, 692

commando *n.* 648

command respect *vb.*
774, 823

commemorate *vb.*
786

commemoration *n.*
786

commemorative *adj.*
448, 786

commence *vb.* 61

commencement *n.*
61

commend *vb.* 825

commendable *adj.*
582, 825

commendation *n.*
825

commendatory *adj.*
825

commensurate *adj.* 9,
19

comment *n.* 429,
528; *vb.* 519

commentary *n.* 462,
519

commentator *n.* 472,
868

comment on *vb.* 462

commerce *n.* 611,
707

commercial *adj.* 611,
707; *n.* 470

commercial traveller
n. 709

commiserate *vb.* 729,
747, 809

commiseration *n.* 809

commissar *n.* 665

commission *n.* 607,
672, 716, 721, 722,
821; *vb.* 672

commissioned *adj.*
672

commissioner *n.* 665

commit *vb.* 473, 607,
672

commit *oneself vb.*
43, 539, 562, 683,
821

commit adultery *vb.*
851

commitment *n.* 43,
473, 539, 562, 683,
715, 821, 872

commit sacrilege *vb.*
873

commit suicide *vb.*
324

committed *adj.* 43,
473, 539, 562, 634,
683, 715, 870, 872

committee *n.* 634,
657, 675

commit to memory
vb. 448

commodious *adj.* 156

commodity *n.* 707

common *adj.* 32, 69,
117, 494, 512, 693,
760, 769, 777; *n.*
313, 693

common aim *n.* 633

commonality *n.* 777

common carrier *n.*
241

commoner *n.* 777

common fraction *n.*
74

common good *n.* 835

common knowledge
n. 470

common-law hus-
band/wife *n.* 797

commonly *adv.* 117

the common man *n.*
27, 777

commonness *n.* 117,
769

common or garden
adj. 72

common people *n.* 69

commonplace *adj.*

27, 442, 509, 549,
762

common practice *n.*
621

common run *n.* 27,
69

commons *n.* 777

common sense *n.*
148, 396, 444, 446

commonsensical *adj.*
396, 444

commonwealth *n.*
331

commotion *n.* 56,
281, 609, 729

communal *adj.* 40,
45, 330, 634, 693

communard *n.* 693

commune *n.* 164, 693

communicable *adj.*
239

communicant *n.* 870,
874

communicate *vb.*
458, 466, 515

communicating *adj.*
874

communication *n.*
40, 466, 494, 515,
533

communications *n.*
472

communicative *adj.*
466, 533

communion *n.* 872,
878

communiqué *n.* 466

communism *n.* 657

communist *adj.* 657

community *n.* 164,
330, 634, 777,
880

community sentence
n. 860

community service *n.*
807, 860

commute *vb.* 119,
236

commuter *n.* 164,
236

compact *adj.* 23, 40,
43, 287, 505; *n.*
633, 636, 684; *vb.*
171

compact disc *n.* 369

compacted *adj.* 171

compaction *n.* 40,
171

compactness *n.* 287

companion *n.* 85,
793

companionable *adj.*
789

companionship *n.*
85, 789, 793

companionway *n.* 42

company *n.* 66, 85,
523, 634, 648, 693

company man *n.* 72

comparability *n.* 17

comparable *adj.* 9,
17, 194

comparative *adj.* 24,
500

comparatively *adv.* 9

compare *vb.* 9, 17,
194

comparison *n.* 9, 194

compartment *n.* 48,
158, 167, 232

compartmentalize *vb.*
57

compartmentalized
adj. 48

compass *n.* 156, 177,
249

compassion *n.* 660,
809, 837

compassionate *adj.*
660, 730, 805, 809

compass point *n.* 249

compatibility *n.* 19,
72, 789, 793

compatible *adj.* 19,
72, 636, 789

compel *vb.* 558, 661,
664, 732

compelling *adj.* 661,
664, 732

compendium *n.* 45,
66, 516

compensate *vb.* 25,
28, 137, 704, 814,
859

compensation *n.* 28,
137, 704, 814, 819,
859

compensatory *adj.*
28, 137, 704, 814

compete *vb.* 643

compete against/with
vb. 632

competence *n.* 141,
573, 624, 854

competent *adj.* 141,
573, 624, 854

competing *adj.* 643

competition *n.* 632,
643, 815

competitive *adj.* 643,
724

competitiveness *n.*
724, 815

competitor *n.* 632,
643, 748, 815

compilation *n.* 45,
66, 520

compile *vb.* 53, 518

complacency *n.* 738

complacent *adj.* 738,
783

complain *vb.* 682,
739, 804, 826, 830

complain of *vb.* 589

complaint *n.* 589,
682, 739, 826, 830

complement *n.* 25,
33, 237, 500, 666;
vb. 85

complementarity *n.*
9, 11

complementary *adj.*
9, 11

complementary
colour *n.* 381

complete *adj.* 47,
584; *vb.* 49, 62,
653

complete change *n.*
127

completed *adj.* 653

completely *adv.* 49

completeness *n.* 47,
49

completion *n.* 62,
653

complex *adj.* 56, 197,
224, 504, 628; *n.*
47, 197, 447

complexion *n.* 5, 68

complexity *n.* 224,
504

compliance *n.* 436,
537, 551, 642, 663,
688, 782

compliant *adj.* 72,
436, 537, 551, 642,
663, 688, 782, 821

complicate *vb.* 56,
461

complicated *adj.* 628

complicate matters
vb. 628

complication *n.* 628

complicity *n.* 633,
840

compliment *n.* 791,
825, 827; *vb.* 791,
825, 827

complimentary *adj.*
667, 698, 724, 786,
825, 827

complimentary
tickets *n.* 724

compliments *n.* 786,
800

comply *vb.* 436, 537,
551, 642, 663, 688,
782

component *adj.* 53; *n.*
48, 53, 282

components *n.* 166

comportment *n.* 621

compose *vb.* 53, 368,
513, 518, 521

compose *oneself vb.*
446

composed *adj.* 131,
148, 733

composer *n.* 149, 368

composite *adj.* 38, 40

composition *n.* 45,
57, 149, 298, 367,
490, 513

compositor *n.* 514

compos mentis *adj.*
446

composure *n.* 131,
148, 446, 733, 760

compound *n.* 38,
158, 210; *vb.* 40

comprehend *vb.* 51,
396, 438, 460

comprehensibility *n.*
460

comprehensible *adj.*
460

comprehension *n.*
396, 438

comprehensive *adj.*
47, 49, 51, 69

comprehensiveness
n. 47, 49, 51, 69

compress *n.* 233, 630;

vb. 66, 171, 179,
287, 505

compressed *adj.* 171,
181, 504, 505

compression *n.* 171,
179, 181, 505

compressor *n.* 171

comprise *vb.* 51, 53

comprising *adj.* 51

compromise *n.* 63,
250, 684, 686; *vb.*
63, 686

compromise solution
n. 686

comps *n.* 724

comptroller *n.* 711

compulsion *n.* 447,
536, 558, 664

compulsive *adj.* 447,
664

compulsorily *adv.*
664

compulsory *adj.* 71,
536, 558, 661, 664,
821

compulsory purchase
n. 703

compunction *n.* 809,
841

computation *n.* 75,
177

computational *adj.*
75

compute *vb.* 75, 177

computer *n.* 75, 568,
570

computer animation
n. 525

computer crime/
fraud *n.* 472, 853

computer dating *n.*
647, 797

computerize *vb.* 75

computer language *n.*
75, 494, 570

computing *n.* 75, 570

comrade *n.* 85, 778,
793

comradely *adj.* 789

comradeship *n.* 789,
793

con *n.* 480, 671, 705;
vb. 480, 626, 705

concatenation *n.* 35

concave *adj.* 221, 227

concavity *n.* 221, 227

conceal *vb.* 166, 202,
373, 378, 467, 469

concealed *adj.* 465,
469

concealment *n.* 373,
465, 467, 469

concede *vb.* 422, 436,
551

conceit *n.* 779, 783

conceited *adj.* 779,
783, 834

conceivable *adj.* 423

conceive *vb.* 22, 149,
152, 396, 398, 457,
557

concentrate *n.* 39; *vb.*
39, 200, 259, 287,
404

concentrated *adj.* 287

concentration *n.* 259,
287, 398, 404, 609

concentration camp
n. 671, 790

concept *n.* 408

conception *n.* 152,
408, 456, 457

conceptual *adj.* 396,
400, 408

conceptualize *vb.*
283, 396

concern *n.* 101, 402,
406, 409, 562, 634,
735, 750; *vb.* 9,
735

concerned *adj.* 750

concerning *prep.* 9

concert *n.* 19, 367,
633

concerted *adj.* 19

concerted effort *n.*
633

concert hall *n.* 761

concertina *vb.* 230

concerto *n.* 367

concession *n.* 422,
551, 677, 722

concessionary *adj.*
422, 722, 724

concessionary fare *n.*
724

concessions on both
sides *n.* 686

concierge *n.* 666, 668

conciliate *vb.* 646,
814

conciliation *n.* 646

corrosive *adj.* 150; *n.* 150

corrugate *vb.* 224, 230, 231, 291

corrugated *adj.* 224, 227, 230

corrugation *n.* 230, 231

corrupt *adj.* 583, 832, 838; *vb.* 838

corruption *n.* 496, 583, 832, 836, 838

corset *n.* 171, 193

cortege *n.* 64, 325

corundum *n.* 321

coruscating *adj.* 374

corvette *n.* 243

cosh *n.* 247, 649

cosmetic *adj.* 50, 187, 198, 766, 785; *n.* 765

cosmetic surgery *n.* 765

cosmic *adj.* 47, 284

cosmography *n.* 284

cosmological *adj.* 284

cosmology *n.* 284

cosmonaut *n.* 238

cosmopolitanism *n.* 69

cosmos *n.* 1, 47, 284

cosset *vb.* 800

cosseted *adj.* 336

cost *vb.* 720, 721, 721

cost price *n.* 721

cost a lot/a packet/a pretty penny/a fortune/a bomb/an arm and a leg *vb.* 723

co-star *n.* 525

costliness *n.* 723

costly *adj.* 723

cost nothing *vb.* 724

costs *n.* 28, 718, 860

cost the earth *vb.* 723

costume *n.* 204, 523

costume drama *n.* 472

costumier *n.* 204

cosy *adj.* 734

cot death *n.* 323

coterie *n.* 52, 66

coterminous *adj.* 176, 207, 211

cottage *n.* 165

cottage industry *n.* 149

cottager *n.* 164

cotton *n.* 569

cotton on *vb.* 460

cottony *adj.* 299

couchant *adj.* 191

cough *n.* 316, 362, 589

cough up *vb.* 716

could do better *adj.* 585

could do with *vb.* 755

could eat a horse *vb.* 755

council *n.* 634, 657, 855, 878

councillor *n.* 657, 665

counsel *n.* 623, 675; *vb.* 623

counselling *n.* 623

counsellor *n.* 623, 631

count *n.* 75, 776, 830; *vb.* 74, 139, 434, 576, 582

countdown *n.* 238

countenance *n.* 212, 394

counter *adj.* 14, 137, 215; *n.* 193, 641; *vb.* 126, 137, 415, 632, 641

counteract *vb.* 14, 137

counteraction *n.* 137

counteractive *adj.* 137

counterargument *n.* 632, 641

counterattack *n.* 137, 258, 459, 641; *vb.* 641

counterbalance *n.* 137; *vb.* 28, 137

counterblast *n.* 137, 415

counterchange *vb.* 393

countercharge *n.* 415

counterclaim *n.* 421, 681

countercurrent *n.* 14

counterevidence *n.* 421

counterfeit *adj.* 21, 481; *n.* 21; *vb.* 21, 481, 711

counterfeiter *n.* 21

counterfeiting *n.* 481

counterfoil *n.* 485, 719

countermand *n.* 673, 678; *vb.* 673, 678

counterpart *n.* 11, 17, 25

counterpoint *n.* 14

counterpoise *n.* 285

counterproductive *adj.* 137

counterrevolution *n.* 137

counterrevolutionary *adj.* 137

countersign *vb.* 485

counterstroke *n.* 258

countertenor *n.* 368

countervailing *adj.* 137

counterweight *n.* 25, 28, 131, 137, 285

countess *n.* 776

count in *vb.* 51

countless *adj.* 86, 89

count on *vb.* 450

count out *vb.* 52

countrified *adj.* 165

country and western *n.* 367

country bumpkin *n.* 164, 777

country cousin *n.* 777

country dance *n.* 524

country sports *n.* 761

count the pennies *vb.* 728

county *adj.* 776; *n.* 157

county council *n.* 657

coup *n.* 161

coup de grâce *n.* 62, 653

coup d'état *n.* 127

coupé *n.* 242

couple *n.* 81; *vb.* 40

couplet *n.* 81, 521

coupling *n.* 40

coupon *n.* 719

courage *n.* 751

the courage of *one's* convictions *n.* 751

courageous *adj.* 751

courier *n.* 241, 466

course *n.* 64, 90, 124, 140, 175, 234, 240, 249, 253, 315, 475, 761; *vb.* 314, 761

course of action *n.* 557

coursing *n.* 761

court *n.* 210, 761, 776, 855; *vb.* 793, 800, 827

court action *n.* 635

court danger *vb.* 599

court disaster *vb.* 753

courteous *adj.* 791, 805, 823

courtesy *n.* 768, 791

courtesy of *prep.* 138

courtesy title *n.* 778

courthouse *n.* 855

courting *n.* 800

courtliness *n.* 791

courtly *adj.* 791

court martial *n.* 673

court-martial *vb.* 673

courtship *n.* 795, 800

courtyard *n.* 158

cousin *n.* 12

couturier *n.* 204

cove *n.* 221, 310, 330

covenant *n.* 683, 684, 687, 698; *vb.* 683, 684

covenanted *adj.* 683, 684

cover *n.* 28, 167, 202, 204, 210, 212, 233, 469, 515, 516, 600, 687; *vb.* 40, 51, 156, 198, 202, 687

cover *oneself* *vb.* 28, 754

coverage *n.* 156, 172

cover charge *n.* 721

covered *adj.* 202, 687

covering *n.* 202, 378

covert *adj.* 465, 467

cover-up *n.* 467

cover up *vb.* 467, 469, 487

cover up for *vb.* 128

covet *vb.* 755, 816

covetous *adj.* 690, 728, 755, 816, 834

covetousness *n.* 728, 755, 816

covey *n.* 66

cow *n.* 326; *vb.* 670, 750

coward *n.* 556, 752

cowardice *n.* 752

cowardliness *n.* 752

cowardly *adj.* 752

cowardy custard *n.* 752

cowboy *n.* 480, 707

cower *vb.* 185, 750, 752

cowering *adj.* 752

cowshed *n.* 165, 328

coy *adj.* 784

coyness *n.* 784

CPU *n.* 570

crabbed *adj.* 513

crabby *adj.* 804

crabwise *adv.* 195, 214

crack *n.* 41, 174, 181, 231, 232, 357, 561, 585, 767, 849; *vb.* 41, 46, 174, 295, 357, 767

crack a joke *vb.* 744

crack down on *vb.* 659

cracked *adj.* 527, 585, 767

cracker *n.* 763

crackers *adj.* 447

crackpot *adj.* 443

crack shot *n.* 255

cracksman *n.* 705

crack up *vb.* 46, 447

cradle *n.* 61, 111, 132, 165, 280; *vb.* 193

craft *n.* 149, 243, 611, 626; *vb.* 149

the craft *n.* 876

craftiness *n.* 480, 626

craftsman *n.* 149, 613, 624

crafty *adj.* 480, 626, 832

crag *n.* 228, 311

cragginess *n.* 291

craggy *adj.* 228, 291

cram *vb.* 49, 66, 166, 846

crammed *adj.* 49

crammer *n.* 477

cramp *n.* 337; *vb.* 171, 181, 630, 668

cramped *adj.* 30, 181, 513

crampedness *n.* 181

cramp one's style *vb.* 630

cramp sb's style *vb.* 142

crane *n.* 192, 276

crank *n.* 73, 447

crankiness *n.* 447

cranky *adj.* 447

cranny *n.* 181, 220, 231

crap *n.* 268, 443; *vb.* 268

crappy *adj.* 268

crash *n.* 34, 123, 150, 247, 355, 357, 717; *vb.* 34, 147, 150, 165, 238, 247, 275, 355, 357, 652, 717

crashland *vb.* 238

crash-landing *n.* 238

crash out *vb.* 619, 848

crass *adj.* 182, 439, 769

crassness *n.* 182, 769

crate *n.* 167, 244

crater *n.* 186, 227

crave *vb.* 681, 755, 816

craven *adj.* 752

craving *n.* 755

crawl *n.* 616; *vb.* 29, 86, 185, 246, 616, 642, 663, 780, 782

crawler *n.* 616, 782, 827

crawling *adj.* 66, 642, 782; *n.* 782

crawling with *adj.* 29

crawl into one's shell *vb.* 784

crawl with *vb.* 573

crayon *n.* 490; *vb.* 381, 490

craze *n.* 544, 755, 770; *vb.* 447

crazed *adj.* 447

craziness *n.* 445

crazy *adj.* 443, 445, 447, 732

crazy about *adj.* 795

crazy for *adj.* 755

crazy paving *n.* 65

creak *vb.* 362

creaky *adj.* 362

cream *n.* 302, 319, 383, 389, 582, 770; *vb.* 302, 319

creaminess *n.* 383

cream off *vb.* 270, 545

creamy *adj.* 319, 383, 389

crease *n.* 230; *vb.* 171, 744

creased *adj.* 230

create *vb.* 22, 132, 149, 216, 457, 732

creation *n.* 1, 3, 132, 149, 216, 284, 322, 862

creationism *or* creation science *n.* 320

creative *adj.* 22, 132, 149, 457

creative accounting *n.* 720

creativity *n.* 22, 457

creator *n.* 22, 132, 149

the Creator *n.* 862

creature *n.* 32, 320, 322, 326, 330

creature comforts *n.* 336

creature of habit *n.* 549

creche *n.* 477

credence *n.* 434

credentials *n.* 420

credibility *n.* 434

credible *adj.* 423, 425, 434

credit *n.* 134, 567, 570, 683, 701, 714, 811, 825; *vb.* 714, 720, 819

creditable *adj.* 582, 825

credit account *n.* 714

credit one's account *vb.* 714

credit card *n.* 702, 711, 714

credit facilities *n.* 714

credit institution *n.* 701

credit note *n.* 714

creditor *n.* 701, 714

credits *n.* 76, 525

credit squeeze *n.* 668

creditworthiness *n.* 712, 714

credo *n.* 434

credulity *n.* 434, 551

credulous *adj.* 434, 551

credulousness *n.* 551

creed *n.* 434, 868

creek *n.* 310, 312

creel *n.* 167

creep *n.* 827; *vb.* 246, 465, 469, 616

the creeps *n.* 750

creep up on *vb.* 469

creepy *adj.* 750

creepy-crawly *n.* 326

cremate *vb.* 325

cremation *n.* 325, 339

crematorium *n.* 325

crème de la crème *n.* 31, 582, 770

crenellated *adj.* 174, 229

crenellation *n.* 229

creole *n.* 38, 494

creosote *vb.* 603

crêpe de chine *n.* 569

crepe paper *n.* 569

crepuscular *adj.* 110

crescendo *n.* 33, 355

crescent *n.* 221, 240

crest *n.* 184, 188, 484; *vb.* 188

crestfallen *adj.* 452, 743

cretin *n.* 397, 445

cretinism *n.* 397

cretinous *adj.* 397

crevasse *n.* 41, 227, 601

crevice *n.* 174, 181, 231

crew *n.* 66, 237, 666

crewcut *n.* 765

crib *n.* 462; *vb.* 21, 702

cricket *n.* 761

crime *n.* 662, 818, 838, 840, 853

crime wave *n.* 853

criminal *adj.* 818,

death camp *n.* 671
death certificate *n.* 323
death chamber *n.* 861
death duties *n.* 721
death knell *n.* 323
deathless *adj.* 95
deathly *adj.* 323, 324
death mask *n.* 492
death notice *n.* 323
death rattle *n.* 323
death row *n.* 671
death sentence *n.* 858, 860
death squad *n.* 147, 324
death throes *n.* 323
death toll *n.* 323
death warrant *n.* 858
deb *n.* 770
débâcle *n.* 275, 652
debar *vb.* 678
debarred *adj.* 52
debarring *adj.* 52
debase *vb.* 277, 583
debasement *n.* 277, 828
debasing *adj.* 277
debatable *adj.* 409, 410, 428
debate *n.* 410, 533, 643; *vb.* 410, 533
debauch *vb.* 851
debauched *adj.* 336, 844, 851
debauchery *n.* 336, 844, 851
debilitate *vb.* 144
debilitated *adj.* 142
debilitating *adj.* 589
debility *n.* 142, 144, 589
debit *n.* 691, 715; *vb.* 720
debouch *vb.* 264
debriefing *n.* 100
debris *n.* 37
deb's delight *n.* 770
debt *n.* 715, 821
debtor *n.* 702, 715
debunk *vb.* 773
debut *n.* 61, 261
debutante *n.* 770
decade *n.* 84, 92
decagon *n.* 84
decalogue *n.* 84

decamp *vb.* 262, 395, 605
decampment *n.* 262, 605
decanter *n.* 167
decapitate *vb.* 36, 324, 860
decapitation *n.* 36, 324, 860
decathlon *n.* 84
decay *n.* 2, 46, 107, 108, 550, 593, 595; *vb.* 2, 46, 107, 593, 595
decayed *adj.* 593, 595
decaying *adj.* 46, 550
decease *n.* 323
deceased *adj.* 323
deceit *n.* 626
deceitful *adj.* 480, 481, 626, 832, 873
deceitfulness *n.* 480, 481
deceive *vb.* 4, 441, 480, 626, 832
deceiver *n.* 480
decelerate *vb.* 34, 246, 668
deceleration *n.* 34, 246, 668
decency *n.* 768, 791, 817, 850
decent *adj.* 204, 582, 791, 817, 821, 850
decentralization *n.* 67
decentralize *vb.* 67
deception *n.* 480, 626
deceptive *adj.* 394, 480, 543
deceptiveness *n.* 480
decibels *n.* 355
decide *vb.* 132, 427, 429, 539, 553
deciduous *adj.* 327
decimal *adj.* 74, 84; *n.* 74, 84
decimalize *vb.* 84
decimate *vb.* 34, 84, 87, 150, 324
decimation *n.* 150
decipher *vb.* 460, 462
decipherable *adj.* 460
decision *n.* 429, 856
deck *vb.* 175
decked out *adj.* 766

deckle edge *n.* 229
deckle-edged *adj.* 209
deck out *vb.* 204, 766
declaim *vb.* 528
declamation *n.* 528
declamatory *adj.* 528
declaration *n.* 473, 683, 868
declarative *adj.* 473
declare *vb.* 468, 473, 528, 683, 856
declare heretical *vb.* 871
declare not guilty *vb.* 857
declare war *vb.* 645
declension *n.* 500
decline *n.* 34, 107, 108, 171, 185, 254, 275, 593; *vb.* 34, 144, 275, 500, 546, 593, 680, 724
declining *adj.* 275
declining years *n.* 112
declutter *vb.* 55
decoction *n.* 303
decode *vb.* 460, 462
décolleté *adj.* 205
decolorant *n.* 382
decolorize *vb.* 382
decommission *vb.* 646
decommissioning *n.* 646
decompose *vb.* 2, 41, 46, 593
decomposed *adj.* 46, 593
decomposition *n.* 41, 46, 593
deconsecrate *vb.* 880
decontamination *n.* 586
decontrol *vb.* 677
decorate *vb.* 510, 766, 859
decorated *adj.* 766
decoration *n.* 510, 650, 766, 859
decorative *adj.* 510, 766
decorator *n.* 613
decorous *adj.* 511, 768, 850
decorum *n.* 511, 768, 850

decoy *n.* 212, 257, 601
decrease *n.* 30, 34, 36, 171; *vb.* 30, 34, 36, 171
decreasing *adj.* 34
decreasingly *adv.* 34
decree *n.* 429, 661; *vb.* 71, 429, 661
decree absolute/nisi *n.* 798
decrement *n.* 36
decrepit *adj.* 144
decrepitude *n.* 144
decrescendo *n.* 34
decruitment *n.* 161
decry *vb.* 828
dedicate *vb.* 872, 881
dedicated *adj.* 43, 540, 833, 872
dedication *n.* 43, 539, 540, 807, 833, 872
deduce *vb.* 400
deduct *vb.* 34, 36, 717, 722
deduction *n.* 34, 36, 400, 717, 722
deductive *adj.* 400
deed *n.* 607
deem *vb.* 434
deep *adj.* 23, 186, 381, 444
the deep *n.* 186, 310
deep down *adv.* 186, 199
deepen *vb.* 186, 741
the deep end *n.* 186
deepening *n.* 741
deep-freeze *n.* 340; *vb.* 340
deeply *adv.* 186
deep-rooted *adj.* 5, 131, 186, 549
deep-sea *adj.* 186, 237, 310
deep-seated *adj.* 5, 131, 186, 199, 549
deep thought *n.* 186
deep vein thrombosis *n.* 233, 238
deface *vb.* 595, 764, 767
defaced *adj.* 764
defacement *n.* 764
defamate *vb.* 604

distraught *adj.* 447, 735

distress *n.* 337, 735, 836; *vb.* 337, 735, 737

distressed *adj.* 107, 735

distressing *adj.* 337, 735, 836

distress signal *n.* 602

distribute *vb.* 23, 57, 67, 470, 698, 700

distribution *n.* 57, 67, 466, 700

district *n.* 157

distrust *n.* 435, 815; *vb.* 435, 815

distrustful *adj.* 435, 815

disturb *vb.* 58, 161, 281, 737

disturbance *n.* 56, 58, 161, 281, 662

disturbed *adj.* 58, 161, 281, 447

disturbing *adj.* 737

disunited *adj.* 635

disunity *n.* 635

disuse *n.* 550, 565

disused *adj.* 107, 550, 565

ditch *n.* 210, 231, 315; *vb.* 238, 546, 563, 565, 696

dither *vb.* 428, 541

ditto *adv.* 13, 21

ditty *n.* 365, 521

ditzy *adj.* 405

diuretic *adj.* 268

diurnal *adj.* 109

diva *n.* 368

dive *n.* 186, 275; *vb.* 186, 245, 275, 761

diver *n.* 275

diverge *vb.* 18, 20, 41, 67, 73, 195, 252, 260

divergence *n.* 18, 20, 41, 67, 195, 252, 260, 871

divergent *adj.* 18, 20, 67, 260, 871

divers *adj.* 16, 80

diverse *adj.* 16, 18

diversify *vb.* 16, 121, 393

diversion *n.* 121, 214, 252, 601, 761

diversity *n.* 16, 18, 393

divert *vb.* 214, 761

diverting *adj.* 761

divest *vb.* 203, 703

divest *oneself vb.* 205

divide *n.* 207; *vb.* 41, 48, 68, 75, 207, 635

divided *adj.* 48, 635

divide fifty-fifty *vb.* 63

dividend *n.* 690, 719

dividing line *n.* 176

divination *n.* 104, 455, 877

divine *adj.* 734, 862, 868; *n.* 868; *vb.* 104, 401, 456, 876, 877

divine manifestation *n.* 862

divineness *n.* 862

diviner *n.* 876

divine task *n.* 862

divine worship *n.* 881

diving *n.* 237, 761

divinity *n.* 862, 868

division *n.* 41, 68, 75, 635, 648, 700, 871

divisive *adj.* 41, 635

divorce *n.* 41, 798; *vb.* 41, 798

divorce court *n.* 798

divorced *adj.* 798

divorcee *n.* 798

divot *n.* 327

divulge *vb.* 203, 464, 468

divvy up *vb.* 700

dizzy *adj.* 405

DJ *n.* 368

DNA *n.* 12, 320

D-notice *n.* 678

do *n.* 786; *vb.* 573, 607

doable *adj.* 423

do a bunk *vb.* 395

do a deal *vb.* 684

do a disservice *vb.* 836

do *sb* a favour *vb.* 805

do a flit *vb.* 605, 717

do *sb* a good turn *vb.* 631, 805

do a job *vb.* 611

do all right *vb.* 712

do a moonlight flit *vb.* 605, 717

do *one* a power of good *vb.* 835

do a roaring trade *vb.* 655, 709

do as *one* is told *vb.* 663

do battle with *vb.* 643

do *one's* best *vb.* 561

do better than expected *vb.* 624

do business *vb.* 611

docile *adj.* 55, 537, 642, 663

docility *n.* 537, 642, 663

dock *n.* 614, 855; *vb.* 36, 41, 160, 179, 237, 238, 261, 717

docker *n.* 613

docket *n.* 485; *vb.* 485

docking *n.* 238

do *oneself* credit *vb.* 774

doctor *n.* 596, 778; *vb.* 121, 481

doctrinaire *adj.* 434

doctrinal *adj.* 868

doctrine *n.* 434, 868

docudrama *n.* 472

document *n.* 486

documentary *adj.* 420, 440; *n.* 3, 521

documentation *n.* 420, 486, 513

documented *adj.* 1

dod *n.* 287

dodder *vb.* 144

doddering *adj.* 112

doddle *n.* 629

dodecahedron *n.* 84

dodge *n.* 480, 556, 626; *vb.* 195, 407, 556

dodger *n.* 556

dodgy *adj.* 428, 599

do *one's* duty *vb.* 663, 688, 821

doe *n.* 333

doer *n.* 607

do evil *vb.* 836

do for *vb.* 666

do *sth* for effect/show *vb.* 785

dog *n.* 326, 332; *vb.* 555

dog days *n.* 108

dog-eared *adj.* 230

dog *sb's* footsteps *vb.* 60, 85, 173

dogged *adj.* 540, 542, 609, 617

doggedness *n.* 540, 542

doggerel *n.* 521

dog-in-the-manger *adj.* 834

dog-leg *n.* 220

dogma *n.* 434, 868

dogmatic *adj.* 430, 434, 542, 783, 868

dogmatism *n.* 434

dognapping *n.* 705

do good *vb.* 582, 805, 807, 835

do-gooder *n.* 805, 807

dogsbody *n.* 613, 666

do *one's* homework *vb.* 559

do in *vb.* 150, 324

do *oneself* in *vb.* 324

doing *n.* 607

the doldrums *n.* 743

dole out *vb.* 698, 700

do less than justice to *vb.* 432

doll *n.* 333, 761

dolled up *adj.* 204

dollop *n.* 700

doll up *vb.* 765

dolly bird *n.* 333, 763

dolour *n.* 735

dolt *n.* 445

do magic *vb.* 876

domain *n.* 157, 854

domain name *n.* 472

dome *n.* 223, 225, 226; *vb.* 225

domed *adj.* 221, 226

domestic *adj.* 164, 199, 326; *n.* 613, 666

domestic animal *n.* 326

granary *n.* 570

grand *adj.* 29, 763, 774; *n.* 84, 369

grandad *n.* 112

grand duke/duchess *n.* 665

grande dame *n.* 112, 776

grandee *n.* 776

grandeur *n.* 29, 763, 785

grandfather *n.* 112

grandfather clock *n.* 97

grandiloquence *n.* 507, 771

grandiloquent *adj.* 507, 510, 771

grandiose *adj.* 785

grandioseness *n.* 510

grand jury *n.* 856

grand larceny *n.* 705

grandmaster *n.* 761

grandmother *n.* 112

grand old man *n.* 112, 774

grandparent *n.* 12

grange *n.* 165

granite *n.* 289, 311

granny *n.* 112

granny flat *n.* 112, 165

grant *n.* 631, 677, 690, 698, 719; *vb.* 434, 436, 697, 698, 859

grant a loan *vb.* 714

grant amnesty to *vb.* 813

grantee *n.* 699

Granth *n.* 868

grant impunity *vb.* 822

grant leave *vb.* 677

grant remission *vb.* 857

granulate *vb.* 300

granulated *adj.* 299, 300

granule *n.* 30, 48, 169, 300

grape *n.* 392

grapeshot *n.* 69, 649

the grapevine *n.* 466, 471

graph *n.* 24, 57

graphic *adj.* 488, 490, 507, 513, 517

graphics *n.* 490

grasp *n.* 43, 141, 438, 692, 695; *vb.* 43, 438, 695, 703

grasping *adj.* 703, 728

grass *n.* 327, 390, 849

grassland *n.* 313

grassroots *n.* 69

grass widow *n.* 798

grassy *adj.* 327, 390

grate *n.* 339, 362; *vb.* 20, 291, 301, 362, 366

grateful *adj.* 811

gratefully *adv.* 811

gratefulness *n.* 811

gratification *n.* 336

gratified *adj.* 734, 811

gratify *vb.* 736, 738

gratifying *adj.* 336

grating *adj.* 20, 291, 301, 362, 366, 517; *n.* 301

gratis *adj.* 667, 698, 724

gratitude *n.* 811, 825

gratuitous *adj.* 135, 820

gratuitousness *n.* 135, 820

gratuity *n.* 667, 698, 859

grave *adj.* 285, 507, 576, 733, 745; *n.* 325

gravel *n.* 311, 569

gravelly *adj.* 291, 311

graven *adj.* 492, 493

graven image *n.* 875

graver *n.* 493

graveyard *n.* 325, 882

gravid *adj.* 152

gravitas *n.* 285, 507

gravitate *vb.* 140

gravitational *adj.* 257

gravity *n.* 257, 285, 576, 733, 745

gravy *n.* 303

graze *n.* 187, 267, 301, 338; *vb.* 173, 187, 301, 338

grease *n.* 302, 319, 587; *vb.* 292, 302, 319

grease paint *n.* 523

greasiness *n.* 292, 302, 319

greasy *adj.* 292, 302, 319, 587

great *adj.* 29, 582

the great and the good *n.* 31

great-aunt *n.* 12

greatest *adj.* 29

greatest part *n.* 29

greatly *adv.* 29

great-nephew *n.* 12

greatness *n.* 29, 582

great-niece *n.* 12

the great outdoors *n.* 198, 306

great quantity *n.* 29

great-uncle *n.* 12

the great unwashed *n.* 777

greed *n.* 728, 755, 834, 846

greediness *n.* 846

greedy *adj.* 690, 728, 755, 834, 846

greedy guts *n.* 846

greedy pig *n.* 846

green *adj.* 50, 106, 111, 346, 390, 439, 627, 839; *n.* 390, 761

greenback *n.* 711

green belt *n.* 157, 313, 390

greenery *n.* 327, 390

greengage *n.* 390

greenhorn *n.* 106, 627

greenhouse *n.* 329

green light *n.* 436, 677

the Green Man *n.* 865

greenness *n.* 50, 106, 390

greenness *n.* 439

greensward *n.* 313

green with envy *adj.* 816

greenwood *n.* 327

greet *vb.* 261, 532, 791, 793, 823

greeting *n.* 261, 532, 791, 823

greetings card *n.* 515

gregarious *adj.* 789

gregariousness *n.* 789

gremlin *n.* 865

grenade *n.* 649

grenadier *n.* 648

grey *adj.* 63, 376, 382, 385; *n.* 385

grey area *n.* 63, 428

greybeard *n.* 112

grey eminence *n.* 139

grey-haired *adj.* 385

greyhound *n.* 245

greyhound-racing *n.* 554

greying *adj.* 385

grey matter *n.* 396

greyness *n.* 382, 385

grid *n.* 24, 177, 197

grief *n.* 735, 739, 747

grief-stricken *adj.* 735, 747

grievance *n.* 739, 818

grieve *vb.* 735, 747

grieve with *vb.* 809

grieving *n.* 735

grievous bodily harm *n.* 147, 639

grill *vb.* 267, 339

grille *n.* 197, 232

grilling *n.* 402

grim *adj.* 539, 737, 745

grimace *n.* 804; *vb.* 219, 484, 804

grime *n.* 587

grimness *n.* 745

grimy *adj.* 587

grin *n.* 744; *vb.* 744

grin and bear it *vb.* 742

grind *n.* 617, 762; *vb.* 296, 300, 301, 362, 617

grind down *vb.* 36

grinder *n.* 300

grinding *n.* 300

grindstone *n.* 296

grip *n.* 43, 167, 624, 695; *vb.* 43, 695

gripe *n.* 337

gripping *adj.* 732

grisly *adj.* 750

gristle *n.* 294

gristly *adj.* 294

grist to the mill *n.* 419

grit *n.* 143, 289, 300

H

habeas corpus *n.* 661
habit *n.* 122, 549,
 688, 849
habitat *n.* 158, 165
habitation *n.* 162
habitual *adj.* 549
habituate *vb.* 549
habituation *n.* 549
habitué *n.* 789
hack *n.* 326; *vb.* 41
hacker *n.* 472
hackney carriage *n.*
 242
hackneyed *adj.* 88,
 442, 508
hack out *vb.* 615
hackwork *n.* 513
had better *vb.* 821
Hades *n.* 323, 862,
 867
haemorrhage *n.* 303
hag *n.* 112
haggard *adj.* 183
haggle *vb.* 685, 707
haggling *n.* 685, 707
ha-ha *n.* 210
haiku *n.* 521
hail *n.* 66, 307, 340;
 vb. 307, 340, 532,
 791, 825
hair *n.* 202
hairbrush *n.* 765
hair cream *n.* 765
hair cut *n.* 765
hairdo *n.* 765
hairdresser *n.* 765
hairdressing *n.* 765
hair dryer *n.* 765
hairgrip *n.* 765
hairiness *n.* 291
hair lacquer *n.* 765
hairless *adj.* 203
hairnet *n.* 765
a hair of the dog that
 bit you *n.* 848
hairpiece *n.* 765
hairpin *n.* 221, 765
hair-raising *adj.* 750
hair-remover *n.* 203
hair's breadth *n.* 173
hair shirt *n.* 841
hair-splitting *adj.*
 411; *n.* 411
hair spray *n.* 765
hairy *adj.* 291, 299

halcyon *adj.* 655
halcyon days *n.* 655
hale and hearty *adj.*
 588
half *n.* 78, 81
half a dozen *n.* 84
half-and-half *adj.* 25
half-baked *adj.* 50,
 399, 560, 654
half-breed *n.* 38
half-brother *n.* 12
half-caste *adj.* 38
half-cut *adj.* 848
half-dead *adj.* 323
half-done *adj.* 273,
 654
half-dressed *adj.* 205
half-finished *adj.* 50,
 654
half-hearted *adj.* 538,
 756
half-heartedness *n.*
 541, 756
half-light *n.* 110, 374,
 376
half measures *n.* 50,
 273
half-moon *n.* 221
half-nelson *n.* 695
half-price *adj.* 724
half-remember *vb.*
 449
half-remembered *adj.*
 449
half-sister *n.* 12
half starved *adj.* 845
half-truth *n.* 479
halfway *adj.* 63; *adv.*
 63, 250; *n.* 27
halfway house *n.* 27,
 63, 165, 250
half-wit *n.* 397
halitosis *n.* 350
hall *n.* 165
hallelujah *n.* 746
hallmark *n.* 70,
 485
halloo *n.* 363
hallow *vb.* 872
hallowed *adj.* 549,
 862
hallucinate *vb.* 4
hallucination *n.* 4,
 394, 447, 457
hallucinatory *adj.* 4
halo *n.* 223, 374

halt *adj.* 144; *n.* 123,
 235; *vb.* 123, 235
halter *n.* 42, 861
halve *vb.* 41, 63, 81
ham *n.* 523
ham-fisted *adj.* 625
ham it up *vb.* 523,
 771
hamlet *n.* 157
hammer *n.* 247, 300,
 568; *vb.* 31, 147,
 247
hammer and tongs
 adv. 147, 617
hammer in *vb.* 475
hammering *n.* 147
hammer into *vb.* 88
hammock *n.* 192
hamper *n.* 167; *vb.*
 628, 630, 668
hamstring *vb.* 630
hamstrung *adj.* 142
ham up *vb.* 744
hand *n.* 97
handcuff *vb.* 40, 668
handcuffed *adj.* 668
handcuffs *n.* 668
hand down *vb.* 697
handful *n.* 30, 87,
 628, 662
handgun *n.* 649
handicap *n.* 26, 32,
 142, 581, 628, 630;
 vb. 26, 142, 630
handicapped *adj.* 142
handicrafts *n.* 149
handiness *n.* 138,
 162, 578
hand in glove *adv.* 40
handing over *n.* 563
hand in hand *adv.* 40
hand in *one's* notice,
 AAA 674
hand it to *vb.* 819
handiwork *n.* 149
handle *n.* 232, 497,
 568, 778; *vb.* 338,
 519, 622
handle roughly *vb.*
 566
handle with kid
 gloves *vb.* 660
handling *n.* 136, 338,
 490, 622
hand-me-downs *n.*
 204

hand of friendship *n.*
 646
handout *n.* 466, 631,
 698
hand out *vb.* 698
handover *n.* 129, 697
hand over *vb.* 129,
 563, 697
hand-picked *adj.* 545,
 582
handrail *n.* 193
handshake *n.* 261,
 791, 793
handsome *adj.* 725,
 763
handsomeness *n.* 763
handwriting *n.* 513
handwritten *adj.* 513
handy *adj.* 115, 138,
 162, 173, 578
handyman *n.* 613,
 666
hang *n.* 192; *vb.* 44,
 133, 192, 324, 766,
 860
hang back *vb.* 32,
 538, 784
hangdog *adj.* 743,
 804
hang, draw and quar-
 ter *vb.* 860
hanger *n.* 192
hanger-on *n.* 85, 827
hang fire *vb.* 114
hang-glider *n.* 244
hang-gliding *n.* 238,
 761
hanging *adj.* 192; *n.*
 192, 324, 860
hang in the balance
 vb. 428
hangman *n.* 324, 860
hang on *vb.* 124, 540,
 695
hang on *sb's* words
 vb. 404
hang-out *n.* 165
hang out at *vb.* 165
hang out the flags *vb.*
 786
hangover *n.* 37, 60,
 848
hang the expense *vb.*
 727
hang together *vb.* 400
hang-up *n.* 447, 735

hurry up *vb.* 615
hurt *adj.* 337, 595, 802; *n.* 337, 566, 595, 604, 802, 836; *vb.* 337, 566, 595, 604, 806, 818
hurtful *adj.* 604, 836
hurtfulness *n.* 604
hurtle *vb.* 147, 245
husband *n.* 332, 797; *vb.* 726
husbandry *n.* 726
hush *n.* 235, 354; *vb.* 354
hushed *adj.* 354, 356
hush-hush *adj.* 467
hush up *vb.* 467
husk *n.* 37, 202; *vb.* 203
huskiness *n.* 362, 527
husky *adj.* 362, 527, 763
hussar *n.* 648
hussy *n.* 838
hustle *vb.* 234, 245, 615
hustling *adj.* 615
hutch *n.* 165, 328
hybrid *adj.* 38, 328; *n.* 38
hydrant *n.* 305
hydrate *vb.* 305
hydrated *adj.* 305
hydration *n.* 305
hydroelectricity *n.* 341
hydrofoil *n.* 243
hydrogen bomb *n.* 649
hydrography *n.* 284, 310
hydrology *n.* 310
hydrotherapy *n.* 305
hygiene *n.* 39, 586, 590
hygienic *adj.* 39, 586, 590, 598
hygienist *n.* 590
hymn *n.* 367, 521, 874
hymn book *n.* 881
hype *n.* 431, 470, 482; *vb.* 431, 470, 482
hyperactive *adj.* 281
hyperactivity *n.* 281

hyperbole *n.* 272, 431, 458, 482
hyperbolic *adj.* 431, 482
hypercorrect *adj.* 501
hypercorrection *n.* 501
hypercritical *adj.* 826
hypermarket *n.* 710
hypersensitive *adj.* 334, 730
hypersensitivity *n.* 334, 401, 730
hypnosis *n.* 731, 877
hypnotic *adj.* 139
hypnotism *n.* 139, 877
hypnotize *vb.* 139, 877
hypnotized *adj.* 731
hypochondria *n.* 750
hypocrisy *n.* 481, 543, 827, 873
hypocrite *n.* 480, 827, 873
hypocritical *adj.* 479, 481, 543, 771, 873
hypothermia *n.* 340
hypothesis *n.* 134, 400, 408, 456
hypothesize *vb.* 134, 398, 400, 416, 456
hypothetical *adj.* 134, 400, 408, 416, 423, 456
hysteria *n.* 447
hysterical *adj.* 147, 447, 729, 732
hysterics *n.* 732

I

ICBM *n.* 649
ice *n.* 305, 340, 379, 603; *vb.* 340, 345
iceberg *n.* 731
icebox *n.* 340
ice-cold *adj.* 340
iced *adj.* 345, 603
ice hockey *n.* 761
ice up *vb.* 340
I Ching *n.* 455
icicle *n.* 192, 340
iciness *n.* 340
icing *n.* 345
icon *n.* 488, 875
iconoclasm *n.* 73

iconoclast *n.* 73
iconoclastic *adj.* 73
iconolatry *n.* 875
icy *adj.* 340
ID *n.* 271
ID card *n.* 485
idea *n.* 408, 456, 457
ideal *adj.* 2, 4, 283, 408, 584; *n.* 584
idealism *n.* 283
idealist *n.* 807
idealistic *adj.* 457, 831
idealize *vb.* 4, 283, 457
ideally *adv.* 4
idée fixe *n.* 408
identical *adj.* 13, 15, 25
identifiable *adj.* 485
identification *n.* 433, 485, 497
identified *adj.* 485
identify *vb.* 68, 433, 485, 497
identifying *adj.* 485
identifying sign *n.* 485
identikit *adj.* 72
identity *n.* 13, 15, 25, 485
identity theft *n.* 488, 705, 853
ideogram *n.* 495, 513
ideology *n.* 434
idiom *n.* 494, 499, 502
idiomatic *adj.* 70, 494
idiosyncrasy *n.* 70, 485
idiosyncratic *adj.* 70, 485, 502
idiot *n.* 397, 445
idiotic *adj.* 445, 772
idle *adj.* 146, 235, 565, 608, 610; *vb.* 90, 136, 146, 610
idleness *n.* 608
idler *n.* 556, 838
idle rich *n.* 610, 712
idol *n.* 763, 795, 862, 875
idolater *n.* 869, 875
idolatrize *vb.* 875
idolatrous *adj.* 869, 875

idolatry *n.* 869, 875
idolism *n.* 875
idolization *n.* 875
idolize *vb.* 874, 875
idolizer *n.* 875
idol-maker *n.* 875
idol-worship *n.* 875
idol-worshipper *n.* 875
idol-worshipping *adj.* 875
ignis fatuus *n.* 4, 370
ignition *n.* 339
ignoble *adj.* 832
ignominious *adj.* 775, 832
ignominy *n.* 775
ignoramus *n.* 439
ignorance *n.* 399, 439
ignorant *adj.* 399, 439, 839
ignore *vb.* 352, 399, 407, 680, 731, 790, 792, 813
ilk *n.* 68
ill *n.* 589, 836; *n.* 604, 836
ill-assorted *adj.* 20
ill-bred *adj.* 792
ill breeding *n.* 792
ill-considered *adj.* 399, 625, 753
ill-digested *adj.* 50
ill-disposed *adj.* 794
illegal *adj.* 678, 818, 820, 853
illegal immigrant *n.* 54, 161, 600, 790
illegality *n.* 840, 853
illegally *adv.* 853
illegibility *n.* 459, 461
illegible *adj.* 461
illegitimacy *n.* 12, 155, 853
illegitimate *adj.* 818, 820, 853
illegitimate child *n.* 853
illegitimately *adv.* 853
ill-equipped *adj.* 560
ill-favoured *adj.* 764
ill feeling *n.* 794, 796
ill-fitting *adj.* 764
ill health *n.* 589

impermanence *n.* 94, 121, 130

impermanent *adj.* 94, 121, 130

impermeability *n.* 143, 233, 287

impermeable *adj.* 143, 233, 287

impersonal *adj.* 756

impersonate *vb.* 21, 128, 488, 498

impersonation *n.* 21, 488, 498

impersonator *n.* 21

impertinence *n.* 781

impertinent *adj.* 781, 792, 824

imperturbability *n.* 731, 733

imperturbable *adj.* 731, 733

impervious *adj.* 233, 731

imperviousness *n.* 233, 287

impetuosity *n.* 407, 548, 732, 753

impetuous *adj.* 407, 548, 732, 753

impetuousness *n.* 732

impetus *n.* 132, 134, 141, 145, 234, 247, 255

impiety *n.* 873

impinge *vb.* 272

impious *adj.* 873

impish *adj.* 865

implacability *n.* 810

implacable *adj.* 539, 810

implant *vb.* 269

implantation *n.* 269

implausibility *n.* 426

implausible *adj.* 424, 426, 435

implement *n.* 568; *vb.* 607

implementation *n.* 136

implicate *vb.* 134, 197, 830

implication *n.* 400, 458

implicit *adj.* 195, 458, 465

implicitness *n.* 195

imploring *adj.* 681

imply *vb.* 400, 458, 465

impolite *adj.* 781, 792, 824

impoliteness *n.* 792, 824

import *n.* 458, 576, 707; *vb.* 54, 239, 707

importance *n.* 200, 576

important *adj.* 139, 576, 823

importation *n.* 239, 263

imported *adj.* 54, 263

importer *n.* 241, 707

impose *vb.* 685, 721, 823

impose a duty *vb.* 821

impose one's will *vb.* 535

imposing *adj.* 576, 774, 823

impossibility *n.* 424, 749

impossible *adj.* 424, 749

impost *n.* 721

impostor *n.* 21, 480, 771, 820, 838

imposture *n.* 498

impotence *n.* 142, 144, 153

impotent *adj.* 142, 144, 153

impound *vb.* 703

impounding *n.* 703

impoverish *vb.* 713

impoverished *adj.* 508, 593, 713

impoverishment *n.* 593, 713

impracticability *n.* 424

impracticable *adj.* 424

impractical *adj.* 565, 625

imprecation *n.* 801

imprecatory *adj.* 681

imprecise *adj.* 441, 504, 818

impreciseness *n.* 504

imprecision *n.* 441

impregnability *n.* 143, 598

impregnable *adj.* 143, 598

impregnate *vb.* 38, 152, 269

impregnation *n.* 269

impress *vb.* 334, 493, 703, 729, 732, 823

impressed *adj.* 729

impression *n.* 227, 334, 488, 514, 516, 729

impressionability *n.* 541

impressionable *adj.* 216, 334, 541, 730

Impressionist *adj.* 490

impressionistic *adj.* 401, 488, 517

impressive *adj.* 823

impressment *n.* 664

imprimatur *n.* 825

imprint *n.* 485

imprison *vb.* 199, 668, 790, 860

imprisoned *adj.* 668

imprisonment *n.* 668

improbability *n.* 426

improbable *adj.* 426

improbity *n.* 832

impromptu *adj.* 548, 560; *n.* 367

improper *adj.* 512, 769, 818, 820

impropriety *n.* 512, 769, 840

improve *vb.* 29, 121, 253, 582, 592, 835

improved *adj.* 592

improvement *n.* 121, 253, 592, 835

improver *n.* 592

improve the appearance of *vb.* 765

improve upon *vb.* 592

improvidence *n.* 454, 727

improvident *adj.* 454, 727

improvisation *n.* 367, 454, 548, 560

improvise *vb.* 96, 416, 454, 548, 560

improvised *adj.* 454, 548, 560

imprudence *n.* 407, 445, 454, 753

imprudent *adj.* 407, 445, 454, 753

impudence *n.* 781, 792

impudent *adj.* 781, 792

impulse *n.* 544, 548

impulse buy *n.* 708

impulsion *n.* 134, 234, 247, 255

impulsive *adj.* 96, 401, 548, 732, 753

impulsiveness *n.* 96, 548, 753

impunity *n.* 822

impure *adj.* 585, 851

impurity *n.* 585, 851

imputation *n.* 134, 830

impute *vb.* 830

in *adj.* 106, 770

in abeyance *adj.* 565, 608

in a big way *adv.* 29

inability *n.* 142, 625

inability to act *n.* 608

in a body *adv.* 66, 85

in one's absence *adv.* 163

in absentia *adv.* 163

inaccessibility *n.* 172

inaccessible *adj.* 172, 233, 424

in accord *adv.* 19

inaccuracy *n.* 407, 441, 479

inaccurate *adj.* 441, 489, 818

inaction *n.* 608

inactive *adj.* 146, 235, 610

inactivity *n.* 146, 610

in addition *adv.* 35, 45

inadequacy *n.* 50, 142, 144, 273, 574, 579, 585

inadequate *adj.* 50, 142, 273, 574, 585

inadmissibility *n.* 546

inform *vb.* 5, 438, 466, 602, 830
informal *adj.* 788
informality *n.* 788
informant *n.* 466
infirmary *n.* 596
informatics *n.* 75
information *n.* 420, 438, 466, 602
information highway/superhighway *n.* 472
information retrieval *n.* 75, 570
information technology *n.* 75
informative *adj.* 466, 468, 471
informed *adj.* 438, 466
informer *n.* 466, 830
inform on *vb.* 466
infotainment *n.* 472
infraction *n.* 272
infra dig *adj.* 775
infrastructure *n.* 189, 216, 298
infrequency *n.* 87, 118, 183, 288
infrequent *adj.* 87, 118, 183, 288
infrequently *adv.* 87, 118
infringe *vb.* 272, 662, 689, 818, 820, 853
infringement *n.* 272, 662, 689, 853
in front *adv.* 59, 212
in full view *adv.* 372
infuriate *vb.* 147, 802
infuriated *adj.* 802
infuriating *adj.* 597
infuse *vb.* 38, 269
infusion *n.* 38, 267, 303
in future *adv.* 104
in general *adv.* 27, 69
ingenious *adj.* 457, 626
ingénue *n.* 627
ingenuity *n.* 457, 626
ingenuous *adj.* 478, 627, 831
ingenuousness *n.* 478, 627

ingest *vb.* 166, 199, 267
ingestion *n.* 199, 265, 267
inglorious *adj.* 775
in good health *adj.* 588
in good heart *adj.* 742
in good taste *adj.* 768
ingrained *adj.* 5, 131, 199, 549
ingratiate *oneself vb.* 782, 827
ingratiating *adj.* 782, 791, 827
ingratiation *n.* 782, 791
ingratitude *n.* 812
ingredient *n.* 35, 48, 53, 282
ingredients *n.* 166
ingress *n.* 263
in-group *n.* 52, 634
ingrown *adj.* 199
inhabit *vb.* 158, 162, 165
inhabitant *n.* 164
inhabited *adj.* 164
inhalation *n.* 316
inhale *vb.* 199, 316, 347
in hand *adj.* 565, 570; *adv.* 37
inharmonious *adj.* 366
in haste *adv.* 245
inhere *vb.* 5, 53
inherent *adj.* 5, 53
inherit *vb.* 690, 697, 699
inheritance *n.* 100, 690, 697, 719
inherited *adj.* 12, 133
inheritor *n.* 100, 699
inherit the mantle of *vb.* 100
inhibit *vb.* 668
inhibited *adj.* 668, 784
inhibition *n.* 784
in hock *adj.* 687
in-house *adj.* 162, 199
inhuman *adj.* 731, 806

inhumanity *n.* 806, 810
inimical *adj.* 794
inimitable *adj.* 22, 70
iniquity *n.* 838
in irons *adj.* 668
initial *adj.* 59, 61; *n.* 495; *vb.* 485, 495
initially *adv.* 61
initials *n.* 485
initiate *vb.* 59, 61, 132, 263, 265, 475
initiation *n.* 59, 61, 263, 265, 475
initiative *n.* 59, 145, 607
initiatory *adj.* 59, 61, 265
inject *vb.* 269, 596, 849
injection *n.* 199, 269, 596
in jeopardy *adj.* 599
in jug *adj.* 668
injunction *n.* 71, 623, 661
injure *vb.* 150, 337, 593, 595, 604, 806, 818
injured *adj.* 337, 593, 595
injured party *n.* 839
injurious *adj.* 150, 604, 818
injury *n.* 337, 593, 595, 604, 818, 836
injustice *n.* 26, 430, 802, 818, 853
ink *n.* 384; *vb.* 490
in keeping *adv.* 15, 19, 72
in kind *adv.* 129
inkiness *n.* 384
inkling *n.* 456
inky *adj.* 375, 384
inlaid *adj.* 766
inland *adj.* 311; *n.* 311
inland revenue *n.* 721
inland sea *n.* 312
in-laws *n.* 12
inlay *n.* 201, 269; *vb.* 201, 269, 766
in league *adj.* 633; *adv.* 40, 45
inlet *n.* 263, 310

in lieu *adv.* 28, 128
in *one's* lifetime *adv.* 1
in limbo *adv.* 161, 198
in line *adv.* 15, 57, 72
in loco parentis *adv.* 154
in love *adj.* 795
inmate *n.* 164, 199, 671
in mind *adv.* 398
in mint condition *adv.* 106
in moderation *adv.* 148
in mothballs *adj.* 565
in motion *adj.* 609; *adv.* 234
inn *n.* 165
in name *adv.* 4
in name only *adj.* 497
innards *n.* 53, 199
innate *adj.* 5
in need *adj.* 558; *adv.* 558
inner *adj.* 199
inner child *n.* 283
inner circle *n.* 52
inner city *n.* 157
inner man *n.* 199
innermost *adj.* 199
innings *n.* 92
innocence *n.* 627, 837, 839, 857
innocent *adj.* 509, 627, 831, 837, 839, 850, 857; *n.* 627, 839
innocent party *n.* 839
innocuous *adj.* 839
innocuousness *n.* 148
innovate *vb.* 106
innovation *n.* 22, 106, 121
innovative *adj.* 22, 59, 106, 121, 132
innovator *n.* 22
innuendo *n.* 465, 744, 828
innumerable *adj.* 86, 89
inoculate *vb.* 269, 590
inoculation *n.* 269, 590, 596

instantaneity *n*. 94, 245

instantaneous *adj*. 96

instantaneousness *n*. 96

instant book *n*. 518

instantly *adv*. 101

instead *adv*. 28, 128, 129

in *one's* stead *adv*. 128

in step *adv*. 19, 103

instigate *vb*. 61, 134

instigation *n*. 61

instil *vb*. 269, 475

instinct *n*. 140, 397, 399, 401, 536

instinctive *adj*. 397, 399, 401, 536, 548

instinctiveness *n*. 548

institute *n*. 477; *vb*. 61, 132

institute of technology *n*. 477

institution *n*. 61, 881

in stock *adj*. 570

in store *adj*. 570

instruct *vb*. 438, 466, 475, 623, 661

instruction *n*. 438, 466, 475, 623, 661

instructive *adj*. 466, 475

instructor *n*. 475

instrument *n*. 132, 568

instrumental *adj*. 132, 138, 367

instrumentalist *n*. 368

instrumentality *n*. 132, 138

instrument of torture *n*. 861

insubordinate *adj*. 637, 662, 824

insubordination *n*. 637, 662

insubstantial *adj*. 2, 4, 283, 286, 295

insubstantiality *n*. 4, 283

in succession *adv*. 60, 64

insufficiency *n*. 30, 50, 273, 574

insufficient *adj*. 30, 50, 169, 179, 574, 826

insufficient funds *n*. 574

insular *adj*. 41, 79, 311, 430

insularity *n*. 41, 430

insulate *vb*. 41

insulation *n*. 201

insult *n*. 792, 802, 824; *vb*. 792, 802, 824

insulting *adj*. 792, 824

in sum *adv*. 179

insuperable *adj*. 424

insupportable *adj*. 285

insurance *n*. 28, 598

insure *vb*. 687

insure against *vb*. 28

insured *adj*. 598, 687

insurgence *n*. 662

insurgency *n*. 127

insurgent *adj*. 127; *n*. 127, 662

insurmountable *adj*. 424

insurrection *n*. 127, 662

insurrectionist *n*. 662

in suspense *adv*. 450

in sympathy with *adj*. 633

in sync *adv*. 103

intact *adj*. 39, 47, 603

intaglio *n*. 493

intake *n*. 263, 265

in tandem *adv*. 45

intangibility *n*. 4, 283

intangible *adj*. 4, 283

integer *n*. 74

integral *adj*. 5, 39, 47, 53

integrate *vb*. 45

integrated *adj*. 40, 79

integrated circuit *n*. 169

integration *n*. 45, 51

integrity *n*. 39, 47, 79, 478, 584, 817, 831, 837, 839

integument *n*. 202

intellect *n*. 283, 396

intellectual *adj*. 396, 398; *n*. 396, 438

intellectual exercise *n*. 398

intellectualize *vb*. 283, 396, 400

intelligence *n*. 396, 466, 471

intelligent *adj*. 396

intelligent design *n*. 1, 132

intelligentsia *n*. 777

intelligibility *n*. 460, 503

intelligible *adj*. 460, 503

intemperance *n*. 844, 846, 848

intemperate *adj*. 844

intend *vb*. 535, 553

intense *adj*. 147, 381

intensely *adv*. 186

intensification *n*. 33, 741

intensify *vb*. 33, 186, 741

intensity *n*. 29, 147, 381

intent *adj*. 404, 539; *n*. 553

intent on *adj*. 553

intention *n*. 535, 553, 557

intentional *adj*. 535, 547, 553

intentness *n*. 404

inter *vb*. 325

interact *vb*. 11

interaction *n*. 11, 129

interbreed *vb*. 12, 38

intercalate *vb*. 207, 269

intercalation *n*. 269

intercede *vb*. 138, 207, 647, 681, 874

interceding *adj*. 874

intercept *vb*. 207

interception *n*. 207

intercession *n*. 138, 207, 647, 681, 862, 874

intercessor *n*. 647, 874

intercessory *adj*. 647

interchange *n*. 11,

129; *vb*. 11, 121, 129, 196

interchangeable *adj*. 11, 13, 128, 129

intercom *n*. 42, 472

interconnect *vb*. 11

interconnected *adj*. 11

interconnectedness *n*. 11

interconnecting *adj*. 176

interdependence *n*. 9, 11

interdependent *adj*. 9, 11

interdict *vb*. 678

interdiction *n*. 678

interest *n*. 35, 402, 466, 690, 694, 732, 761, 835; *vb*. 9, 732, 736

interested *adj*. 402

interesting *adj*. 732

interest rate *n*. 721

interface *n*. 40, 176, 207, 570

interfere *vb*. 58, 207, 402, 630

interference *n*. 58, 207, 630, 678

interfering *adj*. 207, 402

interim *adj*. 63, 121; *n*. 90

interior *adj*. 199; *n*. 199, 311, 490

interior decoration/ design *n*. 766

interjacent *adj*. 207

interject *vb*. 35, 65, 269

interjection *n*. 35, 65, 269, 500

interjectional *adj*. 65, 269, 500

interlace *vb*. 38, 43, 197

interlard *vb*. 38, 207

interleave *vb*. 207

interline *vb*. 201

interlining *n*. 201

interlinked *adj*. 40

interlock *vb*. 43, 197

interlocking *adj*. 197

interloper *n*. 54

keep *one's* head down
vb. 754

keeping *n.* 688, 786

keep in reserve *vb.*
570

keep in step *vb.* 103

keep in the back-
ground *vb.* 784

keep in the dark *vb.*
439

keep late hours *vb.*
114

keep *one's* mouth
shut *vb.* 531

keep *one's* nose clean
vb. 71

keep on *vb.* 117, 124,
253, 540

keep open house *vb.*
789

keep order *vb.* 854

keep out of harm's
way *vb.* 598

keep *one's* pecker up
vb. 742

keepsake *n.* 448

keep secret *vb.* 467

keep *one's* shirt on *vb.*
733

keep smiling *vb.* 742

keep sober *vb.* 843

keep tabs on *vb.* 406

keep *one's* temper *vb.*
733

keep the books *vb.*
720

keep the faith *vb.* 872

keep the peace *vb.*
644

keep the wolf from
the door *vb.* 712

keep to *oneself* *vb.*
834

keep *oneself* to *oneself*
vb. 790

keep to the straight
and narrow *vb.* 71,
837

keep under surveil-
lance *vb.* 406,
598

keep under wraps *vb.*
467

keep up *vb.* 103

keep up appearances
vb. 72

keep up with the Jon-
eses *vb.* 72, 770

keep well *vb.* 588

keep well out of *vb.*
754

keep within bounds
vb. 843

keg *n.* 167

ken *n.* 438

kennel *n.* 165

kerb *n.* 209

kernel *n.* 5, 63, 199

kerosene *n.* 319, 341

ketch *n.* 243

kettle *n.* 167

kettledrum *n.* 369

key *adj.* 200; *n.* 232,
365

keyboard *n.* 570

keyboard instrument
n. 369

keyed up *adj.* 559,
729, 732

keyhole *n.* 232

key moment *n.* 115

khaki *adj.* 386, 390;
n. 204

khan *n.* 776

kibbutz *n.* 328, 693

kibbutznik *n.* 693

kick *n.* 255, 336, 729,
734; *vb.* 247, 255,
682

kick against *vb.* 638

kickback *n.* 248,
859

kick back *vb.* 248

kick *one's* heels *vb.*
608

kick-off *n.* 61

kick off *vb.* 61

kick over the traces
vb. 73, 127, 658

kick the bucket *vb.*
323

kick up a fuss *vb.* 682

kick upstairs *vb.* 161,
673

kid *n.* 111, 155; *vb.*
744, 773

kidnap *n.* 703; *vb.*
395, 703, 705

kidnapper *n.* 703,
705

kidnapping *n.* 703,
705

kidnap victim *n.* 671,
706

kidney *n.* 68

kid's stuff *n.* 629

kill *vb.* 90, 324, 860

kill *oneself* *vb.* 324

killer *n.* 147, 150, 324

killing *adj.* 617, 744;
n. 147, 324

killjoy *n.* 552, 745

kill the fatted calf *vb.*
261, 725, 786

kill with kindness *vb.*
800

kiln *n.* 339

kilo *n.* 23

kind *adj.* 725, 791,
793, 805, 809, 837;
n. 68

kindergarten *n.* 111,
477

kindhearted *adj.* 805

kindheartedness *n.*
805

kindle *n.* 66; *vb.* 132,
145, 339, 341

kindliness *n.* 791

kindling *n.* 341

kindly *adj.* 660, 791,
805, 837

kindness *n.* 660, 791,
793, 805, 837

kind offer *n.* 725

kind person *n.* 805,
807

kindred *adj.* 12

kindred spirit *n.* 17

kinetic *adj.* 234

king *n.* 665, 776

kingdom *n.* 157

kingdom come *n.* 866

the kingdom of God
n. 866

the kingdom of
heaven *n.* 866

kingly *adj.* 776

the King of Kings *n.*
862

king-size *adj.* 29, 168

king's ransom *n.* 712

kink *n.* 224

kinky *adj.* 224, 447

kinship *n.* 9, 12

kiosk *n.* 710

kip *n.* 610

kirby grip *n.* 765

kirk *n.* 882

kiss *n.* 791, 793, 800;
vb. 791, 800

kisser *n.* 212

kiss hands *vb.* 791

the kiss of life *n.* 322

kitbag *n.* 167

kitchen garden *n.* 329

kitchen maid *n.* 666

kitchen-sink *adj.* 523

kitchen-sink drama *n.*
3

kith and kin *n.* 12

kitsch *n.* 769

kitschy *adj.* 769

kitten *n.* 155, 326

kitty *n.* 711

klaxon *n.* 355, 602

kleptomania *n.* 705

kleptomaniac *adj.*
705

knack *n.* 624

knackered *adj.* 619

knackering *adj.* 619

knapsack *n.* 167

knave *n.* 838

knead *vb.* 38, 338

kneecap *vb.* 860

knee-jerk *adj.* 248,
401, 548

knee-jerk reaction/
response *n.* 399,
536

kneel *vb.* 185, 277,
823, 874, 881

kneeling *adj.* 823,
874

knees-up *n.* 524,
789

knife *n.* 296, 568

knife-edge *n.* 181

knight *n.* 648, 776

knit *vb.* 40, 149

knitting *n.* 149, 766

knob *n.* 223, 226, 232

knobbliness *n.* 291

knobbly *adj.* 291

knock *n.* 247, 357; *vb.*
247, 826, 828

knockabout *adj.* 523

knock about *vb.* 236

knock back *vb.* 267

knock back a few *vb.*
848

knock-down *adj.* 724

knock down *vb.* 709

lawlessness n. 658, 662, 853

law-maker n. 852

law-making n. 852

lawn n. 327, 569

law officer n. 854

lawsuit n. 635, 856

lawyer n. 613, 623

lax adj. 407, 658, 689, 788, 809

laxative adj. 268; n. 39, 596

laxity n. 407, 658, 689

lay adj. 880; n. 521; vb. 40

lay aside vb. 565

layabout n. 610, 838

lay at *one's* door vb. 830

lay at the door of vb. 134

lay bare vb. 203, 464, 468

lay brethren n. 880

lay claim to vb. 819

lay down vb. 422, 623, 661

lay down *one's* arms 646

lay down *one's* life vb. 323

lay down the law vb. 71, 661

layer n. 175, 321; vb. 175, 202, 207

layered adj. 175

lay ghosts vb. 876

lay *one's* hands on vb. 690

lay in vb. 570

lay into vb. 147, 639

lay it on thick vb. 482, 827

lay it on with a shovel/trowel vb. 431, 510

lay low vb. 185

layman n. 880

layoff n. 161, 673

lay off vb. 161, 673, 696

layout n. 55, 57, 216, 557

lay out vb. 557, 718

layout artist n. 557

lay people n. 880

lay preacher n. 868, 880

lay reader n. 880

lay siege to vb. 639

lay the foundations vb. 559

lay to rest vb. 325

lay up vb. 570

lay waste vb. 150

lazeabout vb. 610

laziness n. 146, 610, 616

lazy adj. 146, 610, 616

lazy-bones n. 610

lea n. 313

lead n. 31, 285, 385, 569, 651; vb. 31, 59, 212, 622

lead astray vb. 441, 838

a lead balloon n. 285

lead captive vb. 703

leaden adj. 285, 385

leader n. 31, 368, 519, 622, 665

leader of fashion n. 770

leadership n. 31, 622, 657

lead-in n. 61

leading adj. 31, 59, 140, 212, 576, 622, 657, 774

leading lady/man n. 523

leading light n. 774

leading seaman n. 648

lead the fashion vb. 770

lead *sb* up the garden path vb. 480

leaf n. 175, 327

leafiness n. 390

leafless adj. 203

leaflet n. 516

leafy adj. 327, 390

league n. 40, 45, 633, 634, 684

leak n. 264, 468, 605; vb. 232, 264, 308, 314, 466, 468, 572, 605, 691

leakage n. 34, 572, 691

leaky adj. 232, 264

lean adj. 183, 656; vb. 140, 195

leaning n. 140, 757

leanness n. 183

lean on vb. 139, 285, 664

lean times n. 656

lean-to n. 165

lean towards vb. 818

leap n. 66, 253, 274; vb. 274, 524

leap at vb. 537

leap for joy vb. 746

leapfrog n. 761; vb. 65

a leap in the dark n. 753

leap to the eye vb. 372

leap year n. 92, 119

learn vb. 433, 438, 476

learn by heart vb. 448

learned adj. 438, 444, 476

learnedness n. 476

learner n. 61, 476

learning n. 438, 444, 476

learn *one's* lesson vb. 452

learn the hard way vb. 452

learn up vb. 476

lease n. 697, 701; vb. 697, 701, 702

leased adj. 164

leaseholder n. 692

leash n. 42, 668

leasing n. 701, 702

least adj. 30

leather n. 569

leatheriness n. 294

leathery adj. 294

leave n. 612, 618, 677, 822; vb. 262, 556, 563, 674, 697, 698, 798

leave *one* cold vb. 731, 756

leave hanging vb. 50

leave in the lurch vb. 407, 452

leaven n. 121, 276, 286; vb. 286

leavening n. 306

leave no choice vb. 664

leave no stone unturned vb. 49, 414, 555

leave nothing to chance vb. 754

leave of absence n. 163, 612

leave off vb. 50, 65, 123, 550

leave out vb. 52

leavetaking n. 262

leave *sth* to be desired vb. 32, 50, 273, 452

leave *sb* to their own devices vb. 667

leave undone vb. 654

leaving n. 262, 563, 674

leaving present n. 811

leavings n. 37

Lebensraum n. 667

lecher n. 851

lecherous adj. 755, 851

lectern n. 882

lecture n. 532, 826; vb. 475, 528, 532, 826

lecture hall n. 477

lecturer n. 528

ledge n. 191, 193, 228

ledger n. 720

leech n. 43, 702, 703

leer vb. 370, 800

lees n. 37

leeway n. 156, 174, 667

left adj. 214; n. 214

left hand n. 214

leftover adj. 37

leftovers n. 37

left to rot adj. 565

legacy n. 60, 100, 133, 690, 697, 698, 719

legal adj. 71, 817, 819, 852

legal administrator n. 854

legal age *n.* 112

legal battle *n.* 635

legal code *n.* 852

legal eagle *n.* 613

legality *n.* 817, 852

legalization *n.* 658, 677

legalize *vb.* 677

legal learning *n.* 852

legally *adv.* 852

legal proceedings *n.* 856

legal representative *n.* 675

legal right *n.* 819

legate *n.* 675

legatee *n.* 699

legation *n.* 672, 675

legend *n.* 107, 513, 774

legendary *adj.* 457, 479, 774

leggy *adj.* 183

legibility *n.* 460

legible *adj.* 460

legion *n.* 86

legionnaire *n.* 648

legislate *vb.* 622

legislation *n.* 622, 852

legislative *adj.* 622

legislative assembly *n.* 657

legislator *n.* 622, 852

legislature *n.* 634, 657

leg it *vb.* 236

legitimacy *n.* 817, 852

legitimate *adj.* 523, 817, 819, 852

legitimately *adv.* 852

legless *adj.* 848

Lego *n.* 53, 761

leg-pulling *n.* 773

legroom *n.* 156

leg-up *n.* 253, 276

leisure *n.* 580, 608, 612, 616, 761

leisure activities *n.* 612

leisure centre *n.* 612

leisured *adj.* 610, 612

leisured classes *n.* 610

leisureliness *n.* 246

leisurely *adj.* 246, 616

lemon *n.* 346, 389

lend *vb.* 701, 714

lend a hand *vb.* 631

lend an ear *vb.* 351

lender *n.* 571, 701, 714

lending *n.* 701

length *n.* 23, 178

lengthen *vb.* 178

lengthening *n.* 178

lengthily *adv.* 178

lengthways *adv.* 178

lengthy *adj.* 178, 506

leniency *n.* 660

lenient *adj.* 429, 660, 677, 809, 813

lens *n.* 491

Lent *n.* 845, 881

leper *n.* 54, 790

leprechaun *n.* 865

leprosy *n.* 589

lesbian *adj.* 73, 333; *n.* 73

lesbianism *n.* 333

lesion *n.* 595

less *adv.* 36

less and less *adv.* 34

lessee *n.* 692, 699

lessen *vb.* 30, 34, 144, 148, 171

lesson *n.* 475, 476, 602

less than one *n.* 78

let *n.* 701; *vb.* 677, 697, 701

let alone *vb.* 556, 667

let be *vb.* 667

let bygones be bygones *vb.* 449, 646, 813

let down *adj.* 452; *vb.* 452

letdown *n.* 452

let fly *vb.* 147

let fly at *vb.* 639

let go *vb.* 696

let *oneself* go *vb.* 667

let *one's* hair down *vb.* 667, 746

lethal *adj.* 150, 323, 324, 604

lethargic *adj.* 144, 146, 246, 731

lethargy *n.* 144, 146, 246, 610, 731

let *oneself* in for *vb.* 562

let it all hang out *vb.* 667

let-off *n.* 857

let off *vb.* 606, 822, 857; *adj.* 813

let off steam *vb.* 761

let off the lead *vb.* 669

let-out *n.* 264, 422, 605

let out *vb.* 669

let pass *vb.* 813

let sleeping dogs lie *vb.* 608

let slide *vb.* 407

let slip *vb.* 405, 468

let slip through *one's* fingers *vb.* 691

letter *n.* 495, 515; *vb.* 485, 495

letter bomb *n.* 472, 649

letterbox *n.* 232

lettered *adj.* 438, 476

lettering *n.* 495

letter of credit *n.* 711

letter of the law *n.* 659

letterpress *n.* 514

letters *n.* 515

let the cat out of the bag *vb.* 466, 468

let the grass grow under *one's* feet *vb.* 407

let things slide *vb.* 610

letting *n.* 697, 701

letting off *n.* 605

letup *n.* 123

let up *vb.* 246

leukaemia *n.* 589

level *adj.* 185, 191, 222, 292; *n.* 24, 175, 191, 353, 502; *vb.* 15, 150, 185, 191, 222, 249, 277, 292

level down *vb.* 25

level-headed *adj.* 444, 446, 733

level-headedness *n.* 444, 446, 733

levelling *n.* 72, 277

levelness *n.* 191, 292

level pegging *n.* 25

level playing-field *n.* 817

level up *vb.* 25

lever *n.* 132, 193, 276, 568; *vb.* 276

leverage *n.* 31, 139

leveret *n.* 155

leviathan *n.* 168

levitate *vb.* 286

levitation *n.* 274, 276

levity *n.* 445, 742

levy *n.* 699, 721, 819; *vb.* 699, 721

lewd *adj.* 851

lewdness *n.* 851

lexical *adj.* 496

lexicon *n.* 76, 496

LGBT *adj.* 73

liability *n.* 140, 425, 715, 821, 840, 860

liable *adj.* 140, 425, 821, 840, 860

liable to prosecution *adj.* 830

liaison *n.* 795

liar *n.* 480, 838

libel *n.* 604, 775, 828, 830; *vb.* 604, 828, 830

libeller *n.* 828

libellous *adj.* 604, 828

liberal *adj.* 180, 475, 573, 660, 667, 698, 725, 807, 833, 859; *n.* 667

liberalism *n.* 667, 871

liberality *n.* 725, 833

liberalization *n.* 669

liberalize *vb.* 669

liberalness *n.* 180

liberate *vb.* 606, 669, 822

liberated *adj.* 333, 667, 857

liberation *n.* 606, 669, 822

liberator *n.* 606

libertarian *adj.* 667; *n.* 667

libertarianism *n.* 667

libertine *n.* 851

liberty *n.* 667, 677, 822

libidinous *adj.* 851

libido *n.* 851

librarian *n.* 516

loftiness *n.* 184, 276

lofty *adj.* 184, 276, 507, 779

log *n.* 341, 486; *vb.* 76, 97

logarithm *n.* 74

log(book) *n.* 97, 486

logic *n.* 400

logical *adj.* 396, 400, 410

logo *n.* 485

logorrhoea *n.* 530

loins *n.* 152

loiter *vb.* 114, 610, 616

Lolita *n.* 111

loll *vb.* 191

lolly *n.* 711

loneliness *n.* 79, 790

lonely *adj.* 790

lonely hearts column *n.* 797

loner *n.* 790, 808

lone wolf *n.* 73

long *adj.* 23, 178; *adv.* 178; *vb.* 755, 795

long ago *adv.* 105

the long and short of it *n.* 520

longboat *n.* 243

longbow *n.* 649

long dark night of the soul *n.* 656

long-distance *adj.* 172

long distance *n.* 172

long dozen *n.* 84

long-drawn-out *adj.* 93, 178, 506

long dress *n.* 787

longed for *adj.* 450

longevity *n.* 107, 112, 322

long for *vb.* 450, 748

longhand *n.* 513

long-haul *adj.* 93, 172

long haul *n.* 93, 172

long-headed *adj.* 444

longing *n.* 735, 755

long in the tooth *adj.* 112

longitude *n.* 23, 178

longitudinal *adj.* 178

long-lasting *adj.* 93, 294

long-lived *adj.* 322

long odds *n.* 426

long-range *adj.* 172

longship *n.* 243

longshore *adj.* 237

long shot *n.* 10, 416, 426, 456

long-sighted *adj.* 370

long-sightedness *n.* 370

long-standing *adj.* 93, 107, 549

long-suffering *adj.* 540, 660, 733, 813

long-term *adj.* 93

long time *n.* 93

longueur *n.* 178

long-winded *adj.* 93, 178, 251, 459, 506, 530, 762

long-windedness *n.* 506

long word *n.* 496

look *n.* 216, 370, 394; *vb.* 370, 394, 553

look a fright *vb.* 764

look after *vb.* 666

look after number one *vb.* 834

look a gift horse in the mouth *vb.* 546

lookalike *n.* 13

look alike *vb.* 13

look an idiot *vb.* 445

look askance at *vb.* 437

look back *vb.* 105

look before *one* leaps *vb.* 754

look down *one's* nose at *vb.* 824

look down on *vb.* 824

look for *vb.* 555

look forward to *vb.* 425, 450

look in *vb.* 162

look into *vb.* 414

look of disapproval *n.* 826

look on the bright side *vb.* 742, 748

lookout *n.* 104, 184, 370, 450, 668

look out *vb.* 754

look out! *vb.* 602

look out for *vb.* 370, 406

look out for *oneself* *vb.* 834

look right through *vb.* 792

look-see *n.* 370

look to *vb.* 821

look up and down *vb.* 370

look up to *vb.* 774, 823

loom *vb.* 3, 29, 104, 372, 450, 599

loony *adj.* 447; *n.* 447

loop *n.* 221, 223, 251; *vb.* 221, 223, 224, 251, 278

loophole *n.* 232, 264, 422, 605, 685, 853

loopy *adj.* 224

loose *adj.* 44, 67, 192, 300, 501, 504, 658, 788, 851; *vb.* 669, 696

loose cover *n.* 202

loose ends *n.* 50, 407

looseleaf *adj.* 516

loosely *adv.* 180

loosen *vb.* 44

looseness *n.* 44, 192, 300, 407, 504

looseness of morals *n.* 851

loosen up *vb.* 667

loose off *vb.* 255

loosing *n.* 669

loot *n.* 650, 706; *vb.* 705

looter *n.* 705

looting *n.* 705

lop *vb.* 179

lope *vb.* 234

lopsided *adj.* 26, 219

lopsidedness *n.* 26, 219

loquacious *adj.* 530

loquacity *n.* 530

lord *n.* 332, 665

the Lord *n.* 862

lord it *vb.* 781

lord it over *vb.* 657

lordly *adj.* 774

Lord Muck *n.* 779

the Lord of Hosts *n.* 862

the Lord of Lords *n.* 862

the Lord of Misrule *n.* 864

lord of the manor *n.* 665

the Lord's Day *n.* 881

Lordship *n.* 778

lords spiritual *n.* 776

Lord's Supper *n.* 881

lords temporal *n.* 776

lore *n.* 476

Lorelei *n.* 865

lorry *n.* 242

lorryload *n.* 23

lose *vb.* 34, 161, 652, 691

lose *one's* bearings *vb.* 252

lose colour *vb.* 382

lose consciousness *vb.* 335

lose control *vb.* 658

lose face *vb.* 32, 775

lose faith in human nature *vb.* 808

lose heart *vb.* 743

lose *one's* heart *vb.* 795

lose hope *vb.* 749

lose *one's* marbles *vb.* 447

lose *one's* nerve *vb.* 750, 752

lose no time *vb.* 113, 615

lose *its* novelty *vb.* 762

loser *n.* 32, 652

lose *one's* rag *vb.* 802

lose *one's* reputation *vb.* 775

lose *one's* sight *vb.* 371

lose *one's* temper *vb.* 802

lose the thread *vb.* 405

lose track of *vb.* 405

lose *one's* voice *vb.* 527

lose weight *vb.* 845

losing battle *n.* 32

loss *n.* 34, 36, 163, 323, 395, 572, 691

losses *n.* 323

loss of memory *n.* 449

man of means *n.* 712

manacle *n.* 42; *vb.* 40, 668

manacled *adj.* 668

manage *vb.* 31, 567, 571, 621, 622, 726

manageable *adj.* 136, 537, 629

management *n.* 571, 622

manager *n.* 31, 571, 613, 622, 665

managerial *adj.* 136, 622

mañana *n.* 616

man and boy *adv.* 1

man-at-arms *n.* 648

mandarin *n.* 141

mandate *n.* 657, 661, 672; *vb.* 661, 672

mandatory *adj.* 71, 536, 623, 661, 664, 821

mandolin *n.* 369

man Friday *n.* 631

mangle *vb.* 219

manhandle *vb.* 338

man-hater *n.* 808

manhole *n.* 232

manhood *n.* 112, 332

man hour *n.* 90

mania *n.* 447, 729, 755

maniac *n.* 447

maniacal *adj.* 447

manic *adj.* 729

manic-depressive *adj.* 447

manicure *n.* 765

manicurist *n.* 765

manifest *adj.* 394, 464; *n.* 720; *vb.* 394, 464, 484

manifestation *n.* 394, 464

manifold *adj.* 86

manikin *n.* 169

the man in the street *n.* 27, 69, 777

manipulate *vb.* 139, 338

manipulation *n.* 139, 338

manipulative *adj.* 139

mankind *n.* 330

manliness *n.* 143, 332, 751

manly *adj.* 143, 332, 751

man-made *adj.* 149

manner *n.* 7, 68, 240, 502, 621

mannered *adj.* 502, 771

mannerism *n.* 771

manners *n.* 768

mannish *adj.* 332

mannishness *n.* 332

manoeuvre *n.* 607

man of God *n.* 863

man of honour *n.* 831

man of many parts *n.* 624

man of prayer *n.* 863, 872, 874

man of property *n.* 692

man of straw *n.* 4, 142

man of the cloth *n.* 879

the man on the Clapham omnibus *n.* 69, 777

manor *n.* 165

man o' war *n.* 243

manpower *n.* 567, 613

manqué *adj.* 652

man's best friend *n.* 326

manse *n.* 882

manservant *n.* 666

man's estate *n.* 322

mansion *n.* 165

manslaughter *n.* 324

mantissa *n.* 74

mantle *n.* 202; *vb.* 387

mantra *n.* 88, 874

mantrap *n.* 601

manufacture *n.* 149; *vb.* 149

manufacturer *n.* 149, 613

manure *n.* 268; *vb.* 152, 328, 329

manuscript *adj.* 513; *n.* 513, 516

many *adj.* 80, 86

many a time *adv.* 117

many happy returns *n.* 786

map *n.* 249, 488, 557; *vb.* 488, 557

map-maker *n.* 557

map out *vb.* 208

mapreading *n.* 159

maquette *n.* 490, 492

mar *vb.* 585, 764, 767, 775

maracas *n.* 369

marathon *n.* 93, 172, 236

marauding *adj.* 705

marble *n.* 289, 292, 393, 492, 569; *vb.* 393

marbled *adj.* 393

marbles *n.* 761

march *n.* 236, 253, 682; *vb.* 234, 236, 682

marchioness *n.* 776

mare *n.* 326, 333

margin *n.* 20, 156, 174, 209, 214, 667, 722

marginal *adj.* 209; *n.* 73

marginally *adv.* 78

margrave *n.* 665

marigold *n.* 388

marijuana *n.* 849

marimba *n.* 369

marinade *n.* 344; *vb.* 344

marine *adj.* 237, 243, 310; *n.* 648

mariner *n.* 237

marines *n.* 648

marital *adj.* 40, 797

maritime *adj.* 237, 243, 310

mark *n.* 484, 585, 587, 593, 595, 767; *vb.* 5, 587, 593, 595, 767, 786

mark down *vb.* 724

marked *adj.* 464, 585, 587, 593, 595, 767

marked down *adj.* 724

marker *n.* 484

market *n.* 464, 470, 708, 710; *vb.* 709

marketable *adj.* 707, 709

market economy *n.* 667, 710

market gardener *n.* 149, 329

market gardening *n.* 329

marketing *n.* 709

market place *n.* 464

marking *n.* 485

mark off *vb.* 177

mark out *vb.* 211, 484

marksman *n.* 255

mark time *vb.* 90, 122, 235, 608

mark-up *n.* 722

mark up *vb.* 486, 723

marmalade *n.* 388

maroon *adj.* 392; *vb.* 563

marooned *adj.* 311, 563

marque *n.* 68

marquee *n.* 202

marquess *n.* 776

marquetry *n.* 393

marquis *n.* 776

marriage *n.* 40, 45, 797

marriageable *adj.* 797

marriage bureau *n.* 797

marriage ceremony *n.* 797

marriage feast *n.* 797

marriage of convenience *n.* 797

marriage service *n.* 881

married *adj.* 40, 797

married couple *n.* 797

marrow *n.* 5, 63, 166, 199

marry *vb.* 19, 40, 797

marry into *vb.* 797

marry off *vb.* 797

marry up *vb.* 45

marry well *vb.* 797

marsh *n.* 308, 312

marshal *vb.* 57

marshalling yard *n.* 240

marshy *adj.* 308

marsupial *n.* 326

mart *n.* 710

measured *adj.* 119, 507, 843

measurement *n.* 177

measure off *vb.* 24

measures *n.* 240

meaty *adj.* 458

Meccano *n.* 53, 761

mechanic *n.* 613

mechanical *adj.* 401, 536, 568

mechanical engineer *n.* 613

mechanism *n.* 138, 568

mechanize *vb.* 141

mechanized *adj.* 568

medal *n.* 650

medallion *n.* 766

meddle *vb.* 402, 630

meddlesome *adj.* 402

media *n.* 472

media coverage *n.* 470

medial *adj.* 63, 250

median *adj.* 27, 63; *n.* 27, 63, 207, 250

mediate *vb.* 63, 138, 646, 647

mediation *n.* 63, 138, 646, 647, 862

mediator *n.* 63, 148, 647

mediatory *adj.* 647

medical *adj.* 596

medical assistance *n.* 631

medical tourism *n.* 236, 596

medicament *n.* 596

medication *n.* 596

medicinal *adj.* 596

medicine *n.* 596

medicine-man *n.* 876

mediocre *adj.* 27, 32, 583

mediocrity *n.* 27, 583

meditate *vb.* 398, 874

meditating *adj.* 874

meditation *n.* 398, 872, 874

meditative *adj.* 398, 872

medium *n.* 455, 567, 876, 877

medley *n.* 16, 38

meek *adj.* 642, 663, 733, 780, 784, 872

meekness *n.* 642, 733, 780, 784

meet *n.* 761; *vb.* 66, 716, 718

meet an obligation *vb.* 819

meet *sb* halfway *vb.* 63, 436, 686

meeting *n.* 40, 66, 176, 259, 433, 789

meeting-house *n.* 882

meeting point *n.* 200, 207

meet *one's* needs *vb.* 738

meet with approval *vb.* 738, 825

megalomania *n.* 783

megalomaniac *adj.* 783

megaphone *n.* 355

me generation *n.* 70

mela *n.* 761

melancholia *n.* 447

melancholic *adj.* 447

melancholy *adj.* 735, 743, 804; *n.* 447, 735, 743, 804

melange *n.* 38

mêlée *n.* 56, 147, 643

mellifluous *adj.* 365

mellifluousness *n.* 365

mellow *adj.* 290, 342, 736; *vb.* 290

mellowness *n.* 290

melodic *adj.* 365, 367

melodious *adj.* 365, 736

melodiousness *n.* 365

melodrama *n.* 482, 523, 732

melodramatic *adj.* 482, 523, 732

melody *n.* 365, 367, 736

melt *vb.* 2, 4, 44, 94, 183, 217, 290, 303, 809

melt down *vb.* 303

melting pot *n.* 38, 125

melt into thin air *vb.* 395

meltwater *n.* 305

member *n.* 48, 53, 634, 693

member of parliament *n.* 657

membership *n.* 43, 51

memento *n.* 105, 448

memo *n.* 448, 486

memoirs *n.* 517, 518, 522

memo pad *n.* 486

memorable *adj.* 365, 448

memorandum *n.* 448

memorial *n.* 448, 484, 486

memorize *vb.* 438, 448

memory *n.* 75, 105, 448, 570

memsahib *n.* 778

menace *n.* 599, 796, 806; *vb.* 599, 750, 806

menacing *adj.* 599, 806

ménage *n.* 164

menagerie *n.* 326

mend *n.* 594; *vb.* 594, 817

mendable *adj.* 594

mendacious *adj.* 479, 481

mendaciousness *n.* 479, 481

mended *adj.* 594

mender *n.* 594

mend *one's* fences *vb.* 636

mendicancy *n.* 713

mendicant *adj.* 681; *n.* 681, 713

mending *n.* 594

mend *one's* ways *vb.* 592

menhir *n.* 190

menial *adj.* 32, 666; *n.* 613, 666

menopausal *adj.* 112

menopause *n.* 112, 153

menstrual *adj.* 92

menstruation *n.* 119

mensurate *vb.* 177

mensuration *n.* 177

mental *adj.* 396

mental block *n.* 449

mental defective *n.* 397

mental deficiency *n.* 397

mental illness *n.* 447

mental image *n.* 457

mentally deficient *adj.* 397

mentally ill *adj.* 447

mention *n.* 650; *vb.* 70, 404, 458

mentor *n.* 444, 475, 623

Mephistopheles *n.* 864

Mephistopholean *adj.* 864

mercantile *adj.* 707

mercenary *adj.* 728; *n.* 648

merchandise *n.* 149, 707; *vb.* 707

merchandising *n.* 709

merchant *n.* 571, 613, 707

merchantman *n.* 243

merchant navy *n.* 237

merciful *adj.* 660, 805, 809, 813, 862

merciless *adj.* 806, 810

mercilessness *n.* 810

mercurial *adj.* 130, 245, 405, 543, 544, 732

mercury *n.* 130

mercy *n.* 660, 805, 809, 813, 862

mercy killing *n.* 323

mere *n.* 312

merely *adv.* 30, 39, 79

mere shadow *n.* 489

meretricious *adj.* 4, 394, 480, 769

meretriciousness *n.* 480

merge *vb.* 13, 38, 40, 45, 79, 633

merger *n.* 38, 40, 45, 633, 708

meridian *n.* 97, 103

meringue *n.* 306

merit *n.* 582, 837; *vb.* 819

mince *vb.* 234
mind *n.* 283, 396, 535; *vb.* 85, 406
mind-blowing *adj.* 849
mind-boggling *adj.* 732, 759
minder *n.* 85, 598
mindful *adj.* 404, 406
mindfulness *n.* 404, 406
mindless *adj.* 397, 399
mindlessness *n.* 397, 399
mind one's manners *vb.* 791
mind one's Ps and Qs *vb.* 71, 406, 621, 791
mind-reader *n.* 877
mind's eye *n.* 370, 457
mind one's step *vb.* 406
mine *n.* 186, 570, 601, 614, 649; *vb.* 270
minefield *n.* 640
miner *n.* 613
mineral *adj.* 321; *n.* 321, 569
mineralogical *adj.* 321
mineralogy *n.* 321
minginess *n.* 728
mingle *vb.* 38
mingy *adj.* 574, 728
mini *adj.* 169, 205; *n.* 169
miniature *adj.* 30; *n.* 169, 490
miniaturized *adj.* 169
minicab *n.* 242
minicomputer *n.* 75
minimal *adj.* 30, 573
minimalist *n.* 490
minimally *adv.* 30
minimization *n.* 483
minimize *vb.* 30, 432
minimum *n.* 30, 32, 189, 573
mining *n.* 275, 573
minion *n.* 666
minister *n.* 622, 657, 879; *vb.* 881

ministerial *adj.* 878
ministering *adj.* 863
ministering spirit *n.* 863
minister to *vb.* 631, 666
ministration *n.* 878
ministry *n.* 878
minnow *n.* 169
minor *adj.* 30, 32; *n.* 111
minority *n.* 30, 48, 87
minority rule *n.* 657
minster *n.* 882
minstrel *n.* 368, 521
mint *n.* 712; *vb.* 106, 149, 711
minuet *n.* 367, 524
minus *adj.* 2, 163, 273; *adv.* 36
minuscule *n.* 495
minute *adj.* 30, 169, 373; *vb.* 76, 486, 513
minuteness *n.* 30, 169
minutes *n.* 486, 513
minutiae *n.* 70
minx *n.* 111
miracle *n.* 759, 868
miracle-worker *n.* 759, 876
miracle-working *n.* 876
miraculous *adj.* 759
mirage *n.* 4, 370, 394, 457
mire *n.* 308
mirror *n.* 248, 292; *vb.* 13, 17, 81, 88, 248
mirror image *n.* 11, 14
mirth *n.* 742, 744
mirthful *adj.* 742
MIRV *n.* 649
misadventure *n.* 656
misandry *n.* 333
misanthrope *n.* 808
misanthropic *adj.* 808
misanthropize *vb.* 808
misanthropy *n.* 808
misapplication *n.* 566
misapply *vb.* 566

misapprehension *n.* 463
misappropriate *vb.* 566, 705
misappropriation *n.* 705
misbehave *vb.* 621, 662, 838
misbehaviour *n.* 621, 662, 840
miscalculate *vb.* 430, 441
miscalculation *n.* 430, 441
miscall *vb.* 498
miscalling *n.* 498
miscarriage *n.* 152, 323
miscarriage of justice *n.* 853
miscarried *adj.* 652
miscarry *vb.* 153
miscellaneous *adj.* 16, 38
miscellany *n.* 16, 38, 45, 520
mischief *n.* 662, 742, 806, 818, 836
mischief-maker *n.* 662, 838
mischievous *adj.* 662, 742
misconceive *vb.* 430, 441
misconception *n.* 430, 441, 463
misconduct *n.* 621, 792, 840
misconstruction *n.* 441, 463, 489, 501
misconstrue *vb.* 219, 463
miscreant *n.* 838
misdeed *n.* 818
misdemeanour *n.* 840, 853
misdemeanours *n.* 621
miser *n.* 728, 834
miserable *adj.* 735, 743
miserliness *n.* 728
miserly *adj.* 574, 728, 834
misery *n.* 735, 743
misfired *adj.* 652

misfit *n.* 20, 54, 73
misfortune *n.* 554, 604, 656, 806, 836
misgiving *n.* 435
misgivings *n.* 428, 750
misgovern *vb.* 658
misguided *adj.* 430, 441
misguidedness *n.* 441
mishandle *vb.* 566, 625
mishandling *n.* 566, 625
mishit *vb.* 20
mishmash *n.* 38
misinform *vb.* 441
misinformation *n.* 467
misinformed *adj.* 441
misinterpret *vb.* 441, 463
misinterpretation *n.* 463, 489
misjudge *vb.* 116, 430, 441
misjudged *adj.* 116
misjudgement *n.* 116, 430, 441
mislaid *adj.* 161, 691
mislay *vb.* 161, 691
mislead *vb.* 411, 441, 480, 489
misleading *adj.* 411, 441, 489
misled *adj.* 441
mismanage *vb.* 625
mismanagement *n.* 625
mismatch *n.* 20
misname *vb.* 498
misnamed *adj.* 498
misnaming *n.* 498
misnomer *n.* 498
misogynist *n.* 332, 799, 808
misogyny *n.* 808
misplace *vb.* 20, 161
misplaced *adj.* 161
misprint *n.* 441
misread *vb.* 463
misreading *n.* 463, 489
misremember *vb.* 449
misrepresent *vb.* 219, 463, 489

on the road *adv.* 234, 236

on the rocks *adj.* 340, 717, 798; *adv.* 39, 150

on the scrapheap *adj.* 696; *adv.* 150

on the shelf *adv.* 37

on the sly *adv.* 467

on the spot *adv.* 101, 158, 162

on the spur of the moment *adv.* 96, 548

on the stocks *adv.* 50

on the throne *adj.* 657

on the top rung of the ladder *adv.* 188

on the trail *adv.* 236

on the trot *adv.* 64

on the up and up *adj.* 655; *adv.* 33, 274

on the wagon *adj.* 847

on the wane *adv.* 34

on the warpath *adj.* 732

on the way *adv.* 239

on the whole *adv.* 27

on the wing *adv.* 238

on the wrong track *adv.* 58

on time *adv.* 96

on *one's* tod *adv.* 79

on *one's* toes *adj.* 730

ontological *adj.* 1

ontology *n.* 1

on top of that *adv.* 45

on top of the world *adj.* 734, 742

on *one's* uppers *adj.* 713

onus *n.* 821

on vacation *adv.* 163

on view *adv.* 394, 464

onward *adv.* 253

onyx *n.* 766

oodles *n.* 29, 573

oomph *n.* 145

ooze *n.* 308, 317; *vb.* 246, 264, 308, 314

oozy *adj.* 264, 308

opacity *n.* 376, 380

opal *n.* 766

opalescence *n.* 380

opalescent *adj.* 380, 385, 393

opaque *adj.* 376, 380, 459, 461, 504

opaqueness *n.* 380, 459, 461, 504

open *adj.* 232, 265, 464, 468, 478, 627; *n.* 306; *vb.* 232

open-air *adj.* 306

open air *n.* 198, 306

open-and-shut case *n.* 629

open arms *n.* 265

open country *n.* 313

open door *n.* 263

open-ended *adj.* 89, 416

opener *n.* 232

open-handed *adj.* 698, 725, 859

open house *n.* 69, 725

opening *n.* 115, 232, 611

opening gambit *n.* 61

opening night *n.* 523

open letter *n.* 69

openly *adv.* 232, 464

open marriage *n.* 797

open meeting *n.* 69

open *one's* mouth *vb.* 528

open-mouthed *adj.* 232, 759

openness *n.* 232, 265, 478, 627

open *one's* heart *vb.* 478

open prison *n.* 671

open sea *n.* 310

open secret *n.* 470

open sesame *n.* 232, 876

open space *n.* 232

open to the four winds *adv.* 232

open up *vb.* 468

openwork *n.* 197, 232

opera *n.* 367, 761

opera house *n.* 761

operate *vb.* 136, 596

operatic *adj.* 367

operation *n.* 136, 562, 645

operational *adj.* 136, 607

operative *adj.* 136, 141; *n.* 613

operator *n.* 472

operetta *n.* 367

ophthalmic *adj.* 370

opiate *adj.* 849; *n.* 148

opinion *n.* 408, 429, 434

opinionated *adj.* 430, 434, 542, 783

opium *n.* 849

opium den *n.* 849

oppo *n.* 25

opponent *n.* 632, 794, 826

opportune *adj.* 19, 115, 580

opportuneness *n.* 115

opportunism *n.* 543, 580, 834

opportunist *adj.* 580; *n.* 834

opportunity *n.* 115, 423, 580

oppose *vb.* 14, 137, 215, 437, 632, 638, 794, 826

opposed *adj.* 14, 215, 437, 474, 538, 656, 794, 826

opposed to *adj.* 632

opposing *adj.* 137, 632

opposite *adj.* 14, 212, 215; *n.* 14, 215, 632

oppositeness *n.* 14

opposite number *n.* 11, 25

opposite pole *n.* 14

opposition *n.* 14, 137, 215, 437, 632, 638, 656, 826

oppress *vb.* 285, 657, 659, 670, 794, 806

oppressed *adj.* 670

oppression *n.* 659, 670

oppressive *adj.* 285, 659, 737

oppressor *n.* 659

opprobrium *n.* 775

opt for *vb.* 535, 545

optical *adj.* 370

optical device *n.* 370

optical illusion *n.* 4, 370

optimal *adj.* 29

optimism *n.* 450, 742, 748

optimist *n.* 748

optimistic *adj.* 450, 742, 748

optimum *n.* 29

option *n.* 535, 545

optional *adj.* 535, 545

opt out *vb.* 608

opulence *n.* 712

opulent *adj.* 712

opus *n.* 149, 367

oracle *n.* 455, 877

oracular *adj.* 455

oral *adj.* 526, 528

oral history *n.* 107

orange *adj.* 388; *n.* 388

orangery *n.* 329

orangey *adj.* 388

orate *vb.* 528, 532

oration *n.* 528, 532

orator *n.* 528

oratorical *adj.* 502, 528

oratorio *n.* 367

oratory *n.* 502

orb *n.* 223, 225

orbit *n.* 7, 223, 238, 240, 278, 279; *vb.* 223, 238, 278, 279

orbital *adj.* 278; *n.* 278

orbital motion *n.* 278

orbs *n.* 370

orchard *n.* 327, 329

orchestra *n.* 368

orchestral *adj.* 367

orchestrate *vb.* 368, 557

orchestration *n.* 367

ordain *vb.* 71, 661, 672, 878, 881

ordained *adj.* 879

ordeal *n.* 628, 656

order *n.* 55, 57, 68, 68, 622, 634, 650, 661, 881; *vb.* 55, 57, 622, 661, 821, 878

ordered *adj.* 57

peace wall *n.* 52
peach *n.* 388, 763
peachy *adj.* 387
peacock *n.* 770, 783
peak *n.* 29, 31, 62, 184, 188, 584; *vb.* 31, 188
peal *n.* 357, 359; *vb.* 355, 357, 359
pearl *n.* 766
pearliness *n.* 380, 383
pearly *adj.* 380, 383, 385, 393
pear-shaped *adj.* 221
peasant *n.* 164, 328, 777
peashooter *n.* 255
pea-souper *n.* 307
peat *n.* 341
peaty *adj.* 386
pebble *n.* 311
pebbly *adj.* 311
peccadillo *n.* 838, 840
peck at *vb.* 267
pecking order *n.* 55
peckish *adj.* 755
pecs *n.* 42
pectorals *n.* 42
peculiar *adj.* 18, 70, 550
peculiarity *n.* 70
pecuniary *adj.* 711
pedagogic *adj.* 475
pedagogue *n.* 475
pedagogy *n.* 475
pedal *n.* 255
pedal car *n.* 761
pedant *n.* 438, 659
pedantic *adj.* 406, 438, 440, 659, 688
pedantry *n.* 438, 440, 659, 688
peddle *vb.* 681, 709
pedestal *n.* 189, 193
pedestrian *adj.* 508, 522, 762; *n.* 236
pedicure *n.* 765
pedigree *adj.* 39; *n.* 59, 154, 776
pedlar *n.* 681, 707
pee *n.* 268; *vb.* 268
peek *n.* 370; *vb.* 370
peel *n.* 202; *vb.* 175, 203
peeling *adj.* 175

peelings *n.* 175
peel off *vb.* 205
peep *n.* 370; *vb.* 364, 370
peepers *n.* 370
peephole *n.* 232
peeping Tom *n.* 402
peer *n.* 25, 776; *vb.* 370, 370
peerage *n.* 776
peeress *n.* 776
peer group *n.* 66, 101, 103
peerless *adj.* 31, 584
peer of the realm *n.* 776
peeve *vb.* 737
peeved *adj.* 802
peevish *adj.* 739, 803
peg *n.* 42
peg away *vb.* 124, 540
peg out *vb.* 323
pejorative *adj.* 824, 828
pellet *n.* 255, 649
pell-mell *adv.* 38, 56
pellucid *adj.* 379
pellucidity *n.* 379
pelt *n.* 202; *vb.* 96, 147, 245
pen *n.* 158, 210, 328; *vb.* 210, 513
penal *adj.* 860
penalize *vb.* 860
penalty *n.* 685, 860
penance *n.* 814, 841
penchant *n.* 140, 537, 757
pencil *n.* 374; *vb.* 490
pendant *n.* 35, 192, 377, 766
pendency *n.* 192
pendent *adj.* 192
pending *adj.* 90
pendulous *adj.* 192
pendulousness *n.* 192
pendulum *n.* 97, 119, 192, 280
penetrability *n.* 232
penetrate *vb.* 139, 232, 263, 271, 460
penetrating *adj.* 444
penetration *n.* 263, 271, 418, 444
penfriend *n.* 515
peninsula *n.* 311

peninsular *adj.* 311
penis *n.* 152
penitence *n.* 814, 841
penitent *adj.* 814, 841; *n.* 841
penitential *adj.* 814
penitentiary *adj.* 814; *n.* 671
penmanship *n.* 513
pen name *n.* 497, 498
pennant *n.* 484
pennies from heaven *n.* 835
penniless *adj.* 713
pennilessness *n.* 713
penny dreadful *n.* 518
the penny drops *n.* 433
penny-pinching *adj.* 728
penpal *n.* 515
pension *n.* 674, 716, 719, 859
pension off *vb.* 696
pensive *adj.* 398, 405
pensiveness *n.* 398
pentad *n.* 84
pentagon *n.* 84
pentameter *n.* 84
pentangle *n.* 84, 220
Pentateuch *n.* 84, 868
pentathlon *n.* 84
Pentecost *n.* 881
penthouse *n.* 165, 184
penumbra *n.* 376
penurious *adj.* 713
penury *n.* 713
people *n.* 330, 331; *vb.* 165
the people *n.* 777
people's bureau *n.* 672
pep *n.* 145
PEP *n.* 570, 694
pepper *n.* 344; *vb.* 232, 393
pepper-and-salt *adj.* 385, 393
pepperiness *n.* 344
peppery *adj.* 342, 344
pep pill *n.* 849
pep talk *n.* 145, 532
per *prep.* 138
perambulation *n.* 234

per capita *adv.* 700
perceive *vb.* 370, 396
percentage *n.* 35, 48, 78, 722
perceptibility *n.* 372
perceptible *adj.* 372
perception *n.* 334, 370, 396, 729
perceptive *adj.* 334, 370
perceptual *adj.* 396
percolate *vb.* 263, 271
percolation *n.* 271
percussion *n.* 369
perdition *n.* 867
peregrination *n.* 236
peremptory *adj.* 473, 661
perennial *n.* 327; *adj.* 92, 93, 131, 327
perfect *adj.* 584, 837, 839, 850; *vb.* 49, 584, 653
perfectibility *n.* 253
perfection *n.* 31, 584, 653, 850
perfectionism *n.* 406, 440
perfectionist *adj.* 406, 440
perfidious *adj.* 480, 481, 832
perfidy *n.* 480, 543, 832
perforate *vb.* 227, 232
perforated *adj.* 227, 232
perforation *n.* 227, 232
perform *vb.* 136, 368, 488, 523, 607, 688, 786, 821
performance *n.* 136, 367, 488, 523, 607, 688, 786, 821
performer *n.* 368, 523, 607
performing arts *n.* 488
perform ritual *vb.* 881
perfume *n.* 347, 349; *vb.* 349
perfumed *adj.* 347, 349
perfunctoriness *n.* 50, 273

processed *adj.* 559

processing *n.* 125

procession *n.* 64

proclaim *vb.* 464, 468, 470, 661

proclamation *n.* 468, 470, 661

proclivity *n.* 140, 757

proconsul *n.* 665

procrastinate *vb.* 114, 407

procrastination *n.* 114, 616

procreate *vb.* 151, 152

procreation *n.* 151, 152, 322

procreative *adj.* 151, 152

procure *vb.* 571, 690

procurement *n.* 690

prodigal *adj.* 454, 727; *n.* 838

prodigality *n.* 727

prodigal son *n.* 727, 841

prodigious *adj.* 29, 759

prodigy *n.* 759

produce *n.* 133, 149, 328; *vb.* 132, 149, 216, 523, 525

producer *n.* 149

product *n.* 74, 133, 149

production *n.* 149, 216, 523

production line *n.* 15, 614

productive *adj.* 132, 149, 152, 578

productiveness *n.* 152

productivity *n.* 149, 578

profanation *n.* 801

profane *adj.* 801, 869, 873, 880; *vb.* 824, 873

profaneness *n.* 869

profane person *n.* 873

profanity *n.* 801, 873

profess *vb.* 434, 473, 683

professed *adj.* 498

professing *adj.* 688

profession *n.* 434, 473, 611, 683, 821

professional *adj.* 611, 624; *n.* 611, 624

professional classes *n.* 777

professor *n.* 778

proffer *n.* 679; *vb.* 679

proffering *n.* 679

proficiency *n.* 438

proficient *adj.* 438

profile *n.* 208, 214, 216, 517; *vb.* 208

profit *n.* 33, 35, 37, 580, 690, 711, 835, 859; *vb.* 651, 690

profitability *n.* 578

profitable *adj.* 149, 578, 580, 651, 690, 835, 859

profitably *adv.* 859

profit-and-loss account *n.* 720

profit by *vb.* 115

profiteer *vb.* 707, 723

profit-sharing *n.* 693

profligacy *n.* 572, 727

profligate *adj.* 572, 727; *n.* 838

profound *adj.* 186, 444

profoundly *adv.* 186

profundity *n.* 186, 444

profuse *adj.* 86, 573, 727

profusion *n.* 29, 570, 573, 727

progenitor *n.* 154

progeny *n.* 60, 155

prognosis *n.* 59, 455

prognosticate *vb.* 455

program *n.* 75, 570; *vb.* 75

programme *n.* 57, 76, 472, 557, 621; *vb.* 57

programmer *n.* 75

programming language *n.* 75, 494, 570

progress *n.* 124, 234, 253, 592, 651; *vb.* 33, 124, 234, 253, 592, 651

progression *n.* 33, 60

progressive *adj.* 33, 64, 121, 253, 592

progressively *adv.* 253

prohibit *vb.* 52, 424, 630, 668, 678, 680

prohibited *adj.* 678, 853

prohibiting *adj.* 678

prohibition *n.* 52, 630, 668, 678, 680, 847

prohibitionism *n.* 843

prohibitionist *n.* 843, 847

prohibitive *adj.* 52, 630, 678, 723

prohibitory *adj.* 678

project *n.* 476, 553, 557, 562; *vb.* 198, 228, 255, 525, 553, 557

projected *adj.* 557

projectile *n.* 255, 649

projecting *adj.* 228

projection *n.* 6, 228, 457, 488

projector *n.* 491

proletarian *adj.* 777

proletariat *n.* 777

proliferate *vb.* 33, 152, 573

proliferation *n.* 33, 152

prolific *adj.* 149, 151

prolix *adj.* 506, 530, 762

prolixity *n.* 506, 530

prologue *n.* 59, 523

prolong *vb.* 93, 124, 178

prolongation *n.* 93, 124, 178

prolonged *adj.* 178

promenade *n.* 240

prominence *n.* 31, 212, 228, 372, 464, 576, 774

prominent *adj.* 31, 212, 228, 372, 464, 576, 774

promiscuity *n.* 851

promiscuous *adj.* 756

promiscuousness *n.* 756

promise *n.* 104, 423, 425, 473, 562, 683,

748, 821; *vb.* 473, 562, 683

promised *adj.* 683

the promised land *n.* 748

promising *adj.* 104, 425, 655, 748

promissory *adj.* 683

promissory note *n.* 683, 711

promontory *n.* 228, 311

promote *vb.* 132, 138, 253, 470, 576, 592, 631

promoter *n.* 470, 631

promotion *n.* 253, 276, 470, 592

prompt *adj.* 96, 113, 245, 537; *n.* 523; *vb.* 61, 448, 551

promptly *adv.* 245

promptness *n.* 96, 113, 245, 537

promulgate *vb.* 468

promulgation *n.* 468

prone *adj.* 140, 191

proneness *n.* 140, 191

prong *n.* 296

pronoun *n.* 500

pronounce *vb.* 429, 473, 526, 856

pronounced *adj.* 464

pronounce man and wife *vb.* 797

pronouncement *n.* 473

pronto *adv.* 96, 245

pronunciation *n.* 526

proof *adj.* 638; *n.* 412, 417, 420, 514

proof of identity *n.* 485

proofread *vb.* 592

proofreader *n.* 514, 592, 613

proofreading *n.* 592

prop *n.* 131, 193; *vb.* 193

propaganda *n.* 139, 475

propaganda war *n.* 645

propagate *vb.* 67, 149, 152, 329

propagation *n.* 67, 152, 322

propel *vb.* 141, 247, 255, 664

propellant *n.* 255

propellent *adj.* 255

propeller *n.* 255, 279

propensity *n.* 140, 537, 757

proper *adj.* 511, 817, 819, 837

propertied *adj.* 692, 694, 712

property *n.* 5, 694

prophecy *n.* 868

prophesy *n.* 455; *vb.* 453, 455

prophet *n.* 455, 868, 877

prophetic *adj.* 453, 455, 868

prophylactic *adj.* 598, 754; *n.* 754

prophylaxis *n.* 598, 754

propinquity *n.* 173

propitiate *vb.* 646, 738, 814

propitiation *n.* 814, 862

propitiatory *adj.* 646, 814

propitious *adj.* 115

proportion *n.* 9, 24, 48, 78, 218, 511

proportional *adj.* 9, 24, 218

proportionally *adv.* 9

proportionately *adv.* 700

proportions *n.* 156, 168

proposal *n.* 409, 557, 679, 681, 795, 800

propose *vb.* 456, 553, 557, 623, 679, 681, 800

propose conditions *vb.* 685

proposed *adj.* 557

proposer *n.* 557

proposition *n.* 456, 679, 800; *vb.* 800

proprietary *adj.* 694

proprietor *n.* 692

proprietorial *adj.* 692

proprietorship *n.* 692

propriety *n.* 511, 768, 817, 850

props *n.* 523

propulsion *n.* 141, 234, 247, 255

propulsive *adj.* 255

prop up *vb.* 131, 276

pro rata *adv.* 700

prosaic *adj.* 502, 508, 522, 762

prosaicness *n.* 522

pros and cons *n.* 410

proscenium *n.* 523

proscribe *vb.* 678

proscription *n.* 678

prose *n.* 518, 522

prosecute *vb.* 607, 830, 856

prosecution *n.* 555, 830, 856

prosecutor *n.* 830, 856

proselyte *n.* 125

proselytize *vb.* 125, 872

proselytizing *adj.* 125

prose poem *n.* 522

prosiness *n.* 508, 522

prosodic *adj.* 521

prosody *n.* 521

prospect *n.* 104, 425, 450

prospecting *n.* 433

prospective *adj.* 104, 425, 450

prospectus *n.* 76, 516

prosper *vb.* 33, 336, 592, 651, 655, 712, 835

prosperity *n.* 655, 712, 835

prosperous *adj.* 651, 655, 712, 835

prostitute *n.* 851; *vb.* 566

prostitution *n.* 566, 851

prostrate *adj.* 142, 144, 185, 191, 823; *vb.* 142

prostrate *oneself vb.* 874

prostration *n.* 142, 144, 619

prosy *adj.* 506, 508, 522

protean *adj.* 121, 130, 217

protect *vb.* 378, 598, 603, 640

protected *adj.* 378

protection *n.* 598, 603, 640

protectionism *n.* 668

protectionist *adj.* 52, 668

protective *adj.* 598, 603, 640

protective clothing *n.* 640

protector *n.* 598, 640, 807

protectorate *n.* 157, 672

protein *n.* 320

protest *n.* 73, 437, 638, 682, 826; *vb.* 73, 437, 538, 632, 638, 682, 826

protestant *adj.* 682

protester *n.* 682, 739

protesting *adj.* 682

protest meeting *n.* 682

protocol *n.* 549, 787, 791

protoplasm *n.* 320

prototypal *adj.* 22

prototype *n.* 22, 216

protract *vb.* 93, 124, 178, 506

protracted *adj.* 93, 178, 506

protraction *n.* 93, 178

protractor *n.* 177

protrude *vb.* 228

protuberance *n.* 228

protuberant *adj.* 228

proud *adj.* 779

proud person *n.* 779

provable *adj.* 417

prove *vb.* 412, 417, 829

prove accurate *vb.* 440

prove guilty *vb.* 858

prove innocent *vb.* 857

proven *adj.* 417

provender *n.* 267

prosy prove *one's* point *vb.* 412

proverb *n.* 442, 499

proverbial *adj.* 442

prove wrong *vb.* 413

provide *vb.* 559, 571

provided *adj.* 571

provide for *vb.* 453

providence *n.* 835

Providence *n.* 862

provident *adj.* 453

providential *adj.* 115, 862

provider *n.* 571

provide the means *vb.* 567

province *n.* 157

provincial *adj.* 157, 430, 777

provincialism *n.* 430

proving *n.* 416

provision *n.* 453, 559, 570, 571, 685; *vb.* 559, 571

provisional *adj.* 8, 50, 94, 101, 121, 416, 422, 685

provisionally *adv.* 8, 94, 101

provisioning *n.* 559, 571

provisions *n.* 267, 559, 567, 571

proviso *n.* 422, 685

provocation *n.* 132, 637, 732

provocative *adj.* 410, 635, 637, 732

provoke *vb.* 61, 132, 637, 732, 794, 802

provost *n.* 665

prow *n.* 212

prowess *n.* 751

proximity *n.* 104, 173, 176

proxy *n.* 128, 672, 675, 676

prude *n.* 850

prudence *n.* 398, 406, 726, 754

prudent *adj.* 406, 453, 726, 754

prudery *n.* 850

prudish *adj.* 784, 850

prudishness *n.* 784, 850

437, 474, 546, 556, 565, 680, 826

rejects *n.* 724

rejoice *vb.* 734, 746

rejoicing *adj.* 746; *n.* 746

rejoin *vb.* 641

rejoinder *n.* 129, 415, 641

rejuvenate *vb.* 106

rejuvenated *adj.* 151

relapse *n.* 88, 105, 126, 254; *vb.* 88, 126, 254

relate *vb.* 9, 517

related *adj.* 9

relatedness *n.* 9

relation *n.* 9, 42

relationship *n.* 9, 795

relative *adj.* 8, 9, 24

relatively *adv.* 9

relativeness *n.* 9

relatives *n.* 12

relax *vb.* 290, 612, 618, 669, 761, 788, 809

relaxation *n.* 148, 612, 618, 658, 669, 761

relaxed *adj.* 618, 658, 738, 788

relaxing *adj.* 618

relay *n.* 472; *vb.* 470

release *n.* 323, 669, 696, 813, 822, 857; *vb.* 44, 132, 525, 669, 696, 822, 857

released *adj.* 813, 857

relegate *vb.* 161, 266

relegation *n.* 161, 266

relent *vb.* 290, 660, 809, 813

relentless *adj.* 95, 117, 124, 810

relentlessly *adv.* 95

relentlessness *n.* 539, 806, 810

relevance *n.* 9, 200

relevant *adj.* 9

reliability *n.* 119, 131, 425, 427, 714, 774, 831

reliable *adj.* 119, 131, 420, 427, 434, 478, 774, 831

reliance *n.* 434, 748

relic *n.* 37, 105, 107, 448, 486

relict *n.* 37, 798

relief *n.* 16, 128, 148, 208, 228, 492, 596, 620, 631, 673, 740, 809

relieve *vb.* 148, 596, 631, 673, 740, 805

relieve *oneself vb.* 268, 740

relieving *adj.* 740

religion *n.* 634, 868, 877

religiosity *n.* 872

religious *adj.* 688, 862, 868, 874, 877

religious education/ instruction/know-ledge *n.* 868

religious teacher *n.* 868

religious teaching *n.* 868

relinquish *vb.* 563, 674, 696

relinquished *adj.* 563

relinquishment *n.* 563, 674, 696

relish *n.* 145, 342, 344, 734, 757; *vb.* 336, 342, 734, 757

relive *vb.* 448

relocate *vb.* 161

relocation *n.* 161, 239

reluctance *n.* 246, 437, 538, 638, 680, 784

reluctant *adj.* 246, 437, 538, 556, 638, 680, 784

rely *vb.* 434, 748

rely on *vb.* 427, 450

remain *vb.* 1, 37, 93, 122

remainder *n.* 37, 74, 516; *vb.* 709

remaining *adj.* 37

remains *n.* 37, 324, 486

remake *n.* 88, 151, 525; *vb.* 88, 151

remand *n.* 668

remand centre/home *n.* 671

remand in custody *vb.* 668

remark *n.* 528

remarkable *adj.* 29, 759

remarry *vb.* 797

remedial *adj.* 137, 594, 596, 740

remedied *adj.* 594

remedy *n.* 137, 594, 596, 740; *vb.* 137, 594, 596, 740, 817

remember *vb.* 105, 448, 786

remembered *adj.* 448

remembrance *n.* 105, 448, 786

remind *vb.* 448

reminder *n.* 448

reminisce *vb.* 448

reminiscence *n.* 448

reminiscent *adj.* 448

remiss *adj.* 407

remission *n.* 606, 813, 857

remit *vb.* 698, 716, 813

remittance *n.* 716

remixing *n.* 367

remnant *n.* 37

remodel *vb.* 121, 127

remonstrate *vb.* 437, 682

remonstration *n.* 437, 682

remorse *n.* 735, 809, 840, 841

remorseful *adj.* 841

remorseless *adj.* 117, 810

remorselessness *n.* 810

remote *adj.* 172, 790

remote chance *n.* 426

remoteness *n.* 172

removal *n.* 36, 161, 239, 266, 270

removal from office *n.* 673

remove *n.* 24; *vb.* 36, 161, 270

remove from office *vb.* 673

remove from the scene *vb.* 395

remunerate *vb.* 716, 859

remuneration *n.* 690, 711, 716, 719, 859

remunerative *adj.* 690, 859

renaissance *n.* 88, 151

Renaissance man *n.* 49, 80, 438

rend *vb.* 41, 174, 232

render *vb.* 202, 303, 462, 698

render *sb* a service *vb.* 805

render assistance *vb.* 631

rendering *n.* 488, 490

render null and void *vb.* 673

rendezvous *n.* 66; *vb.* 66

rendition *n.* 462

renegade *n.* 44, 73

renege *vb.* 689

renew *vb.* 88, 106, 151

renewal *n.* 88, 151, 620

renounce *vb.* 435, 474, 563, 696, 674

renovate *vb.* 106, 594

renovated *adj.* 594

renovation *n.* 106, 594

renovator *n.* 594

renown *n.* 29, 774

renowned *adj.* 29, 774

rent *adj.* 41; *n.* 41, 719, 721; *vb.* 697, 702

rental *n.* 697, 702, 721

rent-boy *n.* 851

rented *adj.* 164

renunciation *n.* 435, 474, 563, 674, 696

reorganization *n.* 121

reorganize *vb.* 121

rep *n.* 709

repair *n.* 7, 594; *vb.* 594

repaired *adj.* 594

repairer *n.* 594

repairman *n.* 613

reparable *adj.* 594

right of way *n.* 99,
240, 271
Right Reverend *n.*
778
right royal *adj.* 725
rights *n.* 694
right side *n.* 212
right-wing *adj.* 122
right-winger *n.* 122
rigid *adj.* 122, 222,
235, 289, 659
rigidity *n.* 122, 222,
289
rigorous *adj.* 406,
418, 440, 659
rigorousness *n.* 659
rigour *n.* 406, 440,
659
rig-out *n.* 204
rile *vb.* 802
riled *adj.* 802, 803
rill *n.* 314
rim *n.* 208, 209; *vb.*
209
rime *n.* 340, 383; *vb.*
383
rind *n.* 202
ring *n.* 210, 223, 359,
485, 472, 587, 766;
vb. 206, 251, 278,
359, 485
ring a bell *vb.* 448
ring down the cur-
tain *vb.* 62, 123
ringing *adj.* 355, 359
ringlet *n.* 224
ringlets *n.* 765
ring off *vb.* 123
ring out *vb.* 353, 355,
357
ring road *n.* 240, 251,
278
ringside seat *n.* 173
ring the changes *vb.*
121
ringtone *n.* 359
ring true *vb.* 440
rink *n.* 210
rinse *n.* 765; *vb.* 305,
586
riot *n.* 56, 147, 573,
853; *vb.* 56, 147
rioter *n.* 662
rioting *n.* 658
riotous *adj.* 56, 147,
658, 662, 853

rip *n.* 595; *vb.* 595
riparian *adj.* 209, 311
ripen *vb.* 653
ripeness *n.* 107, 653
a ripe old age *n.* 112
rip-off *n.* 480, 705,
723
rip off *vb.* 480, 705,
705, 723
rip-off merchant *n.*
705
riposte *n.* 129, 137,
248, 415, 641; *vb.*
137, 415, 641
ripple *n.* 224, 231; *vb.*
291
ripple effect *n.* 133
rippling *adj.* 224
rise *n.* 33, 184, 274;
vb. 33, 184, 226,
228, 274, 286, 723
rise in the world *vb.*
592
rise up *vb.* 127
risibility *n.* 772
risible *adj.* 772
rising *adj.* 274, 425,
655, 723
rising prices *n.* 723
rising damp *n.* 308
rising generation *n.*
106
rising tide *n.* 33
risk *n.* 554, 599; *vb.*
554, 599
risk *one's* neck *vb.* 753
risky *adj.* 428, 554,
599
risqué *adj.* 744, 851
rite *n.* 874, 881
rite of passage *n.* 265
ritual *adj.* 787, 881; *n.*
549, 786, 787, 881
ritual object *n.* 881
rival *adj.* 643; *n.* 632,
643, 815; *vb.* 632,
643
rivalry *n.* 632, 815
river *n.* 314
riverbank *n.* 311
riverbed *n.* 315
riverboat *n.* 243
riverine *adj.* 311
riverside *adj.* 209
riveted *adj.* 404
rivulet *n.* 314

RK *n.* 868
road *n.* 240
road atlas *n.* 249
roadblock *n.* 233,
630, 668
roadhouse *n.* 165
road map *n.* 249, 557
road pricing *n.* 721
road rage *n.* 802
roadside *adj.* 209; *n.*
209
roadsweeper *n.* 586
road toll *n.* 721
roam *vb.* 234, 236
roan *n.* 386
roar *n.* 355, 363, 526;
vb. 355, 363, 364,
526, 802
roar of laughter *n.* 744
roar with laughter *vb.*
744
roast *vb.* 267, 339
roasting *n.* 826
rob *vb.* 705
robber *n.* 705
robbery *n.* 705
robbery with violence
n. 639, 705
robe *n.* 202; *vb.* 204
robot *n.* 330, 568, 731
robotics *n.* 75
rob Peter to pay Paul
vb. 25
robust *adj.* 143, 588
rock *n.* 289, 311, 321,
367, 849; *vb.* 280
rock-bottom *adj.* 724
rock bottom *n.* 30,
32, 185, 189
rock-climbing *n.* 761
rocker *n.* 280
rockery *n.* 329
rocket *n.* 244, 255,
649, 826; *vb.* 33,
274, 723
rocket motor *n.* 568
rocket-propelled
grenade *n.* 649
rocket scientist *n.* 396
rock-hard *adj.* 289
rock 'n' roll *n.* 524
rock-solid *adj.* 427
rock the boat *vb.* 73
rocky *adj.* 144, 289,
311
rod *n.* 193, 861

rodent *n.* 326
rod of iron *n.* 659
rogation *n.* 874
rogue *n.* 480, 705,
838
roguery *n.* 832, 838
Rohypnol *n.* 849
role *n.* 523
roll *n.* 66, 76, 224,
279, 358, 486; *vb.*
90, 191, 221, 224,
225, 234, 279, 292,
314, 358, 525
roll call *n.* 75, 497
roller *n.* 225, 292, 310
roller coaster *n.* 221
rollers *n.* 765
roller skates *n.* 761
rolling *adj.* 221
rolling in it *adj.* 712
rolling stone *n.* 236
roll in the aisles *vb.*
744
roll into one *vb.* 419
roll out the red carpet
vb. 786
roll up *vb.* 261
roly-poly *adj.* 168
Roma *n.* 236
roman *adj.* 495, 513
romance *n.* 457, 479,
518, 795
romantic *adj.* 367,
457, 518, 729, 730,
732, 795
romanticism *n.* 732
romanticize *vb.* 457
rondo *n.* 367
roof *n.* 188, 202; *vb.*
202
roofing felt *n.* 569
rooftop *n.* 184
rook *vb.* 705
room *n.* 156
roommate *n.* 693, 793
room to manoeuvre
n. 667
roomy *adj.* 29, 156,
180
root *n.* 74, 189, 327,
496
root and branch *adj.*
127; *adv.* 49
rooted to the spot
adj. 235
rootless *adj.* 94, 161

social conscience n. 807

social gathering n. 789

social group n. 66

socialism n. 657

socialist adj. 657

socialize vb. 85

social security n. 631

social services n. 807

social work n. 807

society n. 85, 330, 634, 770

sociological adj. 330

socket n. 227

sod n. 327

sodden adj. 308

sod's law n. 656

soft adj. 144, 290, 292, 356, 381, 658, 660, 730

softback adj. 516

soft drug n. 849

soften vb. 144, 290, 360, 740, 813, 829

soften up vb. 559

soft-hearted adj. 660, 809

soft-heartedness n. 809

softie n. 730

soft in the head adj. 445

softly softly adv. 148, 246

softness n. 144, 290, 292, 352, 356, 660

soft option n. 629

soft pedal n. 360

soft-pedal vb. 432

soft porn n. 851

soft sell n. 139, 470, 709

soft soap n. 827

soft-soap vb. 827

soft-spoken adj. 356

soft spot n. 140, 144, 730, 757

soft touch n. 480, 730

soft voice n. 526

software n. 75, 570

software engineering n. 75

sogginess n. 317

soggy adj. 290, 308, 317

soigné adj. 204, 511

soil n. 311; vb. 268, 587

soirée n. 110, 789

sojourn vb. 165

solace n. 809

solar adj. 284

solar energy n. 341

solarium n. 765

solar panel n. 339

solar system n. 284

solar year n. 92

solder n. 43; vb. 40, 43

soldier n. 648

soldier of fortune n. 648

sold out adj. 709

sole vb. 594

solecism n. 496, 498, 501

solely adv. 79

solemn adj. 507, 576, 745, 787, 872, 874, 881

solemnity n. 507, 576, 745, 787

solemnization n. 786

solemnize vb. 786

solicit vb. 681

solicitation n. 681

solicitor n. 613, 681

solicitous adj. 404, 406

solicitude n. 404, 406

solid adj. 3, 40, 43, 122, 131, 182, 216, 282, 285, 287, 633, 636; n. 287

solidarity n. 19, 40, 43, 633, 636, 793

solidification n. 125, 287

solidify vb. 43, 125, 182, 287, 289

solidity n. 3, 43, 122, 131, 182, 282, 287

solid object n. 282

soliloquize vb. 534

soliloquy n. 79, 534

solipsism n. 70

solipsistic adj. 70

solitaire n. 761

solitariness n. 79

solitary adj. 41, 79, 790; n. 799, 808

solitary confinement n. 860

solitude n. 79, 790

solo adj. 79, 367; n. 524, 534

solo effort n. 79

soloist n. 79, 368

Solomon n. 444

soluble adj. 46, 303, 696

solution n. 303, 305

solve vb. 462

solvent n. 203, 303

solvent abuse n. 849

sombre adj. 375, 384, 804

somebody n. 774

somersault n. 196; vb. 196

something for every-one n. 51, 69

something on one's mind n. 735

sometime adj. 99, 105, 674

some time adv. 102

sometimes adv. 90, 92

somewhat adv. 24, 30

somnolence n. 619

somnolent adj. 610, 619

son n. 12

sonata n. 367

song n. 364, 365, 367, 874

song and dance n. 281, 732

songbook n. 367

song of praise n. 874

songster n. 368

songwriter n. 368

sonic adj. 353

sonic boom n. 357

sonnet n. 521

the Son of God n. 862

the Son of Man n. 862

sonority n. 353, 355

sonorous adj. 353, 355, 359

sonorousness n. 359

soon adv. 90

sooner or later adv. 102

soot n. 384

soothe vb. 148, 596, 736, 740

soothing adj. 148, 596, 736, 740

soothsayer n. 455, 876

sootiness n. 384

sooty adj. 384

sophistical adj. 411

sophisticate n. 768

sophisticated adj. 511, 768

sophistication n. 511, 768

sophistry n. 411

sopping adj. 305

soppy adj. 730, 800

soprano n. 368

sorcerer n. 876

sorcerous adj. 876

sorcery n. 139, 875, 876

sordid adj. 583

sore adj. 334, 337, 737, 802

soreness n. 334, 737

sore point n. 635, 730

sore throat n. 589

sorrel n. 386

sorrow n. 735, 747; vb. 735, 747

sorrowful adj. 735

sorrowing adj. 735

sorry adj. 809, 814, 841

sort n. 68; vb. 24, 55, 57, 68, 418

sorted adj. 57

sortie n. 264, 639; vb. 639

SOS n. 602

so-so adj. 27

so to speak adv. 17, 458

sotto voce adv. 356

sou n. 30

soufflé n. 306

sough vb. 316, 356, 361

sought after adj. 709

soul n. 5, 283, 322, 330, 367

soulmate n. 17, 795

soul-searching n. 398

sound adj. 143, 446, 582, 584, 588, 870;

vat *n.* 167
VAT *n.* 721
the Vatican *n.* 882
vaudeville *n.* 523
vault *n.* 186, 221, 274, 325, 570, 711; *vb.* 221, 274
vaunt *vb.* 771
va-va-voom *n.* 145
VC *n.* 751
VCR *n.* 472
VD *n.* 589
VDU *n.* 570
Vedas *n.* 868
veer *n.* 252; *vb.* 121, 252
vegan *n.* 843
veganism *n.* 843
vegetable *n.* 327
vegetal *adj.* 327
vegetarian *adj.* 267; *n.* 843
vegetarianism *n.* 843
vegetate *vb.* 1, 90, 146
vegetation *n.* 327
vehemence *n.* 147, 473, 507, 732
vehement *adj.* 147, 507
vehicle *n.* 242, 523
vehicular *adj.* 242
veil *n.* 202, 373, 378, 469; *vb.* 373, 378, 469
veiled *adj.* 202, 465
vein *n.* 175, 181, 321, 502, 570; *vb.* 393
veined *adj.* 393
veld *n.* 313
vellum *n.* 513
velocity *n.* 245
velour *n.* 569
velvet *n.* 290, 292, 569
velvety *adj.* 290, 292
venal *adj.* 728
venality *n.* 728
vend *vb.* 709
vendetta *n.* 635, 641, 794
vendor *n.* 709
veneer *n.* 175, 187, 202, 212, 394; *vb.* 175, 187, 202

venerable *adj.* 107, 549, 823
venerate *vb.* 874
veneration *n.* 823, 874
venerator *n.* 874
venereal *adj.* 40
venereal disease *n.* 589
vengeance *n.* 641
vengeful *adj.* 641, 810
venial *adj.* 813
venom *n.* 232, 264
venomous *adj.* 806, 826, 828
vent *n.* 232, 264
ventilate *vb.* 306, 316, 348, 468
ventilation *n.* 306, 348
venture *n.* 611; *vb.* 554, 751
venturesome *adj.* 561, 562
venue *n.* 159
veracious *adj.* 478
veracity *n.* 478
verb *n.* 500
verbal *adj.* 496, 500, 528
verbal diarrhoea *n.* 530
verbalize *vb.* 496, 526, 528
verbatim *adj.* 496; *adv.* 21, 440
verbiage *n.* 459
verbose *adj.* 459, 496, 504, 506, 530, 762
verbosity *n.* 504, 506, 530
verdant *adj.* 327, 390
verdict *n.* 429, 856
verdict of not guilty *n.* 857
verdigris *n.* 390
verdure *n.* 327, 390
verge *n.* 173, 209, 209; *vb.* 140, 173, 209
verger *n.* 880
verifiable *adj.* 412, 417
verification *n.* 416, 417, 420
verified *adj.* 417

verify *vb.* 417, 420
verisimilitude *n.* 3, 440
vermilion *n.* 387
vermin *n.* 326, 597
vernacular *adj.* 69, 164; *n.* 494
vernal *adj.* 108
vernal equinox *n.* 108
versatile *adj.* 16, 69, 80, 125, 130, 578
versatility *n.* 16, 125, 130
verse *n.* 521
versed *adj.* 438
verse form *n.* 521
verses *n.* 521
versification *n.* 521
versifier *n.* 521
versify *vb.* 521
version *n.* 121, 462
verso *n.* 14, 213, 516
vertebral *adj.* 213
vertebrate *n.* 326
vertex *n.* 188
vertical *adj.* 184, 190, 222, 276; *n.* 190, 222
verticality *n.* 184, 190, 222
vertically *adv.* 190
vertiginous *adj.* 184, 190
verve *n.* 145, 322, 507
very *adv.* 29
very much *adv.* 29
Very Reverend *n.* 778
vespers *n.* 110, 881
vessel *n.* 167, 243
vestige *n.* 30, 37, 486
vestigial *adj.* 37
vestment *n.* 881
vestry *n.* 882
veteran *n.* 107, 112, 624
veterinary science *n.* 328
veto *n.* 474, 545, 546, 668, 678, 680; *vb.* 2, 123, 474, 546, 668, 678, 680
vex *vb.* 737, 802
vexation *n.* 737, 739, 802
vexed *adj.* 735, 802

via *prep.* 138
viability *n.* 423
viable *adj.* 322, 423
viaduct *n.* 240
Viagra *n.* 145
vial *n.* 167
vibes *n.* 729
vibrant *adj.* 359
vibraphone *n.* 369
vibrate *vb.* 280, 281, 358, 359
vibrating *adj.* 280
vibration *n.* 234, 280, 281
vibrato *n.* 358
vibrator *n.* 280
vicar *n.* 879
vicarage *n.* 882
vicarious *adj.* 128, 672, 814
the Vicar of Christ *n.* 879
vice- *adj.* 676; *n.* 818, 838
vice admiral *n.* 648
vice-chancellor *n.* 622
vicelike *adj.* 695
viceroy *n.* 665
vice versa *adv.* 11, 121, 196
vicinity *n.* 157, 173, 206
vicious *adj.* 147, 583, 604, 796, 818, 836, 838
vicious circle *n.* 64, 654
viciousness *n.* 604
vicissitudes *n.* 11, 101, 121
victimize *vb.* 604, 737, 806
victor *n.* 31, 651
Victorian *adj.* 850; *n.* 850
victorious *adj.* 31, 651
victory *n.* 651
victuals *n.* 267
video *n.* 472, 761; *vb.* 472, 486
videocassette *n.* 472
videocassette recorder *n.* 472